THE MENTAL PATIENT

Studies in the Sociology of Deviance

The Mental Patient:

STUDIES IN THE SOCIOLOGY OF DEVIANCE

Stephan P. Spitzer and Norman K. Denzin
Associate Professor of Sociology and Assistant Professor of Sociology
University of Iowa and University of Illinois

McGRAW-HILL BOOK COMPANY
New York   St. Louis   San Francisco   Toronto   London   Sydney

THE MENTAL PATIENT:
Studies in the Sociology of Deviance

Library of Congress Catalog Card Number 67–26889

1 2 3 4 5 6 7 8 9 0   MAMM   7 5 4 3 2 1 0 6 9 8

INTRODUCTION

Research concerned with mental illness has proliferated in recent years, but much of it has been conducted in the absence of any consistent theory. The present volume brings together a body of findings in the sociology of mental illness. Using symbolic interactionism, with the related perspective of deviance as a social definition, we seek to impose upon selected research findings a framework which organizes the main currents of knowledge in the area of the sociology of mental illness. It is hoped that this will stimulate future inquiry so that theory and research can be combined to lead to a comprehensive theory of mental illness and other forms of deviant behavior as they appear within and across societal settings.

There is also a practical necessity for this volume. The inaccessibility of growing literature dealing with the sociology of mental illness cannot be denied. Because the study of mental illness is not restricted to any one discipline, its products are scattered throughout a multitude of journals. Some serve specific fields such as abnormal psychology, psychiatry, sociology, and nursing; others penetrate the boundaries of two or more fields. As a result materials are often unavailable or are scattered among numerous branch libraries. In such circumstances effective research and teaching become difficult, if not impossible.

THE SOCIOLOGICAL PERSPECTIVE

Among the several disciplines that have taken mental illness as a subject for study, the most recent has been sociology. Because the sociologist became concerned with this topic after his tradition of inquiry was well established, he was inclined to fuse the subject matter of health and illness with his own viewpoint. Interest in demographic analysis, criminology and deviancy, social structure and personality, and a conception of man as a social being contributed in part to the emergence of a unique perspective on mental illness.

The sociological perspective differs substantially from predominant modes of psychiatric and psychological thought, in which mental illness is regarded as arising from within the individual. During the last ten years there has been a growing recognition among sociologists and some representatives of allied disciplines that "mental illness" could be subsumed under the heading of deviant behavior and treated as an arbitrary label attached to certain forms of behavior. Research stemming from this viewpoint has taken as a point of departure the proposition that mental illness is something ascribed to persons as a function of the definition given certain types of acts by certain audiences. *Attention is focused on defining and labeling persons and on the consequences of being so defined for self-attitudes or interpersonal relations.*

A second way in which the sociological approach differs from the psychological and psychiatric approach is that it concentrates on the circumstances of the ascription process. Who is labeled as mentally ill, when, and under what conditions? In the majority of abnormal psychology, psychiatry, and social work textbooks, one almost always finds a section devoted to the problem of defining "abnormal" or "mentally ill." At least two definitional models are presented: a personal adjustment model (which contends that abnormality is a condition in which the person has difficulty in confronting everyday affairs, i.e., is unhappy) and a normative model (which defines as abnormal, behavior not conforming to some modal pattern). More specifically, the latter definition regards nonconformity, whether expressed as functional mental disorders, organic mental disorders, or social problems, as situations or actions that exceed the tolerance limits of communities, social groups, or individuals. In spite of recognition that there are various ways to define or identify mental illness, work in psychiatry and abnormal psychology has been guided almost exclusively by the personal adjustment definition. Rarely do abnormal psychology or psychiatry texts return to their original formulations and place mental illness in a social context. The normative model provided one other guide for contemporary sociological research.

THE INTERACTIONIST APPROACH

It is possible to delineate various approaches to the study of deviancy within any social science discipline. Within psychiatry there are the Freudians, Sullivanians, and Adlerians, and within psychology there are the behaviorists, neo-Freudians, and Rogerians. Sociology is not immune to sectarian tendencies in thought regarding deviancy. Among the better-known schools of thought from which deviancy has been approached are functionalism and symbolic interactionism. The functionalist view regards mental illness largely as a by-product of social disorganization and in so doing concentrates on problems posed by violations of norms for the continuity and equilibrium of social systems. One basic tenet of symbolic interactionism is that personality is generated through interaction and consists of "self-other" systems. Thus, the interactionist approach is inclined to view deviancy as an outgrowth of interpersonal processes and is concerned primarily with effects on the individual and his associates. Many of the papers in this collection are in the interactionist tradition.

CHARACTERISTICS OF THIS VOLUME

This volume differs from others dealing with the sociology of illness, such as Greenblatt, Levinson, and Williams's The Patient and the Mental Hospital, Jaco's Patients, Physicians, and Illness, Apple's Sociological Studies of Health and Sickness, *Freidson's* The Hospital in Modern Society, *and Freeman, Levine, and Reeder's* Handbook of Medical Sociology.[1] *As a rule, each of these books attempts to make illness behavior amenable to sociological analysis; but their contents deal primarily with the consequences of hospital organization on individual behavior, and the psychological components in health and illness.*

The present volume does not deny the influence of hospital social structure upon patients. Rather it conveys the idea that hospital social structure is only one among many influences impinging upon mentally ill persons. Less attention has been directed to discovering (1) how specific pressures and attitudes from family, friends, and others are related to psychiatric illness, and (2) how social attitudes and responses may lead to the evolution and the stabilization of deviancy before contact with psychiatric treatment centers takes place. Moreover, in earlier volumes the situation of the mentally ill, as opposed to the physically ill, person has not been systematically differentiated. Mental illness is not identical with physical illness in respect to attitudes toward the patient, the type of reactions he elicits, and his acceptance of the sick role. It would be unfair to criticize these compilations for failure to present a body of systematic theory, for serious effort in this direction has come primarily in the last decade. In several respects, the present volume seeks to build upon and continue the type of synthesis provided by Arnold Rose's Mental Health and Mental Disorder, *which appeared thirteen years ago.[2]*

Stephan P. Spitzer
Norman K. Denzin

References

1   Milton Greenblatt, Daniel Levinson, and Richard Williams, *The Patient and the Mental Hospital,* The Free Press, Glencoe, Illinois, 1957; E. Gartly Jaco, *Patients, Physicians, and Illness,* The Free Press, Glencoe, Illinois, 1958; Dorrian Apple, *Sociological Studies of Health and Sickness,* McGraw-Hill Book Company, New York, 1960; Eliot Freidson, *The Hospital in Modern Society,* The Free Press of Glencoe, London, 1963; Howard Freeman, Sol Levine, and Leo Reeder, *Handbook of Medical Sociology,* Prentice-Hall, Inc., Englewood Cliffs, N.J., 1963.

2   Arnold Rose, *Mental Health and Mental Disorder,* W. W. Norton & Company, Inc., New York, 1955.

ACKNOWLEDGMENTS

We would like to thank our research assistants, Susanne Eichler and Martha Reed, for the many tasks they performed in the preparation of this manuscript. Evelyn Denzin and Nancy Spitzer deserve special credit for their excellent editing of the transition material and summary section. Robert M. Swanson's comments and criticisms were helpful. Dr. Paul E. Huston, Director, Psychopathic Hospital, University of Iowa, made funds available through the Iowa Mental Health Authority for an extensive empirical study of the psychiatric patient career. This book is one by-product of that project.

CONTENTS

PART 3   THE PATIENT CAREER—PREPATIENT PHASE

PART 4   THE PATIENT CAREER—INPATIENT PHASE

PART 5   THE PATIENT CAREER—POSTPATIENT PHASE

PART 6 ISSUES AND PROBLEMS IN THE SOCIOLOGY OF MENTAL ILLNESS

THE MENTAL PATIENT

Studies in the Sociology of Deviance

PART ONE

Sociological Approaches toward Deviant Behavior and Mental Illness

The study of mental illness has been approached from the particular perspectives of many disciplines. Theoreticians and researchers in the fields of clinical psychology, psychiatry, physiology, and psychopharmacology have presented conceptualizations and reports dealing with the etiology, treatment, and outcome of mental illness. Classically, the psychiatric and psychological approach has stressed the description and classification of pathological signs and symptoms, and when etiology was considered, illness was accounted for more often than not by individual psychological mechanisms such as anxiety, stress, breakdown of defense mechanisms and ego strength. The failure of these disciplines to provide a sound, empirically tested theory of mental illness can be attributed to the neglect of the social processes involved in the development and resolution of disturbed behavior, as well as to a failure to question some of the fundamental assumptions on which the study of the phenomenon of mental illness is based.

Partly because of the diffusion of psychiatric concepts to the discipline of sociology and the consequent carving-out by the sociologist of the area of psychiatric problems as a legitimate area of inquiry, the last two decades have seen a growing awareness of the social aspects of mental illness. Through the efforts of socially oriented psychiatrists and psychologists, sociologists, and, to an extent, cultural anthropologists, the importance of numerous social variables has been established. Research has demonstrated an association between mental illness and such factors as social class, residential mobility, family dynamics, hospital social structure, and many additional social variables. As a result it is now commonly recognized that the environment of the patient plays a significant role in shaping the characteristics and course of mental illness.

Socially oriented inquiry such as the research mentioned above, as well as the traditional psychiatric perspective, however, has left unquestioned the assumption that the defect or illness is located somewhere in the makeup of the individual. More recently investigators have begun to approach the phenomenon of mental disorder from another perspective, focusing on the larger and more general context of deviant behavior and on the processes by which an individual comes to be identified as deviant. This position is summarized succinctly by Kai Erikson, who states:

Deviance is not a property inherent in certain forms of behavior; it is a property conferred upon these forms by the audiences which directly or indirectly witness them. Sociologically, then, the critical variable in the study of deviance is the social audience rather than the individual person, since it is the audience which eventually decides whether or not any given action or actions will become a visible case of deviation.[1]

A very similar view is stated by Howard S. Becker:

. . . deviance is not a quality of the act a person commits, but rather a consequence of the application by other of rules and sanctions to an "offender." The deviant is one to which that label has successfully been applied; deviant behavior is behavior that people so label.[2]

Examined from this perspective, mental illness is not a consequence of any intrinsic feature or features which characterize the mentally ill. Rather, mental illness is the by-product of the evaluation and labeling by certain persons of certain kinds of behavior.[3] More specifically, mental illness is not a function of the content of an individual's acts (his symptomatology), but is, instead, defined by the reactions to his acts and the categorizations of them by those with whom he is in association. Certain behaviors viewed as violating the rules of conduct imposed by various audience members will earn him the label "mentally ill" and may result in the instigation of steps for the treatment of the "illness." Various aspects of audience reactions, the labeling process, the criteria used in labeling, the extent of consensus on such criteria, the consequences for an individual being so labeled, and other related problems are taken up in the first half of this section.

The second group of papers in this section takes a somewhat different perspective, although it is by no means antithetical to the first group. None of these papers regard "mental illness" as some sort of entity intrinsic to the individual. Focus is less upon the definition by the audience of some behavior than it is upon exactly how the definition of the behavior impinges upon the actor. Specifically, concern is with how one can account for various forms of "mental illness" by analyzing the interplay between the deviant and the audience. Thus, in this respect these papers are as closely integrated with sociological developments in the general area of deviant behavior as they are with the traditional subject matter of social psychology—the person and the social context in which he is embedded. Although each paper is concerned with some specific type of ascribed deviation, the approaches taken can be applied to other diagnostic classifications.

SOCIETAL REACTIONS TO DEVIANT BEHAVIOR

Scheff attempts to show that the causes of the initiation, maintenance, and termination of what is called mental illness are part of the social system in which it occurs and, therefore, that one can account for mental illness by mechanisms other than those internal to the psyche of the individual. Scheff copes with the problem of isolating mental illness as a unique entity and concludes that it is a label given to diverse kinds of deviations which do not fit under any other explicit label. In this regard mental illness can be viewed as a type of "residual deviance."

Although the paper covers various topics such as the origins and prevalence of mental illness, its emphasis is on the role of societal reactions in stabilizing nonconforming behavior. Labeling is identified as the single most important type of societal reaction, since it sets into operation the mechanisms that facilitate entry into deviant roles and restrict exit out of the deviant role.

Drawing analytical materials from diverse sources, Scheff demonstrates that once a person has been labeled as mentally ill, societal reactions are organized so that the nonconforming behavior becomes stabilized. Quite accurately, Scheff observes that this process would not be effective unless societal structure were organized in such a way that there were a place for the residually deviant persons (deviant roles) and that societal reactions impede conformity once deviancy has been ascribed. Rewards accrue for deviancy, and punishments exist for trying to assume old roles. It is also possible that in some instances external types of societal controls are not necessary. Once the labeling of a person as deviant has taken place and once societal reactions have become organized, the deviant may incorporate the definitions of others toward him into his self-concept. When this happens, a deviant has been created, and in many respects the socialization process is complete.

The three papers which follow take up in greater detail various points found in the Scheff article. While Scheff subscribes to the view that mental illness is a residual category of behavior employed when more conventional and delimited classifications are unavailable, Szasz, in "The Myth of Mental Illness," takes up the more basic question of whether it is correct to think of mental illness as illness at all.

Szasz represents a minority opinion among psychiatrists since he feels that the time has come to discard the notion of mental illness as a disease entity and to reconceptualize it in terms of social evaluations. From Szasz's point of view, what is now considered to be mental illness is no more than deviation from social, ethical, and legal standards, which is then evaluated by some social audience or, in some instances, the individual himself. In the former instance the evaluator may be a family member, friend, or medical practitioner who casts the behavior under the rubric of "mental illness." In other instances the evaluator may be the actor himself if he seeks to implement his personal interpretation by seeking *professional assistance. In an extended version of the paper reprinted here, Szasz points to an increasing proclivity among psychiatrists to classify divergent kinds of behavior as mental illness.*[4] *Szasz's proposal that mental illness can be viewed as a form of interpersonal strategy is reviewed in the Scheff paper included in this section.*

The next paper presents a theoretical analysis of mental illness in which the prime antecedent condition is faulty socialization. However, while faulty socialization is an antecedent condition, it is not sufficient cause to lead some persons to be regarded as mentally ill. Before one can say that "mental illness" is present, one must carefully examine the behavior of the actor in conjunction with the interpretation given the behavior by the audience. In this respect, the basic element of analysis is the encounter.

Becker contends that for an individual to interact successfully with persons other than those directly responsible for his socialization, it is necessary that he learn certain rules and norms of propriety. It is necessary that these rules and norms be well learned, for unless they are, the person will be unable to elicit the approving responses of others. In other words, the individual will be unable to command the performance by his behavior. Persons who come to be labeled as mentally ill may be those most guilty of an inability to command their performances.

The central notion in the Kitsuse paper is societal reaction. Kitsuse contends that the study of deviant behavior should not deal with the various forms of deviant behavior but rather should focus on the processes by which persons come to be defined as deviant. Central problems for theory and research then are identification of the behaviors which come to be labeled as deviant and how audience reactions to deviancy are activated and organized. These problems are taken up in detail in conjunction with the case of homosexuality. Specifically, Kitsuse illustrates the steps by which (1) behavior is interpreted as deviant, (2) the person who so behaves comes to be labeled as a homosexual, and (3) he is accorded the reactions considered appropriate to homosexuals.

THEORIES OF SPECIFIC DISORDERS

The Rose, Gough, and Lemert papers account for specific forms of mental illness by the utilization of social-psychological concepts, especially those associated with symbolic-interactionist theory. As conceptualized by classical symbolic interactionists, interaction with other persons provides the individual with definitions of himself and the other objects in his environment.[5] *These definitions are what guide and direct the behavior of the individual as he encounters other individuals and groups. "Each person's orientation toward his human environment is formed and sustained in social interaction. His sentiments, toward himself as well as toward other people, are organized while he is learning to cope with specific people."*[6]

Although the three papers in this section vary in their focus, these assumptions are made by each of them. Together they illustrate vividly the importance of an individual's social relationships in ordering the kinds of behavior he displays.

Rose applies the notions of "self" and "significant other" to the onset of mental illness. He hypothesizes that one factor in the chain of events leading to neurotic behavior is the induction of a negative attitude toward self. Such an attitude, Rose contends, is derived from an evaluation placed on reactions of significant others to one's behavior. Through this sort of interactional process, where one person acts and the audience reacts negatively, a consistent pattern of self-depreciation is established, and the person becomes neurotic. Test of the theory is based on an examination of statistical data on the incidence of involutional melancholia, a disorder sometimes regarded as a neurosis rather than a psychosis. By employing the reactions of significant others as an independent variable, the Rose paper is linked to the preceding papers, which also accord societal reaction a central position in their discussion.

The concepts of self and role-taking ability are given a position of central importance in Gough's view of the psychopathic (i.e. sociopathic) personality. According to Gough, the psychopathic personality is deficient in role-taking abilities. The psychopath is unable to achieve insight into himself and others. The deficiency in self-other insight arises during the childhood socialization process and represents the individual's inability to respond properly to societal rules and prescripts regarding the attention that should be accorded both self and others in daily interaction. By contending that one form of personality disturbance arises out of faulty socialization patterns, Gough's paper relates to Becker's theory, which also focuses upon socialization and sensitivity to others.

As Becker implies, socialization into the rules and norms of conduct of a society entails the learning of a language and the development of the ability to take the role of the other in the situation. The Gough article demonstrates how the inability to accurately take the role of the other can lead to that form of deviant behavior commonly labeled as sociopathic. Cameron, Faris, and Lemert also demonstrate that the failure of persons to develop and use consensual systems of communication and thought can lead to their exclusion and rejection by other group members.[7] Both Faris and Cameron see psychotic behavior as the product of inappropriate responses and interpretations given by the actor to audience behavior. A brief review of Cameron's and Faris's contributions provides the background to Lemert's position.

According to Cameron, paranoid behavior is a product of a private world of experience which is real to the perceiver although it is unshared by others. Because some persons hold unstable or depreciatory attitudes toward themselves as social objects and because some persons are without competence in the social interpretation of motives and intentions of others, they are especially amenable to delusional developments of a paranoid nature. A private world is fabricated in which slights and discriminations, some real and others imaginary, are interpreted to fit a preconception of a uniformly hostile community. As a consequence the paranoid develops a "pseudo-community" which is a product of his unique interpretations of the ordinary behavior of others toward him.

. . . he unintentionally organizes these others into a functional community, a group unified in their supposed reactions, attitudes and plans with respect to him. He in this way organizes individuals, some of whom are actual persons and some only inferred or imagined, into a whole which satisfies for the time being his immediate need for explanation. . . . What he takes to be a functional community is only a *pseudo-community* created by his own unskilled attempts at interpretation, anticipation, and validation of social behavior.[8]

As the delusions of discrimination and persecution grow in extent and intensity, reactions to this supposed community bring the paranoid into open conflict with the real community, which is unable to share in his attitudes and behavior. Forcible restraint or retaliation only serve to reinforce the paranoid's preconceived notion of societal conspiracy.

A very similar view is taken by Faris, although the term pseudo-community is not employed. According to Faris the trouble encountered by the typical schizophrenic results from a long period of partial isolation, precipitated usually by parental treatment and by the reaction of other children to the "resulting personality." The schizophrenic develops a purely private and virtually incommunicable style of cognitive organization as a consequence of societal reactions.

The isolation prevents the development of familiarity with the conventions and necessary principles of primary social relations, so that he slips into a great number of blunders and failures which he does not understand. The reaction of other persons to these experiences further isolates and confuses him. The particular development of the symptoms of the schizophrenic depends on varying circumstances—the common element is an unconventionality so great that other persons can usually perceive no system or order in his behavior, and so judge him to be insane.[9]

Careful case studies, contends Faris, will yield evidence that much of schizophrenic behavior, rather than being disorganized, is merely organization so unconventional that the sense of it is difficult to grasp without intimate knowledge of the person's history.

Lemert challenges the interpretation which involves the notion of a pseudo-community and maintains that the community to which the ill persons react is indeed actual. This is illustrated by demonstrating how the audience may unite in a common effort against the paranoid person. In this respect the paranoid community is real rather than "pseudo," for it is composed of reciprocal relationships and processes whose results are informal and formal exclusion and attenuated communication.

It would be meaningless to conjecture whether the community of responders is or is not "pseudo." From the point of view of the "schizophrenic" it is real if he believes it to be so. More important questions would be about the extent of audience consensus, who are in consensus, and when there is consensus. It might be hypothesized, on the basis of the career notion which is taken up in a later section, that audience conspiracies tend to predominate once a person has been conclusively defined as deviant, but that during the very initial period of the prepatient phase when audience consensus is less firmly established, much of societal reaction is individual in nature and is guided predominantly by common cultural expectations for appropriate behavior.

In any event, Cameron, Faris, and Lemert contribute to an understanding of the effects of the reactions of others and their impact on the self as a social object. All three authors illustrate how certain types of ascribed deviancy develop out of the attempt of the individual to account for situations and happenings on the basis of his own limited resources for explanation. Lemert, however, by stressing the dynamics of exclusion, brings into bolder relief than previous authors the importance of audience reactions for the development and stabilization of delusional states.

References

1 Kai T. Erikson, "Notes on the Sociology of Deviance," *Social Problems,* **9:** 308, 1962.

2 Howard S. Becker, *Outsiders,* The Free Press of Glencoe, New York, 1963, p. 9.

3 For an elaboration and criticism of this perspective see Jack P. Gibbs, "Conceptions of Deviant Behavior: The Old and the New," *Pacific Sociological Review,* **9:** 9–14, 1966.

4 Thomas S. Szasz, *The Myth of Mental Illness,* Paul B. Hoeber, Inc., New York, 1961. See also by the same author *Law, Liberty and Psychiatry,* The Macmillan Company, New York, 1963.

5 George H. Mead, *Mind, Self and Society,* The University of Chicago Press, Chicago, 1934; Charles H. Cooley, *Human Nature and the Social Order,* Charles Scribner's Sons, New York, 1902.

6 Tamotsu Shibutani, *Society and Personality,* Prentice-Hall, Inc., Englewood Cliffs, N.J., 1961, p. 556.

7 Norman Cameron, "The Paranoid Pseudo-Community," *American Journal of Sociology,* **49:** 32–38, 1943; Norman Cameron, *The Psychology of Behavior Disorders,* Houghton Mifflin Company, Boston, 1947; Robert E. L. Faris, *Social Psychology,* The Ronald Press Company, New York, 1952; see also by the same author "Reflections of Social Disorganization in the Behavior of a Schizophrenic Patient," *American Journal of Sociology,* **50:** 134–141, 1944.

8 Cameron, "The Paranoid Pseudo-Community," p. 37.

9 Faris, *Social Psychology,* p. 361.

1

THE ROLE OF THE MENTALLY ILL AND THE DYNAMICS OF MENTAL DISORDER: A RESEARCH FRAMEWORK*

Thomas J. Scheff

Although the last two decades have seen a vast increase in the number of studies of functional mental disorder, there is as yet no substantial, verified body of knowledge in this area. A quotation from a recent symposium on schizophrenia summarizes the present situation: "During the past decade, the problems of chronic schizophrenia have claimed the energy of workers in many fields. Despite significant contributions which reflect continuing progress, *we have yet to learn to ask ourselves the right questions.*"[1] Many investigators apparently agree; systematic studies have not only failed to provide answers to the problem of causation, but there is considerable feeling that the problem itself has not been formulated correctly.

One frequently noted deficiency in psychiatric formulations of the problem is the failure to incorporate social processes into the dynamics of mental disorder. Although the importance of these processes is increasingly recognized by psychiatrists, the conceptual models used in formulating research questions are basically concerned with individual rather than social systems. Genetic, biochemical, and psychological investigations seek different causal agents, but utilize similar models: dynamic systems which are located within the individual. In these investigations, social processes tend to be relegated to a subsidiary role, because the model focuses attention on individual differences, rather than on the social system in which the individuals are involved.

Recently a number of writers have sought to develop an approach which would give more emphasis to social processes. Lemert, Erikson, Goffman, and Szasz have notably contributed to this approach.[2] Lemert, particularly, by rejecting the more conventional concern with the origins of mental deviance, and stressing instead the potential importance of the societal reaction in stabilizing deviance, focuses primarily on mechanisms of social control. The work of all of these authors suggests research avenues which are analytically separable from questions of individual systems and point, therefore, to a theory which would incorporate social processes.

The purpose of the present paper is to contribute to the formulation of such a theory by stating a set of nine propositions which make up basic assumptions

Source: Thomas J. Scheff, "The Role of the Mentally Ill and the Dynamics of Mental Disorder: A Research Framework," *Sociometry,* **26:** 436–453, 1963.

* This project was supported in part by the Graduate Research Committee of the University of Wisconsin. The help of many persons, too numerous to list here, who criticized earlier drafts is gratefully acknowledged.

[1] Nathanial S. Apter, "Our Growing Restlessness with Problems of Chronic Schizophrenia," in Lawrence Appleby, *et al., Chronic Schizophrenia,* Glencoe, Ill.: Free Press, 1958.

[2] Edwin M. Lemert, *Social Pathology,* New York: McGraw-Hill, 1951; Kai T. Erikson, "Patient Role and Social Uncertainty—A Dilemma of the Mentally Ill," *Psychiatry,* **20** (August, 1957), pp. 263–274; Erving Goffman, *Asylums,* New York: Doubleday-Anchor, 1961; Thomas S. Szasz, *The Myth of Mental Illness,* New York: Hoeber-Harper, 1961.

for a social system model of mental disorder. This set is largely derived from the work of the authors listed above, all but two of the propositions (#4 and #5) being suggested, with varying degrees of explicitness, in the cited references. By stating these propositions explicitly, this paper attempts to facilitate testing of basic assumptions, all of which are empirically unverified, or only partly verified. By stating these assumptions in terms of standard sociological concepts, this paper attempts to show the relevance to studies of mental disorder of findings from diverse areas of social science, such as race relations and prestige suggestion. This paper also delineates three problems which are crucial for a sociological theory of mental disorder: what are the conditions in a culture under which diverse kinds of deviance become stable and uniform; to what extent, in different phases of careers of mental patients, are symptoms of mental illness the result of conforming behavior; is there a general set of contingencies which lead to the definition of deviant behavior as a manifestation of mental illness? Finally, this paper attempts to formulate special conceptual tools to deal with these problems, which are directly linked to sociological theory. The social institution of insanity, residual deviance, the social role of the mentally ill, and the bifurcation of the societal reaction into the alternative reactions of denial and labeling, are examples of such conceptual tools.

These conceptual tools are utilized to construct a theory of mental disorder in which psychiatric symptoms are considered to be violations of social norms, and stable "mental illness" to be a social role. The validity of this theory depends upon verification of the nine propositions listed below in future studies, and should, therefore, be applied with caution, and with appreciation for its limitations. One such limitation is that the theory attempts to account for a much narrower class of phenomena than is usually found under the rubric of mental disorder; the discussion that follows will be focused exclusively on stable or recurring mental disorder, and does not explain the causes of single deviant episodes. A second major limitation is that the theory probably distorts the phenomena under discussion. Just as the individual system models under-stress social processes, the model presented here probably exaggerates their importance. The social system model "holds constant" individual differences, in order to articulate the relationship between society and mental disorder. Ultimately, a framework which encompassed both individual and social systems would be desirable. Given the present state of knowledge, however, this framework may prove useful by providing an explicit contrast to the more conventional medical and psychological approaches, and thus assisting in the formulation of sociological studies of mental disorder.

THE SYMPTOMS OF "MENTAL ILLNESS" AS RESIDUALLY DEVIANT BEHAVIOR

One source of immediate embarrassment to any social theory of "mental illness" is that the terms used in referring to these phenomena in our society prejudge the issue. The medical metaphor "mental illness" suggests a determinate process which occurs within the individual: the unfolding and development of disease. It is convenient, therefore, to drop terms derived from the disease metaphor in favor of a standard sociological concept, deviant behavior, which signifies behavior that violates a social norm in a given society.

If the symptoms of mental illness are to be construed as violations of social norms, it is necessary to specify the type of norms involved. Most norm violations do not cause the violator to be labeled as mentally ill, but as ill-mannered, ignorant, sinful, criminal, or perhaps just harried, depending on the type of norm involved. There are innumerable norms, however, over which consensus is so complete that the members of a group appear to take them for granted. A host of such norms surround even the simplest conversation: a person engaged in conversation is expected to face toward his partner, rather than directly away from him; if his gaze is toward the partner, he is expected to look toward his eyes, rather than, say, toward his forehead; to stand at a proper conversational distance, neither one inch away nor across the room, and so on. A person who regularly violated these expectations probably would not be thought to be merely ill-bred, but as strange, bizarre, and frightening, because his behavior violates the assumptive world of the group, the world that is construed to be the only one that is natural, decent, and possible.

The culture of the group provides a vocabulary of terms for categorizing many norm violations: crime, perversion, drunkenness, and bad manners are familiar examples. Each of these terms is derived from the type of norm broken, and ultimately, from the type of behavior involved. After exhausting these categories, however, there is always a residue of the most diverse kinds of violations, for which the culture provides no explicit label. For example, although there is great cultural variation in what is defined as decent or real, each culture tends to reify its definition of decency and reality, and so provide no way of handling violations of its expectations in these areas. The typical norm governing decency or reality, therefore, literally "goes without saying" and its violation is unthinkable for most of its members. For the convenience of the society in construing those instances of unnamable deviance which are called to its attention, these violations may be lumped together into a residual category: witchcraft, spirit possession, or, in our own society, mental illness. In this paper, the diverse kinds of deviation for which our society provides no explicit label, and which, therefore, sometimes lead to the labeling of the violator as mentally ill, will be considered to be technically *residual deviance*.

THE ORIGINS, PREVALENCE AND
COURSE OF RESIDUAL DEVIANCE

The first proposition concerns the origins of residual deviance. *1. Residual deviance arises from fundamentally diverse sources.* It has been demonstrated that some types of mental disorder are the result of organic causes. It appears likely, therefore, that there are genetic, biochemical or physiological origins for residual deviance. It also appears that residual deviance can arise from individual psychological peculiarities and from differences in upbringing and training. Residual deviance can also probably be produced by various kinds of external stress: the sustained fear and hardship of combat, and deprivation of food, sleep, and even sensory experience.[3] Residual deviance, finally, can be a volitional act of innovation or defiance. The kinds of behavior deemed typical of mental illness, such as hallucinations, delusions, depression, and mania, can all arise from these diverse sources.

The second proposition concerns the prevalence of residual deviance which is analogous to the "total" or "true" prevalence of mental disorder (in contrast to the "treated" prevalence). 2. *Relative to the rate of treated mental illness, the rate of unrecorded residual deviance is extremely high.* There is evidence that grossly deviant behavior is often not noticed or, if it is noticed, it is rationalized as eccentricity. Apparently, many persons who are extremely withdrawn, or who "fly off the handle" for extended periods of time, who imagine fantastic events, or who hear voices or see visions, are not labeled as insane either by themselves or others.[4] Their deviance, rather, is unrecognized, ignored, or rationalized. This pattern of inattention and rationalization will be called "denial."[5]

In addition to the kind of evidence cited above there are a number of epidemiological studies of total prevalence. There are numerous problems in interpreting the results of these studies; the major difficulty is that the definition of mental disorder is different in each study, as are the methods used to screen cases. These studies represent, however, the best available information and can be used to estimate total prevalence.

A convenient summary of findings is presented in Plunkett and Gordon.[6] This source compares the methods and populations used in eleven field studies, and lists rates of total prevalence (in percentages) as 1.7, 3.6, 4.5, 4.7, 5.3, 6.1, 10.9, 13.8, 23.2, 23.3, and 33.3.

How do these total rates compare with the rates of treated mental disorder? One of the studies cited by Plunkett and Gordon, the Baltimore study reported by Pasamanick, is useful in this regard since it includes both treated and untreated rates.[7] As compared with the untreated rate of 10.9 per cent, the rate of treatment in state, VA, and private hospitals of Baltimore residents was .5 per cent.[8] That is, for every mental patient there were approximately 20 untreated cases located by the survey. It is possible that the treated rate is too low, however, since patients treated by private physicians were not included. Judging from another study, the New Haven study of treated prevalence, the number of patients treated in private practice is small compared to those hospitalized: over

[3] Philip Solomon, et al. (eds.), *Sensory Deprivation*, Cambridge: Harvard, 1961; E. L. Bliss, et al., "Studies of Sleep Deprivation—Relationship to Schizophrenia," *A.M.A. Archives of Neurology and Psychiatry*, **81** (March, 1959), pp. 348–359.
[4] See, for example, John A. Clausen and Marian R. Yarrow, "Paths to the Mental Hospital," *Journal of Social Issues*, **11** (December, 1955), pp. 25–32; August B. Hollingshead and Frederick C. Redlich, *Social Class and Mental Illness*, New York: Wiley, 1958, pp. 172–176; and Elaine Cumming and John Cumming, *Closed Ranks*, Cambridge: Harvard, 1957, pp. 92–103.
[5] The term "denial" is used in the same sense as in Cumming and Cumming, *ibid.*, Chap. VII.
[6] Richard J. Plunkett and John E. Gordon, *Epidemiology and Mental Illness*, New York: Basic Books, 1960.
[7] Benjamin Pasamanick, "A Survey of Mental Disease in an Urban Population, IV, An Approach to Total Prevalence Rates," *Archives of General Psychiatry*, **5** (August, 1961), pp. 151–155.
[8] *Ibid.*, p. 153.

70 per cent of the patients located in that study were hospitalized even though extensive case-finding techniques were employed. The over-all treated prevalence in the New Haven study was reported as .8 per cent, which is in good agreement with my estimate of .7 per cent for the Baltimore study.[9] If we accept .8 per cent as an estimate of the upper limit of treated prevalence for the Pasamanick study, the ratio of treated to untreated cases is 1/14. That is, for every treated patient we should expect to find 14 untreated cases in the community.

One interpretation of this finding is that the untreated patients in the community represent those cases with less severe disorders, while those patients with severe impairments all fall into the treated group. Some of the findings in the Pasamanick study point in this direction. Of the untreated patients, about half are classified as psychoneurotic. Of the psychoneurotics, in turn, about half again are classified as suffering from minimal impairment. At least a fourth of the untreated group, then, involved very mild disorders.[10]

The evidence from the group diagnosed as psychotic does not support this interpretation, however. Almost all of the cases diagnosed as psychotic were judged to involve severe impairment, yet half of the diagnoses of psychosis occurred in the untreated group. In other words, according to this study there were as many untreated as treated cases of psychoses.[11]

On the basis of the high total prevalence rates cited above and other evidence, it seems plausible that residual deviant behavior is usually transitory, which is the substance of the third proposition. *3. Most residual deviance is "denied" and is transitory.* The high rates of total prevalence suggest that most residual deviancy is unrecognized or rationalized away. For this type of deviance, which is amorphous and uncrystallized, Lemert uses the term "primary deviation."[12] Balint describes similar behavior as "the unorganized phase of illness."[13] Although Balint assumes that patients in this phase ultimately "settle down" to an "organized illness," other outcomes are possible. A person in this stage may "organize" his deviance in other than illness terms, e.g., as eccentricity or genius, or the deviant acts may terminate when situational stress is removed.

The experience of battlefield psychiatrists can be interpreted to support the hypothesis that residual deviance is usually transitory. Glass reports that combat neurosis is often self-terminating if the soldier is kept with his unit and given only the most superficial medical attention.[14] Descriptions of child behavior can be interpreted in the same way. According to these reports, most children go through periods in which at least several of the following kinds of deviance may occur: temper tantrums, head banging, scratching, pinching, biting, fantasy playmates or pets, illusory physical complaints, and fears of sounds, shapes, colors,

---

[9] Hollingshead and Redlich, *op. cit.,* p. 199.
[10] Pasamanick, *op. cit.,* pp. 153–154.
[11] *Ibid.*
[12] Lemert, *op. cit.,* Chap. 4.
[13] Michael Balint, *The Doctor, His Patient, and the Illness,* New York: International Universities Press, 1957, p. 18.
[14] Albert J. Glass, "Psychotherapy in the Combat Zone," in *Symposium on Stress,* Washington, D. C.: Army Medical Service Graduate School, 1953. Cf. Abraham Kardiner and H. Spiegel, *War Stress and Neurotic Illness,* New York: Hoeber, 1947, Chaps. III–IV.

persons, animals, darkness, weather, ghosts, and so on.[15] In the vast majority of instances, however, these behavior patterns do not become stable.

If residual deviance is highly prevalent among ostensibly "normal" persons and is usually transitory, as suggested by the last two propositions, what accounts for the small percentage of residual deviants who go on to deviant careers? To put the question another way, under what conditions is residual deviance stabilized? The conventional hypothesis is that the answer lies in the deviant himself. The hypothesis suggested here is that the most important single factor (but not the only factor) in the stabilization of residual deviance is the societal reaction. Residual deviance may be stabilized if it is defined to be evidence of mental illness, and/or the deviant is placed in a deviant status, and begins to play the role of the mentally ill. In order to avoid the implication that mental disorder is merely role-playing and pretence, it is first necessary to discuss the social institution of insanity.

SOCIAL CONTROL: INDIVIDUAL AND SOCIAL SYSTEMS OF BEHAVIOR

In *The Myth of Mental Illness*, Szasz proposes that mental disorder be viewed within the framework of "the game-playing model of human behavior." He then describes hysteria, schizophrenia, and other mental disorders as the "impersonation" of sick persons by those whose "real" problem concerns "problems of living." Although Szasz states that role-playing by mental patients may not be completely or even mostly voluntary, the implication is that mental disorder be viewed as a strategy chosen by the individual as a way of obtaining help from others. Thus, the term "impersonation" suggests calculated and deliberate shamming by the patient. In his comparisons of hysteria, malingering, and cheating, although he notes differences between these behavior patterns, he suggests that these differences may be mostly a matter of whose point of view is taken in describing the behavior.

The present paper also uses the role-playing model to analyze mental disorder, but places more emphasis on the involuntary aspects of role-playing than Szasz, who tends to treat role-playing as an individual system of behavior. In many social psychological discussions, however, role-playing is considered as a part of a social system. The individual plays his role by articulating his behavior with the cues and actions of other persons involved in the transaction. The proper performance of a role is dependent on having a cooperative audience. This proposition may also be reversed: having an audience which acts toward the individual in a uniform way may lead the actor to play the expected role even if he is not particularly interested in doing so. The "baby of the family" may come to find this role obnoxious, but the uniform pattern of cues and actions which confronts him in the family may lock in with his own vocabulary of re-

[15] Frances L. Ilg and Louise B. Ames, *Child Behavior*, New York: Dell, 1960, pp. 138–188.

sponses so that it is inconvenient and difficult for him not to play the part expected of him. To the degree that alternative roles are closed off, the proffered role may come to be the only way the individual can cope with the situation.

One of Szasz's very apt formulations touches upon the social systemic aspects of role-playing. He draws an analogy between the role of the mentally ill and the "type-casting" of actors.[16] Some actors get a reputation for playing one type of role, and find it difficult to obtain other roles. Although they may be displeased, they may also come to incorporate aspects of the type-cast role into their self-conceptions, and ultimately into their behavior. Findings in several social psychological studies suggest that an individual's role behavior may be shaped by the kinds of "deference" that he regularly receives from others.[17]

One aspect of the voluntariness of role-playing is the extent to which the actor believes in the part he is playing. Although a role may be played cynically, with no belief, or completely sincerely, with whole-hearted belief, many roles are played on the basis of an intricate mixture of belief and disbelief. During the course of a study of a large public mental hospital, several patients told the author in confidence about their cynical use of their symptoms—to frighten new personnel, to escape from unpleasant work details, and so on. Yet these *same* patients, at other times, appear to have been sincere in their symptomatic behavior. Apparently it was sometimes difficult for them to tell whether they were playing the role or the role was playing them. Certain types of symptomatology are quite interesting in this connection. In simulation of previous psychotic states, and in the behavior pattern known to psychiatrists as the Ganser syndrome, it is apparently almost impossible for the observer to separate feigning of symptoms from involuntary acts with any degree of certainty.[18] In accordance with what has been said so far, the difficulty is probably that the patient is just as confused by his own behavior as is the observer.

This discussion suggests that a stable role performance may arise when the actor's role imagery locks in with the type of "deference" which he regularly receives. An extreme example of this process may be taken from anthropological and medical reports concerning the "dead role," as in deaths attributed to "bone-pointing." Death from bone-pointing appears to arise from the conjunction of two fundamental processes which characterize all social behavior. First, all individuals continually orient themselves by means of responses which are perceived in social interaction: the individual's identity and continuity of experience are de-

---

[16] Szasz, op. cit., p. 252. For discussion of type-casting see Orrin E. Klapp, *Heroes, Villains and Fools,* Englewood Cliffs, New Jersey: Prentice-Hall, 1962, pp. 5–8 and *passim.*
[17] Cf. Zena S. Blau, "Changes in Status and Age Identification," *American Sociological Review,* 21 (April, 1956), pp. 198–203; James Benjamins, "Changes in Performance in Relation to Influences upon Self-Conceptualization," *Journal of Abnormal and Social Psychology,* 45 (July, 1950), pp. 473–480; Albert Ellis, "The Sexual Psychology of Human Hermaphrodites," *Psychosomatic Medicine,* 7 (March, 1945), pp. 108–125; S. Liberman, "The Effect of Changes in Roles on the Attitudes of Role Occupants," *Human Relations,* 9 (1956), pp. 385–402. For a review of experimental evidence, see John H. Mann, "Experimental Evaluations of Role Playing," *Psychological Bulletin,* 53 (May, 1956), pp. 227–234. For an interesting demonstration of the inter-relations between the symptoms of patients on the same ward, see Sheppard G. Kellam and J. B. Chassan, "Social Context and Symptom Fluctuation," *Psychiatry,* 25 (November, 1962), pp. 370–381.
[18] Leo Sadow and Alvin Suslick, "Simulation of a Previous Psychotic State," *A.M.A. Archives of General Psychiatry,* 4 (May, 1961), pp. 452–458.

pendent on these cues.[19] Secondly, the individual has his own vocabulary of expectations, which may in a particular situation either agree with or be in conflict with the sanctions to which he is exposed. Entry into a role may be complete when this role is part of the individual's expectations, and when these expectations are reaffirmed in social interaction. In the following pages this principle will be applied to the problem of the causation of mental disorder.

What are the beliefs and practices that constitute the social institution of insanity?[20] And how do they figure in the development of mental disorder? Two propositions concerning beliefs about mental disorder in the general public will now be considered.

4. Stereotyped imagery of mental disorder is learned in early childhood. Although there are no substantiating studies in this area, scattered observations lead the author to conclude that children learn a considerable amount of imagery concerning deviance very early, and that much of the imagery comes from their peers rather than from adults. The literal meaning of "crazy," a term now used in a wide variety of contexts, is probably grasped by children during the first years of elementary school. Since adults are often vague and evasive in their responses to questions in this area, an aura of mystery surrounds it. In this socialization the grossest stereotypes which are heir to childhood fears, e.g., of the "boogie man," survive. These conclusions are quite speculative, of course, and need to be investigated systematically, possibly with techniques similar to those used in studies of the early learning of racial stereotypes.

Assuming, however, that this hypothesis is sound, what effect does early learning have on the shared conceptions of insanity held in the community? There is much fallacious material learned in early childhood which is later discarded when more adequate information replaces it. This question leads to hypothesis No. 5. *5. The stereotypes of insanity are continually reaffirmed, inadvertently, in ordinary social interaction.*

Although many adults become acquainted with medical concepts of mental illness, the traditional stereotypes are not discarded, but continue to exist alongside the medical conceptions, because the stereotypes receive almost continual

---

[19] Generalizing from experimental findings, Blake and Mouton make this statement about the processes of conformity, resistance to influence, and conversion to a new role:

> . . . an individual requires a stable framework, including salient and firm reference points, in order to orient himself and to regulate his interactions with others. This framework consists of external and internal anchorages available to the individual whether he is aware of them or not. With an acceptable framework he can resist giving or accepting information that is inconsistent with that framework or that requires him to relinquish it. In the absence of a stable framework he actively seeks to establish one through his own strivings by making use of significant and relevant information provided within the context of interaction. *By controlling the amount and kind of information available for orientation, he can be led to embrace conforming attitudes which are entirely foreign to his earlier ways of thinking.*

Robert R. Blake and Jane S. Mouton, "Conformity, Resistance and Conversion," in *Conformity and Deviation,* Irwin A. Berg and Bernard M. Bass (eds.), New York: Harper, 1961, pp. 1–2. For a recent and striking demonstration of the effect on social communication in defining internal stimuli, see Stanley Schachter and Jerome E. Singer, "Cognitive, Social, and Physiological Determinants of Emotional State," *Psychological Review,* **69** (September, 1962), pp. 379–399.

[20] The Cummings describe the social institution of insanity (the "patterned response" to deviance) in terms of denial, isolation, and insulation. Cumming and Cumming, *loc. cit.*

support from the mass media and in ordinary social discourse. In newspapers, it is a common practice to mention that a rapist or a murderer was once a mental patient. This negative information, however, is seldom offset by positive reports. An item like the following is almost inconceivable:

Mrs. Ralph Jones, an ex-mental patient, was elected president of the Fairview Home and Garden Society in their meeting last Thursday.

Because of highly biased reporting, the reader is free to make the unwarranted inference that murder and rape occur more frequently among ex-mental patients than among the population at large. Actually, it has been demonstrated that the incidence of crimes of violence, or of any crime, is much lower among ex-mental patients than among the general population.[21] Yet, this is not the picture presented to the public.

Reaffirmation of the stereotype of insanity occurs not only in the mass media, but also in ordinary conversation, in jokes, anecdotes, and even in conventional phrases. Such phrases as "Are you crazy?", or "It would be a madhouse," "It's driving me out of my mind," or "It's driving me distracted," and hundreds of others occur frequently in informal conversations. In this usage insanity itself is seldom the topic of conversation; the phrases are so much a part of ordinary language that only the person who considers each word carefully can eliminate them from his speech. Through verbal usages the stereotypes of insanity are a relatively permanent part of the social structure.

In a recent study Nunnally demonstrated that reaffirmation of stereotypes occurs in the mass media. In a systematic and extensive content analysis of television, radio, newspapers and magazines, including "confession" magazines, they found an image of mental disorder presented which was overwhelmingly stereotyped.

. . . media presentations emphasized the bizarre symptoms of the mentally ill. For example, information relating to Factor I (the conception that mentally ill persons look and act different from "normal" people) was recorded 89 times. Of these, 88 affirmed the factor, that is, indicated or suggested that people with mental-health problems "look and act different": only one item denied Factor I. In television dramas, for example, the afflicted person often enters the scene staring glassy-eyed, with his mouth widely ajar, mumbling incoherent phrases or laughing uncontrollably. Even in what would be considered the milder disorders, neurotic phobias and obsessions, the afflicted person is presented as having bizarre facial expressions and actions.[22]

[21] Henry Brill and Benjamin Malzberg, "Statistical Report Based on the Arrest Record of 5354 Male Ex-patients Released from New York State Mental Hospitals During the Period 1946–48," mimeographed document available from the authors; L. H. Cohen and H. Freeman, "How Dangerous to the Community are State Hospital Patients?", Connecticut State Medical Journal, 9 (September, 1945), pp. 697–701.
[22] Jum C. Nunnally, Jr., Popular Conceptions of Mental Health, New York: Holt, Rinehart and Winston, 1961, p. 74.

DENIAL AND LABELING

According to the analysis presented here, the traditional stereotypes of mental disorder are solidly entrenched in the population because they are learned early in childhood and are continuously reaffirmed in the mass media and in everyday conversation. How do these beliefs function in the processes leading to mental disorder? This question will be considered by first referring to the earlier discussion of the societal reaction to residual deviance.

It was stated that the usual reaction to residual deviance is denial, and that in these cases most residual deviance is transitory. The societal reaction to deviance is not always denial, however. In a small proportion of cases the reaction goes the other way, exaggerating and at times distorting the extent and degree of deviation. This pattern of exaggeration, which we will call "labeling," has been noted by Garfinkel in his discussion of the "degradation" of officially recognized criminals.[23] Goffman makes a similar point in his description of the "discrediting" of mental patients.[24] Apparently under some conditions the societal reaction to deviance is to seek out signs of abnormality in the deviant's history to show that he was always essentially a deviant.

The contrasting social reactions of denial and labeling provide a means of answering two fundamental questions. If deviance arises from diverse sources—physical, psychological, and situational—how does the uniformity of behavior that is associated with insanity develop? Secondly, if deviance is usually transitory, how does it become stabilized in those patients who became chronically deviant? To summarize, what are the sources of uniformity and stability of deviant behavior?

In the approach taken here the answer to this question is based on hypotheses Nos. 4 and 5, that the role imagery of insanity is learned early in childhood, and is reaffirmed in social interaction. In a crisis, when the deviance of an individual becomes a public issue, the traditional stereotype of insanity becomes the guiding imagery for action, both for those reacting to the deviant and, at times, for the deviant himself. When societal agents and persons around the deviant react to him uniformly in terms of the traditional stereotypes of insanity, his amorphous and unstructured deviant behavior tends to crystallize in conformity to these expectations, thus becoming similar to the behavior of other deviants classified as mentally ill, and stable over time. The process of becoming uniform and stable is completed when the traditional imagery becomes a part of the deviant's orientation for guiding his own behavior.

The idea that cultural streotypes may stabilize primary deviance, and tend to produce uniformity in symptoms, is supported by cross-cultural studies of mental disorder. Although some observers insist there are underlying similarities, most agree that there are enormous differences in the manifest symptoms of stable mental disorder *between* societies, and great similarity *within* societies.[25]

[23] Harold Garfinkel, "Conditions of Successful Degradation Ceremonies," *American Journal of Sociology*, **61** (March, 1956), pp. 420–424.
[24] Goffman, "The Moral Career of the Mental Patient," in *Asylums, op. cit.,* pp. 125–171.
[25] P. M. Yap, "Mental Diseases Peculiar to Certain Cultures: A Survey of Comparative Psychiatry," *Journal of Mental Science,* **97** (April, 1951), pp. 313–327; Paul E. Benedict and Irving Jacks, "Mental Illness in Primitive Societies," *Psychiatry,* **17** (November, 1954), pp. 377–389.

These considerations suggest that the labeling process is a crucial contingency in most careers of residual deviance. Thus Glass, who observed that neuro-psychiatric casualties may not become mentally ill if they are kept with their unit, goes on to say that military experience with psychotherapy has been disappointing. Soldiers who are removed from their unit to a hospital, he states, often go on to become chronically impaired.[26] That is, their deviance is stabilized by the labeling process, which is implicit in their removal and hospitalization. A similar interpretation can be made by comparing the observations of childhood disorders among Mexican-Americans with those of "Anglo" children. Childhood disorders such as *susto* (an illness believed to result from fright) sometimes have damaging outcomes in Mexican-American children.[27] Yet the deviant behavior involved is very similar to that which seems to have high incidence among Anglo children, with permanent impairment virtually never occurring. Apparently through cues from his elders the Mexican-American child, behaving initially much like his Anglo counterpart, learns to enter the sick role, at times with serious consequences.[28]

ACCEPTANCE OF THE DEVIANT ROLE

From this point of view, then, most mental disorder can be considered to be a social role. This social role complements and reflects the status of the insane in the social structure. It is through the social processes which maintain the status of the insane that the varied deviancies from which mental disorder arises are made uniform and stable. The stabilization and uniformization of residual deviance are completed when the deviant accepts the role of the insane as the framework within which he organizes his own behavior. Three hypotheses are stated below which suggest some of the processes which cause the deviant to accept such a stigmatized role.

6. *Labeled deviants may be rewarded for playing the stereotyped deviant role.* Ordinarily patients who display "insight" are rewarded by psychiatrists and other personnel. That is, patients who manage to find evidence of "their illness" in their past and present behavior, confirming the medical and societal diagnosis, receive benefits. This pattern of behavior is a special case of a more general pattern that has been called the "apostolic function" by Balint, in which the physician and others inadvertently cause the patient to display symptoms of the illness the physician thinks the patient has.[29] Not only physicians but other hospital personnel and even other patients, reward the deviant for conforming to the stereotypes.[30]

---

[26] Glass, *op. cit.*

[27] Lyle Saunders, *Cultural Differences and Medical Care,* New York: Russell Sage, 1954, p. 142.

[28] For discussion, with many illustrative cases, of the process in which persons play the "dead role" and subsequently die, see Charles C. Herbert, "Life-influencing Interactions," in *The Physiology of Emotions,* Alexander Simon, *et al.,* eds., New York: Charles C. Thomas, 1961.

[29] Balint, *op. cit.,* pp. 215–239. Cf. Thomas J. Scheff, "Decision Rules, Types of Error and Their Consequences in Medical Diagnosis," *Behavioral Science,* 8 (April, 1963), pp. 97–107.

[30] William Caudill, F. C. Redlich, H. R. Gilmore, and E. B. Brody, "Social Structure and the Interaction Processes on a Psychiatric Ward," *American Journal of Orthopsychiatry,* 22 (April, 1952), pp. 314–334.

7. Labeled deviants are punished when they attempt the return to conventional roles. The second process operative is the systematic blockage of entry to nondeviant roles once the label has been publicly applied. Thus the ex-mental patient, although he is urged to rehabilitate himself in the community, usually finds himself discriminated against in seeking to return to his old status, and on trying to find a new one in the occupational, marital, social, and other spheres.[31] Thus, to a degree, the labeled deviant is rewarded for deviating, and punished for attempting to conform.

8. In the crisis occurring when a primary deviant is publicly labeled, the deviant is highly suggestible, and may accept the proferred role of the insane as the only alternative. When gross deviancy is publicly recognized and made an issue, the primary deviant may be profoundly confused, anxious, and ashamed. In this crisis it seems reasonable to assume that the deviant will be suggestible to the cues that he gets from the reactions of others toward him.[32] But those around him are also in a crisis; the incomprehensible nature of the deviance, and the seeming need for immediate action lead them to take collective action against the deviant on the basis of the attitude which all share—the traditional stereotypes of insanity. The deviant is sensitive to the cues provided by these others and begins to think of himself in terms of the stereotyped role of insanity, which is part of his own role vocabulary also, since he, like those reacting to him, learned it early in childhood. In this situation his behavior may begin to follow the pattern suggested by his own stereotypes and the reactions of others. That is, when a primary deviant organizes his behavior within the framework of mental disorder, and when his organization is validated by others, particularly prestigeful others such as physicians, he is "hooked" and will proceed on a career of chronic deviance.

The role of suggestion is noted by Warner in his description of bone-pointing magic:

The effect of (the suggestion of the entire community on the victim) is obviously drastic. An analogous situation in our society is hard to imagine. If all a man's near kin, his father, mother, brothers and sisters, wife, children, business associates, friends and all the other members of the society, should suddenly withdraw themselves because of some dramatic circumstance, refusing to take any attitude but one of taboo . . . and then perform over him a sacred ceremony . . . the enormous suggestive power of this movement . . . of the community after it has had its attitudes (toward the victim) crystallized can be somewhat understood by ourselves.[33]

If we substitute for black magic the taboo that usually accompanies mental disorder, and consider a commitment proceeding or even mental hospital admis-

[31] Lemert, *op. cit.*, provides an extensive discussion of this process under the heading of "Limitation of Participation," pp. 434–440.

[32] This proposition receives support from Erikson's observations: Kai T. Erikson, *loc. cit.*

[33] W. Lloyd Warner, *A Black Civilization*, rev. ed., New York: Harper, 1958, p. 242.

sion as a sacred ceremony, the similarity between Warner's description and the typical events in the development of mental disorder is considerable.

The last three propositions suggest that once a person has been placed in a deviant status there are rewards for conforming to the deviant role, and punishments for not conforming to the deviant role. This is not to imply, however, that the symptomatic behavior of persons occupying a deviant status is always a manifestation of conforming behavior. To explain this point, some discussion of the process of self-control in "normals" is necessary.

In a recent discussion of the process of self-control, Shibutani notes that self-control is not automatic, but is an intricate and delicately balanced process, sustainable only under propitious circumstances.[34] He points out that fatigue, the reaction to narcotics, excessive excitement or tension (such as is generated in mobs), or a number of other conditions interfere with self-control; conversely, conditions which produce normal bodily states, and deliberative processes such as symbolization and imaginative rehearsal before action, facilitate it.

One might argue that a crucially important aspect of imaginative rehearsal is the image of himself that the actor projects into his future action. Certainly in American society, the cultural image of the "normal" adult is that of a person endowed with self-control ("will-power," "back-bone," "strength of character," etc.). For the person who sees himself as endowed with the trait of self-control, self-control is facilitated, since he can imagine himself enduring stress during his imaginative rehearsal, and also while under actual stress.

For a person who has acquired an image of himself as lacking the ability to control his own actions, the process of self-control is likely to break down under stress. Such a person may feel that he has reached his "breaking-point" under circumstances which would be endured by a person with a "normal" self-conception. This is to say, a greater lack of self-control than can be explained by stress tends to appear in those roles for which the culture transmits imagery which emphasizes lack of self-control. In American society such imagery is transmitted for the roles of the very young and very old, drunkards and drug addicts, gamblers, and the mentally ill.

Thus, the social role of the mentally ill has a different significance at different phases of residual deviance. When labeling first occurs, it merely gives a name to primary deviation which has other roots. When (and if) the primary deviance becomes an issue, and is not ignored or rationalized away, labeling may create a social type, a pattern of "symptomatic" behavior in conformity with the stereotyped expectations of others. Finally, to the extent that the deviant role becomes a part of the deviant's self-conception, his ability to control his own behavior may be impaired under stress, resulting in episodes of compulsive behavior.

The preceding eight hypotheses form the basis for the final causal hypothesis.

9. *Among residual deviants, labeling is the single most important cause of careers of residual deviance.* This hypothesis assumes that most residual deviance, if it does not become the basis for entry into the sick role, will not lead to a

---

[34] T. Shibutani, *Society and Personality*, Englewood Cliffs, N. J.: Prentice-Hall, 1961, Chapter 6, "Consciousness and Voluntary Conduct."

deviant career. Most deviant careers, according to this point of view, arise out of career contingencies, and are therefore not directly connected with the origins of the initial deviance.[35] Although there are a wide variety of contingencies which lead to labeling rather than denial, these contingencies can be usefully classified in terms of the nature of the deviant behavior, the person who commits the deviant acts, and the community in which the deviance occurs. Other things being equal, the severity of the societal reaction to deviance is a function of, first, the degree, amount, and visibility of the deviant behavior; second, the power of the deviant, and the social distance between the deviant and the agents of social control; and finally, the tolerance level of the community, and the availability in the culture of the community of alternative nondeviant roles.[36] Particularly crucial for future research is the importance of the first two contingencies (the amount and degree of deviance), which are characteristics of the deviant, relative to the remaining five contingencies, which are characteristics of the social system.[37] To the extent that these five factors are found empirically to be independent determinants of labeling and denial, the status of the mental patient can be considered a partly ascribed rather than a completely achieved status. The dynamics of treated mental illness could then be profitably studied quite apart from the individual dynamics of mental disorder.

CONCLUSION

This paper has presented a sociological theory of the causation of stable mental disorder. Since the evidence advanced in support of the theory was scattered and fragmentary, it can only be suggested as a stimulus to further discussion and research. Among the areas pointed out for further investigation are field studies of the prevalence and duration of residual deviance; investigations of stereotypes of mental disorder in children, the mass media, and adult conversations; studies of the rewarding of stereotyped deviation, blockage of return to conventional roles, and of the suggestibility of primary deviants in crises. The final causal hypothesis suggests studies of the conditions under which denial and labeling of residual deviation occur. The variables which might effect the societal reaction concern the nature of the deviance, the deviant himself, and the community in

[35] It should be noted, however, that these contingencies are causal only because they become part of a dynamic system: the reciprocal and cumulative inter-relation between the deviant's behavior and the societal reaction. For example, the more the deviant enters the role of the mentally ill, the more he is defined by others as mentally ill; but the more he is defined as mentally ill, the more fully he enters the role, and so on. By representing this theory in the form of a flow chart, Walter Buckley pointed out that there are numerous such feedback loops implied here. For an explicit treatment of feedback, see Edwin M. Lemert, "Paranoia and the Dynamics of Exclusion," *Sociometry*, 25 (March, 1962), pp. 2–20.

[36] Cf. Lemert, *op. cit.*, pp. 51–53, 55–68; Goffman, "The Moral Career of the Mental Patient," in *Asylums*, *op. cit.*, pp. 134–135; David Mechanic, "Some Factors in Identifying and Defining Mental Illness," *Mental Hygiene*, 46 (January, 1962), pp. 66–74; for a list of similar factors in the reaction to physical illness, see Earl L. Koos, *The Health of Regionville*, New York: Columbia University Press, 1954, pp. 30–38.

[37] Cf. Thomas J. Scheff, "Psychiatric and Social Contingencies in the Release of Mental Patients in a Midwestern State," forthcoming; Simon Dinitz, Mark Lefton, Shirley Angrist, and Benjamin Pasamanick, "Psychiatric and Social Attributes as Predictors of Case Outcome in Mental Hospitalization," *Social Problems*, 8 (Spring, 1961), pp. 322–328.

which the deviation occurs. Although many of the hypotheses suggested are largely unverified, they suggest avenues for investigating mental disorder different than those that are usually followed, and the rudiments of a general theory of deviant behavior.

2
THE MYTH OF MENTAL ILLNESS
Thomas S. Szasz

My aim in this essay is to raise the question "Is there such a thing as mental illness?" and to argue that there is not. Since the notion of mental illness is extremely widely used nowadays, inquiry into the ways in which this term is employed would seem to be especially indicated. Mental illness, of course, is not literally a "thing"—or physical object—and hence it can "exist" only in the same sort of way in which other theoretical concepts exist. Yet, familiar theories are in the habit of posing, sooner or later—at least to those who come to believe in them—as "objective truths" (or "facts"). During certain historical periods, explanatory conceptions such as deities, witches, and microorganisms appeared not only as theories but as self-evident *causes* of a vast number of events. I submit that today mental illness is widely regarded in a somewhat similar fashion, that is, as the cause of innumerable diverse happenings. As an antidote to the complacent use of the notion of mental illness—whether as a self-evident phenomenon, theory, or cause—let us ask this question: What is meant when it is asserted that someone is mentally ill?

In what follows I shall describe briefly the main uses to which the concept of mental illness has been put. I shall argue that this notion has outlived whatever usefulness it might have had and that it now functions merely as a convenient myth.

MENTAL ILLNESS AS A SIGN OF BRAIN DISEASE

The notion of mental illness derives its main support from such phenomena as syphilis of the brain or delirious conditions—intoxications, for instance—in which persons are known to manifest various peculiarities or disorders of thinking and behavior. Correctly speaking, however, these are diseases of the brain,

Source: Thomas S. Szasz, "The Myth of Mental Illness," *American Psychologist,* **15:** 113–118, 1960.

not of the mind. According to one school of thought, *all* so-called mental illness is of this type. The assumption is made that some neurological defect, perhaps a very subtle one, will ultimately be found for all the disorders of thinking and behavior. Many contemporary psychiatrists, physicians, and other scientists hold this view. This position implies that people *cannot* have troubles—expressed in what are *now called* "mental illnesses"—because of differences in personal needs, opinions, social aspirations, values, and so on. *All problems in living* are attributed to physicochemical processes which in due time will be discovered by medical research.

"Mental illnesses" are thus regarded as basically no different than all other diseases (that is, of the body). The only difference, in this view, between mental and bodily diseases is that the former, affecting the brain, manifest themselves by means of mental symptoms; whereas the latter, affecting other organ systems (for example, the skin, liver, etc.), manifest themselves by means of symptoms referable to those parts of the body. This view rests on and expresses what are, in my opinion, two fundamental errors.

In the first place, what central nervous system symptoms would correspond to a skin eruption or a fracture? It would *not* be some emotion or complex bit of behavior. Rather, it would be blindness or a paralysis of some part of the body. The crux of the matter is that a disease of the brain, analogous to a disease of the skin or bone, is a neurological defect, and not a problem in living. For example, a *defect* in a person's visual field may be satisfactorily explained by correlating it with certain definite lesions in the nervous system. On the other hand, a person's *belief*—whether this be a belief in Christianity, in Communism, or in the idea that his internal organs are "rotting" and that his body is, in fact, already "dead"—cannot be explained by a defect or disease of the nervous system. Explanations of this sort of occurrence—assuming that one is interested in the belief itself and does not regard it simply as a "symptom" or expression of something else that is *more interesting*—must be sought along different lines.

The second error in regarding complex psychosocial behavior, consisting of communications about ourselves and the world about us, as mere symptoms of neurological functioning is *epistemological*. In other words, it is an error pertaining not to any mistakes in observation or reasoning, as such, but rather to the way in which we organize and express our knowledge. In the present case, the error lies in making a symmetrical dualism between mental and physical (or bodily) symptoms, a dualism which is merely a habit of speech and to which no known observations can be found to correspond. Let us see if this is so. In medical practice, when we speak of physical disturbances, we mean either signs (for example, a fever) or symptoms (for example, pain). We speak of mental symptoms, on the other hand, when we refer to a patient's *communications about himself, others, and the world about him.* He might state that he is Napoleon or that he is being persecuted by the Communists. These would be considered mental symptoms *only* if the observer believed that the patient was *not* Napoleon or that he was *not* being persecuted by the Communists. This makes it apparent that the statement that *"X is a mental symptom"* involves rendering a judgment. The judgment entails, moreover, a covert comparison or matching of the patient's ideas, concepts, or beliefs with those of the observer and the society in which they live. The notion of mental symptom is therefore inextricably tied to the *social* (including *ethical*) *context* in which it is made in much the same way as the notion of bodily symptom is tied to an *anatomical* and *genetic context* (Szasz, 1957a, 1957b).

To sum up what has been said thus far: I have tried to show that for those who regard mental symptoms as signs of brain disease, the concept of mental illness is unnecessary and misleading. For what they mean is that people so labeled suffer from diseases of the brain; and, if that is what they mean, it would seem better for the sake of clarity to say that and not something else.

MENTAL ILLNESS AS A NAME FOR PROBLEMS IN LIVING

The term "mental illness" is widely used to describe something which is very different than a disease of the brain. Many people today take it for granted that living is an arduous process. Its hardship for modern man, moreover, derives not so much from a struggle for biological survival as from the stresses and strains inherent in the social intercourse of complex human personalities. In this context, the notion of mental illness is used to identify or describe some feature of an individual's so-called personality. Mental illness—as a deformity of the personality, so to speak—is then regarded as the *cause* of the human disharmony. It is implicit in this view that social intercourse between people is regarded as something *inherently harmonious,* its disturbance being due solely to the presence of "mental illness" in many people. This is obviously fallacious reasoning, for it makes the abstraction "mental illness" into a *cause,* even though this abstraction was created in the first place to serve only as a shorthand expression for certain types of human behavior. It now becomes necessary to ask: "What kinds of behavior are regarded as indicative of mental illness, and by whom?"

The concept of illness, whether bodily or mental, implies *deviation from some clearly defined norm.* In the case of physical illness, the norm is the structural and functional integrity of the human body. Thus, although the desirability of physical health, as such, is an ethical value, what health *is* can be stated in anatomical and physiological terms. What is the norm deviation from which is regarded as mental illness? This question cannot be easily answered. But whatever this norm might be, we can be certain of only one thing: namely, that it is a norm that must be stated in terms of *psychosocial, ethical,* and *legal* concepts. For example, notions such as "excessive repression" or "acting out an unconscious impulse" illustrate the use of psychological concepts for judging (so-called) mental health and illness. The idea that chronic hostility, vengefulness, or divorce are indicative of mental illness would be illustrations of the use of ethical norms (that is, the desirability of love, kindness, and a stable marriage relationship). Finally, the widespread psychiatric opinion that only a mentally ill person would commit homicide illustrates the use of a legal concept as a norm of mental health. The norm from which deviation is measured whenever one speaks of a mental illness is a *psychosocial and ethical one.* Yet, the remedy is sought in terms of *medical* measures which—it is hoped and assumed—are free from wide differences of ethical value. The definition of the disorder and the terms in which its remedy are sought are therefore at serious odds with one another. The practical significance of this covert conflict between the alleged nature of the defect and the remedy can hardly be exaggerated.

Having identified the norms used to measure deviations in cases of mental illness, we will now turn to the question: "Who defines the norms and hence the deviation?" Two basic answers may be offered: (a) It may be the person himself (that is, the patient) who decides that he deviates from a norm. For example, an artist may believe that he suffers from a work inhibition; and he may implement this conclusion by seeking help *for* himself from a psychotherapist. (b) It may be someone other than the patient who decides that the latter is deviant (for example, relatives, physicians, legal authorities, society generally, etc.). In such a case a psychiatrist may be hired by others to do something *to* the patient in order to correct the deviation.

These considerations underscore the importance of asking the question "Whose agent is the psychiatrist?" and of giving a candid answer to it (Szasz, 1956, 1958). The psychiatrist (psychologist or nonmedical psychotherapist), it now develops, may be the agent of the patient, of the relatives, of the school, of the military services, of a business organization, of a court of law, and so forth. In speaking of the psychiatrist as the agent of these persons or organizations, it is not implied that his values concerning norms, or his ideas and aims concerning the proper nature of remedial action, need to coincide exactly with those of his employer. For example, a patient in individual psychotherapy may believe that his salvation lies in a new marriage; his psychotherapist need not share this hypothesis. As the patient's agent, however, he must abstain from bringing social or legal force to bear on the patient which would prevent him from putting his beliefs into action. If his *contract* is with the patient, the psychiatrist (psycho-therapist) may disagree with him or stop his treatment; but he cannot engage others to obstruct the patient's aspirations. Similarly, if a psychiatrist is engaged by a court to determine the sanity of a criminal, he need not fully share the legal authorities' values and intentions in regard to the criminal and the means available for dealing with him. But the psychiatrist is expressly barred from stating, for example, that it is not the criminal who is "insane" but the men who wrote the law on the basis of which the very actions that are being judged are regarded as "criminal." Such an opinion could be voiced, of course, but not in a court-room, and not by a psychiatrist who makes it his practice to assist the court in performing its daily work.

To recapitulate: In actual contemporary social usage, the finding of a mental illness is made by establishing a deviance in behavior from certain psychosocial, ethical, or legal norms. The judgment may be made, as in medicine, by the patient, the physician (psychiatrist), or others. Remedial action, finally, tends to be sought in a therapeutic—or covertly medical—framework, thus creating a situation in which *psychosocial, ethical,* and/or *legal deviations* are claimed to be correctible by (so-called) *medical action.* Since medical action is designed to correct only medical deviations, it seems logically absurd to expect that it will help solve problems whose very existence had been defined and established on nonmedical grounds. I think that these considerations may be fruitfully applied to the present use of tranquilizers and, more generally, to what might be expected of drugs of whatever type in regard to the amelioration or solution of problems in human living.

THE ROLE OF ETHICS IN PSYCHIATRY

Anything that people *do*—in contrast to things that *happen* to them (Peters, 1958)—takes place in a context of value. In this broad sense, no human activity is devoid of ethical implications. When the values underlying certain activities are widely shared, those who participate in their pursuit may lose sight of them altogether. The discipline of medicine, both as a pure science (for example, research) and as a technology (for example, therapy), contains many ethical considerations and judgments. Unfortunately, these are often denied, minimized, or merely kept out of focus; for the ideal of the medical profession as well as of the people whom it serves seems to be having a system of medicine (allegedly) free of ethical value. This sentimental notion is expressed by such things as the doctor's willingness to treat and help patients irrespective of their religious or political beliefs, whether they are rich or poor, etc. While there may be some grounds for this belief—albeit it is a view that is not impressively true even in these regards—the fact remains that ethical considerations encompass a vast range of human affairs. By making the practice of medicine neutral in regard to some specific issues of value need not, and cannot, mean that it can be kept free from all such values. The practice of medicine is intimately tied to ethics; and the first thing that we must do, it seems to me, is to try to make this clear and explicit. I shall let this matter rest here, for it does not concern us specifically in this essay. Lest there be any vagueness, however, about how or where ethics and medicine meet, let me remind the reader of such issues as birth control, abortion, suicide, and euthanasia as only a few of the major areas of current ethicomedical controversy.

   Psychiatry, I submit, is very much more intimately tied to problems of ethics than is medicine. I use the word "psychiatry" here to refer to that contemporary discipline which is concerned with *problems in living* (and not with diseases of the brain, which are problems for neurology). Problems in human relations can be analyzed, interpreted, and given meaning only within given social and ethical contexts. Accordingly, it *does* make a difference—arguments to the contrary notwithstanding—what the psychiatrist's socioethical orientations happen to be; for these will influence his ideas on what is wrong with the patient, what deserves comment or interpretation, in what possible directions change might be desirable, and so forth. Even in medicine proper, these factors play a role, as for instance, in the divergent orientations which physicians, depending on their religious affiliations, have toward such things as birth control and therapeutic abortion. Can anyone really believe that a psychotherapist's ideas concerning religious belief, slavery, or other similar issues play no role in his practical work? If they do make a difference, what are we to infer from it? Does it not seem reasonable that we ought to have different psychiatric therapies—each expressly recognized for the ethical positions which they embody—for, say, Catholics and Jews, religious persons and agnostics, democrats and communists, white supremacists and Negroes, and so on? Indeed, if we look at how psychiatry is actually practiced today (especially in the United States), we find that people do seek psychiatric help in accordance with their social status and ethical beliefs (Hollingshead & Redlich, 1958). This should really not surprise us more than being told that practicing Catholics rarely frequent birth control clinics.

The foregoing position which holds that contemporary psychotherapists deal with problems in living, rather than with mental illnesses and their cures, stands in opposition to a currently prevalent claim, according to which mental illness is just as "real" and "objective" as bodily illness. This is a confusing claim since it is never known exactly what is meant by such words as "real" and "objective." I suspect, however, that what is intended by the proponents of this view is to create the idea in the popular mind that mental illness is some sort of disease entity, like an infection or a malignancy. If this were true, one could *catch* or *get* a "mental illness," one might *have* or *harbor* it, one might *transmit* it to others, and finally one could get *rid* of it. In my opinion, there is not a shred of evidence to support this idea. To the contrary, all the evidence is the other way and supports the view that what people now call mental illnesses are for the most part *communications* expressing unacceptable ideas, often framed, moreover, in an unusual idiom. The scope of this essay allows me to do no more than mention this alternative theoretical approach to this problem (Szasz, 1957c).

This is not the place to consider in detail the similarities and differences between bodily and mental illnesses. It shall suffice for us here to emphasize only one important difference between them: namely, that whereas bodily disease refers to public, physicochemical occurrences, the notion of mental illness is used to codify relatively more private, sociopsychological happenings of which the observer (diagnostician) forms a part. In other words, the psychiatrist does not stand *apart* from what he observes, but is, in Harry Stack Sullivan's apt words, a "participant observer." This means that he is *committed* to some picture of what he considers reality—and to what he thinks society considers reality—and he observes and judges the patient's behavior in the light of these considerations. This touches on our earlier observation that the notion of mental symptom itself implies a comparison between observer and observed, psychiatrist and patient. This is so obvious that I may be charged with belaboring trivialities. Let me therefore say once more that my aim in presenting this argument was expressly to criticize and counter a prevailing contemporary tendency to deny the moral aspects of psychiatry (and psychotherapy) and to substitute for them allegedly value-free medical considerations. Psychotherapy, for example, is being widely practiced as though it entailed nothing other than restoring the patient from a state of mental sickness to one of mental health. While it is generally accepted that mental illness has something to do with man's social (or inter-personal) relations, it is paradoxically maintained that problems of values (that is, of ethics) do not arise in this process.[1] Yet, in one sense, much of psycho-therapy may revolve around nothing other than the elucidation and weighing of goals and value—many of which may be mutually contradictory—and the means whereby they might best be harmonized, realized, or relinquished.

The diversity of human values and the methods by means of which they may be realized is so vast, and many of them remain so unacknowledged, that they cannot fail but lead to conflicts in human relations. Indeed, to say that human relations at all levels—from mother to child, through husband and wife, to nation and nation—are fraught with stress, strain, and disharmony is, once again, making the obvious explicit. Yet, what may be obvious may be also poorly understood. This I think is the case here. For it seems to me that—at least in our scientific theories of behavior—we have failed to *accept* the simple fact that human relations are inherently fraught with difficulties and that to make them even relatively harmonious requires much patience and hard work. I submit that the idea of mental illness is now being put to work to obscure certain difficulties which at present may be inherent—not that they need be unmodifiable—in the social intercourse of persons. If this is true, the concept functions as a disguise; for instead of calling attention to conflicting human needs, aspirations, and values, the notion of mental illness provides an amoral and impersonal "thing" (an "illness") as an explanation for *problems in living* (Szasz, 1959). We may recall in this connection that not so long ago it was devils and witches who were held responsible for men's problems in social living. The belief in mental illness, as something other than man's trouble in getting along with his fellow man, is the proper heir to the belief in demonology and witchcraft. Mental illness exists or is "real" in exactly the same sense in which witches existed or were "real."

CHOICE, RESPONSIBILITY, AND PSYCHIATRY

While I have argued that mental illnesses do not exist, I obviously did not imply that the social and psychological occurrences to which this label is currently being attached also do not exist. Like the personal and social troubles which people had in the Middle Ages, they are real enough. It is the labels we give them that concern us and, having labelled them, what we do about them. While

---

[1] Freud went so far as to say that: "I consider ethics to be taken for granted. Actually I have never done a mean thing" (Jones, 1957, p. 247). This surely is a strange thing to say for someone who has studied man as a social being as closely as did Freud. I mention it here to show how the notion of "illness" (in the case of psychoanalysis, "psychopathology," or "mental illness") was used by Freud—and by most of his followers—as a means for classifying certain forms of human behavior as falling within the scope of medicine, and hence (by *fiat*) outside that of ethics!

I cannot go into the ramified implications of this problem here, it is worth noting that a demonologic conception of problems in living gave rise to therapy along theological lines. Today, a belief in mental illness implies—nay, requires—therapy along medical or psychotherapeutic lines.

What is implied in the line of thought set forth here is something quite different. I do not intend to offer a new conception of "psychiatric illness" nor a new form of "therapy." My aim is more modest and yet also more ambitious. It is to suggest that the phenomena now called mental illnesses be looked at afresh and more simply, that they be removed from the category of illnesses, and that they be regarded as the expressions of man's struggle with the problem of *how* he should live. The last mentioned problem is obviously a vast one, its enormity reflecting not only man's inability to cope with his environment, but even more his increasing self-reflectiveness.

By problems in living, then, I refer to that truly explosive chain reaction which began with man's fall from divine grace by partaking of the fruit of the tree of knowledge. Man's awareness of himself and of the world about him seems to be a steadily expanding one, bringing in its wake an ever larger *burden of understanding* (an expression borrowed from Susanne Langer, 1953). *This burden,* then, *is to be expected and must not be misinterpreted.* Our only *rational* means for lightening it is *more understanding,* and appropriate *action* based on such understanding. The main alternative lies in acting as though the burden were not what in fact we perceive it to be and taking refuge in an outmoded theological view of man. In the latter view, man does not fashion his life and much of his world about him, but merely lives out his fate in a world created by superior beings. This may logically lead to pleading nonresponsibility in the face of seemingly unfathomable problems and difficulties. Yet, if man fails to take increasing responsibility for his actions, individually as well as collectively, it seems unlikely that some higher power or being would assume this task and carry this burden for him. Moreover, this seems hardly the proper time in human history for obscuring the issue of man's responsibility for his actions by hiding it behind the skirt of an all-explaining conception of mental illness.

CONCLUSIONS

I have tried to show that the notion of mental illness has outlived whatever usefulness it might have had and that it now functions merely as a convenient myth. As such, it is a true heir to religious myths in general, and to the belief in witchcraft in particular; the role of all these belief-systems was to act as *social tranquilizers,* thus encouraging the hope that mastery of certain specific problems may be achieved by means of substitutive (symbolic-magical) operations. The notion of mental illness thus serves mainly to obscure the everyday fact that life for most people is a continuous struggle, not for biological survival, but for a "place in the sun," "peace of mind," or some other human value. For man aware of himself and of the world about him, once the needs for preserving the body (and perhaps the race) are more or less satisfied, the problem arises as to what he should do with himself. Sustained adherence to the myth of mental illness allows people to avoid facing this problem, believing that mental health, conceived as the absence of mental illness, automatically insures the making of right and safe choices in one's conduct of life. But the facts are all the other way. It is the making of good choices in life that others regard, retrospectively, as good mental health!

The myth of mental illness encourages us, moreover, to believe in its logical corollary: that social intercourse would be harmonious, satisfying, and the secure basis of a "good life" were it not for the disrupting influences of mental illness or "psychopathology." The potentiality for universal human happiness, in this form at least, seems to me but another example of the I-wish-it-were-true type of fantasy. I do believe that human happiness or well-being on a hitherto unimaginably large scale, and not just for a select few, is possible. This goal could be achieved, however, only at the cost of many men, and not just a few being willing and able to tackle their personal, social, and ethical conflicts. This means having the courage and integrity to forego waging battles on false fronts, finding solutions for substitute problems—for instance, fighting the battle of stomach acid and chronic fatigue instead of facing up to a marital conflict.

Our adversaries are not demons, witches, fate, or mental illness. We have no enemy whom we can fight, exorcise, or dispel by "cure." What we do have are *problems in living*—whether these be biologic, economic, political, or sociopsychological. In this essay I was concerned only with problems belonging in the last mentioned category, and within this group mainly with those pertaining to moral values. The field to which modern psychiatry addresses itself is vast, and I made no effort to encompass it all. My argument was limited to the proposition that mental illness is a myth, whose function it is to disguise and thus render more palatable the bitter pill of moral conflicts in human relations.

References

Hollingshead, A. B., and Redlich, F. C. *Social class and mental illness.* New York: Wiley, 1958.

Jones, E. *The life and work of Sigmund Freud.* Vol. III. New York: Basic Books, 1957.

Langer, S. K. *Philosophy in a new key.* New York: Mentor Books, 1953.

Peters, R. S. *The concept of motivation.* London: Routledge & Kegan Paul, 1958.

Szasz, T. S. Malingering: "Diagnosis" or social condemnation? *AMA Arch. Neurol. Psychiat.*, 1956, **76,** 432–443.

Szasz, T. S. *Pain and pleasure; A study of bodily feelings.* New York: Basic Books, 1957. (a)

Szasz, T. S. The problem of psychiatric nosology: A contribution to a situational analysis of psychiatric operations. *Amer. J. Psychiat.*, 1957, **114,** 405–413. (b)

Szasz, T. S. On the theory of psychoanalytic treatment. *Int. J. Psycho-Anal.*, 1957, **38,** 166–182. (c)

Szasz, T. S. Psychiatry, ethics and the criminal law. *Columbia Law Rev.*, 1958, **58,** 183–198.

Szasz, T. S. Moral conflict and psychiatry, *Yale Rev.*, 1959, in press.

3
SOCIALIZATION, COMMAND OF PERFORMANCE, AND MENTAL ILLNESS
Ernest Becker

The essentials for a sociological understanding of behavioral malfunction presented here underline a crucial but simple consideration which has not been sufficiently stressed in discussions of mental illness.[1] It is clear that whatever the origin of malfunction—in biological substrata or in conventional social definition of desirable norm—there are individuals who will not meet the behavioral requirements of their fellows. But in addition to this consideration, there is a less obvious one, namely, that to a self-reflexive, symbol-using animal, the *purely symbolic, social definition of normative behavior is as crucial to action* as is instinctive patterning to any lower organism. The basis for this conclusion is common knowledge to the clinician. However, recapitulation of several crucial features of man's uniqueness in the animal kingdom is warranted in the present context inasmuch as these features become, as we shall review below, the central problem in negotiating social action.

THE PECULIARITY OF HUMAN ACTION

Freud's genius has been credited with many discoveries, notably the dynamic unconscious and the importance of infantile sexuality, with the multifarious effects of these on human behavior. But it is becoming increasingly obvious—or should be—that a comprehensive theory of human behavior will draw upon those discoveries of Freud which figure less prominently in clinical matters and which are of more general import. I am referring specifically to the genesis of the self and the ego, and to the fact of the Oedipal transition—a transition from biological proximal relationship to a succoring figure, to a distanced, symbolic relationship to the internalized values of that figure. These two general, universal developmental trends are crucial in the humanization of Homo sapiens. It is important to underscore that they are based upon one continuous thread: the change from a stimulus-response reaction to primitive anxiety, to an ego-controlled reaction.[2] The latter interposes a series of complex mechanisms between anxiety and the organism, which we have come to know as the self-

Source: Ernest Becker, "Socialization, Command of Performance, and Mental Illness," *American Journal of Sociology,* **67:** 494–501, 1962.
[1] See, e.g., D. P. Ausubel, "Personality Disorder Is Disease," *American Psychologist,* XVI, No. 2 (February, 1961), 69–74; O. H. Mowrer, " 'Sin,' the Lesser of Two Evils," *American Psychologist,* XV (1960), 301–4; T. S. Szasz, "The Myth of Mental Illness," *American Psychologist,* XV (1960), 113–18, and his *The Myth of Mental Illness: Foundations of a Theory of Personal Conduct* (New York: Paul B. Hoeber, Inc., 1961). See also my forthcoming *The Birth and Death of Meaning: A Perspective in Psychiatric Anthropology* (New York: Free Press of Glencoe).
[2] S. Freud, *The Problem of Anxiety* (New York: W. W. Norton & Co., 1936).

system.[3] The bootstraps, so to speak by which man lifts himself above the other animals are those which enable him to handle primitive animal annihilation-anxiety with a durative defense. The self-system is an anxiety-buffering motor that is always idling.

Now it is well known that this unique development in the animal kingdom is possible for only one reason: the development of language, which permits a self-referential existence. As the infant learns "mine-me-I" in that order, he fixes himself in a space-time world populated by named, identifiable objects. Sullivan referred to the self-system as largely a series of linguistic tricks by which the human conciliates his environment—allays his anxiety, that is. Thus, self-reflexivity and anxiety avoidance are two sides of the same coin. They create symbolic action possibilities by making the world safe for a symbolic, self-reflexive animal.

THE SOCIOLOGICAL VIEW

Sociologists have tended to focus their attention, not on the individual, intra-psychic aspects of the defensive operations of this animal, but rather on the fact that a symbolic animal must be fashioned from the symbols inculcated by other animals. Society co-operates in its instrumental dominance over the natural en-vironment by a joint allegiance to a shared symbolic system of meaning. If the behavioral world of the self-reflexive animal is based on a pronominal "I," then the "I" must be separated from the "not-I." In other words, the motivational goals, and the proper actions for reaching those goals, must be jointly defined as more desirable than other alternatives.[4] The animal must have, in brief, a feeling of primary value in a world of meaningful objects. Culture, in this sense, is a symbolic fiction without which the psychological animal could not act. The basis of this fiction is a pattern of values which gives vital meaning and permits action.

The problem of human behavior in social terms is nothing short of prodigious: How to bring the acutely anxiety-sensitive animals to act together, without endangering the fragile self-system of each. How, in other words, to confront a multitude of individuals with each other, and still permit them all the conviction (the fiction) *that each is an object of primary value in a world of meaningful objects.* In the social encounter, the indispensable internal sentiment of warm self-value that serves as an anxiety buffer is exposed to possible undermining by the very same sentiments of all others. We miss the point completely when we consider "face" an idle preoccupation of a decrepit Chinese culture. The apt term "face" refers to the turning outward for public view, and possible mis-handling, of the anxiety-buffering self-esteem, so laboriously fashioned in the process of humanization. Social interaction, in other words, is a potential anarchy of psychological destruction.

When we say that an individual is properly socialized, we mean simply that the process of formation of the self-system has been secure enough to enable

[3] H. S. Sullivan, *The Interpersonal Theory of Psychiatry* (New York: W. W. Norton & Co., 1953).
[4] A. I. Hallowell, *Culture and Experience* (Philadelphia: University of Pennsylvania Press, 1955).

him to sustain interaction with someone other than the agents of his immediate socialization. If he can do this, society provides him with a conventional code of rules for interaction, by which to sustain his own face and to protect the face of others. The intricacies of this code have been masterfully detailed by Erving Goffman, in a series of landmarking writings.[5] With his two central concepts of deference and demeanor, he has shown how society provides for and even maximizes the primary sense of self-value that the individual brings with him to social encounters.

DEFENSIVE NEEDS VERSUS REQUIREMENTS OF SOCIAL ACTION

The problem, from a social point of view, is to respect the privacy and integrity of the individual and, at the very same time, to include him in social interaction. Society does this by a series of conventions which Goffman includes under two main headings: deferential rituals of avoidance and deferential rituals of presentation. The body privacy, separateness, and the integral self of the individual must be accorded a degree of avoidance behavior. Avoidance implies that everyone has the right to keep others at a certain distance and recognizes that the self is personal. Presentation, on the other hand, implies that everyone has the right to engage others, *if it is done properly;* the self is recognized as social. Thus, all the conventions of salutation, farewell, quick formal smiles of acknowledgment, facile compliments, brief adjustments of another's tie or brushing his clothing, and so on, are presentation rituals which engage his self in social intercourse.[6]

When we are slighted by a "snub" we are simply protesting that someone did not acknowledge the social existence of our self. The "Hi" makes "electric" contact and fuses two discrete selves into a social unity. The problem of deference is an extremely touchy one, precisely because self-esteem is at stake. We must exercise a social claim on each other and yet not seem to manipulate. The simple act of engaging someone by offering him a seat is fraught with possibilities of bungling. Rituals of farewell are delicately sensitive, because here the self is being released from a social situation. The release must be gentle, and not an ejection into isolation. An Italian watching his friends pull away in a train will remain on the platform waving a handkerchief in farewell until they are well out of sight—one must not coarsely break off the social fusion of selves; the magic melting must be sustained until it becomes a thinnest thread. The members of a group long accustomed to being together develop subtle cues for taking leave and will melt apart at a slight signal, perhaps undetectable to an observer.

---

[5] "On Face-Work, an Analysis of Ritual Elements in Social Interaction," *Psychiatry*, XVIII (1955), 213–31; "The Nature of Deference and Demeanor," *American Anthropologist*, LVIII, No. 3 (1956), 473–502; and *The Presentation of Self in Everyday Life* ("Doubleday Anchor Book" [Garden City, N.Y.: Doubleday & Co., 1959]).

[6] The details of these rituals are infinite, and nowhere better conceptualized than by Goffman. Each society, of course, has its own conventions for laying social claim to the personal self. In traditional Japan, for example, the self had to be available to society at almost all times—to close one's door during the day was a community offense.

The further problem is that the gestures of presentation which engage the individuals in social intercourse must not encroach too much on their private selves; "a peculiar tension must be maintained"[7] between avoidance and presentation rituals. The individual, in sum, must be assured that if he intrusts his fallible face to society, it will take good care of it for him: "A social relationship . . . can be seen as a way in which the person is more than ordinarily forced to trust his self-image and face to the tact and good conduct of others."[8] If this all seems axiomatic, its simplicity is deceptive. It is only when we consider the complement to deference, the phenomenon of demeanor, that the fictional fabric of social life becomes transparently clear. Demeanor refers to the problem of social action from the point of view of the individual. Demeanor means proper deportment, dress, bearing—in a word, self-regard. The individual is tasked to respect and maintain a sense of self. For an individual to have a sense of self—and this is of fundamental importance—means sustaining a named, identifiable, locus of symbolic causality, which can be counted on to communicate within the social conventions. Demeanor is the *obligation to have a self,* so that there is something *socially transactable.* But the self-contained locus of communication must behave in an expected manner, so that his inclusion within the larger plot is a matter of facility. Otherwise, people would endanger themselves in undertaking interaction with someone who does not present a socially viable self. They would expose their fragile self-esteem to an entirely capricious monstrosity.

Crucial to our understanding of the delicately staged plot of social actors within a social fiction of learned meanings, goals, and values is this: An individual who engages us by manifesting the proper deference must have an equally appropriate sense of demeanor to make the deference socially meaningful—he must present a credible stage personality. If our interlocutor does not have proper self-regard, he threatens us at the very core of our artificial action. It is fundamental to the implicit rules of social life that there must be no hint or revelation of the *unbelievably flimsy basis* for our impassioned life-and-death actions: the revelation that the self is merely an attitude of self-regard and a learned set of arbitrary conventions designed to facilitate symbolic action. The hopeful enjoinder that upholds the social fiction is: "Let us all protect each other by sincere demeanor and convincing presentations, so that we can carry on the business of living." The self-esteem of plural numbers of anxiety-prone animals must be protected so that symbolic action can continue. Not only must it be protected, it must in fact be enhanced by an intricate web of rituals for delicate handling of the self. Man must make provision for the utmost sensitivity in social intercourse. This fine social sensitivity is, as Goffman observes, largely what we mean when we speak of "universal human nature." That marvelous performer, Goethe, who even in his old age radiated an aura of indomitable selfhood, said that there was a "courtesy of the heart which is akin to love." The courtesy is the delicate handling of other selves. The love is the control of one's self so that social life can go on.

---

[7] Goffman, "The Nature of Deference and Demeanor," *op. cit.,* p. 488.
[8] Goffman, "On Face-Work, an Analysis of Ritual Elements in Social Interaction," *op. cit.,* p. 227.

The culture protects social action in two ways. By providing a strict code of social ritual, it makes available an adaptational device designed to prevent the contamination of social intercourse with private data. The more or less "proper" thing to say in each situation is provided. At the same time, it protects the on-going action situation by ablating the irrelevancies of private data. The socially awkward person is one who is not "successfully" socialized from roughly two points of view: (1) His reaction-sensitivity prevents effective communication, and the forward motion of social action in a situation. (2) He has not learned to use with facility the social ritual rules for interaction. We can ask of an individual in this context: "How much 'reaction-sensitivity' is present in his social presentation of face (of his positive-self valuation)?" "To what extent do his needs and sus-ceptibilities risk contaminating the smooth flow of face-saving ritual that the culture needs in order to function?"[9]

THE LINGUISTIC BASIS OF POWER

It is perhaps in the manipulation of the conversational gambits of politeness that we see best the importance to the individual of learning to use the ritual rules for interaction. It is not widely enough recognized that easy handling of the verbal context of action gives the possibility *of direct exercise of power over others.* The individual who uses with facility "I'm *terribly* sorry," "*Good* show!" "*Good* to see you!" and so on, *creates the context of action* for his interlocutor, by his confident manipulation of the conventional ritual verbiage. The parent's enjoinder "Say 'thank you' to the man" is not an inculcation of obsequiousness so much as it is a training in control. It is now up to "the man" to frame an appropriate response, or to end the social situation gracefully. The proper formula delivered defines the situation for the other and is the most direct means of power. The newly liberated slave's reluctance to relinquish his lifelong pattern of obsequious formulas of deference does not derive from his "degener-ate character." Rather, the formulas are his only tools for confident manipulation of the interpersonal situation—proven methods of control for which substitutes are not easily learned. Furthermore, as mentioned above, by verbally setting the tone for action by the proper ritual formula, we permit complementary action by our interlocutor. Not only do we permit it, we compel it, if mutual face is to be sustained. Thus, the subordinate not only calls the tune for his superior, but by doing his part in permitting action to continue, he infuses the situation with meaning. Finally, since action within shared meaning provides the only frame-work for the continual social validation of the actors, we can understand that deference is the means we have of enhancing one another.[10] The ability to use

[9] For example, a schizophrenic may be overperceptive, unable to shut out irrelevant definitions of the interaction situation. Thus, by his inordinate sensitivity to his interlocutor's genitals, for example, he upsets a comfortably singly defined situation with his own private data.

[10] Goffman, "The Nature of Deference and Demeanor," *op. cit.,* p. 493.

its formulas with facility actually means the power to manipulate others by providing the symbolic context for their action.[11]

Conversely, this power has a central role in the creation of the self. The simplest definition of identity is the experience of one's self as the subject and agent of one's powers.[12] Thus, the person who has not been able to exercise his powers has little experience of self, therefore, little identity. Now, using the deference-demeanor model, we can see how identity and self-experience are *socially created:* only by *exercising demeanor* and *experiencing deference* does the person fashion and renew himself by purposeful action in meaningful contexts. Thus, loneliness is not only a suspension in self-acquaintance, it is a suspension in the very fashioning of identity, because, cut off from one's fellows, one cannot exercise demeanor or experience deference. Therefore, he cannot experience his own powers and come to know himself as agent of them. In this sense, identity is simply the measure of power and participation of the individual in the joint cultural staging of self-enhancing ceremony. One might say that everyone should be a talented *metteur en scène* to get along in social life. But he who is so need-disposition sensitive that he fails to learn to manipulate the ritual rules in his early peer contacts is seriously handicapped in building a strong identity: he never feeds his own power and self-acquaintance with the proper staging of demeanor, as well as with the fuel of deference from his fellows.

It is important to realize that the delicate balance of avoidance and presentation rituals is not an easy one to manipulate. And, in order to have any skill at it at all, one needs a clear definition of the situation. It is precisely this that is obscured by poor socialization. A clear definition of the situation demands an apprehension of one's private self, a sensitivity to needs and expectancies in the interaction, and last but not least, a sure cognizance of self-other discreteness. Thus, in simplest terms, we might say that the basis for social ineptitude is the failure to form an adequate phenomenological self. A feeling of primary value, separation, and de-identification of self from the succoring figure, sure possession of one's body—these have all to be under the individual's control if he is at all to get started in the complicated game of role-playing. Otherwise, we have the familiar gaucheries of an overdoing of avoidance ritual, as, for example, by not allowing oneself to be touched when it is quite in order; or overdoing of presentation ritual by overpersonal manipulations and attentions. (Cf. manic kissing and overly intimate compliments, and so on, so upsetting to his interlocutors. "Oh, there's the doctor who was *so* nice to me! Look everyone, there's the most wonderful doctor in the world; Oh I love him, I do love him, he is so super-wonderful. Here let me straighten your glasses, so you can look as handsome as you are wonderful.")

The notorious attribution to children of "cruelty" is simply a recognition that

---

[11] The manic seems to make a frantic bid for this power. But his exaggerated manipulations of the verbal proprieties are shown to be unnatural by the discomfort they create—in place of the comfort they are supposed to create. Only the manic himself is bemusedly comfortable; and in a social context this discrepancy defines his deviance.

[12] E. Fromm, *The Sane Society* (New York: Rinehart & Co., 1955).

they have not yet learned to use the face-preserving and mutually enhancing social conventions. When a child first steps out into the peer group, the selves of others are not yet recognized except as something to be overcome rather than used. ("Cripple!" "fatty!" "four-eyes!") One still basks in the parental omnipotence and has no need as yet to be socially sustained and created. Actually, the early peer group contacts are crucial in learning the social rituals. One result of role-taking practice is sensitivity in sustaining a constant presentation of self against a variably responsive background. Thus, the child learns to sustain his own sense of value even in the face of negative responses. He learns whose evaluation to discount, who is overly private; he sees others making improperly personal gambits in the social situation. We all remember, hopefully, at least one such person with whom we could compare ourselves favorably in early peer interaction, and feel "properly social" at a very early age. For example, there was always one "sore loser" who filled us with a sense of social righteousness. Furthermore, in early peer contacts, the child may learn that he is justified in refusing a negative response as emanating solely from another's private evaluation, not from his own *improperly presented self:* "Wasn't *I* right?" is a plea for reassurance that one is sustaining the social fiction with proper demeanor. By thus mastering early unjust evaluations in the early peer group, the child learns to sustain a steady self-valuation, without resorting to bolstering paranoid responses. He learns a realistic appraisal of the other's unwarranted privatization of the social context.

In the last analysis, *power over others* consists in presenting an infallible self and in commanding dexterous performance of deference. The power of the "natural leader" resides perhaps in such fortunate socialization that a convincing self is invariably put forth, with sharp separation of personal and reality needs. By putting forth a convincing self, the actor obliges others to a more careful deference. The strong self forces others to make an effort at performance that may often be beyond their means. Thus, the aura of his infallibility is enforced as their performance stumbles or becomes painfully effortful. In this sense, everyone is a potential *metteur en scène* who fashions the plot and provides the cues for proper performance by others.[13] Some are more fortunately endowed to set implicitly the tone for the performance by presenting a model self and an unshakable command of the script.[14]

---

[13] Witness man's enormous expenditure of time in self-torture over having failed to say just the right thing at a particular point in conversation: "If only I had said *that!*" "If *only* I had said that." The implication in this galling preoccupation is that it was at *that* point that one could have exercised majestic control over the interaction.

[14] To follow along with the film analogy: One explanation for "involutional" depression lies simply in the fact that an individual can realistically appraise his life as having fallen far short of hoped-for goals, and give up in the face of a bad job (cf. E. Bibring, "The Mechanism of Depression," in P. Greenacre [ed.], *Affective Disorders* [New York: International Universities Press, 1953]). If a sixty-year span be calculated imaginatively as a fictional saga of sixty minutes, one can imagine the depressed *metteur en scene* who after forty minutes (forty years) of plot sees the whole thing as botched. He simply cannot pin a happy ending within twenty minutes on a forty-minute background which does not support the ending with any credulity. Therefore, the fictional meaning of the whole plot is undermined, and he can give it up as an insurmountable assignment by depressive withdrawal.

SOCIALIZATION AS TRAINING IN
COMMAND OF PERFORMANCE

Socialization, then, is a preparation for *social performance* of the individual actor. Using this scheme (deference-demeanor) we might ask two key sociological questions of this individual preparation, questions familiar to the clinician:

"With what behavioral style has the individual *learned* to get his self-rights respected?" How, in other words, has the child obtained appreciation from significant adults of his discrete social self? The manner of obtaining respect for self would be his basic method of comportment, or demeanor. The other important question has to do with determining his basic pattern of orientation to deference: "How has he learned to react to the hierarchialized status of others?" In other words, what kind of cognizance does he have of the plot, the fiction of social action in which he will be expected to perform? These two sets of questions are separated for conceptual purposes; actually they are part of the same judgment: *How has the actor been trained as a performer?* The social judgment of the individual can be phrased in stark terms of his rule-following ability.

Transference, understood sociologically, is simply rule-following ability as it is constricted within a narrow stylistic range. The artificial crystallization of this stylistic range is what takes place in psychoanalytic therapy. By analyzing it, the analyst hopes to permit performance over a broader range: he presents the patient "with the possibility of a greater number of choices."[15]

The individual we term schizophrenic may well be one who has never learned the simple bases for the possession of real power over his fellows by aptly wielding the verbal armament of social ritual. In Bateson's double-bind theory of schizophrenia, the individual is prevented, by ambiguities and inconsistencies of the environment, from forming a firmly oriented and consistently recognized self. From the outset, therefore, he does not have the wherewithal to play the ritual game on social terms. He has nothing that he can consistently present to confront the potential threats and uncertainties of the environment (except perhaps a certain "unanchored" symbolic dexterity to be satisfied in library halls; or, if illiterate, in shamanistic fantasies). The young schizophrenic may often provide the best example of failure to handle even the simple greeting. With a self-esteem brittle to the core, the threat of an encounter can be overwhelming.

---

[15] In this context, it is worth mentioning the usual fascination of youth for the theater. Goethe, it will be remembered, thought of acting as an indispensable preparation for adult life (Wilhelm Meister). Theatrical acting is a vicarious freedom of acting *control* of a situation. Especially noteworthy of our attention here is that this control is gained merely by *properly saying the right things.* Perfect acting is a unique exercise in omnipotence; by infallible wielding of deference and demeanor, the actor is at one and the same time indisputed director. Those of us who have never performed theatrically have perhaps experienced the sheer power-control aspects of language in learning a foreign tongue. Facility in speaking a foreign language partakes somewhat of a kindred experience in psychotherapy: the individual may find that he is capable of utterances which usher others into appropriate complementary action; but which utterances, because they are new (and in a foreign tongue) he at first experiences as unreal and somewhat ego-alien. It is then that he can best "watch himself perform" and see in action the power aspects of language. When the utterances are finally reduced to habit, the self-critical and the acting individual becomes more fused. One's first sojourn abroad may be a quasi-psychotherapeutic exercise in freedom and power.

One schizophrenic at the beginning of his army career signaled his "queerness" to other soldiers. He learned that a simple greeting used by all never failed to elicit a friendly response. He followed others around, even to the latrine, repeating the greeting again and again. Another learned, perhaps for the first time, a sure ritual of presentation, a reliable way to engage another in social intercourse, without eliciting a hostile response: one had only to offer a cigarette. But even this act has its appropriateness, and the others quickly became embarrassed by his incessant offerings of handfuls of cigarettes, often at inappropriate times.

One cannot overemphasize the fact that the basic pattern of deference-demeanor in a society is the necessary social nutrient for the continuing creation of the personal significance of the social actors—a sort of public mana in which everyone is rejuvenated and supplied. There is a continuing affirmation of meaning in deference-demeanor social transactions which, although purely on a fictional-symbolic level of discourse, seems vital to the very organization of the self. This symbolic sustenance, in other words, seems a *sine qua non* for creating and maintaining an integral symbolic animal. This idea in itself is certainly not new, but its consequences have still not been followed through broadly enough in psychiatry, nor with the requisite theoretical relentlessness: that we cogitate this whole problem on the organism's purely symbolic level of functioning.

Using his idea of deference and demeanor within the framework of a socially self-sustaining fiction, Goffman makes a bold attack upon the label "mental illness." It would refer, simply, to those individuals "who are the least ready to project a sustainable self."[16] Those, in other words, who most directly undermine the mutually sustaining fiction of social ceremonial and who thus prevent the peculiar type of self-justifying action necessary to the continual anxiety-buffering needs of the human animal. It is these individuals who frustrate, by their ineptitude, the best efforts of the other *metteurs en scène* to make the show go on. "One of the bases upon which mental hospitals throughout the world segregate their patients is degree of easily apparent 'mental illness.' By and large this means that patients are graded according to the degree to which they violate ceremonial rules of social intercourse."[17] However, it would be wrong to be misled by words like "ceremonial" into thinking that failure to perform is anything but a vitally serious matter to a symbolic animal. Whether we use the word "fictional" to describe the anxiety-buffering self-system that is created by artificial linguistic symbols, or "ceremonial" to subsume the social means of protecting this fragile self-system, it is plain that we are not talking about inconsequential matters. These fictions are not superfluous creations that could be "put aside" so that the "more serious" business of life could continue. The flesh-and-blood action of lower animals is no more infused with seriousness than is the ethereal, shadowy, symbolic conduct with which man organizes his dominion over nature. We may deal with flimsier coin, but like the abstractness of high finance, the business is perhaps even the more serious for it.

[16] E. Goffman, "The Nature of Deference and Demeanor," *op. cit.*, p. 497.
[17] *Ibid.*

CONCLUSION

The view that social life is a symbolic, fictional nutrient for a self-reflexive, symbolic animal represents one direct, theoretical approach to the problems of behavioral malfunction. Seen from the individual point of view, this problem presents itself in terms of the individual's ability to sustain a self of positive value in a world of meaning and to act according to the social conventions for sustaining and reinforcing that meaning by mutual support. When we realize that the action world of a symbolic animal is fictional and continually fabricated, nourished, and validated, this does not diminish the importance of that world to the behavior of Homo sapiens. There remains the problem of individuals who *cannot follow* the social ritual rules. Questions to which behavioral specialists should be sensitized are: "In what ways is the manner in which this individual has learned to handle anxiety a hindrance in his performance of the ceremonial that permits sustenance of the social fiction of shared meaning?" "What are the rules for performance which society itself projects?" Alertness to questions such as these would lead to a more sensitive understanding of the variations in performance ability of the individual actors, and (as in existing research) the reasons for that variation. Finally, and not least important, it would contribute to a greater flexibility of appraisal of the conditions for social becoming in an open democratic society.[18]

4
SOCIETAL REACTION TO DEVIANT BEHAVIOR: PROBLEMS OF THEORY AND METHOD
John I. Kitsuse

Sociological theory and research in the area traditionally known as "social pathology" have been concerned primarily with the classification and analysis of *deviant forms of behavior* and relatively little attention has been given to societal reactions to deviance.[1] In a recent paper, Merton has noted this lack of a "system-

---

[18] E. Becker, "The Relevance to Psychiatry of Recent Research in Anthropology," *American Journal of Psychotherapy*, Spring, 1962.

Source: John I. Kitsuse, "Societal Reaction to Deviant Behavior: Problems of Theory and Method," *Social Problems*, 9: 247–256, 1962.

I have profited from the critical comments and suggestions of Herbert R. Barringer, Aaron V. Cicourel, Sheldon L. Messinger, and H. Jay Shaffer. Troy S. Duster's valuable assistance in the analysis of the data is gratefully acknowledged.

[1] A notable exception is the work of Edwin M. Lemert who systematically incorporates the concept of societal reaction in his theory of sociopathic behavior. See *Social Pathology*, McGraw-Hill, New York: 1951.

atic *classification* of the responses of the conventional or conforming members of a group to deviant behavior."[2] Similarly, Cohen has observed that "a sociology of deviant behavior-conformity will have to devise ways of conceptualizing responses to deviant behavior from the standpoint of their relevance to the production or extinction of deviant behavior."[3] In this paper, I shall discuss some of the theoretical and methodological issues posed by the problem of societal reactions to deviant behavior and report on a preliminary attempt to formulate a research design which specifically takes them into account.

I propose to shift the focus of theory and research from the forms of deviant behavior to the *processes by which persons come to be defined as deviant by others.* Such a shift requires that the sociologist view as problematic what he generally assumes as given—namely, that certain forms of behavior are *per se* deviant and are so defined by the "conventional or conforming members of a group." This assumption is frequently called into question on empirical grounds when the societal reaction to behaviors defined as deviant by the sociologist is non-existent, indifferent, or at most mildly disapproving. For example, in his discussion of "ritualism" as a form of deviant behavior, Merton states that it is not that such behavior is treated by others as deviant which identifies it as deviant "since the overt behavior is institutionally permitted, though not culturally prescribed."[4] Rather, the behavior is deviant because it "clearly represents a departure from the cultural model in which men are obliged to move onward and upward in the social hierarchy."[5] The discrepancy between the theoretically hypothesized and empirically observable societal reaction is also noted by Lemert: "It is fairly easy to think of situations in which serious offenses against laws commanding public respect have only mild penalty or have gone entirely unpunished. Conversely, cases are easily discovered in which a somewhat minor violation of legal rules has provoked surprisingly stringent penalties."[6]

Clearly, the forms of behavior *per se* do not activate the processes of societal reaction which sociologically differentiate deviants from non-deviants. Thus, a central problem for theory and research in the sociology of deviance may be stated as follows: What are the behaviors which are defined by members of the group, community, or society as deviant, and how do those definitions organize and activate the societal reactions by which persons come to be differentiated and treated as deviants? In formulating the problem in this way, the point of view of those who interpret and define behavior as deviant must explicitly be incorporated into a sociological definition of deviance. Accordingly, deviance may be conceived as a process by which the members of a group, community, or society (1) interpret behavior as deviant, (2) define persons who so behave as a certain kind of deviant, and (3) accord them the treatment considered appropriate to such deviants. In the following pages, this conception of deviance and

[2] Robert K. Merton, "Social Conformity, Deviation, and Opportunity-Structures: A Comment on the Contributions of Dubin and Cloward," *American Sociological Review,* **24** (1959), pp. 177–189.

[3] Albert K. Cohen, "The Study of Social Disorganization and Deviant Behavior," in *Sociology Today,* R. Merton, L. Broom, and L. Cottrell, eds., Basic Books: New York, 1959, pp. 465–466.

[4] Robert K. Merton, *Social Theory and Social Structure,* revised, Free Press: Glencoe, 1957, p. 150.

[5] *Ibid.,* p. 150.

[6] *Op. cit.,* p. 55.

societal reaction will be applied to the processes by which persons come to be defined and treated as homosexuals.

SOCIETAL REACTIONS TO "HOMOSEXUAL BEHAVIOR"

As a form of deviant behavior, homosexuality presents a strategically important theoretical and empirical problem for the study of deviance. In the sociological and anthropological literature[7] homosexual behavior and the societal reactions to it are conceptualized within the framework of ascribed sex statuses and the socialization of individuals to those statuses. The ascription of sex statuses is presumed to provide a complex of culturally prescribed roles and behaviors which individuals are expected to learn and perform. Homosexual roles and behaviors are conceived to be "inappropriate" to the individual's ascribed sex status, and thus theoretically they are defined as deviant.

With reference to American society, Allison Davis states: "Sex-typing of behavior and privileges is even more rigid and lasting in our society than is age-typing. Indeed, sexual status and color-caste status are the only life-long forms of rank. In our society, one can escape them in approved fashion only by death. Whereas sexual mobility is somewhat less rare today than formerly, sex-inappropriate behavior, social or physical, is still one of the most severely punished infractions of our social code."[8] In Lemert's terminology, norms concerning sex-appropriate behavior have a high degree of "compulsiveness" and social disapproval of violations is stringent and effective.[9] Homosexuals themselves appear to share this conception of the societal reaction to their behavior, activities, and subculture.[10]

Such a view of homosexuality would lead one to hypothesize that "sex appropriate" (and conversely "sex-inappropriate") behaviors are unambiguously prescribed, deviations from those prescriptions are invariably interpreted as immoral, and the reactions of the conventional and conforming members of the society to such deviations are uniformly severe and effective. The evidence which apparently supports this hypothesis is not difficult to find, particularly with reference to the definition and treatment of male homosexuals. Individuals who are publicly identified as homosexuals are frequently denied the social, economic, and legal rights of "normal" males. Socially they may be treated as objects of amusement, ridicule, scorn, and often fear; economically they may be

[7] For examples, see Talcott Parsons and Robert F. Bales, *Family Socialization and Interaction Process*, Free Press: Glencoe, 1955, pp. 103–105; Ruth Benedict, "Continuities and Discontinuities in Cultural Conditioning," *Psychiatry*, **1** (1938), pp. 161–167; Abram Kardiner and Associates, *Psychological Frontiers of Society*, Columbia University Press: New York, 1945, pp. 57, 88, etc.; Clifford Kirkpatrick, *The Family*, Ronald Press: New York, 1955, pp. 57–58; Margaret Mead, *Sex and Temperament*, William Morrow: New York, 1955.

[8] Allison Davis, "American Status Systems and the Socialization of the Child," *American Sociological Review*, **6** (1941), p. 350.

[9] *Op. cit.*, Chapter 4.

[10] Evelyn Hooker, "Sequences in Homosexual Identification," read at the meetings of the American Sociological Association, 1960; Donald Webster Cory, *The Homosexual in America*, Greenburg: New York, 1951, esp. Part I.

summarily dismissed from employment; legally they are frequently subject to interrogation and harrassment by police.

In citing such evidence, however, it is important to note that the societal reaction to and the differentiation of homosexuals from the "normal" population is a consequence of the fact that the former are "known" to be homosexuals by some individuals, groups or agencies. Thus, within the framework of the present formulation of homosexuality as a form of deviant behavior, the processes by which individuals come to be "known" and treated as sexually deviant will be viewed as problematic and a problem for empirical investigation. I shall not be concerned here with the so-called "latent homosexual" unless he is so defined by others and differentially treated as a consequence of that definition. Nor will I be concerned with the variety of "internal" conflicts which may form the "clinical" picture of the homosexual except insofar as such conflicts are manifested in behavior leading others to conceive of him as a homosexual. In short, I shall proceed on the principle that it is only when individuals are defined and identified by others as homosexuals and accorded the treatment considered "appropriate" for individuals so defined that a homosexual "population" is produced for sociological investigation.[11] With reference to homosexuality, then, the empirical questions are: What forms of behavior do persons in the social system consider to be "sex-inappropriate," how do they interpret such behaviors, and what are the consequences of those interpretations for their reactions to individuals who are perceived to manifest such behaviors?

In a preliminary attempt to investigate these questions, an interview schedule was constructed[12] and administered to approximately seven hundred individuals, most of whom were college undergraduates. The sample was neither random nor representative of any specified population, and the generalizability of the interview materials is limited except insofar as they are relevant to the previously noted hypothesis that homosexual behavior is uniformly defined, interpreted, and negatively sanctioned. The interview materials will therefore be used for the purpose of illustrating the theory and method of the present conception of deviance and societal reaction.

The objectives of the interview were threefold: It attempted to document (1) the behavior forms which are interpreted as deviant, (2) the processes by which persons who manifest such behaviors are defined and (3) treated as deviant. Thus, in the construction of the interview schedule, what the interviewees considered to be "deviant" behavior, the interpretations of such behavior, and the actions of subjects toward those perceived as deviant were addressed as empirical questions. Labels such as alcoholic, illiterate, illegitimate child, and ex-convict were assumed to be categories employed by persons in everyday life to classify deviants, but the behavioral forms by which they identify individuals as deviants were treated as problematic. "Sexual deviant" was one of ten categories of deviants about which subjects were questioned in the interview. Among

---

[11] This principle has been suggested by Harold Garfinkel. See "Some Sociological Concepts and Methods for Psychiatrists," *Psychiatric Research Reports*, 6 (1956), pp. 181–195.
[12] The interview schedule and methods were conceived and constructed in consultation with Aaron V. Cicourel.

the more than seven hundred subjects interviewed, seventy-five stated they had "known" a homosexual and responded to questions concerning their experiences with such individuals. The data presented below are drawn from the protocols of interviews with this group of subjects.

The interview proceeded as follows:

The subject was asked "Have you ever known anyone who was a sexual deviant?" If he questioned the meaning of "deviant," the subject was asked to consider the question using his own meaning of "sexual deviant."

When the subject stated he had known a sexual deviant—a homosexual in this case—as he defined the term, he was asked to think about the most recent incident involving him in an encounter with such a person. He was then asked "When was the first time you noticed (found out) that this person was a homosexual?" followed by "What was the situation? What did you notice about him? How did he behave?" This line of questioning was focused on the interaction between the subject and the alleged deviant to obtain a detailed description of the situation which led the subject to define the person as homosexual. The subject's description of the person's behavior was systematically probed to clarify the terms of his description, particularly those which were interpretive rather than descriptive.

EVIDENCE OF HOMOSEXUALITY

Responses to the question "When was the first time you noticed (found out) that this person was homosexual?" and the related probes suggest that an individual's sexual "normality" may be called into question with reference to two broad categories of evidence. (a) *Indirect evidence* in the form of a rumor, an acquaintance's experience with the individual in question subsequently communicated to the subject, or general reputational information concerning the individual's behavior, associates, and sexual predilections may be the occasion for suspecting him to be "different." Many subjects reported that they first "found out" or "knew" that the individuals in question were homosexuals through the reports of others or by "reputation." Such information was generally accepted by the subjects without independent verification. Indeed, the information provided a new perspective for their retrospective as well as prospective observations and interpretations of the individuals' behaviors. An example of how hearsay organizes observation and interpretation is the following statement by a 35-year-old male (a draftsman):

I: Then this lieutenant was a homosexual?
S: Yes.
I: How did you find out about it?
S: The guy he approached told me. After that, I watched him. Our company was small and we had a bar for both enlisted men and officers. He would come in and try to be friendly with one or two of the guys.
I: Weren't the other officers friendly?

S: Sure, they would come in for an occasional drink; some of them had been with the company for three years and they would sometimes slap you on the back, but he tried to get over friendly.

I: What do you mean "over friendly"?

S: He had only been there a week. He would try to push himself on a couple of guys— he spent more time with the enlisted personnel than is expected from an officer.

(b) *Direct observation* by the subject of the individual's behavior may be the basis for calling the latter's sexual "normality" into question. The descriptions of behavior which subjects took to be indicative of homosexuality varied widely and were often vague. Most frequently the behaviors cited were those *"which everyone knows"* are indications of homosexuality. For example, a 20-year-old male subject reports an encounter with a stranger at a bar:

I: What happened during your conversation?

S: He asked me if I went to college and I said I did. Then he asked me what I was studying. When I told him psychology he appeared very interested.

I: What do you mean "interested"?

S: Well, you know queers really go for this psychology stuff.

I: Then what happened?

S: Ah, let's see. I'm not exactly sure, but somehow we got into an argument about psychology and to prove my point I told him to pick an area of study. Well, he appeared to be very pensive and after a great thought he said, "Okay, let's take homosexuality."

I: What did you make of that?

S: Well, by now I figured the guy was queer so I got the hell outta there.

The responses of other subjects suggest that an individual is particularly suspect when he is observed to behave in a manner which deviates from the *behaviors-held-in-common* among members of the group to which he belongs. For example, a behavior which is presumed to be held-in-common among sailors in the U. S. Navy is intense and active sexual activity. When a sailor does not affirm, at least verbally, his interest in such activity, his competence as a "male" may be called into question. A 22-year-old engineer, recently discharged from the Navy, responds to the "how did you first know" question as follows:

All of a sudden you just get suspicious of something. I began to wonder about him. He didn't go in for leave activities that most sailors go for. You know, girls and high times. He just never was interested and when you have been out at sea for a month or two, you're interested. That just wasn't Navy, and he was a career man.

Although the responses of our subjects indicate there are many behavioral gestures which "everyone knows" are indicators of homosexuality in males, there are relatively few such gestures that lead persons to suspect females of homosexuality. Following is an excerpt from a 21-year-old college co-ed whose remarks illustrate this lack of definite indicators *prior* to her labeling of an acquaintance as a homosexual:

I: When was the first time you noticed she was a deviant?
S: I didn't notice it. I thought she had a masculine appearance when I first saw her anyway.
I: What do you mean?
S: Oh, her haircut, her heavy eyebrows. She had a rather husky build.
I: Exactly when did you think she had a masculine appearance?
S: It was long after [the first meeting] that I found out that she was "one."
I: How do you define it?
S: Well, a lesbian. I don't know too much about them. It was ——— who told me about her.
I: Did you notice anything else about her [at the first meeting]?
S: No, because you really don't know unless you're looking for those things.

Unlike "effeminate" appearance and gestures in males, "masculine" appearance in females is apparently less likely to be immediately linked to the suspicion or imputation of homosexuality. The statements of the subject quoted above indicate that although "masculine appearance" is an important element in her conception of a lesbian, its significance did not become apparent to her until a third person told her the girl was homosexual. The remarks of other subjects in our sample who state they have "known" female homosexuals reveal a similar ambiguity in their interpretations of what they describe as indicators of sexual deviance.

A third form of evidence by direct observation is behaviors which the subjects interpreted to be *overt sexual propositions*. Descriptions of such propositions ranged from what the subjects considered to be unmistakable evidence of the person's sexual deviance to ambiguous gestures which they did not attempt to question in the situation. The following is an excerpt from an interview with a 24-year-old male school teacher who recounts an experience in a Korean Army barrack:

I: What questions did he [the alleged homosexual] ask?
S: "How long have you been in Korea?" I told him. "What do you think of these Korean girls?" which I answered, "Not too much because they are dirty." I thought he was probably homesick and wanted someone to talk to. I do not remember what he said then until he said, "How much do you have?" I answered him by saying, "I don't know, about average I guess." Then he said, "Can I feel it just once?" To this I responded with, "Get the hell out of here," and I gave him a shove when he reached for me as he asked the question.

In a number of interviews, the subjects' statements indicate that they interpreted the sequence of the alleged deviants' behavior as progressively inappropriate or peculiar in the course of their interaction with them. The link between such behavior and their judgment that a sexual proposition was being made was frequently established by the subjects' growing realization of its deviant character. A 21-year-old male subject recalls the following experience involving his high school tennis coach who had invited him to dinner:

S: Anyway, when I get there he served dinner, and as I think back on it—I didn't notice it at the time—but I remember that he did act sort of effeminate. Finally he got up to change a record and picked up some of my English themes. Then he brought them over and sat down beside me. He began to explain some of my mistakes in my themes, and in the meantime he slipped his arms around me.

I: Would you say that this was done in a friendly manner or with an intent of hugging you or something?

S: Well, no, it was just a friendly gesture of putting his arm around my shoulder. At that time, I didn't think anything of it, but as he continued to explain my mistakes, he started to rub my back. Then he asked me if I wanted a back rub. So I said "No! I don't need one." At this time, I began thinking something was funny anyway. So I said that I had to go. . . .

THE IMPUTATION OF HOMOSEXUALITY

When a detailed description of the subject's evidence concerning the alleged homosexual was obtained, he was asked, "What did you make of that?" to elicit information about how he interpreted the person's observed or reported behavior. This line of questioning yielded data on the inferential process by which the subject linked his information about the individual to the deviant category "homosexual."

A general pattern revealed by the subjects' responses to this section of the interview schedule is that when an individual's sexual "normality" is called into question, by whatever form of evidence, the imputation of homosexuality is documented by *retrospective interpretations* of the deviant's behavior, a process by which the subject re-interprets the individual's past behavior in the light of the new information concerning his sexual deviance. This process is particularly evident in cases where the prior relationship between the subject and the alleged homosexual was more than a chance encounter or casual acquaintanceship. The subjects indicate that they reviewed their past interactions with the individuals in question, searching for subtle cues and nuances of behavior which might give further evidence of the alleged deviance. This retrospective reading generally provided the subjects with just such evidence to support the conclusion that "this is what was going on all the time."

Some of the subjects who were interviewed were themselves aware of their retrospective interpretations in defining individuals as sexually deviant. For example, a 23-year-old female graduate student states:

I: Will you tell me more about the situation?

S: Well, their relationship was a continuous one, although I think that it is a friendship now as I don't see them together as I used to; I don't think it is still homosexual. When I see them together, they don't seem to be displaying the affection openly as they did when I first realized the situation.

I: How do you mean "openly"?

S: Well, they would hold each other's hand in public places.

I: And what did you make of this?

S: Well, I really don't know, because I like to hold people's hands, too! I guess I actually didn't see this as directly connected with the situation. What I mean is that, if I hadn't seen that other incident [she had observed the two girls in bed together] I probably wouldn't have thought of it [i.e., hand-holding] very much. . . . Well, actually, there were a few things that I questioned later on that I hadn't thought really very much about. . . . I can remember her being quite affectionate towards me several times when we were in our room together, like putting her arm around my shoulder. Or I remember one time specifically when she asked me for a kiss. I was shocked at the time, but I laughed it off jokingly.

THE INTERACTIONAL CONTEXTS
OF SOCIETAL REACTIONS

When the description of the alleged deviant's behavior and the subject's interpretations of that behavior were recorded, the subject was asked "What did you do then?" This question was directed toward documenting societal reactions to deviant behavior. Forms of behavior *per se* do not differentiate deviants from non-deviants; it is the responses of the conventional and conforming members of the society who identify and interpret behavior as deviant which sociologically transform persons into deviants. Thus, in the formulation of deviance proposed here, if the subject observes an individual's behavior and defines it as deviant but does not accord him differential treatment as a consequence of that definition, the individual is not sociologically deviant.

The reactions of the subjects to individuals they defined as homosexuals ranged from immediate withdrawal from the scene of interaction and avoidance of further encounters with the alleged deviants to the maintenance of the prior relationship virtually unaltered by the imputation of deviance. The following responses to the question "What did you do then?" illustrate the variation in sanctions directed toward persons defined as homosexuals.

Explicit disapproval and immediate withdrawal.   The most negatively toned and clearly articulated reaction reported by our subjects is that of the previously quoted Korean War veteran. It is interesting to note that extreme physical punishment as a reaction to persons defined as homosexuals, a reaction which is commonly verbalized by "normal" males as proper treatment of "queers," is not reported by any of the subjects. When physical force is used, it is invariably in response to the deviant's direct physical overtures, and even then it is relatively mild, e.g., "I gave him a shove when he reached for me."

Explicit disapproval and subsequent withdrawal.   In the following excerpt, a

20-year-old male college student describes an encounter with a man whom he met in a coffee shop. In the course of their conversation, the man admitted his homosexuality to the subject. The two left the coffee shop and walked together to the subway station.

I: What happened then?

S: We got to the subway whereupon he suggested that he hail a cab and take me up to Times Square—a distance of almost 40 blocks.

I: Did you agree, and what did you think?

S: Yes, I thought he was just being very nice and I had no qualms about getting in a cab with a homosexual since I was quite sure I could protect myself against any advances in a cab.

I: What happened then?

S: When we had ridden a little distance, he put his hand on my knee, and I promptly removed it saying that it just wasn't right and that I wanted nothing of it. However, after a while, he put his hand back. This time I didn't take it away for a while because I was interested in what he would do. It was the funniest thing—he rubbed and caressed my knee the same way in which I would have done this to a girl. This time I took his hand and hit him across the chest with it, telling him to "cut it out." Finally, we got to Times Square, and I got out.

This example and that provided by the Korean War veteran's reaction to behavior interpreted as overt sexual propositions suggest the possibility that responses to persons suspected of homosexuality or defined as homosexuals on the basis of more indirect evidence of appearance, "confessions," hearsay, reputation, or association will vary within an even wider range of applied sanctions. Indeed, the statements of subjects concerning their responses to persons alleged to be deviant on such evidence indicate that the modal reaction is disapproval, implicitly rather than explicitly communicated, and a restriction of interaction through partial withdrawal and avoidance. It should be noted further that although the subject's silent withdrawal from an established relationship with an alleged deviant may represent a stronger disapproval than an explicitly communicated, physically enforced sanction against a stranger, moral indignation or revulsion is not necessarily communicated to the deviant. The subject's prior relationship with the alleged deviant and the demands of propriety in subsequent interactions with him qualify the form and intensity of the sanctions which are applied. Thus, when the organization of the subject's day-to-day activities "forces" him into interaction with the deviant, expressions of disapproval are frequently constrained and diffused by the rules of deference and demeanor.[13] The following excerpts provide illustrations:

Implicit disapproval and partial withdrawal.   A 20-year-old co-ed's reaction to a girl she concluded was a homosexual was expressed as follows:

Well, I didn't want to be alone with X [the homosexual] because the four of us had two

[13] Erving Goffman, "The Nature of Deference and Demeanor," *American Anthropologist,* **58** (1956), pp. 473–502.

connecting rooms and I was in the room with X. As much as I liked the girl and felt sorry for her, I knew she could really wring me through the wringer. So the rest decided that I should tell her that if she and Y wanted to be homos, to do it somewhere else and not in the room.

No disapproval and relationship sustained.   The "live and let live" response to homosexuals, which is implied in the preceding reaction, was not uncommon among the subjects. Some subjects not only affirmed the right of the homosexual to "live his own life" but also reported that their knowledge of the deviance has had little or no effect upon their subsequent relationships with the deviants. In this regard, the mildest reaction, so mild that it might be considered no reaction at all, was that of a 19-year-old male college student:

I: What was your reaction to him?
S: My reactions to him have always been friendly because he seems like a very friendly person. Uh, and he has a very nice sense of humor and I've never been repelled by anything he's said. For one thing, I think he's tremendously interesting because he seems to have such a wide range for background. . . .
I: When was the last time you saw this person?
S: Last night. . . . I was sitting in a restaurant and he walked in with some friends . . . he just stopped in and said hello, and was his usual friendly self.
I: What in particular happened after that?
S: Actually, nothing. He sat down with his friends and we exchanged a few words about the records that were playing on the juke box. But nothing, actually. . . .

The theoretical significance of these data for the conception of deviance and societal reaction presented here is not that the subjects' information is of dubious accuracy or questionable relevance as evidence of homosexuality. Nor is it that the subjects' interpretations of them are unreasonable, unjustifiable, or spurious. They suggest rather that the conceptions of persons in everyday life concerning "sex-appropriate" or "sex-inappropriate" behavior may lead them to interpret a variety of behavioral forms as indications of the same deviation, and the "same" behavioral forms as indications of a variety of deviant as well as "normal" behavior. An individual's sexual "normality" may be made problematic by the interpretations and re-interpretations of his behavior by others, and the interpretive process may be activated by a wide range of situational behaviors which lend new significance to the individual's past and present behavior. His behavior with respect to speech, interests, dress, dating, or relations with other males are not *per se* significant in the deviant-defining process. The data suggest that the critical feature of the deviant-defining process is not the behavior of individuals who are defined as deviant, but rather the interpretations others make of their behaviors, whatever those behaviors may be.

With specific reference to homosexuality as a form of deviant behavior, the interview materials suggest that while reactions toward persons defined as homosexuals tend to be negatively toned, they are far from homogeneous as to the forms or intensity of the sanctions invoked and applied. Indeed, reactions which may appear to the sociological observer or to the deviant himself as negative

sanctions, such as withdrawal or avoidance, may be expressions of embarrassment, a reluctance to share the burden of the deviant's problems, fear of the
deviant, etc., as well as moral indignation or revulsion. In none of the interviews
does the subject react with extreme violence, explicitly define or directly accuse
the deviant of being a "queer," "fairy," or other terms of opprobrium, nor did
any of them initiate legal actions against the deviant. In view of the extreme
negative sanctions against homosexuality which are posited on theoretical
grounds, the generally mild reactions of our subjects are striking.

The relative absence of extreme and overtly expressed negative sanctions
against homosexuals among our subjects may, of course, reflect the higher than
average educational level of the sample. A sample of subjects less biased toward
the highly educated, middle-class segment of the population than was interviewed in this preliminary study may be expected to reflect a more definite
pattern with reference to such negative reactions. We must, therefore, be cautious in generalizing the range of reactions among our subjects to the general
population. It is equally important to note, however, that these data do indicate
that reactions to homosexuals in American society are not *societal* in the sense of
being uniform within a narrow range; rather, they are significantly conditioned
by sub-cultural as well as situational factors. Thus, not only are the processes by
which persons come to be defined as homosexuals contingent upon the interpretations of their behavior by others, but also the sanctions imposed and the
treatment they are accorded as a consequence of that definition vary widely
among conventional members of various sub-cultural groups.

The larger implications of these data are that a sociological theory of deviance
must explicitly take into account the variety and range of conceptions held by
persons, groups, and agencies within the society concerning any form of behavior. The increasing differentiation of groups, institutions, and subcultures in
modern society generates a continually changing range of alternatives and tolerance for the expression of sexual as well as other forms of behavior. Consequently, it is difficult if not impossible to theoretically derive a set of *specific
behavioral prescriptions* which will in fact be normatively supported, uniformly
practiced, and socially enforced by more than a segment of the total population.
Under such conditions, it is not the fact that individuals engage in behaviors
which diverge from some theoretically posited "institutionalized expectations"
or even that such behaviors are defined as deviant by the conventional and conforming members of the society which is of primary significance for the study of
deviance. A sociological theory of deviance must focus specifically upon the
interactions which not only define behaviors as deviant but also organize and
activate the application of sanctions by individuals, groups, or agencies. For in
modern society, the socially significant differentiation of deviants from the non-
deviant population is increasingly contingent upon circumstances of situation,
place, social and personal biography, and the bureaucratically organized activities of agencies of control.[14]

---

[14] For a discussion of such contingencies, see Edwin M. Lemert, *op. cit.*, Chapter 4, and Erving Goffman,
"The Moral Career of the Mental Patient," *Psychiatry*, **22** (1959), pp. 123–142.

5
A SOCIAL-PSYCHOLOGICAL
THEORY OF NEUROSIS
Arnold M. Rose

The analysis of the causes of human behavior of certain types has often been beset by two types of logical difficulties.* One is the monistic explanation in which the search for causation is directed to only one set of determining forces. In the case of pathological behavior (psychosis and neurosis), the monism has most frequently been that of biological determinism or of explanation in terms of disturbances in the transfer of libido (as analyzed by Freud and his followers). The most diverse forms of mental disturbances, in individuals with the most diverse life histories, have been analyzed in terms of the same set of causes. The effort to correct this error by means of a theory involving pluralistic causation has sometimes resulted in the second logical difficulty to be mentioned here. This is the procedure of discovering a list of causes without indicating their relative importance or their manner of interaction. It is not particularly helpful to know that biological, psychological, economic, cultural, and social interactional forces underlie the diverse manifestations of mental disturbances, even though this may be a true statement. Logicians have found that useful causal theories distinguish between the one "sufficient" cause and the several "necessary" causes for a given type of phenomenon—thus gaining some of the advantages of a monistic explanation—and that causation generally involves a complex interplay of forces in which each is effective only when in certain relationship to others.

When now offering a social-psychological theory of neurosis, I wish to avoid both of these errors even though the theory does not yet have sufficient empirical grounding to allow me to be sufficiently detailed concerning the exact relationship of this factor to other causal factors. We must be able to conceive that a given behavioral disturbance has its roots in a given social-personal situation, but that this situation operates to cause the mental disturbance through the creation of physiological unbalances and that it is necessary to restore the physiological balance as well as the social-personal situation to remedy the mental disturbance. To use a perhaps overly simple example: A "worry" induced by relatively insuperable objective social conditions may result in such a deprivation of sleep that the physiological changes ensuing produce mental disturbances. A necessary step in the treatment of this problem might very well be the administration of drugs to induce sleep, even though the "cause" of the problem is a social one. It is difficult to get out of the theological habit of separating the mind from the body and to recognize that all mental processes are also body

Source: Arnold M. Rose, "A Social-Psychological Theory of Neurosis," in Arnold M. Rose, editor, *Human Behavior and Social Processes*, Houghton Mifflin Company, Boston, 1962, pp. 537–549.
* A condensed form of this paper was presented at the Fourth World Congress of Sociology (Stresa, Italy; August 1959), and appears in the *Proceedings* of that Congress (published by the International Sociological Association; Louvain, Belgium, 1960).

processes, so that nothing social or psychological ever happens without biological concomitants. And yet it is proper and necessary to make a social or psychological analysis. In other words, our theory does not claim to exhaust the causal statements that might legitimately be made concerning neurosis; it merely suggests one significant variable which is relatively amenable to control. We must also learn to conceive that a given theory may be highly appropriate for the understanding of one kind of mental disturbance, but quite inappropriate for another kind of mental disturbance. It is not necessary to claim that our hypothesis explains each and every manifestation of neurosis; we merely expect that it helps to explain most forms of neurosis, and we leave the explanation of marginal forms of neurosis to other theorists.

With these cautions before us, a specific social-psychological theory of neurosis will be set forth. Any claim that this theory covers all the varied forms of mental disturbance is specifically denied, although—because the dividing line between neurosis and psychosis is often thin or arbitrary—it might be that such borderline phenomena as "involutional melancholia," at least in its mild form, are capable of being understood in terms of the theory. Our definition of neurosis will simply be "inability to act reasonably effectively[1]—within the material means and limitations present—for the achievement of socially acceptable and personally accepted[2] goals, because of anxiety or because of compulsions which camouflage anxiety." The theory does not rule out the possibility of other factors being important in the etiology of neurosis—as, for example, a traumatic experience which conditions an individual to certain hysterical behavior. The theory further refers to only one social-psychological element in what must necessarily be a complicated matrix of causation. The theory applies only to the behavior covered in our definition of neurosis; if another definition is used the theory may be rendered inappropriate.

Our theory is based on the social psychology of Charles H. Cooley and George H. Mead, who held that a "self," reflecting the reactions of others toward it, is an important intervening variable in human conduct. Observations of human behavior in a variety of settings have supported this conception and recently Manford Kuhn has undertaken laboratory experiments which demonstrate that one's opinion of oneself is significantly influenced by a sharply negative reaction from others concerning oneself.

The hypothesis offered here takes up where Kuhn leaves off. A factor in the chain of events leading to neurotic behavior is the induction of a person's negative attitude toward himself, and this may develop in a variety of ways—not only by sharply negative reactions from others. A significant and consistent pattern of self-deprecation, whether conscious or not, is the independent variable. The repression of this attitude may result in hysterical forms of neurosis, rather

---

[1] What is reasonably effective action is, of course, not precise and somewhat arbitrary. The criterion is what the individual and his associates consider to be reasonably effective action.

[2] By "socially acceptable" is meant acceptance by the valued associates of the individual—that is, his reference membership groups. By using the term "acceptance" rather than "desired" we imply that the groups are at least willing to tolerate the individual's goals, even if they do not always evaluate them highly. By juxtaposing "socially acceptable" and "personally accepted" we imply a modicum of harmony in goals between the individual and his society, not a perfect harmony or conformity.

than the more direct anxiety symptoms. The individual's negative attitude toward himself is related in different degrees and ways to other people's reaction toward him. It is an essential element of Cooley's concept of the "looking-glass self" and of Mead's concept of the "me" that part of the self is a reflection—albeit sometimes distorted—of other people's reactions to the person in question. If the reaction of others is generally negative, and the individual gets a correct perception of this negative reaction, and if he accepts this negative evaluation, our proposition is that the individual becomes neurotic. In other words, an element in the chain of causes leading to neurosis is held to be the social-psychological factor of psychological self-mutilation. The psychoanalyst Carl Jung recognized this in speaking of a sense of "loss of significance" as a major factor in adult neurosis (4). A depreciated or "mutilated" self is a major factor in the development of a neurosis, we hypothesize, because an individual's ability to accept strongly held values of any kind and to act effectively to achieve those values is a function of his conception of himself—a conception that he is an adequate, worth-while, effective, and appreciated person. The mental state is similar to that of the person who commits what Durkheim calls "egoistic" suicide. The difference lies solely in that the individual either retains a compunction against suicide or else is not sufficiently organized to engage in the act of suicide. The psychoanalyst Alfred Adler had a comparaple self-image theory of neurosis, although he tended to limit the concept of a negative self-image to those who had an "organ inferiority."

Certain temporary phenomena should not be confused with the more permanent self-devaluation here considered. Some negative reactions from others, some erroneous interpretations of others' reactions as unfavorable to ourselves, occasional moods of mild depression, are a part of everyday experience and hardly incapacitate an individual except for a very short time. The acceptance of a negative attitude toward oneself has to occur over a period of time to produce a neurosis. There is one significant exception to this: a psychological trauma, a crippling single incident of sharp self-devaluation, may create a neurosis for a significant period of time, although the individual generally recovers if a chain of negative events does not follow.

It is clear that the interactional process is central in this theory of neurosis. Rejection and devaluation by others are probably the most important cause of devaluation of self, provided the individual is not so psychotic or psychopathic that he cannot perceive the opinions of others.[3] Of course, an accurately perceived negative evaluation from others may be rejected by the individual concerned, but in such a case the individual generally has accepted what is for him the higher, more valued opinion of a small select group—perhaps even a group not in immediate social contact with him. The "looking-glass self" is not a mere reflection, it involves selection and evaluation, and hence the resulting self-image is far from being the image of the individual as seen by others with whom the individual interacts.

[3] There are other sources of incorrect perceptions of the opinions of others—including institutionalized sources. We are referring here to grossly incorrect perceptions, which we believe to be associated with psychosis or psychopathy.

This selective and evaluative process can also give rise to a second type of self-disparagement—that in which the individual selects the negative reactions of others and gives them prime importance among the wide range of others' reactions to build his conception of himself. Persons who do this have a perfectionist attitude, and even slight blows to their egos are accorded a subjective importance out of all proportion to their objective importance (in the eyes of a neutral observer). Such a perfectionist or "over-sensitive" attitude probably grows out of certain childhood experiences of a harsh nature, and hence may be thought of as psychogenic. At any rate, the tendency to overrate the negative reactions of others serves to inflict regular blows on one's conception of self. Over the course of time, our hypothesis holds, this is a link in the chain of causes that produce neurosis.

It is to be noted that at first these two types of neurotics are able to communicate with, and receive communications from, others as well as non-neurotic people can. There is no immediate interruption of communication such as is generally associated with psychosis. In fact, it is in the process of communication that the neuroses develop. However, if the self-deprecation persists and becomes greatly exaggerated, communication becomes interrupted and/or distorted. The disturbed individual concentrates his attention on himself to the partial exclusion of all other external stimuli. His very preoccupation with the unworthiness, uselessness, and hopelessness of his self tends to restrict communication with others. Others no longer have to carry on their deprecation from the outside—although they may tend to do so as the individual fails to conform to their social pressures—for the self-deprecatory process comes to be reinforced by itself. The individual's obvious unhappiness, which makes him unattractive to others, and his own concentration of attention on himself, tend to isolate him. Thus there are certain tendencies toward an interruption of communication and a withdrawal from reality which are productive of a psychosis on the border of neurosis—usually called "involutional melancholia," at least in its milder form. On the other hand, unless the individual withdraws himself physically from social relations, the usual stimuli of everyday life intrude on his attention and keep him in some touch with reality. Thus the neurotic is only partly out of touch with reality, insofar as he over-selects the negative responses of others to the relative exclusion of the positive ones and insofar as his attention is concentrated on himself to the partial exclusion of some external stimuli; but if the neurotic further withdraws himself from society and broods almost exclusively on his unhappy self and its psychic pains, an involutional process with melancholia as its external manifestation will result. Karl Menninger describes the similarity of involutional melancholia to the neuroses:

In this condition (melancholia) sufficient contact with reality may be maintained so that the individual, for all his self-destructiveness, does not endanger the lives of others, and may even co-operate in efforts to redirect or reshape his own life. For this reason, melancholia is sometimes described as a neurosis rather than a psychosis. But some victims of melancholia abandon all loyalty to reality and may be extremely deluded and even homicidal. The mechanisms are the same as in the so-called neurotic form, but the surrender of object attachment and of reality testing here is much greater (7, p. 213).

Davidoff expresses the ambiguous distinction between neurosis and involutional melancholia by holding that there is a difference between "the nonpsychotic involutional syndrome" and "the involutional psychosis." (2, p. 189)

The symptoms characteristic of involutional melancholia are those of extreme anxiety and depression. The melancholic individual is able to communicate with others, but in this communication he immediately makes it clear that he has a highly negative attitude toward himself. His inability, failure, and unworthiness are drawn to exaggerated proportions. A melancholic man will typically emphasize his belief that his life has been a failure. A melancholic woman will typically emphasize that she is not capable of doing anything right. The bodily symptoms are appropriate to these attitudes: there is much weeping and whining, wringing of the hands, negative shaking of the head, "long" expression on the face, high body tension. The melancholic's stated belief that nothing is worth while for him (except perhaps for something obviously unobtainable) is reflected in his activity: sometimes futile gestures are made in the direction of doing something constructive, but most of the time the melancholic seems "content" to sit back and contemplate his miserable state in his usual agitated manner. Any slight incident of a mildly unpleasant sort is awarded great importance in the melancholic's thought and conversation; any incident of a pleasant sort is glossed over and quickly forgotten. Attempts at suicide are not uncommon.

Our examination of the statistical incidence of involutional melancholia, even recognizing the great inadequacy of most statistics on mental disorder, reveals two persistent facts: women are more likely to have involutional melancholia in our society than are men, and the women typically have their first onset between the ages of 45 and 55, while men have their onset typically between the ages of 55 and 70 (8). These facts have led many psychiatrists to associate melancholia with glandular changes going on in the body in connection with the loss of sexual powers, particularly with the menopause in women and other physiological changes associated with aging (2, pp. 187–204, esp. 188). But the facts are equally compatible with a social-psychological theory about the changes of life roles. Women in our society typically lose their child-rearing function and much of their household-caring function during the fifth decade of their lives, and men—whose sexual potency has been declining gradually since the age of 20—typically lose their occupational functions at about the age of 65 and begin to foresee this loss about ten years earlier. The "normal" procedure at such a critical juncture is to assume a new life role, which is of course facilitated by some earlier preparation for taking on such a new life role. The process is easier for men, since the socially expected life role for men past the age of 65 is one of leisure (including hobbies, travel, puttering around the house). But it is more difficult for a woman at the age of 45 to assume a new life role, because she is too young to retire (both in terms of her physical strength and in terms of social expectations). Our culture does not specify a "typical" role for the middle-

aged woman whose child-rearing days are over, and the choices before her
involve new efforts and skills on her part: she can find a job commensurate with
her social status and abilities, she can become regularly active in civic or social
affairs, she can play a larger part in the lives of her husband or her now-grown
children (who often do not want her "interference"). Because of lack of previously acquired skill, because of the difficulty in engaging in these activities when
one begins them at the age of 45, because of the outside world's frequent resistance, a woman may often fail to make a satisfactory transition to a new role.
A man between the ages of 55 and 60 may also fail, if he thinks of himself as a
failure in his occupation and finds that he cannot compete with younger men,
and if he has never developed any skills or interests in the uses of leisure, or if
he is especially unhappy about retiring from his occupational role. Our culture
values highly the occupational role for men and the child-rearing role for
women, and when these are lost, the individual's value goes down sharply unless
he can find a new role for himself. In certain other societies a middle-aged person automatically takes on a new role of influence and prestige, and there is no
decline in the individual's sense of his own worth.

The relationship of these facts and interpretations to our theory of neurosis
should now be apparent. People who, for one reason or another, fail to make a
satisfactory role transition (which our culture requires at about the age of 45–50
for women and 60–65 for men), especially if they find that their achievements
have not been up to their expectations and hence cannot retire content with
their laurels, are likely to develop persistent negative attitudes toward themselves. The central element in this negative attitude is that life is meaningless.
This entails a sense of worthlessness, a loss of motivation, a belief in one's inability to achieve anything worth while. Such a complex tends to be persistent,
as our culture does not offer any ready solution of the problem, and no happy
accident is likely to change the situation (as might occur in other difficult problems of life). The individual feels himself aged or aging, and this feeling adds to
the sense of hopelessness. The result is a persistent psychological beating of the
self with a circular intensification of the process. Soon the individual is no longer
able to control his feelings of anxiety and depression. It is as though the individual commits suicide mentally, but forgets to do it, or loses the capacity to do
it, physically. After deciding he is not going to have anything more to do with
life, he finds himself still alive, with the usual sorts of body needs. The latter
naturally become very annoying; hence they tend to become the major object of
attention and chief source of worry. Many such persons do attempt suicide, but
others have certain compunctions against it or fears of it.

This extreme form of neurosis is generally known to psychiatrists as involutional melancholia. Failure to make a subjectively satisfactory transition in life
role is not the sole cause of persistent self-deprecation, of course, but it may very
well be the most frequent cause. Also there seem to be certain types of personalities who are especially susceptible to melancholia, personalities who are especially rigid and hence least able to find new life roles when the culture does
not automatically offer them (1, p. 412; 5; 6, p. 567; 9, p. 19).

The theory applies, of course, to milder forms of neurosis than involutional melancholia. In the case of compulsive-obsessive neuroses, the individual is hypothesized to seek reassurance—to combat his negative attitude toward himself—by some form of repetitive behavior. Repetition of thought or behavior provides a way of "hanging on," of assuring oneself that something is stable even when one does not have confidence in one's perceptions, actions, or thought processes because he conceives of himself as generally inadequate. The specific compulsion or obsession is thus a mere symptom, although the choice of it is undoubtedly related to some significant experience in the life of the neurotic individual.

If reality is persistently bleak, it might be wiser for the individual not to face it completely, at least not for a certain period until a sense of self-confidence can be restored. People have to be taught to avoid persistent self-deprecation, as much as they have to be taught to face reality. Modern Western culture is weak in the social crutches which tend to compensate individuals for personal dissatisfaction with life: the belief in a just hereafter, the belief that God sets trials for people to test them, a strong family and church system which forces people into activity despite their personal disinclination. In the modern Western setting where these things are weak or non-existent, the wise psychiatrist should function partly as a priest, not only in the sense that he can serve as a confessor to relieve guilt feelings and other repressions, but also in that he can help people to turn their minds temporarily from the misery of their personal lot. Such avoidance of reality is necessary if only to let the body restore its physiological balance, which is inevitably unbalanced by the persistent anxiety and depression.

Having a neurotic individual avoid reality is, of course, a temporary device, a first step, since—if our theory is correct—the cure of neurosis must involve changing his situation and/or getting him to redefine his situation. Both of these require contact with reality at least most of the time. If the basis of a neurosis is persistent self-deprecation because the individual is in an objectively unpleasant situation, such as having to face uniformly negative judgments on the part of others or finding oneself without a meaningful life role, a major part of treatment should not be psychotherapeutic but consist of helping the individual move into a more favorable situation. That is, the unfavored individual should be brought into a new social environment, and the roleless individual should be taught a new role. An effective psychotherapy must be allied with these procedures, and should consist in helping the individual to redefine his relationship to his environment. If, on the other hand, the difficulty is not "objective" but results from the neurotic person's tendency to interpret his social situation in personally unflattering terms, there is not any point to changing the situation, and psychotherapy is all-important. Part of the psychotherapy still consists, however, in helping the individual to redefine his situation—in this case, bringing the definition closer to reality. The problem of getting at the sources of the neurotic's tendency to interpret his social situation as more unfavorable to him than it objectively is, cannot be helped by our theory. Freudian or other familiar theories of neurosis would be more successful at this point in guiding psychotherapy. Shock or drug treatment has also been found to be successful in some cases in bringing the melancholic to recognize the social world around him and to realize his relationship to it, and this sometimes aids redefinition and hence at least is a partial "cure." (3) Our own contribution here limits itself to a psychotherapy of redefining the situation, redefining the self through a redefinition of the situation, and to a broader treatment process which involves changing the objective social situation. The goal is the development of a positive attitude toward the self, and a realistic recognition of the attainable ways in which the changing self can continue to function in a changing social environment.

This is not Couéism nor "positive thinking." The individual must *do* those things which are in accord with his own values and which reflect the values of some social group that he rates highly. He must be able to congratulate himself occasionally and receive congratulations from esteemed others. This involves his social actions and not merely his personal thoughts. The therapy, therefore, must include putting him into a situation where he can engage in self-satisfying action with some fair degree of success and where he can receive some degree of recognition by others for this success. If neither changing the situation nor redefining the situation is possible for a given neurotic individual—perhaps because of his advanced age—it may be that "adjustment" can be achieved only by psychologically separating the individual from the stark reality of his life. For such an individual, self-delusion may be the only alternative to complete apathy and depression or suicide. The important thing is to maintain the integrity and the value of the self, even if—in the extreme instance—this means loss of contact with reality.

References

1   Brew, M. F., and Eugene Davidoff. "The Involutional Psychoses, Prepsychotic Personality and Prognosis," *Psychiatric Quarterly,* Vol. 14 (1940).
2   Davidoff, Eugene. "The Involutional Psychoses," in Oscar J. Kaplan (ed.), *Mental Disorders in Later Life.* Stanford University, Calif.: Stanford University Press, 1945.
3   Fishbein, Isadore Leo. "Involutional Melancholia and Convulsive Therapy," *American Journal of Psychiatry,* Vol. 106 (August, 1949), pp. 128–135.
4   Jung, Carl G. *Modern Man in Search of a Soul.* New York: Harcourt, Brace and Co., 1933.
5   Malamud, William, S. L. Sands, and Irene T. Malamud. "The Involutional Psychoses: A Socio-psychiatric Study," *Psychosomatic Medicine,* Vol. 3 (October 1941), pp. 410–426.
6   Malamud, William, S. L. Sands, Irene T. Malamud, and P. J. P. Powers. "The Involutional Psychoses: A Socio-psychiatric Follow-Up Study," *American Journal of Psychiatry,* Vol. 105 (February 1949).
7   Menninger, Karl A. *Man Against Himself.* New York: Harcourt, Brace and Co., 1938.
8   Palatin, Phillip, and James F. MacDonald. "Involutional Psychoses," *Geriatrics,* Vol. 6 (1951).
9   Titley, W. "Prepsychotic Personality of Patients with Involutional Melancholia," *Archives of Neurology and Psychiatry,* Vol. 36 (1936).

6
A SOCIOLOGICAL THEORY OF PSYCHOPATHY
Harrison G. Gough

It is becoming increasingly apparent in modern psychopathology that one of the most heuristic approaches to the study of behavioral disorders is the consideration of social behavior. It is almost a truism that many psychiatric entities are to a large extent dependent upon sociological manifestations for their detection and definition. Thus, for example, schizophrenia may be referred to as a disorder characterized, among other things, by inappropriate social behavior, defection of interpersonal relationships, and meagerness of emotional response. Paranoia is a disorder in which situations are progressively misdefined, occasioning isolation from the social group and inability to communicate successfully with it.[1]

In spite of the interesting possibilities of such an approach, there has been little in the way of formal sociological analysis of the various clinical syndromes.[2] There have been a number of studies of the ecology[3] and of the predisposing or background ʃ tors[4] of mental disease, but the actual conceptualization of these disorders in sociological terms has not received much attention.

The present paper is an attempt to apply sociological concepts and the sociological point of view to the psychopathic personality. In order to clarify the present usage of the concept, a brief survey of the development of the concept will be given.

DEVELOPMENT OF THE CONCEPT

Medical historians have generally traced the concept of psychopathy to Prichard.[5] Prichard classified psychiatric disorders into two broad groups, *moral* and *intellectual* insanity.[6] Moral insanity, or moral imbecility, referred to aberrations

Source: Harrison G. Gough, "A Sociological Theory of Psychopathy," American Journal of Sociology, 53: 359–366, 1948.

[1] Norman Cameron, "The Paranoid Pseudo-Community," American Journal of Sociology, XLIX (1943), 32–38.

[2] Besides Cameron's excellent paper, one should list: Robert E. L. Faris, "Reflections of Social Disorganization in the Behavior of a Schizophrenic Patient," American Journal of Sociology, L (1944), 134–41. Faris delineates the manner in which subgroup identifications are embodied in the psychotic fragmentation of the subject's personality. Also, the paper by G. Devereaux, "A Sociological Theory of Schizophrenia," Psychoanalytical Review, XXVI (1939), 315–42, should be mentioned.

[3] Robert E. L. Faris and H. Warren Dunham, Mental Disorders in Urban Areas (Chicago: University of Chicago Press, 1939); Robert E. L. Faris, "Ecological Factors in Human Behavior," in J. McV. Hunt (ed.), Personality and the Behavior Disorders (New York: Ronald Press, 1944), I, 736–57.

[4] H. Warren Dunham, "The Social Personality of the Catatonic-Schizophrene," American Journal of Sociology, XLIX (1944), 508–18.

[5] G. E. Partridge, "Current Conceptions of Psychopathic Personality," American Journal of Sociology, XLIX (1930), 53–99; D. K. Henderson, Psychopathic States (New York: W. W. Norton Co., 1939), p. 11 (as Henderson states, the term "psychopathic inferiority" was introduced by Koch in 1888 [p. 17]); S. Maughs, "A Concept to Psychopathy and Psychopathic Personality: Its Evolution and Historical Development," Journal of Criminal Psychopathology, II (1941), 329–56 and 465–99.

[6] J. C. Prichard, A Treatise on Insanity (London: Gilbert & Piper, 1835), pp. 6–7.

of the conative and emotional areas; cases were discussed under this heading which may be taken as prototypes of the psychopath as known today.[7]

The dichotomy was vigorously disputed during the remainder of the nineteenth century, with Isaac Ray probably its ablest American defender.[8] The Guiteau trial in 1881 brought the controversy into relief: the exoneration of President Garfield's assassin was sought on the basis of "moral insanity."[9] The contradictory testimony of eminent physicians and alienists led to a repudiation of the concept of moral imbecility.

Various deficiencies in Prichard's treatment were also discovered. Thus, Tredgold now contends that unrecognized cases of mania and early paresis were mistakenly included among the moral imbeciles.[10] The concept became increasingly untenable, and its usage ended about 1900.[11] At this time the designation "psychopathy" was taken up, and it continued in ascendency up to around 1924. The emphasis in this period was primarily on constitutional factors and genetic etiology. At the present time there has been a shift to a more dynamic interpretation, particularly as manifested in the psychoanalytic formulations.[12]

Although the question of etiology is still a polemical one, there is fair agreement concerning symptomatology. Preu's definition is representative:

> The diagnostic labels *psychopathic personality* and *constitutional psychopathic inferiority* designate those individuals who have manifested considerable difficulty in social adjustment over a period of many years or throughout life, but who are not of defective intelligence nor suffering from structural disease of the brain or epilepsy, and whose difficulties in adjustment have not been manifested by the behavioral syndromes which are conventionally referred to as neuroses or psychoses.[13]

Other writers stress similar aspects in most cases. For example, Henry mentions defects of emotional control, inability to profit from experience, impulsiveness,

---

[7] D. K. Henderson and R. D. Gillespie, *A Textbook of Psychiatry* (6th ed.; London: Oxford University Press, 1944), p. 382.

[8] Arthur E. Fink, *Causes of Crime* (Philadelphia: University of Pennsylvania Press, 1938), p. 52.

[9] *Ibid.*, pp. 69–73.

[10] A. F. Tredgold, *A Textbook of Mental Deficiency* (6th ed.; Baltimore: W. Wood, 1937), p. 333.

[11] Maughs, *op. cit.*

[12] There is still an influential body of opinion in psychiatry behind the genetic interpretation of psychopathy (see, e.g., S. B. Maughs, "A Concept of Psychopathy and Psychopathic Personality," *Journal of Criminal Psychopathology*, III [1942], 494–516 and 664–714; and Paul W. Preu, "The Concept of Psychopathic Personality," in J. McV. Hunt [ed.], *Personality and the Behavior Disorders*, p. 928). H. F. Darling ("Definition of Psychopathic Personality," *Journal of Nervous and Mental Diseases*, CI [1945], 121–26) and G. E. Partridge (*op. cit.*) assign greater weight to environmental factors. An incisive developmental analysis is given by Lauretta Bender, "Psychopathic Behavior Disorders in Children," in R. M. Lindner and R. V. Seliger (eds.), *Handbook of Correctional Psychology* (New York: Philosophical Library, 1947), pp. 360–77.

[13] *Op. cit.*, p. 923. Preu is highly critical of the concept, feeling that its persistence in psychiatry is not purely a function of its intrinsic usefulness; rather, its retention may be attributed to, first, its constitutional implications which subtly reject modern environmentalistic trends; second, it is a convenient euphemism when a diagnosis of frank psychosis is inadvisable; and, third, it has a forensic utility in establishing a transition zone between wholly complete and incomplete legal responsibility (pp. 929–30). Others have also objected to the concept recently. J. E. W. Wallin, "Questions and Answers: Mental Deficiency, Psychopathy, and Delinquency," *Journal of Criminal Law and Criminology*, XXXVI (1945), 116–20, states that psychopathy is not a definite nosological entity; and David Abrahamsen, *Crime and the Human Mind* (New York: Columbia University Press, 1944), p. 110, claims that the concept has tended to obscure personality analysis.

and lack of foresight.[14] White suggests an inadequate superego development, which leaves the person unable to control the powerful instinctual drives or to modify infantile standards of conduct.[15] Diethelm emphasizes the lack of self-reliance and unsatisfactory adjustment to the group,[16] whereas Caldwell indicates nomadism, inability to withstand tedium, and irresponsibility as characteristics of psychopathy.[17]

Karpman has objected to the use of psychopathy merely as a synonym for delinquency.[18] He states that, when there is a true lack of ethical and moral principles in the personality, the term "anethopathy" should be used.[19] In a later paper, Karpman distinguished between idiopathic (primary) and symptomatic psychopathy.[20] In the former there is a distinctive personality configuration, but in the latter there is only fortuitous and sporadic antisocial behavior. Lindner feels that the crucial factor is an inadequate resolution of the Oedipal situation.[21]

Cleckley has contributed one of the most searching accounts of this protean disorder.[22] Present legal and medical conceptions are both inadequate, Cleckley contends; the asocial, impulsive psychopath can escape legal retribution for his delinquent acts by pleading insanity and then, after the briefest commitment, can secure release by establishing psychiatric competence. Because of this state of affairs, treatment cannot be imposed upon the psychopath as easily as it can on other mental incompetents.

One of the reasons for this cultural lag is the convincing arguments the psychopath can make on behalf of his own sanity and integration. The psychopath can verbalize all the moral and social rules, but he does not seem to understand them in the way that others do. This verbal façade Cleckley has called the "mask of sanity." The characteristic deterioration is called "semantic dementia."[23] The personality in psychopathy is so completely involved that there are no signs of incongruity, of anxiety, or of self-doubting such as can be found in the psychoneuroses, in psychoses, and in criminality. Nor can factors such as mental defectiveness or cranial pathology be specified. It is almost as if the per-

---

[14] G. W. Henry, *Essentials of Psychiatry* (3d ed.; Baltimore: Williams & Wilkins, 1938), p. 223.

[15] W. A. White, *Outlines of Psychiatry* (14th ed.; Washington, D.C.: Nervous and Mental Disease Publishing Co., 1935), p. 374.

[16] O. Diethelm, "Basic Considerations of the Concept of Psychopathic Personality," in R. M. Lindner and R. V. Seliger (eds.), *Handbook of Correctional Psychology*, pp. 384–94.

[17] J. M. Caldwell, "The Constitutional Psychopathic State," *Journal of Criminal Psychopathology*, III (1941), 171–79.

[18] B. Karpman, *The Individual Criminal* (Washington, D.C.: Nervous and Mental Disease Publishing Co., 1935), pp. 182–83.

[19] "The Problem of the Psychopathies," *Psychiatric Quarterly*, III (1929), 495–526.

[20] "Psychopathy in the Scheme of Human Typology," *Journal of Nervous and Mental Diseases*, CIII (1946), 276–87.

[21] R. M. Lindner, "Psychopathic Personality and the Concept of Homeostasis," *Journal of Clinical Psychopathology*, VI (1945), 517–21; *Rebel without a Cause* (New York: Grune & Stratton, 1944).

[22] H. Cleckley, *The Mask of Sanity* (St. Louis: Mosby, 1941); "The Psychopath Viewed Practically," in R. M. Lindner and R. V. Seliger (eds.), *Handbook of Correctional Psychology*, pp. 395–412.

[23] Wendell Johnson (*People in Quandaries* [New York: Harper & Bros., 1946]), writing from the position of general semantics, concurs with Cleckley on this point. The psychopath, says Johnson, cannot abstract in the technical semantic sense; terms are only vaguely discriminated. His sincerity is an illusion, and his social sense only word-deep (*ibid.*, pp. 321–25).

son were a robot of indescribable ingenuity, able to do everything a healthy personality could except to participate in a social group.[24]

When the various discussions of psychopathy are surveyed, a psychological common denominator is found in a set of attitudes which characterizes the psychopaths as a group. Much of the opposition to the use of the concept refers to the purely symptomatic nature of its definition. However, if a set of attitudes can, in fact, be demonstrated, then there would be some justification for using the diagnostic term "psychopathic personality" with these characteristics as defining properties. Such a concept would enable one to discriminate the adventitious offender against group demands, the intellectually inadequate, etc., from the true psychopathic personalities—persons possessing a characteristic personality configuration.

We may, then, list some of these common attitudes: overevaluation of immediate goals as opposed to remote or deferred ones; unconcern over the rights and privileges of others when recognizing them would interfere with personal satisfaction in any way; impulsive behavior, or apparent incongruity between the strength of the stimulus and the magnitude of the behavioral response; inability to form deep or persistent attachments to other persons or to identify in interpersonal relationships; poor judgment and planning in attaining defined goals; apparent lack of anxiety and distress over social maladjustment and unwillingness or inability to consider maladjustment qua maladjustment; a tendency to project blame onto others and to take no responsibility for failures; meaningless prevarication, often about trivial matters in situations where detection is inevitable; almost complete lack of dependability and willingness to assume responsibility; and, finally, emotional poverty.

None of these attitudes or characteristics, taken alone, would be crucial, but, when seen to converge on a particular person, they constitute strong evidence of psychopathy. Nor is any of these factors explicitly dependent upon illegal or asocial behavior; they may easily be inferred from such behavior, however. Thus a person may be characterized by the above factors, that is, be psychopathic, and still not be institutionalized or guilty of illegal acts; but, on the other hand, the psychopaths would be expected to contribute more than their share to the delinquent and criminal populations.

THE PSYCHOPATH AS DEFICIENT IN ROLE-PLAYING ABILITIES

That part of the personality which links an individual to the social community, often referred to as the "self," is a product of social interaction. Baldwin and Cooley were two of the early writers to call attention to this fact; they contended that self-conceptions are in large part determined by the responses of others.[25]

---

[24] Cleckley, The Mask of Sanity, p. 279.
[25] James Mark Baldwin, Mental Development in the Child and in the Race (New York: Macmillan Co., 1894); Charles Horton Cooley, Human Nature and the Social Order (New York: Charles Scribner's Sons, 1922).

Mead has given what is probably the most acceptable account of this process.[26] According to Mead, the rise of the self depends upon the individual's capacity to look upon himself as an object. Such self-conception is an assumption of the reaction of others. As Mead states:

> The self arises in conduct, when the individual becomes a social object in experience to himself. This takes place when the individual assumes the attitude or uses the gesture which another individual would use and responds to it himself or tends to so respond. . . . The child gradually becomes a social being in his own experience, and he acts toward himself in a manner analogous to that in which he acts towards others.[27]

The self thus has its origin in communication and in taking the role of the other.[28]

In Mead's terminology this role-taking gradually becomes integrated into a number of self-conceptions, each of which is called a "me," each corresponding to the definition of the self by others. During this developmental period the child will often talk to himself as others talk to him.[29] In time a certain communality and consistency in the patterns permit the evolvement of a conception of the "generalized other,"[30] which represents social reality as seen by the self. At this level the personality is able to observe abstract rules and standards, such as occur in formal games.

No matter how thoroughly the societal standards and folkways have been introjected, there will always remain a degree of uncertainty in every expression of the self. This dynamic aspect or feature of the interactive process, as Young has described it, is called the "I."[31] Hence it cannot be predicted precisely how one will react before the action takes place; the "I" constitutes the unpredictable, the unique, the novel element in thought-processes and in behavior.

The importance of these concepts for social interaction can easily be seen. Adaptation, co-operation, and even understanding are functions of the "me's," of the role-taking experiences. Hence, self-criticism as exercised through the "me's" is really social criticism, and behavior modified by self-criticism is really behavior modified socially. As Lee states, "Without the attainment of a *me* there would be no basis for cooperative enterprise."[32]

Whether or not we wish to accept in full Mead's theory and terminology, a clear case is presented for certain fundamental propositions. First of all, the basis for individual sociality is social interaction,[33] and this interaction is effective in so far as the individual can look upon himself as an object or can assume various

---

[26] George H. Mead, *Mind, Self, and Society* (Chicago: University of Chicago Press, 1934).

[27] George H. Mead, "A Behavioristic Account of the Significant Symbol," *Journal of Philosophy*, XIX (1922), 160.

[28] See discussion in Ellsworth Faris, "The Social Psychology of George Mead,"*American Journal of Sociology*, XLIII (1937), 391–403.

[29] Kimball Young, *Personality and Problems of Adjustment* (New York: F. S. Crofts & Co., 1940), p. 169.

[30] Mead, *Mind, Self, and Society*, pp. 150–54.

[31] *Op. cit.*, p. 175.

[32] Grace C. Lee, *George Herbert Mead, Philosopher of the Social Individual* (New York: King's Crown Press, 1945), p. 68.

[33] Cf. e.g., the way "thine" and "mine" proscriptions are learned by the middle-class child (W. A. Davis, and R. J. Havighurst, *Father of the Man* [Boston: Houghton Mifflin Co., 1947], pp. 171–72 *et passim*).

roles. This role-taking ability provides a technique for self-understanding and self-control. Learned prohibitions (and all social interdictions must be learned) may be observed by "telling one's self" not to behave in a certain way. Or speech may be editorially "reviewed" as it is emitted, and the inadmissible deleted. Role-playing, or putting one's self in another's position, enables a person to predict the other's behavior. Finally, role-playing ability makes one sensitive in advance to reactions of others; such prescience may then deter or modify the unexpressed action.

Now if we take the set of attitudes previously described, it would seem desirable to synthesize them into one or more embracing concepts, just as they themselves emerged (were inferred) from discrete bits of behavior. Role-playing is such a concept. Saying that the psychopathic personality is pathologically deficient in role-playing abilities permits the accommodation of the already known facts about psychopathy and also the possibility of predictions in areas where present knowledge is scant. Such deductions could then be submitted to empirical tests.[34] Even without deductive extrapolation of this kind, the concept of the psychopath as one deficient in role-playing ability would be useful to the extent that it resolves and fuses the indeterminate number of descriptive statements, such as those previously made, which could be given.

For our purposes, then, deficiency in role-playing means the incapacity to look upon one's self as an object (Mead) or to identify with another's point of view. The psychopath is unable to foresee the consequences of his own acts, especially their social implications, because he does not know how to judge his own behavior from another's standpoint. What might be called social emotions, such as embarrassment,[35] discomfiture, loyalty, contrition, and gregariousness (group identification), are not experienced by the psychopath.[36]

When confronted with disapproval, the psychopath often expresses surprise

[34] One such deduction would be that on the "Chapin Test of Social Insight" (F. Stuart Chapin, "Preliminary Standardization of a Social Insight Scale," *American Sociological Review*, VII [1942], 214–25) diagnosed psychopaths would secure lower scores than controls matched for intelligence and education. Another would be that an effective scale could be empirically developed to screen psychopaths from normals by use of questions on the responses of hypothetical individuals and groups in described situations. Such a scale would not need to include any ethical or moral decisions or judgments about what would be "right" and "wrong." It would merely ask the subject to predict what such-and-such a person or group would do under such-and-such conditions.

In using tests, however, one must be careful not to set up a self-contained system whose terms are at variance with those of the culture. Lundberg has clearly shown the futility of arguments about the "essential nature" of concepts such as neurosis or psychopathy, or about what a concept "really is" (George A. Lundberg, *Foundations of Sociology* [New York: Macmillan Co., 1939]). The difficulty in using some critical test score as a definition of psychopathy is not that it would be *wrong*, but that the institutionalization of the medical concept requires other users of the term to conform in order to avoid confusion. Actually, what most inventories are trying to do is to *predict the diagnostic behavior of psychiatrists*, and not to establish new meanings for the terms used.

[35] Hathaway has cited an interesting case in this regard. A female psychopath was unable to reply to a question about "humiliating experiences," because she did not understand what such experiences were. She knew what the word meant, but she was not able to tell whether she had ever had such an experience herself (Starke R. Hathaway, "The Personality Inventory as an Aid in the Diagnosis of the Psychopathic Inferior," *Journal of Consulting Psychology*, III [1939], 112–17).

[36] Bender's recent statement should be noted:

The primary defect [of psychopaths] is an inability to identify themselves in a relationship with other people, due to the fact that they experienced no continuous identification during the early infantile period from the first weeks through the period when language and social concepts, and psychosexual and personality development, were proceeding. Related to this lack of capacity to identify or to form

and resentment. He cannot understand the reasons for the observer's objection or disapprobation. The psychopath cannot grant the justice of punishment or deprivation, because this involves an evaluation of his behavior from the standpoint of the "generalized other," or society. The psychopath will violate other's wishes and desires because he does not conceive of his own actions as inimical to their wants. He forms no deep attachments because he does not know how to identify himself with another or to share another's viewpoint. He lacks control because he cannot anticipate objections which others will make to his behavior.

If the psychopath is considered to be lacking in role-playing skills, and socially maladjusted because of this, then therapy should address itself to role-playing. The work of Moreno, and of others, on psychodrama has demonstrated one method of accomplishing this.[37] So far most of the work has been with neurotic persons, inhibited, fearful, and crippled by anxieties which interfere with a clear expression of their basic needs. For them the psychodrama provides an artificial spontaneity wherein unrestricted new approaches may be tested. In the psychopath there is little need for training in spontaneity; what is needed is a situation which will give him practice in disinterested analysis of self, from the viewpoint of others-in-general.[38]

In younger psychopaths foster-home placement undoubtedly contributes somewhat to role-playing ability. Rogers mentions that in cases of behavior-problem children it is permissible to change from one foster-home to another.[39] He points out that such children often adjust fairly well when first transferred but that after a delay the delinquent behavior is again precipitated. It could be said that the child faces the new home with awakened interest and attention and that, as long as this attitude persists, practice in role-playing occurs—practice in foreseeing the effects of one's acts on others. Later, as the novelty of the new home wears off, the disability in role-playing, no longer counterbalanced by deliberate effort, again permits the appearance of unacceptable behavior. Assuming the validity of this admittedly speculative analysis, the prediction would be that more transfers, up to some reasonable limit, of course, would yield relatively more improvement in behavior than continuance in a constant regime.[40]

The entering wedge may be driven home by the severity of the institutional

---

an object-relationship is a lack of anxiety and an inability to feel guilt. It would thus appear that anxiety and guilt are not primarily instinctual qualities, but that they arise in reaction to threats to object relationships and identifications.

(L. Bender, "Psychopathic Behavior Disorders in Children," in R. M. Lindner and R. V. Seliger [eds.], *Handbook of Correctional Psychology*, p. 374).

[37] See J. L. Moreno, *Psychodrama* (New York: Beacon House, 1946).

[38] Sociodrama would presumably fulfil this need if the psychopath carried the part of judge of his own behavior. There is a strong possibility that the psychopath's shallowness of emotional response would preclude ego involvement and hence obstruct therapeutical progress; this is a technical problem, however, and is not a sufficient basis for the rejection of sociodrama as a plausible method. For a brief discussion of ego involvement see Gordon Allport, "The Psychology of Participation," *Psychological Review*, LIII (1945), 117–32.

[39] Carl R. Rogers, *The Clinical Treatment of the Problem Child* (Cambridge, Mass.: Riverside Press, 1939), chap. iv.

[40] That this is what actually does take place is indicated by S. D. Porteus, *The Practice of Clinical Psychology* (New York: American Book Co., 1941). He states: "Then when everything seems to have reached a maximum of satisfactory adjustment, the social worker *should remove the case to another home*" (p. 264). Porteus recommends a rotation of placements for such cases.

discipline in incarcerated cases. The risks taken here are obviously great; the outcome may be favorable, nevertheless, as indicated by Whitaker's results.[41] According to the role-playing hypothesis, such discipline eventually becomes so manifestly incongruous with the psychopath's own definition of the situation, and so detrimental to his personal preferences, that an immediate goal of escape or avoidance is set up whose attainment demands some consideration of the social repercussions of his own behavior.

Knight has found unretaliative permissiveness and indulgence to be highly efficacious in his treatment of irresponsible chronic alcoholics, a group including many psychopaths.[42] If resolutions are made and broken, the therapist refrains from any rebuke or revengeful behavior. In some ways this attitude of the therapist sets up an artificial situation in which failures are not punished, thus giving the subject opportunity to try out new roles without fear of requital. Lippitt has stressed the necessity of establishing permissive "as if" situations where new social skills can be practiced without the fear that attends "playing for keeps."[43] Such practice in role-playing helps the subject to evaluate socially what he had previously done.

It must be remembered that the psychopath does not show intrapsychic conflict, or self-ambivalence, as does the neurotic, and does not ordinarily seek counseling or therapy. The narcissism and complete engulfment of the personality in psychopathy withdraws from the therapist a number of approaches open to him in treating neurotics and some types of psychotics. A neurosis, whatever may be its primary and secondary gains, is distinctly unpleasant (a compromise solution) in some respects, which may motivate the sufferer to seek treatment and welcome improvement.

The self-consistency theory of Lecky may also be mentioned.[44] This theory postulates an evolving, evaluative self-conception as the nucleus of personality and states that integration is the result of unifying attitudes and beliefs (by selection and rejection) in the direction of self-consistency.[45] But the psychopath has no neurotic doubt and perplexity to offer a convenient foothold for the therapist; neither does he show any attitudes or behavior inconsistent with a cherished self-conception, the failure to expel which causes him to seek aid. The psychopath is not at odds with himself; he is at odds with the group because he is deficient in the capacity to evaluate objectively his own behavior against the group's standards.

SUMMARY

The kind of person who seems insensitive to social demands, who refuses to or cannot co-operate, who is untrustworthy, impulsive, and improvident, who

[41] C. A. Whitaker, "Ormsby Village: An Experiment with Forced Psychotherapy in the Rehabilitation of the Delinquent Adolescent," *Psychiatry*, IX (1946), 239–50.

[42] Robert P. Knight, "The Psychodynamics of Chronic Alcoholism," *Journal of Nervous and Mental Diseases*, LXXXVI (1937), 538–48.

[43] Ronald Lippitt, "Techniques for Research in Group Living," *Journal of Social Issues*, II (1946), 55–61.

[44] Prescott Lecky, *Self-consistency: A Theory of Personality* (New York: Island Press, 1945).

[45] F. C. Thorne, "Directive Psychotherapy: II. The Theory of Self-consistency," *Journal of Clinical Psychology*, I (1945), 155–62; "Directive Psychotherapy: IX. Personality Integration and Self-regulation," *ibid.*, II (1946), 371–83.

shows poor judgment and shallow emotionality, and who seems unable to appreciate the reactions of others to his behavior has been discussed in the psychiatric literature for over half a century. Various terms, such as "moral imbecility," "constitutional inferiority," "anethopathy," "sociopathy," and "semantic dementia" have been applied to this class. The designation "psychopathy" is now the most widely accepted term.

Because of the difficulty in clearly specifying the psychopathological implications of the concept and of the resultant confusion in its use, the category has often been used as a sort of psychiatric midden. Many reputable clinicians have preferred to reject the concept altogether. Recently there has been a trend the other way. The concept has been restored, but with more precise demarcation and definition.

There is still opposition to the concept, centered around the contention that psychopathy is just a synonym for delinquency, or social maladjustment. It has been one of the purposes of this paper to show that the essential diagnostic element is not social maladjustment, per se, or even a special kind of social maladjustment such as amorality; rather, it is a deficiency in role-playing ability which is peculiarly liable to manifestation in social relationships.

Finally, the concept of role-playing seems to synthesize a wide range of diagnostic and therapeutical data; in this respect it is useful as a term which intends a set of verifiable facts. Hypotheses may also be deduced from the concept which may be submitted to empirical test. The concept itself is sociological and may be integrated with, and elucidated by, the extensive research that sociologists such as Mead, Cooley, and Kimball Young have already carried out along this line.

7
PARANOIA AND THE DYNAMICS OF EXCLUSION[1]
Edwin M. Lemert

One of the few generalizations about psychotic behavior which sociologists have been able to make with a modicum of agreement and assurance is that such behavior is a result or manifestation of a disorder in communication between the individual and society. The generalization, of course, is a large one, and, while it can be illustrated easily with case history materials, the need for its conceptual refinement and detailing of the process by which disruption of communication occurs in the dynamics of mental disorder has for some time been

Source: Edwin M. Lemert, "Paranoia and the Dynamics of Exclusion," Sociometry, **25**: 2–20, 1962.
[1] The research for this paper was in part supported by a grant from the California State Department of Mental Hygiene, arranged with the assistance of Dr. W. A. Oliver, Associate Superintendent of Napa State Hospital, who also helped as a critical consultant and made the facilities of the hospital available.

apparent. Among the more carefully reasoned attacks upon this problem is Cameron's formulation of the paranoid pseudo-community (1).

In essence, the conception of the paranoid pseudo-community can be stated as follows:[2]

Paranoid persons are those whose inadequate social learning leads them in situations of unusual stress to incompetent social reactions. Out of the fragments of the social behavior of others the paranoid person symbolically organizes a pseudo-community whose functions he perceives as focused on him. His reactions to this *supposed community* of response which he sees loaded with threat to himself bring him into open conflict with the actual community and lead to his temporary or permanent isolation from its affairs. The "real" community, which is unable to share in his attitudes and reactions, takes action through forcible restraint or retaliation *after* the paranoid person "bursts into defensive or vengeful activity" (1).

That the community to which the paranoid reacts is "pseudo" or without existential reality is made unequivocal by Cameron when he says:

As he (the paranoid person) begins attributing to others the attitudes which he has towards himself, he unintentionally organizes these others into a functional community, a group unified in their supposed reactions, attitudes and plans with respect to him. He in this way organizes individuals, some of whom are actual persons and some only inferred or imagined, into a whole which satisfies for the time being his immediate need for explanation but which brings no assurance with it, and usually serves to increase his tensions. The community he forms not only fails to correspond to any organization shared by others but actually contradicts this consensus. More than this, the actions ascribed by him to its personnel are not actually performed or maintained by them; *they are united in no common undertaking against him* (1). (Italics ours.)

The general insightfulness of Cameron's analysis cannot be gainsaid and the usefulness of some of his concepts is easily granted. Yet a serious question must be raised, based upon empirical inquiry, as to whether in actuality the insidious qualities of the community to which the paranoid reacts are pseudo or a symbolic fabrication. There is an alternative point of view, which is the burden of this paper, namely that, while the paranoid person reacts differentially to his social environment, it is also true that "others" react differentially to him and this reaction commonly if not typically involves covertly organized action and conspiratorial behavior in a very real sense. A further extension of our thesis is that these differential reactions are reciprocals of one another, being interwoven and concatenated at each and all phases of a process of exclusion which arises in a special kind of relationship. Delusions and associated behavior must be understood in a context of exclusion which attenuates this relationship and disrupts communication.

By thus shifting the clinical spotlight away from the individual to a relation-

---

[2] In a subsequent article Cameron (2) modified his original conception, but not of the social aspects of paranoia, which mainly concern us.

ship and a process, we make an explicit break with the conception of paranoia as a disease, a state, a condition, or a syndrome of symptoms. Furthermore, we find it unnecessary to postulate trauma of early childhood or arrested psychosexual development to account for the main features of paranoia—although we grant that these and other factors may condition its expression.

This conception of paranoia is neither simple *a priori* theory nor is it a proprietary product of sociology. There is a substantial body of writings and empirical researches in psychiatry and psychology which question the sufficiency of the individual as primary datum for the study of paranoia. Tyhurst, for example, concludes from his survey of this literature that reliance upon intrapsychic mechanisms and the "isolated organism" have been among the chief obstacles to fruitful discoveries about this disorder (18). Significantly, as Milner points out, the more complete the investigation of the cases the more frequently do unendurable external circumstances make their appearance (13). More precisely, a number of studies have ended with the conclusions that external circumstances —changes in norms and values, displacement, strange environments, isolation, and linguistic separation—may create a paranoid disposition in the absence of any special character structure (15). The recognition of paranoid reactions in elderly persons, alcoholics, and the deaf adds to the data generally consistent with our thesis. The finding that displaced persons who withstood a high degree of stress during war and captivity subsequently developed paranoid reactions when they were isolated in a foreign environment commands special attention among data requiring explanation in other than organic or psychodynamic terms (7, 10).

From what has been said thus far, it should be clear that our formulation and analysis will deal primarily with what Tyhurst (18) calls paranoid patterns of behavior rather than with a clinical entity in the classical Kraepelinian sense. Paranoid reactions, paranoid states, paranoid personality disturbances, as well as the seldom-diagnosed "true paranoia," which are found superimposed or associated with a wide variety of individual behavior or "symptoms," all provide a body of data for study so long as they assume priority over other behavior in meaningful social interaction. The elements of behavior upon which paranoid diagnoses are based—delusions, hostility, aggressiveness, suspicion, envy, stubbornness, jealousy, and ideas of reference—are readily comprehended and to some extent empathized by others as social reactions, in contrast to the bizarre, manneristic behavior of schizophrenia or the tempo and affect changes stressed in manic-depressive diagnoses. It is for this reason that paranoia suggests, more than any other forms of mental disorder, the possibility of fruitful sociological analysis.

DATA AND PROCEDURE

The first tentative conclusions which are presented here were drawn from a study of factors influencing decisions to commit mentally disordered persons to hospitals, undertaken with the cooperation of the Los Angeles County Department of Health in 1952. This included interviews by means of schedules with members of 44 families in Los Angeles County who were active petitioners in commitment proceedings and the study of 35 case records of public health officer commitments. In 16 of the former cases and in seven of the latter, paranoid symptoms were conspicuously present. In these cases family members and others had plainly accepted or "normalized" paranoid behavior, in some instances longstanding, until other kinds of behavior or exigencies led to critical judgments that "there was something wrong" with the person in question, and, later, that hospitalization was necessary. Furthermore, these critical judgments seemed to signal changes in the family attitudes and behavior towards the affected persons which could be interpreted as contributing in different ways to the form and intensity of the paranoid symptoms.

In 1958 a more refined and hypothesis-directed study was made of eight cases of persons with prominent paranoid characteristics. Four of these had been admitted to the state hospital at Napa, California, where they were diagnosed as paranoid schizophrenic. Two other cases were located and investigated with the assistance of the district attorney in Martinez, California. One of the persons had previously been committed to a California state hospital, and the other had been held on an insanity petition but was freed after a jury trial. Added to these was one so-called "White House case," which had involved threats to a President of the United States, resulting in the person's commitment to St. Elizabeth's Hospital in Washington, D. C. A final case was that of a professional person with a history of chronic job difficulties, who was designated and regarded by his associates as "brash," "queer," "irritating," "hypercritical," and "thoroughly unlikeable."

In a very rough way the cases made up a continuum ranging from one with very elaborate delusions, through those in which fact and misinterpretation were difficult to separate, down to the last case, which comes closer to what some would call paranoid personality disturbance. A requirement for the selection of the cases was that there be no history or evidence of hallucinations and also that the persons be intellectually unimpaired. Seven of the cases were of males, five of whom were over 40 years of age. Three of the persons had been involved in repeated litigations. One man published a small, independent paper devoted to exposures of psychiatry and mental hospitals. Five of the men had been or were associated with organizations, as follows: a small-town high school, a government research bureau, an association of agricultural producers, a university, and a contracting business.

The investigations of the cases were as exhaustive as it was possible to make them, reaching relatives, work associates, employers, attorneys, police, physicians, public officials and any others who played significant roles in the lives of the persons involved. As many as 200 hours each were given to collecting data on some of the cases. Written materials, legal documents, publications and psychiatric histories were studied in addition to the interview data. Our procedure in the large was to adopt an interactional perspective which sensitized us to sociologically relevant behavior underlying or associated with the more apparent and formal context of mental disorder. In particular we were concerned to establish the order in which delusions and social exclusion occur and to determine whether exclusion takes conspiratorial form.

THE RELEVANT BEHAVIOR

In another paper (8) we have shown that psychotic symptoms as described in formal psychiatry are not relevant bases for predictions about changes in social status and social participation of persons in whom they appear. Apathy, hallucinations, hyperactivity, mood swings, tics, tremors, functional paralysis or tachychardias have no intrinsic social meanings. By the same token, neither do such imputed attributes as "lack of insight," "social incompetence" or "defective role-taking ability" favored by some sociologists as generic starting points for the analysis of mental disorders. Rather, it is behavior which puts strain on social relationships that leads to status changes: informal or formal exclusion from groups, definition as a "crank," or adjudication as insane and commitment to a mental hospital (8). This is true even where the grandiose and highly bizarre delusions of paranoia are present. Definition of the socially stressful aspects of this disorder is a minimum essential, if we are to account for its frequent occurrence in partially compensated or benign form in society, as well as account for its more familiar presence as an official psychiatric problem in a hospital setting.

It is necessary, however, to go beyond these elementary observations to make it pre-eminently clear that strain is an emergent product of a relationship in which the behaviors of two or more persons are relevant factors, and in which the strain is felt both by ego and *alter* or *alters*. The paranoid relationship includes reciprocating behaviors with attached emotions and meanings which, to be fully understood, must be described cubistically from at least two of its perspectives. On one hand the behavior of the individual must be seen from the perspective of others or that of a group, and conversely the behavior of others must be seen from the perspective of the involved individual.

From the vantage of others the individual in the paranoid relationship shows:

1   A disregard for the values and norms of the primary group, revealed by giving priority to verbally definable values over those which are implicit, a lack of loyalty in return for confidences, and victimizing and intimidating persons in positions of weakness.
2   A disregard for the implicit structure of groups, revealed by presuming to privileges not accorded him, and the threat or actual resort to formal means for achieving his goals.

The second items have a higher degree of relevancy than the first in an analysis of exclusion. Stated more simply, they mean that, to the group, the individual is an ambiguous figure whose behavior is uncertain, whose loyalty can't be counted on. In short, he is a person who can't be trusted because he threatens to expose informal power structures. This, we believe, is the essential reason for the frequently encountered idea that the paranoid person is "dangerous" (4).

If we adopt the perceptual set of ego and see others or groups through his eyes, the following aspects of their behavior become relevant:

1   the spurious quality of the interaction between others and himself or between others interacting in his presence;
2   the overt avoidance of himself by others;
3   the structured exclusion of himself from interaction.

The items we have described thus far—playing fast and loose with the primary group values by the individual, and his exclusion from interaction—do not alone generate and maintain paranoia. It is additionally necessary that they emerge in an interdependent relationship which requires trust for its fulfillment. The relationship is a type in which the goals of the individual can be reached only through cooperation from particular others, and in which the ends held by others are realizable if cooperation is forthcoming from ego. This is deduced from the general proposition that cooperation rests upon perceived trust, which in turn is a function of communication (11). When communication is disrupted by exclusion, there is a lack of mutually perceived trust and the relationship becomes dilapidated or paranoid. We will now consider the process of exclusion by which this kind of relationship develops.

THE GENERIC PROCESS OF EXCLUSION

The paranoid process begins with persistent interpersonal difficulties between the individual and his family, or his work associates and superiors, or neighbors, or other persons in the community. These frequently or even typically arise out of bona fide or recognizable issues centering upon some actual or threatened loss of status for the individual. This is related to such things as the death of relatives, loss of a position, loss of professional certification, failure to be promoted, age and physiological life cycle changes, mutilations, and changes in family and marital relationships. The status changes are distinguished by the fact that they leave no alternative acceptable to the individual, from whence comes their "intolerable" or "unendurable" quality. For example: the man trained to be a teacher who loses his certificate, which means he can never teach; or the man of 50 years of age who is faced with loss of a promotion which is a regular order of upward mobility in an organization, who knows that he can't "start over"; or the wife undergoing hysterectomy, which mutilates her image as a woman.

In cases where no dramatic status loss can be discovered, a series of failures often is present, failures which may have been accepted or adjusted to, but with progressive tension as each new status situation is entered. The unendurability of the current status loss, which may appear unimportant to others, is a function of an intensified commitment, in some cases born of an awareness that there is a quota placed on failures in our society. Under some such circumstances, failures have followed the person, and his reputation as a "difficult person" has preceded him. This means that he often has the status of a stranger on trial in each new group he enters, and that the groups or organizations willing to take a chance on him are marginal from the standpoint of their probable tolerance for his actions.

The behavior of the individual—arrogance, insults, presumption of privilege and exploitation of weaknesses in others—initially has a segmental or checkered pattern in that it is confined to status-committing interactions. Outside of these, the person's behavior may be quite acceptable—courteous, considerate, kind, even indulgent. Likewise, other persons and members of groups vary considerably in their tolerance for the relevant behavior, depending on the extent to which it threatens individual and organizational values, impedes functions, or sets in motion embarrassing sequences of social actions. In the early generic period, tolerance by others for the individual's aggressive behavior generally speaking is broad, and it is very likely to be interpreted as a variation of normal behavior, particularly in the absence of biographical knowledge of the person. At most, people observe that "there is something odd about him," or "he must be upset," "or he is just ornery," or "I don't quite understand him" (3).

At some point in the chain of interactions, a new configuration takes place in perceptions others have of the individual, with shifts in figure-ground relations. The individual, as we have already indicated, is an ambiguous figure, comparable to textbook figures of stairs or outlined cubes which reverse themselves when studied intently. From a normal variant the person becomes "unreliable," "untrustworthy," "dangerous," or someone with whom others "do not wish to be involved." An illustration nicely apropos of this came out in the reaction of the head of a music department in a university when he granted an interview to a man who had worked for years on a theory to compose music mathematically: "When he asked to be placed on the staff so that he could use the electronic computers of the University *I shifted my ground* . . . when I offered an objection to his theory, he became disturbed, so I changed my reaction to 'yes and no.' "

As is clear from this, once the perceptual reorientation takes place, either as the outcome of continuous interaction or through the receipt of biographical information, interaction changes qualitatively. In our words it becomes *spurious,* distinguished by patronizing, evasion, "humoring," guiding conversation onto selected topics, underreaction, and silence, all calculated either to prevent intense interaction or to protect individual and group values by restricting access to them. When the interaction is between two or more persons in the individual's presence it is cued by a whole repertoire of subtle expressive signs which are meaningful only to them.

The net effects of spurious interaction are to:

1   stop the flow of information to ego;
2   create a discrepancy between expressed ideas and affect among those with whom he interacts;
3   make the situation or the group image an ambiguous one for ego, much as he is for others.

Needless to say this kind of spurious interaction is one of the most difficult for an adult in our society to cope with, because it complicates or makes decisions impossible for him and also because it is morally invidious.[3]

The process from inclusion to exclusion is by no means an even one. Both individuals and members of groups change their perceptions and reactions, and vacillation is common, depending upon the interplay of values, anxieties and guilt on both sides. Members of an excluding group may decide they have been unfair and seek to bring the individual back into their confidence. This overture may be rejected or used by ego as a means of further attack. We have also found that ego may capitulate, sometimes abjectly, to others and seek group re-entry, only to be rejected. In some cases compromises are struck and a partial reintegration of ego into informal social relations is achieved. The direction which informal exclusion takes depends upon ego's reactions, the degree of communication between his interactors, the composition and structure of the informal groups, and the perceptions of "key others" at points of interaction which directly affect ego's status.

ORGANIZATIONAL CRISIS AND FORMAL EXCLUSION

Thus far we have discussed exclusion as an informal process. Informal exclusion may take place but leave ego's formal status in an organization intact. So long as this status is preserved and rewards are sufficient to validate it on his terms, an uneasy peace between him and others may prevail. Yet *ego's* social isolation and his strong commitments make him an unpredictable factor; furthermore the rate of change and internal power struggles, especially in large and complex organizations, means that preconditions of stability may be short lived.

Organizational crises involving a paranoid relationship arise in several ways. The individual may act in ways which arouse intolerable anxieties in others, who demand that "something be done." Again, by going to higher authority or making appeals outside the organization, he may set in motion procedures which leave those in power no other choice than to take action. In some situations ego remains relatively quiescent and does not openly attack the organization. Action against him is set off by growing anxieties or calculated motives of associates— in some cases his immediate superiors. Finally, regular organizational procedures incidental to promotion, retirement or reassignment may precipitate the crisis.

Assuming a critical situation in which the conflict between the individual and members of the organization leads to action to formally exclude him, several possibilities exist. One is the transfer of ego from one department, branch or division of the organization to another, a device frequently resorted to in the armed services or in large corporations. This requires that the individual be persuaded to make the change and that some department will accept him. While this may be accomplished in different ways, not infrequently artifice, withhold-

---

[3] The interaction in some ways is similar to that used with children, particularly the *"enfant terrible."* The function of language in such interaction was studied by Sapir (16) years ago.

ing information, bribery, or thinly disguised threats figure conspicuously among the means by which the transfer is brought about. Needless to say, there is a limit to which transfers can be employed as a solution to the problem, contingent upon the size of the organization and the previous diffusion of knowledge about the transferee.

Solution number two we call encapsulation, which, in brief, is a reorganization and redefinition of ego's status. This has the effect of isolating him from the organization and making him directly responsible to one or two superiors who act as his intermediators. The change is often made palatable to ego by enhancing some of the material rewards of his status. He may be nominally promoted or "kicked upstairs," given a larger office, or a separate secretary, or relieved of onerous duties. Sometimes a special status is created for him.

This type of solution often works because it is a kind of formal recognition by the organization of ego's intense commitment to his status and in part a victory for him over his enemies. It bypasses them and puts him into direct communication with higher authority who may communicate with him in a more direct manner. It also relieves his associates of further need to connive against him. This solution is sometimes used to dispose of troublesome corporation executives, high-ranking military officers, and academic *personae non gratae* in universities.

A third variety of solutions to the problem of paranoia in an organization is outright discharge, forced resignation or non-renewal of appointment. Finally, there may be an organized move to have the individual in the paranoid relationship placed on sick leave, or to compel him to take psychiatric treatment. The extreme expression of this is pressure (as on the family) or direct action to have the person committed to a mental hospital.

The order of the enumerated solutions to the paranoid problem in a rough way reflects the amount of risk associated with the alternatives, both as to the probabilities of failure and of damaging repercussions to the organization. Generally, organizations seem to show a good deal of resistance to making or carrying out decisions which require expulsion of the individual or forcing hospitalization, regardless of his mental condition. One reason for this is that the person may have power within the organization, based upon his position, or monopolized skills and information,[4] and unless there is a strong coalition against him the general conservatism of administrative judgments will run in his favor. Herman Wouk's novel of *The Caine Mutiny* dramatizes some of the difficulties of cashiering a person from a position of power in an essentially conservative military organization. An extreme of this conservatism is illustrated by one case in which we found a department head retained in his position in an organization even though he was actively hallucinating as well as expressing paranoid delusions.[5] Another factor working on the individual's side is that discharge of a person in a position of power reflects unfavorably upon those who placed him

[4] For a systematic analysis of the organizational difficulties in removing an "unpromotable" person from a position see (9).
[5] One of the cases in the first study.

there. Ingroup solidarity of administrators may be involved, and the methods of the opposition may create sympathy for ego at higher levels.

Even when the person is almost totally excluded and informally isolated within an organization, he may have power outside. This weighs heavily when the external power can be invoked in some way, or when it automatically leads to raising questions as to the internal workings of the organization. This touches upon the more salient reason for reluctance to eject an uncooperative and retaliatory person, even when he is relatively unimportant to the organization. We refer to a kind of negative power derived from the vulnerability of organizations to unfavorable publicity and exposure of their private lives that are likely if the crisis proceeds to formal hearings, case review or litigation. This is an imminent possibility where paranoia exists. If hospital commitment is attempted, there is a possibility that a jury trial will be demanded, which will force leaders of the organization to defend their actions. If the crisis turns into a legal contest of this sort, it is not easy to prove insanity, and there may be damage suits. Even if the facts heavily support the petitioners, such contests can only throw unfavorable light upon the organization.

THE CONSPIRATORIAL NATURE OF EXCLUSION

A conclusion from the foregoing is that organizational vulnerability as well as anticipations of retaliations from the paranoid person lay a functional basis for conspiracy among those seeking to contain or oust him. Probabilities are strong that a coalition will appear within the organization, integrated by a common commitment to oppose the paranoid person. This, the exclusionist group, demands loyalty, solidarity and secrecy from its members; it acts in accord with a common scheme and in varying degrees utilizes techniques of manipulation and misrepresentation.

Conspiracy in rudimentary form can be detected in informal exclusion apart from an organizational crisis. This was illustrated in an office research team in which staff members huddled around a water cooler to discuss the unwanted associate. They also used office telephones to arrange coffee breaks without him and employed symbolic cues in his presence, such as humming the Dragnet theme song when he approached the group. An office rule against extraneous conversation was introduced with the collusion of supervisors, ostensibly for everyone, actually to restrict the behavior of the isolated worker. In another case an interview schedule designed by a researcher was changed at a conference arranged without him. When he sought an explanation at a subsequent conference, his associates pretended to have no knowledge of the changes.

Conspiratorial behavior comes into sharpest focus during organizational crises in which the exclusionists who initiate action become an embattled group. There is a concerted effort to gain consensus for this view, to solidify the group and to halt close interaction with those unwilling to completely join the coalition. Efforts are also made to neutralize those who remain uncommitted but who can't be kept ignorant of the plans afoot. Thus an external appearance of unanimity is given even if it doesn't exist.

Much of the behavior of the group at this time is strategic in nature, with determined calculations as to "what we will do if he does this or that." In one of our cases, a member on a board of trustees spoke of the "game being played" with the person in controversy with them. Planned action may be carried to the length of agreeing upon the exact words to be used when confronted or challenged by the paranoid individual. Above all there is continuous, precise communication among exclusionists, exemplified in one case by mutual exchanging of copies of all letters sent and received from ego.

Concern about secrecy in such groups is revealed by such things as carefully closing doors and lowering of voices when ego is brought under discussion. Meeting places and times may be varied from normal procedures; documents may be filed in unusual places and certain telephones may not be used during a paranoid crisis.

The visibility of the individual's behavior is greatly magnified during this period; often he is the main topic of conversation among the exclusionists, while rumors of the difficulties spread to other groups, which in some cases may be drawn into the controversy. At a certain juncture steps are taken to keep the members of the ingroup continually informed of the individual's movements and, if possible, of his plans. In effect, if not in form, this amounts to spying. Members of one embattled group, for example, hired an outside person unknown to their accuser to take notes on a speech he delivered to enlist a community organization on his side. In another case, a person having an office opening onto that of a department head was persuaded to act as an informant for the nucleus of persons working to depose the head from his position of authority. This group also seriously debated placing an all-night watch in front of their perceived malefactor's house.

Concomitant with the magnified visibility of the paranoid individual, come distortions of his image, most pronounced in the inner coterie of exclusionists. His size, physical strength, cunning, and anecdotes of his outrages are exaggerated, with a central thematic emphasis on the fact that he is dangerous. Some individuals give cause for such beliefs in that previously they have engaged in violence or threats, others do not. One encounters characteristic contradictions in interviews on this point, such as: "No, he has never struck anyone around here—just fought with the policemen at the State Capitol," or "No, I am not afraid of him, but one of these days he will explode."

It can be said parenthetically that the alleged dangerousness of paranoid persons storied in fiction and drama has never been systematically demonstrated. As a matter of fact, the only substantial data on this, from a study of delayed admissions, largely paranoid, to a mental hospital in Norway, disclosed that "neither the paranoiacs nor paranoids have been dangerous, and most not particularly troublesome" (14). Our interpretation of this, as suggested earlier, is that the imputed dangerousness of the paranoid individual does not come from physical fear but from the organizational threat he presents and the need to justify collective action against him.[6]

---

[6] *Supra*, p. 3.

However, this is not entirely tactical behavior—as is demonstrated by anxieties and tensions which mount among those in the coalition during the more critical phases of their interaction. Participants may develop fears quite analogous to those of classic conspirators. One leader in such a group spoke of the period of the paranoid crisis as a "week of terror," during which he was wracked with insomnia and "had to take his stomach pills." Projection was revealed by a trustee who, during a school crisis occasioned by discharge of an aggressive teacher, stated that he "watched his shadows," and "wondered if all would be well when he returned home at night." Such tensional states, working along with a kind of closure of communication within the group, are both a cause and an effect of amplified group interaction which distorts or symbolically rearranges the image of the person against whom they act.

Once the battle is won by the exclusionists, their version of the individual as dangerous becomes a crystallized rationale for official action. At this point misrepresentation becomes part of a more deliberate manipulation of ego. Gross misstatements, most frequently called "pretexts," become justifiable ways of getting his cooperation, for example, to get him to submit to psychiatric examination or detention preliminary to hospital commitment. This aspect of the process has been effectively detailed by Goffman, with his concept of a "betrayal funnel" through which a patient enters a hospital (5). We need not elaborate on this, other than to confirm its occurrence in the exclusion process, complicated in our cases by legal strictures and the ubiquitous risk of litigation.

THE GROWTH OF DELUSION

The general idea that the paranoid person symbolically fabricates the conspiracy against him is in our estimation incorrect or incomplete. Nor can we agree that he lacks insight, as is so frequently claimed. To the contrary, many paranoid persons properly realize that they are being isolated and excluded by concerted interaction, or that they are being manipulated. However, they are at a loss to estimate accurately or realistically the dimensions and form of the coalition arrayed against them.

As channels of communication are closed to the paranoid person, he has no means of getting feedback on consequences of his behavior, which is essential for correcting his interpretations of the social relationships and organization which he must rely on to define his status and give him identity. He can only read overt behavior without the informal context. Although he may properly infer that people are organized against him, he can only use confrontation or formal inquisitorial procedures to try to prove this. The paranoid person must provoke strong feelings in order to receive any kind of meaningful communication from others—hence his accusations, his bluntness, his insults. Ordinarily this is non-deliberate; nevertheless, in one complex case we found the person consciously provoking discussions to get readings from others on his behavior. This man said of himself: "Some people would describe me as very perceptive, others would describe me as very imperceptive."

The need for communication and the identity which goes with it does a good deal to explain the preference of paranoid persons for formal, legalistic, written communications, and the care with which many of them preserve records of their contracts with others. In some ways the resort to litigation is best interpreted as the effort of the individual to compel selected others to interact directly with him as equals, to engineer a situation in which evasion is impossible. The fact that the person is seldom satisfied with the outcome of his letters, his petitions, complaints and writs testifies to their function as devices for establishing contact and interaction with others, as well as "setting the record straight." The wide professional tolerance of lawyers for aggressive behavior in court and the nature of Anglo-Saxon legal institutions, which grew out of a revolt against conspiratorial or star-chamber justice, mean that the individual will be heard. Furthermore his charges must be answered; otherwise he wins by default. Sometimes he wins small victories, even if he loses the big ones. He may earn grudging respect as an adversary, and sometimes shares a kind of legal camaraderie with others in the courts. He gains an identity through notoriety.

REINFORCEMENT OF DELUSION

The accepted psychiatric view is that prognosis for paranoia is poor, that recoveries from "true" paranoia are rare, with the implication that the individual's delusions more or less express an unalterable pathological condition. Granting that the individual's needs and dispositions and his self-imposed isolation are significant factors in perpetuating his delusional reactions, nevertheless there is an important social context of delusions through which they are reinforced or strengthened. This context is readily identifiable in the fixed ideas and institutionalized procedures of protective, custodial, and treatment organizations in our society. They stand out in sharpest relief where paranoid persons have come into contact with law enforcement agencies or have been hospitalized. The cumulative and interlocking impacts of such agencies work strongly to nurture and sustain the massive sense of injustice and need for identity which underlie the delusions and aggressive behavior of the paranoid individual.

Police in most communities have a well-defined concept of cranks, as they call them, although the exact criteria by which persons are so judged are not clear. Their patience is short with such persons: in some cases they investigate their original complaints and if they conclude that the person in question is a crank they tend to ignore him thereafter. His letters may be thrown away unanswered, or phone calls answered with patronizing reassurance or vague promises to take steps which never materialize.

Like the police, offices of district attorneys are frequently forced to deal with persons they refer to as cranks or soreheads. Some offices delegate a special deputy to handle these cases, quaintly referred to in one office as the "insane deputy." Some deputies say they can spot letters of cranks immediately, which means that they are unanswered or discarded. However, family or neighborhood quarrels offer almost insoluble difficulties in this respect, because often it is impossible to determine which of two parties is delusional. In one office some complainants are called "fifty-fifty," which is jargon meaning that it is impossible to say whether they are mentally stable. If one person seems to be persistently causing trouble, deputies may threaten to have him investigated, which, however, is seldom if ever done.

Both police and district attorney staffs operate continuously in situations in which their actions can have damaging legal or political repercussions. They tend to be tightly ingrouped and their initial reaction to outsiders or strangers is one of suspicion or distrust until they are proved harmless or friendly. Many of their office procedures and general manner reflect this—such as carefully recording in a log book names, time, and reason for calling of those who seek official interviews. In some instances a complainant is actually investigated before any business will be transacted with him.

When the paranoid person goes beyond local police and courts to seek redress through appeals to state or national authorities, he may meet with polite evasion, perfunctory treatment of his case or formalized distrust. Letters to administrative people may beget replies up to a certain point, but thereafter they are ignored. If letters to a highly placed authority carry threats, they may lead to an investigation by security agencies, motivated by the knowledge that assassinations are not unknown in American life. Sometimes redress is sought in legislatures, where private bills may be introduced, bills which by their nature can only be empty gestures.

In general, the contacts which the delusional person makes with formal organizations frequently disclose the same elements of shallow response, evasion or distrust which played a part in the generic process of exclusion. They become part of a selective or selected pattern of interaction which creates a social environment of uncertainty and ambiguity for the individual. They do little to correct and much to confirm his suspicion, distrust and delusional interpretations. Moreover, even the environment of treatment agencies may contribute to the furtherance of paranoid delusion, as Stanton and Schwartz have shown in their comments on communication within the mental hospital. They speak pointedly of the "pathology of communication" brought about by staff practices of ignoring explicit meanings in statements or actions of patients and reacting to inferred or imputed meanings, thereby creating a type of environment in which "the paranoid feels quite at home" (17).

Some paranoid or paranoid-like persons become well known locally or even throughout larger areas to some organizations. Persons and groups in the community are found to assume a characteristic stance towards such people—a stance of expectancy and preparedness. In one such case, police continually checked the whereabouts of the man and, when the governor came to speak on the courthouse steps, two officers were assigned the special task of watching the man as he stood in the crowd. Later, whenever he went to the state capitol, a number of state police were delegated to accompany him when he attended committee hearings or sought interviews with state officials.[7] The notoriety this man

---

[7] This technique in even more systematic form is sometimes used in protecting the President of the United States in "White House cases."

acquired because of his reputed great strength in tossing officers around like tenpins was an obvious source of pleasure to him, despite the implications of distrust conveyed by their presence.

It is arguable that occupying the role of the mistrusted person becomes a way of life for these paranoids, providing them with an identity not otherwise possible. Their volatile contentions with public officials, their issuance of writings, publications, litigations in *persona propria,* their overriding tendency to contest issues which other people dismiss as unimportant or as "too much bother" become a central theme for their lives, without which they would probably deteriorate.

If paranoia becomes a way of life for some people, it is also true that the difficult person with grandiose and persecutory ideas may fulfill certain marginal functions in organizations and communities. One is his scapegoat function, being made the subject of humorous by-play or conjectural gossip as people "wonder what he will be up to next." In his scapegoat role, the person may help integrate primary groups within larger organizations by directing aggressions and blame towards him and thus strengthening feelings of homogeneity and consensus of group members.

There are also instances in which the broad, grapeshot charges and accusations of the paranoid person function to articulate dissatisfactions of those who fear openly to criticize the leadership of the community, organization, or state, or of the informal power structures within these. Sometimes the paranoid person is the only one who openly espouses values of inarticulate and politically unrepresented segments of the population (12). The "plots" which attract the paranoid person's attention—dope rings, international communism, monopolistic "interests," popery, Jewry, or "psychopoliticians"—often reflect the vague and ill-formed fears and concerns of peripheral groups, which tend to validate his self-chosen role as a "protector." At times in organizational power plays and community conflicts his role may even be put to canny use by more representative groups as a means of embarrassing their opposition.

THE LARGER SOCIO-CULTURAL CONTEXT

Our comments draw to a close on the same polemic note with which they were begun, namely, that members of communities and organizations do unite in common effort against the paranoid person prior to or apart from any vindictive behavior on his part. The paranoid community is real rather than pseudo in that it is composed of reciprocal relationships and processes whose net results are informal and formal exclusion and attenuated communication.

The dynamics of exclusion of the paranoid person are made understandable in larger perspective by recognizing that decision making in American social organization is carried out in small, informal groups through casual and often subtle male interaction. Entree into such groups is ordinarily treated as a privilege rather than a right, and this privilege tends to be jealously guarded. Crucial decisions, including those to eject persons or to reorganize their status in larger formal organizations, are made secretly. The legal concept of "privileged communication" in part is a formal recognition of the necessity for making secret decisions within organizations.

Added to this is the emphasis placed upon conformity in our organization-oriented society and the growing tendency of organization elites to rely upon direct power for their purposes. This is commonly exercised to isolate and neutralize groups and individuals who oppose their policies both inside and outside of the organization. Formal structures may be manipulated or deliberately reorganized so that resistant groups and individuals are denied or removed from access to power or the available means to promote their deviant goals and values. One of the most readily effective ways of doing this is to interrupt, delay or stop the flow of information.

It is the necessity to rationalize and justify such procedures on a democratic basis which leads to concealment of certain actions, misrepresentation of their underlying meaning and even the resort to unethical or illegal means. The difficulty of securing sociological knowledge about these techniques, which we might call the "controls behind the controls," and the denials by those who use them that they exist are logical consequences of the perceived threat such knowledge and admissions become to informal power structures. The epiphenomena of power thus become a kind of shadowy world of our culture, inviting conjecture and condemnation.

CONCLUDING COMMENT

We have been concerned with a process of social exclusion and with the ways in which it contributes to the development of paranoid patterns of behavior. While the data emphasize the organizational forms of exclusion, we nevertheless believe that these are expressions of a generic process whose correlates will emerge from the study of paranoia in the family and other groups. The differential responses of the individual to the exigencies of organized exclusion are significant in the development of paranoid reactions only insofar as they partially determine the "intolerable" or "unendurable" quality of the status changes confronting him. Idiosyncratic life history factors of the sort stressed in more conventional psychiatric analyses may be involved, but equally important in our estimation are those which inhere in the status changes themselves, age being one of the more salient of these. In either case, once situational intolerability appears, the stage is set for the interactional process we have described.

Our cases, it will be noted, were all people who remained undeteriorated, in contact with others and carrying on militant activities oriented towards recognizable social values and institutions. Generalized suspiciousness in public places and unprovoked aggression against strangers were absent from their experiences. These facts, plus the relative absence of "true paranoia" among mental-hospital populations, leads us to conclude that the "pseudo-community" associated with random aggression (in Cameron's sense) is a sequel rather than an integral part of paranoid patterns. They are likely products of deterioration and fragmentation of personality appearing, when and if they do, in the paranoid person after long or intense periods of stress and complete social isolation.

References

1   Cameron, N., "The Paranoid Pseudo-community," *American Journal of Sociology,* 1943, **46,** 33–38.

2   Cameron, N., "The Paranoid Pseudo-community Revisited," *American Journal of Sociology,* 1959, **65,** 52–58.

3   Cumming, E., and J. Cumming, *Closed Ranks,* Cambridge, Mass.: Harvard Press, 1957, Ch. VI.

4   Dentler, R. A., and K. T. Erikson, "The Functions of Deviance in Groups," *Social Problems,* 1959, **7,** 102.

5   Goffman, E., "The Moral Career of the Mental Patient," *Psychiatry,* 1959, **22,** 127 ff.

6   Jaco, E. G., "Attitudes Toward, and Incidence of Mental Disorder: A Research Note," *Southwestern Social Science Quarterly,* June, 1957, p. 34.

7   Kine, F. F., "Aliens' Paranoid Reaction," *Journal of Mental Science,* 1951, **98,** 589–594.

8   Lemert, E., "Legal Commitment and Social Control," *Sociology and Social Research,* 1946, **30,** 370–378.

9   Levenson, B., "Bureaucratic Succession," in *Complex Organizations,* A. Etzioni, (ed.), New York: Holt, Rinehart and Winston, 1961, 362–395.

10   Listivan, I., "Paranoid States: Social and Cultural Aspects," *Medical Journal of Australia,* 1956, 776–778.

11   Loomis, J. L., "Communications, The Development of Trust, and Cooperative Behavior," *Human Relations,* 1959, **12,** 305–315.

12   Marmor, J., "Science, Health and Group Opposition" (mimeographed paper), 1958.

13   Milner, K. O., "The Environment as a Factor in the Etiology of Criminal Paranoia," *Journal of Mental Science,* 1949, **95,** 124–132.

14   Odegaard, O., "A Clinical Study of Delayed Admissions to a Mental Hospital," *Mental Hygiene,* 1958, **42,** 66–77.

15   Pederson, S., "Psychological Reactions to Extreme Social Displacement (Refugee Neuroses)," *Psychoanalytic Review,* 1946, **36,** 344–354.

16   Sapir, E., "Abnormal Types of Speech in Nootka," *Canada Department of Mines, Memoir 62,* 1915, No. 5.

17   Stanton, A. H., and M. S. Schwartz, *The Mental Hospital,* New York: Basic Books, 1954, 200–210.

18   Tyhurst, J. S., "Paranoid Patterns," in A. H. Leighton, J. A. Clausen, and R. Wilson, (eds.), *Exploration in Social Psychiatry,* New York: Basic Books, 1957, Ch. II.

PART TWO

Social Epidemiology
of Mental Illness

Social epidemiology is the study of the distribution of various forms of illness throughout the social structure. The social epidemiologist attempts to establish valid and reliable estimates of the incidence and prevalence of various types of illness and to determine the influence of certain social and personal variables upon the frequency and onset of illness. Thus the epidemiologist typically works with such personal variables as age and sex and with such social variables as income, education, religion, residence, mobility, and migration. Epidemiological studies serve to highlight the variables which are associated with given forms of illness and which frequently suggest causal or etiological information about psychiatric disturbances. Each paper in this section investigates the relationship of one or more personal and social variables to some aspect of mental illness.

ECOLOGICAL AND SOCIOECONOMIC STATUS
ASPECTS OF MENTAL DISORDER

Human ecology is the study of the distribution of people as determined by various forces in the environment. These forces are presumed to operate in such a way that distinctive patterns of distribution emerge in connection with conditions like juvenile delinquency, crime, drug addiction, and alcoholism.

The relationship between urbanization and social disorganization had been recognized long before the relationship between urbanization and mental illness became evident. Rural-urban comparisons of crime rates, suicide, divorce, and vice have shown these phenomena to be most severe in urban areas, especially in the rapidly growing industrial cities.[1]

As the study of urban sociology advanced in the 1920s, rather striking differen-

tials of social problems in different sections of the city were discovered. While some urban areas were found to be as stable as any well-organized rural neighborhood, other parts of the city were found to be in extreme stages of social disorganization.[2] Disorganization was found to be confined largely to certain areas and not to be characteristic of the city as a whole. Such discoveries led researchers to raise questions and to suggest causal hypotheses for the occurrence and distribution of various types of deviant behavior. One direction this interest took was the exploration of the relationship between mental illness and urban areas.

Dunham examined the spatial or ecological distribution of mental illness within a large urban area, and found an overall pattern which fit the ecological scheme of the city. Rates of hospitalization were highest in Chicago's central business district and decreased regularly as the distance from the center of the city became greater. Schizophrenia, which made up the majority of hospitalizations, fit the general pattern, but rates of manic-depressive psychosis were distributed randomly throughout various ecological areas. Since highest rates were discovered in the most disorganized areas of the city, one major implication of this investigation is that environmental conditions are highly important in the development of schizophrenia. However, since Dunham uncovered some evidence that the diagnosis of manic-depressive psychosis was influenced by social considerations, the hypothesis of environmental influences on this specific type of disorder cannot be ruled out.[3]

Critics have argued that the ecological distribution of disorder described by Dunham can be accounted for in other ways. The "downward drift" hypothesis has been the most popular. This hypothesis assumes that although schizophrenia originates in the population in a random manner, persons who develop schizophrenia cannot maintain normal social obligations, and so drift socially downward, tending to collect in areas of high admission rates. The hypothesis is explored although not supported in a later publication by Faris and Dunham of which the reprinted paper is a part.[4] Nor do data collected by other researchers from New Haven, Connecticut; Buffalo, New York; and Hagerstown, Maryland, reveal evidence for downward drift.[5]

Given the sociologist's traditional interest in social stratification, it is not surprising that this interest took one form in the study of the socioeconomic aspects of mental illness. As early as 1856 a relationship between social position and mental disorder had been reported. Sandifer indicates that Jarvis found that the "pauper" class in Massachusetts furnished proportionately more cases of "insanity" than the "independent" class—sixty-four times as much, to be exact.[6] Additional investigations appeared with increasing frequency during the following decades, although few of the studies were free from various methodological and conceptual shortcomings. Assessment of the stratification system was often impressionistic or, at other times, was inferred indirectly from singular factors assumed to be class-linked. Study populations were rather small and narrowly defined, being limited primarily to hospitalized cases. Analysis of data by diagnostic category was made difficult since standard classification schemes were rarely employed; moreover, they tended to undergo periodic revision. However, it had become apparent by the end of World War II that at least the frequency, if not the type, of mental illness was not distributed throughout a stratified society in a random fashion.

By the time that Hollingshead and Redlich formulated their now classic New Haven study of social stratification and mental disorder, many of the problems associated with conducting valid epidemiological research had been recognized, and efforts could be made to circumvent the most biasing factors.[7] In addition, recent developments within the area of general sociology contributed to the understanding and methods of social class evaluation.[8] The Hollingshead and Redlich study, a portion of which is reprinted here, is distinguished by the fact that it was the first to employ a social class measure which was composed of multiple indicators of status, and which also resulted in meaningful class distinctions. As a result of the New Haven study, the relationship between social class and mental illness could be discussed with more conclusiveness and specificity than previously.

Hollingshead and Redlich found that the prevalence and type of treated mental disorder were related to position in the class structure. Rates of disorder were lowest in the upper classes and highest in the lower classes. Neurotic disorders were more prevalent in the upper classes, but the psychoses characterized the lower classes. The authors stress that their findings are limited in scope since their data are cases of diagnosed (treated) disorder and may not accurately reflect the total distribution of mental disorder in the community.

Subsequently, Kaplan, Reed, and Richardson directed their attention toward social class and rates of "undetected" mental illness.[9] A test of the hypothesis on nonhospitalized and hospitalized psychotics from two distinctly different socioeconomic areas of Boston disclosed that rates of treated psychosis confirmed the Hollingshead and Redlich hypothesis. But rates of untreated psychosis were in the opposite direction, i.e., higher in upper-middle-class than in lower-middle-class areas. It should be noted, however, that this does not imply that psychosis is actually distributed randomly throughout different social classes, for when the authors combined the hospitalized and nonhospitalized rates to arrive at a true or total rate of incidence, psychosis was still most prevalent within the lower socioeconomic class level.

The significance of this study is severalfold. First, the authors have demonstrated a wider applicability of the hypothesis of an inverse relationship between social class and psychosis than the Hollingshead and Redlich data allowed.[10] It appears that for psychotic disorders, at least, the social class and mental illness hypothesis characterizes the United States population as a whole. Second, the data identify one condition when the hypothesis does not apply, e.g., cases of undiagnosed psychosis, and specify the actual direction of the relationship. Third, they have been able to demonstrate something that Hollingshead and Redlich's data could only suggest: a differential social class readiness to exclude potentially ill persons from the household. As such, the study also contributes to the growing body of evidence that attitudes toward and opportunities for hospitalization are more relevant determinants of diagnosed illness than clinical symptoms per se. This latter point is especially salient in the Wanklin et al. paper.

PERSONAL AND SOCIAL CHARACTERISTICS
IN MENTAL ILLNESS

One commonly employed index of the incidence of mental disorder is first admission rates of hospitalization. The Wanklin et al. study analyzes the social and personal characteristics of patients admitted to two Canadian mental hospitals. High rates of hospitalization were associated with urban residence; single, divorced, and separated marital status; less than eight years of education; and recent immigration among the foreign born. One important implication of the paper is that first admission rates of hospitalization are accurate predictors of the actual incidence of mental illness only when acutely psychotic patients are analyzed. Under conditions of less severe disorders, social pressures act as intervening variables between the incidence of the illness and actual hospitalization. Hospitalization under conditions of less severe disorders may only reflect the differential tolerance limits of certain segments of the population for deviant behavior.

Roberts and Myers analyze the data on which the Hollingshead and Redlich investigation is based in terms of racial identity, religious affiliation, ethnic origin, and immigrational status. Some striking diagnostic differentials among the various groupings were observed. The authors' efforts to tie the rates to social conditions, patterns of interaction, and group values provide an excellent demonstration of how epidemiological research can contribute to a better understanding of the etiology of illness. Because the rates of illness found in this investigation were also compared with epidemiological data collected previously, some of the consequences of changing attitudes toward psychiatry and changing social conditions on religious and ethnic groupings can be inferred.

The findings of the previous two investigations in respect to higher rates of mental disorder within the spatially mobile population than within the non-mobile one deserve additional comment. Various investigations, some dealing with international migration and others dealing with migration of a more limited scope (interregional, intercity, intracity, etc.), have usually substantiated the finding of higher rates of disorder among the mobile segments of the population.[11] However, exceptions are contained in the literature. Halevi found lower rates of disorder among immigrants to Israel, and Murphy had similar findings for immigrants to both Israel and Singapore.[12] Odegaard found that, with the exception of migrants to the city of Oslo, migrants had lower rates of psychiatric hospital admission than those who remained in their natal communities.[13] Although lower rates of psychiatric disorder among migrants are more characteristic among European populations than among American ones, at least one study based on native Americans confirms this trend toward higher rates. When a schizophrenic population obtained from a state hospital serving the New Orleans community was compared with a control group of medical patients, it was found that the schizophrenic patients showed significantly less geographic mobility than the controls.[14] Such findings suggest that, in addition to the characteristics of the migrant and stationary segments of various populations, the personal meaning of migration, the relationship between the migrant and the host community, and the characteristics of the host community itself are some of the variables or con-

ditions that need to be taken into account when drawing conclusions about the relationship between spatial mobility and rates of psychiatric disorder.

In almost all modern industrial societies, a large proportion of the population has had to find occupations and a style of life considerably different from those of its parents and grandparents. Investigations that have addressed themselves to the mental health consequences of mobility within the class structure have pointed to difficulties experienced by the mobile segment of the population. Even before the turn of the century, Emile Durkheim had suggested that both upward and downward mobility in the class structure resulted in increased rates of suicide. Mobility was said to increase the number of persons who found themselves in anomic situations, ones in which the definitions of social norms were vague and ambiguous.[15]

Studies of the consequences of interclass mobility have usually revealed that persons moving up or down in the social stratification hierarchy showed higher rates of diagnosed psychotic and psychoneurotic disorders than persons who remained on the same social class level.[16] The paper by Ellis is one such example but differs from several others with the same basic concern in two respects. The sample was not composed of persons presently undergoing psychiatric treatment, and thus reflects the trend to pursue the distribution of unrecognized disorder in the community. But more importantly, perhaps, Ellis goes beyond the usual study in this area by suggesting the interpersonal mechanisms by which status mobility comes to be associated with what is regarded as psychoneurotic symptomatology and behavior.

Looking at groups of upwardly mobile and stationary unmarried career women, Ellis found that neurotic symptoms were more evident among those persons who had risen upward in the class structure. Moreover, a greater percentage of upwardly mobile females reported unsatisfactory family and community relations during childhood and adolescence. Ellis surmises not only that the incentive for upward social mobility lies most probably in unsatisfactory primary group relations but also that achieved status mobility has a disruptive effect on subsequent interpersonal relations and emotional well-being.

Mulford's paper is one of few national surveys which have dealt with the social and personal characteristics associated with the prevalence of alcoholism. Alcoholism is defined as a label attached to certain persons because their patterns of heavy drinking have led to difficulties with employers, spouses, and community officials. The data indicate that alcoholics in the United States tend to be divorced or unmarried, male, Baptist, and in relatively high-status occupations. This paper contributes to our knowledge of alcoholism as a form of deviancy, as well as to the methodology of conducting epidemiological surveys on a nationwide scale.

CROSS-CULTURAL APPROACHES
AND MENTAL ILLNESS

Although it has long been a commonplace assumption that man is strongly influenced by his social and cultural surroundings, only recently have investigators

89

begun systematically to relate variations in cultural and social settings to mental illness. The area which has evolved, in which cultural considerations are of paramount importance, is called cross-cultural psychiatry, although the terms ethnopsychiatry and anthropological psychiatry have also been employed. Cross-cultural psychiatry is a special case of epidemiological research, differing primarily in that the sources of data allow comparisons of a magnitude greater than would ordinarily be found within any one society.

As pointed out by Murphy and Leighton, cross-cultural psychiatry is still in a formative stage, and thus there is still considerable fluidity in defining its problems and research interests.[17] However, the preponderance of work characterizing the area reflects a dual emphasis, an examination of how illness characteristics vary among cultures as well as an effort to discover what factors or combinations of factors in the environment produce or perpetuate various kinds of psychiatric disorders.

The Murphy et al. paper identifies those signs and symptoms which are commonly attached to the label schizophrenia and which consistently appear among divergent national groupings. They also demonstrate that other signs occur with varying frequencies.

Enright and Jaeckle, rather than approaching the problem from the perspective of comparing divergent cultural groupings, concentrate upon two cultural subgroups, Americans of Japanese and Filipino extraction. Their results make quite evident that what is classified as schizophrenia is actually based upon different signs and symptoms. The authors stress that reliance on diagnostic categories developed in the Western world obfuscates clear and important differences, and thus limits the usefulness of psychiatric classification.

Both of these investigations make evident that the behavior called schizophrenia in one culture is not exactly what is called schizophrenia in another culture. In this respect each of these studies supports the contention that if schizophrenia were merely a disease entity, as many persons seem to think it is, one could expect a greater amount of symptomatic uniformity than was actually found. However, neither one of these studies interprets the results from a broader and more sociological perspective, which indicates that one reason differences between cultural groups were observed stemmed from differential tolerance limits for deviancy. For example, the symptoms observed among Japanese, East Indians, or British overseas subjects, if occurring within some other subgroups, would not necessarily lead the audience members to initiate action which would result in psychiatric attention. Such a possibility should not be excluded from consideration.

The Eaton and Weil paper demonstrates that although rates of psychiatric illness are very low among a particular American retreatist subgroup, the Hutterites, what would normally be called mental illness by the majority group culture does indeed exist and that the forms it takes are divergent from the majority group society. This paper is more comprehensive than most cross-cultural studies for several reasons. Not only does it highlight similarities and differences in behavioral forms between the Hutterites and other minority groupings, but it ties together more closely than the preceding papers have been able to do just what cultural characteristics probably precipitate and channel behavioral and cognitive abnormalities. The paper also highlights societal reactions to what is regarded by the group as mental illness. The labeled person is regarded as ill, rather than crazy, and there does not seem to be any stigma upon being so labeled. The Hutterites, unlike the majority of Americans, do not exclude the deviant from the home by sending him off to a mental institution. Rather, when this label is applied to an individual, community support is mustered and care is provided in the home community.[18]

References

1   Robert E. L. Faris, *Social Disorganization,* The Ronald Press Company, New York, 1948; Edwin H. Sutherland and Donald R. Cressey, *Principles of Criminology,* 7th ed., J. B. Lippincott Company, Philadelphia, 1966. See especially chap. 9, "Culture Areas and Crime," pp. 183–215.

2   Faris, *op. cit.*

3   A later study did find higher rates of manic-depressive psychosis in high socioeconomic than low socioeconomic areas of a city. See John A. Clausen and Melvin L. Kohn, "Relation of Schizophrenia to the Social Structure of a Small City," in Benjamin Pasamanick, editor, *Epidemiology of Mental Disorder,* American Association for the Advancement of Science, Publication 60, Washington, 1959, pp. 69–85.

4   Robert E. L. Faris and H. Warren Dunham, *Mental Disorders in Urban Areas,* Chicago: The University of Chicago Press, Chicago, 1939 (reprinted by Hafner Publishing Company, Inc., New York, 1960).

5   August B. Hollingshead and Frederick C. Redlich, "Social Stratification and Schizophrenia," *American Sociological Review,* **19:** 302–306, 1954; R. Lapouse et al., "The Drift Hypothesis and Socioeconomic Differentials in Schizophrenia," *American Journal of Public Health,* **46:** 978–986, 1956; John A. Clausen and Melvin L. Kohn, "Relation of Schizophrenia to the Social Structure of a Small City," in Benjamin Pasamanick, editor, *op. cit.*

6   Myron G. Sandifer, Jr., "Social Psychiatry 100 Years Ago," *American Journal of Psychiatry,* **118:** 749–750, 1962.

7   August B. Hollingshead and Frederick C. Redlich, *Social Class and Mental Illness,* John Wiley & Sons, Inc., New York, 1958.

8   W. Lloyd Warner, *Social Class in America,* Science Research Associates, Inc., Chicago, 1949 (reprinted by Harper & Row, Publishers, Incorporated, New York, 1960).

9   Several earlier "home surveys" are cited in this paper. Some others are Tsung-Yi Lin, "A Study of the Incidence of Mental Disorder in Chinese and Other Cultures," *Psychiatry,* **16:** 313–316, 1953. The term "incidence" is misapplied by Lin, since rates of treated and untreated disorder were combined and yielded what is usually called a "true prevalence rate." See also Alexander Leighton et al., *My Name is Legion,* vol. I of *The Stirling County Study of Psychiatric Disorder and Sociocultural Environment,* Basic Books, Inc., Publishers, New York, 1959; Leo Srole et al., *Mental Health in the Metropolis: The Midtown Manhattan Study,* McGraw-Hill Book Company, New York, 1962.

10   For a critique of the Hollingshead and Redlich study see S. M. Miller and Elliot Mishler, "Social Class, Mental Illness, and American Psychiatry: An Expository Review," in Frank Riessman, Jerome Cohen, and Arthur Pearl, editors, *Mental Health of the Poor,* The Free Press of Glencoe, New York, 1964, pp. 16–36.

11   Benjamin Malzberg and Everett S. See, *Migration and Mental Disease: A Study of First Admissions to Hospitals for Mental Disease 1939–1941,* Social Science Research

Council, New York, 1956; John A. Clausen and Melvin L. Kohn, "Relation of Schizophrenia to the Social Structure of a Small City," in Benjamin Pasamanick, editor, *op. cit.;* the article by Ellis, "Social Psychological Correlates of Upward Social Mobility Among Unmarried Career Women," has some data on this matter. The geographically mobile women (as indexed by intercity, interstate, and international movement) showed a greater prevalence of psychoneurotic traits.

12   H. S. Halevi, "Frequency of Mental Illness among Jews in Israel," *International Journal of Social Psychiatry,* **9:** 268–282, 1963; H. B. M. Murphy, *Social Change and Mental Health in Causes of Mental Disorders: A Review of Epidemiological Knowledge,* Milbank Memorial Fund, New York, 1961.

13   Ornulv Odegaard, "The Distribution of Mental Diseases in Norway, A Contribution to the Ecology of Mental Disorder," *Acta Psychiatrica et Neurologica,* 1945, pp. 270–276.

14   Mary H. Lystad, "Social Mobility among Selected Groups of Schizophrenic Patients," *American Sociological Review,* **22:** 288–292, 1957. See also E. Gartly Jaco, *The Social Epidemiology of Mental Disorders,* Russell Sage Foundation, New York, 1960. An examination of all new admissions for psychoses in Texas for a two-year period disclosed that, in general, migrants to the state showed rates similar to the native-born.

15   Emile Durkheim, *Suicide,* The Free Press of Glencoe, New York, 1951.

16   Lystad, *op. cit.;* Clausen and Kohn, "Relation of Schizophrenia to the Social Structure of a Small City," in Benjamin Pasamanick, editor, *op. cit.;* August B. Hollingshead, R. Ellis, and E. Kirby, "Social Mobility and Mental Illness," *American Sociological Review,* **19:** 557–584, 1954; Srole et al., *op. cit.*

17   Jane M. Murphy and Alexander H. Leighton, *Approaches to Cross-Cultural Psychiatry,* Cornell University Press, Ithaca, N.Y., 1965.

18   Problems in epidemiological research have not been taken up in this section, but they should not be ignored. See August B. Hollingshead, "Some Issues in the Epidemiology of Schizophrenia," *American Sociological Review,* **26:** 5–13, 1964; Victor D. Sanua, "The Etiology and Epidemiology of Mental Illness and Problems of Methodology: With Special Emphasis on Schizophrenia," *Mental Hygiene,* **47:** 607–621, 1963; Bruce P. Dohrenwend and Barbara Snell Dohrenwend, "The Problem of Validity in Field Studies of Psychological Disorder," *Journal of Abnormal Psychology,* **70:** 52–69, 1965.

8
THE ECOLOGY OF THE FUNCTIONAL
PSYCHOSES IN CHICAGO
H. Warren Dunham

Studies of the geographical distribution of social data go back for over a hundred years. Certain it is, that this technique as used by the modern social scientist is hardly a new one. However, improved statistical methods, more adequate, basic population data, and somewhat improved statistical records enable the modern social scientist to get a more accurate picture, quantitatively speaking, of any social phenomona which he may study. Many of those early studies were made by distributing a type of social data within the counties or provinces of a country or nation. Later studies attempted distributions within certain areas of the modern nineteenth century cities. In England, Mayhew attempted some early distribution studies with the city as a unit.[1] It is with Booth who studied economic and social stratification in London, that we get the beginning of the idea of the natural, circular growth of the city,[2] an idea which was later refined and improved by Burgess's attempt to delimit the so-called natural areas of the city and make the scheme applicable to all American cities,[3] with the exception of certain local variations often due to topography.

These nineteenth century social scientists studied by the use of this method practically all of the social problems which are receiving attention by the modern students of social phenomena. However, there was no significant attempt to study insanity by this method, although there were some early statistical studies giving rates by areas or provinces within a country.[4] Otherwise, scientific men of the nineteenth century were definitely concerned with this problem, for there is ample evidence in the literature to prove the scientific interest in the study of mental disorder.[5] The definite determination that the *spirochaeta pallida* was the cause of general paralysis in about 1897[6] was the first great achievement in isolating a definite mental disease. During practically the entire nineteenth century, idiocy, alcoholism, moral insanity, melancholia, mania, dementia, and epilepsy constituted the chief diagnostic categories of mental disorder.[7]

While there were, as pointed out above, some attempts to compute insanity

Source: H. Warren Dunham, "The Ecology of the Functional Psychoses in Chicago," *American Sociological Review,* **2:** 467–479, 1937.
This is part of a more complete study on the ecology of mental disorder which is now being prepared for publication by R. E. Faris and H. W. Dunham. Read at the annual meeting, Chicago, December 29, 1936.

[1] H. Mayhew and J. Benny, *The Criminal Prisons in London,* London, Charles Griffin and Co., 1862.
[2] *Life and Labor of the People of London,* London, Williams and Margate, 1891.
[3] R. E. Park and E. W. Burgess, *The City,* The University of Chicago Press, 1925, p. 50.
[4] *Jour. of the Statist. Soc.* of London, 1851, 49–62; 1852, 250–256.
[5] In this connection, it is interesting to note the establishment of numerous scientific journals in the European countries devoted to scientific inquiry into insanity. *The Journal of Mental Science, London,* was founded in 1855; the *Annales d'hygiene publique et de medicine legale* in Paris in 1829; *The Journal of Nervous and Mental Disease,* in America about 1873.
[6] See A. Rosanoff, *Manual of Psychiatry,* New York, John Wiley and Sons, 6th ed., 1926, p. 270.
[7] J. C. Bucknill and D. H. Tuke, *A Manual of Psychological Medicine,* Philadelphia, Blanchard and Lea, 1858, pp. 88–100.

rates by areas within the countries, it is doubtful if much of this material was ever portrayed on maps. An early study of the geographical distribution of mental disorder was made by J. S. Sutherland[8] in 1901. At about the same time in America, W. A. White presented a paper on the geographical distribution of insanity in the United States.[9] While he presented no actual maps he pointed out, on the basis of his statistics, that the older and longer settled sections of the country had a much higher incidence of insanity than the newer and more recently settled sections. He also found that among the Negroes in the Southern states there was a much lower rate of insanity than among the Negroes in the Northern states. The fact that both men were concerned with all cases of insanity indicates the fact, even at this date, that any diagnostic category of mental disorder in use was hardly of significance for statistical manipulation.[10]

These scattered attempts at presenting and interpreting insanity rates for provinces within a geographical area, were the only studies purporting to investigate insanity in relation to the social milieu in which it developed. In the evolving scientific division of labor the study of mental disease and abnormality had come to be the exclusive concern of the medical men both in Europe and America. This resulted in the very definite tendency to study mental disease by the same methods as had been used in studying physical disease, and consequently this tended to hinder and restrict other approaches to this problem. Since 1930, at the University of Chicago, certain ecological, statistical, and case studies have been made of certain types of mental disorder. This paper has for its purpose the presentation of the ecology of the two main functional psychoses in Chicago and a theoretical discussion of the implications of this ecological analysis.

As is well known, schizophrenia is the most frequently diagnosed mental disorder in the state hospitals throughout the country. This psychosis constitutes between twenty-five and forty percent of the first admissions to hospitals for mental disorders. The percentage varies throughout the United States.[11] Between 1922 and 1931, 7,253 persons from Chicago were admitted to the state hospitals for the first time and given a diagnosis of schizophrenia. Frequency rates for these cases were calculated for the local communities. For the population base of the rates, the estimated adult population of each community[12] in 1927, the

---

[8] "Geographical Distribution of Lunacy in Scotland," *Brit. Assn. for Adv. of Sci.*, Glasgow, September, 1901. See also W. R. McDermott, "The Topographical Distribution of Insanity," *Brit. Med. Jour.*, London, 1908, 1950.

[9] "Geographical Distribution of Insanity in the United States," *Jour. Nerv. and Ment. Disease*, **30**, 1903, 257–279. Also see A. O. Wright, "The Increase of Insanity," *Conference of Charities and Corrections*, 1884, pp. 228–236.

[10] Some statistics on the incidence of insanity by types are to be found in an article by P. Garnier, "La Folie a Paris," *Annales d'hygiene publique et de medicine legale*, **23**, 1890, 5–44.

[11] *Mental Patients in State Hospitals*, 1928, Washington, D.C., Bureau of the Census.

[12] The local communities, as worked out by the Local Community Research Council at the University of Chicago, were used as a basis for these rates. Some of the communities which contained populations too small to be used as a basis for reliable rates were combined with adjoining areas and three of the communities near the center of the city were sub-divided. In this manner, the city was divided so that each community contains reasonably homogeneous characteristics and yet has a sufficiently large population to make possible reliable rates. Rates on some of the maps presented in this paper are distributed in the 120 sub-communities of Chicago which are merely a further refinement of the census tracts. The use of these sub-communities makes possible a somewhat finer discrimination of the differences to be found in the various parts of the city.

middle year, is used.[13] An ecological map of these rates indicates very definitely that schizophrenia shows a great variation in frequency in the different communities. The pattern formed by the rates is a regular and typical one[14] and follows in the gradients of its rates Burgess's scheme of the circular growth of the city. The distribution of rates range from 111 in community 1, at the extreme northeast end of the city, to 1,195 in community 32, the loop, or central business district. The average rate is 289 and the median rate is 322, and these figures indicate that the bulk of the community rates are clustered at the low end of a skewed frequency distribution. In other words, there are a few communities close to the center of the city which have extremely high rates, while the great bulk of the communities have much lower rates. The highest rates for schizophrenia are in the hobohemia, the rooming-house, and the foreign-born communities close to the center of the city. There are no glaring exceptions to this regular pattern. The noticeable rise of the rates in the South Chicago region is consistent with the regular pattern for Chicago, as these communities represent areas of some social disorganization due to their close approximation to the steel factories. In addition to the concentration of the rates in those communities close to the center of the city, it is significant to note the order of the rates in the South Side Negro belt. The three Negro areas in this belt extending south of the loop have rates of 662, 470, and 410 respectively. All of these rates are higher than the average and median rates and decline in a regular manner, similar to the rates on other radial lines from the city's center, and so tend to negate any theories in relation to race as a factor in schizophrenia. If race were a significant factor, there seems to be no legitimate reason why there should be such wide variations in the rates in these communities in which ninety percent of the population are Negroes.

Among these cases of schizophrenia, the males are slightly more numerous than the females, the ratio being 117 males to 100 females.[15] This would indicate that the factor of sex has some significance in connection with schizophrenia. However, in a study of the distribution of the male and female schizophrenic rates separately, there appears to be no radical deviation in the expected pattern.

Of the 7,253 cases, 3,916 are males. The rates range from 79 in community 1, to 1,416 in community 32. These are the same communities which form the extremes in the distribution of total schizophrenia. The average rate is 396 and

---

[13] The use of the adult population is not a perfect adjustment, of course, for age, but since there are few persons under twenty-one years of age in the schizophrenic group, the adjustment is probably adequate for the purpose. It should be noted that in those maps showing the distribution of cases in the 120 subcommunities of the city, there has been a closer refinement for age and these rates are based on the population fifteen years and over. It should also be noted that the rates in the more detailed 120 subcommunities are average rates as contrasted to total rates in the local communities.

[14] The phrase, "a regular and typical pattern" as used in this paper means one in which the high rates for given phenomena are to be found at the center of the city with the rates declining in every direction as one approaches the periphery. For a good example of such a pattern see C. R. Shaw, *Delinquency Areas*, University of Chicago Press, 1929.

[15] The sex ratio in the estimated adult population used as the basis for the rates is 105 males to 100 females. There is, then, a real excess of schizophrenics among the males, a fact which is also true of the total number of schizophrenics in the United States. See *Mental Patients in State Hospitals*, Washington, D.C., Bureau of the Census, 1928, p. 12. See also H. M. Pollock, "Frequency of Schizophrenia in Relation to Sex, Age, Environment, Nativity, and Race," *Schizophrenia—An Investigation of Most Recent Advances*, Reported by the Association for Research in Nervous and Mental Diseases, New York, Paul B. Hoeber, Inc., 1928.

the median rate is 365. This indicates the same type of frequency distribution as was noted in the distribution of the total schizophrenic rates.

The distribution of female rates, based on 3,337 cases, also shows a similar wide range. The lowest rate is 130 in community 8A, the Gold Coast, and the highest rate is 932 in community 28A, a hobohemia community directly west of the central business district. The average rate is 367 and the median rate is 312, and so a similar skewed frequency distribution is in evidence. This distribution of the female schizophrenic rates is typical of the other two, with approximately three exceptions. These three exceptions in the regularity of the pattern are to be found in community 32, which has an extremely low rate, and in communities 17 and $56\pm$[16] which have unexpected high rates. It is difficult to explain away these exceptions. However, it can be noted that in community 32, the central business district, the hobohemia community contributes practically all of the male cases, and that there are practically no desirable places for women to live in this community. The total number of women in the population is extremely low. There were ninety-eight male schizophrenic cases found in this community and only three female schizophrenic cases. These female cases included a maid at an expensive club on Michigan Boulevard, a resident of a first-class hotel, and a resident of a cheap hotel of a disorderly character on Wabash Avenue. The position of these three exceptional communities tends to reduce the resulting coefficient of correlation between the male and female schizophrenic rates to $.59\pm.07$. It is interesting to note that the sex ratio in the total schizophrenic group holds true for the high-rate schizophrenic areas as well as for the city as a whole. In the upper quartile of seventeen communities, the schizophrenic sex ratio is 143 to 100, while the sex ratio of the population in this area is only 130 males to 100 females.

Because of the limitations of space, the distribution of the rates for the separate types of schizophrenia are not discussed here,[17] but it is sufficient to point out that they all show heavy concentration in the disorganized areas of the city and present the familiar skewed frequency distribution, such as was noted in the distribution of the total schizophrenic cases. The paranoid and hebephrenic distributions of rates are similar to the distribution of total schizophrenic rates. However, the catatonic distribution of rates does not follow the pattern of the other types, although it does show a definite concentration of rates in certain of the disorganized areas of the city, notedly the foreign-born and Negro communities.

In addition to the distribution of the above schizophrenic rates, the case data which constitute these distributions, with the addition of three more years, have been distributed in the 120 sub-communities of Chicago.[18] The distribution of

[16] This community, $56\pm$, refers to the fact that the local communities 56, 57, 62, 64, and 65 were combined to form one community.

[17] See H. W. Dunham, *A Study of the Distribution of Six Major Psychoses in the Local Community Areas of Chicago.* (Master's Dissertation), University of Chicago, 1935.

[18] The opportunity to distribute these data in the 120 sub-communities was provided by the setting up of a W.P.A. project to study the trend of mental disease during the depression years. This project is sponsored by the State Psychopathic Institute of the Department of Public Welfare, State of Illinois. Dr. H. D. Singer of the Psychopathic Institute and Drs. Wirth and Burgess of the University of Chicago, served as advisers for the project.

the average yearly rate based on a total of 10,575 schizophrenic cases is shown in Map I.[19] [Map I not reproduced here.] The range of rates in this distribution is from 14 in community 92, an apartment and two flat area, to 150 in community 74, the central business district, with a median rate of 30.1 and an average rate of 34.6. The same skewed frequency distribution, as was noted in the previous distribution of schizophrenic rates, is also in evidence; likewise, the same concentration of rates is noticed, with the high average rates falling at the center of the city and the low rates on the periphery; the highest rates are to be found in the hobohemia, rooming house, foreign-born and Negro communities.

The objective findings in connection with the ecololgy of schizophrenia can be stated as follows: (1) The high rates for total schizophrenia are concentrated in communities of marked social disorganization in Chicago. (2) The distribution of the male and female schizophrenic rates separately shows the same concentration in the disorganized communities of the city. (3) The distribution of rates shows the same pattern and concentration by both local and sub-communities. (4) The high rates for paranoid and hebephrenic schizophrenia are concentrated also in these extremely socially disorganized communities in a similar fashion to the total group. The correlation coefficient between paranoid and hebephrenic schizophrenia is .75±.05. (5) The high rates for catatonic schizophrenia are concentrated mainly in the foreign-born and Negro communities. While this distribution is different from the other types because of the paucity of the catatonics in the rooming-house communities of the city, nevertheless, a definite concentration of rates is noted. (6) The rates for the three types of schizophrenic, as well as the rates for the total schizophrenic series show a skewed frequency distribution, with the bulk of the communities having low rates and a few of the communities at the center of the city having high rates.

While these different distributions of schizophrenic rates present an interesting comparison within themselves, they attain an additional significance when compared with the other main functional psychosis, manic-depressive. Because the diagnostic problems in the functional disorders are so great, a study of the distribution of the manic-depressive group might be significant in ascertaining whether or not any real distinction between them has been made. A preliminary distribution of manic-depressive rates was computed from a base of 734 cases, of which 296 were males and 438 were females. The sex ratio of 68 males to 100 females is very different from the sex ratio in the schizophrenic group. The range of rates is low as compared to any of the schizophrenic distributions, the rates varying from 8 in community 59, an area of second immigrant settlement, to 84 in community 28C,[20] a foreign-born section. The average rate is 37 and the

---

[19] It should be noted that the total case basis in these maps showing distributions by sub-communities include private hospital cases as well as state hospital cases. In the schizophrenic distribution, the private hospital cases are negligible, amounting in all to 13.7 percent of the total, while in the following manic-depressive distribution, the private hospital cases amount to exactly fifty percent of the total, a large enough percentage to affect the character of the distribution pattern. However, while there is a difference in the distribution of manic-depressive rates, when the cases from state and private hospitals are distributed separately (Pearsonian r=−.06±.10), this does not affect the conclusions set forth in this paper.
[20] The female catatonic group with approximately the same number of cases (711) has a much greater range, varying from zero in community 2, to 222 in community 24A. This indicates again the skewed distribution in any schizophrenic sample as contrasted to a manic-depressive sample.

median is 37, and this indicates that the characteristic skewness of the schizo-phrenic distributions is lacking. This distribution shows no marked concentration of the high rates close to the center of the city. In fact, far from being regular, the pattern of rates might be described as random. It is significant to note that while the highest rate is in a community near the center of the city, it is bor-dered by communities which have both low and median rates. This distribution, therefore, is different in many respects from the schizophrenic distributions which have been examined.

Because of the low case basis in the above distribution of manic-depressive rates, it seemed particularly desirable to study a distribution of rates based on a larger number of cases. The distribution of such rates in the sub-communities of Chicago is shown in Map II [Map II not reproduced here.], based on 2,311 cases. As might be expected from the preliminary distribution, there is an absence of the typical pattern. In this distribution, the rates range from 1.5 in community 70, a two-flat and single-home area, to 19.3 in community 74, the central business district. The median rate is 6.9 and the average rate is 7.2. The high rates show no semblance of a pattern in their distribution throughout the city. There are high rates at the center of the city and there are also some high rates on the periphery. This is very much at variance from any of the schizophrenic distribu-tions where, as has been shown, there is a complete absence of high rates in the outlying communities of the city. Again, the very definite lack of skewness in the manic-depressive frequency distribution is to be noted.

When the rates for each sex of the manic-depressive group are distributed in the sub-communities, the same random pattern is in evidence. The patterns are also random to each other as evidenced by a coefficient of correlation of .33±.08. This contrasts quite sharply with the relatively high correlation figure obtained when the schizophrenic rates by sex are considered together.

When the manic-depressive cases are separated into their respective types of manic and depressed, and are distributed in the 120 sub-communities, the dis-tribution of the rates in each type still forms a random pattern, although some-what dissimilar to the random pattern formed when the types are combined together. In other words, not only is there a random pattern formed by the total case basis of the manic-depressive rates, but the pattern is also random when either one of the two chief types in this diagnostic category are considered separately. The distribution of rates for each type is not only random in itself but is random when compared with the other type. In fact, the coefficient of correlation between them is .104±.10. This figure still remains low when the rates by sex, for each type, are correlated together, the coefficient being .15±.09, when the male manic rates are considered with the male depressed rates, and .30±.08 when the female manic rates are correlated with the female depressed rates.[21] These low correlation figures tell a story in themselves when compared

[21] The scantiness of the cases in the manic-depressive group throw some question on the reliability of the rates by sex and by type. See Frank A. Ross, "Ecology and the Statistical Method," *Amer. Jour. Sociol.*, **38,** January 1933, 507–522. Also see the reply to this criticism by C. C. Peters, "Note on a Mis-conception of Statistical Significance," *ibid.*, **39,** September 1933, 231–236. Ross examined Faris's insanity rates for the city of Chicago and pointed out that the number of cases used in the study were too few

with the correlation figures presented for schizophrenia, by sex and type, where high correlations are in evidence.

The objective findings in connection with the ecology of the manic-depressive psychoses can be stated as follows: (1) The pattern formed by the rates is a random one. Both high and low rates are distributed in no systematic fashion throughout the city. (2) The distribution for male and female manic-depressive rates separately shows the same random and unsystematic distribution. (3) The distribution of rates shows the same random pattern for both local and sub-communities. (4) The rates for the separate types of manic and depressed are also extremely random in their distribution. (5) While the addition of the private hospital cases tends to change the distribution of the rates in the city, the elimination of these cases does not change the random pattern of the distribution. (6) All of the distribution of manic-depressive rates shows an absence of skewness in their frequency distribution, with approximately the same number of communities having high rates as low rates.

That there is a vast difference between the distribution of rates in these two main functional psychoses is to be seen again when they are correlated together. The distribution of the rates for these two mental disorders in the 68 local communities of Chicago has a correlation of .37±.10. When the rates of these two psychoses in the 120 sub-communities are correlated, the coefficient figure is .24±.08. In other words, it appears that when any sample of schizophrenic cases is distributed, there is a definite pattern which follows the ecological structure of the city, while when any sample of manic-depressive cases is distributed, there is no pattern formed which fits into this ecological scheme of the city.

Further evidence on this point can be seen when the rates of these two mental disorders are correlated with certain indices of social life. In the second set of distributions of these two functional disorders, a correlation was effected between the respective rates and a housing index for the sub-communities. For this index the percentage ratio of hotels, apartments, and apartment hotels to the total number of dwellings in the sub-communities was used. The manic-depressive distribution correlated with this index .50±.07. When the manic-depressive cases from private hospitals are eliminated, and this index is correlated with the rates based upon a distribution of only manic-depressive state hospital cases, the correlation figure drops to .08±.10. The distribution of schizophrenic rates in the sub-communities of the city correlates with this housing index −.12±.09.

Other indices tend to bring out the differences in the distribution in these two functional psychoses. If one takes as an index of cultural level the median school grade reached by the population in any sub-community and correlates it with the manic-depressive rates, the resulting coefficient is .44±.07. When this index is correlated with the schizophrenic rates, the resulting coefficient figure is

---

and that the distribution pattern might be due to chance. However, when he combined areas and made a test with an error formula for determining the significance or non-significance of rates between different communities, he concluded that the pattern could not be due to chance alone. In the schizophrenic series the case basis has been so increased that it would seem that criticism on this point has been sufficiently answered. In the manic-depressive series, while the case basis is still rather low and the same criticism might be made as to this pattern, it would seem from the other statistical evidence that there is a marked difference in the pattern of the rates as compared to the schizophrenic pattern.

—.47±.07. This would seem to indicate a tendency for the manic-depressive cases to come from those urban areas with a fairly high cultural level. The negative correlation in connection with schizophrenia indicates exactly the opposite. This same situation is noted when correlating these rates with an index of economic level in the sub-communities. For such an index, the median monthly rental paid by families for housing in the community was taken. This index correlates with the manic-depressive rates at .41±.08, and with the schizophrenic rates at —.51±.07.

It was pointed out above in a footnote that in the second sample of manic-depressive cases, exactly fifty percent were admitted to public hospitals and fifty percent were admitted to private hospitals. This high percentage of private hospital cases in the manic-depressive group stands in sharp contrast to the low percentage of schizophrenic cases admitted to private hospitals. This high percentage of private hospital cases in the former group might be explained by either one of two conditions. First, there is a tendency for the private hospital to give the most hopeful diagnosis for the benefit of relatives which, of course, means, according to traditional psychiatry, a manic-depressive diagnosis.[22] Secondly, it is possible that there may be a real selection of manic-depressive cases by the private hospitals. Some psychiatrists in the Chicago area feel that the former condition is the true one. However, there is some evidence in this study to indicate that the second condition is somewhat more than a remote possibility. While the pattern of manic-depressive rates in any distribution of such cases does appear to be extremely random, the correlation coefficients, with certain selective indices, do indicate the tendency of the manic-depressive cases to come from a higher social and economic level in contrast with the schizophrenic cases. Some additional evidence on this point, similar to that presented above, is obtained by contrasting the manic-depressive patients with the schizophrenic patients, in terms of median rentals paid in the sub-communities. Over half of all the manic-depressive cases corrected for the population factor come from communities in the city which pay a median rental of $61.68 or above, while half of the schizophrenic cases, corrected for the population factor, come from communities which pay a median rental of $33.45 or above. There is no doubt that the excessive numbers of private hospital cases in the manic-depressive group tend to increase markedly this median rental figure. When the private hospital cases are eliminated, however, it is found that the remaining manic-depressive cases which are now entirely state hospital cases, come from communities where the median rental is $43.44 or above. This rental figure is still considerably higher than the rental figure of one-half the schizophrenic cases, where the private hospital cases were not eliminated. There is, then, apparently a definite tendency for the manic-depressive patients to come from a higher income group than the schizophrenic patients.

From this comparative study of the distribution of these two main functional psychoses, and their relation to certain indices of social life, the following con-

---

[22] In reference to this point it may be of some significance to note that in the psychoneurotic series 67 percent of the cases were admitted to private hospitals and only 33 percent to the state hospitals.

clusions might be briefly stated: (1) A comparison of the distribution of the rates of the schizophrenic and manic-depressive psychoses shows them to be unlike each other in almost every respect. (2) The schizophrenic rates show the typical ecological pattern and are concentrated in the disorganized areas of the city, while the manic-depressive rates do not show a typical pattern nor any definite concentration in the disorganized and poverty-stricken areas of the city. (3) There is a tendency, although not clearly defined, for the manic-depressive cases to come from a higher cultural and economic level as compared with the schizophrenic cases. (4) The schizophrenic rates show a skewed frequency distribution, while the manic-depressive rates show no such skewness in their distribution.

While this ecological and statistical evidence may not be conclusive, it does appear that there is some real distinction in the distribution of these two functional disorders in Chicago. How far this will hold true of other American cities is problematical. Every psychiatrist realizes that the diagnostic problems in the functional disorders are great, and the question can be raised as to whether anything is gained by making distributions of cases falling in these two categories, when the percent of diagnostic error is so high. The percent of error in the present data probably ranges from 30 to 40 percent—estimates given by the psychiatrists themselves. Even with this high percentage of error, the number of cases is large enough in each sample to assert that the pattern of rates in these two psychoses is a fairly reliable one. While it is necessary to be cautious about interpreting these data, certain implications can, with some justification, be pointed out. The random pattern in the manic-depressive distribution, in juxtaposition to the typical pattern in the schizophrenic distribution, would seem to imply that some valid distinction has been made in classification. From this implication, others follow. Chief of these might be the implication that the environment is a very potent factor in the etiology of the schizophrenic disorder, but that it plays no part in the manic-depressive disorder. It would then follow that, if environmental factors are not significant in manic-depressive, there is a certain justification for asserting the priority of hereditary and constitutional factors. This, of course, would be in line with the statistical studies of heredity in the functional psychoses which universally show that biological inheritance is more significant in manic-depressive than in schizophrenia. Even though there is a great difference between the patterns of rates of the two psychoses, it does not necesarily follow that the schizophrenic psychosis bears a definite relation to the environment and the manic-depressive psychosis does not. Both may be connected with different types of social processes. It is only that in the case of the schizophrenic pattern this connection appears to be more definitely established. A possible sociological explanation of the manic-depressive pattern might be found in the suggestion that precipitating factors are causal ones in relation to these psychoses.[23] Such precipitating factors occur in all social and economic

---

[23] On this point, see C. A. Bonner, "Psychogenic Factors as Causation Agents in Manic-Depressive Psychoses," Manic-Depressive Psychoses—Recent Advances, reported by the Association for Research in Nervous and Mental Disease, vol. XI, pp. 121–130; M. J. Brew, "Precipitating Factors in the Manic-depressive Psychoses," The Psychiatric Quarterly, 7, July, 1933, 401–410; and J. H. Travis, "Precipitating Factors in the Manic-Depressive Psychoses," ibid., 411–418.

levels of life and, consequently, are not so likely to have a definite connection with the community situation, but rather with the interplay of personality and psychological factors of family relationships and intimate personal contacts. An explanation of the high rates of schizophrenia in the extremely disorganized areas of the city has been made by stating that persons with schizophrenic tendencies or pre-dispositions drift down into these areas. If this hypothesis is a correct one, the implication would seem to follow from the evidence presented that the manic-depressives do not drift at all or at least show no tendency to drift into the disorganized areas of city life. These suggested implications are only intended to point the way toward additional research. First, however, it will be necessary to establish beyond a shadow of doubt that there is a difference in the distribution of these two functional disorders as outlined in this paper. Diagnostic problems still make this thesis somewhat uncertain. The study of the distribution of these two functional disorders in other American cities would appear to be the next step in this ecological research.

9

SOCIAL STRATIFICATION
AND PSYCHIATRIC DISORDERS

August B. Hollingshead and Frederick C. Redlich*

The research reported here grew out of the work of a number of men, who, during the last half century, have demonstrated that the social environment in which individuals live is connected in some way, as yet not fully explained, to the development of mental illness.[1] Medical men have approached this problem largely from the viewpoint of epidemiology.[2] Sociologists, on the other hand,

Source: August B. Hollingshead and Frederick C. Redlich, "Social Stratification and Psychiatric Disorders," *American Sociological Review,* **18:** 163–169, 1953.
The research reported here is supported by a grant from the National Institute of Mental Health of the United States Public Health Service to Yale University under the direction of Dr. F. C. Redlich, Chairman, Department of Psychiatry, and Professor August B. Hollingshead, Department of Sociology.

[1] For example, see, A. J. Rosanoff, *Report of a Survey of Mental Disorders in Nassau County, New York,* New York: National Committee for Mental Hygiene, 1916; Ludwig Stern, *Kulturkreis und Form der Geistigen Erkrankung,* (Sammlung Zwanglosen Abhandlungen aus dem Gebiete der Nerven-und-Geisteskrankheiten), X, No. 2, Halle a. S: C Marhold, 1913, pp. 1–62; J. F. Sutherland, "Geographical Distribution of Lunacy in Scotland," *British Association for Advancement of Science,* Glasgow, Sept. 1901; William A. White, "Geographical Distribution of Insanity in the United States," *Journal of Nervous and Mental Disease,* XXX (1903), pp. 257–279.

[2] For example, see: Trygve Braatoy, "Is it Probable that the Sociological Situation is a Factor in Schizophrenia?" *Psychiatrica et Neurologica,* XII (1937), pp. 109–138; Donald L. Gerard and Joseph Siegel, "The Family Background of Schizophrenia," *The Psychiatric Quarterly,* **24** (January, 1950), pp. 47–73; Robert W. Hyde and Lowell V. Kingsley, "Studies in Medical Sociology, 1: The Relation of Mental Disorders to the Community Socio-economic Level," *The New England Journal of Medicine,* **231,** No. 16 (October 19, 1944), pp. 543–548; Robert W. Hyde and Lowell V. Kingsley, "Studies in Medical Sociology, II: The Relation of Mental Disorders to Population Density," *The New England Journal of Medicine,* **231,** No. 17

have analyzed the question in terms of ecology,[3] and of social disorganization.[4] Neither psychiatrists nor sociologists have carried on extensive research into the specific question we are concerned with, namely, interrelations between the class structure and the development of mental illness. However, a few sociologists and psychiatrists have written speculative and research papers in this area.[5]

The present research, therefore, was designed to discover whether a relationship does or does not exist between the class system of our society and mental illnesses. Five general hypotheses were formulated in our research plan to test some dimension of an assumed relationship between the two. These hypotheses were stated positively; they could just as easily have been expressed either negatively or conditionally. They were phrased as follows:

I   The *expectancy* of a psychiatric disorder is related significantly to an individual's position in the class structure of his society.

II   The *types* of psychiatric disorders are connected significantly to the class structure.

III The type of *psychiatric treatment* administered is associated with patient's positions in the class structure.

IV   The *psycho-dynamics* of psychiatric disorders are correlative to an individual's position in the class structure.

V   *Mobility* in the class structure is neurotogenic.

(October 26, 1944), pp. 571—577; Robert W. Hyde and Roderick M. Chisholm, "Studies in Medical Sociology, III: The Relation of Mental Disorders to Race and Nationality," *The New England Journal of Medicine*, **231**, No. 18 (November 2, 1944), pp. 612–618; William Malamud and Irene Malamud, "A Socio-Psychiatric Investigation of Schizophrenia Occurring in the Armed Forces," *Psychosomatic Medicine*, **5** (October, 1943) pp. 364–375; B. Malzberg, *Social and Biological Aspects of Mental Disease*, Utica, N.Y.: State Hospital Press, 1940; William F. Roth and Frank H. Luton, "The Mental Health Program in Tennessee: Statistical Report of a Psychiatric Survey in a Rural County," *American Journal of Psychiatry*, **99** (March, 1943), pp. 662–675; J. Ruesch and Others, *Chronic Disease and Psychological Invalidism*, New York: American Society for Research in Psychosomatic Problems, 1946; J. Ruesch and others, *Duodenal Ulcer: A Sociopsychological Study of Naval Enlisted Personnel and Civilians*, Berkeley and Los Angeles: University of California Press, 1948; Jurgen Ruesch, Annemarie Jacobson, and Martin B. Loeb, "Acculturation and Illness," *Psychological Monographs: General and Applied*, Vol. 62, No. 5, Whole No. 292, 1948 (American Psychological Association, 1515 Massachusetts Ave., N.W., Washington 5, D.C.); C. Tietze, Paul Lemkau and M. Cooper, "A Survey of Statistical Studies on the Prevalence and Incidence of Mental Disorders in Sample Populations," *Public Health Reports*, 1909–27, 58 (December 31, 1943); C. Tietze, P. Lemkau and Marcia Cooper, "Schizophrenia, Manic Depressive Psychosis and Social-Economic Status," *American Journal of Sociology*, XLVII (September, 1941), pp. 167–175.

[3] Robert E. L. Faris, and H. Warren Dunham, *Mental Disorders in Urban Areas*. Chicago: University of Chicago Press, 1939; H. Warren Dunham, "Current Status of Ecological Research in Mental Disorder," *Social Forces*, **25** (March, 1947), pp. 321–326; R. H. Felix and R. V. Bowers, "Mental Hygiene and Socio-Environmental Factors," *The Milbank Memorial Fund Quarterly*, XXVI (April, 1948), pp. 125–147; H. W. Green, *Persons Admitted to the Cleveland State Hospital*, 1928–1937, Cleveland Health Council, 1939.

[4] R. E. L. Faris, "Cultural Isolation and the Schizophrenic Personality," *American Journal of Sociology*, XXXIX (September, 1934), pp. 155–169; R. E. L. Faris, "Reflections of Social Disorganization in the Behavior of a Schizophrenic Patient," *American Journal of Sociology*, L (September, 1944), pp. 134–141.

[5] For example, see: Robert E. Clark, "Psychoses, Income, and Occupational Prestige," *American Journal of Sociology*, **44** (March, 1949), pp. 433–440; Robert E. Clark, "The Relationship of Schizophrenia to Occupational Income and Occupational Prestige," *American Sociological Review*, **13** (June, 1948), pp. 325–330; Kingsley Davis, "Mental Hygiene and the Class Structure," *Psychiatry*, I (February, 1938), pp. 55–56; Talcott Parsons, "Psychoanalysis and the Social Structure," *The Psychoanalytical Quarterly*, XIX, No. 3 (1950), pp. 371–384; John Dollard and Neal Miller, *Personality and Psychotherapy*, New York: McGraw-Hill, 1950; Jurgen Ruesch, "Social Technique, Social Status, and Social Change in Illness," Clyde Kluckhohn and Henry A. Murray (editors), in *Personality in Nature, Society, and Culture*, New York: Alfred A. Knopf, 1949, pp. 117–130; W. L. Warner, "The Society, the Individual and his Mental Disorders," *American Journal of Psychiatry*, **94**, No. 2 (September, 1937), pp. 275–284.

Each hypothesis is linked to the others, and all are subsumed under the theoretical assumption of a functional relationship between stratification in society and the prevalence of particular types of mental disorders among given social classes or strata in a specified population. Although our research was planned around these hypotheses, we have been forced by the nature of the problem of mental illness to study *diagnosed* prevalence of psychiatric disorders, rather than *true* or *total* prevalence.

METHODOLOGICAL PROCEDURE

The research is being done by a team of four psychiatrists,[6] two sociologists,[7] and a clinical psychologist.[8] The data are being assembled in the New Haven urban community, which consists of the city of New Haven and surrounding towns of East Haven, North Haven, West Haven, and Hamden. This community had a population of some 250,000 persons in 1950.[9] The New Haven community was selected because the community's structure has been studied intensively by sociologists over a long period. In addition, it is served by a private psychiatric hospital, three psychiatric clinics, and 27 practicing psychiatrists, as well as the state and Veterans Administration facilities.

Four basic technical operations had to be completed before the hypotheses could be tested. These were: the delineation of the class structure of the community, selection of a cross-sectional control of the community's population, the determination of who was receiving psychiatric care, and the stratification of both the control sample and the psychiatric patients.

August B. Hollingshead and Jerome K. Myers took over the task of delineating the class system. Fortunately, Maurice R. Davie and his students had studied the social structure of the New Haven community in great detail over a long time span.[10] Thus, we had a large body of data we could draw upon to aid us in blocking out the community's social structure.

The community's social structure is differentiated *vertically* along racial, ethnic, and religious lines; each of these vertical cleavages, in turn, is differentiated *horizontally* by a series of strata or classes. Around the socio-biological axis of race two social worlds have evolved: A Negro world and a white world. The white world is divided by ethnic origin and religion into Catholic, Protestant, and Jewish contingents. Within these divisions there are numerous ethnic groups.

[6] F. C. Redlich, B. H. Roberts, L. Z. Freedman, and Leslie Schaffer.
[7] August B. Hollingshead and J. K. Myers.
[8] Harvey A. Robinson.
[9] The population of each component was as follows: New Haven, 164,443; East Haven, 12,212; North Haven, 9,444; West Haven, 32,010; Hamden, 29,715; and Woodbridge, 2,822.
[10] Maurice R. Davie, "The Pattern of Urban Growth," G. P. Murdock (editor), in *Studies in the Science of Society*, New Haven: 1937, pp. 133–162; Ruby J. R. Kennedy, "Single or Triple Melting-Pot: Intermarriage Trends in New Haven, 1870–1940," *American Journal of Sociology*, 39 (January, 1944), pp. 331–339; John W. McConnell, *The Influence of Occupation Upon Social Stratification*, Unpublished Ph.D. thesis, Sterling Memorial Library, Yale University, 1937; Jerome K. Myers, "Assimilation to the Ecological and Social Systems of a Community," *American Sociological Review*, 15 (June, 1950), pp. 367–372; Mhyra Minnis, "The Relationship of Women's Organizations to the Social Structure of a City," Unpublished Ph.D. Thesis, Sterling Memorial Library, Yale University, 1951.

The Irish hold aloof from the Italians, and the Italians move in different circles from the Poles. The Jews maintain a religious and social life separate from the gentiles. The *horizontal* strata that transect each of these vertical divisions are based upon the social values that are attached to occupation, education, place of residence in the community, and associations.

The vertically differentiating factors of race, religion and ethnic origin, when combined with the horizontally differentiating ones of occupation, education, place of residence and so on, produce a social structure that is highly compartmentalized. The integrating factors in this complex are twofold. First, each stratum of each vertical division is similar in its cultural characteristics to the corresponding stratum in the other divisions. Second, the cultural pattern for each stratum or class was set by the "Old Yankee" core group. This core group provided the master cultural mold that has shaped the status system of each sub-group in the community. In short, the social structure of the New Haven community is a parallel class structure within the limits of race, ethnic origin, and religion.

This fact enabled us to stratify the community, for our purposes, with an *Index of Social Position*.[11] This *Index* utilizes three scaled factors to determine an individual's class position within the community's stratificational system: ecological area of residence, occupation, and education. Ecological area of residence is measured by a six point scale; occupation and education are each measured by a seven point scale. To obtain a social class score on an individual we must therefore know his address, his occupation, and the number of years of school he has completed. Each of these factors is given a scale score, and the scale score is multiplied by a factor weight determined by a standard regression equation. The factor weights are as follows: Ecological area of residence, 5; occupation, 8; and education, 6. The three factor scores are summed, and the resultant score is taken as an index of this individual's position in the community's social class system.

This *Index* enabled us to delineate five main social class strata within the horizontal dimension of the social structure. These principal strata or classes may be characterized as follows:

Class I   This stratum is composed of wealthy families whose wealth is often inherited and whose heads are leaders in the community's business and professional pursuits. Its members live in those areas of the community generally regarded as "the best;" the adults are college graduates, usually from famous private institutions, and almost all gentile families are listed in the New Haven *Social Directory*, but few Jewish families are listed. In brief, these people occupy positions of high social prestige.

Class II   Adults in this stratum are almost all college graduates; the males occupy high managerial positions, many are engaged in the lesser ranking professions. These families are well-to-do, but there is no substantial inherited or acquired wealth.

[11] A detailed statement of the procedures used to develop and validate this *Index* will be described in a forthcoming monograph on this research tentatively titled *Psychiatry and Social Class* by August B. Hollingshead and Frederick C. Redlich.

Its members live in the "better" residential areas; about one-half of these families belong to lesser ranking private clubs, but only 5 per cent of Class II families are listed in the New Haven *Social Directory*.

Class III This stratum includes the vast majority of small proprietors, white-collar office and sales workers, and a considerable number of skilled manual workers. Adults are predominately high school graduates, but a considerable percentage have attended business schools and small colleges for a year or two. They live in "good" residential areas; less than 5 per cent belong to private clubs, but they are not included in the *Social Directory*. Their social life tends to be concentrated in the family, the church, and the lodge.

Class IV This stratum consists predominately of semi-skilled factory workers. Its adult members have finished the elementary grades, but the older people have not completed high school. However, adults under thirty-five have generally graduated from high school. Its members comprise almost one-half of the community; and their residences are scattered over wide areas. Social life is centered in the family, the neighborhood, the labor union, and public places.

Class V Occupationally, class V adults are overwhelmingly semi-skilled factory hands and unskilled laborers. Educationally most adults have not completed the elementary grades. The families are concentrated in the "tenement" and "cold-water flat" areas of New Haven. Only a small minority belong to organized community institutions. Their social life takes place in the family flat, on the street, or in neighborhood social agencies.

The second major technical operation in this research was the enumeration of psychiatric patients. A Psychiatric Census was taken to discover the number and kinds of psychiatric patients in the community. Enumeration was limited to residents of the community who were patients of a psychiatrist or a psychiatric clinic, or were in a psychiatric institution on December 1, 1950. To make reasonably certain that all patients were included in the enumeration, the research team gathered data from all public and private psychiatric institutions and clinics in Connecticut and nearby states, and all private practitioners in Connecticut and the metropolitan New York area. It received the cooperation of all clinics and institutions, and of all practitioners except a small number in New York City. It can be reasonably assumed that we have data comprising at least 98 per cent of all individuals who were receiving psychiatric care on December 1, 1950.

Forty-four pertinent items of information were gathered on each patient and placed on a schedule. The psychiatrists gathered material regarding symptomatology and diagnosis, onset of illness and duration, referral to the practitioner and the institution, and the nature and intensity of treatment. The sociologists obtained information on age, sex, occupation, education, religion, race and ethnicity, family history, marital experiences, and so on.

The third technical research operation was the selection of a control sample from the normal population of the community. The sociologists drew a 5 per cent random sample of households in the community from the 1951, New Haven *City Directory*. This directory covers the entire communal area. The names and addresses in it were compiled in October and November, 1950—a period very close to the date of the Psychiatric Census. Therefore there was comparability of residence and date of registry between the two population groups. Each household drawn in the sample was interviewed, and data on the age, sex, occupation, education, religion, and income of family members, as well as other items necessary for our purposes were placed on a schedule. This sample is our Control Population.

Our fourth basic operation was the stratification of the psychiatric patients and of the control population with the *Index of Social Position*. As soon as these tasks were completed, the schedules from the Psychiatric Census and the 5 per cent Control Sample were edited and coded, and their data were placed on Hollerith cards. The analysis of these data is in process.

SELECTED FINDINGS

Before we discuss our findings relative to Hypothesis I, we want to reemphasize that our study is concerned with *diagnosed* or *treated* prevalence rather than *true* or *total* prevalence. Our Psychiatric Census included only psychiatric cases under treatment, diagnostic study, or care. It did not include individuals with psychiatric disorders who were not being treated on December 1, 1950, by a psychiatrist. There are undoubtedly many individuals in the community with psychiatric problems who escaped our net. If we had *true* prevalence figures, many findings from our present study would be more meaningful, perhaps some of our interpretations would be changed, but at present we must limit ourselves to the data we have.

Hypothesis I, as revised by the nature of the problem, stated: *The diagnosed prevalence of psychiatric disorders is related significantly to an individual's position in the class structure.* A test of this hypothesis involves a comparison of the normal population with the psychiatric population. If no significant difference between the distribution of the normal population and the psychiatric patient population by social class is found, Hypothesis I may be abandoned as unproved. However, if a significant difference is found between the two populations by class, Hypothesis I should be entertained until more conclusive data are assembled. Pertinent data for a limited test of Hypothesis I are presented in Table 1. The data included show the number of individuals in the normal population and the psychiatric population, by class level. What we are concerned with in this test is how these two populations are distributed by class.

When we tested the reliability of these population distributions by the use of the chi square method, we found a *very significant* relation between social class and treated prevalence of psychiatric disorders in the New Haven community. A comparison of the percentage distribution of each population by class readily indicates the direction of the class concentration of psychiatric cases. For example, Class I contains 3.1 per cent of the community's population but only 1.0 per cent of the psychiatric cases. Class V, on the other hand, includes 17.8 per cent of the community's population, but contributed 36.8 per cent of the psychiatric patients. On the basis of our data Hypothesis I clearly should be accepted as tenable.

Table 1
Distribution of normal and psychiatric population by social class

Social class	Normal population*		Psychiatric population	
	Number	Per cent	Number	Per cent
I	358	3.1	19	1.0
II	926	8.1	131	6.7
III	2500	22.0	260	13.2
IV	5256	46.0	758	38.6
V	2037	17.8	723	36.8
Unknown**	345	3.0	72	3.7
Total	11,422	100.0	1,963	100.0

$x^2 = 408.16$, P less than .001.
*These figures are preliminary. They do not include Yale students, transients, institutionalized persons, and refusals.
** The unknown cases were not used in the calculation of x^2. They are individuals drawn in the sample, and psychiatric cases whose class level could not be determined because of paucity of data.

Hypothesis II postulated a significant connection between the *type* of psychiatric disorder and social class. This hypothesis involves a test of the idea that there may be a functional relationship between an individual's position in the class system and the type of psychiatric disorder that he may present. This hypothesis depends, in part, on the question of diagnosis. Our psychiatrists based their diagnoses on the classificatory system developed by the Veterans Administration.[12] For the purposes of this paper, all cases are grouped into two categories: the neuroses and the psychoses. The results of this grouping by social class are given in Table 2.

A study of Table 2 will show that the neuroses are concentrated at the higher levels and the psychoses at the lower end of the class structure. Our team advanced a number of theories to explain the sharp differences between the neu-

Table 2
Distribution of neuroses and psychoses by social class

Social class	Neuroses		Psychoses	
	Number	Per cent	Number	Per cent
I	10	52.6	9	47.4
II	88	67.2	43	32.8
III	115	44.2	145	55.8
IV	175	23.1	583	76.9
V	61	8.4	662	91.6
Total	449		1,442	

$x^2 = 296.45$, P less than .001.

[12] *Psychiatric Disorders and Reactions,* Washington: Veterans Administration, Technical Bulletin 10A-78, October, 1947.

roses and psychoses by social class. One suggestion was that the low percentage of neurotics in the lower classes was a direct reaction to the cost of psychiatric treatment. But as we accumulated a series of case studies, for tests of Hypotheses IV and V, we became skeptical of this simple interpretation. Our detailed case records indicate that the social distance between psychiatrist and patient may be more potent than economic considerations in determining the character of psychiatric intervention. This question therefore requires further research.

The high concentration of psychotics in the lower strata is probably the product of a very unequal distribution of psychotics in the total population. To test this idea, Hollingshead selected schizophrenics for special study. Because of the severity of this disease it is probable that very few schizophrenics fail to receive some kind of psychiatric care. This diagnostic group comprises 44.2 per cent of all patients, and 58.7 per cent of the psychotics, in our study. Ninety-seven and six-tenths per cent of these schizophrenic patients had been hospitalized at one time or another, and 94 per cent were hospitalized at the time of our census. When we classify these patients by social class we find that there is a very significant inverse relationship between social class and schizophrenia.

Hollingshead decided to determine, on the basis of these data, what the probability of the prevalence of schizophrenia by social class might be in the general population. To do this he used a proportional index to learn whether or not there were differentials in the distribution of the general population, as represented in our control sample, and the distribution of schizophrenics by social class. If a social class exhibits the same proportion of schizophrenia as it comprises of the general population, the index for that class is 100. If schizophrenia is disproportionately prevalent in a social class the index is above 100; if schizophrenia is disproportionately low in a social class the index is below 100. The index for each social class appears in the last column of Table 3.

The fact that the Index of Prevalence in class I is only one-fifth as great as it would be if schizophrenia were proportionately distributed in this class, and that it is two and one-half times as high in class V as we might expect on the basis of proportional distribution, gives further support to Hypothesis II. The fact that the Index of Prevalence is 11.2 times as great in class V as in class I is particularly impressive.

Table 3
Comparison of the distribution of the normal population with schizophrenics by class, with index of probable prevalence

Social class	Normal population		Schizophrenics		Index of prevalence
	No.	Per cent	No.	Per cent	
I	358	3.2	6	.7	22
II	926	8.4	23	2.7	33
III	2,500	22.6	83	9.8	43
IV	5,256	47.4	352	41.6	88
V	2,037	18.4	383	45.2	246
Total	11,077	100.0	847	100.0	

Hypothesis III stipulated that the type of psychiatric treatment a patient receives is associated with his position in the class structure. A test of this hypothesis involves a comparison of the different types of therapy being used by psychiatrists on patients in the different social classes. We encountered many forms of therapy but they may be grouped under three main types; psychotherapy, organic therapy, and custodial care. The patient population, from the viewpoint of the principal type of therapy received, was divided roughly into three categories: 32.0 per cent received some type of psychotherapy; 31.7 per cent received organic treatments of one kind or another; and 36.3 per cent received custodial care without treatment. The percentage of persons who received no treatment care was greatest in the lower classes. The same finding applies to organic treatment. Psychotherapy, on the other hand, was concentrated in the higher classes. Within the psychotherapy category there were sharp differences between the types of psychotherapy administered to the several classes. For example, psychoanalysis was limited to classes I and II. Patients in class V who received any psychotherapy were treated by group methods in the state hospitals. The number and percentage of patients who received each type of therapy is given in Table 4. The data clearly support Hypothesis III.

At the moment we do not have data available for a test of Hypotheses IV and V. These will be put to a test as soon as we complete work on a series of cases now under close study. Preliminary materials give us the impression that they too will be confirmed.

CONCLUSIONS AND INTERPRETATIONS

This study was designed to throw new light upon the question of how mental illness is related to social environment. It approached this problem from the perspective of social class to determine if an individual's position in the social system was associated significantly with the development of psychiatric disorders. It proceeded on the theoretical assumption that if mental illnesses were distributed randomly in the population, the hypotheses designed to test the idea that psychiatric disorders are connected in some functional way to the class system would not be found to be statistically significant.

Table 4
Distribution of the principal types of therapy by social class

Social class	Psychotherapy		Organic therapy		No treatment	
	Number	Per cent	Number	Per cent	Number	Per cent
I	14	73.7	2	10.5	3	15.8
II	107	81.7	15	11.4	9	6.9
III	136	52.7	74	28.7	48	18.6
IV	237	31.1	288	37.1	242	31.8
V	115	16.1	234	32.7	367	51.2

$x^2 = 336.58$, *P* less than .001.

The data we have assembled demonstrate conclusively that mental illness, as measured by diagnosed prevalence, is not distributed randomly in the population of the New Haven community. On the contrary, psychiatric difficulties of so serious a nature that they reach the attention of a psychiatrist are unequally distributed among the five social classes. In addition, types of psychiatric disorders, and the ways patients are treated, are strongly associated with social class position.

The statistical tests of our hypotheses indicate that there are definite connections between particular types of social environments in which people live, as measured by the social class concept, and the emergence of particular kinds of psychiatric disorders, as measured by psychiatric diagnosis. They do not tell us what these connections are, nor how they are functionally related to a particular type of mental illness in a given individual. The next step, we believe, is to turn from the strictly statistical approach to an intensive study of the social environments associated with particular social classes, on the one hand, and of individuals in these environments who do or do not develop mental illnesses, on the other hand. Currently the research team is engaged in this next step but is not yet ready to make a formal report of its findings.

10
A COMPARISON OF THE INCIDENCE OF
HOSPITALIZED AND NON-HOSPITALIZED CASES
OF PSYCHOSIS IN TWO COMMUNITIES*
Bert Kaplan, Robert B. Reed, and Wyman Richardson

In recent years a number of studies[1] have presented data suggesting that there is an inverse relationship between socio-economic status and mental illness. To workers interested in the epidemiology of mental disorders these findings are of

Source: Bert Kaplan, Robert B. Reed, and Wyman Richardson, "A Comparison of the Incidence of Hospitalized and Non-hospitalized Cases of Psychosis in Two Communities," American Sociological Review, 21: 472–479, 1956.
* The investigation was supported by funds made available to the Harvard School of Public Health by the Commonwealth Fund and the Grant Foundation. The authors are indebted to Dr. Helen Roberts, Director of the Harvard Field Training Unit at the Whittier Street Health Center, and to Dr. Erich Lindemann, Director of the Wellesley Human Relations Service, for their support and guidance. Frederick L. W. Richardson made valuable contributions during the planning phase of the project. Dr. Gerald Caplan of the Harvard School of Public Health gave generously of his time and energies, and Dr. Eric Wright made many important suggestions.

[1] Robert E. Clark, "The Relationship of Schizophrenia to Occupational Income and Occupational Prestige," American Sociological Review, 13 (June, 1948), pp. 325–330; Robert E. L. Faris and H. Warren Dunham, Mental Disorder in Urban Areas, Chicago: University of Chicago Press, 1939; August B. Hollingshead and Frederich C. Redlich, "Social Stratification and Psychiatric Disorders," American Sociological Review, 18 (April, 1953), pp. 163–169; Robert W. Hyde and Lowell V. Kingley, "Studies in Medical Sociology I: The Relation of Mental Disorders to Community Socio-Economic Level," The New England Journal of Medicine, 231 (October, 1944), pp. 543–548; Clarence W. Schroeder, "Mental Disorders in Cities," American Journal of Sociology, 48 (July, 1942), pp. 40–48.

great importance since they imply that certain social patterns play a significant etiological role in the mental illnesses.

Socio-cultural factors, related as they are to psychological development, are precisely the kind of environmental conditions which could explain especially high rates of psychiatric disorders. The suggested relationship between socio-economic level and the occurrence of mental illness is therefore one of the first results of the applications of the epidemiologic method to understanding of the mental disorders. The next step, that of explaining the basis for the relationships, should be a very productive one for both psychiatry and the social sciences.

Before advancing to the phase of theoretical explanations, however, it seems necessary to consider alternate explanations of these findings. One such explanation is that the findings are based on rates of admission to mental hospitals; yet several surveys have indicated that a substantial percentage of those who become psychotic do not enter mental hospitals.[2] It would seem therefore that evidence supporting the hypothesized relationship is based on only a part of the total number of cases of psychosis. Since it cannot be assumed that non-hospitalized cases are distributed in the same way as hospitalized cases, it seems very possible that if the additional cases of non-hospitalized psychotics were also considered, the alleged relationship might be altered.

The specific questions asked in this study were: When only hospitalized cases are considered, does a comparison of incidence at two different socio-economic levels support findings of studies in other regions that there is a lower incidence of hospitalization for psychosis at the higher socio-economic levels? What is the incidence of non-hospitalized cases of psychosis in the two study areas described below? Does this incidence rate vary with socio-economic status in the same way as does the incidence of hospitalized cases? If the hospitalized and non-hospitalized cases are combined, is there still a difference in the incidence rates between the two areas? And finally, is the case finding method used here epidemiologically useful?

PROCEDURES

The comparative values of incidence and prevalence studies have been the subject of much controversy. Since our concern in this study was to investigate the relationship between the factors influencing the occurrence of mental disorder rather than the factors influencing its duration, the incidence figure is clearly more relevant.

Several different periods were used for targets. In Wellesley, a predominantly upper and upper-middle class suburb of Boston, the fifteen year period 1936–1950 was chosen for hospitalized cases. The study did not include the more recent years because records for the last two or three years were incomplete.

---

[2] Paul Lemkau, Christopher Tietze, and Marcia Cooper, "Mental Hygiene Problems in an Urban District," *Mental Hygiene*, 25 (1941), pp. 624–646; Lemkau, *et al.*, "Mental Hygiene Problems in an Urban District, II," *Mental Hygiene*, 26 (1942), pp. 100–119; William F. Roth, Jr. and Frank H. Luton, "The Mental Health Problem in Tennessee," *The American Journal of Psychiatry*, 99 (March, 1943), pp. 662–675.

For the non-hospitalized cases only the last five years (1946–1950) of this period were used because information about earlier years is considerably less reliable and complete. In the Whittier Street area of Roxbury, a lower and lower-middle class neighborhood in Boston, the study of the hospitalized cases covered a one year period, 1949, because this area had a population of about 68,000 and an adequate number of cases could be gathered for comparison in this one year. The search for non-hospitalized cases, however, covered a five year period, 1948–1952, since a large turnover of informants, the main sources of information, made it advisable to study the most recent five year period. To compare rates during these different target periods it was necessary to estimate the number of person-years in each age group by sex. In Wellesley the total population for each year was estimated by counting the yearly List of Residents for every third year, and estimating for the intervening years by straight line interpolation. The percentage distribution by age and sex was estimated for each year by linear interpolation of 1940 and 1950 census figures. On the basis of these two facts, person-years over the fifteen year period were obtained. A similar technique was used to estimate the person-years for the non-hospitalized case study. In the Whittier Street area census findings were utilized. The incidence of hospitalized psychosis was determined by searching admission records of all private and state mental hospitals in Massachusetts.

The community case finding survey was carried on by the senior author, a psychologist. The method consisted of interviewing individuals in the community who were in positions or roles which made it possible for them to know of mentally ill persons. The informants were asked to review their contacts during the target period and describe new cases of mental illness they might have encountered. The clergy, medical practitioners, social workers, public health nurses, welfare department workers, nursing home workers, school nurses, local health officers, and psychiatrists provided potential informants. We reasoned that if a person became mentally ill, most families would seek some kind of outside help. The few who did not seek aid might be known to individuals such as our informants who had a good knowledge of the community and what was happening in it. This method is relatively economical, although it leaves the researcher with some uncertainty whether he has found all the cases. Even if his survey has been fairly complete and accurate, he has no way of knowing or demonstrating it.

In Wellesley work was facilitated greatly by our connection with the Human Relations Service. This agency, under the sponsorship of the Harvard School of Public Health, had been attempting over a five year period to develop a program of preventive psychiatry in Wellesley. Its excellent relations, especially with local physicians and clergy, greatly facilitated the present study. During the interview the informant was asked to describe the symptoms and behavior of persons who had become psychotic for the first time during the years under study. It was explained that our definition of psychosis meant serious mental illness of the kind that might ordinarily lead to hospitalization. It was also made clear that we were not interested in neurosis, in the feeble-minded, in alcoholism or in people who just "had problems."

The problem of diagnosis has been mentioned as one of the great difficulties in doing epidemiological research. It has been thought that since criteria for the diagnosis of psychosis vary so much, it would be difficult to say what any particular incidence figure meant. It is our feeling that this problem did not prove to be a crucial one in the present study. There were, to be sure, a number of cases which seemed borderline. However, they were a relatively small group of cases and our diagnostic procedures with respect to them were standard in the two areas. In the majority of the cases, psychosis was easily recognized by symptoms such as delusions or paranoid trends, which were present in most cases of diagnosed psychotics. There were two diagnostic problems of greater difficulty. One concerned senile psychosis, the other the depressions. Although patients are admitted to mental hospitals with all degrees of senility, it seemed to us good psychiatric practice to differentiate between senility and senile psychosis. The former we defined as intellectual changes of not too great severity accompanying old age. In order to establish the latter diagnosis we looked for severe intellectual deterioration with disorientation, lack of recognition of family, excitements, living in the past, severe emotional upset, or delusions accompanying intellectual changes. The other difficult diagnostic problems involved the depressions. Here we attempted to distinguish between the neurotic and the psychotic depression.

The final decision whether a person was psychotic or not was made by a psychiatrist not connected with the study.[3] He examined the notes of the field worker and on the basis of the evidence contained in them, separated the cases into four categories: the "certain" cases, the "probables," the "improbables," and the "certainly not" cases. He was then asked to examine the "probables" a second time and to divide them into two groups, those he thought had a high degree of probability and those he thought had a lower degree. The former group was then combined with the "certains." We believe this was justifiable because these were not borderline cases, but cases in which it was difficult to get information. The information available strongly suggested the diagnoses which were made.

THE COMMUNITIES

The town of Wellesley (population, about 20,000) is a fast growing suburb of Boston. It is known as one of the three or four wealthiest towns in the area and attracts persons of well above moderate means. The town is, however, by no means homogeneous in this respect and does contain groups of quite different socio-economic levels.

The Whittier Street area is not a political entity but a section of Boston proper. Varying socio-economic and ethnic characteristics of the residents divide the eleven census tracts into three fairly distinct sub-districts: In the "R" area less than 25 per cent of employed persons are "white collar" workers; the majority

---

[3] Gerald Caplan, Lecturer on Mental Health, Harvard School of Public Health.

of people in the area are non-white and are largely native born. About one-fourth of the residents are less than 15 years of age. The median rental in this area is $25, and 37 per cent of the housing is dilapidated. The "S" area is, in its economic characteristics, mid-way between the "R" and "K" sub-districts. Of the resident workers, 30–53 per cent are "white collar" workers; 33–45 per cent of the adults are high school graduates. The population is predominantly Irish in ethnic origin. Median rentals in this area vary from $25 to $41, and there is a marked variation in type of housing from well-maintained, older, single family structures to dilapidated, multi-family structures. The "K" sub-district is the site of many institutions. Compared to the other sub-districts, there are fewer children (families in this economic stratum are known to move to suburban homes when children are born); the residents are predominantly native-born white, and the majority are high-school graduates pursuing white-collar occupations. Median rentals range from $42 to $61; there are many apartment houses in the district and only about 4 per cent of dwellings are dilapidated or without running water. The population for individuals over 15 years of age is 56,303 in the combined eleven census tracts.

RESULTS

Hospitalized cases of psychotics (First Admission).   There were 203 new admissions for psychosis to mental hospitals from the Wellesley area in the 15-year target period, 1936–50, and 90 cases from the Whittier Street area in the one-year target period, 1949.

Analysis of admissions by age and sex (Table 1) shows that in Wellesley there was no significant variation in the age-incidence rate in either sex under 65 years of age, but in both sexes there was a significant increase after the age of 65 years, and this increase was higher in males than in females. In Roxbury, a similar increase in incidence was noted over 65, but the sex incidence in older persons was reversed, in that a higher rate was found among females over 65 years of age. The sex reversal in persons over 65 years of age is not statistically sig-

Table 1
First admissions for psychosis by age and sex

Age	Wellesley, 1936–1950				Whittier Street study area, 1949			
	Male		Female		Male		Female	
	Cases†	Rate*	Cases	Rate*	Cases	Rate*	Cases	Rate*
15–24	13.6	8.4	16	8.6	3.	5.2	6.	9.1
25–44	21.8	7.0	32	7.5	17.	17.4	14.	12.3
45–64	18.4	7.1	32	9.2	9.	13.6	10.	11.2
65 and over	30.0	43.4	36	27.8	9.	31.9	22.	49.9

* Cases per 10,000 person years of exposure.
† Cases appear in fractional numbers because the ages of a small number of cases were unknown. They were distributed among the four age groups in the same proportions as was the population at large.

Table 2
First admissions for psychosis for Wellesley and Whittier Street

	15 and over		15–64		65 and over	
	Cases	Rate*	Cases	Rate*	Cases	Rate*
Wellesley total†	199.8	10.5	133.8	7.9	66.0	32.4
(Wellesley exclusive of the lowest socio-economic areas —						
IIB IIC)	139.6	9.3	92.9	6.9	46.7	30.6
Whittier Street total‡	90.0	16.0	59.0	12.0	31.0	42.9
Whittier Street (minus highest socio-economic areas)	64.	22.8	40.	16.2	24.	70.3

* Cases per 10,000 person years of exposure.
† During 15 year period, 1936–1950.
‡ During one year period, 1949

nificant. Because of the comparative similarity between sexes and between age groups under 65 these cases are grouped in subsequent analysis.

The Whittier Street area shows a higher incidence of hospitalized psychosis than does the Wellesley area. Within each of the two areas, there are also marked differences in incidence rates, apparently associated with socio-economic characteristics. The number of cases in each sub-district in Wellesley is too small to justify statistical comparison, but incidence rates are lower in the sub-districts rated highest socio-economically and highest in those at the lower level of the scale.

The differences in hospitalized psychosis incidence are even more dramatic if the higher socio-economic areas in Wellesley are compared to the lower socio-economic areas in Roxbury, as is shown in Table 2. The same marked difference is found between these populations in all age groups.

Incidence of non-hospitalized psychosis.   A comparison of the incidence of non-hospitalized psychosis in Wellesley and the Whittier Street area (Table 3)

Table 3
Total incidence of new cases of non-hospitalized psychosis, by age for Wellesley and Whittier Street

	15 and over		15–64		65 and over	
	Cases	Rate*	Cases	Rate*	Cases	Rate*
Wellesley New cases of non-hospitalized psychosis‡	47†	6.7	26	4.3	21	21.8
Whittier Street (highest socio-economic areas omitted) New cases of non-hospitalized psychosis§	29†	2.0	12	1.0	17	9.9

* Cases per 10,000 person years of exposure.
† One-half of cases in which we were not certain of year of onset were included. Six were added in Wellesley and five in the Whittier Street Area.
‡ During 5 year period, 1946–1950.
§ During 5 year period, 1948–1952.

Table 4
Total incidence of psychosis and first admissions for psychosis by age for Wellesley and Whittier Street

	15 and over		15–64		65 and over	
	Cases	Rate*	Cases	Rate*	Cases	Rate*
Wellesley						
Total incidence of psychosis†		17.2		12.2		34.7
First admissions for psychosis†	199.8	10.5	133.8	7.9	66.0	32.4
Whittier Street (highest socio-economic areas omitted)						
Total incidence of psychosis‡		24.8		17.2		80.1
First admissions for psychosis§	64	22.8	40	16.2	24	70.3

* Cases per 10,000 person years of exposure.
† During 15 year period, 1936–1950.
‡ Number of cases could not be added since the two categories were based on different time periods, and no totals are given.
§ During 1 year period, 1949.

indicates a reversal of the results shown for hospitalized cases. A lower incidence rate of non-hospitalized psychotics was found in the Whittier Street area than in Wellesley (2.0 cases per 10,000 person years exposure in Whittier Street and 6.7 cases per 10,000 person years of exposure in Wellesley).[4]

If incidence rates for hospitalized and non-hospitalized cases are added (Table 4), total incidence of psychosis in the Whittier Street area is higher than in Wellesley in all adult age groups. (24.8 cases per 10,000 person years of exposure in Whittier Street; 17.2 cases per 10,000 person years of exposure in Wellesley).

DISCUSSION

In summary, we found that when only hospitalized cases of psychosis are considered, incidence rates were considerably higher in a lower and lower-middle class area than they were in an upper-middle and upper class area. Comparisons of sub-areas in Wellesley and Roxbury indicate that for hospitalized cases the same relationship between incidence rate and socio-economic level holds. The incidence of new non-hospitalized cases is much lower in the lower and lower-middle class area than in the upper-middle and upper class area. When both types of cases are combined, the difference between the two areas is reduced. However, a considerable difference remains with the lower socio-economic area revealing a higher psychosis incidence rate.

Before venturing an interpretation of these results, it is necessary to consider whether the fact that a greater incidence of non-hospitalized cases was found in

[4] It will be noted that in Table 3, rates for Wellesley are given excluding sub-areas IIB and IIC, the lowest socio-economic areas, and for the Whittier Street area excluding the census tracts which were at relatively high socio-economic levels. The purpose was to make the groups being compared more homogeneous with respect to socio-economic status. In Tables 3 and 4 the Wellesley rate is given for the whole community since non-hospitalized cases could not be located by sub-areas and therefore a separate rate could not be computed for Wellesley minus the lowest socio-economic areas.

Wellesley than in the Roxbury area is an artifact reflecting a greater difficulty of finding cases in the latter area. Does the paucity of cases in the Roxbury census tracts result from a lack of co-operativeness on the part of our informants? This does not seem to be the case. Although only 29 cases were finally counted, over 175 cases were discussed. Sixty-five of these were judged to be psychotic and not hospitalized, but two-thirds of the cases either began before the five-year period in which we were interested or lived just outside of the area. Our informants in Roxbury were as co-operative as those in Wellesley, but two-thirds of the cases they knew about could not be counted in our study.

There is some reason to suspect, however, that the search in Wellesley was more complete than that in Roxbury. Perhaps the best indication of this is the fact that in Wellesley many cases were known to two, three, four or five informants, while in Roxbury only rarely was a case known to as many as two informants. This suggests that Roxbury informants were each scrutinizing some small part of the whole area, while the Wellesley informants tended to be looking at the same population, because the number of people was smaller and the area was a political entity. It may be seen that there is a much greater chance for gaps in our research to develop in the former situation than the latter. It is entirely possible that even in Wellesley certain groups evaded the scrutiny of any of our informants. In Roxbury we had a strong feeling that this was the case. In the light of these facts it is necessary for us to admit that the search in Roxbury in all probability underestimated the actual incidence rates.

It is difficult to know to what degree our Roxbury count is inaccurate. We would have to have found three times as many cases as we did if the real rates in Roxbury were to approximate those in Wellesley. It is inconceivable to us that this number could be found. Furthermore, we have undoubtedly underestimated the Wellesley rate as well so that to equal it an even greater number should be found in Roxbury.

How can the result that the Roxbury area has twice as high a hospitalization rate as does Wellesley, but a rate of non-hospitalized psychosis which is only about one-third as large, be explained? We believe the answer lies in different attitudes toward hospitalization for mental illness. In Wellesley the field worker frequently encountered the attitude that the mentally ill person should be kept out of the state hospital at any cost. This is partly due to the general perception of the state mental hospital as a "snake pit" and commitment of a relative there, equivalent to abandoning him to the worst possible kind of treatment. In part, also, it is related to a reluctance on the part of upper-middle class families to use public hospital facilities since these are regarded as institutions established to serve the poor rather than those families in the $7–15,000 a year category. Even these levels of income, however, are insufficient to maintain a relative for prolonged periods of time in a high-cost private mental hospital.

In Roxbury, on the other hand, there is a pattern of extensive utilization of public hospital facilities, frequently for illness which private physicians ordinarily handle in homes. Nearby are two large state hospitals which are known to most people in the area, and while it would be an exaggeration to say that there are no barriers between hospitals and the community, there are probably less than in Wellesley where there is no mental hospital. We believe there is a much more casual acceptance of hospitalization in the Whittier Street area than in Wellesley.

Complementing those attitudes toward hospitalization as an explanation of our findings, is the equally important fact that Wellesleyites are better able to care for psychotic individuals in the home. Their households are less crowded and they are better able to afford the extra nursing care needed. It may be easier in Wellesley houses to isolate the mentally ill person on a separate floor or at least in a separate room. In Roxbury there is overcrowding and usually no way for the patient to be isolated. Perhaps most important, in Wellesley it is possible, indeed it is a frequent pattern, to have old people who have become senile cared for in a private nursing home. Roxbury residents could rarely afford such care.

Our explanation, then, of the disparity of incidence rates of non-hospitalized psychosis is that Wellesley residents try, to the limit of their abilities, to keep family members from being committed to mental hospitals, and they have real abilities in this respect. In Roxbury, on the other hand, while somewhat similar attitudes exist, it is our impression that they are not held so strongly, that families are more prone to hospitalize their members when it is indicated. Even where there is a strong desire to keep a family member out of the hospital, it is ordinarily very difficult or impossible to provide the necessary facilities and nursing care.

If we accept this explanation of our results as reasonable and adequate, there is the very strong implication that many cases who in Wellesley might have been found in the non-hospitalized group, were in Roxbury found to be hospitalized. Even when the hospitalized and non-hospitalized cases were combined, the Wellesley community had a lower incidence rate than did the Roxbury area. The discovery of more Roxbury cases would increase this difference. We may say, therefore, that the inverse relationship between the socio-economic status and the incidence of mental disorder is verified, although the inclusion of non-hospitalizd psychotics reduces the height of the correlation.

Let us for a moment assume the language of the statistician and say that any study of the incidence of mental illness is bound to discover a certain amount of variance among groups at different socio-economic levels. If the study has been based on records of hospitalization alone, we can say on the basis of this investigation that a certain amount of the variance can be explained by the fact that a large number of people who become psychotic do not enter mental hospitals and that proportionately more of these cases are found at the upper socio-economic levels than at the lower levels. We believe that another factor explains much of the remainder. The direct consequences of the system of social stratification on the psyche of the individual. Our theory is that the whole network of prerogatives, attitudes, and expectations surrounding any class position has important consequences for the individual ego structure which in turn is an important factor in determining resistance to mental illness. By ego structure is meant the complex of factors concerning the ego—the self picture, self esteem, feelings of adequacy, and most important of all, the ego strength which prescribes on the one hand the amount of impulse control and on the other hand the degrees of successful management of the environment.

A number of considerations lead us to this belief. George Mead and many others have shown the extent to which the individual accepts the public definition of his self. If society says he is superior, he feels that he is superior; if it views him as inferior, then he feels himself to be inferior. While we do not mean to imply that the self picture is given in its entirety by these public definitions, we do maintain they are accepted to a considerable extent by the individual and incorporated into the ego system. If they are of a beneficial bolstering kind, we can expect that the stability and resistance of the individual will be increased. The plain fact of social stratification does not operate alone however; the social superiority feelings of the upper-middle and upper classes are ordinarily accompanied by child rearing and education patterns which have the effect of reinforcing them. It is true that individuals with low self esteem and ego strength are found in great numbers at all class levels and it would be incorrect therefore to hold that these characteristics are determined by class position. Our argument is only that they may sometimes, in some cases, be influenced by it and that if all other factors were constant, or varied randomly, the influence of class position on the ego system and on the resistance to mental illness could be discerned.

SUMMARY AND CONCLUSIONS

Incidence rates of hospitalized psychosis were compared in two communities in the Metropolitan Boston area and were found to be significantly higher in the lower-middle socio-economic area than in the upper level socio-economic community. This finding confirms other studies which suggest an inverse relation between social environment and mental disorder.

An etiological relation between lower socio-economic conditions and mental illness cannot be accepted, however, until we explore the possibility that cases of psychosis may be hospitalized at differing rates in the upper and lower levels of society, so that studies of hospitalized psychosis alone do not give a true picture of incidence.

The lower socio-economic community revealed a significantly lower incidence of non-hospitalized psychosis than did the higher level community. We believe this fact can be explained by differing attitudes toward hospitalization of mental illness in the two communities. Residents in the higher social community resisted hospitalization for their mentally ill family members. Because they had more money and more spacious housing, they were better able to keep ill members of the family at home.

Comparison of sub-areas in the two communities indicates that the same inverse relation between hospitalized psychosis incidence rates and socio-economic levels persists within the individual communities.

A description and discussion of our case-finding procedure for non-hospitalized psychosis is given. The method does not reveal accurately the number of non-hospitalized cases of psychosis in an area but it indicates within the limits of the method, that incidence rates of non-hospitalized psychosis vary differently with socio-economic status than do rates of hospitalized psychosis.

The difference in the incidence of hospitalized psychosis in high socio-economic and low socio-economic communities, found by previous investigators and confirmed by this study, is reduced by including non-hospitalized psychosis in the two areas. But there remains a significant inverse relation between socio-economic circumstances and mental illness. This finding may be the direct consequence of a system of social stratification on the psyche of individuals. In addition the possibility exists that more intensive case-finding methods for non-hospitalized psychosis would reveal even more non-hospitalized cases in the upper level community, thus reducing the differences in total psychosis rates to the point that incidence is the same for the two communities.

11
FACTORS INFLUENCING THE RATE OF
FIRST ADMISSION TO MENTAL HOSPITAL
J. M. Wanklin, D. F. Fleming, C. W. Buck, and G. E. Hobbs

INTRODUCTION

Over the years (2), observed differences in the rate of mental hospital admissions, both between and within countries, have formed the basis for considerable study and speculation. First admission rates have received particular attention and numerous investigators have assumed that differences among these reflect variations in the incidence of mental illness. Others, however, have contended that since many of the differences in rates occur between areas having divergent economic and political structures, they are at least partly explainable on the basis of differences in the availability of hospital services and in attitudes of people toward the hospitalization of the mentally ill.

Anyone who has studied mental illness on the mass level can understand why first admission rates often have been chosen as a measure of incidence. In the first place, the definition of a case becomes objective and straightforward. Alternative definitions (4) usually lead to difficulties in establishing the limits of normal behavior. Secondly, the use of hospital records is more practical than the method of community survey which is laborious and costly even in the most circumscribed population.

Source: Journal of Nervous and Mental Disease, **121:** 103–116, 1955. Copyright © 1955, The Williams & Wilkins Company, Baltimore, Md. 21202 U.S.A.

In view of these advantages of the first admission rate, it is surely unwise to discard the measure prematurely on the basis of objections which, however impressive, have never been established beyond the level of theory. Rather, an attempt should first be made to assess the validity of those objections.

The present study grew from the belief that if factors in addition to the occurrence of an illness influence the likelihood of hospitalization, they should in some way be reflected in hospital statistics. We hoped to find, within patterns of first admission rates, evidence which would permit some evaluation of the extent to which these rates are, on one hand, a reflection of incidence, and on the other, a reflection of the need or desire to hospitalize the mentally ill.

SCOPE AND METHODOLOGY

Area of study

The geographical area chosen for this intensive study of first admission rates was that section of the Province of Ontario consisting of 14 Counties and commonly designated as Western Ontario.

Inhabited by approximately one-quarter of Ontario's four and one-half million residents, Western Ontario includes densely populated industrial areas and rich farm lands near its southern boundaries, and a sparsely settled, rather unproductive northern peninsula. Two of its cities have populations which exceed 100,000. One is a university center and the other is a highly industrialized and cosmopolitan city. So, although the area is not extensive, its diversified characteristics make it almost ideal for a study of this kind.

Period of study

First admission data were assembled for the years 1950 to 1952 inclusive. Each rate was then expressed as the average of the 3 yearly rates for the period, using the 1951 Census of Canada as the base population.

Source and type of information

Information was obtained from complete case records, on file at the hospitals of admission, and made accessible through the active cooperation of the medical staffs of these institutions. This approach allowed more detailed analyses than would be possible from the records of a central statistical office, where many studies of this type originate.

The information was coded on peripheral punch cards to facilitate analysis and was of two types—that which pertained to the patient's life history, and that related to the illness and circumstances leading to hospitalization.

The sample

Funds and personnel were not available to permit the collection of data from all of the hospitals admitting patients from Western Ontario. A compromise, which was somewhat reluctantly adopted, limited the collection of data to two large Provincial Institutions[1] located within 20 miles of the University. The resulting sample included 1,983 first admissions from Western Ontario, admitted to these two hospitals between January 1, 1950 and December 31, 1952.

Excluded were: 1) juvenile mental defectives, epileptic and tuberculous mental patients and the criminally insane who are sent to specialized Provincial institutions, and 2) patients admitted to a Federal Veterans' hospital and to a small private sanitorium. Because of this, most juvenile patients were eliminated from the sample, and a disproportionate number of adult males was excluded.

However, on the basis of a tabulation of all Western Ontario first admissions for 1950, published in the provincial hospitals' annual report (1), it was established that the sample studied for that year was representative of the total admissions in terms of its distribution by county of residence. Since no regional bias was introduced, it is rather unlikely that the sample was distorted with respect to other social variables under consideration. Nevertheless, the observations and conclusions arising from this study pertain, with certainty, only to those forms of mental illness occurring in the civilian population over 15 years of age, and uncomplicated by tuberculosis, epilepsy or serious criminality.

Grouping diagnoses for analysis

Investigators (3) have adequately demonstrated that when specific diagnostic entities are dealt with singly, the rates are often colored by the diagnostic policies of the hospitals involved. We therefore grouped the diagnoses on the basis of a seven-fold classification comparable to that employed by Somner and Harman (7). The more important disorders included under each of the headings are outlined below.

1 Functional psychoses
   a. Schizophrenia
   b. Manic depressive psychosis
   c. Involutional melancholia
2 Psychoneuroses
3 Psychoses with organic disease
   a. Psychosis with mental deficiency
   b. Psychosis with epilepsy
4 Without psychosis
   a. Mental deficiency
   b. Epilepsy
   c. Other (e.g.: simple adult maladjustment)

---

[1] The Ontario Hospitals at London and St. Thomas.

5   Psychoses due to alcohol and drugs
6   Psychoses due to syphilis—general paresis of the insane
7   Psychoses associated with old age
   a. Senile psychosis
   b. Psychosis with cerebral arteriosclerosis

RESULTS

General admission rates from Western Ontario

Age-sex specific rates (Table 1).   Wherever possible, the analyses carried out in this study were age and sex specific, and at all times, rates were expressed per 100,000 population, per year. The over-all distribution of the admission sample on the basis of the two variables is described below.

Rates for both sexes tended to increase with age—notably from a rate of 49.1 at ages 15 to 24, to a rate of 67.6 at ages 25 to 34, and in particular from 72.4 at ages 55 to 64, to 167.4 at ages 65 and over. These points of increase and the intervening plateau correspond to the age curve demonstrated by other studies. The failure of male rates generally to exceed the female, as they are usually reported to do, probably is a reflection of the previously described sex bias of our sample. Throughout the analyses, therefore, sex-differences in the rates were felt to be of questionable significance.

Rates by diagnostic groups, by age and sex (Table 2).   The diagnostic composition of the rates at various ages, and for each sex separately, was revealed in the following analysis.

a. Functional psychoses: Rates for this group were highest at ages 25 to 54 (40.6 to 41.1), where they comprised about 60 per cent of the total admissions. When, in spite of our stated reluctance to do so, schizophrenia and manic depressive psychosis were considered separately, it was found that rates for the former reached a peak at ages 25 to 34, while for the latter, the peak was reached at ages 45 to 64.

Table 1
Rates per 100,000, by age and sex

Age	Male	Female	Male plus female
15–24	50.8	47.3	49.1
25–34	62.0	73.1	67.6
35–44	67.6	69.5	68.5
45–54	65.3	82.0	73.4
55–64	72.8	72.0	72.4
65+	172.2	162.6	167.4
Total*	76.3	81.2	78.7

* Based on population 15 years and over.

Table 2
Rates per 100,000 by diagnostic groups, by ages and sex

Age	M	F	M + F	M	F	M + F	M	F	M + F
	Functional			Schizophrenia†			Manic depressive†		
15–24	24.4	23.4	23.9	20.4	16.6	18.6	2.7	4.5	3.6
25–34	30.6	50.4	40.6	25.6	37.3	31.6	3.4	9.3	6.4
35–44	29.7	47.7	38.5	16.2	29.8	22.8	8.9	10.3	9.6
45–54	33.1	49.4	41.1	11.9	17.4	14.5	13.8	15.3	14.5
55–64	31.5	39.0	35.2	28.9	11.9	20.4	13.8	15.3	14.5
65+	16.6	26.1	21.6	1.3	6.3	3.9	9.6	13.7	11.7
Total*	28.0	39.7	33.8	15.1	21.5	18.3	8.0	10.7	9.4
	With organic disease			Psychoneuroses			Associated with old age		
15–24	0.8	5.7	3.2	2.7	5.2	4.0	0.0	0.0	0.0
25–34	2.3	3.0	2.7	7.2	8.2	7.8	0.0	0.0	0.0
35–44	2.9	4.9	3.9	8.9	9.8	9.3	0.0	0.0	0.0
45–54	2.5	6.3	4.4	5.9	11.5	8.6	1.0	2.1	1.5
55–64	3.3	5.9	4.6	6.5	7.3	6.9	14.4	10.5	12.5
65+	5.7	2.9	4.2	1.3	4.6	3.0	139.1	125.1	131.7
Total*	2.7	4.7	3.7	5.6	7.8	6.7	19.2	19.1	19.1
	Due to alcohol & drugs			Due to syphilis			Without psychosis		
15–24	0.0	0.0	0.0	0.4	0.8	0.6	22.1	11.6	16.9
25–34	1.1	0.8	1.0	0.3	0.3	0.4	19.2	9.0	14.0
35–44	3.4	0.9	2.2	0.4	0.4	0.4	18.7	6.3	12.6
45–54	2.5	3.6	3.1	4.5	0.5	2.5	13.8	6.3	10.2
55–64	2.6	2.6	2.6	5.3	2.0	3.7	8.5	2.3	5.6
65+	2.5	1.2	1.8	1.3	0.5	0.9	3.3	0.5	1.8
Total*	1.9	1.4	1.6	1.7	0.7	1.2	15.5	6.7	11.1

* Based on population 15 years and over.
† Together, compose 84 per cent of functional group.

b. Psychoses with organic disease: Rates for the sexes combined increased with age from 2.7 at ages 25 to 34, to 4.6 at ages 55 to 64. Because the male rate was highest at ages 65 and over (5.7) and the female at ages 45 to 54 (6.3), sex differences in the diagnostic composition of this group were suggested.

c. Psychoneuroses: Ages 25 to 64 predominated in this diagnostic group, with the highest rate of 9.3 occurring at ages 35 to 44.

d. Psychoses associated with old age: Appearing first at ages 45 to 54, the rate for these psychoses was relatively low until ages 65 and over (131.7).

e. Psychoses due to alcohol and drugs: The rate for the sexes combined reached a peak of 3.1 at ages 45 to 54, although the male rate was highest at ages 35 to 44 (3.4). Whether males develop these psychoses earlier in life than the females, or whether they are hospitalized sooner, is not easily determined.

f. Psychoses due to syphilis: Limited almost entirely to ages 45 to 64, the total crude rate (1.2) was lower than that for any other diagnostic group, and arose largely from male admissions.

g. Without psychosis: The rate for the sexes combined was highest at ages

15 to 24 (16.9) and then decreased with age. At all ages, male rates were notably higher than the female, in spite of the known sex bias of the sample.

Three of the diagnostic groups figured most prominently in the composition of the admissions: 1) functional, 2) without psychosis and 3) psychoses associated with old age. Each, in turn, was in greatest evidence within different segments of the age span.

At ages 25 to 64—the plateau of the age curve—the functional group of psychoses predominated; at ages 15 to 24 where the admission rate was comparatively low, the without psychosis group competed with the functional; at ages 65 and over approximately 80 per cent of the admissions were of the group psychoses associated with old age.

The distinctions between the rates of these broad age groups in terms of their diagnostic make-up figured prominently in the conclusions reached on the basis of the following analyses.

Comparison of rural and urban admissions

Rural-urban differences in admission rates were given particular attention. Various associated indices added a measure of substance to the interpretation of the differences observed.

Crude rates by population size—all diagnoses.   The combined rate for the five cities in Western Ontario having populations of 30,000 and over (75.1) was significantly higher than that for rural areas (under 1,000 population) (47.5), and significantly higher, also, than the rate for the smaller urban centres (52.6). The excess of the latter rate over that for rural areas was small and not statistically significant.

Lack of appropriate census data made the age standardization of these rates impossible, but it is unlikely that such a procedure would have greatly modified the relationships. It was therefore concluded that population density influenced the level of admission rates, not only on a rural-urban basis, but among urban areas of varying size.

Age-sex specific rates for rural and urban populations—all diagnoses (Fig. 1). Available census data did not permit the derivation of urban age-sex specific rates by population size. Instead, rates for all urban areas combined (1,000 population and over) were compared with those for the rural areas. On the basis of observations made in the preceding section, it can probably be assumed that if age-sex specific rates for rural areas could have been compared with those for areas of 30,000 and over, the resulting differences would have been exaggerations of those which are to be described.

While it is true that the urban rate was higher than the rural, the excess was not constant from age to age, nor between the sexes. Urban proportionate excesses were greatest among males at ages 15 to 34 (where the difference between rural and urban rates ranged from 59.7 to 61.3 per cent of the rural rate).

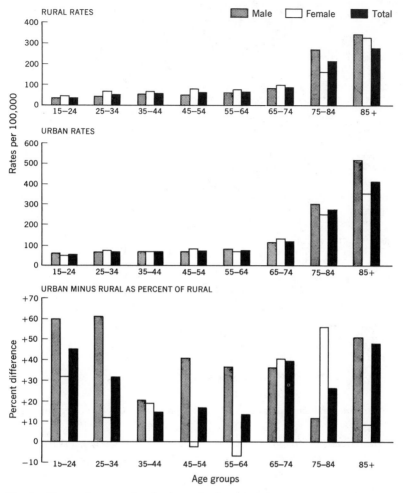

Fig. 1. Comparison: rural and urban rates by age and sex.

Small urban excesses found for males at other ages, were not statistically significant. Rural and urban female rates were more comparable than the male at
most ages, and in only one age group (75 to 84) was an urban excess (56.2 per
cent) statistically significant. Although they usually lacked statistical significance,
urban excesses in the rates for both sexes after age 65 were quite marked. It was
shown, then, that rural-urban differences in rates were greatest among young
adults and the aged, and generally were more extreme among males than among
females.

*Rural and urban comparisons in the upper age group (ages 65 and over); more
detailed analysis by 5-year age groups* (Table 3 and Fig. 2).   The first admission rate for ages 65 and over, at a high level and increasing rapidly over the
years, is thought by many to reflect a growing lack of available home care. If

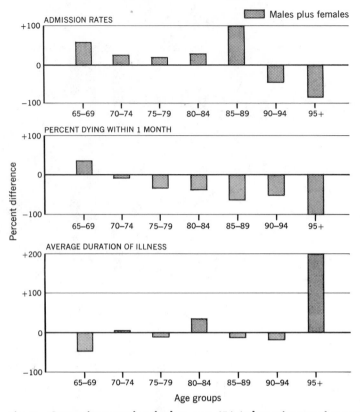

Fig. 2.   Comparison: rural and urban, ages 65+ (urban minus rural as percentage of rural).

this factor influences the hospitalization of the aged, it will likely exert its greatest effect in urban areas characterized by crowded living conditions and by a
relatively high proportion of women with jobs outside the home. Urban excesses
within the old-age group of admissions were therefore assessed as to the extent
to which they suggested, on one hand, real differences in incidence, and on the
other, the effect of varying degrees of pressure for hospitalization.

a. Age specific rates: Urban rates did not exceed the rural at all ages over 65.
Because urban rates reached a peak at ages 85 to 89 (467.3) and then declined,
while rural rates continued to increase until age 95 and over (804.6), rural
excesses occurred at ages 90 and over. These excesses lacked statistical significance, but in view of the regularity of the age curves from which they were
derived, seemed worthy of some consideration.

Here was evidence, then, that after age 65, an urban resident, if he were to
enter hospital, was most likely to do so before age 89, while the probability of
a rural inhabitant entering increased past this age. This observation pointed to:
1) a tendency for urban patients to be hospitalized during an earlier phase of
their illness, or 2) an earlier average age of onset of the degenerative psychoses
among urban patients. Each of these possibilities is considered below.

b. Proportion of patients dying within one month of admission: This was

Table 3
Rural and urban admissions, ages 65 and over by 5-year age groups

	Admission rates per 100,000			Per cent dying within 1 month of admission			Average duration of illness before hospitalization, years		
	Rural	Urban	Diff. as % of rural	Rural	Urban	Diff. as % of rural	Rural	Urban	Diff. as % of rural
65–69	65.9	104.3	58.3*	6.7	9.0	34.3	7.3	3.9	−46.6
70–74	116.8	148.9	27.5	18.6	17.2	−7.5	2.9	3.0	3.4
75–79	203.7	248.5	22.0	24.0	16.1	−32.9	3.0	2.7	−10.0
80–84	238.2	315.6	32.5	20.6	13.4	−35.0	2.8	3.8	35.7
85–89	232.2	467.3	101.2*	57.1	22.0	−61.5†	3.8	3.4	−10.5
90–94	458.2	269.3	−41.2	28.6	14.3	−50.0	6.0	5.0	−16.7
95+	804.6	194.8	−75.8	50.0	0.0	−100.0	0.5	1.5	200.0

* Significant at 0.05 level.
† Significant at 0.01 level.

selected as a rough index of the proportion of patients who were admitted during the terminal phase of their illness.

At all ages except 65 to 69 the proportion dying was higher among rural admissions than among urban, and the difference increased with age due to progressive increases in the rural proportion. This observation, coupled with those concerning the different age trends of rural and urban rates, leads to a speculative kind of conclusion. It may be postulated that the urban rate was higher than the rural up to ages 85 to 89 because of a greater urban tendency to admit early cases; after these ages a backlog of rural patients who had been cared for at home until advanced symptoms made this no longer possible, augmented the rural rate and caused it to exceed the urban.

c. Average duration of illness before hospitalization: It has already been demonstrated that the degenerative psychoses predominated at ages 65 and over. On the basis of our present understanding of the etiology of these illnesses, rural-urban differences in their average age of onset seem about as unlikely as do differences in their true incidence.

Unfortunately, a comparison of the average duration of illness for rural and urban admissions did little to either confirm or negate this opinion. Rural-urban differences showed no consistent trend from age to age and, because of the smallness of the sample and the large variances around mean values, were without statistical significance. But probably the most important defect of this analysis was the fact that since information concerning the onset of symptoms had usually been obtained from the family, attitudes which may determine, in part, the likelihood of hospitalization could have also detracted from the objectiveness of this information.

Rates by the diagnostic groups, functional and without psychosis for rural and urban populations (Table 4). Rural-urban differences among the rates at ages 15 to 64 were examined on the basis of the two diagnostic groups which predominated at these ages.

Table 4
Rural and urban rates per 100,000 by diagnostic groups by age and sex

Age	Rural			Urban			Difference as per cent of rural		
	M	F	M + F	M	F	M + F	M	F	M + F
Functional†									
15–24	16.5	24.4	19.8	30.0	23.1	26.4	81.8‡	−5.3	33.3
25–34	31.4	50.9	40.9	30.2	50.3	40.5	−3.8	−1.4	−1.0
35–44	22.7	49.0	34.8	32.7	47.6	40.2	44.1	−2.9	15.5
45–54	33.7	56.8	44.3	32.7	45.2	39.1	−3.0	−20.4	−11.7
55–64	28.3	39.5	33.5	33.5	38.8	36.3	18.4	7.1	8.4
65+	13.6	20.6	17.0	18.9	29.2	24.6	39.0	41.7	44.7
Total*	24.2	40.6	31.9	30.1	39.3	34.9	24.4	−3.2	9.4
Without psychosis†									
15–24	18.2	8.4	14.0	24.6	13.3	18.8	35.2	58.3	34.3
25–34	6.5	7.8	7.1	26.1	9.5	17.5	301.0§	21.8	146.5§
35–44	15.9	5.0	10.8	20.5	6.7	13.6	29.0	34.0	25.9
45–54	6.4	7.4	6.7	18.9	5.7	12.3	195.0‡	−23.0	83.6
55–64	8.4	5.6	7.1	8.8	0.9	4.7	4.8	−84.0	−33.8
65+	3.2	1.4	2.3	3.3	0.0	1.5	3.1	−100.0	−34.8
Total*	10.4	6.2	8.4	18.8	6.9	12.7	80.8§	11.3	51.2§

* Based on population 15 years and over.
† Together, comprise 57 per cent of all admissions.
‡ Significant at 0.05 level.
§ Significant at 0.01 level.

a. Functional group: Except for males aged 15 to 24, urban excesses within the diagnostic group were neither large, consistent nor statistically significant. There was, in fact, evidence of an over-all rural excess among females.

b. Without psychosis: As with the functional group, an urban excess was largely the result of male differences. These were greatest at ages 25 to 34, and 45 to 54. A moderate female urban excess was reversed at ages 45 and over.

The higher urban rates for the functional group of psychoses among males at the younger ages, could sensibly be related to rural-urban differences in incidence. The stressful aspects of a modern society, which are sometimes thought to influence the occurrence of mental disease, are particularly evident in urban areas; and urban males, because of their economic role, are probably most vulnerable to these stresses.

This interpretation is applied with much more difficulty to the similar, but exaggerated, rural-urban differences found within the diagnostic group without psychosis. At ages 15 to 24, this group included a sizeable proportion of mental defectives; at ages 25 to 64 most of the diagnoses were vague but suggested minor personality abnormalities. For many of these admissions, then, hospitalization hardly seemed to be an appropriate procedure. Some, in fact, were not certified and received no treatment; they had been admitted by court remand following an arrest, and after a period of observation in hospital were returned to court for sentence.

Of the total rural male admissions ages 15 to 64, 20.8 per cent came directly from jail while among the total urban male admissions of the same ages, 29.2 per cent were from this source. In other words, the urban excess in male admission rates at the younger ages was caused, in part, by an excess in the number who entered hospital without clinically recognized psychotic symptoms, but as the result of behavior which could not be tolerated by their society. Urban living, more than rural, may be conducive to the development of these personality types and it may also tend to attract them. But it may be, too, that urban living conditions make their detection and disposition more certain.

The latter interpretation could also be given to rural-urban differences among admissions comprising the functional group since behavior symptoms, often of an asocial variety, are their recognizable feature.

So then, while urban excesses in rates for both sexes at the upper age were more suggestive of a greater urban tendency to dispose of the aged and infirm, the nature of urban excesses among the males at the younger ages could represent rural-urban differences both in incidence and in the likelihood of hospitalization.

Comparison of admissions by marital status

An analysis of first admission rates according to marital status led to general observations which are comparable to those of other studies. This analysis has as yet not proceeded as far as that of the rural-urban differences and, as a result, tentative conclusions must be even more speculative.

Age specific rates—both sexes (Table 5).   Rates for the married were, at all ages, lower than those for any other marital group. Proportionate excesses of the rate for single, divorced and separated combined, were statistically significant at all ages, and reached a maximum at ages 35 to 44 (365.0 per cent). Rates for the widowed, which were calculated only for ages 45 and over, were not as greatly in excess of those for the married as were the rates for the single, divorced and

Table 5
Rates per 100,000 by marital status by age

Age	Married rate	Single, divorced and separated rates	Diff. as % of married	Widowed rate	Diff. as % married
15–24	21.8	57.7	164.7†	0.0	0.0
25–34	43.6	173.3	297.4†	0.0	0.0
35–44	43.5	202.3	365.0†	0.0	0.0
45–54	50.7	240.9	304.1†	74.5	46.9
55–64	52.1	172.7	231.4†	109.4	110.0†
65+	108.7	342.2	214.8†	189.8	74.6†
Total*	50.9	126.7	148.9†	160.4	215.1†

* Based on population 15 years and over.
† Significant at 0.01 level.

separated. However, at ages 55 to 64 where the proportionate difference between widowed and married was greatest (110.0 per cent), and at ages 65 and
over (74.6 per cent), statistical significance was obtained.

Age specific rates by sex (Fig. 3).   To obtain a sample large enough to permit
an analysis by sex, single, divorced and separated admissions were combined
with the widowed and designated as "Other." It should be remembered, however, that before age 50 the single will have predominated, while after this age
the widowed will have been almost entirely responsible for the admission rate
of the group.

Proportionate excesses of rates for the other group over those for the married
were comparable for both sexes at ages 65 and over. However, at ages 25 to 64
the excess was greater among males. Thus, widowhood seemed to have a comparable effect upon the admission rates for both sexes, while the failure to
marry had more influence upon the rates for the males.

Here again, differences among rates had been found which could reflect

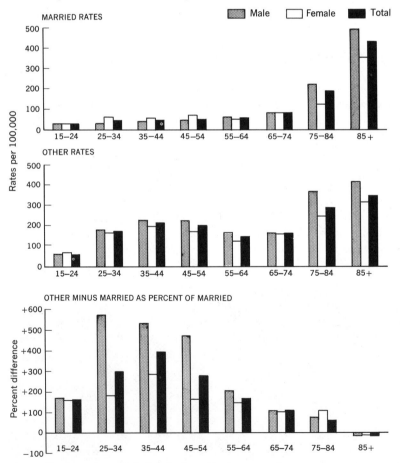

Fig. 3. Comparison: married and other rates by age and sex.

differences both in incidence and in the tendency to hospitalize the mentally ill. Incidence may vary among marital groups because of at least two conditions. First, selection could be involved because the chance of marriage among the unstable, as a group, is almost certainly reduced, and when marriage does occur it will probably have a better than average chance of ending in divorce or separation. Moreover, Odegaard (5) has pointed out that selection may operate, to a lesser extent, in the widowed group through remarriage. Second, an element of psychological protection may be gained through marriage, with the family circle acting as a buffer for some of society's strains and frustrations.

However, protection may also operate in terms of the likelihood of hospitalization. When mental illness occurs, the resources for home care may be most readily at hand among the married.

The tendency for male differences to be greater than female between the married and other groups at ages 15 to 64 is compatible with all of the possible explanations described above. Inadequate mental and personality resources, which handicap social adjustment, probably impede the marriage of males more than of females because of the former's traditional role as the provider in the family; Dayton (3) has suggested that the security of married life in some way benefits the male more than the female; and finally, the single male may be more likely than the female to move from the parental home, leaving behind the resources for home care and protection during a mental illness.

Age specific rates by duration of marriage (Table 6).   The analysis of differences in admission rates among marital groups at the younger ages was carried one step further. Using rather tentative estimates for a base population, rates by duration of marriage were calculated for the married group at ages 25 to 44. Within each age group the rates for each sex were lower for those with the longer duration of marriage. In particular, the results pointed to a remarkably low rate for males who had married at a comparatively early age and whose marriage had been kept intact for more than 10 years. On the other hand, the rate for females who had married rather late in life, although below that for the single, divorced and separated at comparable ages, was noticeably high.

The general trend of rates by duration of marriage supported the belief that marriage offers some degree of psychological protection. However, the differential effect of duration of marriage upon the two sexes seemed to point to an element of selection through marriage. Males who marry early in life and who are able, financially and in other ways, to maintain a successful marriage, probably

Table 6
Rates per 100,000 by duration of marriage

Age	Duration 1–10 years			Duration over 10 years			Difference as per cent of over 10		
	M	F	M + F	M	F	M + F	M	F	M + F
25–34	29.9	67.1	47.9	11.5	41.4	31.5	160.0*	62.1*	52.1*
35–44	94.2	313.5	146.1	28.7	37.2	33.2	228.2*	742.7*	340.1*

* Significant at 0.01 level.

constitute a particularly stable group. On the other hand, females who fail to marry at the younger ages, in spite of an avowed desire on the part of most members of their sex to do so, may in many instances be hampered by personality inadequacies.

Selection through marriage as a factor contributing toward differences between the rates for married and single may be demonstrated further when an analysis by diagnosis has been completed. Preliminary results reveal that virtually all of the mental defective admissions were unmarried. For most of these patients marriage must have been impossible because of the mental retardation which eventually brought them to hospital.

The upper age group (ages 65 and over); a more detailed analysis by 5-year age groups for married and other populations (Table 7 and Fig. 4).   a. Age specific rates: Here, comparisons between married and other rates were made, keeping in mind the rural-urban relationships observed at these ages. The rural-urban differences were thought to be suggestive of a tendency to care for the rural mentally ill at home as long as possible, and it has already been postulated that the desire and capacity for home care may operate favourably among the married group as well.

Striking similarities between the two comparisons did, in fact, emerge. Like urban rates, those for the other group reached a peak at ages 85 to 89 (336.4) and then declined, while married rates resembled the rural in their tendency to increase with age until ages 90 and over (3043.5). As a result of these trends, moreover, statistically significant excesses in rates for the other group at ages 65 to 79 were reduced, or replaced by married excesses, at ages 80 and over. The latter, however, were not statistically significant.

b. Proportion of patients dying within one month of admission: This proportion was higher among the married group, especially at ages 90 and over, and could again have reflected the tendency to keep the mentally disabled members of that group at home as long as possible.

Table 7
Marital groups (married and other)

Age	Admission rates per 100,000			Per cent dying within one month of admission		
	Married	Other	Diff. as % of married	Married	Other	Diff. as % of married
65–69	59.7	146.8	145.9†	8.5	8.2	−3.5
70–74	108.5	170.6	57.2*	21.4	14.9	−30.4
75–79	156.5	285.1	82.2†	31.7	11.8	−62.8†
80–84	254.7	297.8	16.9	17.9	15.1	−15.6
85–89	391.9	366.4	−6.5	36.4	31.8	−12.6
90–94	234.4	350.2	49.0	100.0	15.4	−84.6†
95+	3043.5	0.0	−100.0	50.0	0.0	−100.0
Total	108.7	227.1	108.9†	21.5	12.3	−42.8†

* Significant at 0.05 level.
† Significant at 0.01 level.

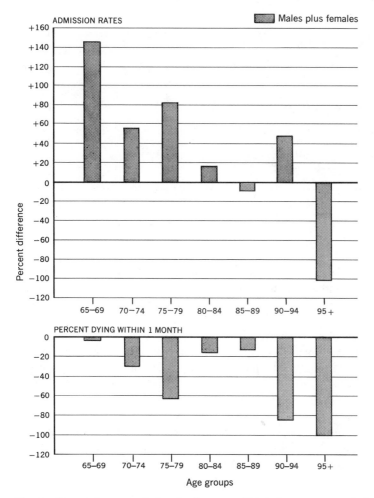

Fig. 4. Comparison: married and other, ages 65+ (other minus married as percentage of married).

The analyses which are now to be described were less extensive than the preceding ones and the results are merely presented in summary form. Their primary significance lies in the fact that the patterns of rates closely resemble those pertaining to rural and urban environment and marital status.

Comparison of admission rates by duration of schooling (Table 8)

Age-sex specific rates for those out of school at the time of admission.   Those with 8 years of schooling or less were more likely to have been admitted to a Provincial hospital than were those with a more extensive education. This ap-

Table 8
Rates per 100,000 by duration of schooling by age and sex:
those not attending school on admission

Age	Schooling—8 years and under			Schooling—over 8 years			Difference as per cent of over 8 years		
	M	F	M + F	M	F	M + F	M	F	M + F
15–24	99.7	119.9	110.0	28.7	24.6	25.7	247.4‡	387.4‡	328.0‡
25–34	92.8	90.9	91.8	38.4	61.0	50.2	141.7‡	49.0†	82.9‡
35–44	88.3	87.7	88.0	44.4	52.7	48.8	98.9‡	66.4‡	80.3‡
45–54	79.1	91.0	84.4	30.2	68.5	51.2	161.9‡	32.8	64.8‡
55–64	84.6	85.0	84.8	31.3	48.2	40.7	170.3‡	76.3‡	108.4‡
65+	182.2	176.2	180.3	126.3	127.0	126.7	44.3†	38.7†	42.3‡
Total*	105.5	110.9	108.0	41.6	56.9	50.0	153.6‡	94.9‡	116.0‡

* Based on population 15 years and over.
† Significant at 0.05 level.
‡ Significant at 0.01 level.

plied at all ages, but especially at ages 15 to 24. At these ages schooling may have been terminated, in many instances, because of the onset of psychotic symptoms. More important, mental defectives without psychosis, who comprised 17 per cent of the admissions aged 15 to 24, could not have proceeded far in school.

The rates at ages 25 to 54 showed that lack of education was a greater handicap to males than to females from the point of view of admission to mental hospital. The duration of schooling among males, being influenced by occupational goals, could be an expression of personality stability as well as of intellectual capacity. If this is so, selection of the more stable into the better educated group could have occurred.

The extent of education determines economic status to some extent. Among males, those with less education will more likely be at the lower end of the economic scale where they will experience, in material terms at least, more of society's viscissitudes than those whose financial resources are more adequate. A possible etiological effect upon incidence is thus suggested. However, marginal living conditions will probably make it less feasible to care for the mentally ill wage-earner outside of a mental institution, and so the familiar factor of home care is again invoked as a possible explanation for differences among the rates.

Obviously, it was impossible to distinguish between the relative influence of schooling upon incidence and upon the need or desire for hospitalization at this stage in the investigation.

Comparison of age-sex specific rates of native and foreign-born admissions (Table 9)

Comparison of the rates for native and foreign-born was hampered because of a fault in the assembly of the data. Patients born in the United States were included with the native-born admissions, without taking note of the fact that they were defined as foreign-born in the census population used as a base for the calculation of rates. This error could no longer be corrected at the time of its discovery. Even though the native-born rates were artificially high, and the foreign-born rates too low because of the misplacement of American-born admissions, foreign-born excesses prevailed at certain ages. It can safely be assumed that these excesses would have been increased in size and number had the error not been made. Moreover, re-allocation of American-born admissions likely would not have altered greatly the relationship between rates by age or sex, or by time in Canada.

Foreign-born excesses occurred most often among the rates for those in Canada 5 years or less, most regularly among males and to a marked extent among males aged 15 to 44. Odegaard (6) and others have made similar observations and their explanations are usually related to selection, environmental stress and lack of available home care and protection.

Table 9
Rates per 100,000 native and foreign-born

Age	Admission rates			Difference as per cent of native-born		
	M	F	M + F	M	F	M + F
Native-born						
15–24	49.3	46.9	48.1			
25–34	61.4	76.3	68.9			
35–44	66.3	68.3	67.3			
45–54	62.8	91.1	76.8			
55–64	72.5	78.8	75.8			
65+	185.0	173.3	178.7			
Total*	75.4	83.7	79.6			
Foreign-born — in Canada more than 10 years						
15–24	33.9	81.1	55.3	−31.2	72.9	15.0
25–34	32.7	47.1	40.1	−46.7†	−38.3	−41.8†
35–44	70.8	55.7	63.4	6.8	−18.4	−5.8
45–54	74.5	56.4	66.2	18.6	−38.1†	−13.8
55–64	70.1	57.0	64.1	−3.3	−27.7	−15.4
65+	137.1	124.4	130.9	−25.9†	−28.2†	−26.7‡
Total*	83.3	69.6	74.9	10.5	−16.8†	−5.9
Foreign-born — in Canada 5 years or less						
15–24	85.5	42.1	65.4	73.4	−10.2	36.0
25–34	95.2	66.8	80.3	55.0	−12.5	16.5
35–44	80.4	137.1	105.5	21.3	100.7‡	56.8
45–54	33.5	112.6	72.6	−46.7	23.6	−5.5
55–64	167.8	0.0	73.5	131.4	−100.0‡	−3.0
65+	82.4	54.6	76.7	−55.5	−68.5†	−57.1
Total*	84.2	77.4	80.9	11.7	−7.5	1.6

* Based on population 15 years and over.
† Significant at 0.05 level.
‡ Significant at 0.01 level.

Knowledge of Canadian immigration policy, especially since World War II, did not encourage the speculation that immigrants represent a basically inferior sample of foreign populations, and the "selection theory" was thought to have dubious merit. The possible effect of the environment upon incidence should, however, be given consideration. Many of these people suffered grave hardships in their native lands during the war and when the added stress of readjustment to a new environment is superimposed, the likelihood of a mental breakdown could be expected to be high. Moreover, if an illness occurs, lack of available home care and protection could increase the necessity for hospitalization, especially among males who often migrate without their families. These unfavorable conditions surrounding the recent immigrant could be expected to diminish with time as indeed was suggested by the lower admission rates for the Foreign-born with longer residence in Canada.

SUMMARY

1. An analysis was made of first admission rates involving 1,983 patients from Western Ontario who were admitted to two Provincial mental institutions during the years 1950 to 1952.

2. The general findings were comparable to those proceeding from other studies of this kind. Higher rates tended to be associated with urban residence; with single, divorced and separated marital status; with lack of more than 8 years' schooling and with recent immigration among the foreign born.

3. An attempt was then made to assess the possible influence of these variables, both upon the incidence of mental illness, and upon the need or desire to hospitalize the mentally ill. Because of their nature, some of the differences between rates could sensibly have been the reflection of variations in incidence, resulting from differences in the group levels of environmental stress and from a process of selection which may determine the general degree of stability among persons characterized by a particular variable. However, the evidence pointing to this kind of interpretation never became so convincing that the possible influence of differences in social pressure could be ignored. Among the aged, in fact, the latter explanation was favoured.

AN OUTLINE OF FURTHER RESEARCH

On the basis of certain observations made throughout the analyses, together with a general understanding of the nature of mental illness, it has been concluded that if social pressure for hospitalization causes one rate to exceed another, it does so, not simply through the creation of more admissions generally, but through the addition of *different kinds* of patients to the admission number. The behavioral symptoms of mental illness vary greatly in type and in severity. Some gross symptoms demand institutional care regardless of attendant environmental circumstances; others, under certain conditions, could be tolerated and either treated outside of a hospital or ignored. Social pressure is almost surely limited in its influences upon admission rates to those among the mentally ill who exhibit the latter type of symptoms. Admission rates for the more acutely psychotic probably measure quite accurately the incidence of illnesses of this kind.

A detailed symptom analysis based upon this hypothesis currently is being made. Admission rates related to symptoms, and symptom clusters, are being compared among population groups and it is hoped that the results will add to an understanding of the factors which lead to the hospitalization of the mentally ill.

References

1 Annual Report of the Hospital Division, Department of Health, upon Ontario Hospitals for the Mentally Ill, Mentally Defective, Epileptic and Habituate Patients, of the Province of Ontario.

2 Dawson, W. R.: The Presidential Address on the relation between the geographical distribution of insanity and that of certain social and other conditions in Ireland. *J. Ment. Sc.,* **99:** 571–597, 1911.

3 Dayton, N. A.: *New Facts on Mental Disorders.* Springfield, Ill.: C. C. Thomas, 1940.

4 Leighton, Alexander H., et al.: Definition of a case for purposes of research in social psychiatry, in *Interrelations Between the Social Environment and Psychiatric Disorders.* New York: Milbank Memorial Fund, 1953.

5 Odegaard, O.: New data on marriage and mental disease: The incidence of the psychoses in the widowed and the divorced. *J. Ment. Sc.,* **99:** 778–785, 1953.

6 Odegaard, O.: Emigration and mental health. *Ment. Hyg.,* **20:** 546–553, 1936.

7 Somner, C., and Harman, H. H.: Trend in mental diseases in Illinois, 1922–1943. *Am. Psychopath. A. Proc.,* **33:** 56–91, 1944.

12
RELIGION, NATIONAL ORIGIN, IMMIGRATION, AND MENTAL ILLNESS[1]
Bertram H. Roberts and Jerome K. Myers

In the midst of the current dynamic orientation in psychiatric theory, the investigators in this study have reapproached some of the major social variables that have been part of the basic etiological data of clinical psychiatry. These are long-

Source: Bertram H. Roberts and Jerome K. Myers, "Religion, National Origin, Immigration, and Mental Illness," *American Journal of Psychiatry,* **110:** 759–764, 1954.
[1] The authors were aided by USPHS Mental Health Act Grant MH 263 (R), "Relationship of Psychiatric Disorder to Social Structure." Also participating in this research were F. C. Redlich, A. B. Hollingshead, H. A. Robinson, and L. Z. Freedman.

standing regularities which must either be included in psychodynamic theory or dismissed as artefacts. The distribution of mental illness among religious and nationality groups is a subject of special interest since these factors undoubtedly create a great deal of personal conflict. People still tend to type themselves according to these labels even though this form of differentiation is very much discredited in the American ideology. Beyond this rejection based upon our system of values the scientist cannot disregard certain empirical findings in the distribution of mental illness which have turned up with considerable regularity.

It has been pointed out in previous studies that the diagnostic categories of mental illness are not proportionately distributed among the religious and nationality groups; also, that immigration into the United States has a determining effect upon the occurrence of mental illness. Most of the preceding investigations have dealt with the numbers of first admissions to mental hospitals (2, 6, 7). There have also been surveys of Selective Service examinations which represent random samples of the male population within certain age limits (4). In this study, we have examined the distribution of psychiatric illness according to religion, national origin, and immigration in an urban center with a population of approximately 250,000. Since the previous studies were carried out 10 to 30 years ago, our findings can be expected to reflect some of the trends brought about by advancement in psychiatric treatment and also some of the effects of changing social conditions.

DESIGN OF THE SURVEY

A survey was made of all patients with residence in the metropolitan area of New Haven under the treatment of a psychiatrist on December 1, 1950. For each patient a schedule was addressed to his psychiatrist or filled out from his record in a mental hospital or outpatient clinic. The effort to cover the entire population under psychiatric treatment on this particular date involved contacting all the practitioners, clinics, and hospitals in the state and nearby regions, as well as national hospitals treating New Haven patients. In the total, 1,963 cases were found with 1,393 located in public hospitals, 37 in private hospitals, 159 in clinics, and 374 being treated by private practitioners.

A direct inquiry was made about the patient's place of birth, rearing, and religion; also the nationality of his parents in order to determine his national origin. The psychiatric diagnosis proposed by the practitioner or the record was converted into the Veterans Administration diagnostic scheme after agreement with the opinion of members of our psychiatric team.[2] Since consensus was difficult in certain of the subcategories, the differences were resolved by combining the subcategories under a more general heading. This was necessary for the psychoneurotic, psychosomatic, and character disorders. Alcohol and drug addictions were grouped together as were the affective disorders and the illnesses of senescence. The small number of organic mental illnesses necessitated their

[2] Adapted from the Veterans Administration Nomenclature: TB 10A-78.

inclusion under one heading. The final form of the diagnostic scheme which has been carried through the entire study is presented in Table 1.

FINDINGS

Religion and mental illness. The analysis of the population broken down into the 3 major religious groupings is shown in Table 1. Comparison of this psychiatric population with a control group consisting of a 5% systematic sample of the general population reveals a significant statistical difference in the distribution of total mental illness, the psychoneurotic disorders, and alcohol and drug addiction among the religious groups.[3] In addition, significance is approached in the distribution of the organic illnesses. However, it was found that schizophrenia, the affective disorders, psychosis with mental deficiency and illnesses of senescence were distributed in the same proportions as in the general population. Since it was found in a previous analysis that social class is also a determining factor in the distribution of mental illness, this possibility was checked in all of the significant findings in this study (8). This was of importance in the finding that psychoneurotic disorder among Jews was 2-1/2 times above expectation. Our check brought out that social class accounted for this skewed religious distribution in the lowest socio-economic level; however, only 10% of the neurotic patients were in this level. The Catholic group was found to be inordinately high for alcohol and drug addiction, and it is remarkable that there were no Jews with this form of illness. Social class was of no importance in this instance.

Our findings have been compared with those of Malzberg and Dayton, using first hospital admissions (2, 6). As would be expected, our rates were higher for psychoneurotic disorders since we had included ambulatory patients. In all other categories our findings are substantially the same as those of other investigators. In contrast to what is stated in 2 textbooks of psychiatry (3, 9), we did not find

Table 1
Distribution of psychiatric and general population according to diagnosis and religious affiliation

	Catholic		Protestant		Jewish	
	No.	%	No.	%	No.	%
General population	6,736	57.5	3,869	33.0	1,108	9.5
Total psychiatric population	1,059	57.0	576	31.0	223	12.0
Psychoneurotic and character disorder	189	46.2	122	29.8	98	24.0
Alcohol and drug addiction	61	68.5	28	31.5	0	0.0
Schizophrenia	506	60.8	245	29.4	81	9.7
Affective disorders	86	55.1	53	34.0	17	10.9
Psychosis with mental deficiency	56	61.5	23	25.3	12	13.2
Disorders of senescence	100	55.9	67	37.4	12	6.8
Epilepsy	25	71.5	9	25.7	1	2.9
Other organic	36	53.8	29	43.4	2	2.8

[3] The Chi Square test for difference was utilized in all calculations in this paper and significance is defined at the .05 level, although in most cases it was less than .01.

a higher rate of affective disorders among Jews. This observation was also made by Malzberg (5) in 1930.

National origin and mental illness.   The response to the question regarding national origin cannot be taken as an entirely valid indication of nationality. It is merely the respondent's subjective impression of the patient's origin. Since our data on this item were crudely defined, analysis was limited to 4 categories representing relatively distinct groups—the Irish, Italian, Negro, and Jewish.[4] As national origin of the parents differed in only 10% of the cases, that of the father was used as the index. As there are no general population figures dealing with national origin, it was necessary to compare the distribution of diagnoses within each nationality group (See Table 2).

Significant differences were found in the distribution of mental illness among these 4 groups. Within the individual groups Jews were high for psychoneurotic disorder (Table 1). The Italians were low for alcohol and drug addiction while the Irish were high. Clearly the high rate of alcoholism among Catholics mentioned previously actually is to be found in the Irish group since these 2 nationalities make up the majority of Catholics in this city. A unique finding is that Negroes were extremely low in their proportion of affective disorders (10). Six of the 8 Negroes with organic disease had general paresis; however, this represents a dramatic decline in total numbers in comparison with earlier studies (2, 6). All other findings are substantially the same as previously presented.

Immigration and mental illness.   Since immigration into the United States has been very low during the last 2 decades, the average age of the foreign-born population is considerably higher than the native-born. For this reason, analysis was limited to a comparison of the psychiatric and general population over 21 years of age.[5] These findings are presented in Table 3. There is a significant

Table 2
Distribution of psychiatric population according to selected ethnic groups and diagnosis

	Irish		Italian		Jewish		Negro	
	No.	%	No.	%	No.	%	No.	%
Psychoneurotic and character disorders	50	15.5	93	23.4	98	43.9	10	11.1
Alcohol and drug addictions	35	10.9	3	0.8	0	0.0	8	8.9
Schizophrenia	153	47.5	192	48.4	81	36.3	50	55.6
Affective disorders	23	7.1	35	8.8	17	7.6	1	1.1
Psychosis with mental deficiency	12	3.7	21	5.3	12	5.4	3	3.3
Disorders of senescence	42	13.0	36	9.1	12	5.4	9	10.0
Epilepsy	0	0.0	3	0.8	1	0.4	1	1.1
Other organic	7	2.2	14	3.5	2	0.9	8	8.9
Total	322	99.9	397	100.1	223	99.9	90	100.0

[4] Negroes are included although strictly speaking they represent a racial group.
[5] The data on the country of birth of the general population were obtained in 1950 United States Census reports.

difference in the distribution of native- and foreign-born with a higher proportion of foreign-born in the total psychiatric population and in the diagnostic
categories of affective disorder, illnesses of senescence, and the organic illnesses.
A significantly higher occurrence of psychoneurosis is found among the native-
born. In the remaining diagnostic categories there are no significant differences
between the native- and foreign-born. The similarity between these findings and
those of Dayton (2) is remarkable if neurosis is excluded from the computation.

The foreign-born population was broken down into specific national groups
(Table 4). It was found that the Italians were high for affective disorders and
illnesses of senescence. The Irish were high for illnesses of senescence and the
addictions but devoid of any psychoneurotic disorders. Northwest Europe was
high for illnesses of senescence; Poland and Russia for affective disorders and
schizophrenia. These findings show the same relative trend reported by other
investigators.

GENERAL DISCUSSION

It is important to note that this survey is not a true prevalency study of psychiatric illness: it is limited to those people with mental illness who are under the
treatment of a psychiatrist. It would be inaccurate to infer that the distribution
found here is a direct reflection of what might be found if the community were
surveyed on a random door-to-door basis since the present findings refer to a
selected population. It is therefore necessary to speculate on factors that might
differentiate this psychiatric population from such a prevalency sample. For
example, there may be significant differences among the religious and nationality
groups in their recognition of psychiatric symptoms. A similar exclusion from
psychiatric treatment would arise from a difference between the cultural groups
with regard to their acceptance of psychiatry as the optimal treatment for mental
symptoms. These general implications of this treated prevalency sample must be
held in mind in reviewing the details of this study.

Table 3
Distribution of psychiatric and general population, 21 years of age and over,
by nativity and psychiatric diagnosis

	Native-born		Foreign-born	
	No.	%	No.	%
General population	135,568	79.5	34,900	20.5
Total psychiatric population	1,363	77.0	408	23.0
Psychoneurotic and character disorders	313	93.2	23	6.8
Alcohol and drug addictions	70	85.4	12	14.6
Schizophrenia	643	76.9	193	23.1
Affective disorders	102	65.4	54	34.6
Psychosis with mental deficiency	67	84.8	12	15.2
Disorders of senescence	91	50.3	90	49.7
Epilepsy	32	91.4	3	8.6
Other organic	45	68.2	21	31.8

Table 4
Distribution of psychiatric and general population, 21 years of age and over, by country of birth and psychiatric diagnosis

	Italy		Ireland		N.W. Europe		Poland and Russia		Other for.-born		Native-born	
	No.	%	No.	%	No.	%	No.	%	No.	%	No.	%
General population	13,369	7.8	3,357	2.0	5,723	3.4	7,252	4.3	5,199	3.0	135,568	79.5
Total psychiatric population	135	7.6	51	2.9	64	3.6	97	5.5	6	3.4	1,363	77.0
Psychoneurotic and character disorder	5	1.5	0	0.0	6	1.8	5	1.5	7	2.1	313	93.2
Alcohol and drug addictions	1	1.2	4	4.9	3	3.7	2	2.4	2	2.4	70	85.4
Schizophrenia	56	6.7	23	2.8	27	3.2	60	7.2	27	3.2	643	76.9
Affective disorders	25	16.0	5	3.2	6	3.8	14	9.0	4	2.6	102	65.4
Psychosis with mental deficiency	6	7.6	0	0.0	1	1.3	1	1.3	4	5.1	67	84.8
Disorders of senescence	35	19.3	16	8.8	16	8.8	10	5.5	13	7.2	91	50.3
Epilepsy	1	2.9	1	2.9	1	2.9	0	0.0	0	0.0	32	91.4
Other organic	6	9.1	2	3.0	4	6.1	5	7.6	4	6.1	45	68.2

The negative findings are of some interest; for example the social variables under consideration had no effect on the distribution of schizophrenia or psychosis with mental deficiency. Among the positive findings this investigation showed an increased frequency of psychoneurotic disorders. Part of this can be immediately credited to the inclusion of ambulatory patients. The acceptance of psychiatry and psychotherapeutic treatment, however, is undoubtedly a growing trend in the United States. As a new development requiring some informed intellectual comprehension, it would be expected that the better educated would have first exposure to the trend. This would explain the higher rate of psychoneurotic disorder among the native-born who have reached a higher educational level.

It is our opinion that the acceptance of psychiatry probably accounts for the inordinately high rate of psychoneurosis among Jews. The explanation for this must be considered in terms of the ethnic structure and the tradition of the Jewish group in addition to its religious organization. Among Jews it is generally accepted that there is no conflict between religious doctrine and psychoanalytic theory. This is in contrast to a partially supported opposition among Catholics. From the standpoint of community attitude, the Jews exhibit a high level of acceptance of psychoanalytic psychiatry with a minimum of disturbance of their social values. The Jewish attitude is widely divergent from the Irish as is substantiated by our finding that not a single patient of Irish birth was receiving psychotherapy for psychoneurosis. Although this explanation of the rates of psychoneurosis in terms of the acceptance of modern psychiatry appears plausible, we cannot definitely state that the actual occurrence of the illness is not higher among Jews.

In this study there was found a general diminution in organic mental disease. Probably this is due to the fact that general paresis is a vanishing clinical entity as a result of improved chemotherapy. This trend also is dependent upon an enlightened acceptance of modern medicine. Our findings show that this has particularly benefited the Negro group. Considering the mental illnesses of senescence among foreign-born, it would be our speculation that this might be explained by the specific type of deficiency caused by this illness. The loss of recent memory erases the skill, learned later in life, essential to an adjustment in the American culture. This would create a more pervading difficulty for those who have immigrated to this country than for those reared in its practices.

The high rate of alcoholism among the Irish population and its absence among Jews has repeatedly been found (1). If this finding is compared with the rates of psychoneurosis it appears that there is some kind of cultural determination in the formation of symptoms. This poses a challenging question to the conceptual framework of psychodynamic theory. A second finding of similar challenge is in the distribution of affective disorder. This illness was found to be higher among the foreign-born and apparently of diminishing frequency in the Jewish group. The trend in affective illness, which is one of the major forms of psychosis, is not easily explained in terms of our knowledge of etiological factors.

The explanation for these cultural psychological phenomena must be in terms of the manner in which the external environment impinges upon the psychological mechanism. There are two important junctures at which this is conceived to occur. The first is the manner in which social factors color the childhood experiences, and the second is in terms of the ego's reaction to external reality. The conception of the ego's relationship with external reality implies its capacity to control the social manifestations of internal impulses in deference to external pressures. Just as behavior is modified in this way, it can be expected that neurotic symptoms which are also interpersonal communications will be influenced by social pressures. There is considerable acceptance by the Irish of alcohol as a means of tension relaxation. From the psychodynamic standpoint, it is remarkable that the Irish can find an outlet for many diverse forms of psychic conflict in this single form of escape. On the other hand, the Jewish disapproval of inebriety precludes this means for the Jewish neurotic. Our findings represent an example of cultural conditions expressing a suppressive and displacing effect upon the symptomatic manifestations of psychic disorder.

To explain the distribution of affective disorder we must seek it in the direction of the developmental process. According to psychoanalytic theory, the affective illness is based upon a fixation in the first four years of life. Hence, if social forces have some effect upon the formation of this illness, it must be that they are brought to bear upon the dynamics of the family. More concretely, this would mean the role and responsibility assumed by various members of the family and the quality of the parent-child relationship. If this is the case, it is conceivable that since the American family structure differs from the European there would be a different etiological force operating to produce affective illness. This is plausible since early childhood experience in America differs from other cultures. It has been suggested elsewhere that the accentuation of feeding has been an important factor in the causation of affective illness among Jews. The acculturation of the Jewish family to America has tended to play down this practice. We can only speculate that such changes as these operating within the family dynamics have brought about the diminution of affective illness among Jews and native-born Americans.

SUMMARY

A survey of the prevalency of patients with mental illness who were under treatment in New Haven was analyzed according to religion, national origin, and immigrational status. It was found that psychoneurotic disorders were more frequent among Jews whereas the rate of affective disorder in this group had fallen to the average of the population. Alcoholism is most prevalent among the Irish Catholics. There has been a general fall in the rate of organic mental disease, particularly in that of general paresis among Negroes. The illness of senescence and the affective illnesses are higher in the foreign-born while psychoneurotic disorders are more frequent in the native-born. Schizophrenia and psychosis with mental deficiency are not related to the social variables.

Comparisons were made between these findings and previous studies. Speculative explanations are offered to explain the trends and disproportions.

Bibliographies

1   Bacon, S. D., et al. *Studies of Drinking in Jewish Culture.* New Haven: Laboratory of Applied Physiology, Yale University, 1951.

2   Dayton, A. N. *New Facts on Mental Disorders.* Springfield: Charles C. Thomas, 1940.

3   Henderson, D. K., and Gillespie, R. D. *A Textbook of Psychiatry,* 7th ed. London: Oxford University Press, 1950.

4   Hyde, R. M., and Chisholm, R. M. Studies in medical sociology, III: The relation of mental disorder to race and nationality. *New England J. of Med.,* **23:** 612, 1944.

5   Malzberg, B. The prevalence of mental disease among Jews, *Ment. Hyg.,* **14:** 926, 1930.

6   Malzberg, B. *Social and Biological Aspects of Mental Disease.* Utica: State Hospital Press, 1940.

7   Pollock, H. M., et al. *Hereditary and Environmental Factors in the Causation of Manic-depressive Psychoses and Dementia Praecox.* Utica: State Hospital Press, 1939.

8   Redlich, F. C., et al. Social structure and psychiatric disorder. *Am. J. Psychiat.,* **109:** 729, Apr. 1953.

9   Rosanoff, A. J. *Manual of Psychiatry and Mental Hygiene,* 7th ed. New York: John Wiley and Sons, Inc., 1944.

10   Tooth, G. *Studies in Mental Illness in the Gold Coast,* Colonial Research Publications (No. 6). London: His Majesty's Stationery Office, 1950.

13
SOCIAL PSYCHOLOGICAL CORRELATES OF UPWARD SOCIAL MOBILITY AMONG UNMARRIED CAREER WOMEN
Evelyn Ellis

The rags to riches success story has long captivated the imagination of the American people. Few other themes have been so glorified or so enduringly popular. But despite its familiarity, the upward climb has been more admired and envied than understood. There has been comparatively little scientific study of the motivations of the mobile person, the methods of achieving mobility, or the effects of status changes upon the individual. Upward social mobility has usually been accepted rather uncritically as a natural and desirable part of a democratic, open-class society, and with reference to the individual, mobility has often been regarded as a coveted prize awarded almost automatically to the able and energetic.

Certain social scientists, however, have suspected that the rags to riches story is not always an entirely happy one for the person who lives it. Some of the

Source: Evelyn Ellis, "Social Psychological Correlates of Upward Mobility Among Unmarried Career Women," *American Sociological Review,* **17:** 558–563, 1952.

social scientific literature regarding vertical mobility has hinted that the experience is often a traumatic one for the individual, growing out of neurotic drives and resulting in further neurotic tendencies. Such a view of mobility is implicit in the writings of Karen Horney,[1] Pitirim Sorokin,[2] and John Dollard.[3]

This paper is a report on an attempt to make an empiric test, with female subjects, of that largely unverified theory. The major underlying hypothesis, suggested particularly by Horney and Sorokin, is that mobility frequently is inspired at least partly by emotional drives generated by unsatisfactory early primary group relations, and that mobility leads to further deterioration of primary group relations with accompanying neurotic symptoms. The early primary group relations would have been characterized by a lack of affection from others and by a series of humiliating experiences which wounded the child's self-esteem.

DESIGN OF THE STUDY

The basic plan of the investigation was to compare a selected group of mobile persons with a comparable group of non-mobile persons in regard to a number of factors thought to be associated with upward social mobility. The groups were kept as homogeneous as possible with respect to such important variables as marital status and occupational status, so that statistically significant differences between the two groups could be assumed to be associated with upward mobility. The sample included sixty outstanding unmarried career women now living in one city, Montgomery, Alabama.

Although there was an interest in overall social mobility, in this study movement was defined in terms of a single dimension—that of occupation, which has been regarded by leading students of social stratification as the most easily determined and probably most valid single index of social status.[4]

Respondents were divided into mobile and non-mobile sub-samples on the basis of a comparison of each respondent's occupational status with the occupational status of her father. Occupational status was reduced to numerical scores suitable for comparisons by a method developed by Cecil C. North and Paul K. Hatt.[5] The method was based on ratings of occupations made by a cross-section of the American population during interviews conducted by the National Opinion Research Center. Persons interviewed were asked to evaluate ninety jobs at all status levels by giving their "own personal opinion" of the "general standing" of each job. Possible ratings were 5 (excellent), 4 (good), 3 (average),

---

[1] Karen Horney, *The Neurotic Personality of Our Time*, New York: Norton and Co., Inc., 1937, pp. 80–82, 178–179.

[2] Pitirim Sorokin, *Social Mobility*, New York: Harper and Brothers, 1927, pp. 510, 515, 522–525. Most of Sorokin's hypotheses were expressed in terms of the characteristics of a mobile society. The implication was, however, that the societal characteristics are largely a reflection of the personal characteristics of mobile individuals.

[3] John Dollard, "The Life History in Community Studies," *American Sociological Review*, 3 (1938), p. 735.

[4] W. Lloyd Warner, Marchia Meeker, and Kenneth Eells, *Social Class in America*, Chicago: Science Research Associates, Inc., 1949, p. 40; and Cecil C. North and Paul K. Hatt, "Jobs and Occupations: A Popular Evaluation," in Logan Wilson and William L. Kolb, *Sociological Analysis*, New York: Harcourt, Brace & Co., 1949, p. 464.

[5] *Ibid.*, pp. 464–474.

2 (fair), and 1 (poor). Final rating of each job was the average of the individual ratings made by all persons interviewed. The resulting averages were reported on a scale with possible ratings ranging from 20 to 100. A separate scale for each major geographical region of the country also was computed by averaging the ratings of interviewees living in the section.

The North-Hatt method was modified to take into consideration the fact that occupations of both men and women were important in this study, while North and Hatt were concerned only with occupations of men. It was believed that, because of the different social expectations for men and women, ratings of specific jobs would vary somewhat with the sex of the holder.

The North-Hatt ratings for the Southern region were used for men's occupations listed in that study. Final ratings of all women's occupations and of men's occupations not appearing on the North-Hatt scale were the average of individual ratings made by twenty persons, ten sociologists now living in Alabama and ten residents of Montgomery. Occupations for the two sexes were listed on separate sheets, with directions asking the rater's personal opinion of the "general standing" of each job as an occupation for the sex indicated. As in the North-Hatt scale, individual ratings were on a five-point scale and final average ratings had a possible range of 20 to 100.

The sample was comprised of women whose occupations received ratings of 75 or more. Since no refusals were encountered, the group included virtually all unmarried women in the city with such occupations. A mobile person was defined as one whose occupational rating exceeded that of her father's major occupation by more than ten points. A non-mobile person was defined as one whose occupational rating exceeded that of her father's major occupation by ten points or less, or whose rating was lower than that of her father. The sample included 27 mobile women and 33 non-mobile. Occupational ratings of the mobile respondents were an average of 26 points above father's occupational rating, while ratings of non-mobile respondents averaged about 2 points below father's rating.

The research was done through intensive personal interviews, guided by a schedule composed largely of broad open-end questions. Factors studied were based chiefly upon hypotheses found in current social scientific literature. The variables fell into three major categories: (1) presumed causes of upward social mobility, (2) presumed effects of upward social mobility, and (3) steps and methods in achieving high status.

EARLY PRIMARY GROUP RELATIONS

Probably the most complete treatment of the presumed role of deep-seated personality factors in the drive for upward mobility is given by Horney[6] in her discussion of neurotic quests for power, prestige and wealth. The invariable basic cause, she says, is a "lack of genuine warmth and affection" from others during the child's early years. Referring to those in whom the desire for prestige is

[6] Horney, op. cit.

paramount, Horney says that the underlying motivation is a hostility, usually taking the form of a desire to humiliate others. That desire, she says, is uppermost in "those persons whose own self-esteem has been wounded by humiliation and who have thus become vindictive." Such persons, she asserts, usually have gone through a "series of humiliating experiences in childhood." Horney lists among the possible contributing factors parental preference for other children, unjust reproaches, rejection by parents, jealousy of a parent or of siblings, minority group membership, and being poor but having wealthy relatives.

Accordingly, in attempting to isolate presumed causes of upward social mobility, the major emphasis of the present study is upon early primary group relations. Results indicate that the proportion of respondents having had a series of humiliating experiences during childhood is significantly larger among mobile women than among non-mobile. Larger proportions of mobile women had experienced both rejection by the general community and at least a partial rejection by parents who had showed favoritism toward a sibling or siblings. Marked preference for a sibling or siblings was reported by 56 per cent of the mobile respondents, but by only 27 per cent of the non-mobile. Percentages having experienced relatively complete rejection by the general community were 20 for mobile women and 0 for non-mobile. Both differences are statistically significant at the five per cent level. Critical ratios are 2.32 for parental favoritism and 2.50 for community rejection. Another interesting point is that within the mobile group the women reporting parental or community rejection were more highly mobile than those with neither background factor. Those whose parents had preferred another child had risen an average of 32 points, while those not reporting favoritism had risen an average of 22 points. Despite the smallness of the numbers involved, the difference was statistically significant (C.R.=2.35). Similarly, those reporting community rejection had risen an average of 31 points.

One further specific indication of a lack of the affection apparently necessary for emotional security in our society was found among mobile women. A significantly larger proportion of mobile respondents rated their attachment to parents during childhood and adolescence as "less than average" (see Table 1).

Table 1
Self-rating of degree of attachment to parents during childhood and adolescence by 58* career women

Self-rating of attachment	Percentage of mobile women (N = 25)	Percentage of non-mobile women (N = 33)
More than average**	36	61
Average	28	33
Less than average†	36	6
Total	100	100

* Two respondents were orphaned during childhood or early adolescence.
** C.R. = 1.92.
† C.R. = 2.24.

CHARACTERISTICS DURING ADULTHOOD

The basic hypothesis regarding characteristics during adulthood is that the mobile woman would continue to have unsatisfactory primary group relations and would exhibit generally neurotic tendencies. The assumption, suggested particularly by Sorokin, was that the mobile person as a result of childhood conditioning is less than normally capable of achieving lasting, satisfactory primary group relations. That incapacity would then be further encouraged by movement through different social class sub-cultures with conflicting values and customs. Sorokin also suggested that in an attempt to alleviate the resulting loneliness the mobile person might turn to a frantic "hunt for pleasure."[7]

The plan of the study, of course, did not permit determination either of the extent to which the mobile woman's adult characteristics were simply the result of a continuation of personality traits developed in childhood, or of the extent to which the already existing characteristics were further aggravated by upward movement.

In general, the theory that mobile persons are more socially isolated than non-mobile is supported by the findings. Significant differences between mobile and non-mobile women are found with respect to number of intimate friends, length of friendships, and conflict with parents during adulthood (see Tables 2 and 3).

Sorokin's theory that the mobile person may turn to a mad "hunt for pleasure" in an attempt to overcome loneliness also received some support. A statistically significant difference (C.R.=2.26) was found in the proportions of mobile and non-mobile women who named as their major leisure-time activities drinking and going to parties and night clubs. Percentages were 22 for mobile respondents, and 3 for non-mobile.

Another hypothesis regarding attempts to alleviate loneliness was that a disproportionately large number of mobile women acquire pets as outlets for affection. A highly significant group difference in the ownership of pets was found (C.R.=3.05). Percentages were 40 for mobile women, and 15 for non-mobile.

In an attempt to find at least crude indications of neurotic tendencies, each respondent was asked for a description of any of her own health problems, and

Table 2
Number of intimate friends reported by 60 career women

Item	Mobile women (N = 27)	Non-mobile women (N = 33)
Mean number of intimate friends*	8.9	17.8
Mean number of intimate friends in Montgomery**	5.6	9.4
Mean number of friendships of more than five years duration†	3.2	8.2

* C R = 3.21.
** C.R. = 3.72.
† C.R. = 3.50.

[7] Sorokin, op. cit., pp. 522–525.

Table 3
Incidence of serious conflict with parents in four areas of
behavior reported by 58* career women

Area of behavior	Percentage reporting conflict	
	Mobile women (N = 25)	Non-mobile women (N = 33)
Religion	16	3
Politics	20	12
Respondent's career**	40	18
Respondent's personal conduct†	40	12

* Two respondents were orphaned during childhood or early adolescence.
** C.R. = 1.82.
† C.R. = 2.47.

for a self-rating of happiness during adulthood. The assumption was, of course, that the neurotic tends to be less happy than the well-adjusted person and is thus more likely to have psychosomatic and similar ailments.

A significantly larger proportion of mobile women did have relatively severe psychosomatic symptoms of the types generally regarded as emotionally based. Percentages were 32 for mobile women, and 9 for non-mobile (C.R.=2.10). No one in the non-mobile group had more than one type of psychosomatic illness, while in the mobile group half of those with such complaints had more than one type of disorder.

Self-ratings of happiness during adulthood did not show statistically significant differences between the mobile and non-mobile groups. It perhaps is noteworthy, however, that the answers of both groups had a more or less normal distribution rather than the heavy majority of "very happy" replies frequently found in happiness ratings.[8] Self-ratings given by respondents in this study appear in Table 4.

One interesting question was the extent to which respondents' careers were actually major ends or only second-choice substitutes for marriage. Answers to two questions offered some evidence that successful careers were major ends for mobile women more often than for non-mobile. A significantly larger proportion of mobile women indicated a desire to continue working in the event of their marriage, and, among those previously married and now widowed or divorced, a significantly larger proportion of mobile women actually did continue working during marriage. Percentages of respondents wishing to continue careers if married were 52 for mobile, and 27 for non-mobile (C.R.=2.00). Of those previously married, 75 per cent of the mobile and 8 per cent of the non-mobile worked during marriage (C.R.=3.10).

[8] For example, two well-known marriage prediction studies report that more than 50 per cent of the wives in the samples rated their marriages as unusually happy. See Ernest W. Burgess and Leonard S. Cottrell, Jr., *Predicting Success or Failure in Marriage*, New York: Prentice-Hall, Inc., 1939, p. 39; and Lewis Terman, *Psychological Factors in Marital Happiness*, New York: McGraw-Hill Book Co., Inc., 1938, p. 203.

Table 4
Self-ratings of happiness during adulthood
by 58* career women

Rating	Percentage of mobile women** (N = 25)	Percentage of non-mobile women (N = 33)
Very happy	16	33.3
Happy	48	30.2
Average	20	30.3
Unhappy	12	6.1
Very unhappy	4	0.0
Total	100	100.0

* Two respondents said they were unable to answer the question.
** Differences between mobile and non-mobile groups were not statistically significant.

METHODS OF ACHIEVING HIGH STATUS

The study included questions dealing with four major hypotheses regarding steps and methods in achieving high occupational status. Two of the hypotheses, formulated especially by Warner and his associates, are that advanced education[9] and geographical mobility[10] are factors facilitating upward mobility. Geographical movement is said to be helpful because it makes determination of a person's background more difficult and the prejudicial effect of former status, therefore, becomes less definitive. The other hypotheses are that the mobile person requires a longer time period than the non-mobile to reach a high-status position, and that, with the "maturing" of the American economy, the professions have offered a better road to mobility than has business.

Statistically significant differences were not found regarding any of these hypotheses. Mobile and non-mobile groups are almost identical with respect to mean age at reaching present high status, and in proportions in business and professional occupations.

Average educational level is the same for mobile and non-mobile sub-samples. The mean number of years in college is 3.7 for each group. Attempts to measure the influence of education in the rise of mobile women, however, should be based partly upon comparison of the respondent's education with parents' education. In this study the mobile women were unable to give sufficiently exact information about parents' schooling to permit such a comparison. Other available information about parents, particularly occupational status, hints that the educational attainment of the mobile women was considerably higher than that of their parents. It seems very probable that advanced education is one of the important factors facilitating upward mobility.

[9] W. Lloyd Warner and Paul S. Lunt, *The Social Life of a Modern Community*, New Haven: Yale University Press, 1941, p. 119.
[10] *Ibid.*, p. 436.

While no specific question regarding geographical mobility yielded statistically significant group differences, there are numerous small differences, without exception pointing in the direction of more geographical movement among mobile women. Although the evidence is inconclusive, it seems doubtful that chance alone would result in so many small differences in the same direction, and it appears probable that the occupationally mobile women do tend to be somewhat more geographically mobile (see Table 5).

SUMMARY AND CONCLUSIONS

The evidence is consistent with the theory that upward social mobility is likely to be an outgrowth of basically neurotic drives resulting from unsatisfactory early primary group relations, and that mobility leads to a continuation of superficial, impermanent primary group relations and other overt manifestations of emotional maladjustment.

A comparison of mobile and non-mobile career women reveals that significantly larger proportions of mobile individuals had experienced both rejection by parents and by the over-all community during childhood. The mobile women continued to be more socially isolated than the non-mobile during adulthood. A further indication of the relative maladjustment of the mobile women was the significantly greater incidence of psychosomatic ailments.

The group differences, however, are not as marked as those suggested in the original hypotheses. It appears that in regard to upward social mobility, as with most other complex social phenomena, no single explanation is entirely adequate. But since the presumed indicators of maladjustment in general have the greater incidence in the more highly mobile half of the mobile sub-sample, it is possible that larger differences in the anticipated directions are somewhat obscured by the inclusion of cases of only moderate mobility. A more crucial test of the hypotheses probably would be furnished by a more extensive study of very highly mobile persons.

Table 5
Statistics regarding geographical movements of 60 career women

Item	Mobile women (N = 27)	Non-mobile women (N = 33)
Per cent born in Alabama or an adjacent state	66.7	78.8
Mean number of years residence in Montgomery	10.8	14.8
Mean number of jobs held in Montgomery	1.7	2.1
Mean number of cities worked in	3.5	2.7
Mean number of states worked in	2.4	1.8
Mean number of cities lived in before working	2.0	1.6
Mean number of states lived in before working	1.7	1.2
Per cent having worked outside the United States	22.2	9.9

Differences between mobile and non-mobile groups are not statistically significant.

14
DRINKING AND DEVIANT
DRINKING, U. S. A., 1963[1]
Harold A. Mulford

The purpose of this study is to obtain current information on the patterns of beverage alcohol use in the United States. So long as "alcoholics" are defined and reacted to in terms of their deviant drinking behavior, knowledge of the prevailing drinking practices of the general population and various social segments should be of value for the design and administration of action programs to alleviate the alcoholism problem and should provide clues for further research on the genesis and prevention of extreme deviant drinking.

The only previous scientific investigation of the nation's drinking patterns was conducted nearly a generation ago. In 1946 Riley and Marden, in cooperation with the National Opinion Research Center, studied the prevalence of drinkers, their social characteristics, what and how often they drank, and their reasons for drinking (1, 2). Since then, studies have been made in two states (3, 4, 5), and one major community survey (6) of drinking practices has been carried out. In addition, commercial pollsters have from time to time asked relevant questions. The present study investigates the prevalence of drinkers, ex-drinkers, and "deviant" drinkers in the national population and in selected social segments.

METHODS

The sample consisted of 1515 respondents chosen by modified random sampling procedures to represent the total noninstitutional population of the United States aged 21 years and over. A standard multistage area probability sample to the block or segment level was used; and, at the block level, certain quotas were set on sex, age and race, and on the employed–unemployed status of women. Approximately 200 interviewers, using a structured questionnaire, conducted the field work in the summer of 1963.

Sampling and interviewing as potential sources of bias

When the sample was checked against the 1960 U. S. Census data (7) only minor discrepancies were detected with regard to sex, age, residence, education, and income distribution. If educational attainment was not overstated by some re-

Source: Harold A. Mulford, "Drinking and Deviant Drinking, U.S.A., 1963," Quarterly Journal of Studies on Alcohol, 25: 634–650, 1964 (abridged).
[1] This study was financed by the State Psychopathic Hospital and the Department of Psychiatry, College of Medicine, State University of Iowa, Iowa City. The sampling and field work were done by the National Opinion Research Center, using questions prepared by the author. Special thanks for assistance with data processing are due to Richard Ingersoll, Research Associate, Department of Psychiatry, University of Iowa.

spondents, as may well have been the case (8, *p. 147*) then the lower educational categories may have been underrepresented in the sample to an extent that could inflate the over-all prevalence value by a maximum of 3 percentage points.

Table 1
Distribution of the adult population and of selected social segments by
certain measures of drinking behavior, U.S.A. 1963

	(1)	(2)	(3)	(4)	(5)	(6)
	Entire sample			Drinkers only		
	N	% Drink	% Quit[a]	N	% Q-F 5	% Troubles[b]
Totals	1509	71	8	1068	11	10
Regions[c]						
New England	85	81	2	69	12	6
Mid Atlantic	283	88	4	249	12	8
E. N. Central	292	75	6	220	15	12
W. N. Central	139	74	6	103	9	4
S. Atlantic	196	64	10	126	6	11
E. S. Central	86	33	17	28	7	11
W. S. Central	182	48	9	87	7	13
Mountain	31	55	26	17	0	12
Pacific	215	79	9	169	9	11
Sex:						
Male	737	79	9	580	16	16
Female	772	63	7	488	4	2
Age, years:						
21–39	641	79	4	505	10	10
40–59	551	70	9	386	12	10
60 and over	308	56	12	171	9	8
Education, years[d]:						
0–7	182	46	17	83	7	16
8	197	60	13	118	10	11
9–11	298	70	9	208	13	11
12	433	79	5	340	10	9
13–15	229	76	4	175	6	9
16	95	89	3	85	15	4
More than 16	71	79	3	56	21	13
Residence community size:						
Under 2,500	261	60	8	157	5	6
2,500–9,999	293	69	9	201	12	8
10,000–74,999	427	76	7	323	11	8
75,000–499,999	278	71	7	198	10	13
500,000 and over	250	76	8	189	13	13
Religion:						
Jewish	50	90	2	45	7	7
Catholic	378	89	5	336	12	10
Lutheran	136	85	4	116	13	5
Other large Prot. den.[e]	156	81	6	127	12	6
Protestant den. unsp.[f]	46	78	9	36	17	14
Other non-Prot. relig.	46	76	7	35	14	9
Methodists	218	61	8	133	5	8
Small Prot. denoms.	191	53	14	102	10	15
Baptists	289	48	11	138	9	16

	(1)	(2)	(3)	(4)	(5)	(6)
		Entire sample			Drinkers only	
					%	%
	N	% Drink	% Quit[a]	N	Q-F 5	Troubles[b]
Income, annual:						
Under $3,000	279	54	14	151	8	7
$3,000–4,999	307	64	5	195	5	12
$5,000–6,999	349	68	9	236	11	9
$7,000–9,999	290	85	3	247	12	10
$10,000 and over	237	87	4	207	14	9
Marital status:						
Single	121	79	2	95	18	16
Married	1211	72	8	871	10	9
Divorced	62	69	8	43	9	19
Widowed	113	51	12	58	5	2
Occupation[g]:						
00–09	99	69	11	68	10	16
10–19	270	67	12	182	11	15
20–29	109	76	8	83	19	19
30–39	101	73	9	74	11	12
40–49	139	83	5	115	13	9
50–59	76	76	4	58	12	7
60–69	106	84	6	89	15	6
70–79	76	80	3	61	11	5
80–89	47	87	9	41	24	17
90–99	5	100	0	5	0	20

[a] Abstainers now who drank formerly.
[b] Had one or more "troubles" (see text) because of drinking.
[c] The states comprising each region are as follows: *New England:* Connecticut, Maine, Massachusetts, New Hampshire, Rhode Island, Vermont. *Middle Atlantic:* New Jersey, New York, Pennsylvania. *East North Central:* Indiana, Illinois, Michigan, Ohio, Wisconsin. *West North Central:* Iowa, Kansas, Minnesota, Missouri, Nebraska, North Dakota, South Dakota. *South Atlantic:* Delaware, Florida, Georgia, Maryland, North Carolina, South Carolina, Virginia, West Virginia, District of Columbia. *East South Central:* Alabama, Mississippi, Kentucky, Tennessee. *West South Central* Arkansas, Louisiana, Oklahoma, Texas. *Mountain:* Arizona, Colorado, Idaho, Nevada, New Mexico, Utah, Wyoming. *Pacific:* Alaska, California, Hawaii, Oregon, Washington.
[d] Completions: 8 years = grade school, 12 years = high school, 16 years = college.
[e] "Other large Protestant denominations" includes Congregationalists, Presbyterians and Episcopalians. The prevalence rates in these three denominations varied little, ranging from 79 to 86%, but these rates were based on N's ranging from 29 Congregationalists to 82 Presbyterians.
[f] Protestants of unspecified denomination.
[g] This occupational classification is based on work originally done by the National Opinion Research Center (11) and attempts to arrange occupation according to socioeconomic status. Much of the original work was done by P. K. Hatt and C. C. North. More recent work by O. D. Duncan can be found in Reiss (12, *especially ch. 6 and 7*). It is important to note that "housewives" are omitted, hence the rates of drinkers, etc., by occupation are not computed on the same base as is used for all other social segments. The following occupations illustrate the types in each category: 00–09, laborers, private household workers, janitors; 10–19, farmers, carpenters, painters; 20–29, shipping clerks, cabinet makers, mechanics; 30–39, machinists, salesmen, small business proprietors and managers; 40–49, electricians, construction foremen, nurses; 50–59, musicians, bookkeepers, manufacturing foremen; 60–69, real estate and insurance agents, secretaries, draftsmen; 70–79, buyers and store department heads, veterinarians, designers; 80–89, college professors, scientists, engineers; 90–99, dentists, lawyers, judges, physicians.

The Iowa studies (3, 4) found that drinking interviewers reported proportionately more drinkers than did abstaining interviewers. In the present study, drinking interviewers interviewed 1,272 persons and found that 74% of them drink.

Abstaining interviewers interviewed 243 respondents and reported that 51% were drinkers.

In the Iowa studies the source of this discrepancy was sought in (a) interviewer selection of respondents for their drinking habits or (b) the interviewing situation, or both. However, the results of the search were inconclusive (3, 4).

In the present study interviewer selection of respondents on the basis of their drinking habits or some related factor is highly unlikely. Although the quota sampling procedures that were employed permitted the interviewers some discretion in the selection of respondents, the freedom of choice was greatly restricted: interviewers were instructed to begin at a designated point on a specified block and proceed along a designated route until their quota was filled. These procedures greatly reduced the likelihood that interviewers could have had prior knowledge about potential respondents. Moreover, the considerable homogeneity among persons living on the same block would also restrict the ability of interviewers to choose respondents for their drinking habits. The possibility that drinking and abstaining interviewers differentially influenced the responses of their respective respondents could not be checked with available data.

There is a third and much more likely explanation of the differences. They may be mainly a matter of ecology. Interviewers living, as they do, in the same general locale as their respondents are likely to share many habits and attitudes, including those relating to alcohol. For example, in a rural, southern, predominantly Baptist area it would not be surprising if the interviewer and most of his respondents were abstaining Baptists.

Support for this hypothesis is seen in the fact that within geographic regions the differences in results reported by the two groups of interviewers were reduced to approximately 10 percentage points. When respondents' religion was controlled, the differences were similarly reduced. Thus the discrepancy between the prevalence rates reported by drinking and abstaining interviewers is substantially reduced when either of these variables is controlled. If there were enough cases to control simultaneously both religion and geographic region, the difference probably would be further reduced.

To measure prevalence of drinkers, the following question was employed: "Do you ever have occasion to use alcoholic beverages such as liquor, wine, or beer, or are you a total abstainer?" This wording was borrowed from the Gallup Poll, which has used it repeatedly (9, 10).

FINDINGS

Quantity—frequency of drinking

Not only the fact of alcohol use but also a relatively high quantity and frequency of consumption are necessary conditions for the kind of drinking behavior which identifies the "alcoholic." Therefore knowledge of the extent of drinking in the population and its social segments becomes important.

Table 2 shows the distribution of the sample according to the quantity–

Table 2
Distribution of U.S.A. adults by Q-F Index types (in per cent)

Q-F Index type	Quantity	Frequency	Total* (N = 1469)	Male (N = 718)	Female (N = 751)
Light drinkers					
Type 1	Small	Once a month or less	28	24	32
Type 2	Medium or large	Once a month or less	4	4	4
Moderate drinkers					
Type 3	Small	More than once a month	23	28	19
Type 4	Medium or large	2–4 times a month	7	9	4
Heavy drinkers					
Type 5	Medium or large	More than once a month	8	13	3
Abstainers					
Type 0			30	22	38

* Most of the 40 drinkers who could not be given Q-F Index scores drank less than once a year or for medicinal purposes only, or otherwise indicated very low consumption.

frequency of consumption as measured by the Q–F Index, originally developed by Straus and Bacon (13).[2] The distribution in the nation is similar to the distribution observed in the Iowa studies, except that in Iowa there were one-third more drinkers classified as Q–F type "0," i.e., abstainers (4, p. 47). The additional drinkers at the national level are light and moderate rather than heavy drinkers. The Iowa studies found approximately three men to one woman among heavy drinkers. The national ratio is four to one. If inference can be drawn from this about the sex ratio among "alcoholics," it hardly supports the widespread assertions that there are as many women as men alcoholics.

Drinkers with a Q–F Index score of 1, who make up 28% of the sample, drink a maximum of one or two drinks (no more than 1.6 ounces of absolute alcohol) no more often than once a month. Q–F Index type 3 drinkers consume small amounts more than once a month and constitute 23% of the sample. Together, these two Q–F Index types (1 and 3) when added to type "0" (abstainers) constitute 81% of the population. This major portion of the nation's adults are either abstainers or have such a low consumption level that they can hardly contribute to the "alcoholism problem."

Moreover, only a fraction of the remaining 19% of the population (Q–F types 2, 4, and 5) are "alcoholics" by any commonly accepted definition. The Q–F types 2 and 4, constituting 11% of the population, infrequently (less than once a week) consume a medium or large quantity (more than two drinks). However,

[2] For a detailed description of the Q–F Index as used here and the definition of the several quantities of consumption, see Mulford and Miller (4). There is need for an improved quantity–frequency measure which would collect all of the most likely candidates for the label "alcoholic" into one Q–F category.

since there is no limit on the quantity of consumption of these two Q–F types, it is possible that some of them are periodic "binge" drinkers and candidates for the label "alcoholic."

Q–F type 5 defines persons who consume medium or large amounts of alcohol more than once a week and probably contain a higher proportion of "alcoholics" than any of the other types. In any case, the Quantity–Frequency level of the type 5's exceeds that of 92% of all drinkers and they are, therefore, deviant drinkers. Assuming that, except for a few periodic binge drinkers, "alcoholics" are concentrated in this category, the type 5 drinkers will be given closer scrutiny below.

Deviant drinking.   The proportions in the last two columns of Table 1 represent two different indicators of deviant drinking and are based only on the drinkers in the sample. Column 5 shows the proportion of drinkers in each segment who received a Q–F Index score of 5. These persons reported consuming three or more drinks two or more times a week and will be referred to as "heavy drinkers." Column 6 shows the proportion of drinkers who reported having had trouble with wife, police, employer, or in health because of their own drinking.

Approximately 10% of all drinkers in the sample reported themselves as either heavy drinkers, or as having had trouble due to drinking, or both. While there is some overlap between the heavy drinkers and persons reporting trouble, the overlap is far from complete. Actually 26% of the 113 heavy drinkers reported one or more troubles, and 9% reported two or more. On the other hand, 28% of the 104 persons who reported trouble were heavy drinkers. Table 5 compares trouble-due-to-drinking with Q–F Index scores. It can be seen that the Q–F type 4's differ little from the 5's with respect to the proportion reporting trouble. As mentioned earlier, the type 4's consume either medium or large amounts of alcohol, as do the type 5's, but less frequently. Among the type 4's we might expect a relatively high proportion of "binge" drinkers rather than steady drinkers. In any case the type 4 drinkers appear to encounter just as much difficulty as do the type 5's.

Heavy drinking.   From Table 1, Column 5, it is apparent that heavy drinkers occur most frequently in the three northeastern regions—the New England,

Table 3
Relationship between Q-F Index scores and trouble due to drinking (drinkers only, in per cent)

Troubles	Q-F Index scores					
	1	**2**	**3**	**4**	**5**	**Total**
0	96	90	92	76	74	90
1	3	8	8	17	17	8
2	*	*	*	6	6	2
3	*	2	*	1	3	*
Total *N*'s	416	60	340	99	113	1028

* Less than 1%.

Middle Atlantic, and East North Central states—while the southern states have the lowest rates of heavy drinkers. The Mountain region stands out with a rate of zero but this is based on only 17 cases.

The heavy drinkers tend to be concentrated in the following social segments: males, the college educated, the cities, the above $5,000 income group, the next-to-highest and the third-from-lowest status occupations, and the unmarried Among the religious categories the Protestants who did not specify a denomination have the highest rate of heavy drinkers while the Methodists, Baptists and Jews stand out with low rates. The small age differences show drinkers over 60 to have the lowest rates of both heavy drinkers and trouble due to drinking. Segments with the highest rates of heavy drinkers are generally the same as those having the highest rates of drinkers. A noteworthy exception to this is the Jews, who had the highest rates of drinkers of any religion but, next to the Methodists, the lowest rates of heavy drinkers. This is consistent with the finding of the infrequency of alcoholism among the Jews (14).

Trouble due to drinking.   Drinking and relatively heavy drinking are necessary conditions of "alcoholism"; but, beyond this, most current definitions of alcoholism include some kind of personal or interpersonal trouble that can be attributed to drinking. While it is not reasonable to equate the trouble-due-to-drinking measure in the present study with "alcoholism," it is reasonable to suppose that any subpopulation composed of persons who have encountered such trouble contains a high concentration of "alcoholics." For the present, this is as close as we can get to comparing "alcoholics" with "nonalcoholics."

Column 6 of Table 1 shows the proportion of drinkers who reported having encountered one or more of the following troubles because of their drinking (the proportion of the drinkers reporting each type of trouble is shown in parentheses): (a) an employer had fired or threatened to fire the person if he did not reduce or quit drinking (0.3%); (b) his spouse had left or threatened to leave him if he would not do something about his drinking (0.8%); (c) his spouse or other family member had complained of the money he was spending on alcoholic beverages (5.4%); (d) he had been arrested for intoxication or on other charges involving alcoholic beverages (2.9%); and (e) a physician had told him that drinking was injuring his health (3.9%). Thus, the most frequent difficulty due to drinking involved complaints about the money spent for alcohol, followed by injury to health and trouble with the police. Only three respondents reported trouble with their employers and only eight reported marital separation or the threat of it.

The social segments also vary on this measure of deviant drinking. The West South Central region, where the rate of drinkers is relatively low, has the highest rate of persons encountering trouble. This is followed by the East North Central region, where there is a relatively high rate of drinkers. (The Mountain states also have a high rate of trouble, but this is based on very few cases.) The lowest rates of trouble are found in the West North Central followed by the New England and Middle Atlantic regions. The latter two have relatively high rates of drinkers and of heavy drinkers.

Persons encountering trouble due to drinking occur most often among males, and have either the least or the most schooling. They also tend to be residents of the largest cities (over 75,000 population), and to be Baptists or members of "small" or unspecified Protestant denominations. They are also more frequent in the next-to-lowest income group, among divorced and unmarried persons, and in the three lowest status and the two highest status occupational categories. There is a hint in these findings that the drinker in a group where drinkers are less prevalent is more likely to encounter trouble because of his drinking. This suggests the hypothesis that whether an individual's drinking leads to trouble depends as much or more upon the reactions of others as it does upon his own actions. On the other hand, there is the fact that males, the highest educational category, the next-to-highest if not the highest occupational categories, and the largest cities have relatively high rates of both drinkers and trouble-due-to-drinking as well as high rates of heavy drinkers.

Deviant drinking among ex-drinkers

The reasons for giving up alcohol cannot be deeply probed with the data at hand but certain inferences can be made from the two measures of deviant drinking. A first thought is that persons who have quit drinking are mostly deviant drinkers who have encountered trouble and then yielded to the negative reactions of others. But this seems to be true only to a limited degree. The proportions of ex-drinkers who had once been heavy drinkers or who had encountered trouble did not greatly exceed the proportion among currently practicing drinkers. There were 116 respondents (7.7% of the sample) who said that they had quit; approximately 14% of these ex-drinkers met the criteria for heavy drinking and about 15% of them reported having encountered one or more troubles due to drinking. Thus, approximately 15% of the ex-drinkers were "deviant" drinkers compared with approximately 10% of persons who are currently drinkers. It is worth further investigation to discover how many ex-drinkers may be "recovered alcoholics."

DISCUSSION

This study, aimed at the ultimate understanding and control of the kind of drinking behavior that identifies the "alcoholic," has provided knowledge concerning the relative occurrence of drinkers, ex-drinkers and deviant drinkers in certain major social segments of the population of the United States. Although the conclusion that individual drinking patterns, including deviant drinking patterns, are socially determined has been strengthened, the interpersonal processes by which this is accomplished and the thoughts and values underlying the behavior remain to be determined. A first step, however, is to describe the behavior to be explained, and this has been the burden of the present work. The findings provide clues for future research and should be of value to alcoholism program administrators for identifying target populations and designing and evaluating action programs of education and treatment.

The evidence that drinking and heavy drinking—two necessary conditions for "alcoholism"—vary from one social segment to another reaffirms the findings of previous studies and raises important questions for further research. What is there, for example, about the three South Central regions of the country which gives them a rate of drinkers approximately half that of the North Eastern regions? Why do so many drinkers in the South Central regions give up the practice? What success do these subpopulations have in modifying the "alcoholic's" drinking? How is the rate of heavy drinkers among women restricted to only one-fourth that of men?

Drinking behavior, including the extreme deviant drinking that renders the actor a likely candidate for the label "alcoholic," will probably be understood eventually in terms of prevailing public definitions—definitions of alcohol, of drinkers, of what we now call "alcoholics," not to mention definitions of self. There is need for explanatory research using measures of attitudinal variables intervening between the dependent behavioral measures and independent sociocultural factors. For example, identification of the kinds of definitions that discourage the use of alcohol and make for moderation among those who do drink would be a long step toward establishing alcohol education programs on a rational footing. Sex differences (or the lack of differences) in rates of ex-drinkers may be an especially fruitful area of investigation. One of the largest and most consistently reported differences in drinking behavior is that between the sexes. Yet the present survey found that men and women drinkers abandon the practice in essentially the same proportion.

The social segments in which different types of drinkers are concentrated could be more precisely located in future research if the sample were large enough to make additional cross-tabulation feasible. For example, both the age and educational differences in drinking behavior found in the present work might look quite different if the one could be controlled with respect to the other. Cross-tabulations of sex and education in the Iowa studies indicated that heavy drinking increases with increased education among men but decreases among women.

Considering that some cultures, e.g., the Italian (15) and Jewish (14), have evolved a set of drinking norms and definitions which curb deviant drinking and in view of the findings of this study that some segments of the United States population are more restrained than others in their use of alcohol, it is conceivable that this nation may also evolve a set of norms which would reduce the kind of drinking that renders the drinker a likely candidate for the label "alcoholic." The process could be expedited by well-designed educational programs. However, it is hardly possible to identify target populations, or intelligently design educational messages, or decide what means of communication should be used, until more is known about existing drinking habits and attitudes.

References

1   Riley, J. W., Jr. and Marden, C. F. The social pattern of alcoholic drinking. *Quart. J. Stud. Alc.* **8:** 265–273, 1947.

2   Riley, J. W., Jr., Marden, C. F., and Lifshitz, M. The motivational pattern of drinking. *Quart. J. Stud. Alc.* **9:** 353–362, 1948.

3   Mulford, H. A. and Miller, D. E. Drinking in Iowa. *I.* Sociocultural distribution of drinkers. *Quart. J. Stud. Alc.* **20:** 704–726, 1959.

4   Mulford, H. A. and Miller, D. E. The prevalence and extent of drinking in Iowa, 1961; a replication and an evaluation of methods. *Quart. J. Stud. Alc.* **24:** 39–53, 1963.

5   Maxwell, M. A. Drinking behavior in the State of Washington. *Quart. J. Stud. Alc.* **13:** 219–239, 1952.

6   California State Department of Public Health, Division of Alcoholic Rehabilitation. The California Drinking Practices Study. Berkeley, Calif.; 1961.

7   U. S. Bureau of the Census. U. S. Census of Population, 1960. Detailed Characteristics. U. S. Summary; Table 173. (Final Report PC[1]–ID.) Washington; U. S. Government Printing Office; 1963.

8   Stephan, F. F. and McCarthy, P. J. *Sampling Opinions.* New York; Wiley; 1958.

9   American Institute of Public Opinion. Princeton, N. J., Press Release, 5 Feb. 1964.

10   Cantril, H., ed. *Public Opinion, 1935–1946.* Princeton; Princeton University Press; 1951.

11   National Opinion Research Center. Jobs and occupations. *Opinion News* **9:** 4–5, 1947.

12   Reiss, A. J., Jr. *Occupations and Social Status.* Glencoe, Ill.; Free Press; 1961.

13   Straus, R. and Bacon, S. D. *Drinking in College.* New Haven; Yale University Press; 1953.

14   Snyder, C. R. *Alcohol and the Jews; a Cultural Study of Drinking and Sobriety.* New Brunswick, N. J.; Publications Division, Rutgers Center of Alcohol Studies; 1958.

15   Lolli, G., Serianni, E., Golder, G. M. and Luzzatto-Fegiz, P. *Alcohol in Italian Culture; Food and Wine in Relation to Sobriety among Italians and Italian Americans.* New Brunswick, N. J.; Publications Division, Rutgers Center of Alcohol Studies; 1958.

15
A CROSS-CULTURAL SURVEY OF
SCHIZOPHRENIC SYMPTOMATOLOGY

H. B. M. Murphy, E. D. Wittkower, J. Fried, and H. Ellenberger

For many years the present writers, individually and collectively, have been engaged in studies of the relationship between mental disorder and cultural environment. In the course of these studies contact was established with many psychiatrists and social scientists throughout the world, and through the estab-

Source: H. B. M. Murphy, E. D. Wittkower, J. Fried, and H. Ellenberger, "A Cross-cultural Survey of Schizophrenic Symptomatology," *International Journal of Social Psychiatry,* **9:** 237–249, 1963.

lishment of a twice-yearly *Transcultural Psychiatric Review and News-letter* a regular network of correspondents developed. In 1958 it was decided to explore whether this network could be used for research. From the start it was clear that there would be problems, not only with reference to the time and effort which our correspondents could spare, but more particularly with respect to the comparability of the data thus obtained. This problem of comparability arises at all times in cross-cultural psychiatry, since the meaning of behavioural acts varies from one culture to another and the meaning of symptoms may vary likewise; but when the observers have themselves come from different cultures, have been trained in different schools, have been working in extremely varied settings, and when they have never met, the problem becomes especially great. Nevertheless, it was decided that a trial of such research would be worth while, and the symptomatology of schizophrenia was chosen as the first subject.

The tool for the research was a questionnaire containing a list of twenty-six symptoms or signs, and also inquiring into the main locale of observation, the psychiatrist's opinion with respect to four borderline types of patient, the relative distribution of the main schizophrenia sub-types, and some information on the culture or people to which the patients belonged. One such report was requested for each main cultural group that the respondent thought he could distinguish among his patients, and for this cultural group he was asked to rate each symptom or sign along a five-point scale ranging from "very frequent" to "very infrequent." Such ratings were obviously much less satisfactory than actual symptom counts obtained from large patient samples would have been, but we did not think that the busy and often single-handed psychiatrists to whom we were appealing would have the time or the means to study large samples of patients especially for this research. It therefore seemed better to try to tap the general body of impressions which these psychiatrists had amassed than to ask for figures which would probably relate to a handful of patients only. Our assumption in asking for these ratings was that experienced psychiatrists throughout the world would have roughly similar expectations regarding the frequency of different signs and symptoms in schizophrenia, and that the ratings would be made with reference to these expectations. This assumption appears to have been correct; but it might not have been and we cannot prove that it was. In consequence, it is intended in any future research to be more specific at this point.

The questionnaires were sent to some 120 individuals or psychiatric centres. Replies were received from forty of these, representing twenty-seven countries and supplying information on over ninety "cultural samples". The countries from which information was obtained are listed in Table 1. Regarding the "cultural samples," these did not always represent what an anthropologist would have called cultural entities, but they were obviously distinct enough to be regarded so by the reporting psychiatrists, and as such were grist for our mill. Not all of them have been included in the following analyses, since a few were incomplete or arrived too late for inclusion; but the total was still quite satisfactory for the purposes we had in mind.

Table 1
Countries from which reports were secured

Africa:
   Kenya, Union of South Africa, Nigeria, Uganda.
Asia:
   Formosa, Japan, Java, Hong Kong, Korea (South), India, Thailand.
Australasia:
   Australia, New Zealand.
North America:
   Canada, United States.
South America:
   Brazil, Colombia, Chile, Peru, Ecuador.
Middle East:
   Kuwait, Turkey.
Europe:
   Bulgaria, Germany, Czechoslovakia, Norway.
Caribbean:
   Barbados, Martinique.

THE AGREED FEATURES OF SCHIZOPHRENIA

The goal of our inquiry was to reveal and explore relations between culture and symptomatology, but before that could be done it was desirable to investigate to what extent the answers received reflected a common viewpoint towards schizophrenia. If this were not so reflected then one would have to suspect either that greater differences in conceptualizing the disease existed than had been expected or, more probably, that our method of research was defective. A common viewpoint was expected to show itself in the minimal criteria which were demanded before a diagnosis of schizophrenia could be made at all, and also with respect to certain included symptoms which modern psychiatry does not regard as deriving from the disease process proper.

On both points the results were satisfactory. Four of our twenty-six signs and symptoms—but only four—were never reported as infrequent for any sample, and hence could be inferred to constitute the minimal criteria for diagnosis. These were *social and emotional withdrawal, auditory hallucinations, delusions* (in general), and *flatness of affect.* Conversely, *echolalia, echopraxia, bowel incontinence* and *bladder incontinence* were rarely reported as anything but infrequent, and never from locations where our knowledge of conditions suggested that the hospital psychiatrist was permitted to apply modern policies. (This was in accord with the view that such symptoms stem from custodial hospital policies rather than from the disease itself.) Some other items in our list which might have been expected to be included in the minimal criteria category apparently are not viewed thus throughout the world. For instance, inappropriateness of affect was reported as infrequent for 15 cultures, depersonalization as infrequent for 38, and hypochondriacal ideas for 18. These unexpected findings, however, do not detract from the fact that the questionnaire results do reflect a common, agreed method of viewing and reporting on schizophrenia.

SYMPTOM PATTERNS IN CULTURAL GROUPINGS

While the core pattern of schizophrenia symptomatology was immediately apparent from the questionnaires, the influence of culture on other symptoms or
signs was not. The reports showed an abundance of variation from one sample
to another, but these differences were not so marked—or so in accordance with
some theory—that it could be said that they must derive definitely from the
patients' cultural backgrounds and definitely not from the limitations of our
instrument or from observer bias. Furthermore, the "cultures" selected by our
respondents for sampling were often not entities such as a cultural anthropologist
would recognize or about which a literature existed. Thus, it was not possible to
say that certain findings were indubitably a result of the sample's culture, nor
was it possible to match individual questionnaire findings against sound anthropological descriptions of the relevant peoples.

Our first attempt to overcome this difficulty was to search for groups of three
or more questionnaires dealing with what could broadly be called the same
culture, with a view to seeing whether they agreed with each other and disagreed to some extent with the averaged reports of the other groups. Five such
groups could be isolated and, as Table 2 shows, the reports within each group
agreed much more than they disagreed, and much more than would have been
expected by chance, when a difference of not more than one step in the five-
point scale was defined as "agreement" and a difference of more than three such
steps as "disagreement." However, these five groups of reports covered only a
minority of the ninety which had been sent us, and clear differences between
the averaged ratings of one group on a particular symptom and the averaged
ratings of all the others were few. It was therefore decided that a quite different
approach, enabling us to make use of all or nearly all the reports, was required.
After some experimentation such an approach was found.

This new approach was to take all the ratings on a particular symptom or sign,
and see whether it appeared to be randomly distributed or to have some association with one of the various observational and socio-cultural variables which we

Table 2
**Frequency of "agreement" and of "disagreement" observed between psychiatrists
reporting on patient samples drawn from the same or similar cultures, as
compared with the frequencies expected by chance**

| Culture | Number of psychiatrists reporting | For thirty items | | | |
| | | "Agreement" | | "Disagreement" | |
		Observed	Expected	Observed	Expected
Japanese	4 reports	14	2	5	14
East Indians	5 reports	8	2	3	19
Jewish	4 reports	12	2	3	14
British Overseas	6 reports	7	1	10	24
	5 out of the 6 reports	10	2	6	19
"Old U.S."	3 reports	20	4	5	9

had in mind. The results from this technique of analysis were much more fruitful, and are summarized in Table 3 under two categories of variable, the observational and the socio-cultural.

Table 3
Factors found to affect the distribution of reported symptoms in schizophrenic patients throughout the world

Item	Observational factors	p.	Socio-cultural factors	p.
A. Types of schizophrenic process				
1. Paranoid	Nil		*Most* frequent in urban middle classes; *least* frequent in rural groups.	**
2. Catatonic	*Least* frequently noted by psychiatrists requiring chronicity as criterion of schizophrenia.	*	*Least* frequently reported in Euro-Americans.	**
3. Hebephrenic	*Most* frequently noted by those who exclude confusional cases from schizophrenia group; and by those working only *outside* mental hospital.	** / **	*Most* frequently reported in Japanese and Okinawans.	**
4. Simplex	*Least* frequently reported by those requiring delusions and hallucinations as criteria of diagnosis; *most* by those working only *inside* mental hospitals.	* / *	*Most* frequently reported in Asians; *least* frequently in Euro-Americans.	*** / *
B. Disturbances of reality contact				
5. Visual hallucinations	Nil		*Least* frequently reported in *urban* Euro-Americans; most frequently in peoples of Africa and Near East.	*** / **
6. Tactile hallucinations	Nil		*Most* frequently reported in peoples of Africa and Near East.	*
7. Delusions of grandeur	Nil		*Most* frequently reported in rural groups.	****
8. Delusions of destruction	Nil		*Most* frequently reported in Christian samples.	***
9. Religious delusions	Nil		*Most* frequently reported in Christian samples; *least* in Buddhist, Hindu and Shintoist samples.	*** / ***
10. Delusions involving jealousy	Nil		*Most* frequently reported in Asian groups.	**
11. Depersonalisation	Nil		*Least* frequently reported in rural groups.	***
C. Disturbances of affect				
12. Social and emotional withdrawal	*Least* frequently noted by psychiatrists working only in mental hospital.	*	*Most* uniformly frequent in Japanese and Okinawans.	***

Item	Observational factors	p.	Socio-cultural factors	p.
13. Flatness of affect	*Most* frequently reported by those working only *outside* mental hospital.	****	*Most* frequently reported in Japanese and Okinawans; and after them in peoples of South America.	*** **
D. Types of catatonic disturbance				
14. Catatonic mannerisms	*Most* frequently noted by those requiring chronicity as criterion of schizophrenia.	***	*Most* frequently reported from rural groups.	**
15. Catatonic negativism	*Most* frequently noted by those requiring chronicity as criterion of schizophrenia.	***	*Most* frequently reported from peoples of India and of South America.	****
16. Catatonic excitement	*More* frequently reported by those working only *outside*; and *less* frequently by those working only *inside* mental hospital.	* *	*Most* frequently reported in peoples of Africa and S. America; *least* in peoples of Anglo-Saxon origin.	** **
17. Catatonic stupor	*Least* frequently reported by those insisting on delusions and hallucinations as criteria for diagnosis.	**	*Most* frequently reported in rural groups.	**
18. Stereotypy	*Least* frequently noted by those excluding confusional cases from schizophrenic category.	***	*Most* frequently reported in East Indians; *least* frequently in Euro-Americans.	** ****
19. Catatonic rigidity	Nil		*Most* frequently reported in East Indians.	***
E. Other behavioral disturbances				
20. Bowel and bladder incontinence	*Least infrequently* noted by psychiatrists insisting on chronicity as criterion for schizophrenia.	***	Nil	
21. Temper outbursts	*Most* frequently noted by those working only *outside*; *least* by those working only *inside* mental hospitals.	* *	*Most* frequently reported in Christian groups.	**
22. Sexual assault	Nil		*Least* frequently reported in Euro-Americans.	***
23. Suicide	Nil		*Most* frequently reported in Japanese.	****

Notes: 1. Significance of socio-cultural factors was re-calculated after allowing for observational factors' influence.
2. Levels of significance as calculated by χ^2 modified for small N.s are: ****, beyond 0.001; ***, 0.01–0.001; **, 0.01–0.05; *, 0.05–0.10.

OBSERVATIONAL VARIABLES

To appraise the relevance of observational variables in our findings we had included in the inquiry, as mentioned previously, questions concerning one category of situational variable, and questions concerning one category of conceptual. The situational one related to the location of observation in terms of hospital ward, O.P. clinic, private office, etc.; the conceptual one concerned four borderline categories of patient such as are sometimes included within the schizophrenia concept, and sometimes not. Analysis of the responses to these questions revealed the following points.

With respect to the setting of observations, the majority of our respondents saw patients in more than one major type of situation and hence, presumably, were seeing both the early and the later forms of the disease. However, six respondents saw patients only within mental hospitals—so that their samples would presumably be weighted on the chronic side—while six more saw their patients only outside—so that presumably they would be seeing mainly the earlier stages. These two latter groups of respondents present average pictures of schizophrenia which differ significantly both from each other and from the co-ordinated picture presented by the remaining majority, and hence it may be inferred that their setting of observation truly had an influence on their findings. As Table 3 shows, the symptom whose reporting is most markedly affected by this difference in setting is *flatness of affect*, but the *hebephrenic* sub-group appears also to be involved and, if the numbers of respondents in each minority position had been greater, some further items (those marked with one * in the table) might also prove to need inclusion. However, the degree to which reporting appeared affected by this question was not marked, and it is of interest to note that the ratings for disturbances of reality contact (e.g. delusions and hallucinations) were not affected at all. It may therefore be said that this variable is not likely to interfere much with the reporting of culturally-specific symptom complexes. Naturally, other situational variables—notably those relating to treatment and hospital régime—may have more of an effect on the reporting; but these could not be explored at this time.

For the differences in conceptual outlook, Table 4 gives the questions which we asked and the various combinations of answers which were received. It must be stressed that both our approach and our reporting on this point oversimplify the matter, for many respondents qualified their answers in ways that it has not been convenient to summarize here. (For instance, where a respondent answered "Yes" to each of the four questions, this often meant not that his concept of schizophrenia was a loose and all-embracing one, but that he preferred to put most weight on criteria we had not mentioned.) Nevertheless, the great majority of respondents proved subsumable under four headings, in this matter, and when these four groups were compared the further results under Observational Factors in Table 3 were obtained. *Incontinence* and two types of *catatonic* trait were, as one might have expected, perceived most often by those who exclude from their schizophrenia samples patients whose episodes are of short duration. However, *stupor, stereotypy* and the *hebephrenic sub-type* also seem to have their reported frequencies affected by the conceptual viewpoints under discussion, while, on the contrary, hallucinations and delusions do not appear to be affected.

Table 5, using catatonic stupor as the example, illustrates the manner in which the above associations have been deduced, and the actual differences involved.

Table 4
Borderline diagnostic criteria explored, and numbers of respondents answering "yes" for each combination of categories

The questions	No. of respondents answering "yes"					
	to A+B +C+D	to A+B +C	to B+C +D	to A+B only	to A+C only	Other combi- nations
In making a diagnosis of schizo- phrenia do you include patients: A. *Without* hallucinations or delusions?	13	12	—	5	4	—
B. *With* marked affective disturbance?	13	12	3	5	—	1
C. Whose psychotic episode(s) is of *short duration*?	13	12	3	—	4	3
D. *With* much confusion and slight organic-type symptoms for which no organic cause can be found?	13	—	3	—	—	1

Once more, the results indicate that differences in the conditions governing the observations—in this case differences in conceptual viewpoint—do influence the reporting of the schizophrenic picture. However, it can also be said again that this is an influence which is not of such great relevance when answers from many psychiatrists are grouped together. Where reports from single psychiatrists —such as comprise the bulk of the literature in the cross-cultural field—are being used, or evaluated, then our findings here suggest that the author's viewpoint must be given very full consideration. In the present instance, the variations which the four main categories of viewpoint showed were considered each time an apparent association between a symptom and a socio-cultural variable was uncovered, and if it seemed that what was presented as a socio-cultural influence might have been a conceptual one, then the apparent association was excluded from further consideration. Where associations between symptoms and socio-

Table 5
Relation between conceptual boundaries and frequency with which stupor is reported in schizophrenia patients

Division of questionnaires in terms of answers to item (A) in Table 4	Stupor reported infrequent or very infrequent	Stupor reported common, frequent or very frequent
Culture samples reported on by respondents *not* diagnosing schizophrenia in absence of hallucinations or delusions.	12	3
Culture samples reported on by respondents accepting possibility of schizophrenia without hallucinations or delusions.	29	37

$x^2 = 5.01; n = 1; p. = 0.05$–$0.02$; using the formula

$$x^2 = \frac{(ad-bc-\frac{1}{2}(a + b + c + d))^2 \, (a + b + c + d)}{(a + b)\,(c + d)\,(a + c)\,(b + d)}$$

cultural variables are posited, it can be assumed that explanations in terms of the above situational and conceptual factors have been excluded.

SOCIAL VARIABLES

Respondents were asked to indicate whether their patients were predominantly from a rural background or from an urban one, or from one particular social class. In many cases the patients came from too mixed backgrounds to type in such fashion, but in almost half of the questionnaires it was possible, either from the respondent's notes or from our own knowledge of the local situation, to say that the patients must have been predominantly rural, predominantly urban middle class, etc. When the samples belonging to each of these rough categories were grouped and their modal symptomatologies compared, two most interesting and quite significant groups of associations appeared.

As is shown in Table 6, *delusions of grandeur* and *mannerisms* are rated, on average, much higher for rural samples than for urban ones, while *depersonalization* is the reverse. This correlation of depersonalization with urban life, and delusions of grandeur and mannerisms with rural life, is something which is not easy to explain in terms of psychoanalytic theory, but in terms of social science theory a tentative explanation is available.

One of the main ways in which rural life differs from urban, irrespective of culture, relates to community size, and community size, in turn, has an important effect on the separation of social rôles. In large communities, and especially in modern urban life, there is considerable separation and isolation of an individual's different social rôles. His life at home is probably unknown to the group with which he interacts at his work-place; the way he performs his work rôle is probably unknown to the people with whom he plays cards or goes hunting, etc. So great is this separation that one rôle can become drastically disturbed or even abandoned without the other rôles being manifestly affected, and it might therefore be said that urban life teaches the individual to isolate rôles from each other as a means of protecting the rest of his personality from disturbances affecting one facet. If this is accepted, then it can probably be seen that there is a certain

Table 6
Comparative frequencies with which delusions of grandeur, mannerisms, and depersonalisation are reported in schizophrenic samples from rural and urban backgrounds (for levels of significance see Table 3)

(N)	Rural (21)	Urban (27)
Grandeur (%age rated v. frequent or frequent)	63%	11%
Mannerisms (%age rated v. frequent or frequent)	40%	8%
Depersonalisation (%age rated v. frequent, frequent, common)	29%	70%

analogy here to the process which is believed to take place in depersonalisation, a process of defensive isolation or repression of a disturbed, over-cathected part of the personality. The urban dweller is likely to try to isolate his failure as a husband from affecting his rôles as workman or as sportsman by the device of suppressing all mention of the former rôle; the urban schizophrenic, according to our data, is particularly likely to try to isolate a narcissistically over-cathected part of his personality from other parts by repressing and counter-cathecting the former.

In rural, smaller communities the same separation of rôles is less likely to be effective, and hence unlikely to be tried as frequently. The rural doctor knows that his relationship with his patients will be affected by what he does in his leisure time and by how he treats his children, and the labourer who changes his religion knows that it may affect his employment or his tenancy. Failure in one rôle cannot be isolated or hidden; it can only be compensated for by extra success or prestige acquired in other rôles. And where such compensation cannot be obtained legitimately and has to be fantasied, the tendency is likely to be towards megalomania. By adopting such a view of urban and rural life, therefore, it becomes possible in terms of social science theory to see depersonalization as the pathological reflection of a social device particularly to be found in urban societies, and to see megalomania as the pathological reflection of a device more likely to be found in rural communities. If the mannerisms especially found in rural patients were of the snobbish, theatrical type which not infrequently accompany delusions of grandeur, then their association with that rural background might similarly be explained.

The above argument is difficult to harmonize with current psychiatric teaching, but for the other main finding in a social sphere such harmonizing is easier. As Table 3 shows, the paranoid sub-type of schizophrenia was more frequently reported for urban middle-class samples than for urban lower class, and least frequently reported for rural groups. Harry Stack Sullivan has interpreted the paranoid state as an unconscious attempt at "making sense" of a chaotic, frightening experience. However, such "making sense" is something most encouraged, and most easy for which to strive, in a middle-class urban setting where higher education stresses long-range planning, and where one is apparently in control of one's own destiny. It is less encouraged, and less striven for, in rural and lower-class settings where formal education is shorter and where one's destiny appears to be at the mercy of the weather, the economic cycle, or of some unknown employer a thousand miles away. Hence, again looking at the matter in terms of social science rather than of psychiatric theory, it might be expected that social strata where planning and organization are highly stressed would tend to produce schizophrenics who use a paranoid type of defence, while sectors of society where planning and organization are less emphasized—perhaps because too much is outside personal control—would produce patients who use the paranoid defence less. In line with the same argument, one would expect in the former sectors less hallucination and more delusion, and, as Table 3 shows, this was found.

CULTURAL VARIABLES

The social and observational variables which have been discussed above, all fell into fairly sharp and obvious categories, and associations could thus be found simply by contrasting one of the given categories with another. When it comes to cultures, however, there are, as was remarked earlier, no obvious categories to use. Accordingly, a different procedure had to be used, and with this procedure the logic of the categories and the significance of the findings is affected. What was done was to note, for each symptom or sign in turn, which cultural samples got a rating of "very frequent," which of "frequent," etc. These lists were then studied to see whether a majority of the samples at one or the other end of the scale appeared to have something in common, and if such did suggest itself the facts were then tested statistically.[1] However, in looking for qualities in common we were most regrettably limited to such elementary matters as geographic propinquity, unity of historic origin, and religion. It would have been more desirable to think in terms of categories of child-rearing practices, types of social integration, or discrepancy between aspirations and attainments; but the literature from which to derive such classifications hardly exists today, and the "cultures" reported on were too often ones which the anthropologist in our team (J. F.) did not recognize as entities. Thus what presented itself to us by this method was often not particularly meaningful psychiatrically. Nevertheless, from the items noted in Table 3 certain constellations do appear about which something can be said.

The most notable finding, though not entirely an original one, relates to *delusions of destruction* and *religious delusions*. Both of these symptoms are so very frequently met with in the classical European descriptions of schizophrenia that it has rather been assumed that this type of disturbance was an intrinsic, though not inevitable, part of the schizophrenic process. Table 7 shows that this is not true, since in East Asian schizophrenics who have not been converted to Christianity or to Mohammedanism such symptoms are reported to be quite infrequent. Moreover, if one follows the succession of increasing frequencies, then with one notable exception it would appear that the frequency of these delusions increases in step with the guilt-evoking character of the religions. The exception is Judaism, which one would expect to be near the top of the frequency table for religious delusions, along with the other apocalyptic religions, but which is at the bottom. The number of Jewish samples is only five, so that there is scope for quite a large chance error in the attributed average frequency, and their position in the delusions of destruction rankings is as expected; but one would still like to have a better explanation. Certainly, both the general association suggested by data, and the apparent exception, call for fuller investi-

---

[1] The method of selecting items obviously increases the likelihood of chance associations appearing. Unfortunately, it was not possible to find a method of allowing statistically for this increased chance. In consequence, statistically the significance of the associations reported in Table 3 is probably somewhat less than that indicated by the asterisks. This has no practical relevance for the stronger associations, but makes the weaker more doubtful.

Table 7
Relation of frequency of religious delusions and delusions of destruction to religion

Predominant religion of sample	No. of samples	Percentage of samples rated "very frequent", "frequent" or "common" with respect to:	
		Religious delusions	Delusions of destruction*
Christianity (R.C.)	22	91%	56%
Christianity (other)	18	78%	53%
Mohammedanism	10	60%	20%
Hinduism	5	40%	0%
Buddhism, Shintoism and other East Asian religions	15	27%	0%
Judaism	5	20%	40%
Pagan religions	6	50%	17%

* Corrected from original (editors).

gation. From this material the association appears to be with religion rather than with any other social variable tending to share the same type of world distribution—industrialization or broad cultural grouping, for instance.

The next clusters of findings which are suggestive of an underlying process are those relating to the Japanese and Okinawans on the one hand, and the East Indians on the other. Both these groups are taught, through Hinduism, Buddhism and their offshoots, that withdrawal is an acceptable mode of reacting to difficulties; and hence if one expected such cultural teachings to play any part in the symptomatology of schizophrenia, one should also expect that these peoples, and others of East Asia, would show a raised frequency of emotional withdrawal and other symptoms carrying a related connotation. This we found, since the reported frequency of *social and emotional withdrawal* is significantly higher for the Japanese and Okinawan samples than for others, and slightly higher for Indian samples than for Euro-American or African. However, the two groups of peoples show, through our material, notable differences in the symptoms associated with this withdrawal. The Japanese and Okinawans, in addition to withdrawal itself, have *flatness of exhibited affect, suicidal tendencies* and *the hebephrenic sub-type* reported as significantly more frequent than average, whereas the Indians have *catatonic rigidity, negativism* and *stereotypy* as the items in which they appear to show excess. The possibility suggests itself that these differences in symptomatology may be related to differences in normative attitudes towards withdrawal in the two culture complexes. Submissiveness to superiors and to Fate, intrapunitiveness and restraint in the expression of emotion are the ways in which Japanese traditionally have been taught to meet a personal blow such as severe loss of face. For Indians, on the contrary, withdrawal has tended to be of a dramatic, public character; is expected to take the individual right out of social life; and represents not a submission of the individual to society (as in the Japanese case) but a rejection of society. Moreover, in India certain types of social withdrawal—those followed by certain sanyasi or yogi—are associated with bizarre or unusual posturing and immobility not unlike the catatonic rigidity and stereotypy of the Indian schizophrenic, whereas such postures are much less culturally accepted or encouraged in Japan.

A number of other notable features of schizophrenia prove to have similarly skewed distributions. Thus, *delusions of jealousy* prove to be much more frequently reported for Asian samples than for Euro-American, so that their distribution roughly reverses that of delusions of destruction. *Schizophrenia simplex* is also highest in Asians, but with a pattern which is quite different from that of either of the delusional systems just mentioned, since it tends to be highest in those Asian samples that can be inferred to have the least education. (However, there seems to be no direct association with education or richness of culture as such, since this sub-type is not reported particularly frequently either for African or for Amerindian groups.) *Catatonic* signs appear with excess reported frequency not only for East Indians, as noted before, but also for Amerindians and mestizos. *Visual and tactile hallucinations* are reported in excess frequency for Arabian and some African groups. It is not intended to offer hypotheses for these apparent associations here, and neither is it intended to relate these findings to earlier ones in the same field. The literature on the character which schizophrenia seems to adopt in different peoples is vast and often contradictory. What we have tried to offer here is not a survey of the subject, but the first results of applying a new technique to its investigation.

SUMMARY

In twenty-three of the thirty schizophrenic symptoms, signs and sub-types whose distribution was explored through our questionnaire, it was found that their reported frequencies varied in a non-random fashion when the material was ordered in certain apparently independent ways. For a majority of these instances the ordering was according to some social or cultural schema; for a minority it was according to variables thought likely to affect the observation or interpretation of the data. The inference is therefore that the reported distribution of schizophrenic symptoms appears to vary in association with social, cultural, observational and conceptual factors, since even though the instrument and criteria for comparison were imprecise, non-randomness should not occur as often as we found.

The main goal of our inquiry was to establish in what directions, if any, patients' cultural backgrounds influenced their symptomatology. Apparently the goal has been considerably achieved in the associations which have been uncovered; but this is not necessarily so. In calculating the relevant associations care was taken to ensure that the two ascertained observational and conceptual factors were not accidentally associated with a social or cultural one, but there are many more observational and conceptual variables which we could have explored but did not, and the question arises whether these could be the hidden explanations for our findings. The matter has been looked into as far as our material and our knowledge of the people and places went, and for a majority of the findings it seems very unlikely that such hidden explanations would exist. Such explanations would have been possible and even probable if, say, all the psychiatrists reporting on the Japanese and Okinawans had been Japanese themselves and trained in the same schools, or if all the reports on East Indians had come from Indian psychiatrists trained in London, but the Japanese reports included one by a U.S. psychiatrist and one from Brazil, while those on East Indians included two from different centres in Africa. It is not to be assumed that the distribution of psychiatrists in terms of their backgrounds, outlook and opportunities for observation should be entirely random with respect to the social and cultural schema used here, but in the instances where a marked deviation from random expectancy is found (e.g. those with a p. of 0.01 or more) it is highly improbable that the findings would wholly be accountable on such grounds.

Given that associations do exist between schizophrenic symptomatology and social or cultural variables, the next question is: what do they mean? The main alternative answers are that culture can affect the basic schizophrenic process, or that it affects not the basic process itself but the personality's reaction to that process. Our inquiry was not directed towards obtaining information on the comparative incidence of schizophrenia in different cultures, and without such information the first alternative can neither be proved nor disproved, but even if it is assumed not to be true the second alternative is not without importance. The main significance of our findings at this stage is that doubt has been thrown on the picture which Euro-American psychiatry has built up of the schizophrenic process. For instance, considering the high percentages of the simplex and catatonic sub-types of schizophrenia reported for certain Asian samples (in some instances our respondents kindly sent actual figures) and the low percentages of the paranoid sub-type, it might be questioned whether the delusional systems which are the most familiar feature of chronic schizophrenia in Euro-American hospitals are an essential part of the disease process. Might they not be culturally conditioned attempts by the personality to "make sense" of that process, attempts which Eastern cultures inspire to a much lesser degree?

In resolving such doubts it is clear that cross-cultural psychiatry has a major rôle to play, and it would seem that the technique which has been used in the present inquiry holds considerable promise to that end. There are a number of improvements needed, notably in finding means of identifying and codifying the cultures being reported. Also, there are aspects of the question—or related questions—which this approach is quite unsuited to answer, the most important being that of true incidence or prevalence of a disease. In other directions, and not necessarily cross-culturally, the technique seems admirably suited for exploring the influence of different conceptual and observational variables on the descriptions which psychiatrists provide of their patients. A similar inquiry, for instance, might be made among the members of a single city or centre, provided only that the number of respondents was large enough to permit analysis along more than one variable. Mainly, however, the approach seems suited to international studies where wide coverage is required and where marked differences in setting or viewpoint may exist that are difficult to define or measure.

16
PSYCHIATRIC SYMPTOMS AND
DIAGNOSIS IN TWO SUBCULTURES
John B. Enright and Walter R. Jaeckle

INTRODUCTION AND STATEMENT OF THE PROBLEM

The psychiatric diagnostic system first developed by Kraepelin and widely used in many modified forms has been criticized from a variety of standpoints. Many of these criticisms are summarized by Zigler and Phillips.[7] They do not stress, however, an objection that seems of importance to the present authors: that the diagnostic system is based on the symptoms of patients from one general cultural background—Western European. No single culture exhibits the whole range of variability of any psychological, social or biological factor; further, the relationships between such factors may differ in different cultural contexts. There is no reason to believe that the phenomena of psychopathology are exempt from such limitations of variability. Thus psychiatric symptoms might occur with very different frequencies in different cultures or might fall together into different patterns of syndromes. A diagnostic system developed in one culture, and appropriate for use with patients from that background, would lead to errors of classification of two general kinds when applied to patients from a different ethnic group. Patients quite different from each other with respect to symptoms important in their culture might be grouped as similar by the criteria of a foreign diagnostic system that did not recognize or give adequate weight to these symptoms; and patients quite similar by culturally appropriate standards might be classified as different by this system.

The likelihood of distortion and misclassification would seem to be even greater if a culture-bound diagnostic system were used to compare patients from a variety of cultural backgrounds which were different from each other as well as from the culture in which the diagnostic system originated. Yet such applications are made in cross-cultural research and multi-cultural clinical settings. The purpose of the present paper is to investigate empirically the distortion occurring in a situation in which a derivative of the Kraepelinian system, the American Psychiatric Association Standard Diagnostic Nomenclature,[1] is applied to individuals from different non-Western ethnic backgrounds.

In the state of Hawaii several different ethnic groups are represented. Two of the largest groups are Americans of Japanese and of Filipino extraction.* Both of

Source: John B. Enright and Walter R. Jaeckle, "Psychiatric Symptoms and Diagnosis in Two Subcultures, International Journal of Social Psychiatry, 9: 12–17, 1963.
* Hereafter, the word "Japanese" will be used to refer to individuals of Japanese origin or ancestry now residing in Hawaii. The majority are American citizens born and raised here. In spite of the long residence of this group in America it has retained many characteristics of Japanese culture, in modified form. Males of Japanese extraction constitute about 34 per cent of the non-military male population of the Hawaiian Islands. The word "Filipino" will be used to refer to individuals of Philippine birth or ancestry now residing in Hawaii. The majority of Filipinos were born in the Philippine Islands and are immigrants to Hawaii. In general, the Filipinos are less acculturated to Amercan society than the Japanese. Filipino men constitute about 16 per cent of the non-military male population of the Hawaiian Islands.

these groups are non-Western in origin, yet culturally very different from each other. Each retains considerable ethnic identity, yet both share the same broader social and physical environment. Most important from the standpoint of this study, both share the same state mental hospital where diagnoses of all committed patients are made by the same clinical staff.

Clinicians at Hawaii State Hospital have long had the impression that patients from Japanese and Filipino backgrounds have shown many differences in the form their psychopathology takes. Attempts to document this impression by comparing the frequency of occurrence of each of the American Psychiatric Association diagnostic categories in the two groups of patients[2, 3, 5, 6] did show some frequency differences, but these were not extensive. One finding of these studies was that, in spite of the impression of differences between the two groups, the diagnosis of Schizophrenic Reaction, Paranoid Type occurred with exceptionally high frequency in both. This finding suggested to the authors that there might be differences between the groups that were not revealed by the diagnostic system used, and seemed to present an opportunity to investigate the distortion introduced by applying the American Psychiatric Association diagnostic system to patients from different cultural backgrounds.†

This paper presents a comparison of the actual presenting symptoms of Japanese and Filipino patients who received the same diagnosis of Schizophrenic Reaction, Paranoid Type. Our hypothesis is that at the level of concrete psychiatric symptoms clear and consistent differences between patients from these two ethnic groups exist, in spite of their being classified as psychiatrically identical by the American Psychiatric Association system.

METHOD

Subjects in the present study consisted of all male Filipino and Japanese patients admitted for the first time to Hawaii State Hospital during the six-year period beginning July 1, 1954 and diagnosed Schizophrenic Reaction, Paranoid Type. The study was limited to men because of the uneven sex distribution in the Filipino population. There were sixty-five Filipinos and fifty-eight Japanese in all. The source of data on each patient was the legal commitment paper filled out by a relative or acquaintance of the patient in collaboration with a physician. In the few cases of voluntary admissions or transfers from prison equivalent documents filed at the time of admission were used. The commitment paper is by no means a complete psychiatric evaluation, but it offered distinct advantages for the purposes of this study. The descriptions of the patient that are contained in this paper pertain to the time of the most acute episode and stress the most salient symptoms which require the patient to be hospitalized. What makes the commitment paper especially valuable for research purposes is that symptoms

---

† It is fairly rare that patients from different ethnic backgrounds share the same psychiatric facilities, thus bypassing the many problems of different diagnostic practices and the unreliability that exists when different facilities are involved. To the authors' knowledge the study of Irish and Italian men by Opler and Singer[4] is the only other systematic study that shares this adventure.

are described very concretely, with the actual behaviour and verbalization of the patient reported in some detail.

The commitment papers for all subjects were read by both investigators first independently, then jointly and every statement that could be construed as a description of the patient or his behaviour was written down. Categories of symptoms induced from the data first independently, then jointly were agreed upon. Each investigator then went through the data and assigned each statement to one of these categories. Agreement about assignment of statement to category ranged from perfect in some categories to fairly low agreement in one of the categories. The final assignment of statements over which there were disagreements was arrived at by consultation. Formal statistical analyses (chi-square) were applied to each category separately to determine whether the proportion of Japanese and Filipino patients in the category was significantly different from what would be expected if there were no relationship between symptom category and ethnic group membership. In addition qualitative analyses were made by both investigators independently and jointly to determine whether trends could be noticed which were not amenable to statistical test.

RESULTS

Table 1 summarizes the symptom clusters in which significant differences were found between Japanese and Filipino patients. Included are examples of the types of statements categorized within each symptom cluster. The total frequencies noted in the table for each symptom cluster indicate the number of patients with any symptoms in that cluster. The subtotals indicate the number of patients showing the specific symptoms mentioned. The subtotals do not sum to equal the totals for the symptom cluster, since some individuals show more than one specific symptom within the cluster.

It might be most meaningful to discuss these results in the context of the definition of Schizophrenic Reaction, Paranoid Type. The Diagnostic and Statistical Manual[1] says of this diagnosis, in part:

> This type of reaction is characterized by autistic, unrealistic thinking, with mental content composed chiefly of delusions of persecution, and/or of grandeur, ideas of reference and often hallucinations. It is often characterized by unpredictable behaviour, with a fairly consistent attitude of hostility and aggression.

Taking up these symptoms in order we find that:

a. The Japanese show significantly more disturbance of thinking. Such terms as "preoccupied", "confused" and "obsessed" are applied much more frequently to Japanese patients than Filipino.
b. Delusions of persecution are common in both groups. Examining the content of these delusions, however, it is clear that Filipinos often are convinced that someone wishes

Table 1
Chi-square analyses of symptom clusters

Symptom	Frequency of occurrence	
	Japanese	Filipino
1. Thinking disturbance (Preoccupied, obsessed, confused, cannot concentrate, obsessed with ideas, disoriented, poor reality testing)	37*	18
2. Delusions of persecution		
(a) Others wish to kill	5	19*
(b) All other (e.g. cursed by Kahuna, somebody chasing him	28	26
Total	31	37
3. Ideas of reference		
(a) Influenced, controlled, hypnotized or mind read	15*	1
(b) All other (e.g. laughed at, talked about)	19	13
Total	27*	13
4. Disturbing behaviour		
(a) Violent (e.g. uncontrollable, police called, had to be restrained)	4	12†
(b) Excitement (e.g. noisy, talks loudly, agitated)	7	13
Total	11	19
5. Hostility		
(a) Suspicious, irritable, hostile (without indication of directly hostile action)	19†	9
(b) Menacing (e.g. threatening or frightening others, carrying weapons)	14	25†
Total	33	34
6. Depression	17*	7
7. Withdrawal from activity		
(a) Difficulties with work (e.g. unable to work, lazy in work, refused to work)	20*	5
(b) Withdrawn (e.g. seclusive, quiet, introverted, hiding in closet)	31†	25
(c) Apathy (e.g. interest loss, does nothing, assumed catatonia, mute)	18†	5
Total	42*	27

* Significant at or beyond the .01 level of confidence.
† Significant at or beyond the .10 level of confidence.

to kill them while the delusions of the Japanese are confined to less drastic forms of persecution.

c. Japanese more frequently have ideas of reference—that is, that natural events or behaviour of others have special reference and meaning for them. These ideas are particularly evident in delusions that one is being influenced, hypnotized or controlled; this is almost exclusively a Japanese delusion.

d. The category of "unpredictable behaviour" did not emerge clearly in our data, but a possible related category, "behaviour disturbing to others", did. Both groups contributed about the same number of patients to this category, but the disturbing behaviour of the Filipinos tended to be more violent, wild and uncontrollable than that of the Japanese.

e. Both groups showed an "attitude of hostility and aggression" with equal frequency. However, the Japanese showed this more commonly in a passive or ideational way, while the Filipinos tended to do something direct with their anger. Thus the Japanese were more often described as "suspicious", "guarded", "irritable", etc., while the

Filipinos more frequently threatened others, carried weapons with them or were described as menacing or frightening to others.

f. The most striking differences were in two symptomatic areas not considered part of Paranoid Schizophrenia, although their presence does not contradict that diagnosis. These were depression and a general area of withdrawal from daily activity. In the latter, Japanese much more frequently exhibited apathy, loss of interest in their surroundings and social isolation. Japanese were also more frequently noted as having difficulty in their work adjustment.

In addition to the above statistically significant differences between the two groups, there were some trends which did not achieve significance, but deserve brief mention. One of these trends was in the area of withdrawal and seclusiveness already mentioned. As indicated, the Filipinos withdrew less often than the Japanese, but there was a different quality to their withdrawal that eluded statistical tests. This trend was for the Filipinos to be more active in their withdrawal. The withdrawing Japanese tended to stay in his room; the withdrawing Filipino was more likely to go out and hide in the cane fields. Incidentally it was in this area of withdrawal and seclusiveness that the inter-rater disagreement mentioned earlier occurred and it was this elusive qualitative difference that caused the disagreement.

Another non-significant trend occurred in the category of delusions of grandeur. These delusions occurred equally in both groups, but the Filipinos tended to be more extreme in the content of theirs. For instance, they believed themselves to be God, believed they commanded the moon and stars and felt they could fly around the world in a few minutes. In contrast, the Japanese only went as far as talking to God or Jesus in their religious delusions, and concentrated their grandiosity on achieving social recognition and prestige. For example, they felt they were more intelligent than anyone else, possessed honorary scholastic degrees, read minds and knew famous people. In another area two contrasting trends appeared. Japanese patients tended more frequently to be described as worried or anxious. However, when a Filipino was described as showing this emotion it was usually more extreme—afraid rather than anxious, and terrified rather than worried.

Still another tendency was for Filipinos to show more behaviour described as bizarre. They slightly more often talked to themselves or to animals or made strange gestures. Finally, the Japanese tended to report more physical symptoms, such as headaches.

There were, of course, many symptom categories in which no differences appeared. Hallucinations were common in both groups. Sleep disturbances, bodily delusions, guilt, restlessness, destructiveness and disturbances of emotions—other than those mentioned—occurred with moderate and equal frequency in both groups.

DISCUSSION OF RESULTS

The hypothesis of this study seems to be supported. Patient groups from two different non-Western ethnic backgrounds, defined as psychiatrically identical by the American Psychiatric Association diagnostic system, showed distinct differences in the frequency of occurrence of concrete symptoms. It is important to note that there is no question of accuracy of diagnosis. All symptoms described are legitimate features of the diagnosis, or at least not contradictory to it. Potentially important differences between the two groups were concealed, however, by the application of an inappropriate diagnostic system.

It was not the purpose of this paper to explore Japanese-Filipino symptomatic differences definitively. By narrowing our focus to comparisons in only one diagnostic category, and by limiting our statistical analyses to comparisons of the groups on a series of separate symptoms, we can only justify the conclusion that Japanese and Filipino paranoid patients do differ in several specific ways. It is tempting, however, to speculate beyond this conclusion, assuming that apparent general differences between Japanese and Filipino patients would emerge again in a more exhaustive study.

Recognizing the tentative nature of any generalizations, we would nonetheless like to present what we feel might be a valid and succinct way of summarizing our data. The observed differences can be viewed in terms of one or both of two dimensions. One of these might be called the expressive-restrained dimension. The Filipino patients tend to express feelings freely and directly, frequently motorically, while the Japanese patients tend to be more inhibited and restrained and to respond ideationally rather than openly.

The other proposed dimension has to do with the direction of behaviour. The Filipino patients tend to act on the world or on others. Their behaviour is directed outward in the attempt to resolve conflicts by removing environmental obstacles or in some other way changing the world. In psychoanalytic theory such outward directed behaviour has been given the name *alloplastic*. Japanese behaviour, in contrast, is *autoplastic,* that is, directed inward. The Japanese patients tend to act on themselves in the attempt to.resolve conflicts by internalization—by modifying their behaviour rather than by trying to change the external world.

CONCLUSIONS AND SUMMARY

The central finding of this paper is that, in comparison of psychiatric symptoms in two non-Western ethnic groups, reliance on diagnostic categories developed in a Western culture concealed clear and important differences. Only by collecting actual symptomatic and behavioural descriptions could these differences be explicated. This finding suggests that the usefulness of the Kraepelinian diagnostic system and its derivatives is limited by its culturally narrow origins. Also this finding casts doubt on the meaningfulness of cross-cultural comparisons of psychopathology that employ the Kraepelinian system, and suggests that serious effort should be made to include representative cross-cultural psychiatric data in future revisions or modifications of the Kraepelinian system.

Findings with respect to the two groups studied are that Japanese paranoid schizophrenic patients differed from Filipino patients with the same diagnosis in being more restrained and inhibited, with a greater tendency toward auto-plastic behaviour.

References

1 American Psychiatric Association: *Diagnostic and Statistical Manual of Mental Disorders.* Washington; American Psychiatric Association, 1952.

2 Hawaii State Hospital: *Psychology Research Reports,* Vol. I, No. 8, unpublished.

3 Kimmich, R. A.: "Ethnic aspects of schizophrenia in Hawaii." *Psychiat.,* 1960, **23,** 97–102.

4 Opler, M. K., and Singer, J. L.: "Ethnic differences in behaviour and psychopathology: Italian and Irish." *Int. J. Soc. Psychiat.,* 1956, **2,** 11–23.

5 Schmidt, R. C.: "Psychosis and race in Hawaii." *Hawaii Med. J.,* 1956, **16,** 144–146.

6 Wedge, B. and Abe, S.: "Racial incidence of mental disease in Hawaii." *Hawaii Med. J.,* 1949, **8,** 337–338.

7 Zigler, E. and Phillips, L.: "Psychiatric diagnosis: a critique." *J. Abnormal and Soc. Psychol.* In press.

17
THE MENTAL HEALTH OF THE HUTTERITES
Joseph W. Eaton and Robert J. Weil

Is modern life driving many people insane? Would insanity diminish or disappear if mankind could return to a simpler life? From Virgil to Thoreau the philosophers have had little doubt about the answer to these questions, and some modern anthropologists have offered data which seem to bear them out. They say they have found mental disorders rare among technologically primitive peoples. For instance, recent cursory studies of the people on Okinawa and of the natives of Kenya have suggested that these groups are virtually free of some psychoses. Contrasted with this picture is the civilized U. S., where some authorities have estimated that one person in 10 suffers an incapacitating mental illness at one time or another during his life.

Whether a culture can cause psychoses is not easy to discover, but one way to get at the question is to examine the mental health of a secure, stable society. The Hutterites, an isolated Anabaptist religious sect who inhabit a section of the North American Middle West, provide an ideal social laboratory of this kind. These people live a simple, rural life, have a harmonious social order and provide

Source: Joseph Eaton and Robert J. Weil: "The Mental Health of the Hutterites," *Scientific American,* **189:** 31–37, 1953.

every member with a high level of economic security from the womb to the tomb. They are a homogeneous group, free from many of the tensions of the American melting-pot culture. And they have long been considered almost immune to mental disorders. In a study during the 1930s Lee Emerson Deets said that psychoses were almost nonexistent among them. The Manitoba Provincial Legislature received in 1947 a report which said that the Hutterites "do not contribute to the overcrowding of mental hospitals, since the mental security derived from their system results in a complete absence of mental illness."

Three years ago a research team consisting of the writers of this article—a sociologist and a psychiatrist—and the Harvard University clinical psychologists Bert Kaplan and Thomas Plant undertook a more intensive study of the Hutterites' mental health. The investigation was administered by Wayne University and financed largely by the National Institute for Mental Health. The Hutterite people cooperated generously. In the interest of science they opened their "family closets" and helped us to obtain a census of every person in their community who was then or had ever been mentally ill.

The Hutterites, whose origin as a sect goes back to 1528, are a closely knit group of German stock who had lived together in neighboring villages in Europe for a long time before they migrated to the U. S. from southern Russia between 1874 and 1877. The immigrants—101 married couples and their children—settled in eastern South Dakota. Their descendants have now spread over a wide area in the Dakotas, Montana and the prairie provinces of Canada. They live in 98 hamlets, which they call colonies. But they remain a remarkably cohesive group; each grown-up is intimately acquainted with hundreds of other members in the settlements. The Hutterites believe it sinful to marry outside the sect, and all of the present descendants (8,542 in 1950) stem from the original 101 couples.

Cardinal principles of the Hutterites are pacifism, adult baptism, the communal ownership of all property and simple living. Jewelry, art and over-stuffed chairs are regarded as sinful luxuries. Radio sets and the movies are taboo. Children are the only possessions to which there is no limit: the average completed family has more than 10. The Hutterites cling to their own customs and are considered "different" by their neighbors. But they are not primitive in the ethnographic sense. They get a grammar-school education and speak English fluently. They read daily newspapers, have a telephone in most colonies and own trucks. Since their own members are not encouraged to seek formal education beyond the primary grades, there are no doctors or lawyers among them, but they utilize such professional services from outside. Each hamlet engages in a highly mechanized form of agriculture. Their business with the "outside world," as Hutterites are apt to refer to their neighbors, usually exceeds $100,000 per year per colony.

On the surface it seemed that the Hutterites did indeed enjoy extraordinary freedom from mental illness. We did not find a single Hutterite in a mental hospital. The 55 outside doctors patronized by these people said they showed fewer psychosomatic and nervous symptoms than their neighbors of other faiths. But this appearance of unusual mental health did not stand the test of an intensive screening of the inhabitants, carried out colony by colony. Among the 8,542 Hutterites we discovered a total of 199 (one in 43) who either had active symp-

Staff diagnosis of illness	Lifetime morbidity	Active case morbidity		Other cases	
	Total number ever ill	Ill in summer 1951	Ill but improved on August 31, 1951	Recovered by or before August 31, 1951	Status unknown
Psychoses:					
Schizophrenia	9	7	1	1	0
Manic-depressive reaction	39	3	5	27	4
Acute and chronic brain disorders	5	4	0	1	0
Total	53	14	6	29	4
Neuroses:					
Psychoneurotic disorders	53	24	15	12	2
Psychophysiological, auto- nomic and visceral disorders	16	7	3	5	1
Total	69	31	18	17	3
Mental deficiency:					
Mild	14	14	0	0	0
Moderate	23	23	0	0	0
Severe	14	14	0	0	0
Total	51	51	0	0	0
Epilepsy	20	12	5	3	0
Personality disorders	6	6	0	0	0
Total cases	199	114	29	49	7

Mental illness among U.S. and Canadian Hutterites living in the summer of 1951 is classified in this table. The total Hutterite population on December 31, 1950, was 8,542.

toms of a mental disorder or had recovered from such an illness. Of these illnesses 53 were diagnosed as psychoses, all but five of them of a functional (non-organic) character.

In short, the Hutterite culture provides no immunity to mental disorders. The existence of these illnesses in so secure and stable a social order suggests that there may be genetic, organic or constitutional predispositions to psychosis which will cause breakdowns among individuals in any society, no matter how protective and well integrated.

The distribution of symptoms among the Hutterites was quite unusual. There were few cases diagnosed as schizophrenia, although elsewhere this is the most common psychosis. Only nine Hutterites had ever manifested the pattern of delusions, hallucinations and other recognized symptoms of schizophrenia; the group lifetime rate was 2.1 per 1,000 persons aged 15 and over. On the other hand, the proportion of manic-depressive reactions among those with mental disorders was unusual; this disorder accounted for 39 of the 53 psychoses, and the rate was 9.3 per 1,000 aged 15 and over. The name of the disorder is misleading; manic-depressives often are not dangerous to other persons, and none of the Hutterite patients was. Ther symptoms were predominantly depressive. There was much evidence of irrational guilt feelings, self-blame, withdrawal from normal social relations and marked slowing of mental and motor activities. Five of the patients had suicidal impulses. Two Hutterites had actually killed themselves.

The fact that in the Hutterite society manic-depression is more common than schizophrenia, reversing the situation in all other populations for whom comparable data have been obtained, suggests that cultural factors do have some influence on the manifestation of psychoses. A Johns Hopkins University team of researchers who recently made an extensive analysis of mental hospital statistics concluded that schizophrenic symptoms are most common among unskilled laborers, farmers, urban residents in rooming-house sections and other persons who are relatively isolated socially, while manic-depressive reactions are more prevalent among professional, socially prominent and religious persons, who have a stronger need to live up to social expectations. Our data fits this theory well. Religion is the focus of the Hutterite way of life. Their whole educational system, beginning with nursery school, orients the people to look for blame and guilt within themselves rather than in others. Physical aggression is taboo. Like the Catholic orders, Hutterites own everything in the name of their church. They eat in a common dining room, pay medical bills from the communal treasury and work at jobs assigned to them by managers elected by the males of the colony. The group, rather than the individual, comes first.

In projective psychological tests the Hutterites, like other groups, show antisocial and aggressive impulses, but in their daily lives they repress these effectively. Their history showed no case of murder, arson, severe physical assault or sex crime. No individual warranted the diagnosis of psychopath. Divorce, desertion, separation or chronic marital discord were rare. Only five marriages were known to have gone on the rocks since 1875. Personal violence and childish or amoral forms of behavior among adults were uncommon, even in persons with psychotic episodes. There were no psychoses stemming from drug addiction, alcoholism or syphilis, although these disorders account for approximately 10 per cent of all first admissions to state mental hospitals in the U. S. In general our study tends to confirm the theory of many social scientists and public health officials that a favorable cultural setting can largely prevent these forms of social maladjustment.

All this does not entirely rule out the possibility that genetic factors play some part in the unusual proportions of manic-depression and schizophrenia symptoms among the Hutterites. There is some evidence that these disorders tend to run in families. The Hutterites are biologically inbred. Three surnames—Hofer, Waldner and Wipt—accounted for nearly half of all families in 1950. It is possible that the Hutterite group has a disproportionate number of persons genetically prone to becoming depressed—if there is such a predisposition. A team of Harvard University workers is planning to make a follow-up genetic study of the Hutterites.

The question of the relation of mental disorders to culture is difficult to investigate quantitatively. No country has a really complete record of mental disorders among its population. Censuses of patients in mental hospitals are almost worthless for this purpose; they leave out patients who have recovered and mentally ill persons who have never come to the attention of doctors.

Study	Number of cases diagnosed	Per cent of cases diagnosed			
		Schizo-phrenia	Manic depres-sion	All other diag-noses	Total
Ethnic Hutterites	53	17	74	9	100
North Swedish area	107	87	2	11	100
West Swedish island of Abo	94	43	27	30	100
Bornholm Island	481	31	25	43	100
Williamson County, Tenn.	156	27	26	47	100
Baltimore Eastern Health District	367	43	11	46	100
Thuringian villages	200	37	10	53	100
Bavarian villages, Rosenheim area	21	38	10	52	100

Eight groups investigated by independent studies, including the one described here, are analyzed for percentage of each major diagnositc category among their psychotics.

The Hutterite study attempted to track down every case of a mental disorder, past or present, hospitalized or not, in the whole living population. It probably succeeded in finding virtually all the cases of psychosis. Similar studies have been made of seven other communities in various parts of the world, and the results are shown in the tables on this page. They give the comparative rates of psychosis, as standardized by the Hutterite lifetime rate and corrected for variations in age and sex distribution. (The Hutterite population is predominantly youthful— 50 per cent under 15 years of age.)

On this basis the Hutterites apparently rank second highest among the eight populations in the rate of psychosis, being exceeded only by an area in the north of Sweden. But there is considerable evidence that the count of mental disorders was less complete in the other seven groups; that is, in those studies many cases were missed because their illness was not a matter of public record, while the Hutterite population was thoroughly screened. It is probable that the psychosis rate among the Hutterites is actually low compared with that in other populations. It seems to be only one third as high as the rate in New York State, for instance, taking into consideration the common estimate that even in that State (where mental hospital facilities are among the most extensive) there is at least one undetected psychotic person for every one in an institution.

Survey	Total popu-lation	Actual number of cases found	Expected number of cases by Hutterites norms	Expec-tancy ratio
North Swedish area	8,651	107	94	1.14
Ethnic Hutterites	8,542	53	53	1.00
Bornholm Island	45,694	481	773	.62
Baltimore Eastern Health District	55,129	507	822	.62
Williamson County, Tenn.	24,804	156	271	.58
West Swedish island of Abo	8,735	94	186	.51
Bavarian villages, Rosenheim area	3,203	21	49	.43
Thuringian villages	37,546	200	617	.32

One group, the Hutterites, is compared to the other seven by the standard expectancy method. The frequency of *diagnosed* cases of psychosis among Hutterites is relatively high.

The statistical comparison of mental disorder rates has many limitations, but it does offer several promising leads to the puzzle that the problem of functional psychoses presents to modern science. Among the Hutterites, as in all the other populations, the frequency of psychoses increases rapidly with age. Among those who showed manic-depressive reactions, females predominated. The social biology of the aging process and of sex probably holds worthwhile clues to some of the problems of cause and treatment.

Neuroses were more common than psychoses among the Hutterites, as elsewhere. Four fifths of the 69 discovered neurotics were female. Melancholy moods were regarded by teachers as the number one emotional problem of Hutterite school children. Hutterite neurotics showed the same tendency as psychotics to take out mental stress on themselves instead of on others. Self-blame and remorse were common, as were psychosomatic headaches, backaches and hysteric paralysis of a limb. There was little scapegoating or projection of hostile feelings by imputing them to others.

There is no evidence of any unusual concentration of hereditary mental defects in the Hutterite population. A total of 51 persons was diagnosed as mentally deficient, and 20 normal persons had suffered epileptic attacks. These epilepsy and mental deficiency rates are not high in comparison with other groups.

How does the Hutterite culture deal with mental illness? Although it does not prevent mental disorders, it provides a highly therapeutic atmosphere for their treatment. The onset of a symptom serves as a signal to the entire community to demonstrate support and love for the patient. Hutterites do not approve of the removal of any member to a "strange" hospital, except for short periods to try shock treatments. All patients are looked after by the immediate family. They are treated as ill rather than "crazy." They are encouraged to participate in the normal life of their family and community, and most are able to do some useful work. Most of the manic-depressive patients get well, but among neurotic patients recovery is less common. Most of the epileptics were either cured or took drugs which greatly relieved the condition. No permanent stigma is attached to patients after recovery. The traumatic social consequences which a mental disorder usually brings to the patient, his family and sometimes his community are kept to a minimum by the patience and tolerance with which most Hutterites regard these conditions. This finding supports the theory that at least some of the severely antisocial forms of behavior usually displayed by psychotic and disturbed patients are not an inherent attribute. They may be reflections of the impersonal manner of handling patients in most mental hospitals, of their emotional rejection by the family and of their stigmatization in the community.

In the Hutterite social order people are exposed to a large number of common experiences. Their indoctrination begins in infancy and is continued by daily religious instruction and later by daily church-going. Hutterites spend their entire life within a small and stable group. Their homes consist only of bedrooms, all furnished in an almost identical manner. The women take turns cooking and baking for everybody. Everyone wears the same kind of clothes; the women, for example, all let their hair grow without cutting, part it in the middle and cover it with a black kerchief with white polka dots. The Hutterite religion provides definite answers for many of the problems that come up.

Despite this uniformity in the externals of living, Hutterites are not stereotyped personalities. Differences in genetic, organic and psychological factors seem to be sufficiently powerful to produce an infinite variety of behavior, even in a social order as rigid as this one. It appears that the nightmare of uniformity sketched in George Orwell's *Nineteen Eighty-four* is actually unachievable in a living society. At least our study in depth disclosed no simple standardization of personality structure among Hutterites.

There is considerable objective evidence that the great majority of Hutterites have a high level of psychological adjustment. Their misfortunes and accidents are alleviated greatly by the group's system of mutual aid. The sick, the aged, the widows and orphans are well taken care of. In the last three decades only about 100 persons (most of them male) have left the community permanently. During World War II about one third of the men between the ages of 20 and 40 served in camps for conscientious objectors; more than 98 per cent of them ultimately returned to their colonies.

There has not, however, been any rush of applicants from outside to join the Hutterite sect. Mental health involves value judgments and depends on what people want from life. Only 19 adults have joined the sect in America during the last few decades. The austere and puritanical customs of the sect impose restrictions which even the members, who learn to accept them, regard as a "narrow path." Their culture is therapeutic only for conformists. There are occasional rebels; the more able ones find a means of expressing themselves by becoming leaders, the less brilliant have difficulties.

The survival of this 16th-century peasant culture in the heart of the most 20th-century-minded continent is a vivid demonstration of the power of values and beliefs. Although our data on the Hutterites' mental disorders clearly demonstrate the inadequacy of a purely cultural approach to the problem of mental health, they do show that culture has a large influence in shaping personality. Psychiatrists who work exclusively in hospitals or clinics cannot see the whole patient as he functions in his total environment. Our findings lead us to conclude that the social relations of the patient and his culture, including the things in which he believes, deserve more attention from psychiatric researchers and clinicians than is commonly given to them.

PART THREE

The Patient Career—
Prepatient Phase

It is possible to conceptualize the experience of persons defined and treated as mentally ill as a temporal sequence of events or "career." The concept of career encompasses at least two notions. First, it refers to the sequence of movements from a position in any particular network of social relations to another position in the same, or in a different, social network by any given person, and second, the sequence of individual adjustments accompanying the movement.[1] The career of the mental patient may be thought of as having three distinct phases: a prepatient phase, which describes the patient in the community prior to hospitalization; an inpatient phase, which describes the patient in the psychiatric treatment center; and a posthospital phase, which describes the patient as he is back in the community after the experience of hospitalization.

In recent years a number of investigations have begun to focus on various aspects of the patient career. The papers in this section deal explicitly with the prepatient phase of the career and all, either explicitly or implicitly, approach the prepatient phase from the perspective of the social psychological theories set forth in Part 1.

DEFINING A PERSON AS MENTALLY ILL

This section begins with a paper by Mechanic which attempts to conceptualize the labeling process which goes on between the prepatient and his definers. In contrast to the Scheff paper, which took as problematic the attachment of the label "mentally ill," Mechanic questions the very processes which make a potential deviant act visible. He notes that the process whereby the deviant label is applied is often quite unclear and can most frequently be traced to characteristics of the social situation in which the deviant and his labelers interact, as opposed to actual characteristics of the deviant. Thus he argues, quite similarly to Ernest Becker and Gough, that deviance may arise out of the inability of the deviant to accurately respond to interpersonal demands of the other in the situation. Variables which appear to influence the visibility of such acts include (1) the act being labeled by "professional" outsiders, (2) the seriousness of the act itself, (3) the frequency of occurrence of the act, and (4) structural characteristics of the community.

Previous investigators argue that it is the violation of group norms which leads to immediate rejection; e.g., the person is hospitalized when his behavior exceeds the tolerance limits of the family. Sampson, Messinger, and Towne imply that labeling of a person as mentally ill—and not necessarily rejection—follows the violation of situational norms. This paper demonstrates that once behavior has been labeled mentally ill, family members develop elaborate accommodation mechanisms to keep the deviant within the home setting. It is when these mechanisms fail that action is taken to move (e.g., reject) the "ill person" out of the family and into the hospital. Intrusion of a third person into the husband-wife relationship and public visibility of the deviant behavior are two of several factors which disrupt the accommodation patterns between the prepatient and his family.

The Goffman paper delineates the personal experiences of those defined as mentally ill before they enter hospitals for treatment. The Goffman work is outstanding because it highlights the stigma associated with the label "mentally ill" and the consequences of this ascription process upon family relations. Like Sampson, Messinger, and Towne, Goffman notes the accommodative processes which may arise between the deviant and his labelers, but his main attention is given to the contingencies surrounding the labeling process and the alienation which arises between the prepatient and his significant others when a family member is responsible for hospitalizing the patient. Under these circumstances Goffman argues that the patient will often deny his relationship to the family member—feeling that he has been betrayed and rejected by those he formerly trusted most.

Taking as given the fact that a person has been labeled as mentally ill, Phillips examines the relationship between the utilization of various mental health help sources and rejection by societal members. Seeking a psychiatric help source involves both a cost and a reward to the person labeled as mentally ill. The findings indicate that persons exhibiting "disturbed" behavior are rejected by members of the community more readily if they seek a psychiatric help source, as opposed to seeking a clergyman or no help source at all. However, among respondents with first-hand experiences with mental illness, greater rejection occurred under the circumstances of seeking no help or going only to a clergyman. Phillips's findings point to the dilemma of those persons labeled as mentally ill. A person cannot avoid rejection by some members of society once he has been defined as mentally ill. If he seeks psychiatric help, he will be rejected by the community; and if he seeks no help at all, he may well be rejected by relatives more than if some help source is consulted.

THE HOSPITALIZATION PROCESS

The beginning of the inpatient career represents the conclusion of several events that had taken place during the prepatient phase. Before the patient enters the mental hospital, at least four major events have occurred. The first event, here called the behavioral event, *consists of an individual engaging in some public action or set of actions. The second event, called the* definitional event, *represents the process whereby the behavior is evaluated and defined as deviant, unacceptable, and within the category of disturbed behavior called mental illness. The third event is a* treatment decision *which comes about if the individual fails to adjust his behavior to conform to the expectations of those persons who have defined the behavior as unacceptable. It becomes highly probable that persuasive pressures will be directed toward the individual to leave his present setting and to move into an institution created to deal with psychiatric disturbances. Persuasive pressures may stem from the primary groups to which the deviant individual belongs or from secondary groupings such as community social agencies or courts. Sometimes, the individual may recognize the deviancy of his behavior and decide to seek psychiatric help without pressures from others. The fourth and final event in the prepatient career phase is the attachment of a* legalistic definition *to the patient's hospital entry status. While some patients are legally committed, other patients gain entry to the hospital upon application for voluntary admission.*[2]

The Hammer paper as well as the Wood, Rakusin, and Morse work describes the processes which move persons into mental hospitals. Hammer examines the first three phases in the movement process into the hospital. Her data suggest that persons occupying critical positions in tightly bound interpersonal networks are more rapidly moved into the hospital than are persons who occupy positions of less importance, such as membership in loosely structured interpersonal networks. Thus for persons occupying such roles as head of the household, the stabilization and evolution of the patient career may occur much more rapidly than for the person in a truncated family role position such as mother-in-law, cousin, or nephew. With persons in the former positions, the decision to enter the hospital is more likely to arise within the family than to come from external social agencies. Similarly, the interaction surrounding the definitional event is more likely to focus on the particular costs and consequences to the family of moving the labeled deviant into the hospital.

By identifying those variables which determine whether or not a person will be allowed to enter any one of two psychiatric hospitals, Mishler and Waxler focus on decisions made during the last step of the prepatient phase of the patient career. They indicate that a medical referral increases the likelihood of acceptance to both hospitals for the voluntary patient. Certain patient background characteristics also serve as important filtering variables when decisions about hospital entry are made. While some background characteristics may increase a person's chances for admission in one hospital, the same characteristics may decrease his chances in another.

The Scheff study describes the final steps in the prepatient career phase. His data suggest that psychiatric screening by court-appointed psychiatrists is usually perfunctory and that the diagnosis of mental illness almost always follows accusation, regardless of solid evidence of actual illness behavior.

The implication from these two studies is that quite different decision-making models operate for voluntary and involuntary patients. In the case of the voluntary patient, the path to the hospital and his own personal background characteristics enter into the decision-making process. For the involuntary patient, however, these variables seem to be largely inconsequential. The prime consideration for such patients is refuting the charge of mental illness. Taken together these two studies illustrate a paradox. If a patient voluntarily presents himself for psychiatric treatment, he has no assurance of gaining hospital admission; but if illness is ascribed, avoidance is virtually impossible.

References

1 As first used by Hughes the notion of career embodied a formal and a subjective component. Career referred both to the sequence of movements from one office or status to another within an occupational organization and to "the moving perspective in which the person sees his life as a whole and interprets the meaning of his various attributes, actions, and the things which happen to him." (pp. 409–410). Everett C. Hughes, "Institutional Office and the Person," *American Journal of Sociology*, **43:** 404–413, 1937. Subsequent uses of the concept of career usually incorporate both components, by describing a sequence of movements accompanied or followed by a series of personal adjustments. See Oswald Hall, "The Stages of a Medical Career," *American Journal of Sociology*, **53:** 327–336, 1948; Howard S. Becker, *Outsiders,* The Free Press of Glencoe, New York, 1963; Erving Goffman, *Asylums,* Doubleday & Company, Inc., Garden City, N.Y., 1961.

2 Norman K. Denzin and Stephan P. Spitzer, "Paths to the Mental Hospital and Staff Predictions of Patient Role Behavior," *Journal of Health and Human Behavior,* **7:** 265–271, 1966.

18
SOME FACTORS IN IDENTIFYING
AND DEFINING MENTAL ILLNESS*
David Mechanic

The procedures through which persons in need of psychiatric treatment are identified and treated are frequently unclear. On some occasions persons exhibiting relatively mild symptoms are identified as psychiatric problems and appear for treatment, while persons with more serious psychiatric symptoms go unrecognized and untreated.

Yet the routes taken by patients who are brought to or appear at the hospital, clinic, or office of the private psychiatrist, provide the sociologist with an opportunity to illuminate the processes of patient selection and treatment.

A number of studies along these lines[1] have contributed richly to our understanding of these processes. These studies have pointed to the varying definitions of illness that are made at various locations in the social structure.[2] For example, the patient may view his own illness in terms of his feeling state; his employer might evaluate his symptoms in terms of his apparent deviation from group requirements; and his family may adjudge him "ill" on the basis of the attitude he professes or his situational behavior.

Yet definitions *are* made; patients *do* appear for treatment—although at times by rather devious routes—and psychiatric aid *is* administered. It is the major purpose of this paper to consider some of the definitions that are made, the conflicts that occur, the manner in which resolutions are attempted, and the effects of the definitional process on the eventual decisions as to who receives treatment.

In essence, I will draw a descriptive model of the definitional processes by which persons within a community are adjudged "mentally ill" by family, friends, community authorities and even by themselves, based on observations made at admission wards in two California mental hospitals and other reported research results.

The early definitions of mental illness, especially in middle-class populations,

Source: David Mechanic, "Some Factors in Identifying and Defining Mental Illness," *Mental Hygiene,* **46:** 66–74, 1962.
* The impressions reported here stem, in part, from exploratory interviews and observations at two California hospitals. These observations were carried out with the assistance of Research Grant MF–8516 of the National Institute of Mental Health.

[1] Hollingshead, A. B. and F. C. Redlich, *Social Class and Mental Illness* (New York: John Wiley & Sons, 1958); Myers, J. K. and B. H. Roberts, *Family and Class Dynamics in Mental Illness* (New York: John Wiley & Sons, 1959); Clausen, J. A. and Marion R. Yarrow, eds., "The Impact of Mental Illness on the Family," *Journal of Social Issues,* **11** (December, 1955); Cumming, Elaine and John Cumming, *Closed Ranks* (Cambridge, Mass.: Harvard University Press, 1957).

For an excellent study of the relationship between social class status and mode of treatment received, see Myers, J. K. and L. Schaffer, "Social Stratification and Psychiatric Practice: A Study of an Outpatient Clinic," *American Sociological Review,* **19** (June, 1954), 307–10.

[2] For some reviews of the problems of definition, see Jahoda, Marie, *Current Concepts of Positive Mental Health* (New York: Basic Books, Inc., 1958); Redlich, F. C., "The Concept of Health in Psychiatry," in Leighton, A. H., J. Clausen and R. Wilson, eds., *Explorations in Social Psychiatry* (New York: Basic Books, Inc., 1957); and Cumming and Cumming. *op. cit.*

are likely to take place in the groups within which the person primarily operates; evaluations are made by family, fellow employees, friends, and employers. If symptoms appear and are not recognized as such by members of the individual's more primary groups, it is unlikely that he will become accessible to psychiatric personnel unless his symptoms become visible, and disturbing enough to lead to his commitment to some treatment center by external authorities.

On other occasions, it is the person himself, who, in comparing his feelings and behavior with how he thinks others feel and behave or with how he has felt and behaved in the past, defines himself as ill and seeks what he regards as competent help.

Finally, when patients appear for psychiatric treatment, either on their own volition or under pressure of significant others, the physician evaluates the symptoms and then comes to some decision about the "illness." These various evaluations by the person himself, by his social group, by community agencies, and by psychiatric experts may be more or less consistent. However, discrepancies often occur, and when they arise, adequate solutions for resolving these differences are not always readily available.

Problems of definition arise, in part, because all behaviors occur within specific group contexts, and the frames of reference of the evaluators are not always comparable. Also, since the evaluators may be located at different foci of interaction with the person, the behavior they see may differ significantly.

The behaviors defined as symptoms of "illness" may be as much characteristic of some particular situation or group setting as they are enduring attributes of persons. For example, even with purely physiological symptoms, social definitions are applied which have important consequences for the patient and the course of his illness. The symptom may be defined as a sign of "illness" and receive the usual considerations of the sick role, or it may be viewed as an unjustifiable attempt to seek relief from legitimate expectations. It may be evaluated as a symbol of high prestige and community status (as a battle wound) or it may be seen as a consequence of promiscuous and shameful activities (as might be the case with venereal disease). The symptom, in sum, may be worthy of group consideration, sympathy and support, or it may be punished, criticized, or ignored.

Persons with intangible neurotic symptoms which might be interpreted as signs of weakness and excessive self-concern are reacted to quite differently from, for example, persons who have difficulties during such stressful situations as bereavement.

Although seemingly obvious, it is important to state that what may be viewed as deviant in one social group may be tolerated in another, and rewarded in still other groups. How group members view a particular behavior is likely to influence both the frequency with which it occurs and the extent to which it is exhibited. In other words, all groups exercise considerable control over their members.

"Mental illness" and other forms of deviancy become visible when persons in the participant's group recognize his inability and reluctance to make the proper responses in his network of interpersonal relations. How a particular deviant behavior is to be evaluated depends largely on the frame of reference the evaluators assume. Whether a deviant act is seen as evidence of "crime," "corruption," "illness," and so on, will be contingent on the criteria with which the evaluator operates and how he applies them.

It is hypothesized that the evaluator attempts to understand the motivation of the actor. In the language of Mead, he assumes the role of the other and attempts to empathize. If the empathy process is successful, the evaluator is likely to feel that he has some basis for labeling the deviant act as "delinquency," "undependability," or whatever.[3] It is primarily in those cases where the evaluator feels at a loss in adequately empathizing with the actor and where he finds it difficult to understand what attributed to the response that the behavior is more likely to be labeled "queer," "strange," "odd," or "sick."

There are behaviors, however, where the distinction is unclear; where, for example, an understandable crime is committed, but the expressed motive makes little sense; it thus becomes difficult to decide whether the actor is a "criminal," a potential "mental patient," or both.[4] In general, however, mental illness is regarded usually as a residual category for deviant behavior having no clearly specified label.

Of course the physician trained in the treatment of the mentally ill, applies different criteria to behavior than does the layman. The criteria he applies to deviant behavior are more closely related to the theory of pathology he holds than to his own ability or inability to take the role of the other. The criteria he holds, however, are at times indefinite and the physician who practices in large treatment centers often must assume the illness of the patient who appears before him and then proceed to prescribe treatment. Both the abstract nature of the physician's theories and the time limitations imposed upon him by the institutional structure of which he is a part make it impossible for him to make a

---

[3] In an interesting experimental study Jones and deCharms found that the degree to which a confederate is seen as responsible for his behavior when he causes the group to fail is a definite factor in evaluating his dependability. If he causes the group to fail, but is viewed as lacking the necessary ability to perform the necessary task, he is less likely to be defined as "undependable" than if he is viewed as lacking motivation.

See Jones, E. E. and R. deCharms, "Changes in Social Perception as a Function of the Personal Relevance of Behavior," *Sociometry*, **20** (March, 1957), 75–85. Kingsley Davis also presents an argument similar to the one offered in the text of this paper. *See* Davis, K., *Human Society* (New York: Macmillan Co., 1958), Chap. 10.

[4] Public health programs attempt, in some measure, to change the lay evaluation of what constitutes "mental illness." A study by Woodward, J. L., "Changing Ideas on Mental Illness and Its Treatment," *American Sociological Review*, **16** (August, 1951), 443–54, indicates that in at least one community persons are becoming more sensitive to what physicians regard as signs of "mental illness." However, more recently, Shirley Star, in the analysis of data from a National Opinion Research Center survey, points out that for most people "mental illness" is associated with violent, unpredictable behavior.

The Cummings, *op. cit.*, found that persons in the community they studied had fairly simple notions about "mental illness," and that they were relatively immune to the influence of an educational mental health program. In their book they attempt to analyze why this program failed.

As the public image of "mental illness" slowly changes to conform more closely to that held by the professional psychiatrist, predictability and the ability to take the role of the other may become less important in the evaluation made by lay persons.

R. T. LaPiere, in *The Freudian Ethic* (New York, Duell, Sloan & Pearce, Inc., 1959) argues that the therapeutic ethic has influenced many segments of social action and that the consequences are that deviant persons are absolved from responsibility for their actions regardless of the direction of deviancy and the abilities of the evaluators to understand the motivation for deviancy. From this, argues LaPiere, stems the ideology of permissive and nonpunishing prisons, therapeutic schools for delinquents, etc.

rapid study of the patient's illness or even to ascertain if illness, in fact, exists. Instead, it becomes necessary for him to assume the illness of the patient and to apply some label to the alleged if not recognizable symptoms. The consequences are that the basic decision about illness usually occurs prior to the patient's admission to the hospital and this decision is more or less made by non-professional members of the community. It therefore becomes a matter of considerable interest to understand how these nonprofessional members of the community define "mental illness."

Before moving on to discuss the variables affecting community definitions of "mental illness," it is important to emphasize in more detail the preceding point: that the basic decision about illness is usually made by community members and *not professional personnel.* Although the very "sick" are usually found in mental hospitals, there are occasions when very "sick" persons go unattended while moderately "sick" persons receive treatment. This selection is clearly based on social criteria, not on psychiatric ones.

The layman usually assumes that his conception of "mental illness" is not the important definition since the psychiatrist is the expert and presumably makes the final decision. On the contrary, community persons are brought to the hospital on the basis of lay definitions, and once they arrive, their appearance alone is usually regarded as sufficient evidence of "illness."

In the crowded state or county hospitals, which is the most typical situation, the psychiatrist does not have sufficient time to make a very complete psychiatric diagnosis, nor do his psychiatric tools provide him with the equipment for an expeditious screening of the patient. If he is a psychiatrist trained in the more orthodox psychoanalytic notions, his belief system makes it impossible to determine the "sickness" or "wellness" of the patient, since the classical theories assume that all people have unconscious drives which interfere with optimal functioning, and no clear practical criteria are provided for judging the "sick" from the "well."

In the two mental hospitals studied over a period of three months, the investigator never observed a case where the psychiatrist advised the patient that he did not need treatment. Rather, all persons who appeared at the hospital were absorbed into the patient population regardless of their ability to function adequately outside the hospital.

In this regard, it is important to note that mental hospitals care for more than the mentally ill. The unwanted, the aged, the indigent, the lonely, and others often enter public mental hospitals voluntarily. For example, on an alcoholic ward in a hospital studied by the author, staff generally recognized that as weather became cold and as snow began falling, indigent alcoholics would enter the hospital voluntarily, only to return to their usual patterns of life when the weather improved.

Psychiatric hospitals filled well over capacity will attempt to control more carefully those they will accept for treatment. But should beds be available, as was the case with the hospitals studied, it is likely that they will absorb whoever appears, at least for a time. This suggests that the definition of "mental illness" made by the lay public is crucial with regard to who is treated, and comprehension of medical care programs requires an understanding of how such definitions are made.

Intervention in a situation of "assumed mental illness" by family, friends, and others in the community is highly dependent on the visibility of symptoms.[5] Persons recognized and treated may not be those most in need of treatment by psychiatric criteria. Rather, it is at the point at which deviancy is most easily and clearly recognized—and most disturbing to the group—that pressures of various sorts are brought to bear on the person. Intervention, then, is likely to occur only after the person becomes a problem to himself or others, or gives definite indications that he will soon be a problem.

In evaluating the criteria by which visible symptoms might be judged, one practical basis is the extent to which the person failed to fulfill expectations adequately in performing his primary social roles (especially his familial and occupational roles), and the extent to which he violated legal and moral norms and highly important values of the group.

Whether a definition of deviancy is made and acted upon will depend largely on how serious the consequences of this deviation are for the group.[6] Some deviant behaviors are rewarded and tolerated. Others have some idiosyncratic function for the group, as is often the case with the "comic." Perhaps the deviant may be thought of as "eccentric," "queer," or "strange" but not sufficiently so to merit a definition of illness. However, should the deviancy begin to have serious consequences, because it is damaging or harmful to the individual, a group, or both, or because it becomes so visible to external groups that the family suffers loss of status, it might be redefined as "mental illness" and the person sent for treatment.

In some groups, of course, the stigma attached to a definition of mental illness is sufficiently great to bring about group resistance to such a definition.[7] However, other factors being constant, a definition of "mental illness" is more likely to be made as the serious consequences of the deviancy increase.[8]

The size and form of social structure characteristic of a community can affect the visibility of symptomatology, hence its consequences and definition. The data

[5] Lemert has pointed out that when an "ill" person deviates from role expectancies, his social visibility increases and others are constrained to respond accordingly to his behavior. In cases of violence and disorderly conduct, police action more often is taken. Where less violent behaviors occur—delusion, hallucinations, restlessness—if action is to be taken at all, it is likely to be taken by more primary associates. See Lemert, E., "Legal Commitment and Social Control," *Sociology and Social Research*, **30** (May–June, 1946), 370–78.

[6] In this regard, Jones and deCharms, *op. cit.*, found that behavior does not appear to have a constant meaning, and that the attribution of stable characteristics to behavior is dependent on the significance of the behavior for the perceiver's own value-maintenance or goal attainment.

[7] In his research, Clausen, et al., *op. cit.*, reports large differences in the degrees to which primary group members are willing to support and tolerate persons displaying schizophrenic symptoms. For excellent general reviews of the sociological mental health literature, see Clausen, J. A., "The Sociology of Mental Health," in Merton, R. K., L. Broom, and L. S. Cottrell, Jr., eds., *Sociology Today*, (New York: Basic Books, Inc., 1959), 485–508; and Clausen, J. A., *Sociology and the Field of Mental Health*, (New York: Russell Sage Foundation, 1956).

[8] From time to time, situations do occur where the social group uses the label "mental illness" as an excuse to rid itself of one of its members, if his presence or behavior are becoming annoying. This seems to occur relatively frequently with aged members in our society.

The absence of a strong familial feeling of responsibility to the aged often leads to hospitalization, especially in cases where the person makes more than the usual demands for care and attention. Often it becomes convenient for the family to view increasing demands as symptoms of "mental illness."

relevant to this area, however, are not very clear. It appears that in the autonomy of a large and impersonal network of relationships, the social visibility of persons lessens and symptoms may not be defined as readily as in more intimate communities. However, in the latter case, where the demands of social life may not be as rigorous and the deviant may not be as much of an inconvenience, the behavior is more likely to be ignored or tolerated, and the deviant can perform useful social roles more readily. In the larger and more impersonal structures, the abilities required to obtain sufficient life gratifications may be greater, and the person handicapped in his interpersonal responses may have a more difficult time making a satisfactory adjustment to life demands.[9]

The visibility and consequences of deviancy also increase as the deviant act increases in frequency. Other factors being equal, the frequency of a deviant act will affect how likely it is to be noticed, defined, and acted upon. Moreover, as the deviant act increases in frequency, it becomes more annoying to the group and some sanction is more likely to follow.

Depending upon life circumstances, groups—both family and community— differ in the kinds and degree of toleration they have for various behaviors. When the vulnerability of the group increases, its toleration for deviancy decreases.[10] During stress situations and crises, vulnerability increases, group soli-

---

[9] The data in this general area lead to difficult problems of interpretation. Clausen writes:

> To explain, in part, the differential distribution of rates of hospitalization found by Faris and Dunham, Owen suggested that mentally ill persons are perceived and dealt with differently in different settings. Thus far, no one has demonstrated that the areas of the city and segments of the population with the highest rates of hospitalization are characterized by a higher rate of recognition of mental illness than are other areas. Several studies suggest that, if anything, the reverse is true. There is substantial documentation, however, of the fact that the social status of the mentally ill person tends to influence the perception by his family and others of the nature of his problem, their modes of dealing with him prior to his entering medical-psychiatric channels, and the kinds of services offered to him by psychiatric clinics or hospitals. (*Sociology Today, op. cit.*, 494–95.)

The difficulties with the available data stem from the fact that important effects work at cross-purposes, and the studies, thus far, have not adequately controlled for these effects. One such factor is the varying toleration levels in the different kinds of communities reported by Eaton, J. and R. J. Weil, *Culture and Mental Disorders: A Comparative Study of the Hutterites and Other Populations* (Glencoe, Ill.: The Free Press, 1955). They report that the Hutterite culture, which seemingly had little mental illness, in fact, had prevalence rates similar to those found in other groups, but that in this culture mental illness was handled differently from the way it was handled among other groups.

Thus, while there may be lesser visibility in larger social structures, group toleration or the ability to make use of the psychologically handicapped may be more limited. Further research is needed in this general area, with a clearer delineation and control of visibility, tolerance, and role variables.

[10] In this respect, the data reported by Glass are especially interesting. See Glass, A. J., "Psychotherapy in the Combat Zone," in *Symposium on Stress* (Washington, D.C.: Army Medical Service Graduate School, Walter Reed Army Medical Hospital, 1953). He reports that when psychiatry casualties were evacuated to psychiatric facilities during the North African and Sicilian campaigns, few patients were salvaged for combat duty.

The psychiatrist usually assumed the patient was "ill" and "sought to uncover basic emotional conflicts or attempted to relate current behavior and symptoms with past personality patterns," which seemingly provided patients with "rational" reasons for their combat failure. Both patient and therapist were often readily convinced that the limit of combat endurance had been reached.

On the other hand, when patients were subsequently treated in the combat zone with such interpersonal devices as suggestion, influence, etc., a much higher percentage were returned to combat.

As Clausen points out, "maintaining ties with their outfits and preserving a conception of themselves as somehow being able to cope seem to have given many men the strength to do exactly that. . . . A good deal of research is needed to learn under what circumstances withholding the label 'mental illness' may lead to more effective coping than would combining, labeling and therapy." (See Clausen, *Sociology Today, op. cit.* 503.)

Clausen's comments are especially interesting because we have some evidence that during periods of

darity becomes more essential, and deviation is treated more harshly, especially where the deviation exacerbates the crisis and further increases group vulnerability.

Moreover, during periods of family and community stress, deviancy may increase because already handicapped persons find themselves unable to cope with the new and rigorous demands made upon them.

There are occasions when a person's behaviors, while tolerated in the primary group, become visible to authorities in the person's secondary groups who may have different values and standards. Hence there are different toleration levels for various behaviors, and those who define these behaviors as signs of "mental illness" may forcefully bring the patient to a treatment center.[11]

When this occurs, the primary group sometimes resists the definition placed upon its member by the secondary authorities; and it is not unusual for conflicting definitions to arise among the patient, his family, the courts, and the hospital physician. While the court is likely to accept the professional opinion of the physician, there are occasions when the psychiatrist—who by independent criteria has either assumed or decided that serious pathology exists—insists that a patient is ill, while the patient and his family strongly resist this definition. In such cases, the physician is often reluctant to press his definition and urge court commitment, since this requires him to argue in some states that the patient is dangerous to himself and others, a contention which is very difficult to support in many cases. In these state institutions, when the physician does decide to press such a petition for the commitment of an unwilling patient, his decision is usually made on the basis of whether there is sufficient evidence to convince the court that the patient should be lawfully detained, even when the family is reluctant.

Often the patient is released from the hospital without detailed judicial consideration, not because the psychiatrist finds him free of serious pathology, but rather because the psychiatrist has anticipated what the court decision would be. if the psychiatrist is to gain commitment of an unwilling patient, he must usually convince the family that the patient is indeed seriously ill and in

---

stress—with increasing social, psychological, and physical demands—rates of psychotic breakdown increase. However, if group solidarity is essential and group vulnerability is high, the sick role is not easily accorded to persons with neurotic-type symptoms, and considerable pressure is placed upon them to continue in their social roles.

See, Mechanic, D., "Illness and Social Disability: Some Problems in Analysis," *Pacific Sociological Review*, **2** (Spring, 1959), 37–41; and Schneider, D. M., "Social Dynamics of Physical Disability in Army Basic Training," in Kluckhohn, C., H. A. Murray, and D. M. Schneider, eds., *Personality in Nature, Society, and Culture, second edition* (New York: Alfred A. Knopf, 1956), 386–92.

The observations by Groen, C., "Psychogenesis and Psychotherapy of Ulcerative Colitis," *Psychosomatic Medicine*, **9** (May–June, 1947), 151–74, that the ulcer symptoms of his patients disappeared during the stress conditions of concentration camp life and often reappeared after leaving the concentration camp, raises some interesting questions, as W. Caudill has observed. *See* Caudill, W., *Effects of Social and Cultural Systems in Reactions to Stress* (New York: Social Science Research Council, 1958).

Whether the change during incarceration is a reaction to the change in the stressors, or is tied with shifts in the physiological, psychological, and social systems accompanying camp life, is a question for further and better-controlled research. Also, Groen's observations that the wives were providing their husbands with more emotional support than formerly is an important variable.

[11] The data collected by Hollingshead and Redlich, *op. cit.*, indicate that members of the lower strata are most likely to take this path to treatment centers.

need of treatment, and bring them around to support his definition of the situation.

In any case, the psychiatrist treating a patient implicitly, if not explicitly, recognizes that it is important to communicate his perception of pathology to the patient and to his family. He also realizes that he must convince the patient that he is indeed "sick" and in serious need of treatment. The necessity of having the patient accept the psychiatric definition of his case is especially apparent in the early hospital experience, where the patient must become socialized to a "patient-role," accepting the definition of his symptoms placed upon him by the hospital population, including staff and other patients. Should the patient refuse to accept the patient-role and deny his illness, this resistance is viewed as a further symptom of the "illness," and he is told that if he is to get well, he must recognize the fact that he is ill.

Should the patient continue to reject the psychiatric definition of his illness, the psychiatrist is likely to report that the patient is a poor treatment risk. Furthermore, ancillary hospital staff and other patients also apply similar definitions of illness to the patient and expect him to accept these definitions. The patient's denials create social difficulties for him within the hospital, difficulties of adaptation to ward life which can be further viewed as indications that the patient is seriously ill and which reinforce the original impressions and definitions placed upon him by physicians, aides and other patients. Unless the patient begins to see himself through the eyes of the psychiatrist, hospital personnel, and other patients, he will remain a problem to the ward,[12] and his therapy and progress are likely to be viewed as inconsequential.

The foregoing suggests that if we are to understand the "mentally ill" patient, we must understand the situation from which he comes and the circumstances that led to the definition that he needs treatment. If the patient is to be effectively treated in regard to his life situation, we must understand what demands were made upon him and why he failed to meet these demands. Was it because he was unable to perceive the expectations of others accurately? Was it because he was unable to make proper responses? Or were there other reasons for his failure to meet expectations? Furthermore, we should want to inquire about the expectations he faced, the conflicts he perceived, and the cross-currents of expectations and behaviors that led to the societal response and definitions of mental illness.

From a theoretical point of view, what has been attempted is a descriptive model of the definitional processes by which persons within a community are adjudged as mentally ill. If we are to expand our understanding of definitions of deviancy and mental illness, a logical step is to move in the direction of axiomatic models, utilizing relevant variables and encouraging systematic empirical investigation. It is with the constant interplay of exploratory observations,

---

[12] A similar argument has been presented by Goffman, E., "The Moral Career of the Mental Patient," *Psychiatry*, 22 (May, 1959), 123–42, and Erikson, K. T., "Patient Role and Social Uncertainty—a Dilemma of the Mentally Ill," in Cohen, Mabel B., ed., *Advances in Psychiatry* (New York: W. W. Norton Co., 1959), 102–23.

systematic theory, and rigorous empirical tests that our knowledge will develop in a useful fashion.

ACKNOWLEDGMENT: The author wishes to express his thanks to Edmund Volkart and Thomas Scheff for their helpful comments.

19
FAMILY PROCESSES AND
BECOMING A MENTAL PATIENT[1]

Harold Sampson, Sheldon L. Messinger, and Robert D. Towne[2]

Becoming a mental patient is not a simple and direct outcome of "mental illness"; nor is hospitalization in a mental institution, when and if it comes, the automatic result of a professional opinion. Persons who are, by clinical standards, grossly disturbed, severely impaired in their functioning, and even overtly psychotic may remain in the community for long periods without being "recognized" as "mentally ill" and without benefit of psychiatric or other professional attention. It is clear that becoming a mental patient is a socially structured event.[3] The research reported here is directed to increasing our understanding of the nature and significance of this structuring as it mediates the relations between individuals and the more formal means of social control. The research explores (a) the relationship between patterns of family means for coping with the deviant behavior of a member who later becomes a mental patient and (b) efforts of the future patient or members of his family to secure professional help.

The broad nature of this latter relationship may be inferred from a number of published findings. Yarrow and her colleagues have documented the monumental capacity of family members, before hospitalization, to overlook, minimize, and explain away evidence of profound disturbance in an intimate.[4] The

Source: Harold Sampson, Sheldon L. Messinger, and Robert D. Towne, "Family Processes and Becoming a Mental Patient," *American Journal of Sociology,* **68:** 88–96, 1962.
[1] This report is based on a study carried out by the California Department of Mental Hygiene and partially supported by Grant No. 3M-9124 from the National Institute of Mental Health.
[2] Thanks are due to David Ross, Florine Livson, Mary-Dee Bowers, Lester Cohen, and Kate S. Dorst for their substantial contributions to the research for this study.
[3] Erving Goffman, in "The Moral Career of the Mental Patient," *Psychiatry,* XXII (May, 1959), 123–42, discusses a variety of "career contingencies" that may intervene between deviant behavior and hospitalization for mental illness. Also see the articles in *Journal of Social Issues,* XI (1955), ed. John A. Clausen and Marian Radke Yarrow, under the general title of "The Impact of Mental Illness on the Family." August B. Hollingshead and Frederick C. Redlich (*Social Class and Mental Illness: A Community Study* [New York: John Wiley & Sons, Inc., 1958], chap. vi, "Paths to the Psychiatrist") also emphasize this point.
[4] Marian Radke Yarrow, Charlotte Green Schwartz, Harriet S. Murphy, and Leila Calhoun Deasy, "The Psychological Meaning of Mental Illness in the Family," *Journal of Social Issues,* XI (1955), 12–24. Also see Charlotte Green Schwartz, "Perspectives on Deviance—Wives' Definitions of Their Husbands' Mental Illness," *Psychiatry,* XX (August, 1957), 275–91; Hollingshead and Redlich, *op. cit.,* esp. pp. 172–79; and Elaine Cumming and John Cumming, *Closed Ranks* (Cambridge, Mass.: Harvard University Press, 1957), esp. pp. 91–108.

post-hospital studies of the Simmons group have suggested that high "tolerance for deviance" in certain types of families is a critical determinant of the likelihood of poorly functioning and sometimes frankly psychotic former patients avoiding rehospitalization.[5] Myers and Roberts found that few mental patients or their families sought or used professional assistance before hospitalization until the problems they encountered became unmanageable.[6] Whitmer and Conover reported that the occasion for hospitalization was ordinarily not recognition of "mental illness" by the patient or his family but inability to cope with disturbed behavior within the family.[7]

These observations and our own permit two inferences. First, both before and after hospitalization some type of accommodative pattern ordinarily evolves between a disturbed person and his family which permits or forces him to remain in the community in spite of severe difficulties. Second, it is the disruption of this pattern which eventually brings a disturbed person to psychiatric attention.[8] An investigation of typical family accommodations to the deviant behavior of future patients, and how these accommodations collapse, should therefore contribute to our understanding of the ways in which individuals and the intimate social networks of which they are members are rendered less and more accessible to institutionalized devices of social control. Specifically, it should provide us with a glimpse of those dynamic family processes which determine a future mental patient's accessibility to community, particularly psychiatric intervention; these same processes determine the accessibility of the family. It should also contribute to our understanding of the meaning of such intervention to the future patient and his family. Such family accommodations pose strategic problems for the persons who constitute and man community remedial facilities. These are problems seldom taken into explicit or systematic account by such persons—problems beyond but related to the pathology of the patient.

We shall be concerned here with two phases in the relationship between the future patient and his family and with the connections between these phases and the course of events leading to hospitalization. The first phase consists of the evolution of a pattern of accommodation within the family to behavioral deviance on the part of the future patient.[9] The second phase consists in the

---

[5] See Ozzie G. Simmons, *After Hospitalization: The Mental Patient and His Family* (Hogg Foundation for Mental Health, n.d.) and the several studies by the Simmons group cited there.

[6] Jerome K. Myers and Bertram H. Roberts, *Family and Class Dynamics* (New York: John Wiley & Sons, Inc., 1959), pp. 213–20. These findings also suggest that lower-class families are better able to contain an extremely disturbed person for long periods of time than are middle-class families; the latter call on outside help more rapidly when "major psychotic decompensation" occurs. This would follow from the argument presented by Talcott Parsons and Renee Fox in "Illness, Therapy, and the Modern Urban American Family," *Journal of Social Issues*, VIII (1953), 31–44.

[7] Carroll A. Whitmer and Glenn C. Conover, "A Study of Critical Incidents in the Hospitalization of the Mentally Ill," *Journal of the National Association of Social Work*, IV (January, 1959), 89–94 (see also Edwin C. Wood, John M. Rakusin, and Emanuel Morse, "Interpersonal Aspects of Psychiatric Hospitalization," *Archives of General Psychiatry*, III [December, 1960], 632–41).

[8] Another inference we have made, and which we discuss elsewhere, is that an important set of effects of community devices of social control pertain to family patterns of accommodation. In important ways, it is through these that individuals are controlled, rather than by direct action (Harold Sampson, Sheldon L. Messinger, and Robert D. Towne, "The Mental Hospital and Family Accommodations" [unpublished manuscript, 1962]).

[9] This phase emphasizes one side of a complicated reciprocity between family relations and the deviance of family members. We have focused on the other side of this reciprocity—family relations as they sus-

disruption of this pattern of accommodation. Our observations are derived from a study of seventeen families in which the wife-mother was hospitalized for the first time in a large state mental institution and therein diagnosed as schizophrenic.[10] We established a research relationship with both patient and spouse at the time of admission and continued to see them regularly and frequently throughout hospitalization, and for varying periods extending to more than two years following first release. We conducted about fifty interviews with the members of each marital pair, including typically one or more joint interviews. Other relatives, psychiatrists, physicians, hospital personnel, and other remedial agents who had become involved with the patient or family over the years were also interviewed. Interview materials were supplemented by direct observation at home and in the hospital, and by such medical and social records as we could locate and gain permission to abstract.

These methods, which are described more fully elsewhere,[11] enabled us to reconstruct the vicissitudes of these marital families from courtship through marriage, child-bearing and child-rearing, eventual hospitalization of the wife, and well into the period following the patient's first release. We shall focus here on a longitudinal analysis of two patterns of accommodation which evolved between these women and their families prior to hospitalization and the disruption of these patterns. The patterns are exemplified by eleven and four cases, respectively; two of the seventeen families do not appear to be adequately characterized by either pattern. In order to present the patterns in some detail, our analysis will be developed in terms of selected families exhibiting each type of accommodation. This does not exhaust the empirical variety to be found even in the limited number of cases studied here. In the concluding section, however, emphasis will be placed on common patterns of relationship between future mental patients and their immediate interpersonal communities, as well as on the conditions under which these patterns deteriorate and collapse.

THE UNINVOLVED HUSBAND AND SEPARATE WORLDS

In the first situation, exemplified by eleven families, the marital partners and their children lived together as a relatively independent, self-contained nuclear family, but the marital relationship was characterized by mutual withdrawal and

---

tain and promote deviant behavior—elsewhere (see Robert D. Towne, Sheldon L. Messinger, and Harold Sampson, "Schizophrenia and the Marital Family: Accommodations to Symbiosis," *Family Process* (forthcoming), and Robert D. Towne, Harold Sampson, and Sheldon L. Messinger, "Schizophrenia and the Marital Family: Identification Crises," *Journal of Nervous and Mental Diseases*, CXXXIII [November, 1961], 423–29). There is a large and growing literature on this topic, particularly as it concerns schizophrenia, much of which is referred to in the various citations to be found in *The Etiology of Schizophrenia*, ed. by Don D. Jackson (New York: Basic Books, Inc., 1960).

[10] Detailed characteristics of the families studied may be found in Harold Sampson, Sheldon L. Messinger, and Robert D. Towne, "The Mental Hospital and Marital Family Ties," *Social Problems*, IX (Fall, 1961), 141–55. In two of seventeen cases, a brief psychiatric hospitalization in a county hospital had occurred earlier; in a third case, the woman had been hospitalized in a private sanitarium for one month earlier in the same year she entered the state institution.

[11] *Ibid.*

the construction of separate worlds of compensatory involvement. At some point during the marriage, usually quite early, one or both of the partners had experienced extreme dissatisfaction with the marriage. This was ordinarily accompanied by a period of violent, open discord, although in other cases, the dissatisfaction was expressed only indirectly, through reduced communication with the marital partner. Whatever the means of managing the dissatisfaction when it occurred, in each of these families the partners withdrew and each gradually instituted a separate world. The husband became increasingly involved in his work or in other interests outside the marital relationship. The wife became absorbed in private concerns about herself and her children. The partners would rarely go out together, rarely participate together in dealing with personal or family problems, and seldom communicate to each other about their more pressing interests, wishes, and concerns. The marriage would continue in this way for some time without divorce, without separation, and without movement toward greater closeness. The partners had achieved a type of marital accommodation based on interpersonal isolation, emotional distance, and lack of explicit demands upon each other. This accommodation represented an alternative to both divorce and a greater degree of marital integration.

It is a particularly important characteristic of this type of family organization that pathological developments in the wives were for a time self-sustaining. The wife's distress, withdrawal, or deviant behavior did not lead to immediate changes of family life but rather to an intensification of mutual withdrawal. In this setting, the wives became acutely disturbed or even psychotic, without, for a time, very much affecting the pre-existing pattern of family life. This is exemplified in the following cases:

In the evenings, Mr. Urey worked on his car in the basement while his wife remained upstairs, alone with her sleeping children, engaged in conversations and arguments with imaginary others. This situation continued for at least two years before Mrs. Urey saw a psychiatrist on the recommendation of her family physician. Another two years elapsed before Mrs. Urey was hospitalized. During this period, Mr. Urey became ever less concerned with his wife's behavior, accepting it as a matter of course, and concerned himself with "getting ahead" in his job.

For two years prior to hospitalization, Mrs. Rand was troubled by various somatic complaints, persistent tension, difficulty in sleeping, a vague but disturbing conviction that she was a sinner, and intermittent states of acute panic. Mr. Rand was minimally aware of her distress. He worked up to fourteen hours a day, including weekends, in his store, and eventually a second job took him out of the home three evenings a week. On those infrequent occasions when his wife's worries forced themselves on his attention, he dismissed them curtly as absurd, and turned once again to his own affairs.

In these families the patterned response to distress, withdrawal, or illness in the wife was further withdrawal by the husband, resulting in increasing distance between, and disengagement of, the marital partners. These developments were neither abrupt nor entirely consistent, but the trend of interaction in these families was toward mutual alienation and inaccessibility of each partner to the other. In this situation, early involvement of the wife in a professional treatment situation was limited by her own withdrawal and difficulty in taking the initiative for any sustained course of action in the real world, as well as by the husband's detachment.

This pattern of mutual withdrawal eventually became intolerable to one or the other partner, pressure for a change was brought to bear, and the family suffered an acute crisis. In some cases, pressure for change was initiated by the husband. In other cases, such pressure was initiated by the wife in the form of increasing agitation, somatic and psychic complaints, and repeated verbal and behavioral communications that she was unable to go on. However the pre-hospital crisis was initiated, and whether it signaled a desire for increased or reduced involvement by the initiating partner, the change indicated an incipient collapse of the former pattern of accommodation.

In four of the eleven cases considered here, the pre-hospital crisis was primarily precipitated by a shift in the husband's "tolerance for deviance." In two of these cases, the wives had been chronically and pervasively withdrawn from role performances and at least periodically psychotic. One husband, in the midst of job insecurities and a desire to move to another state to make a new start, pressed his wife to assume more responsibility. Another husband, approaching forty years of age, reassessed his life and decided that the time had come to rid himself of a wife whom he had long considered "a millstone around my neck." These husbands sought medical or psychiatric assistance specifically to exclude their wives from the family; the two wives were passively resistant to hospitalization. The explicit attitude of the husbands was that they wished the hospital to take their wives off their hands.

In the other two cases, the disruption of the earlier accommodation was associated with the establishment, by the husband, of a serious extra-marital liaison. Here, as in the two cases referred to above, there appeared to be no marked change in the wife's conduct prior to this indication of a desire by the husband for total withdrawal.

Virtually identical family processes were apparent in those cases where the manifest illness of the wife was itself the source of pressure for change, the harbinger of the collapse of the prior marital accommodation. The wife's illness intruded itself into family life, at first with limited impact, but then more insistently, like a claim which has not been paid or a message that must be repeated until it is acknowledged. The wife's "complaints" came to be experienced by the husband as, literally, complaints to him, as demands upon him for interest, concern, and involvement. These husbands, however, uniformly initially struggled to preserve the earlier pattern, that is, to maintain uninvolvement in the face of demands which implicitly pressed for their active concern. Thus, as the pre-hospital crisis unfolded, the wife's manifest illness assumed the interpersonal significance of a demand for involvement, and the husband's difficulty in recognizing her as seriously disturbed had the interpersonal significance of a resistance to that demand. The excerpt cited earlier from the Rand case illustrates this process if we add to it the observation that during these two years Mrs. Rand's difficulties recurrently came to the husband's attention in the form of momentary crises which compelled at least the response of curt dismissal.

In this situation, the husband initially assumed a passive or indifferent attitude toward his wife's obtaining professional help. But if she became involved with a psychiatrist, physician, minister, or social worker who took some interest in her life situation, the husband became concerned with the treatment in a negative way. The treatment "wasn't necessary," it "wasn't helping," it "cost too much money." In addition to these deprecations was a hint of alarm that the treatment would challenge the husband's pattern of uninvolvement.[12] For example, Mr. Rand, whose working schedule was mentioned earlier, worried that his wife's psychiatrist might support her complaint that he did not spend enough time at home. Thus the involvement of the wife with a psychiatrically oriented helper was experienced by the husband, at least initially, as a claim upon himself—for money, for concern, and most centrally, for reinvolvement. We have reported elsewhere[13] that there is some basis for this feeling. The treatment process, especially during hospitalization, does tend to induct the husband into the role of the responsible relative, and thereby presses for the re-establishment of reciprocal expectations which had been eroded in the earlier family accommodation.

In most of these cases, these processes led to more extreme deviance on the part of the wife which eventually came to the attention of the larger community, thereby resulting in hospitalization. For example, Mrs. Urey, who had been actively psychotic for some time, was hospitalized only after she set fire to her home. In brief, the wife's distress is at first experienced by the husband as an unwarranted demand for his reinvolvement in the marital relationship, he withdraws further, and her behavior becomes more deviant.

We may conclude this section with a few more general remarks. The prehospital crisis, in each of these cases, marked, and was part of, the disruption of a pattern of accommodation which had been established between the marital partners. The disruption was in effect initiated by one of the partners and resisted by the other.[14] The former accommodation and the way in which it came to be disrupted were important determinants of the processes of "recognizing" the wife as mentally ill, of seeking and using professional help, and of moving the wife from the status of a distressed and behaviorally deviant person within the community to that of a mental patient. These processes, in fact, can only be understood within the context of these family patterns. The problems of early intervention in cases of serious mental illness and of effective intervention in the later crises which ordinarily do come to psychiatric attention cannot even be formulated meaningfully without consideration of these interpersonal processes which determine when, why, and how sick persons become psychiatric patients.

[12] In one case, the psychiatrist urged the husband to seek treatment for himself.

[13] Sampson et al., "The Mental Hospital and Marital Family Ties," op. cit.

[14] Wood, Rakusin, and Morse, op. cit., have arrived at a related conclusion on the basis of an analysis of the circumstances of admission of forty-eight patients to a Veterans Administration hospital. "There is also evidence to suggest that hospitalization can for some patients be a way of demanding that those close to them change their behavior, just as it can be an expression by relatives that they are dissatisfied with the patient's behavior."

THE OVERINVOLVED MOTHER AND
THE MARITAL FAMILY TRIAD

In a contrasting situation found in four cases, the marital partners and their children did not establish a relatively self-contained nuclear family. Rather, family life was organized chronically or periodically around the presence of a maternal figure who took over the wife's domestic and child-rearing functions.[15]

This organization of family life was a conjoint solution to interlocking conflicts of the wife, husband, and mother. In brief, these mothers were possessive and intrusive, motivated to perpetuate their daughters' dependency, and characteristically disposed to assume the "helpful" role in a symbiotic integration with her. The daughters ambivalently pressed for the establishment or maintenance of a dependent relationship with their mothers and struggled to break the inner and outer claims of the maternal attachment. The husbands responded to anxieties of their own about the demands of heterosexual intimacy and marital responsibility, as well as their own ambivalent strivings toward maternal figures, by alternately supporting and protesting the wives' dependence on the maternal figure. The resulting family organization, in which the mother was intermittently or continuously called upon for major assistance, represented an alternative to both a relatively self-contained, independent nuclear family and to marital disruption with the wife returning to live within the parental family.

In direct contrast to the family accommodation described in the preceding section, the wives in "triadic" families did not quietly drift into increasing isolation and autism. Here, sickness or withdrawal by the wife were occasions for intense maternal concern and involvement. This development was ordinarily abetted by the husband. The resulting situation, however, would come to be experienced as threatening by the wife. She would come to view her mother as interfering with her marriage and her fulfilment of her own maternal responsibilities, as restricting her freedom, and as preventing her from growing up. At this point a small but often violent rebellion would ensue, and the husband would now participate with his wife to exclude the mother from family life. Such cycles of reliance on the mother followed by repudiation of her recurred over the years with only minor variations.

This accommodation complicated seeking and using professional help, but in a distinctively different way than in the family setting depicted earlier. Here, the family accommodation included this patterned response to withdrawal, illness, or distress in the wife: the mother replaced the wife in her domestic and child-care functions, and established with the wife a characteristic integration involving a helpless one who needs care and a helpful one who administers it; the husband withdrew to the periphery of the family system, leaving the wife and mother bound in a symbiotic interdependency.

In this patterned response, outside help was not simply superfluous but constituted an actual threat to the existing interdependency of mother and daughter

---

[15] This person was the wife's mother in three cases, her mother-in-law in the fourth. This distinction is not critical in the present context, and we shall refer to "the wife's mother," etc.

(by implying that it was inadequate, unnecessary, or even harmful), whereas in the type of family accommodation previously described, treatment was experienced as a threat to the husband's uninvolvement; here, treatment was a threat to the mother's involvement.

It was the failure of this family accommodation which led to the wife's contact with the physician or psychiatrist. This failure occurred when, simultaneously, the wife rebelled against the maternal attachment but could not establish with her husband the previously effective alternative of temporary repudiation of that attachment. The following example demonstrates these processes:

Mrs. Yale became anxious, confused, and unable to cope with the demands of daily life in the context of increasing withdrawal by her husband combined with increasing inner and outer pressure for reinvolvement with her mother. Her mother, Mrs. Brown, was living with the marital family, tending the house, caring for the child, and remaining by the side of her troubled daughter night and day. Mr. Yale had become increasingly involved in shared interests with a circle of male friends, and felt disaffected from family life.

Mrs. Brown later characterized this period to the research interviewer: "I think Mary resented me because I tried to help and do things for her. She didn't want me to help with her work. She didn't seem to want me around—sort of resented me. She kept saying she wanted to be on her own and that she didn't have confidence because I was always doing things for her. She even resented me doing the dishes. I just wanted to help out." At this point, Mrs. Brown considered her daughter to be seriously emotionally disturbed, and thought psychiatric help would be advisable.

In such cases, the behavior which led family members to doubt the young woman's sanity consisted of hostility, resentment, and accusatory outbursts directed toward the mother. In these violent outbursts toward the maternal figure, the daughter was indeed "not herself." It was at just this point that the daughter's behavior constituted a disruption of the former family pattern of accommodation and led toward involvement with outside helpers. The mother might now view outside helpers as potential allies in re-establishing the earlier interdependency. The psychiatrist, however, was unlikely to fulfil the mother's expectations in this regard, and then he became an heir to the husband in the triadic situation, a potential rival to the mother-daughter symbiosis.

Shortly after outpatient treatment began, Mrs. Brown took her daughter on an extended vacation which effectively interrupted the treatment, detached the daughter from her incipient attachment to the psychiatrist, and re-established the pattern of mother-daughter interdependency with the husband at the periphery of involvement.

We may summarize, then, certain connections between this type of family accommodation and the use of professional help prior to hospitalization. The initial response of the family to the wife's distress was to attempt to reinstate a familiar pattern: a drawing together of mother and daughter in symbiotic interdependency, and a withdrawal of the husband to the periphery of the family. This accommodation was disrupted by the eruption of the daughter's formerly ego-alien resentment toward her mother, and at this point the latter was likely to view physicians or psychiatrists as potential allies in restoring the former equilibrium. The psychiatrist, however, was unlikely to play this part and became, for the mother, a rival to the interdependency. For the daughter, also, this meaning of treatment invested it with the dangerous promise of a possible separation from the maternal figure. In this drama, the husband was likely to play a relatively passive if not a discouraging role, affording the wife little if any support in what she experienced as a threatening and disloyal involvement outside the family.

The way in which the hospitalization of the wife came about, in the collapse of this family accommodation, also provided contrasts to the processes depicted in the preceding section. As the pre-hospital crisis developed, the wife sought to withdraw from continuing intolerable conflict in the triadic situation. At first, the wife felt impelled to choose between regressive dependency on a maternal figure and the claims of her marital family, but was unable to either relinquish the former or achieve inner and outer support for the latter. Both alternatives were transiently affirmed and repudiated in the period preceding hospitalization, but in time she came to feel alienated from *both* mother and husband, and driven toward increasing *psychic* withdrawal. This process did not resolve her conflicts or remove her from the triadic field, and in time she herself pushed for physical removal.

Thus, in two of the four triadic cases, the wife herself, with a feeling of desperation, explicitly requested hospitalization. In a third case, the disturbed wife was brought to a psychiatrist in the company of both mother and husband, refused to return home with them after the appointment, and was thereupon hospitalized. In the fourth case, the wife was initially cooperative to a hospitalization plan, but equivocation by the husband and psychiatrist delayed action, and the wife gave herself and her daughter an overdose of drugs, thereby precipitating the hospitalization. This last case resembles the most common pattern described in the preceding section, in which the wife is driven to extreme deviance which comes to the attention of the larger community and compels hospitalization. But the secondary pattern, in which a husband takes primary initiative for hospitalizing a reluctant wife because she has become a "millstone around my neck," was entirely absent.

DISCUSSION

The career of the mental patient and his family ordinarily comes to the attention of treatment personnel during the course of an "unmanageable" emergency and fades from view when that emergency is in some way resolved. Prior to this public phase of the crisis, and often again after it, the disturbance of the patient is contained within a community setting. It is the collapse of accommodative patterns *between* the future patient and his interpersonal community which renders the situation unmanageable and ushers in the public phase of the pre-hospital (or rehospitalization) crisis.

Our analysis has been addressed to ways in which two particular organizations of family life have contained pathological processes, to the ways in which these organizations were disrupted, and to the links between family dynamics and recognition of illness, seeking and using professional help, and the circumstances of mental hospitalization. The analysis carries us beyond the observations that families often "tolerate" deviant behavior, may resist "recognition" that the future patient is seriously disturbed, and may be reluctant to use help, toward a systematic view of "typical" accommodations around deviance and typical patterns of crisis.

It is, of course, by no means evident how typical the patterns we have described may be. Although the analysis is confined to certain marital family organizations and does not entirely exhaust our own empirical materials, we suggest that the presentation does touch upon two common situations encountered in work with the mentally ill and their families. In the first situation, the future patient and his immediate interpersonal community move from each other, effect patterns of uninvolvement, and reciprocate withdrawal by withdrawal. The future patient moves, and is moved, toward exclusion from interpersonal ties and from any meaningful links to a position in communal reality. This situation, as we have seen, is compatible with very high "tolerance for deviant behavior," which may permit an actively psychotic patient to remain *in* the community while not psychosocially *of* it.

The accommodation may be disrupted by a shift in the "tolerance" of the interpersonal community, however determined,[16] or from the side of the future patient by increasing agitation which signals an attempt to break out of inner and outer isolation. Here, hospitalization is a possible route toward further disengagement of the patient from his interpersonal community, or conversely, toward re-establishment of reciprocal expectations compatible with re-engagement. Whatever the outcome, a strategic therapeutic problem is posed by the chronic pattern of mutual disinvolvement and withdrawal.

In the second situation, the future patient and a member of his immediate interpersonal community become locked in mutual involvement, effect patterns of intense interdependency, and reciprocate withdrawal by concern. The future patient moves and is moved toward a bond in which interlocking needs tie the participants together rather than isolate them. This situation is also compatible with high tolerance for deviant behavior, but here because the deviance has become a necessary component of the family integration. It is this type of family process, rather than the first type, which has attracted most psychiatric interest,[17] although there is no reason from our data to suppose that it is the more common.

In the cases observed the disruption of this accommodation took the form of an ego-alien movement by the future patient against the claims of the over-

---

[16] The determinants may be extraneous to inherent family processes. Thus, in a case not included in the present sample, the movement of a family from farm to city altered the family's capacity to retain a psychotic young man and precipitated his hospitalization.

[17] See Jackson (ed.), *op. cit.*

whelming attachment. Here, hospitalization is at once a route of escape from intolerable conflict in the interpersonal community, and a potential pathway toward re-establishing the earlier pattern of accommodation. The strategic therapeutic problem posed is the contrasting one of modification of a chronic pattern of intense involvement.

The observations reported do not yield precise knowledge as to how psychiatric intervention might routinely be brought about early in the development of a serious mental illness, whether or when this is advisable, and how intervention might be more effective later on. The observations indicate, rather, that we must confront these questions in their real complexity, and investigate more closely and persistently than heretofore the characteristic ways in which families cope with severe psychiatric disturbances, the ways in which these intra-family mechanisms are disrupted, and the significance of the family dynamics which form the crucial background of the eventual encounter between patient and clinician.

20

REJECTION: A POSSIBLE CONSEQUENCE OF SEEKING HELP FOR MENTAL DISORDERS*

Derek L. Phillips

The nonconformist, whether he be foreigner or "odd ball," intellectual or idiot, genius or jester, individualist or hobo, physically or mentally abnormal—pays a price for "being different" unless his peculiarity is considered acceptable for his particular group, or unless he lives in a place or period of particularly high tolerance or enlightenment.[1]

The penalty that *mentally ill* persons pay for "being different" is often rejection by others in the community. Following the increased interest of social scientists in the public's attitudes toward the mentally ill,[2] this research investigates some of the factors involved in the rejection of mentally ill individuals.

Source: Derek L. Phillips, "Rejection: A Possible Consequence of Seeking Help for Mental Disorders," *American Sociological Review*, **28:** 963–972, 1963.
* This investigation was carried out during the tenure of a Predoctoral Fellowship from the National Institute of Mental Health. The writer wishes to thank C. Richard Fletcher, Phillip S. Hammond, and Elton F. Jackson for their helpful suggestions.
[1] Joint Commission on Mental Illness and Health, *Action for Mental Health*, New York: Science Editions, 1961, p. 69.
[2] See, for example, John A. Clausen and Marian R. Yarrow, "Paths to the Mental Hospital," *The Journal of Social Issues*, **11** (November, 1955), pp. 25–32; Elaine and John Cumming, *Closed Ranks: An Experiment in Mental Health Education.* Cambridge: Harvard University Press, 1957; Bruce P. Dohrenwend, Viola W. Bernard, and Lawrence C. Kolb, "The Orientations of Leaders in an Urban Area Toward Problems of Mental Illness," *The American Journal of Psychiatry*, **118** (February, 1962), pp. 683–691; Howard E. Freeman and Ozzie G. Simmons, "Mental Patients in the Community," *American Sociological Review*, **23** (April, 1958), pp. 147–154; Gerald Gurin, Joseph Veroff, and Sheila Feld, *Americans View Their Mental Health*, New York: Basic Books, 1960; E. Gartly Jaco, *The Social Epidemiology of Mental Disorders*, New York: Russell Sage Foundation, 1960; Paul V. Lemkau and Guido M. Crocetti, "An Urban Population's Opinion

This paper presents the results of a controlled experiment in influencing people's attitudes toward individuals exhibiting symptoms of mental illness. The research attempts to determine the extent to which people's attitudes toward an individual exhibiting disturbed behavior are related to their knowledge of the particular help-source that the individual is using or has used. The term "help-source" here refers to such community resources as clergymen, physicians, psychiatrists, marriage counselors, mental hygiene clinics, alcohol clinics, and mental hospitals, each of which is frequently concerned with persons having emotional problems.

Most studies concerned with attitudes toward the mentally ill have focused on the individual's behavior as the sole factor determining whether or not he is rejected by others. Other research has considered the importance of psychiatric treatment or hospitalization in *identifying* the individual as mentally ill and, subsequently, leading to his rejection.[3] But as far as could be determined, no study has been made of the importance of utilizing other help-sources in determining or influencing public attitudes toward individuals exhibiting disturbed behavior.

In a number of studies respondents have been asked whether they considered various *descriptions* to be those of mentally ill persons, and some respondents were found unable to recognize certain serious symptoms of disturbed behavior. Star, for example, asking 3500 respondents about six case abstracts of mentally ill persons, found that 17 per cent of the sample said that none of these imaginary persons was sufficiently deviant to represent what they meant by mental illness. Another 28 per cent limited their concept of mental illness to the paranoid, the only description where violence was a prominent feature of the behavior.[4] Elaine and John Cumming, asking questions about the same six descriptions of deviant behavior, found that the majority of people dismissed the descriptions, even when they were clinically grave, as normal, with such comments as "It's just a quirk, it's nothing serious."[5]

Sharply in disagreement with these findings, however, are the results of studies by Lemkau and Crocetti, and by Dohrenwend, Bernard and Kolb. Using three of the Star abstracts, Lemkau and Crocetti found that 91 per cent of their sample identified the paranoid as mentally ill, 78 per cent identified the simple schizophrenic, and 62 per cent identified the alcoholic.[6] Dohrenwend and his associates, interviewing "leaders in an urban area," used the six Star abstracts. They report that "all saw mental illness in the description of paranoid schizophrenia; 72 per cent saw it in the example of simple schizophrenia; 63 per cent in the

and Knowledge about Mental Illness," *The American Journal of Psychiatry,* **118** (February, 1962), pp. 692–700; Jum C. Nunnally, Jr., *Popular Conceptions of Mental Health,* New York: Holt, Rinehart and Winston, 1961; Glen V. Ramsey and Melita Seipp, "Public Opinions and Information Concerning Mental Health," *Journal of Clinical Psychology,* **4** (October, 1948), pp. 397–406; Charlotte Green Schwartz, "Perspectives on Deviance—Wives' Definitions of Their Husbands' Mental Illness," *Psychiatry,* **20** (August, 1957), pp. 275–291; Shirley Star, "The Place of Psychiatry in Popular Thinking," paper presented at the meeting of the American Association for Public Opinion Research, Washington, D.C., May, 1957; Julian L. Woodward, "Changing Ideas on Mental Illness and Its Treatment," *American Sociological Review,* **16** (August, 1951), pp. 443–454.

[3] See Clausen and Yarrow, *op. cit.,* and Cumming and Cumming, *op. cit.*

[4] Star, *op. cit.*

[5] Elaine and John Cumming, "Affective Symbolism, Social Norms, and Mental Illness," *Psychiatry,* **19** (February, 1956), pp. 77–85.

[6] Lemkau and Crocetti, *op. cit.,* p. 694.

alcoholic; about 50 per cent in the anxiety neurosis and in the juvenile character disorder; and 40 per cent in the compulsive-phobic."[7] These findings, although somewhat inconsistent, do indicate some public ignorance concerning the signs and symptoms of mental illness. More important here, they tell us nothing about how the public *feels* toward the individuals in these case abstracts.

Hospitalization is another cue that has been found to influence recognition of a person as mentally ill. The Cummings state, "Mental illness, it seems, is a condition which afflicts people who must go to a mental institution, but up until they go almost anything they do is fairly normal."[8]

Apparently some people can correctly identify symptoms of mental illness and others cannot, while for some the mentally ill are only those who have been in a mental hospital. But it seems equally important to ask whether people *reject* individuals displaying symptoms of mental illness or those who have been hospitalized. In part, the task of this research was to determine the extent to which people reject various descriptions of disturbed behavior. An additional cue—the *help-source* that the individual described is utilizing—was presented to the respondents in order to ascertain the importance of the help-source in determining rejection of mentally ill individuals. Four help-sources that people with mental disorders often consult[9]—the clergyman, the physician, the psychiatrist, and the mental hospital—were represented.

Several recent studies have been concerned with the help-sources that people suggest using for mental disorders, as well as the ones they actually have used.[10] Considerable evidence from these studies indicates that people have strong negative attitudes toward psychiatrists and mental hospitals and toward individuals using either of these help-sources.[11] But there seems to be no evidence of negative attitudes toward clergymen or physicians, or toward people consulting these two help-sources. Further, the fact that people with emotional problems are more likely to consult clergymen and physicians than psychiatrists and mental hospitals[12] suggests the absence of strong negative attitudes toward the latter and those utilizing them. Gurin points out that they ". . . are the areas most people turn to with their personal problems; they are the major 'gatekeepers' in the treatment process, either doing the treating themselves or referring to a more specialized professional resource."[13] Both the clergyman and the physician are professionally involved in what are usually defined as "the private affairs" of others. They have, what Naegele calls ". . . legitimate access to realms beyond public discussion."[14]

Although it is probably true that the public does not hold negative attitudes toward clergymen and physicians, I suggest that an individual consulting either of these help-sources may more often lose face, and more often be regarded as

[7] Dohrenwend, Bernard and Kolb, *op. cit.,* p. 685.

[8] Cumming and Cumming, *Closed Ranks, op. cit.,* p. 102.

[9] See, for example, Gurin, *et al., op. cit.*

[10] Dohrenwend, *et al., op. cit.;* Gurin, *et al., op. cit.;* Ramsey and Seipp, *op. cit.;* Woodward, *op. cit.*

[11] Clausen and Yarrow, *op. cit.;* Cumming and Cumming, *op cit.;* Frederick C. Redlich, "What the Citizen Knows About Psychiatry," *Mental Hygiene,* **34** (January, 1950), pp. 64–70; Star, *op. cit.*

[12] Gurin, *et al., op. cit.,* p. 307.

[13] *Ibid.,* p. 400.

[14] Kasper D. Naegele, "Clergymen, Teachers, and Psychiatrists: A Study in Roles and Socialization," *The Canadian Journal of Economic and Political Science,* **22** (February, 1956), p. 48.

deviant, than an individual exhibiting the same behavior who does not consult one of these professional resources. How does this come to be so?

As Clausen and Yarrow point out, "There is an ethic of being able to handle one's own problems by oneself, which applies not only to psychiatric problems."[15] Similarly, Ewalt says, "One value in American culture compatible with most approaches to a definition of positive mental health appears to be this: An individual should be able to stand on his own two feet without making undue demands or impositions on others."[16] In another statement of this view, Kadushin reports that, in answer to the question "Would you tell people in general that you came here?" (the Peale-Blanton Religio-Psychiatric Clinic), a respondent replied ". . . I wouldn't tell people in general. I know that there's still a stigma attached to people who seek psychiatric aid, and I guess I'm ashamed that I couldn't manage my own problem."[17]

Thus, an outside observer's knowledge that a person is consulting any of the four help-sources discussed may have at least two important consequences for the individual with a behavior problem: (1) He is defined as someone who *has* a problem. Moreover, the further along the continuum from clergyman to mental hospital the individual moves, the more his problem is seen as a serious one, and individuals consulting a psychiatrist or a mental hospital are very often defined as "mentally ill" or "insane." (2) The individual is defined as unable to handle his problem by himself.

I am suggesting that the reported inability of some persons to recognize certain serious symptoms of disturbed behavior is due to difficulty in evaluating an individual's behavior, and that knowledge about what help-source the individual is utilizing helps others decide whether he is "deviant" or has a problem that he cannot cope with himself. And an important social consequence for the person who, because of his behavior or choice of help-source, is defined as deviant may be *rejection*.

These considerations led to formulation of the following hypothesis: Individuals exhibiting identical behavior will be increasingly rejected as they are described as not seeking any help, as utilizing a clergyman, a physician, a psychiatrist, or a mental hospital.

METHOD

To test this hypothesis, interviews were conducted with a systematic sample[18] of 300 married white females selected from the address section of the City Di-

[15] Clausen and Yarrow, *op. cit.*, p. 63.

[16] Jack K. Ewalt, intro., Marie Jahoda, *Current Concepts of Positive Mental Health*, New York: Basic Books, 1958, p. xi.

[17] Charles Kadushin, "Individual Decisions to Undertake Psychotherapy," *Administrative Science Quarterly*, 3 (December, 1958), p. 389.

Gurin, *et al.*, report that 25 per cent of their respondents who had problems but did not utilize help tried to solve the problems by themselves, *op. cit.*, pp. 350–351.

[18] The sample was drawn from the address section of the Directory, with every 15th address marked for interview. The first address was drawn randomly from the first 15 entries; thereafter every 15th address was included until the total sample of 300 was obtained.

rectory of Branford, a southern New England town of approximately 17,000 population.[19] The sample was so small that the need to control for a number of variables was obvious. Thus, males,[20] non-whites, and unmarried respondents were excluded from the sample.

The interviews took place in the respondents' homes and were of 20 to 40 minutes duration. Each respondent was given five cards, one at a time, describing different behaviors. The interviewer read each description aloud from the interview schedule as the respondent followed by reading the card.

Case abstract (A) was a description of a paranoid schizophrenic, (B) an individual suffering from simple schizophrenia, (C) an anxious-depressed person, (D) a phobic individual with compulsive features, and (E) a "normal" person. The first four abstracts were, in the main, the same as those developed by Shirley Star, formerly of the National Opinion Research Center in Chicago.[21] The fifth abstract, that of the "normal"[22] individual, was developed expressly for this research.[23]

The five case abstracts were presented in combination with information about what help-source an individual was utilizing, in the following manner:

1   Nothing was added to the description of the behavior—this was, of course, the absence of any help.
2   Affixed to the description was the statement: "He has been going to see his clergyman regularly about the way he is getting along."
3   Affixed to the description was the statement: "He has been going to see his physician regularly about the way he is getting along."
4   Affixed to the description was the statement: "He has been going to see his psychiatrist regularly about the way he is getting along."
5   Affixed to the description was the statement: "He has been in a mental hospital because of the way he was getting along."

This research required an experimental design permitting classification of each

---

[19] Twenty-eight of the households drawn in the original sample refused to be interviewed. In each of these cases, a substitution was made by selecting an address at random from the same street. Four of these substitutes refused to be interviewed, necessitating further substitution. Also requiring substitution were three addresses that could not be located and six wives of household heads who were divorced, separated, or widowed, rather than married. Selecting substitutes from the same neighborhood was done on the assumption that persons living in the same neighborhood would resemble one another in certain important ways; they were more likely, than people living in different neighborhoods, to be of similar socio-economic status. Although the possibility of bias still exists, so few substitutions were necessary that, hopefully, the effect is minimal.
[20] In a pre-test with a sample of 32 women and 28 men, no significant differences were found between the rejection rates of men and women.
[21] Star, op. cit.
[22] The normal person was described as follows:
    Here is a description of a man. Imagine that he is a respectable person living in your neighborhood. He is happy and cheerful, has a good enough job and is fairly well satisfied with it. He is always busy and has quite a few friends who think he is easy to get along with most of the time. Within the next few months he plans to marry a nice young woman he is engaged to.
[23] My purpose was to determine (a) whether the rejection of the mentally ill descriptions might in part be accounted for by individuals who rejected everyone regardless of behavior; and (b) whether the utilization of a help-source alone could influence rejection, or whether it was the "combination" of deviant behavior and the use of a help-source that led to rejection.

of the two independent variables (behavior and help-source) in five categories.[24] Observations for all possible combinations of the values of the two variables would have been desirable, but this clearly was not feasible. Hence the observations were arranged in the form of a Graeco-Latin Square[25] so as to obtain a large amount of information from a relatively small number of observations. Specifically, this type of design enables us to discover: (a) the influence of different types of behavior in determining rejection, and (b) the influence of different help-sources in determining rejection.

The 300 respondents were divided at random into five groups of 60 individuals each. Every individual in each group saw five combinations of behavior and help-source, but no group or individual saw any given behavior or any given help-source more than once. In order to assure that the rejection rates were not affected by the *order* in which individuals saw the combinations, the experiment was designed so that each behavior and each help-source was seen first by one group, second by another, third by another, fourth by another, and last by the remaining group.[26]

Thus, in the Graeco-Latin Square design, three variables were considered (behavior, help-source, and order). The data were classified in five categories on each of these variables. See Figure 1, where the letters in each cell indicate a description of behavior, and the numbers in each cell indicate the help-source utilized. In the top left-hand cell, for example, the letter A indicates that the paranoid schizophrenic was the description seen first by Group 1, and that he was described as seeing help-source 1 (that is, he was not described as seeking any help). Similarly, in the bottom right-hand cell, the letter D indicates that the phobic-compulsive person was the abstract seen fifth by Group 5, and that he was described as consulting help-source 3 (a physician).

After reading each combination of behavior and help-source, the respondents were asked a uniform series of questions. These questions made up a social distance scale, indicating how close a relation the respondent was willing to tolerate with the individuals in the case abstracts. This scale was used as the measure of *rejection,* the dependent variable in the research.

The social distance scale consisted of the following items: (1) "Would you discourage your children from marrying someone like this?" (2) "If you had a

[24] The advantages of including tests of different combinations of two or more variables within one experiment have been cited by several writers concerned with experimental design. For example, D. J. Finney, *The Theory of Experimental Design,* Chicago: The University of Chicago Press, 1960, p. 68, notes the following advantages: "(1) To broaden the basis of inferences relating to one factor by testing that factor under various conditions of others; (2) To assess the extent to which the effects of one factor are modified by the level of others; (3) To economize in experimental material by obtaining information on several factors without increasing the size of the experiment beyond what would be required for one or two factors alone."

[25] For two excellent explanations of the Graeco-Latin Square design see, Finney, *op. cit.,* and E. F. Lindquist, *Design of Experiments in Psychology and Education,* Boston: Houghton Mifflin, 1953.

[26] In addition, to 50 per cent of the respondents, the paranoid, the depressed individual, and the "normal" person were presented as males, with the simple schizophrenic and the phobic-compulsive individual presented as females. The other half of the sample saw a reversed order—the simple schizophrenic and the compulsive individuals as males, and the paranoid, depressed, and "normal" persons as females. Since both the male case abstracts and the female case abstracts were rejected in accordance with the pattern shown in Table 1, they will not be discussed further in this paper. The findings for the *differences* in the *absolute* rejection of males and females exhibiting a given behavior and utilizing the same help-source will be the subject of a forthcoming paper.

Figure 1
The Graeco-Latin square design[a]

	Order				
	1	**2**	**3**	**4**	**5**
Group 1	A1	B2	C3	D4	E5
Group 2	B3	C4	D5	E1	A2
Group 3	C5	D1	E2	A3	B4
Group 4	D2	E3	A4	B5	C1
Group 5	E4	A5	B1	C2	D3

[a] *N* for each cell in the table is 60.

room to rent in your home, would you be willing to rent it to someone like this?" (3) "Would you be willing to work on a job with someone like this?" (4) "Would you be willing to have someone like this join a favorite club or organization of yours?" (5) "Would you object to having a person like this as a neighbor?"[27]

The range of possible scores for each combination of help-source and behavior was from zero (when no items indicated rejection) through five (when all items indicated rejection). A test of reproducibility was applied and the resulting co-efficient was .97, indicating that the scale met acceptable standards; i.e., was a unidimensional scale.

It should be emphasized that each combination of behavior and help-source was seen by 60 respondents. It also bears repeating that each respondent was presented with five combinations of behavior and help-source. Thus, each re-spondent contributed a rejection score (on the social distance scale) to each of five cells out of the 25 cells in Figure 1. An analysis of variance of the form gen-erally applied to planned experiments was carried out.[28]

RESULTS AND DISCUSSION

Table 1 presents the mean rejection rate for each combination of behavior and help-source. An individual exhibiting a given type of behavior is increasingly re-jected as he is described as seeking no help, as seeing a clergyman, as seeing a physician, as seeing a psychiatrist, or as having been in a mental hospital. The relation between the independent variable (help-source) and the dependent variable (rejection) is statistically significant at the .001 level. Futhermore, the reversal in the "paranoid schizophrenic" row is the only one among 25 combi-nations.[29]

The relation between the other independent variable (behavior) and rejection

[27] The above order duplicates the order of "closeness" represented by the scale. The items, however, were administered to each respondent in a random fashion.
[28] See, for example, Lindquist, *op. cit.*, chs. 12 and 13.
[29] Following Lindquist, neither orders nor interaction was found to be statistically significant at the .20 level. See Lindquist, *op. cit.*, pp. 273–281.

Table 1
Rejection scores[a] for each help-source and behavior combination[b]

Behavior	Help-source utilized					
	No help	Clergy-man	Physi-cian	Psychia-trist	Mental hospital	Total
Paranoid schizophrenic	3.65	3.33	3.77	4.12	4.33	3.84
Simple schizophrenic	1.10	1.57	1.83	2.85	3.68	2.21
Depressed-neurotic	1.45	1.62	2.07	2.70	3.28	2.22
Phobic-compulsive	.53	1.12	1.18	1.87	2.27	1.39
Normal individual	.02	.22	.50	1.25	1.63	.72
Total	1.35	1.57	1.87	2.56	3.04	—

$F = 23.53, p < .001$
[a] Rejection scores are represented by the mean number of items rejected on the Social Distance Scale.
[b] N for each cell in the table is 60.

is also significant at the .001 level. In fact, the F obtained for the relation between behavior and rejection ($F=64.52$) is much higher than the F obtained for the relation between help-source and rejection ($F=23.53$). In other words, when a respondent was confronted with a case abstract containing both a description of their individual's behavior and information about what help-source he was utilizing, the description of behavior played a greater part (i.e., accounted for more variance) than the help-source in determining how strongly she rejected the individual described.

As was indicated earlier, the main purpose of this presentation is to show the extent to which attitudes toward an individual exhibiting symptoms of mental illness are related to knowledge of the particular help-source that he is utilizing. The importance of the type of behavior is of secondary interest here; I have investigated the relation between behavior and rejection mainly to ascertain the *relative* importance of each of the two elements presented in the case abstracts. The relation between behavior and rejection will be fully treated in a future paper.

The totals at the bottom of Table 1 show that the largest increase in the rejection rates occurs when an individual sees a psychiatrist. That is, the rejection rate for individuals described as consulting a physician (1.87) differs from the rejection rate for individuals described as consulting a psychiatrist (2.56) to a degree greater than for any other comparison between two adjacent help-sources. The second largest over-all increase in rejection occurs when the individual is described as having been in a mental hospital, and the smallest net increase (.20) occurs when the individual sees a clergyman, compared to seeking no help at all.

Probably the most significant aspect of the effect of help-source on rejection rates is that, for four of the five case abstracts, the biggest increase in rejection occurs when the individual is described as consulting a psychiatrist, and in three of the five abstracts the second largest increase occurs when the individual is depicted as having been in a mental hospital. Not only are individuals increasingly rejected as they are described as seeking no help, as seeing a clergyman, a physician, a psychiatrist, or a mental hospital, but they are *disproportionately* rejected when described as utilizing the latter two help-sources. This supports the suggestion made earlier that individuals utilizing psychiatrists and mental hospitals may be rejected not only because they have a health problem, and because they are unable to handle the problem themselves, but also because contact with a psychiatrist or a mental hospital defines them as "mentally ill" or "insane."

Despite the fact that the "normal" person is more an "ideal type" than a normal person, when he is described as having been in a mental hospital he is rejected more than a psychotic individual described as not seeking help or as seeing a clergyman, and more than a depressed-neurotic seeing a clergyman. Even when the normal person is described as seeing a psychiatrist, he is rejected more than a simple schizophrenic who seeks no help, more than a phobic-compulsive individual seeking no help or seeing a clergyman or physician.

As was noted previously, there is one reversal in Table 1. The paranoid schizophrenic, unlike the other descriptions, was rejected more strongly when he was described as not utilizing any help-source than when he was described as utilizing a clergyman. The paranoid was described in the case abstract as suspicious, as picking fights with people who did not even know him, and as cursing his wife. His behavior may be so threatening and so obviously deviates from normal behavior, that the respondents feel that he is socially less objectionable when he takes a step to help himself. In other words, the individual *obviously* in need of professional help is in a sense "rewarded" for seeking at least one kind of help, that of the clergyman. And though the paranoid schizophrenic is increasingly rejected when he is described as utilizing a physician, a psychiatrist, and a mental hospital, the relative amount of increase is much less than for the other four case abstracts.

Mentally ill persons whose behavior does not deviate markedly from normal role-expectations may be assigned responsibility for their own behavior. If so, seeking any professional help is an admission of inability to meet this responsibility. An individual whose behavior is markedly abnormal (in this instance, the paranoid schizophrenic) may not, however, be considered responsible for his behavior or for his recovery, and is, therefore, rejected less than other individuals when he seeks professional help.

CONTROLS

To determine whether the findings were spurious, the relation between help-source and rejection was observed under several different controls. The association was maintained within age groups, within religious affiliation groups, within educational attainment groups, and within groups occupying different positions

Table 2
Rejection scores[a] for all cases by help-source and acquaintance with help-seekers

Help-source utilized	Acquaintance		
	Relative (N = 37)	Friend (N = 73)	No one (N = 190)
No help-source	2.35	1.45	1.12
Clergyman	2.06	1.45	1.51
Physician	1.30	1.58	2.09
Psychiatrist	2.08	2.53	2.66
Mental hospital	2.38	2.82	3.25

[a] Rejection scores are represented by the mean number of items rejected on the Social Distance Scale.

in the status hierarchy.[30] The association was also maintained within groups differing in authoritarianism.[31]

But when (1) experience with someone who had sought help for emotional problems[32] and (2) attitude toward the norm of self-reliance,[33] were controlled, the relation between help-source and rejection was specified.

Table 2 presents the rejection rates for respondents reporting a relative who sought help, those reporting a friend who sought help, and those who knew no one who sought help for emotional problems. For ease of presentation and interpretation, the rejection rates for the five case abstracts have been combined.[34]

There are two points of interest in Table 2. One is the difference in rejection rates *among* the three groups of respondents. But because these interesting differences are peripheral to the central concern here, I will focus, instead, on the second point of interest. This is the consistent increase—*within* two of the three groups of respondents—in rejection scores for persons not seeking any help, utilizing a clergyman, a physician, a psychiatrist, or a mental hospital.

Respondents *not* acquainted with a help-seeker as well as those acquainted with a help-seeking *friend* adhere to the pattern of rejection previously demonstrated in Table 1. But respondents with a help-seeking *relative* deviate markedly from this pattern. They reject persons not seeking help more than they do persons consulting a clergyman, physician, or psychiatrist, and almost as much as those utilizing a mental hospital. And they reject persons consulting a clergyman more than those consulting a physician.

[30] For details of the classification procedures, see pp. 82–88 of the author's doctoral dissertation, of which this research is a part: "Help-Sources and Rejection of the Mentally Ill," unpublished Ph.D. Dissertation, Yale University, 1962.

[31] For details of the authoritarian scale, see *ibid.*, p. 77.

[32] The question was: "We've been talking about people with worries and problems. Have any of your close friends or relatives had any psychiatric treatment or gone to a hospital or professional person, or community agency, regarding emotional problems?" If the respondent answered in the affirmative, she was asked who this person was.

[33] Attitude toward self-reliance was measured by the respondent's reaction to the following statement: "People should be expected to handle their own problems," with a choice of four responses—strongly agree, agree somewhat, disagree somewhat, and strongly disagree.

[34] Because our primary interest is in the effect of help-source rather than behavior, rejection rates will hereafter be presented in combined form only.

Table 3
Rejection scores[a] for all mentally ill cases by help-source
and acquaintance with help-seekers

Help-source utilized	Acquaintance		
	Relative (N = 37)	Friend (N = 73)	No one (N = 190)
No help-source	2.81	1.64	1.16
Clergyman	2.20	1.65	1.86
Physician	1.51	1.91	2.46
Psychiatrist	2.45	2.88	2.90
Mental hospital	3.04	3.14	3.51

[a] Rejection scores are represented by the mean number of items rejected on the Social Distance Scale.

Perhaps respondents with help-seeking relatives are more able to recognize the behavior in the abstracts as that of persons who *need* help and therefore they reject them strongly when they do not seek help. A similar explanation may apply to the rejection of persons using a clergyman. That is, these respondents may see the clergyman as not being what Parsons calls "technically competent help"[35] and equate seeing him with not seeking help. The comparatively low rejection of persons consulting a physician may reflect the respondents' belief that a physician is one of the professional resources that one *should* utilize for emotional problems, and that a physician brings the least stigma to the user; whereas the psychiatrist and the mental hospital, though both competent resources, tend to stigmatize the user much more.[36]

The reader will recall that one of the case abstracts presented to the respondents was that of a "normal" individual. Since respondents with a help-seeking relative may reject the non-help-seeking cases because they are recognized as needing help, including the description of the normal person may "distort" the findings. The rejection rates for the four mentally ill abstracts have, therefore, been separated from those for the normal person and presented in Table 3. Inspection of this table reveals the same pattern found in Table 2, except that the rejection rate for persons utilizing each help-source is somewhat higher than in Table 2.[37]

Turning now to the relation between adherence to the norm of self-reliance and rejection of persons described as using the various help-sources, the data in Table 4 indicate that the association between help-source and rejection is maintained even among those who do not strongly adhere to the norm of self-

[35] Talcott Parsons, *The Social System*, Glencoe, Ill.: The Free Press, 1950, p. 437. Parsons states that ". . . the fourth closely related element [in the sick role] is the obligation—in proportion to the severity of the condition, of course—to seek *technically competent* help, namely in the most usual case, that of a physician and to *cooperate* with him in the process of trying to get well." He makes this point again in "Definitions of Health and Illness in the Light of American Values and Social Structure," in E. Gartly Jaco (ed.), *Patients, Physicians and Illness*, Glencoe, Ill.: The Free Press, 1958, pp. 165–187.

[36] We might expect those with help-seeking friends to reject in the same pattern as those with help-seeking relatives. Although both groups of respondents have had experience with someone who sought help, those whose experience was with friends probably were not so involved in the other's welfare and therefore had less intimate a knowledge of the help-sources people consult for emotional problems.

[37] This is not surprising in light of the generally low rejection of the "normal" person.

Table 4
Rejection scores[a] for all cases by help-source and adherence to the norm of self-reliance

Help-source utilized	Adherence to norm of self-reliance		
	Disagree (N = 28)	Agree somewhat (N = 128)	Agree strongly (N = 144)
No help-source	1.79	1.39	1.22
Clergyman	1.68	1.56	1.52
Physician	1.67	1.87	2.00
Psychiatrist	2.43	2.52	2.65
Mental hospital	2.64	3.09	3.23

a Rejection scores are represented by the mean number of items rejected on the Social Distance Scale.

reliance.[38] Among respondents agreeing either strongly or somewhat to the norm of self-reliance there is a consistent increase in rejection of persons as they moved from no help to the mental hospital. Respondents *not* adhering to the norm of self-reliance, however, reject persons not seeking help more than they do persons seeing a clergyman or a physician.[39]

This pattern is similar to the one followed by respondents who had help-seeking relatives (see Table 2),[40] and the same general interpretation may be appropriate. Respondents who do not agree that people should handle their own problems may view people seeing a clergyman as "handling their own problems." If this is true, then those not adhering to the norm of self-reliance would be expected to reject persons who see a clergyman, as well as those who seek no help.

Thus, for the great majority of respondents, who either (1) have not had experience with a relative who sought help for emotional problems, or (2) adhere to the norm of self-reliance, help-source and rejection are strongly associated.[41]

On the other hand, respondents who have had experience with a help-seeking relative deviate quite sharply from the rejection pattern of the majority, as do those who do not adhere to the norm of self-reliance. Nevertheless, this deviant pattern appears to make sense theoretically. Those acquainted with a help-seeking relative, having had more exposure to sick-role prescriptions, may be highly rejecting of persons not seeking help because they feel that people should seek "technically competent help." Respondents not adhering to the norm of self-reliance may reject non-help-seekers for a similar reason. They too may feel

38 Only 9 per cent disagreed (either somewhat or strongly) with the statement about people handling their own problems. This finding lends support to the proposition that people in our society are expected to handle their own problems.
39 Again we ignore differences *among* the various groups of respondents. Our primary interest is in determining whether the relation between help-source and rejection is maintained *within* each group.
40 It should be recalled that the latter respondents also rejected persons not seeking help more than persons seeing a psychiatrist; the findings with respect to experience with a help-seeking relative and nonadherence to the norm of self-reliance are not entirely similar.
41 It would have been desirable to control for experience and attitude toward self-reliance simultaneously, but there were too few (13) respondents who reported experience with a help-seeking relative *and* did not adhere to the norm of self-reliance.

that handling one's own problems is inappropriate, and that people should seek competent help. And, as suggested previously, both groups may equate help from a clergyman with no help at all.[42]

CONCLUSIONS AND IMPLICATIONS

On the basis of these findings from a southern New England town, the source of help sought by mentally disturbed individuals appears to be strongly related to the degree to which others in the community reject them. Individuals are increasingly rejected as they are described as utilizing no help, as utilizing a clergyman, a physician, a psychiatrist, or a mental hospital.

Controls for age, religion, education, social class, and authoritarianism failed to diminish the relationship, but controls for experience with an emotionally disturbed help-seeker and for adherence to the norm of self-reliance tended to specify it. Respondents who had had experience with a help-seeking relative deviated markedly from the pattern followed by the rest of the sample, as did respondents not adhering to the norm of self-reliance. Both of these groups rejected people seeking no help more than they did those consulting a clergyman or a physician, and respondents with help-seeking relatives also reject non-help-seekers more than those consulting a psychiatrist. Both groups rejected persons seeing a clergyman more than those seeing a physician.

The evidence presented here suggests that a mentally ill person who seeks help may be rejected by others in the community. The findings also have implications for what Mechanic and Volkart call "the inclination to adopt the sick role."[43] We can easily imagine an individual who, because he fears the stigma attached to the help-seeker, does not utilize a professional resource for his problems. Avoiding the possibility of rejection, he also denies himself technically competent help.[44]

Thus the utilization of certain help-sources involves not only a *reward* (positive mental health), but also a *cost* (rejection by others and, consequently, a negative self-image);[45] we need to assess the net balance of gains and losses resulting from seeking help for problems of disturbed behavior.

The present analysis has been concerned with the rejection of help-seekers in hypothetical situations. Future research should be designed so that it would be possible to examine the rejection of help-seekers in "real" situations. Hopefully, the present research will provide some understanding and raise significant questions about the consequences of seeking help for problems of disturbed behavior in our society.

---

[42] The small number of respondents with a help-seeking relative (37), and the small number not adhering to the norm of self-reliance (28), make these findings, as well as their interpretation, highly tentative.

[43] David Mechanic and Edmund A. Volkart, "Stress, Illness, and the Sick Role," *American Sociological Review,* 26 (February, 1961), pp. 51–58.

[44] Jaco, *op. cit.,* points out that "If mental disease carries a stigma in a particular community, it is likely that many families will use extreme measures to conceal the fact that a member is mentally ill; even to the extent of preventing him from obtaining psychiatric treatment in that area." (p. 18)

[45] For an interesting presentation of cost and reward, see George C. Homans, *Social Behavior: Its Elementary Forms,* New York: Harcourt, Brace & World, 1961, ch. 5.

21
THE MORAL CAREER OF THE MENTAL PATIENT
Erving Goffman

THE PREPATIENT PHASE

A relatively small group of prepatients come into the mental hospital willingly, because of their own idea of what will be good for them, or because of whole-hearted agreement with the relevant members of their family. Presumably these recruits have found themselves acting in a way which is evidence to them that they are losing their minds or losing control of themselves. This view of oneself would seem to be one of the most pervasively threatening things that can happen to the self in our society, especially since it is likely to occur at a time when the person is in any case sufficiently troubled to exhibit the kind of symptom which he himself can see. As Sullivan described it,

What we discover in the self-system of a person undergoing schizophrenic changes or schizophrenic processes, is then, in its simplest form, an extremely fear-marked puzzlement, consisting of the use of rather generalized and anything but exquisitely refined referential processes in an attempt to cope with what is essentially a failure at being human—a failure at being anything that one could respect as worth being.[1]

Coupled with the person's disintegrative re-evaluation of himself will be the new, almost equally pervasive circumstance of attempting to conceal from others what he takes to be the new fundamental facts about himself, and attempting to discover whether others too have discovered them.[2] Here I want to stress that perception of losing one's mind is based on culturally derived and socially engrained stereotypes as to the significance of symptoms such as hearing voices, losing temporal and spatial orientation, and sensing that one is being followed, and that many of the most spectacular and convincing of these symptoms in some instances psychiatrically signify merely a temporary emotional upset in a stressful situation, however terrifying to the person at the time. Similarly, the anxiety consequent upon this perception of oneself, and the strategies devised to reduce this anxiety, are not a product of abnormal psychology, but would be exhibited by any person socialized into our culture who came to conceive of himself as someone losing his mind. Interestingly, subcultures in American society apparently differ in the amount of ready imagery and encouragement they

Source: Erving Goffman, "The Moral Career of the Mental Patient," Psychiatry, 22: 125–131, 1959 (excerpt).
[1] Harry Stack Sullivan, Clinical Studies in Psychiatry; edited by Helen Swick Perry, Mary Ladd Gawel, and Martha Gibbon; New York, Norton, 1956; pp. 184–185.
[2] This moral experience can be contrasted with that of a person learning to become a marihuana addict, whose discovery that he can be 'high' and still 'op' effectively without being detected apparently leads to a new level of use. See Howard S. Becker, "Marihuana Use and Social Control," Social Problems (1955) 3: 35–44; see especially pp. 40–41.

supply for such self-views, leading to differential rates of *self*-referral; the capacity to take this disintegrative view of oneself without psychiatric prompting seems to be one of the questionable cultural privileges of the upper classes.[3]

For the person who has come to see himself—with whatever justification—as mentally unbalanced, entrance to the mental hospital can sometimes bring relief, perhaps in part because of the sudden transformation in the structure of his basic social situations; instead of being to himself a questionable person trying to maintain a role as a full one, he can become an officially questioned person known to himself to be not so questionable as that. In other cases, hospitalization can make matters worse for the willing patient, confirming by the objective situation what has theretofore been a matter of the private experience of self.

Once the willing prepatient enters the hospital, he may go through the same routine of experiences as do those who enter unwillingly. In any case, it is the latter that I mainly want to consider, since in America at present these are by far the more numerous kind.[4] Their approach to the institution takes one of three classic forms: they come because they have been implored by their family or threatened with the abrogation of family ties unless they go "willingly"; they come by force under police escort; they come under misapprehension purposely induced by others, this last restricted mainly to youthful prepatients.

The prepatient's career may be seen in terms of an extrusory model; he starts out with relationships and rights, and ends up, at the beginning of his hospital stay, with hardly any of either. The moral aspects of this career, then, typically begin with the experience of abandonment, disloyalty, and embitterment. This is the case even though to others it may be obvious that he was in need of treatment, and even though in the hospital he may soon come to agree.

The case histories of most mental patients document offense against some arrangement for face-to-face living—a domestic establishment, a work place, a semipublic organization such as a church or store, a public region such as a street or park. Often there is also a record of some *complainant,* some figure who takes that action against the offender which eventually leads to his hospitalization. This may not be the person who makes the first move, but it is the person who makes what turns out to be the first effective move. Here is the *social* beginning of the patient's career, regardless of where one might locate the psychological beginning of his mental illness.

The kinds of offenses which lead to hospitalization are felt to differ in nature from those which lead to other extrusory consequences—to imprisonment, divorce, loss of job, disownment, regional exile, noninstitutional psychiatric treatment, and so forth. But little seems known about these differentiating factors; and when one studies actual commitments, alternate outcomes frequently appear to have been possible. It seems true, moreover, that for every offense that leads

---

[3] August B. Hollingshead and Frederick C. Redlich, *Social Class and Mental Illness;* New York, Wiley, 1958; p. 187, Table 6, where relative frequency is given of self-referral by social class grouping.
[4] The distinction employed here between willing and unwilling patients cuts across the legal one, of voluntary and committed, since some persons who are glad to come to the mental hospital may be legally committed, and of those who come only because of strong familial pressure, some may sign themselves in as voluntary patients.

to an effective complaint, there are many psychiatrically similar ones that never do. No action is taken; or action is taken which leads to other extrusory outcomes; or ineffective action is taken, leading to the mere pacifying or putting off of the person who complains. Thus, as Clausen and Yarrow have nicely shown, even offenders who are eventually hospitalized are likely to have had a long series of ineffective actions taken against them.[5]

Separating those offenses which could have been used as grounds for hospitalizing the offender from those that are so used, one finds a vast number of what students of occupation call career contingencies.[6] Some of these contingencies in the mental patient's career have been suggested, if not explored, such as socio-economic status, visibility of the offense, proximity to a mental hospital, amount of treatment facilities available, community regard for the type of treatment given in available hospitals, and so on.[7] For information about other contingencies one must rely on atrocity tales: a psychotic man is tolerated by his wife until she finds herself a boy friend, or by his adult children until they move from a house to an apartment; an alcoholic is sent to a mental hospital because the jail is full, and a drug addict because he declines to avail himself of psychiatric treatment on the outside; a rebellious adolescent daughter can no longer be managed at home because she now threatens to have an open affair with an unsuitable companion; and so on. Correspondingly there is an equally important set of contingencies causing the person to by-pass this fate. And should the person enter the hospital, still another set of contingencies will help determine when he is to obtain a discharge—such as the desire of his family for his return, the availability of a "manageable" job, and so on. The society's official view is that inmates of mental hospitals are there primarily because they are suffering from mental illness. However, in the degree that the "mentally ill" outside hospitals numerically approach or surpass those inside hospitals, one could say that mental patients *distinctively* suffer not from mental illness, but from contingencies.

Career contingencies occur in conjunction with a second feature of the prepatient's career—the *circuit of agents*—and agencies—that participate fatefully in his passage from civilian to patient status.[8] Here is an instance of that increasingly important class of social system whose elements are agents and agencies, which are brought into systemic connection through having to take up and send on the same persons. Some of these agent-roles will be cited now, with the understanding that in any concrete circuit a role may be filled more than once, and a single person may fill more than one of them.

First is the *next-of-relation*—the person whom the prepatient sees as the most

---

[5] John A. Clausen and Marion Radke Yarrow, "Paths to the Mental Hospital," *J. Social Issues* (1955) **11:** 25–32.

[6] An explicit application of this notion to the field of mental health may be found in Edwin M. Lemert, "Legal Commitment and Social Control," *Sociology and Social Research* (1946) **30:** 370–378.

[7] For example, Jerome K. Myers and Leslie Schaffer, "Social Stratification and Psychiatric Practice: A Study of an Outpatient Clinic," *Amer. Sociological Rev.* (1954) **19:** 307–310. Lemert, see footnote 5; pp. 402–403. *Patients in Mental Institutions, 1941;* Washington, D.C., Department of Commerce, Bureau of the Census, 1941; p. 2.

[8] For one circuit of agents and its bearing on career contingencies, see Oswald Hall, "The Stages of a Medical Career," *Amer. J. Sociology* (1948) **53:** 227–336.

available of those upon whom he should be able to most depend in times of trouble; in this instance the last to doubt his sanity and the first to have done everything to save him from the fate which, it transpires, he has been approaching. The patient's next-of-relation is usually his next of kin; the special term is introduced because he need not be. Second is the *complainant,* the person who retrospectively appears to have started the person on his way to the hospital. Third are the *mediators*—the sequence of agents and agencies to which the prepatient is referred and through which he is relayed and processed on his way to the hospital. Here are included police, clergy, general medical practitioners, office psychiatrists, personnel in public clinics, lawyers, social service workers, school teachers, and so on. One of these agents will have the legal mandate to sanction commitment and will exercise it, and so those agents who precede him in the process will be involved in something whose outcome is not yet settled. When the mediators retire from the scene, the prepatient has become an inpatient, and the significant agent has become the hospital administrator.

While the complainant usually takes action in a lay capacity as a citizen, an employer, a neighbor, or a kinsman, mediators tend to be specialists and differ from those they serve in significant ways. They have experience in handling trouble, and some professional distance from what they handle. Except in the case of policemen, and perhaps some clergy, they tend to be more psychiatrically oriented than the lay public, and will see the need for treatment at times when the public does not.[9]

An interesting feature of these roles is the functional effects of their interdigitation. For example, the feelings of the patient will be influenced by whether or not the person who fills the role of complainant also has the role of next-of-relation—an embarrassing combination more prevalent, apparently, in the higher classes than in the lower.[10] Some of these emergent effects will be considered now.[11]

In the prepatient's progress from home to the hospital he may participate as a third person in what he may come to experience as a kind of *alienative coalition.* His next-of-relation presses him into coming to "talk things over" with a medical practitioner, an office psychiatrist, or some other counselor. Disinclination on his part may be met by threatening him with desertion, disownment, or other legal action, or by stressing the joint and explorative nature of the interview. But typically the next-of-relation will have set the interview up, in the sense of selecting the professional, arranging for time, telling the professional something about the case, and so on. This move effectively tends to establish the next-of-relation as the responsible person to whom pertinent findings can be divulged, while effectively establishing the other as the patient. The prepatient often goes

[9] Elaine and John Cumming, *Closed Ranks;* Cambridge, Commonwealth Fund, Harvard University Press, 1957; p. 92.

[10] Hollingshead and Redlich, footnote 3, p. 187.

[11] For an analysis of some of these circuit implications for the inpatient, see Leila C. Deasy and Olive W. Quinn, "The Wife of the Mental Patient and the Hospital Psychiatrist," *J. Social Issues* (1955) **11:** 49–60. An interesting illustration of this kind of analysis may also be found in Alan G. Gowman, "Blindness and the Role of Companion," *Social Problems* (1956) **4:** 68–75. A general statement may be found in Robert Merton, "The Role Set: Problems in Sociological Theory," *British J. Sociology* (1957) **8:** 106–120.

to the interview with the understanding that he is going as an equal of someone who is so bound together with him that a third person could not come between them in fundamental matters; this, after all, is one way in which close relationships are defined in our society. Upon arrival at the office the prepatient suddenly finds that he and his next-of-relation have not been accorded the same roles, and apparently that a prior understanding between the professional and the next-of-relation has been put in operation against him. In the extreme but common case the professional first sees the prepatient alone, in the role of examiner and diagnostician, and then sees the next-of-relation alone, in the role of advisor, while carefully avoiding talking things over seriously with them both together.[12] And even in those nonconsultative cases where public officials must forcibly extract a person from a family that wants to tolerate him, the next-of-relation is likely to be induced to "go along" with the official action, so that even here the prepatient may feel that an alienative coalition has been formed against him.

The moral experience of being third man in such a coalition is likely to embitter the prepatient, especially since his troubles have already probably led to some estrangement from his next-of-relation. After he enters the hospital, continued visits by his next-of-relation can give the patient the "insight" that his own best interests were being served. But the initial visits may temporarily strengthen his feeling of abandonment; he is likely to beg his visitor to get him out or at least to get him more privileges and to sympathize with the monstrousness of his plight—to which the visitor ordinarily can respond only by trying to maintain a hopeful note, by not "hearing" the requests, or by assuring the patient that the medical authorities know about these things and are doing what is medically best. The visitor then nonchalantly goes back into a world that the patient has learned is incredibly thick with freedom and privileges, causing the patient to feel that his next-of-relation is merely adding a pious gloss to a clear case of traitorous desertion.

The depth to which the patient may feel betrayed by his next-of-relation seems to be increased by the fact that another witnesses his betrayal—a factor which is apparently significant in many three-party situations. An offended person may well act forbearantly and accommodatively toward an offender when the two are alone, choosing peace ahead of justice. The presence of a witness, however, seems to add something to the implications of the offense. For then it is beyond the power of the offended and offender to forget about, erase, or suppress what has happened; the offense has become a public social fact.[13] When the witness is a mental health commission, as is sometimes the case, the witnessed betrayal can verge on a "degradation ceremony."[14] In such circumstances, the offended patient may feel that some kind of extensive reparative action is required before witnesses, if his honor and social weight are to be restored.

[12] I have one case record of a man who claims he thought *he* was taking his wife to see the psychiatrist, not realizing until too late that his wife had made the arrangements.
[13] A paraphrase from Kurt Riezler, "The Social Psychology of Shame," *Amer. J. Sociology* (1943) **48:** 458.
[14] See Harold Garfinkel, "Conditions of Successful Degradation Ceremonies," *Amer. J. Sociology* (1956) **61:** 420–424.

Two other aspects of sensed betrayal should be mentioned. First, those who suggest the possibility of another's entering a mental hospital are not likely to provide a realistic picture of how in fact it may strike him when he arrives. Often he is told that he will get required medical treatment and a rest, and may well be out in a few months or so. In some cases they may thus be concealing what they know, but I think, in general, they will be telling what they see as the truth. For here there is a quite relevant difference between patients and mediating professionals; mediators, more so than the public at large, may conceive of mental hospitals as short-term medical establishments where required rest and attention can be voluntarily obtained, and not as places of coerced exile. When the prepatient finally arrives he is likely to learn quite quickly, quite differently. He then finds that the information given him about life in the hospital has had the effect of his having put up less resistance to entering than he now sees he would have put up had he known the facts. Whatever the intentions of those who participated in his transition from person to patient, he may sense they have in effect "conned" him into his present predicament.

I am suggesting that the prepatient starts out with at least a portion of the rights, liberties, and satisfactions of the civilian and ends up on a psychiatric ward stripped of almost everything. The question here is *how* this stripping is managed. This is the second aspect of betrayal I want to consider.

As the prepatient may see it, the circuit of significant figures can function as a kind of *betrayal funnel*. Passage from person to patient may be effected through a series of linked stages, each managed by a different agent. While each stage tends to bring a sharp decrease in adult free status, each agent may try to maintain the fiction that no further decrease will occur. He may even manage to turn the prepatient over to the next agent while sustaining this note. Further, through words, cues, and gestures, the prepatient is implicitly asked by the current agent to join with him in sustaining a running line of polite small talk that tactfully avoids the administrative facts of the situation, becoming with each stage, progressively more at odds with these facts. The spouse would rather not have to cry to get the prepatient to visit a psychiatrist; psychiatrists would rather not have a scene when the prepatient learns that he and his spouse are being seen separately and in different ways; the police infrequently bring a prepatient to the hospital in a strait jacket, finding it much easier all around to give him a cigarette, some kindly words, and freedom to relax in the back seat of the patrol car; and finally, the admitting psychiatrist finds he can do his work better in the relative quiet and luxury of the "admission suite" where, as an incidental consequence, the notion can survive that a mental hospital is indeed a comforting place. If the prepatient heeds all of these implied requests and is reasonably decent about the whole thing, he can travel the whole circuit from home to hospital without forcing anyone to look directly at what is happening or to deal with the raw emotion that his situation might well cause him to express. His showing consideration for those who are moving him toward the hospital allows them to show consideration for him, with the joint result that these interactions can be sustained with some of the protective harmony characteristic of ordinary face-to-face dealings. But should the new patient cast his mind back over the sequence of steps leading to hospitalization, he may feel that everyone's *current* comfort was being busily sustained while his long-range welfare was being undermined. This realization may constitute a moral experience that further separates him for the time from the people on the outside.[15]

I would now like to look at the circuit of career agents from the point of view of the agents themselves. Mediators in the person's transition from civil to patient status—as well as his keepers, once he is in the hospital—have an interest in establishing a responsible next-of-relation as the patient's deputy or *guardian;* should there be no obvious candidate for the role, someone may be sought out and pressed into it. Thus while a person is gradually being transformed into a patient, a next-of-relation is gradually being transformed into a guardian. With a guardian on the scene, the whole transition process can be kept tidy. He is likely to be familiar with the prepatient's civil involvements and business, and can tie up loose ends that might otherwise be left to entangle the hospital. Some of the prepatient's abrogated civil rights can be transferred to him, thus helping to sustain the legal fiction that while the prepatient does not actually have his rights he somehow actually has not lost them.

Inpatients commonly sense, at least for a time, that hospitalization is a massive unjust deprivation, and sometimes succeed in convincing a few persons on the outside that this is the case. It often turns out to be useful, then, for those identified with inflicting these deprivations, however justifiably, to be able to point to the cooperation and agreement of someone whose relationship to the patient places him above suspicion, firmly defining him as the person most likely to have the patient's personal interest at heart. If the guardian is satisfied with what is happening to the new inpatient, the world ought to be.[16]

Now it would seem that the greater the legitimate personal stake one party has in another, the better he can take the role of guardian to the other. But the structural arrangements in society which lead to the acknowledged merging of two persons' interests lead to additional consequences. For the person to whom the patient turns for help—for protection against such threats as involuntary commitment—is just the person to whom the mediators and hospital administrators logically turn for authorization. It is understandable, then, that some patients will come to sense, at least for a time, that the closeness of a relationship tells nothing of its trustworthiness.

There are still other functional effects emerging from this complement of roles. If and when the next-of-relation appeals to mediators for help in the trouble he is having with the prepatient, hospitalization may not, in fact, be in

[15] Concentration camp practices provide a good example of the function of the betrayal funnel in inducing cooperation and reducing struggle and fuss, although here the mediators could not be said to be acting in the best interests of the inmates. Police picking up persons from their homes would sometimes joke good-naturedly and offer to wait while coffee was being served. Gas chambers were fitted out like delousing rooms, and victims taking off their clothes were told to note where they were leaving them. The sick, aged, weak, or insane who were selected for extermination were sometimes driven away in Red Cross ambulances to camps referred to by terms such as "observation hospital." See David Boder, *I Did Not Interview the Dead;* Urbana, Univ. of Illinois Press, 1949; p. 81; and Elie A. Cohen, *Human Behavior in the Concentration Camp;* London, Cape, 1954; pp. 32, 37, 107.

[16] Interviews collected by the Clausen group at NIMH suggest that when a wife comes to be a guardian, the responsibility may disrupt previous distance from in-laws, leading either to a new supportive coalition with them or to a marked withdrawal from them.

his mind. He may not even perceive the prepatient as mentally sick, or, if he does, he may not consistently hold to this view.[17] It is the circuit of mediators, with their greater psychiatric sophistication and their belief in the medical character of mental hospitals, that will often define the situation for the next-of-relation, assuring him that hospitalization is a possible solution and a good one, that it involves no betrayal, but is rather a medical action taken in the best interests of the prepatient. Here the next-of-relation may learn that doing his duty to the prepatient may cause the prepatient to distrust and even hate him for the time. But the fact that this course of action may have had to be pointed out and prescribed by professionals, and be defined by them as a moral duty, relieves the next-of-relation of some of the guilt he may feel.[18] It is a poignant fact that an adult son or daughter may be pressed into the role of mediator; so that the hostility that might otherwise be directed against the spouse is passed on to the child.[19]

Once the prepatient is in the hospital, the same guilt-carrying function may become a significant part of the staff's job in regard to the next-of-relation.[20] These reasons for feeling that he himself has not betrayed the patient, even though the patient may then think so, can later provide the next-of-relation with a defensible line to take when visiting the patient in the hospital and a basis for hoping that the relationship can be re-established after its hospital moratorium. And of course this position, when sensed by the patient, can provide him with excuses for the next-of-relation, when and if he comes to look for them.[21]

Thus while the next-of-relation can perform important functions for the mediators and hospital administrators, they in turn can perform important functions for him. One finds, then, an emergent unintended exchange or reciprocation of functions, these functions themselves being often unintended.

The final point I want to consider about the prepatient's moral career is its peculiarly *retroactive* character. Until a person actually arrives at the hospital there usually seems no way of knowing for sure that he is destined to do so, given the determinative role of career contingencies. And until the point of hospitalization is reached, he or others may not conceive of him as a person who is becoming a mental patient. However, since he will be held against his will in the hospital, his next-of-relation and the hospital staff will be in great need of

---

[17] For an analysis of these nonpsychiatric kinds of perception, see Marian Radke Yarrow, Charlotte Green Schwartz, Harriet S. Murphy, and Leila Calhoun Deasy, "The Psychological Meaning of Mental Illness in the Family," *J. Social Issues* (1955) **11:** 12–24; Charlotte Green Schwartz, "Perspectives on Deviance: Wives' Definitions of their Husbands' Mental Illness," *Psychiatry* (1957) **20:** 275–291.

[18] This guilt-carrying function is found, of course, in other role-complexes. Thus, when a middle-class couple engages in the process of legal separation or divorce, each of their lawyers usually takes the position that his job is to acquaint his client with all of the potential claims and rights, pressing his client into demanding these, in spite of any nicety of feelings about the rights and honorableness of the ex-partner. The client, in all good faith, can then say to self and to the ex-partner that the demands are being made only because the lawyer insists it is best to do so.

[19] Recorded in the Clausen data.

[20] This point is made by Cumming, see footnote 9; p. 129.

[21] There is an interesting contrast here with the moral career of the tuberculosis patient. I am told by Julius Roth that tuberculous patients are likely to come to the hospital willingly, agreeing with their next-of-relation about treatment. Later in their hospital career, when they learn how long they yet have to stay and how depriving and irrational some of the hospital rulings are, they may seek to leave, be advised against this by the staff and by relatives, and only then begin to feel betrayed.

a rationale for the hardships they are sponsoring. The medical elements of the staff will also need evidence that they are still in the trade they were trained for. These problems are eased, no doubt unintentionally, by the case-history construction that is placed on the patient's past life, this having the effect of demonstrating that all along he had been becoming sick, that he finally became very sick, and that if he had not been hospitalized much worse things would have happened to him—all of which, of course, may be true. Incidentally, if the patient wants to make sense out of his stay in the hospital, and, as already suggested, keep alive the possibility of once again conceiving of his next-of-relation as a decent, well-meaning person, then he too will have reason to believe some of this psychiatric work-up of his past.

Here is a very ticklish point for the sociology of careers. An important aspect of every career is the view the person constructs when he looks backward over his progress; in a sense, however, the whole of the prepatient career derives from this reconstruction. The fact of having had a prepatient career, starting with an effective complaint, becomes an important part of the mental patient's orientation, but this part can begin to be played only after hospitalization proves that what he had been having, but no longer has, is a career as a prepatient.

22
INFLUENCE OF SMALL SOCIAL NETWORKS AS FACTORS ON MENTAL HOSPITAL ADMISSION
Muriel Hammer*

INTRODUCTION

The phenomena referred to by the phrase "mental illness" may be studied at several different levels—biochemical, psychological, sociocultural. At the cultural level, an individual is "mentally ill" when his behavior ceases to have the kind of predictability which is necessary for incorporation into the structure of social units in which he holds positions. All social interaction rests to some degree on classification of the participants in terms of their position in a social structure.

Source: Muriel Hammer, "Influence of Small Social Networks as Factors in Mental Hospital Admission," Human Organization, 22: 243–251, 1963–64.
* This research was supported in part by funds from Grant M1541 from the National Institute of Mental Health. The author is indebted to Dr. Joseph Zubin and Dr. Conrad Arensberg for helpful interest throughout the study, to Dr. Arthur Zitrin and the staff of Bellevue psychiatric wards for making available the sample of patients studied, to Dr. Donald Carmichael for his assistance in facilitating contact with the patients' families, to Dr. Henry Brill for his kind cooperation in making the many administrative contacts that were necessary, to Mr. Martin Smolin, Mr. Sherman Patrick, Miss Verna Schmauder, and Mr. Victor Bergenn, who assisted with various phases of this work.

For a given social structure there will be appropriate ways of behaving toward persons occupying given categories, such as "brother," "employee," "pedestrian," etc., and there will be ways of interpreting their behavior in terms of these categories. It is characteristic of mental illness, however, that the individual's behavior ceases to be within the range of the usual expectancies, or in fact, within the range of the defining properties of the positions he holds. Although social relationships are modified by the particular characteristics of the persons involved, this modification never is such that the social or "positional" category becomes irrelevant. For effective social interaction, the participants must share ways of receiving and interpreting information, and ways of executing and anticipating behavior. The sharing need not be complete but must be sufficient to enable the participants to operate in terms of the same set of social expectancies. People's expectancies for a given individual's behavior are based on their experience of the behavior of others in the same social category as this individual. Mentally ill individuals, however, appear to be less responsive to social sanctions than normal persons.[1] Thus, normal expectancies for their behavior will often be misleading.

The mentally ill individual tends to disrupt the social structures in which he holds positions. To maintain these structures, some adjustment must be made. Since any position is part of a system of relationships, it has associated with it certain kinds of behavior without which the system either ceases to operate or must operate differently. Thus, if the mentally ill individual violates the behavioral requirements of the position he occupies, then the characteristics of this position must be altered, or he must be removed from occupancy of the position. By one or the other means, his field of contacts must be restructured in such a way as to make prediction of his behavior depend relatively less on his social category and relatively more on his personal idiosyncratic characteristics; or he must be removed to a situation in which predictability can be externally imposed (e.g., hospitalization).

Evidence from epidemiological studies indicates that whether or not mental illness has a social etiology, treatment rates vary with differences in social conditions.[2] To understand the bases of such variation in rates, more intensive investigations are necessary of the social factors which may affect these rates.

The focus of this study is the impact of the behavior of the mental patient on the structure of certain social units in which he participates, and some of the characteristics of these structures which may determine the responses made to his behavior. Primary attention is given to the most intimate unit of which the patient is a member—usually a nuclear family. The material for the study is based

[1] Discussions relevant to this view of mental illness may be found in Ralph Linton, *Culture and Mental Disorder*, G. Devereux, (Ed.), Charles C. Thomas, Springfield, Ill., 1956. See also, Anthony F. C. Wallace, *Culture and Personality*, Random House, New York, 1961, and G. Devereux, "Normal and Abnormal: The Key Problem of Psychiatric Anthropology," in *Some Uses of Anthropology: Theoretical and Applied*. The Anthropological Society of Washington, Washington, D.C., 1956.

[2] See Herbert Goldhamer and Andrew W. Marshall, *Psychosis and Civilization*, The Free Press, Glencoe, Ill., 1950; Eleanor Leacock, "Three Social Variables and the Occurrence of Mental Disorder," in Leighton, Clausen, and Wilson, (Eds.), *Explorations in Social Psychiatry*, Basic Books, New York, 1957; Muriel Hammer and Eleanor Leacock, "Source Material on the Epidemiology of Mental Illness," in J. Zubin (Ed.), *Field Studies in Mental Disorders*, Grune and Stratton, New York, 1961.

on the sequences of events leading to the hospitalization for mental illness of a sample of Negro and Jewish patients hospitalized in New York City.

The patients' backgrounds were analyzed in terms of a particular conception of the nature of social ties. This conception will be set forth briefly in the following section.

CHARACTERISTICS OF SOCIAL NETWORKS

The network of ties in which any person or social unit is involved is seen both as a major force for maintenance of existing forms of interaction and as a major factor in the determination of the kind of change which will occur when the existing forms cannot be maintained unchanged. To the extent that a given interaction has necessary implications beyond the immediate situation, it must involve, indirectly, other individuals with whom each of the original participants interacts at other times. A divorce, for example, does not merely alter the relationship between one man and one woman. It also alters their relationships with landlords, neighbors, and other family members, decreases the frequency of contact with some of the people they generally saw together, increases the frequency of contact with some of the people each of them saw separately, and so on.

It is suggested here that such chains or networks of interaction largely determine the responses that will be made to the mentally ill individual by the other members of his social unit.[3] The members of the patient's social unit will be affected by the actual or anticipated responses that their behavior concerning the patient may elicit from the other people they interact with, who in turn are affected by their own networks of interaction. Such interrelations create a strong pressure to respond to any new situation in ways which are very similar to previously used forms of interaction, since changes in one part of a network of interactions are likely to require changes in other parts, some of which may conflict with each other. Thus, despite the fact that the mentally ill person's behavior departs from that which is appropriate to the situation, others in the situation tend to restructure the interaction in such a way as to enable themselves to respond with behavior appropriate to their own *total* situations. In doing this, they tend to make the smallest available changes, and only evolve "new" behavior as external pressures and the "real" behavior of the patient force further alterations of responses. Often their new behavior is not seen as new, having developed quite gradually—e.g., a wife or mother may become the sole link between a patient and all other individuals by a series of very small successive alterations in her behavior. Even hospitalization may "develop gradually," from family doctor to outpatient clinic to legal commitment. Only transgressions of

---

[3] For some interesting work on the effect of differences in the structure of small groups on the solution of problems involving communication within the group, see Lee S. Christie, R. Duncan Luce, and Josiah Macy, Jr., *Communication and Learning in Task-Oriented Groups*, Massachusetts Institute of Technology, Research Laboratory of Electronics, Technical Report #231, May 13, 1952.

clearly formulated cultural prohibitions seem to be responded to in our society by going sharply outside the range of prior behavior.

The characteristics of the ties in a social network which seem most important in determining whether aberrant behavior will produce a reorganization of the network are (1) distance, (2) degree of inter-connectedness, and (3) narrowness of definition of the behavior relevant to the interactions.

1. This *"distance"* is of two kinds. First, direct ties are closer than ties mediated through others. For example, in our society, a husband-wife relationship is direct, whereas an in-law relationship is usually indirect. Second, ties involving a number of areas of activity are closer than ties which involve fewer areas of activity. In general, alterations in the behavior of one individual will affect another individual more if their ties are close than if they are distant.

In the intimate social unit, ties are usually direct and therefore "close" in the first meaning of the term. They also tend to be "close" in the second meaning of the term since relationships within the intimate social unit usually involve broad areas of interaction. Another dimension is added to closeness when there is also "symmetry" in a relationship, i.e., when the two persons involved in a relationship have no other relationships which are closer. Thus, the behavior of a patient in a symmetrical relationship has a much more profound effect on the other member of the relationship than it would have if the patient's relationship, though equally close, were not symmetrical. Someone with a symmetrical relationship to the patient is more likely to respond to the patient's disturbing behavior by attempting to alter that behavior (through informal advice or psychiatric therapy, including hospitalization), or to alter his own behavior to minimize the impact on the relationship.

2. *"Interconnectedness"* means that ties between two members are "joined" by ties between each of these and a third. For example, if A lives with B whose friend C is unknown to A, the tie between A and B is not connected to the tie between B and C. This is an open unit, composed of "linear" ties. If C then comes to live with A and B, the ties become interconnected, or "triangular." (These ties need not be equivalent—if A and B are siblings, and C is independently close to each, the three ties are not identical, but form a triangular network.) In interconnected units, there is greater freedom of substitution in performance not vital to the maintenance of ties than in relatively open units. In our example of the open unit, B's absence—or an illness or a broken arm— might impose on A incompatible requirements of support and maintenance of the household. In the interconnected unit these new requirements could be shared between A and C. There is, however, less freedom of substitution of the ties themselves. D cannot as readily be substituted for C in the A-B-C (triangular) relationship as in the B-C (linear) relationship, since simultaneous changes A-C to A-D and B-C to B-D would be required.

Where the structure of the intimate social unit is triangular—a relatively closed or interconnected network—the effects of the patient's behavior may be "shared," thus creating less pressure for severance of ties; and since severance implies complete reorganization for a triangular network, there is strong pressure against it.

3. *"Narrow definition"* of an aspect of behavior means that little variation in performance is allowed, whereas "broad definition" means more variation is allowed.[4] The variations in performance appropriate to a storekeeper's conversation with a customer are relatively few compared with those appropriate to his conversation with his son. Broadness of definition will vary for different positions in a network, and for different kinds of behavior. Generally behavior which is most critical to the maintenance of the network will be most narrowly defined. Deviations in performance in such areas of behavior must elicit rapid response by the other individuals composing the network.

Where the patient's usual behavior is essential to the maintenance of the unit (a "critical" position), it is narrowly defined, and there is little room for minor alterations. Substantial change (hospitalization, severance of ties, positional redefinition) must therefore occur more rapidly.

PROCEDURES

The data were drawn from interviews with patients and their relatives and from hospital records.

In order to reduce somewhat the possible sources of variation, data were collected only for patients from two ethnic groups and only for patients diagnosed as having a functional psychosis. Negro and Jewish subcultural groups were selected because they have fairly large populations in New York, they are recognized as groups by both members and outsiders, and they are in many ways quite different from each other culturally. The purpose of using two groups rather than one was that if the variables found to be useful in the analysis of one group are the basic structural variables in the situation rather than "accidental" aspects of that particular group, the hypotheses considered should also be demonstrable for other groups. Thus, the analysis of a second group serves as a partial check on the generality of the conclusions.

Selection of sample

The patients were selected from card files and case records at the Bellevue Psychiatric Hospital. Patients meeting the following criteria were interviewed: age 17 to 59; diagnosis schizophrenic or manic depressive; residence Manhattan; ethnic background, either Negro with patient and parents born in the United States, or Jewish with patient born in the United States and one or both parents born in Eastern Europe;[5] psychiatric history, no record of a previous hospitalization in adulthood of more than a year's duration. Information from the patient's

[4] This is probably not independent of the interconnections among ties: the open network with high substitutability should tend to narrow definitions of behavior essential to the tie and broad definitions not essential to the tie; whereas the closed network should define much broader areas of behavior as essential, but with less narrow definition of most aspects of this "essential" behavior.

[5] Eastern Europe was considered to include Russia, Poland, Lithuania, Latvia, Hungary, Romania, and Czechoslovakia.

record and from an interview with the patient was used to select the person who appeared to have had closest recent contact with the patient. If an interview with this person did not appear to yield sufficient information, further informants were selected and interviewed about the same patient.

The sample was selected during several periods in 1958 and 1959 to allow time for interviewing the families and friends of the patients already selected before adding to the sample. The general procedure followed was to select from the records of each ward visited those patients who met the sample criteria, and to interview them before they left the hospital. All adult wards except those for medical, surgical, prison, and senile cases were visited in rotation for this purpose. Because of the relatively low rate of admission of Jewish patients who met the criteria for the sample, this procedure involved a great expenditure of time in the selection of patients. The sample was therefore supplemented by selection, on the basis of records in a central file, of patients who had just been discharged from Bellevue. These patients were not interviewed although their families were interviewed.

The total number in this sample, after excluding those patients who turned out not to meet all the criteria, was 55. Table 1 shows the breakdown of this sample by sex and ethnic group.

Information obtained on each patient

There were three major areas of interest on which data were sought. These were (1) positions occupied by the patient in any structures in which he participated; (2) kinds of behavior eliciting hospitalization; and (3) kinds of responses to the patient, other than hospitalization.

Interview procedures

The writer interviewed all of the patients and some of the families from each ethnic group. The other family interviews were conducted by two other interviewers. The interviewer began the interview by identifying himself or herself as associated with the New York State Department of Mental Hygiene, and stated that the information asked for was desired for the purpose of finding out more about mental hospital patients, and would not be used in the patient's personal

Table 1
Number of patients in the interview sample by ethnic group and sex

	Negro	Jewish	Total
Men	19	11	30
Women	16	9	25
Total	35	20	55

records. In most cases interviews were recorded on small portable recording machines. Handwritten notes were also taken. Questions about the patient's behavior were asked in general terms (e.g., "Will you tell me about 'X' going to the hospital?") early in the interview, and later, specific questions were asked about such things as hallucinations and violence if they had not already been mentioned. Where possible, additional interviews were conducted when it was felt that the information from the first interview or the first informant was inadequate.

For administrative reasons, interviews could not be conducted with the families of three patients who were not transferred to other hospitals from Bellevue. (There were actually six such patients but interviews were conducted for three of them before the administrative regulation was made.) The families of two Negro patients could not be located, and the families of two Jewish patients refused to be interviewed—for one of these two, however, a brief interview was conducted before the refusal. Thus, there were six patients for whom no relative or friend was interviewed. There were also twelve patients who were not interviewed because of difficulties in scheduling. Hospital records were used for all patients.

Combining all sources of data used, information was available, directly or indirectly, from several informants and more than one interviewer for all patients. Interviews were conducted with most patients and with members of their families, and the patients' case records were consulted at the admissions hospital and at the hospitals to which the patients were subsequently transferred. The case records generally include reports on interviews that hospital psychiatrists and social workers have held with members of the patients' families. Although there were a number of discrepancies among the different sources of information, very few discrepancies occurred which were relevant to this analysis. The interview or interviews with the informant who was closest to the patient were considered to be the basic source of information; other sources were used for corroboration and supplementing of information, except in the few cases mentioned above where interviews could not be conducted with such an informant.

Representativeness of samples

Since the patients studied here were all selected from Bellevue Psychiatric Division any selective bias involved in the use of this institution will introduce selective bias into the samples studied. Precautions were taken to avoid adding other sources of bias, by including in the analysis all patients who had been selected. Patients for whom it was not possible to get adequate interviews from family or friends were included in the analysis by relying on the data from their case records.

The major precaution against bias due to unrepresentativeness of the samples was the structural analysis, which does not require samples representative of the subcultural groups. For example, in testing the effect of criticalness of the position of the patient in his social unit on the speed with which his deviant behavior is responded to by the social unit, lack of representativeness in the distribution of patients in critical and non-critical positions will not affect the results.

RESULTS

Classification of the patient's behavior in terms of the universality of responses elicited

It will be useful to make a distinction between two components of the behavior which constitutes a symptom of illness. The behavior may have directly disturbing effects or may be a sign that future disturbances are likely. The former will be called here a "disturbance-symptom," the latter a "sign-symptom." In physical illness, symptoms like pain or faintness have both characteristics. The discomfort of an identified, temporary, short-term disturbance like a cold or a minor burn is primarily of the "disturbance" type. A small growth like a mole is of the "sign" type, having no directly disturbing effects, but often associated with potential severe disturbance.

Both kinds of symptoms occur in mental illness. Violent attacks on another person, or complete cessation of activity, are directly disturbing to the social unit in which they occur; whereas certain bizarre mannerisms, or the expression of some delusional ideas may be primarily signs, not directly disruptive of the social unit. Hospitalization seems to be elicited by symptoms involving direct disturbance when these symptoms are also accompanied by some signs indicative of illness. The first kind of symptom produces the pressure to act; the second identifies the appropriate channel for action. When sign-symptoms occur without disturbance-symptoms, they appear to elicit non-hospital medical care rather than hospitalization. In the analyses which follow we are primarily concerned with disturbance symptoms and only incidentally with sign symptoms.

It was stated earlier that the responses made to the patient's behavior tend to be those involving the least immediate change in the organization of the social unit affected by his behavior. Thus, for most kinds of disturbing behavior, responses made by differently organized units will not be the same since the least immediate change in one form of organization need not be the least immediate change in another. Only behavior which is quite generally disturbing and for which there are no available "lesser" responses should be responded to by a wide variety of referral agents, and should consistently elicit hospitalization.

The kinds of disturbances which are handled as emergencies in the subcultures dealt with in this study are active immediate threats to life or substantial property, or marked interference with the necessary activities of some unit or institution. These kinds of behavior are responded to rapidly regardless of the patient's position or subculture, and they may even elicit action from exposed persons not otherwise connected with the patient. Uncodified violence and grossly bizarre behavior interfere with the ordinary performance of any person connected at the time of these events to the actor. Potential consequences are not precisely predictable, but are extreme—involving permanent injury, loss of property, inability to carry out tasks, etc. Such action elicits rapid removal of the actor from the situation—usually by means of arrest or hospitalization—since there is no other available reorganization or therapy that could control the immediate situation.

Thirteen patients were hospitalized for violent behavior, and seven for grossly bizarre behavior. All twenty of these patients were hospitalized immediately after the occurrence of this behavior. The referral agents for these patients included family, friends, neighbors, a landlady, a Welfare department employee, general hospital personnel, police, the crew of a tug boat, a storekeeper, a bank guard, and church officials.

Although only four of these twenty hospitalizations were initiated by police, police were regularly called in for the other sixteen by the initiating agents mentioned above.

The opposite type of behavior—withdrawal, non-performance—may be equally disturbing, but not in so broad a range of situations. It is only disturbing to individuals who have close ties with the patient (particularly if the patient has occupied a position critical to the maintenance of the social unit). Non-performance or poor performance were the main reasons for hospitalization for ten patients (although all of them showed other symptoms as well). The three who ceased virtually all activity were hospitalized by spouses; of the seven who continued some activity, but functioned poorly, six were self-referrals and one was hospitalized by his sister. Although non-performance may elicit rapid structural response, poor performance does not. Generally, non-performance or poor performance is associated with the development of marginal and dependent relationship and occasionally, severance of relationships.

Other symptoms seem more dependent on context for determination of the kind of response made, and the length of time allowed to elapse between the onset of symptoms and a clear response to them.

Position in the intimate social unit

1 *Narrowness of definition: critical versus non-critical positions.*   One relevant axis of the difference in responses made by others to the behavior of a patient is the criticalness of the position of the patient in the social unit. Critical positions within the unit are those whose structural norms involve performance significant for the maintenance of the unit. Performance in such positions tends to be narrowly defined. In this study, criticalness generally meant regular financial contribution or care of the household or children in a unit involving at least one other adult. Since the existing organization requires the performances defining the critical position, there must be rapid reaction to violation of structural norms by the occupant of a critical position. Furthermore, permanent reorganization without such a position-occupant is difficult, so that rapid hospitalization (for the purpose of therapy, rather than for the purpose of severance of ties with

the individual) is a likely reaction. *Stated as a hypothesis, patients in critical positions are hospitalized more rapidly than those in non-critical positions.*

Tables 2 through 7 show the relationship of duration of symptoms prior to hospitalization to the criticalness of the patient's position in his intimate social unit.[6] Because of difficulties in estimating duration of symptoms, a gross dichotomy of "less than one year" and "a year or more" was used rather than finer categories.[7] Some patients had hospitalizations preceding the one during which they were selected for this sample. For these patients, the earliest manifestation of clear symptoms since the last hospitalization was used, unless the period between hospitalizations was less than one year, in which case duration of symptoms prior to the first hospitalization within the year was used. Classification of the patient as critical or non-critical refers to the position of the patient in the unit at the first indication of symptoms prior to this hospitalization.

Significantly more "critical" than "non-critical" patients are hospitalized within a year of the manifestation of symptoms. The Negro "critical" patients, and both the Negro and Jewish "non-critical" patients, show the expected tendency. However, only four Jewish patients were "critical," and these four were evenly divided on the duration measure.

Two methodological difficulties (in addition to the problem of classification) must be considered in treating this hypothesis, i.e., that "critical" patients are hospitalized sooner than "non-critical" patients. The first question is the measurement of duration from onset of symptoms till hospitalization; the second concerns the problem of patients whose hospitalization was not initiated by their intimate unit.

Measuring duration from the first reported symptoms involves, in some cases, measuring from the first indication of poor performance. There is, thus, some problem of contamination, since "criticalness" is also defined by performance. It was in order to avoid this source of contamination that patients were classified as to criticalness of position not at the time of hospitalization but rather at the

Table 2
Relationship of criticalness of position to duration of symptoms prior to hospitalization: all symptoms

Duration	Negro		Jewish		Total		
	Critical	Non-critical	Critical	Non-critical	Critical	Non-critical	Both
Less than one year	15	3	2	1	17	4	21
One year or more	0	17	2	15	2	32	34
Total	15	20	4	16	19	36	55

$x^2 = 29.12 \, p < .001$ (x^2 computed for total group.)

[6] Throughout this section, tables will be presented for all patients combined and for Negro and Jewish patients separately. Results of significance tests will only be shown for the combined sample, because of the small size of the subgroups. Direction of difference, however, is consistent for both groups in all these tables.
[7] The use of finer categories—such as "within a week," "within a month," etc.—seems to strengthen the relationship, but they have not been used here because of the problem of making such fine judgments reliably.

Table 3
Relationship of criticalness of position to duration of symptoms prior to
hospitalization: "specific" symptoms only

Duration	Negro		Jewish		Total		
	Critical	Non-critical	Critical	Non-critical	Critical	Non-critical	Both
Less than one year	15	6	3	4	18	10	28
One year or more	0	14	1	12	1	26	27
Total	15	20	4	16	19	36	55

$x^2 = 20.64$ $p < .001$ (x^2 computed for total group.)

time of the first indication of symptoms prior to this hospitalization. However, as a further check, a separate criterion of duration of symptoms prior to hospitalization will be used. Some specific psychiatric symptoms, such as hallucinations, delusions, clearly bizarre behavior, and attempted suicide, do not seem to be involved in the definitions of criticalness and non-criticalness of position in the unit. They may tentatively be considered as indicative of the question under examination, even though it is not certain they are an adequate indication of duration of other symptoms. To test this, we would need better evidence than seems to be available about the relationship, in time, between performance-disturbances and the specific symptoms of hallucinations, delusions, etc. Table 3 uses a duration beginning with the first evidence of such specific symptoms and ending with hospitalization.

Considering only these specific symptoms, the relationship still holds between criticalness of position and duration of symptoms before hospitalization.

Not all patients were hospitalized by members of their intimate social unit. In order to test the effect of criticalness of position on responses made directly by the patient's intimate unit, some cases must be excluded from the analysis. The following tables (measuring duration from earliest symptoms reported) exclude cases where outside agents initiated hospitalization within the first year of manifestation of symptoms. Thus, cases where the patient was hospitalized by a member of his intimate unit within a year of the onset of symptoms are contrasted with those where the patient was not hospitalized by any agent within the year, whether the unit later hospitalized him or he was later hospitalized by another agent. The four patients judged to have no intimate unit (isolates) have been excluded, since they could not have been hospitalized by an intimate unit.

As shown in Table 4, "critical" patients are hospitalized within a year of appearance of symptoms by members of their intimate social units significantly more often than are "non-critical" patients.[8] As in Table 2 the relationship is clear for Negro "critical" patients and for all "non-critical" patients, but not for the Jewish "critical" patients.

Finally, because of the difficulty in estimating duration of symptoms, the same

[8] Actually the relationship is probably even stronger than indicated in Table 4 since in some cases, rapid hospitalization by other agents may be "used" by the unit to avoid the necessity of direct action.

Table 4
Criticalness of position for patients hospitalized by their unit within a year, or by any agent more than a year after reported symptoms began

Agent duration	Negro		Jewish		Total		
	Critical	Non-critical	Critical	Non-critical	Critical	Non-critical	Both
Unit: Less than one year	7	2	2	0	9	2	11
Any: One year or more	0	17	2	15	2	32	34
Total	7	19	4	15	11	34	45

$\chi^2 = 22.00\ p < .001$ (χ^2 computed for total group.)
(Note that patients hospitalized by agents other than members of their intimate social unit within one year of manifestation of symptoms are excluded.)

tests were applied to the thirty patients who had no history of prior hospitalization on the assumption that prior hospitalization could have biased reports on duration of symptoms.

Among patients never previously hospitalized (as among all patients), those in critical positions at the time symptoms become apparent are hospitalized more rapidly than those in non-critical positions whether one disregards the question of agent of hospitalization, or compares hospitalizations initiated by the patients' units within a year with those initiated by any agent after a year has elapsed. However, when only specific psychiatric symptoms are considered rather than all symptoms, the relationship is not statistically significant.

2 *Distance: symmetrical versus non-symmetrical relationships.* A second characteristic of the relationship of the patient to his most intimate unit which is relevant to the ways in which the unit responds to him, is the symmetry of his closest tie. As discussed earlier, the closer the patient's relationship to some member of the unit (as compared with the other relationships of that member), the more his behavior will affect the unit, and the more likely it is that the unit will respond directly to such behavior. *Thus, patients with non-symmetrical ties are not as likely to be given assistance in ways which may disturb the functioning of the other members of the unit (such as personal care and help in performance of the patient's tasks). Nor are they as likely to be hospitalized by their units or to have non-hospital therapy initiated by some member of the unit.* (The four isolates are excluded from this analysis.) The following tables show this relation-

Table 5
Duration from earliest symptoms, any agent of hospitalization: first admissions only

Duration	Negro		Jewish		Total		
	Critical	Non-critical	Critical	Non-critical	Critical	Non-critical	Both
Less than one year	9	2	2	1	11	3	14
One year or more	0	9	1	6	1	15	16
Total	9	11	3	7	12	18	30

$\chi^2 = 13.39\ p < .001$ (χ^2 computed for total group.)

Table 6
Duration from first specific symptoms, any agent of hospitalization: first admissions only

Duration	Negro		Jewish		Total		
	Critical	Non-critical	Critical	Non-critical	Critical	Non-critical	Both
Less than one year	9	5	2	3	11	8	19
One year or more	0	6	1	4	1	10	11
Total	9	11	3	7	12	18	30

$x^2 = 2.52$ $.20 > p > .10$ N. S. (x^2 computed for total group.)

Table 7
Duration from earliest symptoms, "within the year by the unit" against "more than a year by any agent": first admissions only (excluding 2 isolates)

Duration	Negro		Jewish		Total		
	Critical	Non-critical	Critical	Non-critical	Critical	Non-critical	Both
Unit: Less than one year	4	2	2	0	6	2	8
Any agent: One year or more	0	9	1	6	1	15	16
Total	4	11	3	6	7	17	24

$p < .002*$ (computed for total group.)
(Note that patients hospitalized by agents other than members of their intimate social unit within one year of manifestation of symptoms are excluded.)
* Fisher's exact test.

ship to be significant for the giving of assistance, not quite significant for attempted therapy and hospitalization, and significant when both kinds of action are considered together. Table 8 shows that about half of the "symmetrical" patients in both ethnic groups received aid from their units, while only one of six Jewish patients and one of twelve Negro patients who were "non-symmetrical" received aid. As shown in Table 9, therapy or hospitalization was initiated by the units of most of the "symmetrical" patients, but by less than half of the units of the "non-symmetrical" patients. When aid and initiation of therapy or hospitalization are all considered, as in Table 10, we see that the units of most

Table 8
Relation of symmetry of relationship to frequency of receiving aid

	Negro		Jewish		Total		
	Sym	Non-sym	Sym	Non-sym	Sym	Non-sym	Both
Aid	10	1	6	1	16	2	18
No aid*	10	11	7	5	17	16	33
Total	20	12	13	6	33	18	51

$x^2 = 5.58$ $p < .02$ (x^2 computed for total group.)
* Aid refers only to personal care and/or performance for the patient of his regular tasks. Thus, "no aid" does not imply total lack of assistance (e.g. a place to stay, loans of money, etc.) but lack of those forms of assistance which necessitate reorganization of the tasks of others.

Table 9
Relation of symmetry of relationship to frequency of having therapy or
hospitalization initiated by the unit

	Negro		Jewish		Total		
	Sym	Non-sym	Sym	Non-sym	Sym	Non-sym	Both
Attempted therapy or hospitalization initiated by unit	13	5	10	2	23	7*	30
Neither initiated by unit	7	7	3	4	10	11	21
	—	—	—	—	—	—	—
Total	20	12	13	6	33	18	51

$x^2 = 3.38$ .10 $> p >$ .05 N. S. (x^2 computed for total group.)
* It should be noted that two of the "non-symmetrical" patients, but none of the "symmetrical,"
were apparently brought to the hospital as a means of severing ties rather than for therapy. If
these two patients were not included in the category of positive responses, the association would,
of course, be stronger, and the result would be significant.

"symmetrical" patients made such responses while the units of less than half of
the "non-symmetrical" patients made any of these responses.

Greater frequency of contact is generally associated with symmetry of ties, and
may also be expected to affect the likelihood of receiving assistance or the initiation of therapy or hospitalization. An attempt was made to consider whether
the above relationships (Tables 8, 9, 10) simply reflect differences in frequency
of contact. The closest ties of the patients were, therefore, classified according
to whether contact was "daily" or "less than daily."

Table 11 shows the distribution of aid and/or attempted therapy or hospitalization for the combined groups.

Thus it appears that where there is daily contact, the distinction between symmetrical and non-symmetrical ties has no effect on the responses to the patients
considered here. When there is less frequent contact, however, aid, attempted
therapy, or hospitalization are more often initiated by the unit if the relationship is symmetrical than if it is not. If frequency of contact is interpreted as an

Table 10
Relation of symmetry of relationship to frequency of receiving aid or
having therapy or hospitalization initiated by the unit

	Negro		Jewish		Total		
	Sym	Non-sym	Sym	Non-sym	Sym	Non-sym	Both
Aid** and/or attempted therapy or hospitalization initiated by unit	16	5	10	2	26	7	33
None of these actions initiated by unit	4	7	3	4	7	11	18
	—	—	—	—	—	—	—
Total	20	12	13	6	33	18	51

$x^2 = 6.48$ $p <$ .02 (x^2 computed for total group.)
** Aid refers only to personal care and/or performance for the patient of his regular tasks. Thus,
"no aid" does not imply total lack of assistance (e.g., a place to stay, loans of money, etc.) but
lack of those forms of assistance which necessitate reorganization of the tasks of others.

Table 11

	Daily contact		Less frequent contact	
	Sym	Non-sym	Sym	Non-sym
Aid and/or attempted therapy or hospitalization initiated by unit	18	4	8	3
None of these actions initiated by unit	4	1	3	10

$p. = 34\ p. < .05$
(Fisher's exact test.)

alternative criterion of closeness, and comparison is made between patients with either daily contact or symmetrical ties and patients who neither have symmetrical ties nor are in daily contact with their most intimate unit, the association between the response in question and closeness is quite strong. (See Table 12.)
3   *Interconnectedness: triangular versus linear relationships.*   *Finally, it was suggested above that severance of ties, i.e., cessation or sharp diminution of contact, is less likely for triangular than for linear ties.* As shown in Table 13, severance occurs significantly less often when there are triangular than when there are only linear ties. All except one case of severance of most recent close ties—whether initiated by the patient or the unit—were "linear." (The four isolates were, of course, excluded.)

The hypotheses proposed here are generally supported by the tests made on this sample. It is obvious, however, that there is a great deal of overlap, empirically, among the criteria of criticalness, symmetry, and triangularity—although they are not equivalent. It would require a larger sample to ascertain whether the results are independent of each other, or whether, for example, symmetry and criticalness are linked and some of the results here are a function of a combination of these criteria.

In general, the patient seems first to elicit responses which involve no structural change in his unit, although there may be some changes in personal interaction. He or she receives advice. Relatives avoid situations which will disturb the patient, and make fewer demands than they do on others. However, in at least three-quarters of the cases studied, structural changes had finally occurred in the patient's ties with those closest to him. Prior to the hospitalization observed in the present study, most of the patients' units had been reorganized, either to exclude the patient or to maintain him in a marginal position. At the time of hospitalization, most patients had some personal unit which would permit their return to it but only sixteen had units to which they could return as

Table 12
Relation between closeness* of relationship and initiation of aid, therapy, or hospitalization

	Daily or symmetrical	Neither
Aid, therapy, hospitalization	30	3
None	8	10

$\chi^2 = 10.91\ p < .001$
* Symmetrical relationships and relationships involving daily contact are combined.

Table 13
Relationship between form of network of ties and frequency of severance

	Negro		Jewish		Total		
	Triangular ties	Linear ties	Triangular ties	Linear ties	Triangular ties	Linear ties	Both
Severance	0	7	1	4	1	11	12
No severance	16	9	10	4	26	13	39
Total	16	16	11	8	27	24	51

$x^2 = 10.30 \, p < .01$ (x^2 computed for total group.)

fully participant members, and only four of these sixteen had units whose organization during the period of hospitalization was such as to require the return of the patient.

Responses to the patient's behavior by non-intimate agencies

These responses included firing, eviction, arrest, and financial support (by welfare agencies), as well as hospitalization.

Responses by non-intimate agencies always follow the institutional definitions of relevant behavior and relevant responses except in those cases where the institutional definition is contaminated by other ties irrelevant to that definition. Thus, there are histories of severance by employers for thirteen patients, and eviction by landlords for three patients. Police arrested, or began to arrest eleven patients, and hospitalized or helped to hospitalize an additional fourteen.

Welfare agents initiated hospitalization for five patients, three who seemed incapable of maintaining themselves in accord with welfare practices (e.g., eviction because of non-payment of rent), one who threatened to stop caring for her children, and one who threatened the case-worker. In one case where the patient violated no welfare-agency policies, she was not hospitalized, although hospitalization was recommended by one of their psychiatrists.

Exceptional action was taken by one employer (actually, a supervisor) who had independent ties with the patient's adoptive sister. In this case, the supervisor recommended vacation rather than firing the patient. Exceptional action was also taken by two landlords. One lived in the same building as the patient, with whom she was friendly, and had her hospitalized. The other landlord lived near the patient and was friendly with the patient's wife, whom he helped in bringing the patient to the hospital.

Summary of results

The nature of this study was such that the data were obtained from retrospective reports. While it is believed that the particular analyses made do not rest, in any obvious way, on consistent retrospective bias, such data are known to be unreliable, and therefore any conclusions based on them must be considered quite tentative.

The only kinds of symptom pattern which appeared consistently to elicit immediate hospitalization (sometimes preceded by arrest) were violent and grossly bizarre behavior. Non-performance of tasks might also elicit hospitalization soon after the onset of symptoms, but only by persons close to the patient. Responses made to other symptoms seemed to depend on situational differences, such as the patient's position in a social unit.

Patients in critical positions were brought to the hospital more rapidly than those in non-critical positions. Patients with symmetrical ties or ties with whom they had daily contact, were more likely to receive personal care, help in the performance of tasks, attempts at non-hospital medical therapy and initiation of hospitalization by those close to them than were patients with less frequent contact and non-symmetrical ties. Severance of ties with the patient occurred almost exclusively in linear rather than triangular relationships.

Responses to the patient by non-intimate agencies, such as police, landlords, employers, etc., tended to be those generally typical for those agencies—arrest, eviction, firing, etc.—except in cases where there was an incidental personal tie as well.

In general, the processes leading to the hospitalization of the mental patient involved changes of several kinds: attempts at modification of the patient's behavior, altered interpretations of such behavior, alterations in the relationships with the patient and sometimes with others besides the patient. It is, of course, not possible to consider all the factors which may be relevant to the determination of a particular course of events for particular patients, but some of the interrelations between characteristics of the patient's behavior and the socio-cultural context have been selected as being significant determinants.

23
INTERPERSONAL ASPECTS OF PSYCHIATRIC HOSPITALIZATION: I. THE ADMISSION
Edwin C. Wood, John M. Rakusin, and Emanuel Morse

INTRODUCTION

Patients have various reasons for seeking psychiatric care in a hospital setting. In this paper we direct our attention to 1 phase of this complex problem: the interpersonal aspects of hospital admission. By this we mean to suggest that just as hospitalization may affect a number of people who are emotionally close to

Source: Edwin C. Wood, John M. Rakusin, and Emanuel Morse, "Interpersonal Aspects of Psychiatric Hospitalization," Archives of General Psychiatry, 3: 632–641, 1960.
Submitted for publication July 8, 1960.

the patient, so may these same people have influenced the patient's coming to the hospital. We further take it as our hypothesis that a study of the steps leading to admission will be diagnostically and therapeutically useful to the clinician.

We became interested in this question when it was noted that the psychiatric residents tended to overlook quite completely the importance of certain admission data.

To help ascertain the extent to which factors surrounding the admission of patients had or had not been explored, written summaries of discharged patients were reviewed and discussions were held with residents about a number of their presumably thoroughly understood cases. The results of our inquiries were noticeably unrewarding. Beyond their knowledge of the the symptoms presented by their patients for the purpose of seeking hospital admission, the residents were able to offer little about other forces at work that may have prompted the need for hospitalization.

The literature in this regard is also far from complete. The majority of the publications which deal with the factors that play a role in the admission of patients to mental hospitals are concerned essentially with gross statistical or public health data such as age, place of residence, and diagnostic categories.[1,2] There is relatively little reference to individual patients and families in these studies. One such paper by Stanton and Schwartz[3] which made such reference, however, was quite influential in directing our attention to the problem under study. It pays particular heed to the way a patient's behavior changed in conjunction with the changes experienced in his relationships with 2 nurses in the hospital, each of whom felt quite differently about him and were as a result in conflict with one another.

Stanton and Schwartz reasoned that such a disagreement between persons with power over the patient was a necessary condition for prolonged excitement by the patient.

In a comment on the paper, Harry Stack Sullivan raised the question of whether the same pattern might not exist at home in the period immediately prior to hospitalization. Stanton and Schwartz agreed with this inference. They referred to the situation in which a patient seemed "to serve as an unfortunate intermediary in a conflict between 2 other persons," and expressed the belief that "this type of process occurs in excited patients before admission to the hospital."

In a series of publications, Clausen, Yarrow, Schwartz, Deasy, and others explored the wife's understanding and reaction to the husband's illness and made reference to her important and ambivalent attitudes toward the early signs of his mental illness and his need for hospitalization.[4-6] In one specific paper, they discuss the mechanics of the referral of the patient to the hospital.[7] On a theoretical plane, J. Spiegel developed a frame of reference for the understanding of the conflict of roles within the family group.[8] Though he is not discussing hospitalization per se, many of his conceptualizations have direct bearing on our thinking that admission to the hospital is a complex move involving a group of people and that it frequently represents a modification of role of one or several group members.

In our own initial inquiry into the problem we posed the following questions: 1. What is known about the people with whom the patient discussed hospitalization? 2. Was their role significant in the hospitalization process? 3. Was the environment from which the patient came a friendly one or was it a place from which he wished to escape? 4. Were there conflicted relationships at home, on the job, with friends, which seemed to precipitate the need for hospitalization?

Since those responsible for patients whom we thought were involved in intensive treatment could shed little, if any, light on these issues, our study was begun in an effort to determine the relevance of the admission phenomena to the diagnostic and treatment purposes of psychiatric hospitalization.

The setting of our study is an open psychiatric ward of the West Haven, Connecticut, Veterans Administration General Medical and Surgical Hospital. Affiliated with the Yale University School of Medicine, the hospital conducts an active research and training program. This study was designed to cover the 6-month period from July 1, 1957, to Dec. 31, 1957.

On this open ward to which 60 male patients were admitted in the course of the study there were, at any one time, an average of 25 patients. Staffing this ward were a psychiatrist who was also its administrative head, a clinical psychologist, and a clinical social worker able to serve on a part-time basis only. These 3 are responsible for this study. Three first year psychiatric residents were responsible for the total care of the patients on the ward. Three third year medical students, a psychology trainee, a ward nurse, and nursing assistants were also integral members of the ward staff. Rehabilitation personnel such as occupational therapists, manual arts therapists, and educational therapists were also available.

Dynamically oriented psychotherapy characterized the major treatment effort as it did for the rest of the Psychiatric Service which was made up of a second such open ward, 2 acute closed wards on which there was a total of 41 patients, and 2 wards with 70 chronic, long-term patients. Free interchange between open and closed wards could and did take place.

Of the 60 patients admitted, 12 were not studied for administrative reasons. Our study population thus consisted of 48 patients. We made a point of seeing each of these patients as soon after admission as possible. The interview usually took place within 24 hours. Either the psychologist or the psychiatrist conducted this interview which was generally about an hour's duration. In about one-fifth of our cases, for purposes of checking techniques, joint interviews were held. The purpose of the interview was to gather as much detailed information as possible concerning the circumstances leading to hospital admission.

We devised a questionnaire to guide us after a 5-week pilot study during which we interviewed all admissions (see Appendix). The results of this trial run are not part of the data we present below.

The research nature of the interview was made clear to the patient at the outset. He knew that his therapist if not already assigned was to be another member of the staff and that our emphasis on admission circumstances had no direct bearing on the treatment he was to receive. To help round out our picture by getting a participant's point of view it had been our intention at first to have the social worker routinely interview the person or persons who had accompanied the patient to the hospital. For administrative reasons, however, this could not be consistently done. When such interviews were not held and when the patient was unaccompanied, decisions about whether to write asking a family member to come in were made in the initial research interview with the patient. That decision was based on the belief that the particular family member was dynamically important from the patient's view of his family and could shed light on events which seemed to be related to the need for hospitalization. The patient always knew that the social worker was having this interview. The questionnaire indicated above was also used as the point of reference for this interview. In 23 of our 48 cases family members were seen.

RESULTS

We attempted to quantify as much of the data from our interviews as seemed fruitful to us. In presenting the results, we shall give quantitative data as well as short case reports that suggest a relationship between seeking hospital admission and changes in interactions between the patients and significant people in their lives.

First, a few general characteristics of our patients should be noted. The patients in this population were diagnosed as having a variety of psychiatric disorders. The following table gives distribution of patients according to discharge diagnosis:

Distribution of diagnoses at time of discharge

Psychosis	19	40%
Psychoneurosis	18	38%
Personality trait and pattern disturbance	10	20%
Chronic brain syndrome	1	2%
	48	100%

This distribution is not significantly different from the distribution of diagnoses for the Psychiatric Service of this hospital during the entire year that the study was conducted.

Our evidence indicates that the majority of patients had been ill for some time. Thirty-one (65%) reported that they had been ill for longer than 1 year prior to admission. Most of these patients stated that they had been ill "for years." One patient gave a history of periodic hallucinations for the past 40 years, though less than a year was spent in a psychiatric hospital during that time. Twenty-seven (57%) reported previous psychiatric hospitalizations.

The above findings show how our open ward patient population encompasses the major diagnostic categories and that the patients vary in the length of time they report having symptoms, the majority longer than a year. Certainly, we would consider all of these patients psychiatrically ill, but this study is concerned with trying to account for the event of hospital admission within this illness. The majority of these patients were living outside the hospital with symptoms. Our concern is with the question, "Why apply for admission to the hospital at this time?" To this end, we focused our attention on the patients' relationships to significant people in their environment.

The marital status of our patients at the time of admission breaks down as follows: 29 (61%) were married; 7 (14%) were divorced, separated, or widowed; 12 (25%) were single. But when we determine with whom the patients were living at the time of admission, some discrepancies appear. Only 20 of the 29 married patients were living with their spouses. Thirteen others were living with 1 or both of their parents. Fifteen patients were living alone. Of the 15 patients who were living alone, 7 were married, 4 were single, and 4 had been divorced or legally separated.

The most impressive findings in the above were that 9 of the 29 married patients were not living with their wives and that 7 of these 9 were living alone just prior to admission. These findings imply that at least one-third of our married patients were involved in conflicts that led to separation. Study of these individual cases revealed the fact that these were people who were isolated from their families at the time of admission.

The group of patients living alone were of special interest to us, since they represented almost one-third of our total population. They were people who were living out of the family setting, and we were curious about how relations with other people might affect their decisions to come to the hospital. The following 2 histories illustrate some of the diverse ways that interpersonal factors influence patients to seek hospitalization, though the patients are living alone.

One patient had been separated from his wife for about 18 months. He had been in arrears in his payments to her for the support of their children, and she had sought legal assistance. Their respective attorneys suggested reconciliation as a way of settling his obligations. The wife—who was an aide in the hospital—readily consented, providing the patient would agree to come to the hospital, "for him to find out what was wrong with him." The patient had been abusive and quite suspicious of her since his discharge from service in the last 10 years. He agreed to come into the hospital, "to prove she was wrong." His wife arranged his admission.

A second patient, age 58, had been divorced for many years and was living a marginal life in a cheap hotel. About 2 years prior to this admission he had been discharged from the tuberculosis unit at this hospital. Over a period of about 3 months he became increasingly anxious, complaining of being unable to concentrate. Upon reporting for a routine tuberculosis evaluation, he requested admission for his anxiety symptoms. On admission he reported 2 events which had caused his concern. One was a recent occasion in which he had stolen 50 dollars from an intoxicated friend, and as a consequence reported suffering a great deal of guilt. The second event was his concern about not hearing from his daughter for about a month prior to admission. Their only contact for many years had been the exchange of occasional letters.

Though the first patient was living alone, his wife was the instigator of hospitalization and asked the hospital to convince the patient that he was ill. The patient in turn saw his hospitalization as an opportunity to convince his wife that he was healthy, in order to effect a return to the family. The second patient sought hospital admission following a threat to 2 relationhips, however tenuous they were. Hospitalization for him seemed to be an opportunity to reestablish a relationship with an interested interpersonal environment to make up for the loss.

One of the characteristics of the first patient referred to above was that he did not initiate a request for help. It was clearly his wife who seemed much more concerned about his behavior than he was. In our interviews we attempted to identify the first person we heard about who initiated a request for help. Of the 48 patients studied, 8 were judged as having someone other than themselves initiate a request for help for them. These requests came from a court, The American Red Cross, a father, and wives in several instances. In the remaining 40 admissions, the patient seemed to be the first person to ask directly for help.

The first person or agency to whom the initial request for help was directed was also identified. A VA agency was the most frequent recipient of this request; 26 (54%) of the patients or their families turned to it directly. The next most frequent source of help was the local medical doctor, who was approached by 9 (19%) of the patients. Only 4 patients turned to a non-VA psychiatric source for help. For the remaining 9 patients, wives, siblings, a friend, and the court were approached. In 2 instances we identified the patient as the person who was approached to get help for himself. These findings highlight the fact that half the patients immediately turned to the VA as a source of help. The other half eventually were directed to it, or considered it themselves.

The fact that these patients do turn to the hospital more frequently than other medical sources of help is revealed by the fact that only 14 (29%) of the patients considered or actually had some form of outpatient treatment for the complaints which they presented to the hospital. Reasons given for not considering out-patient treatment included feeling too sick and in need of constant contact with doctors, inability to wait for an appointment, being advised specifically by a physician to seek hospital admission. A few patients stated clearly that they had no place else to go when they were disturbed or that they were helped on a previous admission and immediately thought of returning to the hospital when they realized the need of further treatment. The fact that 34 (71%) of these patients did not even consider outpatient treatment suggested that hospitaliza-tion is an end in itself—over and above the question of getting help for the complaints. The existence of a hospital facility in a metropolitan area, with an interest in and an obligation to treat these patients, makes it possible for patients to turn quite readily to the hospital when faced with certain serious inter-personal conflicts.

Since our interest was in the status of the patients' relations with significant people in their lives, we attempted to estimate the extent to which the patients involved other people in their decision to come to the hospital. For this purpose we counted the number of participants in the patients' decisions to come to the hospital. A participant is defined as someone or some agency who either was sought out by the patients or sought them out and took a stand relative to the patients' interest in getting help. These data are based on the detailed interviews

The median number of participants other than the patient was two. But there were 2 patients who presented themselves at the hospital door, presumably without conferring with anyone about coming to the hospital. There were 14 patients involving 3 or more participants. We believe that we have some evidence that the more participants, the greater the likelihood that the patients' admissions are in response to pressures from significant people in their environment.

In the above data, we have made several references to the involvement of a varied number of people in the patient's admission. We sought to determine how these people felt about the patient's admission in terms of its effect on the family and the patient's work, and to compare their responses to those of the patients. Twenty-seven (57%) of the patients said with little hesitation that it was a good thing for their families that they decided to come to the hospital. By "a good thing" they included a variety of elements. In some situations, it was good because their symptoms or poorly controlled behavior interrupted the normal living patterns at home. Sometimes the patients felt if they could get well, they and their wives could live a more meaningful life together. Only 4 (8%) of the patients felt hospitalization would be bad for the family, but 17 (35%) felt it would have no effect on the family at all. It is of interest to note that in only 2 instances did patients state that they thought hospitalization would adversely affect their job in any way.

A rather different picture of the effect of hospitalization on the family is obtained from the caseworker's interviews with the 23 family members. Their responses were equally distributed among the 3 categories indicated above.

The family's uncertainty seems mirrored here. Often at the time of admission there is a real perplexity about whether the patient can be helped in a hospital, anxiety about the economic aspects of the hospitalization, and guilt often related to some recognition of the part they play in the patient's emotional turmoil.

The complexity of the relationships of patient and family is further underlined by our findings of no correlation between the patient's and the family's stated view of the effect the hospitalization will have on the family.

From the above remarks it seems clear that patients come to the hospital from a variety of situations and under many different circumstances. It would not be surprising, then, to find that they came to the hospital for any number of reasons and had rather varied expectations as to the outcome of their hospital treatment. However, in looking over the responses to questions in these areas, one is impressed with a general agreement among the patients. It was not usual for patients to see their environment at fault, or even specific people with whom they felt in conflict. Rather they focused the problem more on themselves, though in a rather definite way. Generally, the patients stated that they came to the hospital for the relief of symptoms. The spectrum of symptomatology was quite wide including vague complaints such as headache or upset stomach. There were some patients who stated their reasons for coming to the hospital in more sophisticated terms indicating awareness of emotional conflict playing a role in the production of their symptoms, but this was unusual. The symptoms and the manner in which they were presented were so varied that any more specific categorization seemed useless.

When the patients discussed their expectations of hospital treatment in this early interview, they showed little variation in their responses. What they wanted was relief from symptoms. They were not particular as to the way in which this relief was to be brought about (i.e., drugs, rest, psychotherapy), nor did they have anything to say about how long they expected the treatment to take. In fact, only 2 patients made a major point of stressing the need for a brief hospitalization.

An integral part of our interest is that patients come to the hospital at a certain phase of their involvement in conflictual personal relationships, or at times when there are changes in certain important aspects of their living situations. To explore these areas we asked these recently admitted patients directly or indirectly about their relationships with people and changes in their lives prior to admission. It is important to keep in mind here as well as in other parts of this section of the paper that if these patients had been interviewed later in their hospital course they may have provided more information revealing a wider scope of conflictual areas in their lives.

Our criteria for conflict and change are quite gross. By conflict, we refer to open disagreements and arguments and by changes we refer to such things as change in work, loss of work, loss of a family member. Thirty-one (65%) of this patient group reported emotional conflicts with people close to them, almost always family members. These conflicts seemed to be over a variety of manifest issues, and it did not seem to be useful to try to categorize them. It was usual that if a patient reported a conflict, he also indicated that some change had occurred in his life prior to admission. However, there are some exceptions, so that some patients reported conflicts and no changes and others indicated changes and no emotional conflicts. A total of 37 (77%) of the patients indicated conflicts or changes. It should be recognized that these categories overlap and depend on each other. A certain conflict at home may lead to a change in a job or a move. On the other hand, loss of a job might intensify certain conflict situations in the home.

Patients tended to be more specific in talking about changes in their lives prior to hospitalization. Thirty (63%) of the patients reported such changes. Eighteen of these 30 patients reported such changes as marriages, separations from their wives, birth of a child, employer becoming more critical.

It is seen, then, that the majority of patients give evidence of conflict or change in their lives just prior to hospital admission. Of course at this point we cannot say that these changes or these conflicts brought about hospitalization. However, it is our impression that in many instances these circumstances were of major importance and that they had certain implications for the hospital treatment, its course, and eventual outcome.

COMMENT

What impressed us about our data were the patterns which emerged from our study of the circumstances surrounding admission. As we began to look at the patients' attitudes toward hospitalization, we were struck by their lack of concern about length of hospitalization, for the welfare of their families, or for the protection of their employment while in the hospital. Only 2 patients expressed concern about length of hospitalization, and 2 expressed concern about losing their jobs. As indicated, 27 (57%) of the patients expressed the opinion that it was to the family's benefit that they be in the hospital.

On the other hand families tend to take a somewhat different view of this state of affairs. Only one-third of the family members stated that it was good for the family that the patient was being hospitalized. When this is coupled with the lack of correlation between the patient's opinions about the effect on the family, and the family member's opinion about the same thing, it becomes clear that patients and family members are in conflict about the patients' hospitalization. The evidence for conflict in general is apparent in the fact that 31 (65%) of the patients report conflict with someone in the environment.

These findings suggested to us that a closer examination of the circumstances leading to hospitalization would be profitable. As we focused our attention on this problem it was especially notable that hospital admission seemed to follow demands by some other person for the patient to change his behavior. This was striking enough for us to begin to think of admission as being initiated in some patients by the action of some family member. We examined our data from this point of view; and the 3 authors agreed that 13 of the 48 patients' admissions followed some action on the part of some other person. This was a family member in every instance except one. In 8 patients the family member explicitly refused to continue living with the patient under existing circumstances.

We called this group of 13 patients the "Family Group," to highlight the manifest demands of a family member for the patient to change his behavior, as a condition of his remaining at home. The other group of 35 patients we called the "Patient Group," to point up the fact that hospital admission was initiated by the patient without specific pressure from the family being discerned by us.

With this distinction in mind we compared these 2 groups to determine the extent to which membership in 1 of the 2 groups differentiated patients on all of the variables indicated in the previous parts of the paper. Chi Square procedures were applied to test the statistical significance of our findings.

The "Family Group" was found to be significantly different from the "Patient Group" in the following ways:

1   Someone other than the patient is more likely to initiate the request for help for the patient.
2   This request for help is less likely to be directed toward the VA initially.
3   Significantly more people participate in the patients' decisions to come to the hospital.
4   Patients remain in the hospital a significantly shorter period of time.

The first 3 findings in some way represent the criteria we used to select people for this group. Thus 7 patients in the Family Group did not initiate the request for help; but a wife, and a court requested help for these patients. In 6 admissions the request for help came from the patient only after the family member took some kind of action. The number of participants in the Family Group involved 2 people more frequently than the Patient Group. This finding highlights the interpersonal involvement of these patients, though its significance is not clear. The last finding that the length of hospitalization is less for this group is an entirely independent finding, since it was not known at the time of the assignment of patients to the 2 groups. Only 1 patient in the Family Group stayed longer than 4 months, while 17 patients in the Patient Group remained longer than that.

In no other respect could we find a statistically significant difference between these two groups. In a future study we will investigate the extent to which treatment procedures and outcomes differ for patients in the 2 groups. We are interested in examining this concept of family demand for modification of behavior as a factor in hospital admission. By the same token it is our impression that patients in our patient group utilize hospital admission to influence family members to modify their behavior. The extent to which these 2 views contribute to our understanding will be illustrated by the following 2 histories, one from each group.

An example of the Family Group is a 23-year-old married man with a history of ill-defined "seizures," previously considered epilepsy. There was indication of considerable turmoil between patient and wife, and patient had sought female companionship outside his marriage. Prior to his admission the patient gave a history of increasingly frequent "blackout spells" and feelings of inadequacy and inability to work followed by a series of poorly coordinated medical consultations and requests for hospital care. His wife refused to let him in the house and changed the locks on the doors. His admission here was further characterized by his confession that he would like to maintain the marriage and his willingness to forego his relationship with his girl friends. He also came to reveal that his "blackout spells" were feigned and an indication that he simply did not know what to do because his life seemed to be in such turmoil. The wife clearly indicated that if hospitalization could help him resolve his emotional distress that their marriage could continue. His admission seemed to say to her that he was willing to try to resolve his difficulties and attempt to continue the marriage.

The reverse situation seemed to apply for some of the patients in the "Patient Group." They appeared to be saying that until certain family relationships changed, their place was not at home but in the hospital.

Illustrative of this was a 36-year-old married man with a history of impotence and intense marital conflict, culminating in his admission to our open ward with the diagnosis of "anxiety reaction, acute." He indicated that he had reason to believe that his wife had been unfaithful to him and that this had been almost too much for him to bear. His maladjustment found expression in an inability to continue the work he had been doing as a skilled factory employee for many years. His wife immediately prior to admission had, at an outing conducted by the company, involved the factory foreman in an attempt to convince the patient to give up his concern about the problem and to give up the idea of getting help with it. These pressures notwithstanding, the patient still sought hospital admission, in part, it seems to us, as an expression of his unwillingness to tolerate a relationship in which his wife's conduct was unacceptable to him. He made several attempts to enter the hospital, refusing the opportunity to enter when it was offered. Each time, he returned to his wife trying to force her to confess her infidelity. During his hospitalization after considerable badgering by him, she acknowledged the fact that in truth she had been unfaithful. He was thus able to communicate to her his attitude that his return home from the hospital required her confession of infidelity.

We are interested in pursuing the distinction between family initiated and patient initiated hospital admission from the point of view of how patients are treated and the outcomes of that treatment. We are also investigating the extent to which return to the family requires modification of the behavior of either the patient or a family member. It is not the thesis of this paper that psychiatric admissions are unrelated to psychopathology. But we view hospital admission as an event taking place in an interpersonal setting frequently as a response to threatening demands for someone to change his behavior. We were able to demonstrate to some degree the function of hospitalization as a demand from the patient for someone else to change. In at least one-fourth of our patients, we believe we identified a clear demand for the patient to change his behavior through psychiatric hospitalization.

SUMMARY

The admission circumstances of 48 patients on an open psychiatric ward of a general-medical and surgical training Veterans Administration Hospital were studied on the assumption that understanding these circumstances would be diagnostically and therapeutically useful to the clinician. Special attention was paid to the role of relatives in the period immediately prior to admission.

In 13 of the 48 cases the admission did follow some action by another person. Of these 13 it was explicitly indicated to 8 that under prevailing conditions, they could not continue to live in their household. Our understanding of these 13 patients led to the concept of a "Family Group" in which there seemed to be a relationship between the family's demands and the patient's hospitalization, and a "Patient Group" in which hospitalization was initiated by the patient without apparent specific family pressure.

The "Family Group" was found to be significantly different from the "Patient Group" in the following ways:

1 Someone other than the patient is more likely to initiate the request for help for the patient.
2 This request for help is less likely to be directed toward the Veterans Administration initially.
3 Significantly more people participate in the patients' decisions to come to the hospital.
4 Patients remain in the hospital a significantly shorter period of time.

There is also evidence to suggest that hospitalization can for some patients be a way of demanding that those close to them change their behavior, just as it can be an expression by relatives that they are dissatisfied with the patient's behavior. Seventy-one per cent of the patients did not even consider outpatient treatment prior to seeking admission, lending further support to the hypothesis that hospitalization is an end in itself over and above the question of getting help with symptoms. As viewed by the patient, his purpose in coming to the hospital generally was to obtain symptom relief. It was the rare patient who verbalized an awareness of his need for psychological aid.

Conflictual relations at home or changes in some aspect of their living situation characterized the preadmission status of 77% of our total group. In only 2 of our 48 cases did the patients think hospitalization for psychiatric treatment would adversely effect their job in any way.

Studies awaiting publication report the hospital treatment experience and post-discharge adjustment of this same patient population.

Psychiatric Section, West Side Veterans Administration Hospital (16).

References

1   Wanklin, J. M.; Fleming, D. F.; Buck, C. W., and Hobbs, G. E.: Factors Influencing Rate of First Admissions to Mental Hospitals, *J. Nerv. & Ment. Dis.* **121:** 103–116 (Feb.) 1955.

2   Buck, C.; Wanklin, J. M., and Hobbs, G. E.: Analysis of Regional Differences in Mental Illness, *J. Nerv. & Ment. Dis.* **122:** 73–79 (July) 1955.

3   Stanton, A. H., and Schwartz, M. D.: The Management of A Type of Institutional Participation in Mental Illness, *Psychiatry* **12:** 13–26 (Feb.) 1949.

4   Yarrow, M. R.; Clausen, J. A., and Robbins, P. R.: The Social Meaning of Mental Illness, *J. Social Issues* **11:** 33–48, 1955.

5   Yarrow, M. R.; Schwartz, C. G.; Murphy, H., and Deasy, L.: Psychological Meaning of Mental Illness in the Family, *J. Social Issues* **11:** 12–25, 1955.

6   Deasy, L., and Quinn, O. W.: The Wife of the Mental Patient and the Hospital Psychiatrist, *J. Social Issues* **11:** 49–61, 1955.

7   Clausen, J. A., and Yarrow, M. R.: Paths to the Mental Hospital, *J. Social Issues* **11:** 25–33, 1955.

8   Spiegel, J. P.: The Resolution of Role Conflict Within the Family, *Psychiatry* **20:** 1–16 (Feb.) 1957.

9   Coleman, J.; Fleck, S.; Janowicz, and Norton, N.: A Comparative Study of Psychiatric Clinic and Family Agency: Part I, *Social Casework* **38:** 3–8 (Jan.) 1957.

10 Coleman, J.; Fleck, S.; Janowicz, and Norton, N.: A Comparative Study of Psychiatric Clinic and Family Agency: Part II, *Social Casework* **38:** 74–80 (Jan.) 1957.

Appendix

Admission Questionnaire

1.   Name
2.   Age
3.   Sex

4.   Race—W. N.

5.   Birthplace of parents (country)

6.   Marital status: 1. Single   2. Married   3. Divorced   4. Separated   5. Widowed

7.   With whom does patient live? (List all persons by relationship to patient.)

8.   Where was patient living prior to hospitalization? (City)

9.   When did patient decide to come to the hospital? (Number of days prior to hos.)

10.   Who were people who participated in this decision? (List all people by relationship to patient, including LMD, VA Psychiatrist, VA Agency, NVA Psychiatrist, and others as specified)

11.   How long has patient had complaints? (In months, or parts of months)

12.   How long prior to hospitalization does patient claim his complaints have become worse? (In weeks, or parts of weeks)

13.   Who initiated request for help for the patient?

14.   To whom was this request directed?

15.   List each of the participants in the decision to come to the hospital in chronological order, and specify the position each took with respect to influencing the patient's admission to the hospital.

16.   Who accompanied patient to the hospital, and why, and what is the relationship of this person to the patient?

17.   Why didn't patient seek or accept outpatient treatment?

18.   Did person admitting patient to the hospital raise some objection to the patient about admitting him?

24
DECISION PROCESSES IN PSYCHIATRIC HOSPITALIZATION: PATIENTS REFERRED, ACCEPTED, AND ADMITTED TO A PSYCHIATRIC HOSPITAL*

Elliot G. Mishler and Nancy E. Waxler

Recent studies of the treatment histories of psychiatric patients have documented the strong influence of social factors, such as social class or family role expectations, on both the type of treatment offered patients and on their re-

Source: Elliot G. Mishler, and Nancy E. Waxler, "Decision Processes in Psychiatric Hospitalization: Patients Referred, Accepted, and Admitted to a Psychiatric Hospital," American Sociological Review, 28: 576–587, 1963.

* This is the first report of a study of the decisions to refer and admit patients to psychiatric hospitals. The study involved both a follow-up of inquiries for admission received at two psychiatric hospitals and intensive interviews with the referring physicians and mothers or wives of a sub-sample of male patients referred to the hospital. This paper includes findings from the follow-up inquiries; other papers will discuss some of the factors entering into the referral decision as determined from the field interviews. The authors wish to acknowledge the active cooperation and interest of the superintendents, admitting officers, and staffs of the hospitals involved: at the Massachusetts Mental Health Center—Jack R. Ewalt, M.D., Superintendent; Halim Mitry, M.D., Executive Officer; Mrs. H. Hunnefeld and Mrs. Patricia Kary of the Admitting Office; at the McLean Hospital—Alfred H. Stanton, M.D., Psychiatrist-in-Chief; Francis de Marneffe, M.D., Director of Hospital Affairs; Miss Golda M. Edinburg, Director of the Department of Social Work; and Mrs. Hope N. MacDonald, Social Work Supervisor. This study was supported in part by a grant from the Department of Psychiatry of the Harvard Medical School.

sponse to treatment.[1] These studies have focused on in-treatment populations which have already been subjected to a variety of selective influences. We know very little about either the determinants of the decision to enter treatment or about the ways that social factors enter into the process at different points along the path to treatment.

We see the psychiatric patient's path into, through, and out of treatment as a selection problem.[2] From this perspective it is necessary, first, to define an initial "legitimate demand" population; that is, the group of persons making a claim on the services of the treatment facility from which group are drawn the sub-populations of those who are accepted for and eventually enter treatment. Second, we must specify the sequence of "selection operations" by which the original demand population becomes a later "in-treatment" population. Finally, a clear understanding of the selection "rules" and of the relationship between initial and later populations requires comparisons between the sub-populations selected "in" and "out" at each selection point in the sequence. (Figure 1 gives a schematic representation of the process.)

Specifically, this paper will examine the "fates" of persons referred for psychiatric hospitalization as their respective fates are associated with selected social characteristics. The rules governing decisions to accept or admit patients to treatment will be made explicit through analysis of differences within a cohort of referred patients between those who are accepted or not accepted, and admitted or not admitted to a psychiatric hospital. A major aim of the paper is the description and illustration of a conceptual approach and a method of analysis that is particularly appropriate to the study of selection decisions.

PROCEDURE

The study was conducted at the Massachusetts Mental Health Center and the McLean Hospital. The first is state-supported, the second a private mental hospital. Both hospitals are small, about 160 and 225 beds, respectively, and are intensive treatment institutions.

The initial "legitimate demand" population was defined for purposes of the study as all persons for whom hospitalization was requested or inquired about of the hospital's Admissions Officers (or their representatives). The Admissions Officer has the authority to accept patients; all admissions to the hospital must at some point be accepted or approved by him. Requests may be from the patient himself although in most instances in the hospitals under study the requests came from physicians or family members. We will refer to this group as the

[1] August B. Hollingshead and Fredrick C. Redlich, *Social Class and Mental Illness*, New York: Wiley, 1958; John A. Clausen and Marian Radke Yarrow (eds.), "The Impact of Mental Illness on the Family," *Journal of Social Issues*, XI, 4 (1955); Howard E. Freeman and Ozzie G. Simmons, "Mental Patients in the Community: Family Settings and Performance Levels," *American Sociological Review*, 23 (April, 1950), pp. 147–54; L. Schaffer and J. Myers, "Psychotherapy and Social Stratification: An Empirical Study of Practices in a Psychiatric Outpatient Clinic," *Psychiatry*, 17 (1954), pp. 83–93.

[2] Harold Garfinkel, Harry R. Brickman, and Egon Bittner, "Methodological Adequacy in the Quantitative Study of Selection Criteria and Selection Activities in Psychiatric Out-patient Clinics," Unpublished Manuscript, Revised November, 1959, 35 pp. and Appendices, (Ditto). The basic theoretical approach and method of analysis used in the present study are taken directly from Garfinkel's work. In addition to his published and unpublished materials, the senior author has had the benefit of extended discussions with him of many of the questions involved in the development of this study. His help and advice are gratefully acknowledged.

"inquiry" population since it is composed of those making inquiries about admission. The procedures for collecting these names varied in detail between the two hospitals, but the aim was to record all inquiries related to hospitalization that came into the hospital Admissions Office. Our inquiry population consists of all referrals for hospitalization during an eleven-week period in the spring of 1961.

Admissions Officers were asked to obtain as much of the following information as was possible on each call: (a) name of the referring person, (b) profession of the referring person, (c) presence or absence of a relative, (d) familial relationship of closest relative, (e) patient's sex, (f) patient's age, (g) whether and where previously hospitalized, (h) time of day of inquiry, (i) Admitting Officer receiving the call, (j) nature of the hospital's response to the call, that is, whether the patient was accepted, rejected, or referred elsewhere. All of these items of information are inquired about routinely. Thus, they were not being asked to change their usual procedures but only to make a more systematic attempt to secure this information even for cases that were not accepted.

If a patient was accepted for admission by the Massachusetts Mental Health Center, his name was placed on a waiting list and he was routinely given an appointment for admission for between a few days to two weeks after the inquiry; at McLean Hospital, a waiting list procedure was not used at the time of the study. Acceptance required medical approval and usually involved making an appointment at the time of the inquiry for the patient's admission.

Being accepted and placed on the waiting list or being given an appointment for admission did not mean that the individual automatically entered the hospital as a patient. One major aim of the current study is to determine the nature of the differences between those who did and those who did not enter the hospital. Information on actual admission was obtained from a search of the hospital admission records. All patients who had been accepted at the point of inquiry were traced and classified as admitted if they appeared on the admission records within a period of four weeks following the inquiry date.

Finally, all patients who did not enter the hospital, including those originally accepted as well as those not accepted for admission at the point of inquiry, were traced through the Massachusetts Department of Mental Health files, which record admissions to all public and private hospitals in the state. Patients were classified according to whether they had or had not been admitted to a psychiatric hospital during the six month period following their original inquiry to our two study hospitals.

To answer the basic question of the study—namely, whether there are differences along social variables between populations that are sorted into different paths—the most appropriate comparisons are between the complementary subgroups that emerge after each decision point. Thus, one first compares the group accepted with that not accepted for admission (the stage immediately after inquiry on Figure 1); then within the accepted group, those admitted are compared with those not admitted to the hospital; and similarly for the other comparisons. Thus, at each decision point in the path we will compare the patients who continue "in" the path with those who drop "out" of this particular treatment path.

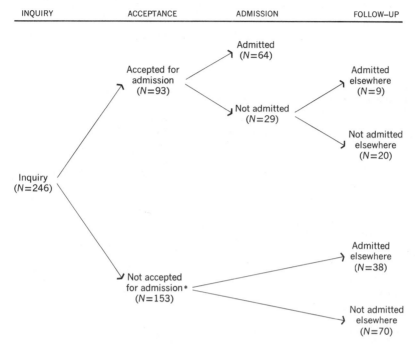

| INQUIRY | ACCEPTANCE | ADMISSION | FOLLOW–UP |

Inquiry
(*N*=246)

Accepted for
admission
(*N*=93)

Admitted
(*N*=64)

Not admitted
(*N*=29)

Admitted
elsewhere
(*N*=9)

Not admitted
elsewhere
(*N*=20)

Not accepted
for admission*
(*N*=153)

Admitted
elsewhere
(*N*=38)

Not admitted
elsewhere
(*N*=70)

*No names were available for 45 of these cases, and no follow-up was possible for these individuals.

Note: During an eleven-week period in the Spring of 1961, a total of 246 requests for admission were received by the Admissions Office of the Massachusetts Mental Health Center. The numbers in parentheses record how this initial population was distributed and the points where patients were selectively accepted or admitted.

Fig. 1   Model for representing decision points in the hospitalization of psychiatric patients.

This form of analysis permits the use of statistical tests that assume independence since the sub-samples being compared in each case are independent samples. Further, it allows us to pin-point precisely at which point in the sequence of selection operations particular variables exert their influence. Finally, the basic theoretical idea of the sequence of selection operations is retained in the statistical analysis since later populations being compared are selected subpopulations of the original cohort.[3]

RESULTS

The model for analyzing the data is presented in Figure 1. The original demand population for the Massachusetts Mental Health Center consisted of 246 requests for admission. Of these, 93 (or 39 per cent) were accepted for admission; of the

[3] Garfinkel's paper, *op. cit.*, should be referred to for a detailed examination of other possible comparisons such as between two successive "in" populations as, for example, the accepted and admitted groups; or, between two different "out" populations, such as those not admitted to the study hospital and those not admitted elsewhere. Each of these possible comparisons is shown to be either illegitimate because the samples are not independent of each other, or inappropriate to the basic question because the sequential character of the process is ignored.

93 accepted, 64 (or 69 per cent) were actually admitted. The group admitted represents 26 per cent of the group who requested admission.

The distributions of the original cohort and the sub-populations along the de-

Table 1
Frequency and percentage distributions of original inquiry cohort and cohorts accepted and admitted to the Massachusetts Mental Health Center

Attribute	Original inquiry cohort	Accepted by the hospital		Admitted to the hospital	
	N	N	%	N	%
Total	246	93	39	64	27
Referral source:					
M.D.	137**	80**	58	55	40
Non-M.D.	103	13	13	9	9
Unknown[a]	6	0	0	0	0
Specialty of referral agent:					
Psychiatrist	66	42	64	30	45
Psychiat. resident	33	23	70	16	50
Specialist	11	8	73	3	27
G.P.	5	2	40	1	20
Other M.D.	22	7	32	5	23
Non-M.D. and unknown	109	13	12	10	9
Presence of relative:					
Mentioned	110**	54**	49	38	35
Not mentioned	136	39	29	26	19
Relative relationship:					
Spouse	49	27	55	19	39
Parent	61	27	44	19	31
Unknown	136	39	29	26	19
Sex of patient:					
Male	99	41	41	32	32
Female	144	52	36	32	22
Unknown	3	0	0	0	0
Age of patient:					
10–19	29*	9**	31	6	21
20–29	54	34	63	22	41
30–39	36	17	47	13	36
40–49	20	13	65	8	40
50 plus	34	9	26	4	12
Unknown	73	11	15	11	15
Previous hospitalization:					
None	68*	35*	51	22	32
Here	61	17	28	14	23
Other	61	28	46	20	33
Unknown	56	13	23	8	14
Hospital decision maker:					
Non-M.D.	147	56	38	40	27
M.D.	95	35	37	23	24
Unknown	4	2	50	1	25
Time of inquiry:					
Day	179	73	41	50	28
Night	67	20	30	14	21

Note: Percentage figures refer to the number of persons out of the original cohort who are accepted or admitted to the hospital; e.g., 58% of those referred by M.D.s are accepted and 40% admitted to the hospital.
[a] "Unknown" means the information was not determined at the time of inquiry.
** Two-tailed χ^2 with $p < .01$.
* Two-tailed χ^2 with $p < .05$.

scriptive variables on which information was collected can be determined by examining Table 1. The degree and nature of attrition in the original population after each of the two decision points is evident from a comparison of the second and third columns with the first column of the table.

Chi square has been used as a summary statistic to evaluate the level of statistical significance of differences on each variable between patients sorted "in" and "out" at each of the two decision points.[4] In Tables 1, 2, and 3 the levels of significance noted in the first column (Original Inquiry Cohort) tell us whether there is a significant overall difference on a particular variable across the full selection process from beginning to end, without regard for whether this difference occurred at either one or both of the decision points. The probability values in the other two columns, Accepted and Admitted to the Hospital, tell us whether there are any significant differences between groups of patients at either of the specific decision points; that is, whether those accepted differ from those not accepted and whether those admitted differ from those not admitted to the hospital. Following Garfinkel and the usual convention, a difference at either one of the decision points will be accepted as significant only if the overall chi square value for that variable is also significant.

In the overall comparisons, four of the nine variables differentiate significantly between groups sorted "in" or "out" of the path into the hospital. These are: whether the referring person is or is not a physician, whether a relative of the patient is mentioned at the time of inquiry, the age of the patient, and whether the patient has been previously hospitalized. These results tell us that there are significant differences on these particular variables between groups sorted "in" or "out" at one or more points in time.

The sub-table comparison in Table 1 of Accepted vs. Non-Accepted cohorts examines differences between the persons sorted "in" and "out" at the inquiry decision point (refer to Figure 1). At the point of inquiry to the hospital the decision to accept or reject a particular patient reflects the hospital's implicit and explicit rules for acceptance. At this decision point we find that the type of referral agent, whether a relative is mentioned, the age of the patient, and the hospitalization history of the patient all discriminate between those groups accepted by the hospital and those groups not accepted. All four of these were also significant in the overall comparisons.

The second set of sub-table comparisons in Table 1 refers to differences between groups of patients actually admitted to the hospital after having been accepted and those accepted but not admitted. In this instance the decision process is centered outside of the hospital in the referring person, the patient, and other people. None of the variables recorded by the hospital at inquiry discriminates significantly between these two groups.

---

[4] As would be true of any summary statistic, chi square may over- or under-emphasize certain differences as compared to others, for example, as a function of different sample size, the numbers of categories used, or the distributions of cases through categories. While it seemed the most generally useful statistic for the comparisons made in this paper, the reader should also refer directly to the absolute percentage differences as shown in the tables for a more complete picture of the effects of different variables. Chi squares were corrected for continuity where expected cell frequencies were small and in a few cases categories were collapsed. For reasons of space, tables showing all chi squares have been omitted from the paper but are available from the authors.

Of the several variables that distinguish between accepted and non-accepted patients, it is clear from Table 1 that whether the referring person is or is not a physician is by far the most important one. This is reflected in the markedly high chi square value ($\chi^2 = 55.02, 1$ df, $p < .001$) and perhaps more importantly in the actual distribution of accepted and admitted patients. Thus, while referrals from physicians represent only 56 per cent of all inquiries, 86 per cent of those accepted and a similar proportion of those admitted are referred by physicians.

This finding is not surprising. It is the explicit policy of the hospital to accept as "legitimate" requests for admission only those inquiries that come from physicians and on the basis of this policy one might have expected an even higher relative rate of acceptance. However, the presence of a single strong variable makes it difficult to evaluate the meaning of relationships found with other variables. For example, the significant differences in age or previous hospitalization between accepted and non-accepted patients that appear in Table 1 may reflect the association of these variables with the likelihood of referral by physicians rather than a further and different aspect of the hospital's selection process. For this reason, a second analysis was conducted with the referral source controlled. That is, the same comparisons as those reported in Table 1 were made within that sub-group of the original cohort that had been referred to the hospital by a physician. (The number of accepted cases not referred by physicians is too small to permit the parallel comparisons that would constitute a complete control analysis.)

Table 2 reports the frequency and percentage distributions of the physician-referred inquiry cohort at the acceptance and admission points. Within the physician-referred group three variables reach a level of statistical significance in the overall comparison between groups sorted "in" and "out" at some point in the selection process. These are whether a relative is mentioned at the time of referral, the sex of the patient, and whether the patient had been previously hospitalized. The sub-table comparisons in the Accepted and Admitted columns of Table 2 tell us whether these variables distinguish between the "in" and "out" groups at the acceptance or admission point. At inquiry, when the hospital makes the decision to accept or reject the patient, mention of a relative, the sex of the patient, and the hospitalization history of the patient are all significant in differentiating between "ins" and "outs." At admission, when the patient, his physician, and others involved in the case decide whether the patient will enter the hospital, none of the variables is significant.

In summary, for the Massachusetts Mental Health Center, we have found that whether the referral agent is or is not a physician is significantly related to whether the patient is accepted by the hospital; although once the patient is accepted, whether he is admitted does not depend on the source of the referral. Further, for the entire group of inquiries, the patient's age, previous hospitalization, and the mention of a relative at the time of inquiry also discriminate significantly between accepted and non-accepted patients. Finally, the latter two variables also discriminate significantly, as does the sex of the patient, between accepted and non-accepted patients within that sub-group of inquiries referred to the hospital by physicians.

Table 2
Frequency and percentage distributions of original inquiry cohort and
cohorts accepted and admitted to the Massachusetts Mental Health Center:
persons referred to the hospital by physicians

Attribute	Original inquiry cohort: physician-referred	Accepted by the hospital		Admitted to the hospital	
	N	N	%	N	%
Total	136	80	59	54	40
M.D. specialty:					
Psychiatrist	66	42	64	30	45
Psychiat. res.	32	22	69	16	50
Specialist	11	8	73	3	27
G.P.	5	2	40	1	20
Other M.D.	22	6	27	4	18
Presence of relative:					
Mentioned	57**	48**	84	33	58
Not mentioned	79	32	41	21	27
Relative relationship:					
Spouse	27	23	85	16	59
Parent	30	25	83	17	23
Unknown	79	32	41	21	27
Sex of patient:					
Male	47**	35*	74	27	57
Female	88	45	51	27	31
Unknown	1	0	0	0	0
Age of patient:					
10–19	14	7	50	4	29
20–29	38	31	82	21	55
30–39	21	15	71	11	52
40–49	15	12	80	7	47
50 plus	11	7	64	3	27
Unknown	36	8	22	8	22
Previous hospitalization:					
None	32*	32**	74	21	49
Here	27	11	41	8	30
Other	35	26	74	19	54
Unknown	31	11	35	6	19
Hospital decision maker:					
Non-M.D.	87	48	55	34	39
M.D.	46	30	65	19	41
Unknown	3	2	66	1	33
Time of inquiry:					
Day	111	62	56	41	37
Night	25	18	72	13	52

** Two-tailed χ^2 with $p < .01$
* Two-tailed χ^2 with $p < .05$

From the point of view of the variables we have been concerned with, the
point of acceptance or rejection by the hospital would appear to be the critical
decision point in the selection process. Once a patient is accepted by the hospital, these particular variables do not discriminate among patients who are
admitted or not admitted whether we take the entire cohort of inquiries or the
physician-referred group as our base population.

These findings for the Massachusetts Mental Health Center may be compared with those for the McLean Hospital. The procedures for handling referrals differ between the two hospitals. At McLean no separate acceptance and admission points are easily discriminated. Negotiations for admission may continue over a period, and whether it is the hospital, the referral agent, or the patient who makes the decision against admission is not recorded in a way that permits us to distinguish between the two points of acceptance and admission as was done for the Massachusetts Mental Health Center. For this reason, we are able at McLean to compare only admitted and non-admitted groups with each other and we cannot locate whether the decision reflected the hospital's operating procedure or the patient's situation since they are intermingled.

This inability to make the separation between points of acceptance and admission means that a comparison with the previous findings is both arbitrary and somewhat ambiguous. This is so since we may choose whether to compare the differences found at McLean with those found at the Massachusetts Mental Health Center either at the point of acceptance or the point of admission or for the full overall comparison. (That these different points provided different findings has been shown in Tables 1 and 2. The McLean findings will stand by themselves as reflecting the admission patterns at that institution; in relating them to the previous findings we will use the overall results for the full inquiry cohort as the most appropriate point of comparison.

Table 3 presents the findings for the McLean Hospital.

Two of the variables that previously showed significant differences between admitted and non-admitted groups reappear in the findings for McLean. Referrals from physicians are more likely to be admitted than other referrals; and whether or not a relative's name is recorded is also associated with admission. These variables seem to reflect fairly directly both hospital policy and admitting procedures. As for the non-significant differences we find three variables that repeat those noted previously. That is, who the hospital decision maker is, the time of day at which the inquiry is received, and the sex of the patient do not distinguish between admitted and non-admitted patients at either hospital.

Two variables show significant differences at both hospitals but the direction of the relationship is different. Age of the patient is a significant discriminator but whereas at the Massachusetts Mental Health Center the age groups 20–29 were accepted in disproportionately greater numbers than their numbers in the population of referrals, at McLean Hospital it is the age group 30–39 that is admitted at a disproportionately higher rate. The previous hospitalization history of the patient is also a strong discriminating variable at both hospitals. However, while we found that at the Massachusetts Mental Health Center patients who were previously hospitalized there had a lower chance for admission, at the McLean Hospital we find that their ex-patients have a disproportionately greater chance for admission and those hospitalized elsewhere fare better than those with no previous record of hospitalization.

At the McLean Hospital, if the relationship of the relative involved is that of spouse the admission rate is higher than that found with other relationships; no differences among different types of relatives involved were found at the Massachusetts Mental Health Center.

Table 3
Frequency and percentage distributions of original inquiry and physician-referred cohorts and cohorts admitted to McLean Hospital

Attribute	Original inquiry cohort	Admitted to the hospital		Physician-referred cohort	Admitted to the hospital	
	N	N	%	N	N	%
Total	137	79	58	94	69	73
Referral source:						
M.D.	94	69**	73	—	—	—
Non-M.D.	36	6	17	—	—	—
Unknown	7	4	57	—	—	—
Presence of relative:						
Mentioned	114	78**	68	84	68**	81
Not mentioned	23	1	4	10	1	10
Relative relationship:						
Spouse	50	40*	80	42	37	88
Parent	38	26	68	28	22	79
Other	26	12	46	14	9	64
Unknown	23	1	4	10	1	10
Sex of patient:						
Male	66	36	54	46	31	67
Female	60	33	55	48	38	79
Unknown	1	0	0	0	0	0
Age of patient:						
10–19	16	8**	50	12	8	67
20–29	29	20	69	21	18	86
30–39	23	19	83	18	15	83
40–49	14	9	64	12	9	75
50 plus	38	22	58	22	19	86
Unknown	17	1	6	9	0	0
Previous hospitalization:						
None	57	28**	49	42	26*	62
McLean	26	22	85	22	19	86
Other	48	29	60	28	24	86
Unknown	5	29	0	2	0	0
Hospital decision maker:						
Non-M.D.	91	43	47	58	38	66
M.D.	17	7	24	10	5	50
Unknown	29	29	100	26	26	100
Time of inquiry:						
Day	92	43	47	59	38	64
Night	13	5	38	6	3	50
Unknown	32	31	97	29	28	97

** Two-tailed χ^2 with $p < .01$
* Two-tailed χ^2 with $p < .05$

Whether or not the referral came from a physician is the strongest variable discriminating between admitted and non-admitted groups ($\chi^2 = 32.04$, 1 df; $p < .001$). For this reason, a second analysis was conducted within the physician-referred cohort as was done previously. These findings are in the last two columns of Table 3. Two variables, whether a relative is mentioned and whether the patient was previously hospitalized, retain discriminating power within this control variable. While a relationship with previous hospitalization had also held for our analysis at the Massachusetts Mental Health Center, it must be remembered that the direction of the relationship is different. Here, at the McLean Hospital, it is the patients who had been previously hospitalized there, and next in rank those who had been hospitalized elsewhere, who have higher rates of admission.

We have examined selection criteria, as they are manifest in comparisons of accepted and admitted patients, for two hospitals that are different from each other in some important respects and similar to each other in still other important respects. The findings suggest that there are some criteria and rules they share, such as a tendency to accept physician-referred patients at disproportionately higher rates than patients not so referred. There are also some rules and criteria on which they differ that reflect their particular policies and referral populations. For example, the different ways in which they handle their own ex-patients seem to fall into this category.

So far the analysis has centered on whether persons referred to a particular psychiatric hospital are admitted to it or not. Whether those not admitted enter another hospital is also of considerable interest. Is referral to one hospital part of a "shopping around" process or is it a selective and specific act? In the first instance, a high rate of admission to other hospitals might be expected among the non-admitted group; in the second, a low rate of admissions to other hospitals. Further, differences found among patients admitted or not admitted to other hospitals will suggest the kinds of considerations that entered into the first referral and into the decision not to enter the hospital after having been accepted.

Whether an individual in the original inquiry cohort is admitted to any psychiatric hospital in Massachusetts during the six month period following the inquiry to the Massachusetts Mental Health Center is shown in Table 4. Forty-five per cent of the referred population is actually admitted to some hospital following this inquiry. Of this group of admissions about 60 per cent are ad-

Table 4
Follow-up of inquiries to the Massachusetts Mental Health Center: frequency and percentage distributions of admissions to inquiry or other hospital

Admission status	Admission from time of inquiry					
	Within four weeks		After four weeks		Total	
	N	%	N	%	N	%
Admitted to:						
Inquiry hospital	61	25	3	1	64	27
Other state hospital	19	8	9	4	28	12
Private hospital	13	5	3	1	16	7
Total admitted	93	38	15	6	108	45
Not admitted					93	39
Status unknown					38	16
Total inquiry cohort					239*	100

* The total N is 7 cases less than the total inquiry N since duplicate inquiries were followed up only once.

mitted to the original referral hospital. Eighty-six per cent of the patients admitted to any hospital enter within four weeks of the initial inquiry.[5]

While the findings suggest that other hospitals are not adequate substitutes for the Massachusetts Mental Health Center—among those whose fates are known, only 32 per cent of those not admitted to the latter are admitted to any hospital —nevertheless, the meaning of this finding remains ambiguous with regard to the factors taken into account in the referral decision. This ambiguity arises from the fact that this percentage of eventually admitted cases is strikingly similar to the percentage of all original inquiries admitted to the Massachusetts Mental Health Center itself—27 per cent.

If the prime consideration involved in a patient's admission to a hospital is the severity of his illness, we would expect that most referred patients would be admitted to some hospital soon after their referral. That more than half of the referred patients are not admitted to any hospital points to the importance of other factors in referral and admission. Social factors such as the degree of the physician's control over the patient, the nature of the family's role in the hospitalization decision, and the degree to which the patient has power over the treatment decision may all be relevant. These factors are explored directly in the field interview survey of relatives and referral physicians, from which findings will be reported in other papers.

However, some leads to understanding this process may be found in comparisons, within the accepted and non-accepted cohorts, of patients admitted and not admitted to other hospitals. Of these patients on whom we have follow-up information who are originally rejected at the hospital's admission office, there are only two variables that approach statistical significance in distinguishing between those admitted and those not admitted elsewhere. First, patients who are referred by physicians are more likely to stay out of other hospitals if they are not accepted by the original referral hospital; in contrast, patients referred by relatives are more likely to enter another hospital ($\chi^2=2.70$, 1 df, $p<.20$). Family members appear to be taking a general step toward hospitalization for the patient; if the patient is not accepted in one hospital he is referred to another. Physicians who refer patients to the original hospital seem to be making a more selective decision that reflects their knowledge of the hospital's particular treatment program.

The second variable distinguishing between patients originally rejected and then admitted elsewhere and those rejected and not admitted elsewhere is the age of the patient. The relationship is curvilinear with those in the 30–49 age group more likely to stay out of the hospital ($\chi^2=5.81$, 2 df, $p<.10$). This may reflect differences both in the types of social support available and the prevalent diagnoses in the different age groups.

The second cohort of patients followed up after inquiry to the original hospital consists of those patients who were accepted for admission, put on the

---

[5] Two limitations with regard to these findings must be kept in mind. First, 16 per cent of the original cohort fall into a "status unknown" group which is largely composed of referred patients where the exact name was not determined at inquiry; second, some of the general hospitals in Massachusetts that accept psychiatric patients, usually for very brief stays, do not report their admissions to the Department of Mental Health. The figures on admission are, therefore, the minimum estimate for actual admissions.

waiting list, and then were not admitted either because they or their physicians cancelled the appointment or they did not show up at the appointed time. Of the total group of 29 (representing about 30 per cent of all originally accepted patients) nine patients are admitted to another hospital.

Only one significant difference occurs between those admitted elsewhere and those who are not. This is whether the decision maker who accepted the patient at the referral hospital was a physician. Patients accepted by non-physicians in the referral hospital admission office and who are not actually admitted are also unlikely to be admitted to any other hospital ($\chi^2=4.67$, 1 df, $p<.05$). The sex of the patient approaches significance with males more likely than females to be admitted to another hospital ($\chi^2=2.15$, 1 df, $p<.20$).

DISCUSSION

A primary objective of this paper has been to demonstrate the applicability of a particular model to the analysis of a selection problem; that is, the acceptance and admission of referred patients to a psychiatric hospital. Essentially, the model involves a comparison of the sub-groups of persons sorted "in" or "out" at each selection point, the two groups together comprising the total group arriving to this point. The model directs attention to the separate decision points that constitute the overall selection process and sensitizes us to the possibility that specific variables may have different effects at different points in this process.

The importance of this differentiated view of the selection process is shown in the findings presented from the Massachusetts Mental Health Center. For those variables on which we had information, it appears that the point of acceptance by the hospital is more critical in distinguishing between "ins" and "outs" than the later point of actual admission. Thus, within the physician-referred cohort, the patient's sex, previous hospitalization, and whether or not the presence of a relative is mentioned at the time of inquiry all differentiate accepted from non-accepted patients at a statistically significant level. But, none of these variables discriminates between admitted and non-admitted patients.

The differences found between patients admitted and not admitted to this hospital are thus seen to be largely a function of the decision made at the point of inquiry. The power over this decision resides in the hospital; the power over the decision to enter the hospital is more diffused and is centered out in the community. It is the hospital, through its admitting procedures and selective orientation, that disproportionately accepts males and persons with no record of previous hospitalization and not persons with these characteristics that disproportionately select themselves for admission.

One additional caution is necessary in interpreting this set of findings. The analysis has been restricted to standard information collected routinely by the hospital admitting office at the point of inquiry. Other variables such as the patient's diagnosis, the degree of incapacity, social class, the "tolerance for deviance" of family members may all be more critical in discriminating "ins" and "outs" at the point of admission. Information on these variables was not available for both accepted and non-accepted patients in a standard form for comparison purposes.

The model has also permitted us to compare selection processes in two different institutions. It was possible to indicate both how the processes differ qualitatively and vary in the criteria used for selecting or rejecting patients. For example, in applying the model to the McLean Hospital we found that we could not separate for analytic purposes the acceptance and admission decision points in the way we had at the Massachusetts Mental Health Center. Further, even when the same variable proved to be important this did not mean that it functioned in the same way. For example, to be previously hospitalized at the McLean increased an applicant's chance of admission to it; to be previously hospitalized at the Massachusetts Mental Health Center decreased an applicant's chance of admission there.

Some limitations of the findings may be reviewed briefly. First, the analysis has been restricted to an examination of each variable taken one at a time. This assumes a high degree of independence among the variables. A multi-variate analysis was carried out that explored the degrees of association among the variables in each of the successive cohorts. The results add to but do not negate the findings reported here and since their inclusion would have severely complicated the presentation they have been reserved for a later paper.

Second, the restriction to routine administrative data is a serious limitation to our understanding of the role of other potentially important variables in this process. In the field interviews, considerable attention was given to social and psychological factors as they entered into the referral decision. Emphasis will be placed on these variables in reporting the findings from the field study.

Third, these data do not permit a direct inference to how these variables are actually taken into account by the hospital or community decision makers when the decision is made to accept or admit the patient. Interpretations of the way these variables enter into the decisions require information beyond that contained in these comparisons and levels of statistical significance. For example, our other information about these hospitals suggests that the powerful effect of being referred by a physician on a patient's likelihood of acceptance by the hospital is a function of explicit hospital policy. This is not the only possible explanation. The findings would fit as easily within a scheme of interpretation that pushes the selection mechanism back to the referral agent's judgment. That is, physicians may be more acquainted with the types of patients preferred by the hospital and therefore tend to select patients for referral that are more likely to be accepted, than are non-physicians who have less experience and less knowledge of the system.

In this connection a non-significant difference does not mean that the variable is not being taken into account by the decision maker. We found no significant differences among physician-referred patients between "ins" and "outs" on the variable of age. However, this may reflect a conscious attempt on the part of the admitting officers to accept patients proportional to their appearance at the point of inquiry. It might reflect a procedure that explicitly randomizes for age; or, a procedure where age is irrelevant to the decision. Our point is that a choice from among these interpretations requires more than a finding of significant or non-significant differences. With this model of the selection process and its associated method of analysis, non-significant differences are as important a source of information about the selection criteria as are significant differences. Other information is needed for the statistical findings to be made theoretically meaningful.[6]

Finally, there is an important implication of these findings for studies that are restricted to populations of patients who are "in treatment" whether the locus of treatment be the office of the private practitioner or the ward of the mental hospital. Our data not only permit but force the conclusion that the patients in treatment, in this instance "admitted" to the hospital, are not a representative sample of patients referred and accepted for hospitalization, nor of all patients seeking such care, nor, by implication, of all mentally ill persons.

If, for example, we were to make this assumption of representativeness with regard to the admitted group of patients we would be obscuring the fact that this group comes through a referral pathway of a physician. This may make them more likely to define their problems in medical terms; the probability of prior contact with physicians may be related to education or ethnicity. Other variables found associated with selection into treatment such as age or previous hospitalization may also be associated in complex ways with characteristics of the patient's illness.

When the social characteristics of patients in treatment are viewed as if they were valid correlates of the illness itself, this ignores the important role played by these variables in the selection process. A method for the analysis of this process has been described and illustrated in this paper.

25
THE SOCIETAL REACTION TO DEVIANCE: ASCRIPTIVE ELEMENTS IN THE PSYCHIATRIC SCREENING OF MENTAL PATIENTS IN A MIDWESTERN STATE
Thomas J. Scheff (with the assistance of Daniel M. Culver)

The case for making the societal reaction to deviance a major independent variable in studies of deviant behavior has been succinctly stated by Kitsuse:

[6] See Garfinkel, op. cit., for an extended discussion of the problem of interpretation.
Source: Thomas J. Scheff, "The Societal Reaction to Deviance: Ascriptive Elements in the Psychiatric Screening of Mental Patients in a Midwestern State," Social Problems, 11: 401–413, 1964.
This report is part of a larger study, made possible by a grant from The Advisory Mental Health Committee of Midwestern State. By prior agreement, the state in which the study was conducted is not identified in publications.

A sociological theory of deviance must focus specifically upon the interactions which not only define behaviors as deviant but also organize and activate the application of sanctions by individuals, groups, or agencies. For in modern society, the socially significant differentiation of deviants from the non-deviant population is increasingly contingent upon circumstances of situation, place, social and personal biography, and the bureaucratically organized activities of agencies of control.[1]

In the case of mental disorder, psychiatric diagnosis is one of the crucial steps which "organizes and activates" the societal reaction, since the state is legally empowered to segregate and isolate those persons whom psychiatrists find to be committable because of mental illness.

Recently, however, it has been argued that mental illness may be more usefully considered to be a social status than a disease, since the symptoms of mental illness are vaguely defined and widely distributed, and the definition of behavior as symptomatic of mental illness is usually dependent upon social rather than medical contingencies.[2] Furthermore, the argument continues, the status of the mental patient is more often an ascribed status, with conditions for status entry external to the patient, than an achieved status with conditions for status entry dependent upon the patient's own behavior. According to this argument, the societal reaction is a fundamentally important variable in all stages of a deviant career.

The actual usefulness of a theory of mental disorder based on the societal reaction is largely an empirical question: to what extent is entry to the status of mental patient independent of the behavior or "condition" of the patient? The present paper will explore this question for one phase of the societal reaction: the legal screening of persons alleged to be mentally ill. This screening represents the official phase of the societal reaction, which occurs after the alleged deviance has been called to the attention of the community by a complainant. This report will make no reference to the initial deviance or other situation which resulted in the complaint, but will deal entirely with procedures used by the courts after the complaint has occurred.

The purpose of the description that follows is to determine the extent of uncertainty that exists concerning new patients' qualifications for involuntary confinement in a mental hospital, and the reactions of the courts to this type of uncertainty. The data presented here indicate that, in the face of uncertainty, there is a strong presumption of illness by the court and the court psychiatrists.[3] In the discussion that follows the presentation of findings, some of the causes, consequences and implications of the presumption of illness are suggested.

The data upon which this report is based were drawn from psychiatrists' ratings of a sample of patients newly admitted to the public mental hospitals in a Midwestern state, official court records, interviews with court officials and

---

[1] John I. Kitsuse, "Societal Reaction to Deviant Behavior: Problems of Theory and Method," *Social Problems,* **9** (Winter, 1962), pp. 247–257.

[2] Edwin M. Lemert, *Social Pathology,* New York: McGraw-Hill, 1951; Erving Goffman, *Asylums,* Chicago: Aldine, 1962.

[3] For a more general discussion of the presumption of illness in medicine, and some of its possible causes and consequences, see the author's "Decision Rules, Types of Error and Their Consequences in Medical Diagnosis," *Behavioral Science,* **8** (April, 1963), pp. 97–107.

psychiatrists, and our observations of psychiatric examinations in four courts. The psychiatrists' ratings of new patients will be considered first.

In order to obtain a rough measure of the incoming patient's qualifications for involuntary confinement, a survey of newly admitted patients was conducted with the cooperation of the hospital psychiatrists. All psychiatrists who made admission examinations in the three large mental hospitals in the state filled out a questionnaire for the first ten consecutive patients they examined in the month of June, 1962. A total of 223 questionnaires were returned by the 25 admission psychiatrists. Although these returns do not constitute a probability sample of all new patients admitted during the year, there were no obvious biases in the drawing of the sample. For this reason, this group of patients will be taken to be typical of the newly admitted patients in Midwestern State.

The two principal legal grounds for involuntary confinement in the United States are the police power of the state (the state's right to protect itself from dangerous persons) and *parens patriae* (the state's right to assist those persons who, because of their own incapacity, may not be able to assist themselves.)[4] As a measure of the first ground, the potential dangerousness of the patient, the questionnaire contained this item: "In your opinion, if this patient were released at the present time, is it likely he would harm himself or others?" The psychiatrists were given six options, ranging from Very Likely to Very Unlikely. Their responses were: Very Likely, 5%; Likely, 4%; Somewhat Likely, 14%; Somewhat Unlikely, 20%; Unlikely, 37%; Very Unlikely, 18%. (Three patients were not rated [1%].)

As a measure of the second ground, *parens patriae,* the questionnaire contained the item: "Based on your observations of the patient's behavior, his present degree of mental impairment is:

None............................ Minimal................................
Mild............................ Moderate................................
Severe..........................."

The psychiatrists' responses were: None, 2%; Minimal, 12%; Mild, 25%; Moderate, 42%; Severe, 17%. (Three patients were not rated [1%].)

To be clearly qualified for involuntary confinement, a patient should be rated as likely to harm self or others (Very Likely, Likely, or Somewhat Likely) and/or as Severely Mentally Impaired. However, voluntary patients should be excluded from this analysis, since the court is not required to assess their qualifications for confinement. Excluding the 59 voluntary admissions (26% of the sample), leaves a sample of 164 involuntary confined patients. Of these patients, 10 were rated as meeting both qualifications for involuntary confinement, 21 were rated as being severely mentally impaired, but not dangerous, 28 were rated as dangerous but not severely mentally impaired, and 102 were rated as not dangerous nor as severely mentally impaired. (Three patients were not rated.)

[4] Hugh Allen Ross, "Commitment of the Mentally Ill: Problems of Law and Policy," *Michigan Law Review,* 57 (May, 1959), pp. 945–1018.

According to these ratings, there is considerable uncertainty connected with the screening of newly admitted involuntary patients in the state, since a substantial majority (63%) of the patients did not clearly meet the statutory requirements for involuntary confinement. How does the agency responsible for assessing the qualifications for confinement, the court, react in the large numbers of cases involving uncertainty?

On the one hand, the legal rulings on this point by higher courts are quite clear. They have repeatedly held that there should be a presumption of sanity. The burden of proof of insanity is to be on the petitioners, there must be a preponderance of evidence, and the evidence should be of a "clear and unexceptionable" nature.[5]

On the other hand, existing studies suggest that there is a presumption of illness by mental health officials. In a discussion of the "discrediting" of patients by the hospital staff, based on observations at St. Elizabeth's Hospital, Washington, D. C., Goffman states:

[The patient's case record] is apparently not regularly used to record occasions when the patient showed capacity to cope honorably and effectively with difficult life situations. Nor is the case record typically used to provide a rough average or sampling of his past conduct. [Rather, it extracts] from his whole life course a list of those incidents that have or might have had "symptomatic" significance. . . . I think that most of the information gathered in case records is quite true, although it might seem also to be true that almost anyone's life course could yield up enough denigrating facts to provide grounds for the record's justification of commitment.[6]

Mechanic makes a similar statement in his discussion of two large mental hospitals located in an urban area in California:

In the crowded state or county hospitals, which is the most typical situation, the psychiatrist does not have sufficient time to make a very complete psychiatric diagnosis, nor do his psychiatric tools provide him with the equipment for an expeditious screening of the patient . . .

In the two mental hospitals studied over a period of three months, the investigator never observed a case where the psychiatrist advised the patient that he did not need treatment. Rather, all persons who appeared at the hospital were absorbed into the patient population regardless of their ability to function adequately outside the hospital.[7]

A comment by Brown suggests that it is a fairly general understanding among mental health workers that state mental hospitals in the U. S. accept all comers.[8]

---

[5] This is the typical phrasing in cases in the *Dicennial Legal Digest,* found under the heading "Mental Illness."

[6] Goffman, *op. cit.,* pp. 155, 159.

[7] David Mechanic, "Some Factors in Identifying and Defining Mental Illness," *Mental Hygiene,* **46** (January, 1962), pp. 66–74.

[8] Esther Lucile Brown, *Newer Dimensions of Patient Care,* Part I, New York: Russell Sage, 1961, p. 60, fn.

Kutner, describing commitment procedures in Chicago in 1962, also reports a strong presumption of illness by the staff of the Cook County Mental Health Clinic:

Certificates are signed as a matter of course by staff physicians after little or no examination . . . The so-called examinations are made on an assembly-line basis, often being completed in two or three minutes, and never taking more than ten minutes. Although psychiatrists agree that it is practically impossible to determine a person's sanity on the basis of such a short and hurried interview, the doctors recommend confinement in 77% of the cases. It appears in practice that the alleged-mentally-ill is presumed to be insane and bears the burden of proving his sanity in the few minutes allotted to him . . .[9]

These citations suggest that mental health officials handle uncertainty by presuming illness. To ascertain if the presumption of illness occurred in Midwestern State, intensive observations of screening procedures were conducted in the four courts with the largest volume of mental cases in the state. These courts were located in the two most populous cities in the state. Before giving the results of these observations, it is necessary to describe the steps in the legal procedures for hospitalization and commitment.

STEPS IN THE SCREENING OF PERSONS ALLEGED TO BE MENTALLY ILL

The process of screening can be visualized as containing five steps in Midwestern State:

1 The application for judicial inquiry, made by three citizens. This application is heard by deputy clerks in two of the courts (C and D), by a court reporter in the third court, and by a court commissioner in the fourth court.
2 The intake examination, conducted by a hospital psychiatrist.
3 The psychiatric examination, conducted by two psychiatrists appointed by the court.
4 The interview of the patient by the guardian *ad litem,* a lawyer appointed in three of the courts to represent the patient. (Court A did not use guardians *ad litem.*)
5 The judicial hearing, conducted by a judge.

These five steps take place roughly in the order listed, although in many cases (those cases designated as emergencies) step No. 2, the intake examination, may occur before step No. 1. Steps No. 1 and No. 2 usually take place on the same day or the day after hospitalization. Steps No. 3, No. 4, and No. 5 usually take place within a week of hospitalization. (In courts C and D, however, the judicial hearing is held only once a month.)

This series of steps would seem to provide ample opportunity for the presumption of health, and a thorough assessment, therefore, of the patient's

[9] Luis Kutner, "The Illusion of Due Process in Commitment Proceedings," *Northwestern University Law Review,* **57** (Sept. 1962), pp. 383–399.

qualifications for involuntary confinement, since there are five separate points at which discharge could occur. According to our findings, however, these procedures usually do not serve the function of screening out persons who do not meet statutory requirements. At most of these decision points, in most of the courts, retention of the patient in the hospital was virtually automatic. A notable exception to this pattern was found in one of the three state hospitals; this hospital attempted to use step No. 2, the intake examination, as a screening point to discharge patients that the superintendent described as "illegitimate," i.e., patients who do not qualify for involuntary confinement.[10] In the other two hospitals, however, this examination was perfunctory and virtually never resulted in a finding of health and a recommendation of discharge. In a similar manner, the other steps were largely ceremonial in character. For example, in court B, we observed twenty-two judicial hearings, all of which were conducted perfunctorily and with lightning rapidity. (The mean time of these hearings was 1.6 minutes.) The judge asked each patient two or three routine questions. Whatever the patient answered, however, the judge always ended the hearings and retained the patient in the hospital.

What appeared to be the key role in justifying these procedures was played by step No. 3, the examination by the court-appointed psychiatrists. In our informal discussions of screening with the judges and other court officials, these officials made it clear that although the statutes give the court the responsibility for the decision to confine or release persons alleged to be mentally ill, they would rarely if ever take the responsibility for releasing a mental patient without a medical recommendation to that effect. The question which is crucial, therefore, for the entire screening process is whether or not the court-appointed psychiatric examiners presume illness. The remainder of the paper will consider this question.

Our observations of 116 judicial hearings raised the question of the adequacy of the psychiatric examination. Eighty-six of the hearings failed to establish that the patients were "mentally ill" (according to the criteria stated by the judges in interviews).[11] Indeed, the behavior and responses of 48 of the patients at the hearings seemed completely unexceptionable. Yet the psychiatric examiners had not recommended the release of a single one of these patients. Examining the court records of 80 additional cases, there was still not a single recommendation for release.

Although the recommendation for treatment of 196 out of 196 consecutive cases strongly suggests that the psychiatric examiners were presuming illness, particularly when we observed 48 of these patients to be responding appropriately, it is conceivable that this is not the case. The observer for this study was not a psychiatrist (he was a first year graduate student in social work) and it is

[10] Other exceptions occurred as follows: the deputy clerks in course C and D appeared to exercise some discretion in turning away applications they considered improper or incomplete, at step No. 1; the judge in Court D appeared also to perform some screening at step No. 5. For further description of these exceptions see "Rural-Urban Differences in the Judicial Screening of the Mentally Ill in a Midwestern State." (In press)

[11] In interviews with the judges, the following criteria were named: Appropriateness of behavior and speech, understanding of the situation, and orientation.

possible that he could have missed evidence of disorder which a psychiatrist might have seen. It was therefore arranged for the observer to be present at a series of psychiatric examinations, in order to determine whether the examinations appeared to be merely formalities or whether, on the other hand, through careful examination and interrogation, the psychiatrists were able to establish illness even in patients whose appearance and responses were not obviously disordered. The observer was instructed to note the examiner's procedures, the criteria they appeared to use in arriving at their decision, and their reaction to uncertainty.

Each of the courts discussed here employs the services of a panel of physicians as medical examiners. The physicians are paid a flat fee of ten dollars per examination, and are usually assigned from three to five patients for eacn trip to the hospital. In court A, most of the examinations are performed by two psychiatrists, who went to the hospital once a week, seeing from five to ten patients a trip. In court B, C and D, a panel of local physicians was used. These courts seek to arrange the examinations so that one of the examiners is a psychiatrist, the other a general practitioner. Court B has a list of four such pairs, and appoints each pair for a month at a time. Courts C and D have a similar list, apparently with some of the same names as court B.

To obtain physicians who were representative of the panel used in these courts, we arranged to observe the examinations of the two psychiatrists employed by court A, and one of the four pairs of physicians used in court B, one a psychiatrist, the other a general practitioner. We observed 13 examinations in court A and 13 examinations in court B. The judges in courts C and D refused to give us the names of the physicians on their panels, and we were unable to observe examinations in these courts. (The judge in court D stated that he did not want these physicians harassed in their work, since it was difficult to obtain their services even under the best of circumstances.) In addition to observing the examinations by four psychiatrists, three other psychiatrists used by these courts were interviewed.

The medical examiners followed two lines of questioning. One line was to inquire about the circumstances which led to the patient's hospitalization, the other was to ask standard questions to test the patient's orientation and his capacity for abstract thinking by asking him the date, the President, Governor, proverbs, and problems requiring arithmetic calculation. These questions were often asked very rapidly, and the patient was usually allowed only a very brief time to answer.

It should be noted that the psychiatrists in these courts had access to the patient's record (which usually contained the Application for Judicial Inquiry and the hospital chart notes on the patient's behavior), and that several of the psychiatrists stated that they almost always familiarized themselves with this record before making the examination. To the extent that they were familiar with the patient's circumstances from such outside information, it is possible that the psychiatrists were basing their diagnoses of illness less on the rapid and peremptory examination than on this other information. Although this was true to some extent, the importance of the record can easily be exaggerated, both because of the deficiencies in the typical record, and because of the way it is usually utilized by the examiners.

The deficiencies of the typical record were easily discerned in the approximately one hundred applications and hospital charts which the author read. Both the applications and charts were extremely brief and sometimes garbled. Moreover, in some of the cases where the author and interviewer were familiar with the circumstances involved in the hospitalization, it was not clear that the complainant's testimony was any more accurate than the version presented by the patient. Often the original complaint was so paraphrased and condensed that the application seemed to have little meaning.

The attitude of the examiners toward the record was such that even in those cases where the record was ample, it often did not figure prominently in their decision. Disparaging remarks about the quality and usefulness of the record were made by several of the psychiatrists. One of the examiners was apologetic about his use of the record, giving us the impression that he thought that a good psychiatrist would not need to resort to any information outside his own personal examination of the patient. A casual attitude toward the record was openly displayed in 6 of the 26 examinations we observed. In these 6 examinations, the psychiatrist could not (or in 3 cases, did not bother to) locate the record and conducted the examination without it, with one psychiatrist making it a point of pride that he could easily diagnose most cases "blind".

In his observations of the examinations, the interviewer was instructed to rate how well the patient responded by noting his behavior during the interview, whether he answered the orientation and concept questions correctly, and whether he denied and explained the allegations which resulted in his hospitalization. If the patient's behavior during the interview obviously departed from conventional social standards (e.g., in one case the patient refused to speak), if he answered the orientation questions incorrectly, or if he did not deny and explain the petitioners' allegations, the case was rated as meeting the statutory requirements for hospitalization. Of the 26 examinations observed, eight were rated as Criteria Met.

If, on the other hand, the patient's behavior was appropriate, his answers correct, and he denied and explained the petitioners' allegations, the interviewer rated the case as not meeting the statutory criteria. Of the 26 cases, seven were rated as Criteria Not Met. Finally, if the examination was inconclusive, but the interviewer felt that more extensive investigation might have established that the criteria were met, he rated the cases as Criteria Possibly Met. Of the 26 examined, 11 were rated in this way. The interviewer's instructions were that whenever he was in doubt he should avoid using the rating Criteria Not Met.

Even giving the examiners the benefit of the doubt, the interviewer's ratings were that in a substantial majority of the cases he observed, the examination failed to establish that the statutory criteria were met. The relationship between the examiners' recommendations and the interviewer's ratings are shown in the following table.

Table 1
Observer's ratings and examiners' recommendations

Observer's ratings:		Criteria met	Criteria possibly met	Criteria not met	Total
Examiners' Recommendations	Commitment	7	9	2	18
	30-day observation	1	2	3	6
	Release	0	0	2	2
Total		8	11	7	26

The interviewer's ratings suggest that the examinations established that the statutory criteria were met in only eight cases, but the examiners recommended that the patient be retained in the hospital in 24 cases, leaving 16 cases which the interviewer rated as uncertain, and in which retention was recommended by the examiners. The observer also rated the patient's expressed desires regarding staying in the hospital, and the time taken by the examination. The ratings of the patient's desire concerning staying or leaving the hospital were: Leave, 14 cases; Indifferent, 1 case; Stay, 9 cases; and Not Ascertained, 2 cases. In only one of the 14 cases in which the patient wished to leave was the interviewer's rating Criteria Met.

The interviews ranged in length from five minutes to 17 minutes, with the mean time being 10.2 minutes. Most of the interviews were hurried, with the questions of the examiners coming so rapidly that the examiner often interrupted the patient, or one examiner interrupted the other. All of the examiners seemed quite hurried. One psychiatrist, after stating in an interview (before we observed his examinations) that he usually took about thirty minutes, stated: "It's not remunerative. I'm taking a hell of a cut. I can't spend 45 minutes with a patient. I don't have the time, it doesn't pay." In the examinations that we observed, this physician actually spent 8, 10, 5, 8, 8, 7, 17, and 11 minutes with the patients, or an average of 9.2 minutes.

In these short time periods, it is virtually impossible for the examiner to extend his investigation beyond the standard orientation questions, and a short discussion of the circumstances which brought the patient to the hospital. In those cases where the patient answered the orientation questions correctly, behaved appropriately, and explained his presence at the hospital satisfactorily, the examiners did not attempt to assess the reliability of the petitioner's complaints, or to probe further into the patient's answers. Given the fact that in most of these instances the examiners were faced with borderline cases, that they took little time in the examinations, and that they usually recommended commitment, we can only conclude that their decisions were based largely on a presumption of illness. Supplementary observations reported by the interviewer support this conclusion.

After each examination, the observer asked the examiner to explain the criteria he used in arriving at his decision. The observer also had access to the examiner's official report, so that he could compare what the examiner said about the case with the record of what actually occurred during the interview. This supplementary information supports the conclusion that the examiner's decisions are based on the presumption of illness, and sheds light on the manner in which these decisions are reached:

1 The "evidence" upon which the examiners based their decision to retain often seemed arbitrary.
2 In some cases, the decision to retain was made even when no evidence could be found.
3 Some of the psychiatrists' remarks suggest prejudgment of the cases.
4 Many of the examinations were characterized by carelessness and haste. The first question, concerning the arbitrariness of the psychiatric evidence, will now be considered.

In the weighing of the patient's responses during the interview, the physician appeared not to give the patient credit for the large number of correct answers he gave. In the typical interview, the examiner might ask the patient fifteen or twenty questions: the date, time, place, who is President, Governor, etc., what is 11×10, 11×11, etc., explain "Don't put all your eggs in one basket," "A rolling stone gathers no moss," etc. The examiners appeared to feel that a wrong answer established lack of orientation, even when it was preceded by a series of correct answers. In other words, the examiners do not establish any standard score on the orientation questions, which would give an objective picture of the degree to which the patient answered the questions correctly, but seem at times to search until they find an incorrect answer.

For those questions which were answered incorrectly, it was not always clear whether the incorrect answers were due to the patient's "mental illness," or to the time pressure in the interview, the patient's lack of education, or other causes. Some of the questions used to establish orientation were sufficiently difficult that persons not mentally ill might have difficulty with them. Thus one of the examiners always asked, in a rapid-fire manner: "What year is it? What year was it seven years ago? Seventeen years before that?" etc. Only two of the five patients who were asked this series of questions were able to answer it correctly. However, it is a moot question whether a higher percentage of persons in a household survey would be able to do any better. To my knowledge, none of the orientation questions that are used have been checked in a normal population.

Finally, the interpretations of some of the evidence as showing mental illness seemed capricious. Thus one of the patients, when asked, "In what way are a banana, an orange, and an apple alike?" answered, "They are all something to eat." This answer was used by the examiner in explaining his recommendation to commit. The observer had noted that the patient's behavior and responses seemed appropriate and asked why the recommendation to commit had been made. The doctor stated that her behavior had been bizarre (possibly referring to her alleged promiscuity), her affect inappropriate ("When she talked about being pregnant, it was without feeling,") and with regard to the question above: "She wasn't able to say a banana and an orange were fruit. She couldn't take it one step further, she had to say it was something to eat." In other words, this psychiatrist was suggesting that the patient manifested concreteness in her thinking, which is held to be a symptom of mental illness. Yet in her other answers to classification questions, and to proverb interpretations, concreteness was not apparent, suggesting that the examiner's application of this test was arbitrary. In another case, the physician stated that he thought the patient was suspicious and distrustful, because he had asked about the possibility of being represented by counsel at the judicial hearing. The observer felt that these and other similar interpretations might possibly be correct, but that further investigation of the supposedly incorrect responses would be needed to establish that they were manifestations of disorientation.

In several cases where even this type of evidence was not available, the examiners still recommended retention in the hospital. Thus, one examiner, employed by court A stated that he had recommended 30-day observation for a patient whom he had thought *not* to be mentally ill, on the grounds that the patient, a young man, could not get along with his parents, and "might get into trouble." This examiner went on to say:

We always take the conservative side. [Commitment or observation] Suppose a patient should commit suicide. We always make the conservative decision. I had rather play it safe. There's no harm in doing it that way.

It appeared to the observer that "playing safe" meant that even in those cases where the examination established nothing, the psychiatrists did not consider recommending release. Thus in one case the examination had established that the patient had a very good memory, was oriented and spoke quietly and seriously. The observer recorded his discussion with the physician after the examination as follows:

When the doctor told me he was recommending commitment for this patient too (he had also recommended commitment in the two examinations held earlier that day) he laughed because he could see what my next question was going to be. He said, "I already recommended the release of two patients this month." This sounded like it was the maximum amount the way he said it.

Apparently this examiner felt that he had a very limited quota on the number of patients he could recommend for release (less than two percent of those examined).

The language used by these physicians tends to intimate that mental illness was found, even when reporting the opposite. Thus in one case the recommendation stated: "No gross evidence of delusions or hallucinations." This statement is misleading, since not only was there no gross evidence, there was not any evidence, not even the slightest suggestion of delusions or hallucinations, brought out by the interview.

These remarks suggest that the examiners prejudge the cases they examine. Several further comments indicate prejudgment. One physician stated that he thought that most crimes of violence were committed by patients released too early from mental hospitals. (This is an erroneous belief.)[12] He went on to say that he thought that all mental patients should be kept in the hospital at least three months, indicating prejudgment concerning his examinations. Another physician, after a very short interview (8 minutes), told the observer:

On the schizophrenics, I don't bother asking them more questions when I can see they're schizophrenic because I *know what they are going to say.* You could talk to them another half hour and not learn any more.

Another physician, finally, contrasted cases in which the patient's family or others initiated hospitalization ("petition cases," the great majority of cases) with those cases initiated by the court: "The petition cases are pretty *automatic.* If the patient's own family wants to get rid of him you know there is something wrong."

The lack of care which characterized the examinations is evident in the forms on which the examiners make their recommendations. On most of these forms, whole sections have been left unanswered. Others are answered in a peremptory and uninformative way. For example, in the section entitled Physical Examination, the question is asked: "Have you made a physical examination of the patient? State fully what is the present physical condition.", a typical answer is "Yes. Fair.", or, "Is apparently in good health." Since in none of the examinations we observed was the patient actually physically examined, these answers appear to be mere guesses. One of the examiners used regularly in court B, to the question "On what subject or in what way is derangement now manifested?" always wrote in "Is mentally ill." The omissions, and the almost flippant brevity of these forms, together with the arbitrariness, lack of evidence, and prejudicial character of the examinations, discussed above, all support the observer's conclusion that, except in very unusual cases, the psychiatric examiner's recommendation to retain the patient is virtually automatic.

Lest it be thought that these results are unique to a particularly backward Midwestern State, it should be pointed out that this state is noted for its progressive psychiatric practices. It will be recalled that a number of the psychiatrists employed by the court as examiners had finished their psychiatric residencies, which is not always the case in many other states. A still common practice in other states is to employ, as members of the "Lunacy Panel," partially retired physicians with no psychiatric training whatever. This was the case in Stockton,

[12] The rate of crimes of violence, or any crime, appears to be less among ex-mental patients than in the general population. Henry Brill and Benjamin Malzberg, "Statistical Report Based on the Arrest Record of 5354 Ex-patients Released from New York State Mental Hospitals During the Period 1946–48." Mimeo available from the authors; Louis H. Cohen and Henry Freeman, "How Dangerous to the Community Are State Hospital Patients?", *Connecticut State Medical Journal,* 9 (Sept., 1945), pp. 697–700; Donald W. Hastings, "Follow-up Results in Psychiatric Illness," *Amer. Journal of Psychiatry,* 118 (June 1962), pp. 1078–1086.

California, in 1959, where the author observed hundreds of hearings at which these physicians were present. It may be indicative of some of the larger issues underlying the question of civil commitment that, in these hearings, the physicians played very little part; the judge controlled the questioning of the relatives and patients, and the hearings were often a model of impartial and thorough investigation.

DISCUSSION

Ratings of the qualifications for involuntary confinement of patients newly admitted to the public mental hospital in a Midwestern state, together wih observations of judicial hearings and psychiatric examinations by the observer connected with the present study, both suggest that the decision as to the mental condition of a majority of the patients is an uncertain one. The fact that the courts seldom release patients, and the perfunctory manner in which the legal and medical procedures are carried out, suggest that the judicial decision to retain patients in the hospital for treatment is routine and largely based on the presumption of illness. Three reasons for this presumption will be discussed: financial, ideological, and political.

Our discussions with the examiners indicated that one reason that they perform biased "examinations" is that their rate of pay is determined by the length of time spent with the patient. In recommending retention, the examiners are refraining from interrupting the hospitalization and commitment procedures already in progress, and thereby allowing someone else, usually the hospital, to make the effective decision to release or commit. In order to recommend release, however, they would have to build a case showing why these procedures should be interrupted. Building such a case would take much more time than is presently expended by the examiners, thereby reducing their rate of pay.

A more fundamental reason for the presumption of illness by the examiners, and perhaps the reason why this practice is allowed by the courts, is the interpretation of current psychiatric doctrine by the examiners and court officials. These officials make a number of assumptions, which are now thought to be of doubtful validity:

1 The condition of mentally ill persons deteriorates rapidly without psychiatric assistance.

2 Effective psychiatric treatments exist for most mental illnesses.

3 Unlike surgery, there are no risks involved in involuntary psychiatric treatment: it either helps or is neutral, it can't hurt.

4 Exposing a prospective mental patient to questioning, cross-examination, and other screening procedures exposes him to the unnecessary stigma of trial-like procedures, and may do further damage to his mental condition.

5 There is an element of danger to self or others in most mental illness. It is better to risk unnecessary hospitalization than the harm the patient might do himself or others.

Many psychiatrists and others now argue that none of these assumptions are necessarily correct.

1   The assumption that psychiatric disorders usually get worse without treatment rests on very little other than evidence of an anecdotal character. There is just as much evidence that most acute psychological and emotional upsets are self-terminating.[13]

2   It is still not clear, according to systematic studies evaluating psychotherepy, drugs, etc., that most psychiatric interventions are any more effective, on the average, than no treatment at all.[14]

3   There is very good evidence that involuntary hospitalization and social isolation may affect the patient's life: his job, his family affairs, etc. There is some evidence that too hasty exposure to psychiatric treatment may convince the patient that he is "sick," prolonging what may have been an otherwise transitory episode.[15]

4   This assumption is correct, as far as it goes. But it is misleading because it fails to consider what occurs when the patient who does not wish to be hospitalized is forcibly treated. Such patients often become extremely indignant and angry, particularly in the case, as often happens, when they are deceived into coming to the hospital on some pretext.

5   The element of danger is usually exaggerated both in amount and degree. In the psychiatric survey of new patients in state mental hospitals, danger to self or others was mentioned in about a fourth of the cases. Furthermore, in those cases where danger is mentioned, it is not always clear that the risks involved are greater than those encountered in ordinary social life. This issue has been discussed by Ross, an attorney:

> A truck driver with a mild neurosis who is "accident prone" is probably a greater danger to society than most psychotics; yet, he will not be committed for treatment, even if he would be benefited. The community expects a certain amount of dangerous activity. I suspect that as a class, drinking drivers are a greater danger than the mentally ill, and yet the drivers are tolerated or punished with small fines rather than indeterminate imprisonment.[16]

From our observations of the medical examinations and other commitment procedures, we formed a very strong impression that the doctrines of danger to self or others, early treatment, and the avoidance of stigma were invoked partly because the officials believed them to be true, and partly because they provided convenient justification for a pre-existing policy of summary action, minimal investigation, avoidance of responsibility and, after the patient is in the hospital, indecisiveness and delay.

The policy of presuming illness is probably both cause and effect of political pressure on the court from the community. The judge, an elected official, runs

[13] For a review of epidemiological studies of mental disorder see Richard J. Plunkett and John E. Gordon, *Epidemiology and Mental Illness*. New York: Basic Books, 1960. Most of these studies suggest that at any given point in time, psychiatrists find a substantial proportion of persons in normal populations to be "mentally ill." One interpretation of this finding is that much of the deviance detected in these studies is self-limiting.

[14] For an assessment of the evidence regarding the effectiveness of electroshock, drugs, psychotherapy, and other psychiatric treatments, see H. J. Eysenck, *Handbook of Abnormal Psychology*, New York: Basic Books, 1961, Part III.

[15] For examples from military psychiatry, see Albert J. Glass, "Psychotherapy in the Combat Zone," in *Symposium on Stress*, Washington, D.C., Army Medical Service Graduate School, 1953, and B. L. Bushard, "The U.S. Army's Mental Hygiene Consultation Service," in *Symposium on Preventive and Social Psychiatry*, 15–17 (April 1957), Washington, D.C.: Walter Reed Army Institute of Research, pp. 431–43. For a discussion of essentially the same problem in the context of a civilian mental hospital, cf. Kai T. Erikson, "Patient Role and Social Uncertainty—A Dilemma of the Mentally Ill," *Psychiatry*, **20** (August 1957), pp. 263–275.

[16] Ross, *op. cit.*, p. 962.

the risk of being more heavily penalized for erroneously releasing than for erroneously retaining patients. Since the judge personally appoints the panel of psychiatrists to serve as examiners, he can easily transmit the community pressure to them, by failing to reappoint a psychiatrist whose examinations were inconveniently thorough.

Some of the implications of these findings for the sociology of deviant behavior will be briefly summarized. The discussion above, of the reasons that the psychiatrists tend to presume illness, suggests that the motivations of the key decision-makers in the screening process may be significant in determining the extent and direction of the societal reaction. In the case of psychiatric screening of persons alleged to be mentally ill, the social differentiation of the deviant from the non-deviant population appears to be materially affected by the financial, ideological, and political position of the psychiatrists, who are in this instance the key agents of social control.

Under these circumstances, the character of the societal reaction appears to undergo a marked change from the pattern of denial which occurs in the community. The official societal reaction appears to reverse the presumption of normality reported by the Cummings as a characteristic of informal societal reaction, and instead exaggerates both the amount and degree of deviance.[17] Thus, one extremely important contingency influencing the severity of the societal reaction may be whether or not the original deviance comes to official notice. This paper suggests that in the area of mental disorder, perhaps in contrast to other areas of deviant behavior, if the official societal reaction is invoked, for whatever reason, social differentiation of the deviant from the non-deviant population will usually occur.

CONCLUSION

This paper has described the screening of patients who were admitted to public mental hospitals in early June, 1962, in a Midwestern state. The data presented here suggest that the screening is usually perfunctory, and that in the crucial screening examination by the court-appointed psychiatrists, there is a presumption of illness. Since most court decisions appear to hinge on the recommendation of these psychiatrists, there appears to be a large element of status ascription in the official societal reaction to persons alleged to be mentally ill, as exemplified by the court's actions. This finding points to the importance of lay definitions of mental illness in the community, since the "diagnosis" of mental illness by laymen in the community initiates the official societal reaction, and to the necessity of analyzing social processes connected with the recognition and reaction to the deviant behavior that is called mental illness in our society.

[17] Elaine Cumming and John Cumming, *Closed Ranks*, Cambridge, Mass.: Harvard University Press, 1957, 102; for further discussion of the bipolarization of the societal reaction into denial and labeling, see the author's "The Role of the Mentally Ill and the Dynamics of Mental Disorder: A Research Framework," *Sociometry*, **26** (December, 1963), pp. 436–453.

PART FOUR

The Patient Career—
Inpatient Phase

CHARACTERISTICS OF THE MENTAL HOSPITAL

This section opens with a paper in which Goffman describes the characteristics of total institutions. According to Goffman a total institution is a "place of residence and work where a large number of like-situated individuals, cut off from the wider society for an appreciable period of time, together lead an enclosed, formally administered round of life."[1] Mental hospitals, prisons, and monasteries serve as clear examples. In the essay he describes the culture of the total institution by examining several aspects of its social organization and the position and experiences of its members. A paper by Angrist attempts to place the mental hospital in a historical perspective. She not only shows how the mental hospital has changed throughout the centuries but also points to the linkage between public conceptions of illness and the characteristics of institutions responsible for dealing with mental illness. The paper by Loeb looks at the mental hospital from the perspective of its most salient cultural themes. He points to the symbolism of keys and locks and to the expectations that staff hold for psychiatric hospital inmates. Taken together, these three papers illustrate many of the major characteristics of the environment which confront the incoming patient.

PATIENT BEHAVIOR IN THE HOSPITAL

Entry into the mental hospital means that the patient is exposed to various prescriptions for behavior. According to Smith and Thrasher the psychiatric hospital provides the context for the enactment of a number of patient roles. They point to a common role which is shared by all as a function of the status of

291

patient and to several secondary roles for which acceptance is not mandatory. The ways in which the roles are assumed and enacted illustrate the idiosyncratic patterns of adjustment to the hospital environment by various types of patients. The second Goffman paper in this section is related to the Smith and Thrasher work because it focuses on the more minor and personalized roles of patients. Goffman also describes, from a somewhat different point of view, the various types of patterns of patient accommodation to institutional life. The Sobel and Ingalls paper may be regarded as an intensive analysis of the shared aspects of the psychiatric patient role. It also indicates how the psychiatric patient role differs from the role of medical patient, a point which is usually given insufficient consideration.

STAFF RESPONSES TO THE PATIENT

When the patient enters the mental hospital, staff members respond to him on the basis of certain preconceived attitudes and opinions. These expectations are based on the assumption that patients with certain personal and social characteristics will think and act in predictable ways.

Denzin and Spitzer demonstrate that the routes taken to psychiatric hospitals influence the expectations that hospital personnel hold for patients. The results of their study show that staff members did anticipate that the patients who entered the hospital voluntarily would be more attractive and conforming than those who entered involuntarily. Staff members also showed a tendency to anticipate that patients who entered because of a family decision would be better patients than those who entered as a result of interference by an outside agency.

The other papers in this section test the hypothesis that the type of psychiatric treatment accorded a patient is associated with his social and personal characteristics. The Hollingshead and Redlich paper in Part 2 briefly demonstrated how therapy varied with the social class of the patient. Psychotherapy was concentrated in the upper classes, and organic therapies and custodial care without therapy were concentrated in the lower classes. In an extended presentation of the same study it was also reported that the higher an individual's social class position, the more likely he was to gain admission, to be assigned to highly trained personnel, and to be treated intensively over a long period of time.[2] The Siegel et al. paper also examines the diagnostic and therapeutic consequences of social class, but in this investigation data were collected in therapeutically oriented research hospitals. It was found in this type of setting that the social class of the patient was less intimately related to diagnosis and type of treatment accorded than to the predominant forms of treatment of a given hospital tends to employ. The direct implication of the Siegel et al. study is quite obvious; it is necessary to take into account the place of treatment when considering the relationship between social class and psychiatric policy.

The Denzin paper explores the hypothesis that the processes which underlie patient-therapist interaction during psychiatric treatment have a greater impact upon the outcome of treatment than does the degree of illness exhibited by the patient at the time of hospitalization. Treatment is conceptualized from the per-

292

spective of the "self-fulfilling prophecy," and it is argued that initial definitions of the therapist become translated into responses made by the patient during treatment. Consequently, patients defined as initially good treatment cases actually become good treatment cases because of the initial definitions attributed them. This paper has implications for the hospital's treatment goals, and if patients are accorded rights and privileges on the basis of how they present themselves and not in terms of how ill they are, only those patients who have undergone prehospital socialization into the "psychiatric line" will receive the most favored forms of treatment and return to the community most rapidly.

THE INPATIENT AND HIS FAMILY

When a person enters a mental hospital, there is a carry-over of relationships and attitudes established during the prepatient phase. Although these relationships and attitudes are subject to change and modification throughout the course of hospitalization, the initial state of affairs and the type and direction of change appear to have important implications for the unfolding of the patient career. The last three papers illustrate the importance of taking a "career approach" to the study of psychiatric patients.

The paper by Alivisatos and Lyketsos is one of the few that examines the attitudes of family members of hospitalized patients and shows the alienation that arises between relatives and patients as the result of hospitalization. Various theorists have suggested that disorganization in, or absence of, primary group relations is an antecedent condition of mental disorder. It is quite likely that the additional isolation which comes from hospitalization may, in some instances, detract from, rather than contribute to, the process of patient recovery.

Dinitz, Mangus, and Pasamanick focus on the self-concept of hospitalized psychiatric patients, drawing special attention to the relationship between self-attitudes and concepts held of patients by spouses and other relatives. Patients tended to view their relatives, notably their spouses, differently from how these persons viewed themselves. If we assume that congruence in self-other perceptions is one prerequisite for successful social interaction, the implication is that the very problems in interpersonal relations that existed prior to hospitalization persist throughout the inpatient, and perhaps even the postpatient phase of the patient career.

The final paper in this section, by Simmons, Davis, and Spencer, is unusual because it is one of the few investigations in the literature concerned with variables leading to patient release. The data show how the relationships established between patients, families, and therapists enter into the decision to release patients from psychiatric treatment centers.

References

1   Erving Goffman, *Asylums,* Doubleday & Company, Inc., Garden City, N.Y., 1961, p. xiii.
2   August B. Hollingshead and Frederick C. Redlich, *Social Class and Mental Illness,* John Wiley & Sons, Inc., New York, 1958.

26
CHARACTERISTICS OF TOTAL INSTITUTIONS
Erving Goffman

INTRODUCTION

Institutions

Social establishments—institutions in the everyday sense of that term—are buildings or plants in which activity of a particular kind regularly goes on. In sociology we do not have an apt way of classifying them. Some, like Grand Central Station, are open to anyone who is decently behaved. Others, like the Union League Club of New York or the laboratories at Los Alamos, are felt to be somewhat "snippy" about the matter of whom they let in. Some institutions, like shops and post offices, are the locus of a continuous flow of service relationships. Others, like homes and factories, provide a less changing set of persons with whom the member can relate. Some institutions provide the place for what is felt to be the kind of pursuits from which the individual draws his social status, however enjoyable or lax these pursuits may be. Other institutions, in contrast, provide a home for associations in which membership is felt to be elective and unserious, calling for a contribution of time that is fitted in to more serious demands.

In this paper another category of institutions is recommended and claimed as a natural and fruitful one because its members appear to have so much in common—so much, in fact, that if you would learn about one of these institutions you would be well advised to look at the others. My own special purpose in examining these institutions is to find a natural frame of reference for studying the social experience of patients in mental hospitals. Whatever else psychiatry and medicine tell us, their happy way of sometimes viewing an insane asylum as if it were a treatment hospital does not help us very much in determining just what these places are and just what goes on in them.

Total institutions

Every institution captures something of the time and interest of its members and provides something of a world for them; in brief, every institution has encompassing tendencies. When we review the different institutions in our Western society we find a class of them which seems to be encompassing to a degree discontinuously greater than the ones next in line. Their encompassing or total character is symbolized by the barrier to social intercourse with the outside that is often built right into the physical plant: locked doors, high walls, barbed wire, cliffs and water, open terrain, and so forth. These I am calling total institutions,

Source: Erving Goffman, "Characteristics of Total Institutions: The Inmate World," *Symposium on Preventive and Social Psychiatry,* U.S. Government Printing Office, 1958, pp. 49, 56–62 (excerpt).

and it is their general characteristics I want to explore.[1] This exploration will be phrased as if securely based on findings but will in fact be speculative.

The total institutions of our society can be listed for convenience in five rough groupings. *First,* there are institutions established to care for persons thought to be both incapable and harmless; these are the homes for the blind, the aged, the orphaned, and the indigent. *Second,* there are places established to care for persons thought to be at once incapable of looking after themselves and a threat to the community, albeit an unintended one: TB sanitoriums, mental hospitals, and leprosoriums. *Third,* another type of total institution is organized to protect the community against what are thought to be intentional dangers to it; here the welfare of the persons thus sequestered is not the immediate issue. Examples are: Jails, penitentiaries, POW camps, and concentration camps. *Fourth,* we find institutions purportedly established the better to pursue some technical task and justifying themselves only on these instrumental grounds: Army barracks, ships, boarding schools, work camps, colonial compounds, large mansions from the point of view of those who live in the servants' quarters, and so forth. *Finally,* there are those establishments designed as retreats from the world or as training stations for the religious: Abbeys, monasteries, convents, and other cloisters. This sublisting of total institutions is neither neat nor exhaustive, but the listing itself provides an empirical starting point for a purely denotative definition of the category. By anchoring the initial definition of total institutions in this way, I hope to be able to discuss the general characteristics of the type without becoming tautological.

Before attempting to extract a general profile from this list of establishments, one conceptual peculiarity must be mentioned. None of the elements I will extract seems entirely exclusive to total institutions, and none seems shared by every one of them. What is shared and unique about total· institutions is that each exhibits many items in this family of attributes to an intense degree. In speaking of "common characteristics," then, I will be using this phrase in a weakened, but I think logically defensible, way.

Totalistic features

A basic social arrangement in modern society is that we tend to sleep, play and work in different places, in each case with a different set of coparticipants, under a different authority, and without an overall rational plan. The central feature of total institutions can be described as a breakdown of the kinds of barriers ordinarily separating these three spheres of life. *First,* all aspects of life are conducted in the same place and under the same single authority. *Second,* each phase of the member's daily activity will be carried out in the immediate company of a large batch of others, all of whom are treated alike and required to do the same thing together. *Third,* all phases of the day's activities are tightly

---

[1] The category of total institutions has been pointed out from time to time in the sociological literature under a variety of names, and some of the characteristics of the class have been suggested, most notably perhaps in Howard Roland's neglected paper, "Segregated Communities and Mental Health," in *Mental Health Publication of the American Association for the Advancement of Science,* No. 9, edited by F. R. Moulton, 1939. A preliminary statement of the present paper is reported in the *Third Group Processes Proceedings,* Josiah Macy Foundation, edited by Bertram Schaffner, 1957.

scheduled, with one activity leading at a prearranged time into the next, the whole circle of activities being imposed from above through a system of explicit formal rulings and a body of officials. *Finally,* the contents of the various enforced activities are brought together as parts of a single overall rational plan purportedly designed to fulfill the official aims of the institution.

Individually, these totalistic features are found, of course, in places other than total institutions. Increasingly, for example, our large commercial, industrial and educational establishments provide cafeterias, minor services and off-hour recreation for their members. But while this is a tendency in the direction of total institutions, these extended facilities remain voluntary in many particulars of their use, and special care is taken to see that the ordinary line of authority does not extend to these situations. Similarly, housewives or farm families can find all their major spheres of life within the same fenced-in area, but these persons are not collectively regimented and do not march through the day's steps in the immediate company of a batch of similar others.

The handling of many human needs by the bureaucratic organization of whole blocks of people—whether or not this is a necessary or effective means of social organization in the circumstances—can be taken, then, as the key fact of total institutions. From this, certain important implications can be drawn.

Given the fact that blocks of people are caused to move in time, it becomes possible to use a relatively small number of supervisory personnel where the central relationship is not guidance or periodic checking, as in many employer-employee relations, but rather surveillance—a seeing to it that everyone does what he has been clearly told is required of him, and this under conditions where one person's infraction is likely to stand out in relief against the visible, constantly examined, compliance of the others. Which comes first, the large block of managed people or the small supervisory staff, is not here at issue; the point is that each is made for the other.

In total institutions, as we would then suspect, there is a basic split between a large class of individuals who live in and who have restricted contact with the world outside the walls, conveniently called *inmates,* and the small class that supervises them, conveniently called *staff,* who often operate on an 8-hour day and are socially integrated into the outside world.[2] Each grouping tends to conceive of members of the other in terms of narrow hostile stereotypes, staff often seeing inmates as bitter, secretive and untrustworthy, while inmates often see staff as condescending, high-handed and mean. Staff tends to feel superior and righteous; inmates tend, in some ways at least, to feel inferior, weak, blameworthy and guilty.[3] Social mobility between the two strata is grossly restricted;

[2] The binary character of total institutions was pointed out to me by Gregory Bateson, and proves to be noted in the literature. See, for example, Lloyd E. Ohlin, *Sociology and the Field of Corrections,* Russell Sage Foundation, New York, 1956, pp. 14, 20. In those special situations where staff too is required to live in, we may expect staff members to feel they are suffering from special hardships and to have brought home to them a status-dependency on life on the inside which they did not expect. See, Jane Cassels Record, "The Marine Radioman's Struggle for Status," *American Journal of Sociology,* Vol. LXII, 1957, p. 359.

[3] For the prison version, see, S. Kirson Weinburg, "Aspects of the Prison's Social Structure," *American Journal of Sociology,* Vol. 47, 1942, pp. 717–726.

social distance is typically great and often formally prescribed; even talk across the boundaries may be conducted in a special tone of voice.[4] These restrictions on contact presumably help to maintain the antagonistic stereotypes.[5] In any case, two different social and cultural worlds develop, tending to jog along beside each other, with points of official contact but little mutual penetration. It is important to add that the institutional plant and name comes to be identified by both staff and inmates as somehow belonging to staff, so that when either grouping refers to the views or interests of "the institution," by implication they are referring (as I shall also) to the views and concerns of the staff.

The staff-inmate split is one major implication of the central features of total institutions; a second one pertains to work. In the ordinary arrangements of living in our society, the authority of the workplace stops with the worker's receipt of a money payment; the spending of this in a domestic and recreational setting is at the discretion of the worker and is the mechanism through which the authority of the workplace is kept within strict bounds. However, to say that inmates in total institutions have their full day scheduled for them is to say that some version of all basic needs will have to be planned for, too. In other words, total institutions take over "responsibility" for the inmate and must guarantee to have everything that is defined as essential "layed on." It follows, then, that whatever incentive is given for work, this will not have the structural significance it has on the outside. Different attitudes and incentives regarding this central feature of our life will have to prevail.

Here, then, is one basic adjustment required of those who work in total institutions and of those who must induce these people to work. In some cases, no work or little is required, and inmates, untrained often in leisurely ways of life, suffer extremes of boredom. In other cases, some work is required but is carried on at an extremely slow pace, being geared into a system of minor, often ceremonial payments, as in the case of weekly tobacco ration and annual Christmas presents, which cause some mental patients to stay on their job. In some total institutions, such as logging camps and merchant ships, something of the usual relation to the world that money can buy is obtained through the practice of "forced saving"; all needs are organized by the institution, and payment is given only after a work season is over and the men leave the premises. And in some total institutions, of course, more than a full day's work is required and is induced not by reward, but by threat of dire punishment. In all such cases, the

---

[4] An illustration may be found in Mary Jane Ward's fictionalized record of her sojourn in a mental hospital. *The Snake Pit,* Signet Books, New York, 1955, p. 72.

"I tell you what," said Miss Hart when they were crossing the dayroom. "You do everything Miss Davis says. Don't think about it, just do it. You'll get along all right."

As soon as she heard the name, Virginia knew what was terrible about Ward One. Miss Davis. "Is she head nurse?"

"And how," muttered Miss Hart. And then she raised her voice. The nurses had a way of acting as if the patients were unable to hear anything that was not shouted. Frequently they said things in normal voices that the ladies were not supposed to hear; if they had not been nurses, you would have said they frequently talked to themselves. "A most competent and efficient person, Miss Davis," announced Miss Hart.

[5] Suggested in Ohlin, *op. cit.,* p. 20.

work-oriented individual may tend to become somewhat demoralized by the system.[6]

In addition to the fact that total institutions are incompatible with the basic work-payment structure of our society, it must be seen that these establishments are also incompatible with another crucial element of our society, the family. The family is sometimes contrasted to solitary living, but in fact the more pertinent contrast to family life might be with batch living. For it seems that those who eat and sleep at work, with a group of fellow workers, can hardly sustain a meaningful domestic existence.[7] Correspondingly, the extent to which a staff retains its integration in the outside community and escapes the encompassing tendencies of total institutions is often linked up with the maintenance of a family off the grounds.

Whether a particular total institution acts as a good or bad force in civil society, force it may well have, and this will depend on the suppression of a whole circle of actual or potential households. Conversely, the formation of households provides a structural guarantee that total institutions will not arise. The incompatibility between these two forms of social organization should tell us, then, something about the wider social functions of them both.

Total institutions, then, are social hybrids, part residential community, part formal organization, and therein lies their special sociological interest. There are other reasons, alas, for being interested in them, too. These establishments are the forcing houses for changing persons in our society. Each is a natural experiment, typically harsh, on what can be done to the self.

Having suggested some of the key features of total institutions, we can move on now to consider them from the special perspectives that seem natural to take. I will consider the inmate world, then the staff world, and then something about contacts between the two.

27
THE MENTAL HOSPITAL: ITS HISTORY AND DESTINY
Shirley S. Angrist*

Throughout history, the treatment of the mentally ill, like other aspects of life, has reflected the predominant values of the time. For a long period in the history

---

[6] An interesting reflection of the no-payment world of total institutions is found in the culture of State mental hospitals in the practice of "bumming" or "working someone for" a nickel or dime to spend in the canteen. This practice is indulged in, often with some defiance, by persons who would consider such actions beneath their self-respect were they on the outside. Staff persons, interpreting this begging pattern in terms of their own outsider's orientation to earning, tend to see it as a symptom of psychological sickness and one further bit of evidence that inmates really are unwell persons.

[7] An interesting marginal case here is the Israeli kibbutz. See, Melford E. Spiro, *Kibbutz: Venture in Utopia*, Harvard University Press, Cambridge, 1956.

Source: Shirley S. Angrist, "The Mental Hospital: Its History and Destiny," *Perspectives in Psychiatric Care*, 1: 20–26, 1963.

* I am grateful to Simon Dinitz, Professor of Sociology at the Ohio State University for his editorial comments and suggestions.

of the West, the acutely or chronically deviant—the criminals, the sexual offenders, the mentally ill, and the physically handicapped—shared the fate of the dependent, noncontributing members of society, such as the widows, the orphans, and the illegitimate children, and remained largely the responsibility of the family and the local community.

It is true that some forms of the public care of the insane date back as far as the temples of healing in Greece, which were at their height in the sixth century B.C. Ancient Rome had public provisions for its sick by the fourth century B.C. The first known mental institution was a house for lunatics in Byzantium during the fourth century A.D. Thereafter, history records the sporadic appearance of institutions or other community provisions for the care of the insane. For example, in the city of Cologne, monks began to take care of insane men in the year 560 A.D. Asylums for the insane existed in the Middle East and in England prior to 700 A.D., and by the thirteenth century, Spain and Germany had such institutions.

Such facilities, however, were rare and the conditions in them terrible as judged by present-day standards. By and large, the mentally ill were the lees of society, doomed to be wanderers, pariahs: to be mocked, tortured, burned, and beaten; to be regarded as hopeless victims of incurable "natural" afflictions—the work of demons. At their worst, Christian doctrines of free will and individual responsibility outweighed the Calvinist notion of predestination; this intensified the prevalent European image of deviants as dangerous creatures and, in extreme instances, as bedeviled witches and sorcerers. Such a conception of the mentally ill often led to their elimination by burning. Occasional notes of humane concern for the mentally sick were sounded, but the prevailing obsessions with devils and sorcery prevented the isolated voices from being heard.

With the coming of the industrial revolution and its resultant urbanization, increased complexity of community organization, and weakening of the family and the local community—responsibility for the mentally ill, as for other deviants and dependents, was shifted more directly to the larger community. Supporting the practical impossibility of maintaining such persons locally or in the family was the prevalent Christian conception that they were consumed with the devil, the victims of sin and punishment, and therefore subhuman and dangerous.

Elimination of deviants from the rounds of everyday life became the major recourse of urban communities. This policy was carried out in a variety of ways. One way, which was widespread, was the use of older methods: capital punishment or banishment. Another newer method was the development by the state of various institutions—the prison, the asylum, the poor farm, the workhouse—whereby the nearly permanent removal of the burdensome member from society was accomplished.

These methods for managing deviants were imported to America by the early colonists. At first, the idiot, the thief, and the insane, if nonviolent, could be controlled in the village, and the violent could be sent out to wander and be forbidden readmission to the community. But the growth of the colonies with their pioneering mentality, their ethic of hard work and frugality, made systematic community handling necessary. The burdensome liability of noncontributing members necessitated the establishment of larger scale facilities such as were common in the mother country. Thence arose the town jail and almshouse to house a miscellany of social misfits. These institutions were "total" institutions —institutions in which every activity of an inmate's life was carried out in the same place, under the same authority, and in the company of a large group of other inmates and in which each day's activities were tightly scheduled according to an overall plan that was thought to fulfill the institution's goals.[1]

Once initiated and diffused, the total institution in Europe and America became highly resistant to change. Indeed, in view of the stigma conferred by institutionalization and the absence of concern with care, treatment, or return to society, it is hardly surprising that such institutions remained primarily a custodial repository for persons whom society wished to banish.

Reaction to the inhuman dimensions of industrialization began in the eighteenth century. The philosophies that brought forth the French Revolution and the period of the Enlightenment were expressed in a humanitarianism that reached into all corners of society. Deviants came to be viewed as victims of social conditions or of illness; by the mid-nineteenth century the insane were actually considered human, albeit sick, human beings. Incarceration in the total institution continued but in a more specialized form, inmates of conglomerate institutions were segregated, so that the insane, for instance, were now separately housed.

Advances in science were reflected in the medical concern with organic lesions to explain mental as well as physical illness. France's Pinel, England's Tuke, and America's Benjamin Rush were influential in spreading the doctrine of "moral treatment," which was based on the view that mental illness was treatable, even curable, by humane methods. Thus, for a time, mechanical restraints and barbaric forms of treatment, such as the saddle and bleeding, were minimized.

In America, the separate housing of the mentally sick was undertaken in French Catholic Quebec in 1714. The first American hospital, the Pennsylvania Hospital, opened to patients in 1752 in Philadelphia, made provisions for mental as well as other patients. In 1773, the first institution designed solely for the care of the mentally ill was opened at Williamsburg, Virginia. During the next fifty years, new mental institutions burgeoned rapidly as at first private groups and then the states undertook to house and treat their mentally ill. Dorothea Lynde Dix, the most famous of the American reformers in the field of mental illness, campaigned for more and larger institutions for the insane.

The reform movements for separate institutions and "moral treatment" had the effect of humanizing the institution and of providing a modicum of amenities for its inmates. But the third quarter of the nineteenth century saw a growing confusion of earlier enlightened views. The enthusiasm for state hospitals had culminated in overcrowding and administrative problems. Even though psychiatry was taking shape as a field and was earning academic recognition in America, the rugged individualism of an entrepreneurial society and the popularity of survival-of-the-fittest notions which stressed the inheritability of taints adversely affected the care of society's failures, the sick and the weak. A widespread feeling of hopelessness about recovery permeated mental institutions, and in many, the mentally ill were again considered less than human. The use of restraint was revived. William Alanson White described the abominable conditions he found at St. Elizabeth's Hospital in 1903:

I found certain parts of the institution in a rather primitive condition. The overcrowding had necessitated something like four hundred patients sleeping on the floor on straw mattresses . . . mechanical restraints in the form of camisoles and the bed saddle, which I had never before seen or heard of, were in use.[2]

A combination of events and ideas served to rehumanize noticeably the care of mental patients by the second decade of the twentieth century. Mesmerism, and later psychoanalysis, shed new light on the psychological dimensions of insanity, with focus on the unconscious. Clifford Beers's exposé of mental institutions, which stemmed from his personal experience, contributed directly to the organization of the mental hygiene movement, which crusaded for reform. By the 1930's, improvement in the care of mental patients had begun to be reflected in a decrease in the use of restraint, in attempts at family care of released patients, and in an increase in prepared personnel especially social workers and nurses, trained in the care and rehabilitation of the mentally ill.

This progress, though certain, was for several years slow and by no means universal. Abominable conditions in some American mental institutions were described as recently as the 1950's. Undoubtedly this lag in institutional treatment had roots in the discrepant theories concerning mental illness and the professional uncertainty as to causes and cures.

Within the past few years, however, certain trends have revitalized the situation. The elimination, or at least the control, of many of the infectious diseases; the early detection of many of the chronic ailments by better diagnosis and their alleviation by newer drugs; the increasing number of aged and chronically impaired persons that has resulted from the lengthening of the average life span; the rise in crime and delinquency—all these factors have contributed to a renewal of interest in and investigation of the noncontributing deviant. The result has been a major shift in thinking. After years of resisting change, the total institution has begun to give ground. In an almost complete reversal, the belief that persons who do not conform or contribute to society should be banished from it is rapidly giving way to the idea that they should and can be reintegrated into society. Hope is replacing despair, action is replacing passivity; therapy is replacing confinement; small institutions are replacing large ones; professional personnel are replacing custodial personnel; home visits, trial visits, probation, parole, family placement, and community reintegration are replacing uninterrupted and permanent confinement. The short-term treatment hospitals, which now exist in most large urban areas, represent an important step in the evolution of the care of the mentally ill.

SHORT-TERM PSYCHIATRIC CARE

Short-term treatment has a history that can be traced at least to the mid-nineteenth century. At that time, in France, England, and Germany a distinction was made between the acutely and the chronically insane, with the consequent separation of these two classes of patients within the same institution or in specialized institutions. This separation of patients by the chronicity or acuteness of their illness was an early but important step in the refinement of facilities specifically for the mentally ill. Parallel conceptions in America, intensified by the added burden on state institutions of the "immigrant pauper insane," led to a similar movement in favor of two distinct kinds of state institutions. In 1865, the Willard Act in New York State brought into being the Willard Asylum for the Chronic Insane to provide for the removal of chronically ill patients from county almshouses and bring them under state jurisdiction. There was strong reaction against this trend, since one could argue, as many physicians did at the time, that separation put the stamp of incurability on chronic patients.

The issue was responsible for several further developments. A number of states, including Massachusetts and Rhode Island, built separate institutions; other states continued to keep hospitals "mixed." But the major outcome was the growth of the "cottage" and "colony" systems, in which specialization of treatment has its roots. The cottage system usually provided central housing for patients considered curable, with separate houses for each of several patient categories: convalescents, severely disturbed, chronic patients. Illinois State Hospital, built in 1877 at Kankakee, was an example of the new pattern. The colony system—first introduced at Kalamazoo State Hospital in 1855, was characterized by the conjunction of a state hospital with a tract of farm land thereby providing both for the segregation of patient categories and for the occupational utilization of patients.

The distinction between chronic and acute cases connoted more than a differentiation between long-term and short-term care. It also implied a sorting of patients according to the recency of the illness. By the end of the nineteenth century, many states (Iowa and Wisconsin most notably), still suffering from the pressures of overpopulated institutions, began to return harmless chronic cases to county custodial institutions and to designate state hospitals as centers for "recent" cases.

Short-term psychiatric treatment received its greatest boost from the mental hygiene movement's crusade for prevention and early treatment of disorders and the concomitant interest in research by multidisciplinary groups. The early 1920's saw the opening of pre-school and school-affiliated clinics to treat behavior and personality problems of children. At the same time, the possible connection between criminal behavior and mental disorder was considered reasonable cause for operating mental hygiene clinics in prisons. The growth and expansion of such services occurred after World War II, which had heightened public and professional sensitivity to the effects of psychological stress and the widespread need for the rehabilitation of veterans. By 1947, ninety-one mental hygiene clinics were operated by the Veterans Administration alone.

The growing acceptance of the mentally ill as persons in need of medical care was expressed in the elaboration of treatment facilities for the general population, in the growth of professionally trained personnel (social workers, nurses, occupational therapists), and in the further specialization of treatment facilities. The minimum standards for mental hospitals adopted by the American Psychiatric Association in 1945 specified that each institution provide a receiving ward to which patients would be admitted for a maximum of two weeks and in which they would be sorted according to their treatment needs. The concept of short-term treatment has taken such strong hold that the past decade witnessed the establishment of state receiving hospitals specifically for this purpose, along with the spreading practice of providing psychiatric wards in general hospitals.

THE EFFICACY OF HOSPITALIZATION

From this brief history, there are discernible three major stages through which the mental hospital has passed. From subhuman, custodial, bastille origins, it went through a humanizing phase which was characterized by long-term treatment, then, more recently, through a more scientific phase, which stresses short-term, intensive care. The progress to more humanistic values has naturally led us to look back on former attitudes toward mentally disturbed persons with smug condemnation and to assume, without question, that things are surely much better today. Such contemporary self-righteousness must be tempered by the knowledge that facilities for the care of mental patients are still quantitatively and qualitatively needed.

Further, we must face the fact that mental disease is as yet subject to neither prevention nor control. In an age of scientific triumph in the conquest of various diseases, it is still assumed that more institutions with pleasant surroundings and greater kindness to mental patients are in themselves aids in conquering mental illness. Thus, humanitarian goals are considered adequate criteria of patient care.

We need to realize that treatment methods must be judged by their consequences rather than by their intent. The numerous reformers in the history of psychiatric care took pains to elucidate this point. For example, Pinel argued that the medical-scientific value of "moral treatment" must rest upon objective research of the

distinction between the various kinds of mental derangement, the exact history of the precursory symptoms . . . the careful definition of those circumstances which make certain remedies necessary and of those which make them superfluous.[3]

He went on to stress the need in medical science for

the orderly spirit of research which rules in all parts of natural history. It should be dictated neither by individual prejudices nor by the flights of keen imagination but by a truly sincere love of mankind, or rather by the honest desire to contribute to the general welfare.[4]

Insofar as we are presently committed to certain modes of treatment we must ask the question: How effective are our institutions and the prevailing types of patient care? Since we stand on the threshold of new developments in the care of the mentally ill, we need to know what their implications are. What is the value of community care as compared with institutional care? Is home care effective? For which types of patients? What role will institutional treatment play? We submit that during this ultra-scientific age, our role as concerned participants in the field of mental health and illness is to assess scientifically the outcome of our care programs with a view to altering them on scientific as well as on humanitarian grounds.

These questions have motivated some of the recent research on the outcome of hospitalization in both England and America.

In a Central Ohio study of women who had been in a short-term intensive therapy mental hospital, it was found that the various treatment modes (chemotherapy, shock therapy and psychotherapy) do not lead to significantly different levels of posthospital adjustment. However, some personal and family characteristics were shown to be related to the former patient's ability to perform well in the community.[5] In families where the former patient is the only one available to carry out the responsibilities of the woman's role, her performance is likely to be satisfactory. It was also shown, however, that certain aspects of the illness play a part in outcome. Thus, patients diagnosed with acute or chronic brain syndromes or patients with a history of alcoholism or drug addiction have the poorest chance to succeed. Relatives of these former patients report that it is primarily when bizarre, frightening or unmanageable behaviors occur that the patient is rehospitalized.[6] Finally, comparison of these patients with women who have never been treated for mental disorder, and who are similar in background characteristics, indicated that many former patients can perform as well as nonpatients socially and domestically.

These findings were corroborated for both male and female former patients in a second study of former patients with psychotic diagnoses which was carried out in the Boston area. Those who conducted this research emphasize the influence of family attitudes on the patient's functioning in the community.[7] An English study points to the composition of the household to which the patient returns as crucial to the outcome.[8]

The potential of such scientific evaluations of psychiatric hospitalization appears great. Continuing research on the efficacy of the various therapies practiced both in hospitals and in community settings may gradually lead to important changes in care of the mentally ill. Some of these changes have already been implemented in a few places, and many others will surely follow. On the basis of such trends, one might predict that future care of the mentally ill will take this pattern:

The mental hospital as it has been known and operating since the eighteenth century will disappear as an institution for all but the small proportion of patients who are so severely impaired as to warrant detention for the remainder of their lives. For the vast bulk of disordered and disturbed persons permanent or even lengthy confinement will become as antiquated as blood-letting. Many of them will remain at home or elsewhere in the community, retaining employment and functioning in more or less accustomed roles. They will be scientifically evaluated and clinically treated. With drugs and other still-to-be developed therapeutic aids, under medical care, and in suitable community settings, their behavioral impairments will seem no more critical than physical impediments.

Some future patients will be in half-way houses, in day hospitals, and in outpatient clinics. Others will perhaps be the recipients of conditioning and sleep therapies and of many other forms of treatment which none of us can as yet imagine. The patient will no longer be alienated, isolated, confined, and stigmatized. His status, at worst, will be comparable to that of the celebrated psychoneurotic of the middle or upper class whose private personal psychiatrist or analyst is as much a mark of his "salvation" as is his ulcer testimony to his success.

References

1 Goffman, Erving, "On the Characteristics of Total Institutions," *Asylums,* New York: Anchor Books, (1961), pp. 3–124.
2 White, William Alanson, *Forty Years of Psychiatry,* New York: Nervous and Mental Disease Publishing Company, (1933), p. 29.
3 Zilboorg, Gregory, *A History of Medical Psychology,* New York: Norton, (1941), p. 337.
4 *Ibid.,* p. 341.
5 Dinitz, Simon, Lefton, Mark, Angrist, Shirley, and Pasamanick, Benjamin, "Psychiatric and Social Attributes as Predictors of Case Outcome in Mental Hospitalization," *Social Problems,* Spring 1961, pp. 322–328.
6 Angrist, Shirley, Dinitz, Simon, Lefton, Mark, Pasamanick, Benjamin, "Rehospitalization of Female Mental Patients," *Archives of General Psychiatry,* (1961), **4:** 363–370.
7 Freeman, Howard and Simmons, Ozzie, *The Mental Patient Comes Home,* New York: John Wiley, (1963).
8 Brown, George W., "Experiences of Discharged Chronic Schizophrenic Patients in Various Types of Living Groups," *Milbank Memorial Fund Quarterly,* (1959), **37:** 105–131.

28
SOME DOMINANT CULTURAL THEMES
IN A PSYCHIATRIC HOSPITAL*
Martin B. Loeb

This report derives from a study of social interaction patterns in a small psychiatric hospital in Kansas City, Missouri, under a grant from the National Institute

Source: Martin B. Loeb, "Some Dominant Cultural Themes in a Psychiatric Hospital," *Social Problems,* **4:** 17–20, 1956.
* This investigation is being supported by a research grant (M-815R) from the National Institute of Mental Health, of the National Institutes of Health, Public Health Service.

of Mental Health. I should like to look at this hospital as if it were a society with a culture of its own and I should like to try and characterize it by a few of its more dominant cultural themes. The social structure of this hospital is very complicated. As in other hospitals, there is a professional status system which ranges from the physician at the top through social workers, psychologists and nurses to the lowly maintenance and kitchen help. In addition, there is a departmental status system. In the hospital there are several departments, for example: adult in-patient, business office, child guidance, etc. The adult in-patient has the highest status as a department but other departments jockey for position and occasionally individuals get caught in status conflict between occupational and departmental hierarchies. For instance, how does the head psychiatrist of the rather low status Child Guidance Department relate to a staff psychiatrist in the higher status Adult In-patient Department? Inasmuch as the hospital we are studying opened a year ago, we have been able to study how these status systems develop. This has been complicated because the hospital is run by a private social agency for the city on a contractual basis. Most of the professional staff are on the agency payroll and the rest of the staff is on the city payroll. There are differences in personnel practices and how one gets a job, etc., which complicates any status structure. There is another status system which I presume is present in any hospital and which is sometimes very clear to us in this hospital, namely, the *personal status system*. By this I mean the way in which an individual relates to the head of the whole outfit.

The status of an individual or a department is often signified by the location of the office in a building. One may think of this hospital as a community with neighborhoods differing from one another in terms of prestige. The first floor is upper class. Most of the administrative and professional offices are there and in general the closer one's office is to the director, the higher status is the office. The second and third floors, where the patients live, are the middle class neighborhoods of which the social leaders are residents and head nurses. And the basement is the lower class neighborhood which has the admissions department, the kitchen and maintenance people. It is within this social structural scheme that I would like to discuss some cultural themes.

THE KEY

The key is a very important symbol in a mental hospital. All possibilities of ingress and egress are controlled by a key. Doors, windows, screens, closets, cupboards, and bathrooms can only be entered or left if one has a key. So the problem is: Who gets the key? One group of people in this community, the patients, never get keys. Other groups get keys which open some doors but not other doors. Some people get keys that open the screens and some do not. The highest status people have keys that open all doors. In the development of what I have called the personal status system, giving out the key was one way of showing how close one was to the top, that is, in terms of personal relationships. Furthermore, keys were distributed more widely and readily in the departments which had higher status in the hospital hierarchy. Of course, you also got a key if you had a right to one. But in the development of this hospital there were many arguments about who had a right to the key. Thus, there was an altercation between the business office which gets the keys made and the administration which feels that it is responsible for handing them out. But the key is a property with value, so when the business office officials saw a key going away in somebody's pocket, they wanted a record for inventory and regulatory purposes.

The key is not only a social status symbol but is a basic symbol of hospital life. There are two worlds: "inside" and "outside." Those who relate to the "outside" are key-bearers and healthy, responsible people while those who are confined "inside" are sick and irresponsible. A person such as a maintenance man or a clerk may not have a key and hence may be unsure of his health status.

The key is an essential term of the care and custodial function of the hospital but plays no part in the therapeutic function which is sometimes referred to by the slogan "opening the closed doors of the mind."

NURTURANCE

When a person is brought to the hospital, the first major lesson he learns is that he is "sick." As the admitting psychiatrist will say, "I want you to understand why you are here. You are sick and I am a doctor." Until the person learns this, he is not really acculturated as a patient. Once he is convinced that he is sick, however, he may want to be treated as if he were sick. Most patients are ambulatory; they are asked to look after themselves. It is difficult to find a way in such a hospital to provide nurturance in any usually understood way. But there are many programs in the hospital which are designed to do just this, such as occupational therapy and recreational activities. If they perform their roles properly, a rather large number of nursing students, nurses, aides, and orderlies are nurturers rather than guards. (Nurses and aides are known to bring food in on their own for evening snacks.) I am, however, impressed how seldom food is used as a way of expressing nurturance. Meals are served because people have to eat and special diets are made up because the doctors say so. In other words, food is another care and custodial function. But there is very little use of food and eating as a therapeutic device. It is so much so that in this hospital the dietitian was not until recently included in meetings of the professional staff. Our interviews show, however, that patients and food handlers are quite intimate with one another and, inasmuch as the food handlers move from the basement to the second and third floors, they provide the best grapevine for gossip and discussion.

Moreover, the most frequent and relaxed occasions when patients and some staff—nurses, attendants, etc.—interact together informally is meal time. This is true even though meals are only served on trays in an efficient cafeteria style. I should like to see some experiments on the use of food and meal times as a therapeutic procedure.

THE PERSONALISTIC OR DIAGNOSTIC CULTURE

What I have said about the key and nurturance is subordinate to what can be said about the most dominant cultural theme in a psychiatric hospital, namely, the persistent tendency for each participant who feels identified with the psychiatric aspect of the hospital to relate to others by diagnosing their inner feelings and to try to deal with them accordingly. This has been described by Stanton and Schwartz as follows:

> Restriction of attention to "deep" interpretation was not, of course, confined to dealing with patients; on the contrary, many psychiatrists seemed to pride themselves on ignoring the face value of what their colleagues said to them, focusing instead on what they believed to be "really going on." This decreased somewhat as the general interest in formalities increased, with the corollary interest in the face value of statements. Nevertheless, information was frequently lost in this manner, particularly when a junior staff member protested to a senior about certain aspects of the hospital; the protest was likely to be interpreted as a transference rebellion. This interpretation was rarely made when the younger staff members agreed with the older. Because of these pseudo-deep interpretations, communication sometimes became so complex that the situation could almost be summarized by the statement, "If you disagree with me, you need to see a psychiatrist." Certainly modern psychiatrists and psychologists make up one of the few groups in history where *ad hominem* argument may be treated with greater prestige than an argument confined to the subject matter of the discussion. (1)

I might add that the "good" patient also participates in this activity not only with other patients but with the staff. We have observed that patients are both diagnostic and therapeutic in their interaction and that to be a "good" patient in the sense of performing well on the ward requires more sensitivity than to be a staff member. It has been noted in other places as well as in our own studies that for one patient to ask another patient the ritualistic question, "How do you feel today?" evokes an impatient reply inasmuch as this is the kind of question one can ask only if one is really interested and concerning which the questioner can do something if the respondent says "I feel terrible."

As seen among the staff, this diagnostic or interpretive interaction is one way of trying to deny status or role in a given interpersonal situation. Very frequently, when an individual tries to assert his status or define his role, the impact is diminished by giving such action the diagnostic treatment. For example, when a psychiatrist tries to assert his role and status with a psychiatric social worker, we may hear later, "Well, you know he is in that stage of his analysis," or "He is a little paranoid anyway," or "He just never can get along with professional women." In this community, status and role are frequently thought of as a result of some irrational social system and it is believed that a more rational system would be one in which people would relate on a purely personal basis. When an individual tries to assert his status prerogatives and role responsibilities, it is relatively simple in this culture affectively to diminish the impact by projecting onto or into such a person feelings of hostility. It is assumed by the participants that in this culture any time a person is put in the position of feeling subordinated or frustrated, it is done as an expression of someone else's hostility.

It is relatively easy to participate in this culture. It requires the knowledge of a special vocabulary and it also requires a kind of emphatic insight so that one does know enough to make some pretty good guesses as to what is going on inside of other people and enough about what is going on inside of one's self so that one may receive as well as give within the culture. One has to know for instance how to participate in an interchange such as: "It seems to me there was a lot of hostility in that statement you just made." To which the reply might be, "I didn't really mean it that way. I only meant etc., etc., etc." Within a given psychiatric community, diagnostic stereotypes develop and do interfere with communication. One psychiatrist, for instance, insists that nurses are all passive dependents and in a staff meeting will operate on this basis. He may tell us that nurses never speak up. In our tape recordings of a staff meeting, however, we find that nurses have been speaking up throughout the meeting but the psychiatrist has been paying no attention to what they say. And the acculturated nurses will say that he does not like nurses or is hostile to women. One can say that diagnostic stereotypes are in themselves a kind of self-fulfilling prophecy and work within the staff group as well as between staff patients.

When one looks at this as a cultural pattern, one also sees that the way to become a full-fledged member of the psychiatric community is to become acculturated or to learn the language and behavior. The old guard of such a community consists of the psychiatrists and the psychiatric social workers. A "good" clinical psychologist is one who has learned how to live within this interaction pattern as differentiated from the psychometrician. When looking at the nurses, one sees it more clearly. Many of the nurses in the hospital have not been trained as psychiatric nurses and hence are outside of this cultural pattern. Their success in a hospital depends upon their ability to participate in this cultural pattern and already several nurses have either left or have been fired partly because they could not participate appropriately. The business manager and his staff give us a good example of people in the hospital but not of it. The business manager, for example, is trained as a hospital administrator and before coming to this hospital he had nothing to do with the psychiatric culture and therefore is unable to participate. He has a role in this culture similar to that of a colonial administrator who brings with him a foreign and largely unwanted set of values and ways of relating to other people. He likes tables of organization and systematic ways of handling the various transactions that are required in maintaining a hospital. Those who participate fully in the diagnostic culture have many ways and channels for direct and informal communication, but the business manager has none of these and, unless a situation is formally established, he does not participate in the activities of the hospital community. The business manager, for instance, likes birthdays and ritual festive occasions for which he is quite willing to loosen the purse strings for cakes and candles. It is the only time he ever feels that he is part of the group.

The study of this diagnostic culture has two aspects of importance: (a) Only by understanding it can one understand the interpersonal relationships in the social structure of the hospital. The rigidities of social organization tend to deprive professional people of their professional dignity, but the diagnostic defense is designed to overcome the feelings of subordination. (b) It presents the problem of studying how the "good" patient who has been acculturated in this "inside" culture moves from it back to the outside world. It has already been noted by others that professional people immersed in this culture do not relate well on an informal basis with people who have not had this experience so that friendship patterns of psychiatrists, clinical psychologists, and social workers are primarily among their own ilk. However, patients on leaving the hospital as recovered may not have people in the outside community with whom they can share their new-found way of life which may make rehabilitation very difficult. This is a process to which further research should be devoted.

References

1 Stanton, Alfred H., and Schwartz, Morris S., *The Mental Hospital* (New York: Basic Books, 1954), p. 205

29
CHARACTERISTICS OF TOTAL INSTITUTIONS
Erving Goffman

THE INMATE WORLD

Mortification processes

It is characteristic of inmates that they come to the institution as members, already full-fledged, of a *home world,* that is, a way of life and a round of activities taken for granted up to the point of admission to the institution.[1] It is useful to look at this culture that the recruit brings with him to the institution's door—his *presenting culture,* to modify a psychiatric phrase—in terms especially designed to highlight what it is the total institution will do to him. Whatever the stability of his personal organization, we can assume it was part of a wider supporting framework lodged in his current social environment, a round of experience that somewhat confirms a conception of self that is somewhat acceptable

Source: Erving Goffman, "Characteristics of Total Institutions: Introduction," *Symposium on Preventive and Social Psychiatry,* U.S. Government Printing Office, 1958. pp. 43–49 (excerpt).
[1] There is reason then to exclude orphanages and foundling homes from the list of total institutions, except insofar as the orphan comes to be socialized into the outside world by some process of cultural osmosis, even while this world is being systematically denied him.

to him and a set of defensive maneuvers exercisable at his own discretion as a means of coping with conflicts, discreditings and failures.

Now it appears that total institutions do not substitute their own unique culture for something already formed. We do not deal with acculturation or assimilation but with something more restricted than these. In a sense, total institutions do not look for cultural victory. They effectively create and sustain a particular kind of tension between the home world and the institutional world and use this persistent tension as strategic leverage in the management of men. The full meaning for the inmate of being "in" or "on the inside" does not exist apart from the special meaning to him of "getting out" or "getting on the outside."

The recruit comes into the institution with a self and with attachments to supports which had allowed this self to survive. Upon entrance, he is immediately stripped of his wonted supports, and his self is systematically, if often unintentionally, mortified. In the accurate language of some of our oldest total institutions, he is led into a series of abasements, degradations, humiliations, and profanations of self. He begins, in other words, some radical shifts in his *moral career*, a career laying out the progressive changes that occur in the beliefs that he has concerning himself and significant others.

In total institutions there will also be a system of what might be called *secondary adjustments*, namely, technics which do not directly challenge staff management but which allow inmates to obtain disallowed satisfactions or allowed ones by disallowed means. These practices are variously referred to as: the angles, knowing the ropes, conniving, gimmicks, deals, ins, etc. Such adaptations apparently reach their finest flower in prisons, but of course other total institutions are overrun with them too.[2] It seems apparent that an important aspect of secondary adjustments is that they provide the inmate with some evidence that he is still, as it were, his own man and still has some protective distance, under his own control, between himself and the institution. In some cases, then, a secondary adjustment becomes almost a kind of lodgment for the self, a churinga in which the soul is felt to reside.[3]

The occurrence of secondary adjustments correctly allows us to assume that the inmate group will have some kind of a *code* and some means of informal social control evolved to prevent one inmate from informing staff about the secondary adjustments of another. On the same grounds we can expect that one dimension of social typing among inmates will turn upon this question of security, leading to persons defined as "squealers," "finks," or "stoolies" on one hand, and persons defined as "right guys" on the other.[4] It should be added that

---

[2] See, for example, Norman S. Hayner and Ellis Ash, "The Prisoner Community as a Social Group," *American Sociological Review*, Vol. 4, 1939, p. 364 ff. under "Conniving Processes;" also, Morris G. Caldwell, "Group Dynamics in the Prison Community," *Journal of Criminal Law*, Criminology and Police Science, Vol. 46, pp. 650–651.

[3] See, for example, Melville's extended description of the fight his fellow seamen put up to prevent the clipping of their beards in full accordance with Navy regulations. Herman Melville, *White Jacket*, New York, Grove Press, n.d., pp. 333–347.

[4] See, for example, Donald Clemmer, "Leadership Phenomenon in a Prison Community," *Journal of Criminal Law, Criminology and Police Science*, Vol. 28, 1938, p. 868.

where new inmates can play a role in the system of secondary adjustments, as in providing new faction members or new sexual objects, then their "welcome" may indeed be a sequence of initial indulgences and enticements, instead of exaggerated deprivations.[5] Because of secondary adjustments we also find *kitchen strata,* namely, a kind of rudimentary, largely informal, stratification of inmates on the basis of each one's differential access to disposable illicit commodities; so also we find social typing to designate the powerful persons in the informal market system.[6]

While the privilege system provides the chief framework within which reassembly of the self takes place, other factors characteristically lead by different routes in the same general direction. Relief from economic and social responsibilities—much touted as part of the therapy in mental hospitals—is one, although in many cases it would seem that the disorganizing effect of this moratorium is more significant than its organizing effect. More important as a reorganizing influence is the *fraternalization process,* namely, the process through which socially distant persons find themselves developing mutual support and common *counter-mores* in opposition to a system that has forced them into intimacy and into a single, equalitarian community of fate.[7] It seems that the new recruit frequently starts out with something like the staff's popular misconceptions of the character of the inmates and then comes to find that most of his fellows have all the properties of ordinary decent human beings and that the stereotypes associated with their condition or offense are not a reasonable ground for judgment of inmates.[8]

If the inmates are persons who are accused by staff and society of having committed some kind of a crime against society, then the new inmate, even though sometimes in fact quite guiltless, may come to share the guilty feelings of his fellows and, thereafter, their well-elaborated defenses against these feelings. A sense of common injustice and a sense of bitterness against the outside world tends to develop, marking an important movement in the inmate's moral career. This response to felt guilt and massive deprivation is most clearly illustrated perhaps in prison life:[9]

By their reasoning, after an offender has been subjected to unfair or excessive punishment and treatment more degrading than that prescribed by law, he comes to justify his

[5] See, for example, Ida Ann Harper, "The Role of the 'Fringer' in a State Prison for Women," *Social Forces,* Vol. 31, 1952, pp. 53–60.

[6] For concentration camps, see the discussion of "Prominents" throughout Elie A. Cohen, *Human Behavior in the Concentration Camp,* London, Jonathan Cape, 1954; for mental hospitals, see Ivan Belknap, *Human Problems of a State Mental Hospital,* New York, McGraw-Hill, 1956, p. 189. For prisons, see the discussion of "Politicos" in Donald Clemmer, *The Prison Community,* Christopher Publishing House, Boston, 1940, pp. 277–279, 298–309; also Hayner, *op. cit.,* p. 367; and Caldwell, *op. cit.,* pp. 651–653.

[7] For the version of this inmate solidarity to be found in military academies, see, Sanford M. Dornbush, "The Military Academy as an Assimilating Institution," *Social Forces,* Vol. 33, 1955, p. 318.

[8] An interesting example of this re-evaluation may be found in a conscientious objector's experience with nonpolitical prisoners, see Alfred Hassler, *Diary of a Self-Made Convict,* Henry Regnery, Chicago, 1954, p. 74, 117. In mental hospitals, of course, the patient's antagonism to staff obtains one of its supports from the discovery that, like himself, many other patients are more like ordinary persons than like anything else.

[9] Richard McCleery, *The Strange Journey,* University of North Carolina Extension Bulletin, Vol. 32, 1953, p. 24. Italics are McCleery's.

act which he could not have justified when he committed it. He decides to "get even" for his unjust treatment in prison and takes reprisals through further crime at the first opportunity. *With that decision he becomes a criminal.*

A more general statement[10] may be taken from two other students of the same kind of total institution: "In many ways, the inmate social system may be viewed as providing a way of life which enables the inmates to avoid the devastating psychological effects of internalizing and converting social rejection into self rejection. In effect, it permits the inmate to reject his rejectors rather than himself."

Adaptation alignments

The mortifying processes that have been discussed and the privilege system represent the conditions that the inmate must adapt to in some way, but however pressing, these conditions allow for different ways of meeting them. We find, in fact, that the same inmate will employ different lines of adaptation or tacks at different phases in his moral career and may even fluctuate between different tacks at the same time.

First, there is the process of *situational withdrawal.* The inmate withdraws apparent attention from everything except events immediately around his body and sees these in a perspective not employed by others present. This drastic curtailment of involvement in interactional events is best known, of course, in mental hospitals, under the title of "regression." Aspects of "prison psychosis" or "stir simpleness" represent the same adjustment, as do some forms of "acute depersonalization" described in concentration camps. I do not think it is known whether this line of adaptation forms a single continuum of varying degrees of withdrawal or whether there are standard discontinuous plateaus of disinvolvement. It does seem to be the case, however, that, given the pressures apparently required to dislodge an inmate from this status, as well as the currently limited facilities for doing so, we frequently find here, effectively speaking, an irreversible line of adaptation.

Second, there is the *rebellious line.* The inmate intentionally challenges the institution by flagrantly refusing to cooperate with staff in almost any way.[11] The result is a constantly communicated intransigency and sometimes high rebel-morale. Most large mental hospitals, for example, seem to have wards where this spirit strongly prevails. Interestingly enough, there are many circumstances in which sustained rejection of a total institution requires sustained orientation to its formal organization and hence, paradoxically, a deep kind of commitment to the establishment. Similarly, when total institutions take the line (as they sometimes do in the case of mental hospitals prescribing lobotomy[12] or army

[10] Lloyd W. McCorkle and Richard Korn, "Resocialization Within Walls," *The Annals,* May 1954, p. 88. See also p. 95.

[11] See, for example, the discussion of "The Resisters," in Edgar H. Schein, "The Chinese Indoctrination Program for Prisoners of War," *Psychiatry,* Vol. 19, 1956, pp. 166–167.

[12] See, for example, Belknap, *op. cit.,* p. 192.

barracks prescribing the stockade) that the recalcitrant inmate must be broken, then, in their way, they must show as much special devotion to the rebel as he has shown to them. It should be added, finally, that while prisoners of war have been known staunchly to take a rebellious stance throughout their incarceration, this stance is typically a temporary and initial phase of reaction, emerging from this to situational withdrawal or some other line of adaptation.

Third, another standard alignment in the institutional world takes the form of a kind of *colonization.* The sampling of the outside world provided by the establishment is taken by the inmate as the whole, and a stable, relatively contented existence is built up out of the maximum satisfactions procurable within the institution.[13] Experience of the outside world is used as a point of reference to demonstrate the desirability of life on the inside; and the usual tension between the two worlds collapses, thwarting the social arrangements based upon this felt discrepancy. Characteristically, the individual who too obviously takes this line may be accused by his fellow inmates of "having found a home" or of "never having had it so good." Staff itself may become vaguely embarrassed by this use that is being made of the institution, sensing that the benign possibilities in the situation are somehow being misused. Colonizers themselves may feel obliged to deny their satisfaction with the institution, if only in the interest of sustaining the counter-mores supporting inmate solidarity. They may find it necessary to mess up just prior to their slated discharge, thereby allowing themselves to present involuntary reasons for continued incarceration. It should be incidentally noted that any humanistic effort to make life in total institutions more bearable must face the possibility that doing so may increase the attractiveness and likelihood of colonization.

Fourth, one mode of adaptation to the setting of a total institution is that of *conversion.* The inmate appears to take over completely the official or staff view of himself and tries to act out the role of the perfect inmate. While the colonized inmate builds as much of a free community as possible for himself by using the limited facilities available, the convert takes a more disciplined, moralistic, monochromatic line, presenting himself as someone whose institutional enthusiasm is always at the disposal of the staff. In Chinese POW camps, we find Americans who became "pros" and fully espoused the Communist view of the world.[14] In army barracks there are enlisted men who give the impression that they are always "sucking around" and always "bucking for promotion." In prisons there are "square johns." In German concentration camps, longtime prisoners sometimes came to adapt the vocabulary, recreation, posture, expressions of aggression, and clothing style of the Gestapo, executing their role of straw-boss with military strictness.[15] Some mental hospitals have the distinction of providing two quite different conversion possibilities—one for the new admis-

[13] In the case of mental hospitals, those who take this line are sometimes called "institutional cures" or are said to suffer from "hospitalitis."

[14] Schein, *op. cit.,* pp. 167–169.

[15] See, Bruno Bettelheim, "Individual and Mass Behavior in Extreme Situations," *Journal of Abnormal and Social Psychology,* Vol. 38, 1943, pp. 447–451. It should be added that in concentration camps, colonization and conversion often seemed to go together. See, Cohen, *op. cit.,* pp. 200–203, where the role of the "Kapo" is discussed.

sion who can see the light after an appropriate struggle and adapt the psychiatric view of himself, and another for the chronic ward patient who adopts the manner and dress of attendants while helping them to manage the other ward patients with a stringency excelling that of the attendants themselves.

Here, it should be noted, is a significant way in which total institutions differ. Many, like progressive mental hospitals, merchant ships, TB sanitariums and brainwashing camps, offer the inmate an opportunity to live up to a model of conduct that is at once ideal and staff-sponsored—a model felt by its advocates to be in the supreme interests of the very persons to whom it is applied. Other total institutions, like some concentration camps and some prisons, do not officially sponsor an ideal that the inmate is expected to incorporate as a means of judging himself.

While the alignments that have been mentioned represent coherent courses to pursue, few inmates, it seems, carry these pursuits very far. In most total institutions, what we seem to find is that most inmates take the tack of what they call *playing it cool*. This involves a somewhat opportunistic combination of secondary adjustments, conversion, colonization and loyalty to the inmate group, so that in the particular circumstances the inmate will have a maximum chance of eventually getting out physically and psychically undamaged.[16] Typically, the inmate will support the counter-mores when with fellow inmates and be silent to them on how tractably he acts when alone in the presence of staff.[17] Inmates taking this line tend to subordinate contacts with their fellows to the higher claim of "keeping out of trouble." They tend to volunteer for nothing, and they may even learn to cut their ties to the outside world sufficiently to give cultural reality to the world inside but not enough to lead to colonization.

I have suggested some of the lines of adaptation that inmates can take to the pressures that play in total institutions. Each represents a way of managing the tension between the home world and the institutional world. However, there are circumstances in which the home world of the inmate was such, in fact, as to *immunize* him against the bleak world on the inside, and for such persons no particular scheme of adaptation need be carried very far. Thus, some lower-class mental hospital patients who have lived all their previous life in orphanages, reformatories and jails, tend to see the hospital as just another total institution to which it is possible to apply the adaptive technics learned and perfected in other total instituations. "Playing it cool" represents for such persons, not a shift in their moral career, but an alignment that is already second nature.

The professional criminal element in the early periods of German concentration camps displayed something of the same immunity to their surroundings

---

[16] See the discussion in Schein, *op. cit.*, pp. 165–166 of the "Get-Alongers," and Robert J. Lifton, "Home by Ship: Reaction Patterns of American Prisoners of War Repatriated From North Korea," *American Journal of Psychiatry*, Vol. 110, 1954, p. 734.

[17] This two-facedness, of course, is very commonly found in total institutions. In the state-type mental hospital studied by the writer, even the few elite patients selected for individual psychotherapy, and hence in the best position for espousal of the psychiatric approach to self, tended to present their favorable view of psychotherapy only to the members of their intimate cliques. For a report on the way in which Army prisoners concealed from fellow offenders their interest in "restoration" to the Army, see the comments by Richard Cloward in Session 4 of *New Perspectives for Research on Juvenile Delinquency*, ed. by Helen L. Witmer and Ruth Kotinsky, U.S. Department of Health, Education and Welfare, Children's Bureau Bulletin, 1955, especially p. 90.

or even found new satisfactions through fraternization with middle-class political prisoners.[18] Similarly, Shetland youths recruited into the British merchant marine are not apparently threatened much by the cramped arduous life on board because island life is even more stunted; they make uncomplaining sailors because from their point of view they have nothing much to complain about. Strong religious and political convictions may also serve perhaps to immunize the true believer against the assaults of a total institution, and even a failure to speak the language of the staff may cause the staff to give up its efforts at reformation, allowing the nonspeaker immunity to certain pressures.[19]

30
ROLES, CLIQUES AND SANCTIONS: DIMENSIONS OF PATIENT SOCIETY
Harvey L. Smith and Jean Thrasher

In recent years psychiatrists and social scientists have shown an increasing interest in the organization and functions of patient society. For psychiatrists this concern has resulted from the realization that the ward is the actual living situation of the hospitalized patient, the need to develop additional types of therapy, and from the problems of management and administration which arise as a result of the group living situation of the patients. Social scientists have recognized patient society as a special type of social organization, existing within certain well-defined limits, in which social processes can be observed in greater detail and depth than in social systems characterized by greater complexity. The study reviewed in this paper[6] had a two-fold purpose: to describe the informal social organization of the patients in one short-term treatment hospital, and to evaluate, in the short-term setting, the utility of the concept "patient society" which has proven so valuable in the study of other types of hospitals.[2, 5, 8, 10]

Two wards of the psychiatric in-patient service of a large general hospital were selected for study. One of these was an open ward for neurotic and alcoholic patients, the other a locked ward for psychotic patients. For both wards the most frequent diagnoses were depressive reaction and schizophrenic reaction. The patients were not segregated by age or sex. All of the patients were white. Each ward housed a maximum of eighteen patients, and the actual number of patients varied from seven to eighteen.

The primary research method was that of direct observation of the patients

---

[18] Bettelheim, op. cit., p. 425.

[19] Thus, Schein, op. cit., p. 165 fn., suggests that Puerto Ricans and other non-English-speaking prisoners of war in China were given up on and allowed to work out a viable routine of menial chores.

Source: Harvey L. Smith and Jean Thrasher, "Roles, Cliques and Sanctions: Dimensions of Patient Society," International Journal of Social Psychiatry, 9: 184–191, 1963.

in the ward setting. For a period of six months the observer mingled with the patients and joined in their activities and conversations. This direct observation was coupled with some formal interviewing of patients concerning their associations and activities.

Despite the short length of hospitalization—an average of about three weeks —the patients on each ward have an observable society. This society can be seen as existing on a number of levels. This paper will first consider the larger patient society as it is reflected in the attitudes, social rôles and sanctions of the patient group. The different types of cliques will then be discussed in terms of their organization and functions. The paper will conclude with a re-evaluation of the concept "patient society" and some suggestions for further research.

The larger patient society is characterized by a set of norms which the patients consider binding upon them, and by a number of expectations which they have of each other. Conformity to these norms is encouraged through a number of sanctions, both positive and negative, which are applied either in support of, or in disapproval of, the behavior of individual patients. These norms become manifest in a number of social rôles which are recognized and utilized by the patients. The expectations of the patients involve attitudes towards each group of significant others in the hospital, as well as attitudes towards illness.

Towards his therapist, the patient is expected to have an attitude of complete faith, confidence, trust and reliance. The stated or assumed wishes of the therapist are taken as the primary guide for the behaviour of the patient and no criticism of the therapist is permitted within the context of the larger society. Refusal to see the therapist evokes the strongest of negative sanctions, and any expression of doubt or dislike elicits a strong defence of the therapist from the other patients.

The other categories of hospital personnel do not enjoy the immunity from criticism reserved for the therapists; complaint and criticism are permitted, and to some extent expected, as long as they do not reach the proportions of constant complaining. The patients realize that certain demands are placed upon them by the staff and expect each other to observe the ward rules, at least most of the rules most of the time, but at the same time there is some resentment. There appears to be some ambivalence in the relations of the patients to the ward staff. On the one hand, the patients expect to co-operate with the staff and to avoid making trouble for them, to observe the ward rules and generally to keep the relationship as free from conflict as possible. On the other hand, the patients resent the fact that the staff sometimes talk down to them, occasionally show indifference and at times do not permit sufficient self-direction in the patients' activities. This feeling is reflected in the group norms which prescribe that patients do not inform the staff of the behaviour of another patient. This in turn reinforces the feeling of the patients as being a group apart from the staff and to some extent insulates the group from the staff.

The attitudes which the patients hold towards each other reflect an attempt to maintain a sympathetic and supportive atmosphere on the ward, as well as the primary goal of all the patients, to go home. The patient is expected to behave as normally as he is able and to avoid upsetting the other patients as much as possible. There is a tendency to define the behaviour of another patient as a function of his illness and to withhold any judgment of that behaviour; at the same time the patient is expected to attempt to abandon his own "sick" behaviour. However, if the behaviour of another patient is not defined as a part of the illness the withholding of judgment is abandoned. For example, a delusional or hallucinating patient will be treated with an unusual amount of sympathy and support, while similar behaviour which is not delusional will be criticized. In less obvious instances of upsetting behaviour, those harder to define, the degree to which the patient in question has accepted the general rôle of patient appears to be an important factor in determining whether or not his behaviour will be defined as "sick" or "not sick". The more closely the patient conforms to the expectations of the patient rôle, the more likely his occasional deviations will be defined as illness. A similar process was found by Fonseca,[4] who indicates that the privileges of the sick rôle may be lost by a patient who deviates from the dominant rôle definition of the patient.

There are very definite limits set upon the topics of conversation within the total patient group. The patient is permitted to talk about himself but not to tell the intimate details of his life or his illness. To a certain extent, it is permissible to complain about the staff, hospital and somatic ailments, but such complaining is negatively sanctioned when it becomes constant or comes to monopolize the conversation. Reasons given by the patients for this limiting of conversation include the feeling that they should avoid upsetting the other patients, that they should get their minds off themselves and that other patients might be bored. Whatever the importance of the stated reasons, they do reflect the desire on the part of the patients to maintain a supportive and non-threatening milieu.

The last category of attitudes involves the attitudes of the patient towards himself and his illness. The strongest expectation in this area is that the patient should realize and admit that he is in a psychiatric hospital, and that he should be in such a hospital. While the patient is permitted to complain that he was brought to the hospital against his will, he is not permitted to say that he is in the wrong hospital or that he was hospitalized by mistake. The patients develop a set of indices which are perceived as reflecting stages of improvement, and the patient is expected to work for these tangible indications of recovery. These revolve primarily around the privilege system, the possession of privileges being highly valued by the patients and important as an indication of recovery. The privileges are themselves graded, extending from no privilege to full access to the hospital and town. Between are several gradations dealing primarily with space and time limitations.

In summary, the patient is expected to perceive himself and the other patients as sick and in need of hospitalization. At the same time the patient is expected to be optimistic about his own, and others', chances for recovery, and to concentrate his efforts towards the goal of leaving the hospital.

From these considerations, it can be seen that the patients share a rather complex normative system. This system is evidenced in behaviour through a number of social rôles. The shared rôle of psychiatric patient, the major features of which have been discussed above, is but one of the social rôles commonly found in patient society, the others being less general and not played by all the patients. These more specific rôles are of three types and contribute in different ways to the total organization of patient society.

The first major category may be called "social activity rôles" and includes those rôles which contribute directly to the social activities or the increase of interaction among the patients. For the most part, these rôles reflect an adaptation of outside behaviour patterns to the hospital situation. One such rôle is that of "organizer". Often one patient will take it upon himself to organize activities for other patients which help to reduce the boredom on the ward. Another social activity rôle is that of the clown, or jester. This patient, tolerated for his amusement value, is permitted to make joking attacks directed against members of the staff and other patients without evoking criticism. Rôles which involve special talents, such as musical ability, are also placed in the category of social activity rôles.

The second major category of rôles may be called "hospital specific rôles". These do not represent rôle behaviour imported from outside the hospital but are differentiations of the more general patient rôle already discussed. These rôles relate directly to the needs of the patients as a group, needs which arise as they attempt to cope with their current living situation within the hospital. The many forms of patient leadership fall in this category, as do those patients who take it upon themselves to greet and orient new patients to the ward, and those who make suggestions to the staff.

Some of the rôles played by the patients appear to be carried over with little alteration from rôles played in the family or work situation. These are "outside rôles", the third major category of specific rôles, and are direct reflections of the patients' outside statuses. The clearest examples of work rôles brought into the hospital occurred when teachers or physicians were on the wards as patients. Often these persons related to the other patients in terms of the occupational rôles rather than the mutual patient rôles. Family rôles were most apparent when children were on the ward, but parental and sibling relationships were also observed among the adult patients. Age and sex rôles were also carried over into the hospital situation and were reflected in the flirtations which sometimes developed among adolescent or young adult patients. The presence and prevalence of these outside rôles reflect a continued orientation to the outside community, which is one of the most important differences in patient society between the short- and long-term treatment settings. Studies of long-term hospitals indicate that patients tend to lose their orientation to the outside community and become much more involved with factors within the hospital.[3, 5, 9]

It must be emphasized that, with the exception of the common rôle of psychiatric patient, these rôles are not present at all times; one or all of them may be absent. However, the particular rôle configuration of the group at any time does affect the operation of patient society, and changes in the patient structure or "ward atmosphere" may be attributable to the presence or absence of certain of these rôles.

To summarize briefly, the psychiatric ward provides the context for a number of social rôles. There is a common rôle shared by all as a result of their common status of psychiatric patient. In addition there are a number of rôles which relate to the common activities on the ward, other rôles which relate to the needs of the patients as a group, and still others which reflect the outside statuses of individual patients. All these rôles are recognized and utilized within the total organization of the larger patient society.

It has already been mentioned that the patients encourage conformity to their norms through a number of positive and negative sanctions. The positive sanctions, through which the patients reward approved behaviour, include social support, coaxing, sympathy and encouragement. For the most part, the positive sanctions are built into the patient rôle and reflect the dominant patient values. That is, patients are generally expected to be supportive and sympathetic towards one another. The negative sanctions include kidding, joking, ignoring, avoidance, criticism and enforced social isolation. All of these sanctions vary in intensity and duration, and at times the positive and negative sanctions are used in combination, i.e. first coaxing and then avoiding the offending patient. The use of sanctions can be seen as serving a manifest and a latent function; on the one hand they operate to change the behaviour which is disapproved, and at the same time reinforce the dominant values and norms of the group.

The larger patient society, which has been briefly described, is only one type of association among the patients. It is well known that cliques and other small social groupings arise within the larger patient group. The cliques observed in this study were of two distinct types, confidence cliques and activity cliques. Confidence cliques were usually quite small, dyads or triads, and were characterized by a high degree of intimacy among the members. The members of these cliques tended to isolate themselves from the rest of the patient group and retain an air of secrecy, both tendencies reflecting the confidential nature of the cliques.

If the different types of association are viewed on a continuum of intimacy, the larger patient group appears at one pole and the confidence cliques at the opposite pole. In fact, most of the generalizations just reviewed concerning the larger group appear to be reversed in the confidence cliques. In the total group, patients do not discuss the intimate details of their lives and illnesses, but this is the primary characteristic of the confidence cliques where the patients express many misgivings concerning leaving the hospital and readjusting to the outside community. Within the larger group there is a norm of non-judgment concerning most behaviour, but this also breaks down in the confidence cliques, and patients freely criticize other patients. Criticism of the therapists, which is immediately negatively sanctioned in the larger group, is quite common within the small cliques. The general picture presented by confidence clique relationships is one of great intimacy, in which the patients speak freely about their feelings and doubts concerning themselves, their therapists, the hospital and the other patients. This is the private area within the social structure of the ward and remains fairly stable and free from conflict. This private sphere exists within a larger social context, the public sphere of the total patient group, in which the expression of these feelings is restricted.

In both size and degree of intimacy the activity cliques stand between the larger patient group and the confidence cliques. Activity cliques tended to be rather large, four to ten members, and centred around some activity on the ward, usually cards. Activity cliques tended to persist longer than confidence cliques since a member who had been discharged could be replaced without great difficulty. Often the members of activity cliques resisted the planned activities of the hospital, such as occupational and recreational therapy, perhaps because they did not need this activity to provide amusement, and the formal activities often tended to break up the ongoing informal associations.

In intimacy, too, the activity cliques are between the public and private spheres of patient organization. They do not approach the intimacy of the confidence cliques but neither are they as free from judgment nor restrictive of conversation as the total patient group. In informal situations, activity cliques maintained an atmosphere of easy camaraderie centred around a commonly enjoyed activity.

The activity cliques are of particular importance in understanding the operation of the total patient society. Standing on the continuum of intimacy between the private sphere of the confidence cliques and the public sphere of the larger patient group, the activity cliques are both a point of contact and a point of conflict. However, any conflict remained covert as long as the clique members remained in an informal situation. It became quite apparent in the behaviour of members of activity cliques only in formal situations, when there was a change in the organization and orientation of the group.

During the course of the study there were a number of patient meetings in which all the patients on the ward met the chief resident and sometimes the head nurse. These meetings have been called formal situations because they were called by members of the staff for stated purposes (therapy, to hear complaints and suggestions, etc.), and because they represent a possible shift in the orientation of the patients from the horizontal, peer-group relations to an orientation along doctor-patient, vertical lines. These meetings were the only situation in which a member of the staff came in contact with the patient group as a group. It was found that although the supportive, non-conflictual atmosphere which characterized both the larger patient group and the confidence cliques tended to carry over into the formal situation, this was not true among activity clique members. These patients often became quite critical and verbally abusive of one another in the formal, more public patient meetings. This took the form of open criticism, "interpretations", or "telling off" the offending patient. The important thing to note is that such criticism would not be voiced directly to the offending patient in any informal situation and occurred almost exclusively among patients who were members of the same activity cliques. The presence of the physician served to redefine the usual situation from a peer-group organization to a vertical organization, with the result that the usual sanctioning system ceased to be operative. In short, with the entrance of the physician into the system, patient society became reorganized along a different axis; when the physician withdrew, it returned to its customary organization.

To summarize this point, the change of orientation evidenced in these meetings casts interesting light upon the total organization of patient society. In informal situations, there is primarily a patient-patient orientation; when the physician comes into contact with the total patient society there is a change to a physician-patient orientation, with the result that there is disruption of the usual functioning of the society. This disruption occurred at the weakest point in the organization of patient society, the point of contact between the more stable spheres of patient organization. Parsons'[7] analogy between the doctor-patient and parent-child relationships may be useful in understanding the changes in social organization following the introduction of an authority figure.

There are three distinct types of association found among the patients and these may be placed along a continuum of intimacy. The public sphere of the larger patient group and the private sphere of the confidence cliques remain relatively free from conflict although they are characterized by different, and sometimes contradictory, norms and expectations. The activity cliques are a point of contact and conflict between these two spheres, and with a change in the orientation of the patients from the informal to the formal this conflict becomes overt.

Patient society, in all its aspects, was found to serve a number of functions for its members. Function, in this study, was defined as observed consequences, or processes, which contributed to the adaptation and adjustment of the patients to the hospital situation. Complete discussion of these functions is outside the scope of this paper, but some of the major ones should be mentioned. First, the organization of patient society permits the patients to help each other in ways which would not otherwise be possible. This can be seen in the number of favours which the patients do for each other and the co-operative enterprises which often arise spontaneously. Second, it helps to combat the boredom which the patients consider one of the primary problems of ward living. Third, it provides the patient with a comparative reference group which he can utilize to judge his own illness and recovery. Fourth, it provides a bridge between the hospital and the outside community, thus minimizing the discontinuity of the hospital experience.[1, 5] Fifth, patient society provides a supportive and ego-sustaining milieu which closely parallels the therapeutic goals of the staff; and sixth, it provides means to assert independence and self-identity within a total context of dependence and enforced association.

A second focus of this study was to evaluate the utility of the concept "patient society" in the study of the short-term hospital. This concept was developed in the study of long-term treatment settings, and has proven quite useful in that situation. It must be admitted, however, that the concept "patient society" proved to be of limited utility in this study. The concept, as utilized in the studies of long-term treatment settings, provided only a partial view of the meaningful processes and relationships among the patients. It was necessary to employ other concepts, which altered the focus of observation, in order to gain a more complete picture of the organization and behaviour of the patients, and to place the larger patient group in a better perspective with regard to the total operation and organization of the ward. For example, the analysis of the types and functions of cliques, a smaller social unit than patient society, proved very useful in explaining some of the confusing and inconsistent aspects of that society. In addition, the analysis of cliques revealed an area of conflict and a different set of norms and attitudes. Patient society in formation lacks a tradition and a history. The staff, representing the permanent aspect of the total ward structure, is a group which does have established definitions and expectations of the patients. The patient group, lacking this stability and tradition, may accept and perpetuate these definitions on the level of the larger patient society. Another set of definitions, developed in the more intimate clique relationships, does not emerge as dominant in the larger group because of the transitory nature of the cliques. Using only the concept "patient society" as it is usually used in studies of long-term hospitals, these important aspects of patient organization would not have been revealed.

This study would indicate that the concept is valid, but of limited usefulness in the study of the short-term hospital. In addition, this study indicates that additional concepts and foci of observation, i.e. patient orientation (whether inside or outside the hospital), rôle differentiation and cliques, must be utilized to implement the concept "patient society" in the investigation of the short-term, rapid-turnover situation.

In concluding this paper, mention should be made of a number of areas requiring additional research. The shared rôle of psychiatric patient, and the implications of the rôle, is one such area. The findings of this study indicate that to some extent the patient definition of this rôle comes from the staff definition. Research is needed to determine to what extent the staff does influence the specific content of this rôle, and to what extent modification of patient society could be accomplished by changing the staff's expectation of the patient rôle. A study is in progress which has as its focus the process of rôle definition and the resultant rôle-images of the patients on these same wards.

The individual social rôles, and their various combinations, also require further research. It is not known which of these rôles are essential for the formation and continuation of patient society, and which others are not essential but affect the overall structure and functioning of the society. In general, research is needed to determine how the presence or absence of certain rôles, the various rôle combinations which develop, and the means of learning these rôles all combine to contribute to the various forms and functions of patient societies in different hospitals.

Several questions arise in this study which reflect upon conceptions of the ward structure and upon the possibilities of a therapeutic milieu. The psychiatric ward is usually perceived as a very permissive situation. This is the appearance on the surface, but with further study it becomes apparent that in fact patient society is very restrictive in many of its aspects. This raises some questions as to whether or not the atmosphere maintained by the patients is really non-threatening. Perhaps the best formulation is that the patients maintain an environment which minimizes threat to the patients as a group, but the restrictiveness necessitated by this attempt poses some threat to the individual patients. It can be hypothesized that different aspects of the total milieu vary in their importance to different patients. If a therapeutic milieu is to be established it must be determined what aspects of patient society are therapeutic, to what patients they are therapeutic, and to what patients they are non-therapeutic. The degree of actual and perceived restrictiveness is one such aspect requiring research.

References

1   Bierer, Joshua (ed.): *Therapeutic Social Clubs. London:* H. K. Lewis, 1948.

2   Caudill, William, Redlich, Frederick C., Gilmore, Helen, and Brody, Eugene: "Social structure and interaction process on a psychiatric ward." *Amer. J. Orthopsychiatry*, 1952, **22,** 314–331.

3   Dunham, H. Warren, and Weinberg, S. Kirson: *The Culture of the State Mental Hospital.* Detroit: Wayne State University Press, 1960.

4   Fonseca, O. W.: "Emergent social structure among short-term psychiatric patients." *Internat. J. Social Psychiatry*, 1956, **2,** 134–141.

5   Goffman, Erving: "The characteristics of total institutions." *Symposium on Preventive and Social Psychiatry.* Washington: U.S. Government Printing Office, 1958, pp. 43–85.

6   Harmon, Jean: "The functions of patient society in a short-term psychiatric setting." Unpublished M.A. Thesis, University of North Carolina, 1959.

7   Parsons, Talcott, and Fox, Renée: "Illness, therapy, and the modern urban American family." *J. Social Issues*, 1952, **9,** 31–44.

8   Rowland, Howard: "Friendship patterns in the state mental hospital: a sociological approach." *Psychiatry*, 1939, **2,** 363–373.

9   Rowland, Howard: "Interaction process in the state mental hospital." *Psychiatry*, 1938, **1,** 322–331.

10 Stanton, Alfred H., and Schwartz, Morris: *The Mental Hospital.* New York: Basic Books, 1954.

31
RESISTANCE TO TREATMENT: EXPLORATIONS OF THE PATIENT'S SICK ROLE*
Raymond Sobel and Ardis Ingalls

THE PROBLEM

Over the past several years we have been struck by the existence of a common thread that can be observed in a variety of difficulties encountered in all doctor-patient relationships. Though not unique to psychiatry, it can be seen in the

Source: Raymond Sobel, and Ardis Ingalls, "Resistance to Treatment: Explorations of the Patient's Sick Role," *American Journal of Psychotherapy*, **18:** 562–573, 1964.
* This study was supported by the State of Washington Initiative 171 Funds for Research in Biology and Medicine.

interaction of the psychiatrist and his patient in the form of resistance to psychiatric treatment. Much of this resistance, which includes failure to keep appointments and to take prescribed medicines, may be traced to doctor-patient disagreement regarding the patient's sick role. By sick role we mean the behavior and attitudes expected of the patient to which he tacitly or explicitly agrees when he becomes a patient. Every society defines the expectations placed upon the behavior of both doctor and patient and ensures that they are complementary and congruous. Neither time nor complexity of civilization seems to make any difference, for in every society the doctor and the patient are expected to fulfill certain duties, rights, and obligations. These apply to the healer, be he a listerian surgeon, present-day *curandero* of New Mexico, or a witch doctor of Nyasaland.

For the patient, likewise, it does not seem to matter whether he undergoes surgery or exorcism . . . he is expected to behave in a certain predictable fashion congruous with the behavior and actions of his doctor or practitioner. Should he fail to exercise these rights and obligations or should the healer's behavior conflict with his own, it is likely that the healing process will be impeded and that tension between himself and his doctor will develop (1).

In the United States as elsewhere, the initiation into the successful practice of the sick role is begun early in the socialization process. Just as one learns to become a law-abiding citizen or a good wife, one learns to become a good patient. Unfortunately, little is known about how this occurs save that it begins early in life with the first illnesses, is taught by the parents and is reinforced by the physician. It seems relatively well crystallized by the time puberty sets in.

Other investigators have shown that social class is significantly related not only to the outcome but also to the type of treatment selected, and the choice of the doctor (2–6). Social class is definitely related to the patient's concept of his sick role (7). This is attested to by the common difficulties of medical students and residents in treating patients from the lowest socioeconomic stratum, since these patients often prove uncooperative to the physician's regimen. These social class factors are characteristically encountered in the field of psychiatry, where the house officer tends to shun lower-class patients not because of snobbery but because the patient wants something other than talking (8). These residents frequently institute therapeutic endeavors which are self-fulfilled failures.

Our present concern is to report the results of our attempts to measure the sick role as seen by a variety of participants in the doctor-patient relationship and to speculate on the meaning of the data for the relationship.

THEORETICAL CONSIDERATIONS

The social sciences provide a wealth of information regarding social roles and their analysis (9, 10, 11). Parsons and Coser furnish useful models for the medical patient's sick role and describe the mutual expectations inherent in the doctor-patient relationship (12, 13). They state, in essence, that the medical patient is expected to be passive and dependent, to seek help, and to be helpless to a major degree. He is not held responsible for his illness and it is expected that he will seek competent professional help rather than attempt self-cure. Often the choice of physician is best determined by others than himself and he is expected to be unable or incompetent to judge his doctor's expertness. Furthermore, the medical patient may be expected to delegate the ultimate responsibility for his care to another person (usually a relative) since he feels in no position to make major decisions when ill.

Mauksch et al. show that the type of illness and the sex of the patient may be related to different sick role expectations. For example, they report that patients with gastrointestinal disorders feel it most important to have confidence in the physician, whereas patients with cardiovascular diseases consider cooperation with the doctor as a paramount expectation (14). Mechanic reports that it is easier for a patient to feel not responsible for the demands of others when the illness is relatively common, predictable, and nonthreatening (15).

In a less scientific vein, an article entitled "How to be a Good Patient" that appeared in Today's Health, an official publication of the American Medical Association, gently tells the reader to be passive, submissive, and uncomplaining. For example, "Should you ask your doctor to prescribe a specific drug or medicine because you've heard it 'worked wonders' for someone with an ailment which you think is the same as yours?" The author answers as follows: "Few things annoy doctors more than this request. If your doctor refuses—as he most likely will—to prescribe the remedy of your choice, he will do so for sound scientific reasons. . . ." The author then continues to put the patient in his place, or, to be more accurate, to assign him to his appropriate sick role (16).

In a previous article I have pointed out that "In the practice of medicine the patient is expected to deliver himself passively to the doctor's ministrations, to submit to his manipulations and to complain of the discomfort and inconvenience as little as possible. Behavior initiated in the doctor's office is not to be carried on outside the office unless the doctor gives permission and suggests it. . . . The 'good' patient is the one who waits to be told what to do and who does exactly what he is told: no more, no less, since he may injure himself by independent activity. The contrast to the psychiatric patient is most obvious and needs no belaboring. In fact, failure to take initiative is usually considered as further evidence of unfulfilled dependency needs and of a 'magic helper' transference. Similarly, dependency, helplessness, and submissiveness which are essential features of the medical patient's expected behavior emerge as undesirable activities for the psychiatric patient" (17).

In addition, the psychiatric patient cannot use his psychiatrist to make decisions for him or to be a final court of appeal, particularly if the problem is excessive dependency on others. Ideally, the psychiatrist confronts such a dependent person with his irrational need to have someone else live his life for him. The doctor also points out the consequences of such behavior, using the data gleaned in previous interviews. Should the patient cling to a medical model of doctor-patient relationship, the anticipated change toward greater independence will not occur or will be delayed. It is essential that the doctor's and the patient's expectations are congruous and are aimed at a mutual goal of increased self-determination.

It is well known that when social roles are well defined and congruous, a minimum of tension will exist between the participants in the interaction (18). Since clinical experience suggested that the expectations placed upon psychiatric patients tend to be ambiguous and to conflict with the previously learned sick role, three hypotheses were made and subjected to experimental verification:

1. Medical and psychiatric patient roles demand different behavior with respect to passivity, dependency, and submission.

2. Psychiatric patients tend to perceive their role as more closely allied to the role of the medical patient than do their psychiatrists.

3. Medical patients and their doctors are more in agreement regarding the patient's role than are their counterparts in the psychiatric transaction.

METHODOLOGY

Using Parson's definition of the sick role, a reliable scale† of 38 statements was constructed to describe behavior entailed in passivity, dependency, helplessness, submission, and loyalty to the doctor, all items characteristic of the medical sick role. The questionnaire was administered to a variety of patients and doctors. The respondents were asked to judge each statement according to a four-point scale ranging from strong agreement to strong disagreement. Typical items may be found in Table 1.

The lowest possible score, 38, represents the medical patient role as described previously. The highest possible score, 152, represents the psychiatric patient's role which is hypothesized as more active, independent, and inner-directed. Thus the scale can be considered to be a continuum between two extremes of relationship to the doctor.

It appears that the questionnaire taps the patient's view of how he should behave vis-à-vis the doctor. However, when the doctor is asked to reveal his

† Retest $r = .87$.

Table 1
Typical statements from the sick role questionnaire

	Strong agreement			Strong disagreement
1 A good patient does exactly what the doctor tells him to do	1	2	3	4
2 The patient should experiment on his own with methods for improving his condition	1	2	3	4
3 A patient cannot get well without the doctor's advice and care	1	2	3	4
4 The doctor is always right	1	2	3	4

perception of the patient's role, his answer may be influenced by the element of social desirability and thus the questionnaire may not give an accurate portrayal of his views. This is illustrated by item 4 of Table 1 "The doctor is always right." Ninety per cent of the doctors disagreed with this statement, whereas over 50 per cent of medical and psychiatric patients of all types agreed with it. Unsolicited comments indicated that many medical respondents did not feel comfortable admitting to an authoritarian kind of role, even though it may be rationally required. To some doctors, the questionnaire might represent an authoritarian scale on which he may appear to be a martinet. Thus, he may prefer the least authoritarian judgments since they might seem more democratic and therefore more socially desirable.

SAMPLING

The 588 subjects were drawn from four populations: 133 psychiatrists, 229 psychiatric patients, 156 physicians and surgeons, and 70 medical and surgical patients. The sample of psychiatrists represents those in private outpatient practice as well as those practicing in institutions and state hospitals. The psychiatric patients were drawn from the private practice of psychiatrists and from the psychiatric wards of the University of Washington Hospital, King County Hospital, Seattle Veterans Administration Hospital, and Western Washington State Hospital. The sample of physicians and surgeons represents doctors in private practice, members of the house and attending staff of the University Hospital, and nonpsychiatric staff from the state mental hospitals in Washington, Oregon, and Idaho. The medical and surgical patients were selected from the wards and outpatient departments of the University Hospital. An attempt was made to obtain responses from doctors and patients with complementary role interactions, that is private patients—private practitioners; state hospital patients—state hospital physicians.

A score was obtained for each subject based upon the sum of his responses to the questionnaire. Means were computed for each group and subgroup of patients and doctors and were compared, using the t-test.

RESULTS

Patient's role conception

The results of the initial sample are shown in Table 2.

Medical patients perceive their role in a manner which adheres most closely to the medical role as hypothesized by Parsons. Physicians and surgeons perceive the patient's role as less representative of the hypothesized medical role. Psychiatrists agree least of all with this view. The psychiatrists receive the patient's role as being least passive and dependent. Psychiatric patients, however, perceive their role much as a medical patient would.

Table 2

Group	n	$\bar{x}$	s^2
Medical patients	70	72*	173
Physicians and surgeons	74	91*	99†
Psychiatric patients	90	83*	244
Psychiatrists	92	102*	194

* Significantly different from all other means at level of $p < 0.01$.
† Significantly different from all other variances at level of $p <$ 0.01.

The initial results indicate that there are significant differences between the four groups sampled. The relative positions of these groups are in agreement with our predictions. However, we felt that two of our samples were biased. First, the psychiatric patient sample consisted of a conglomeration of inpatients, outpatients, psychotics, neurotics, and alcoholics. This group showed the largest degree of variance in their perception of the patient's role. Suspecting that this wide variation was a result of the patient's milieu, degree of illness, and social class, we obtained two additional samples which we felt might control for these factors. The first was drawn from the Western Washington State Hospital and included acute and chronic psychotics as well as severe neurotics. All came from predominantly lower-class backgrounds. The second sample was drawn from the private practices of psychiatrists and included ambulatory patients being treated for psychoneuroses and personality disorders. All of these were from the middle or upper class. Comparing the state hospital psychiatric patients with private psychiatric patients, we find significant differences (Table 3).

However, state hospital patients do not differ in their role perception from medical patients. This similarity may be interpreted from several points of view.

The state hospital patients live in an authoritarian social milieu. Additionally, as has been shown by Goffman in *Asylums,* the state hospital patient learns to assume the medical model of disease (19). He knows he is supposed to be sick and acts accordingly in relationship to the doctor. Finally, the institutionalized psychiatric patients come from a lower socioeconomic group than our sample of private psychiatric patients. It has been established elsewhere that lower-class patients more readily assume a submissive and dependent role in their transactions with their physicians (6). In contrast, psychiatric outpatients do not perceive their sick role in a similar fashion. They see the patient's role as more egalitarian, independent, and less bound to the authority of the doctor.

The private psychiatric patient's view is in closer agreement with the psychi-

Table 3

Group	n	$\bar{x}$	s^2
Psychiatric patients: State hospital	57	75*	177
Psychiatric patients: Private practice	82	93*	183

* Significantly different at level of $p < 0.01$.

atrist's view. Private patients are generally from higher socio-economic levels and have had more education. These individuals either come to psychotherapy with considerable foreknowledge of its behavorial requirements or, as we suspect in the case of the patients in our series, they have been educated in the different role requirements of the psychiatric method as a result of their own treatment. They are also seen in a relatively nonmedical milieu. Psychiatrists in private practice are less apt to conduct physical examinations or engage in drug or medically oriented therapy.

Physicians' and surgeons' role conceptions

Physicians and surgeons showed exceptional consensus regarding the patient's role as evidenced by their variance which was significantly different from any of the three other groups.‡ We suspected that such a high degree of consensus was a function of the particular setting from which the sample was drawn, namely the teaching hospital of the University of Washington School of Medicine.

Accordingly, two additional samples were collected consisting of 52 private practitioners from the Seattle area and 30 physicians employed at state mental hospitals in Washington, Oregon, and Idaho.

The results as shown by Table 4 indicate that the three groups of physicians and surgeons have similar perceptions of the patient's role and show the same high consensus both within as well as among the groups.

This is not surprising since these doctors expect patient behavior which is congruous with their training and which is well defined by tradition. They are *medical* doctors treating *medical* patients.

Psychiatrists' role conceptions

Two samples of psychiatrists were collected in an attempt to make more meaningful comparisons with the two groups of psychiatric patients. The means for psychiatrists at the University Center and in private practice and psychiatrists employed at state mental hospitals are compared in Table 5. Although state hospital psychiatrists require their patients to display behavior more appropriate to medical patients than do psychiatrists in the University Center and in private practice, this difference is not statistically significant.

Table 4

Group	n	$\bar{x}$	s^2
University physicians & surgeons	74	91	99
Private practitioners	52	90	147
State hospital physicians (medical)	30	88	236

No significant differences between groups.
‡ Variance: 99
$p < .01$.

Table 5

Psychiatrists	n	x̄	s²
University and private practice	92	102	194
State hospital	41	97	199

No significant differences between groups.

CONCLUSIONS

The results indicate that on the parameters of helplessness, passivity, submission, and dependency, the psychiatric role tends to be in opposition to the medical role. This finding is in agreement with our first hypothesis. We also found that psychiatric patients cannot be viewed as a homogeneous group in considering their sick roles.

The second hypothesis, that psychiatric patients tend to perceive their role as more closely allied to the role of the medical patient than do their psychiatrists was found to be borne out. However, it is much more characteristic of state hospital patients than of ambulatory private patients, for reasons described previously.

The last hypothesis, that medical patients and their physicians are more in agreement regarding the patient's sick role than are their counterparts in the psychiatric transaction, was partially supported, as the data indicate. On the other hand, there was a surprising tendency, namely, that physicians and surgeons saw the patient's role in a less authoritative light than did medical and surgical patients. According to our results, the patient demands a more submissive role than the physician would deem appropriate. The social desirability factor may account for this choice on the part of the physician.

The effects of these disparities in role perception can only be conjectured at the present time. We believe that our studies tend to confirm our suspicion that psychiatrists expect referred medical patients to be more independent and active in their treatment than the patients consider to be appropriate. It seems likely that this role conflict is at the root of many difficulties encountered in the psychiatric treatment of patients with organic disorders. Typically, such a patient believes the psychiatrist should be doing more for him, prescribing or telling him what to do, whereas the psychiatrist feels the patient is resisting psychiatric treatment by demanding such an authoritative approach. Although there is ample evidence that this phenomenon is characteristic of psychiatric patients from lower socioeconomic classes, the data suggest that it is not specific to them but may be a feature of the medical sick role. Possibly middle-class and upper-class patients can shift from a submissive medical to a permissive psychiatric patient role more easily than lower-class patients.

The medical role, though consensually valid for the customary doctor-patient relationship, does not work well in the psychiatric transaction. Another example is seen in the case of internists who begin modified psychotherapy at the request of their patient. Usually it is a patient whose psychosomatic disorder has failed to respond to conventional organic treatment. Often the enterprise fails abysmally despite the best of intentions on both sides. We suspect that although the doctor's old role did not meet the medical patient's needs, his new psychiatrically oriented role is unacceptable. The patient wants to be a medical patient but cannot accept the changed role of the physician. Role conflict results with the inevitable deterioration of relationship and results.

Finally, our findings may shed some light on why physicians and surgeons tend to be so critical of their psychiatric colleagues: They do not play the game according to the medical rules!

The role perceptions of the four major groups can best be presented in terms of a continuum (Table 6). At one extreme we have the hypothesized medical role and at the other extreme the hypothesized psychiatric role with regard to the specific characteristics of passivity, submission, dependency, and helplessness. Medical patients perceive their role as most closely conforming to the medical role as hypothesized. State hospital psychiatric patients do not differ significantly from medical patients in their perception of the patient's role.

Physicians and surgeons perceive the patients' role as significantly less passive, dependent, helpless, and submissive. Their perceptions of the patient's role do not differ significantly from that of psychiatric patients.

Finally, psychiatrists perceive the patient's role as being the least submissive, dependent, helpless and passive. They perceive the patient's role as characterized by more independence, activity, and self-direction in the treatment relationship. The psychiatrists' perception of the patient's role differed significantly from that of all other groups.

Table 6

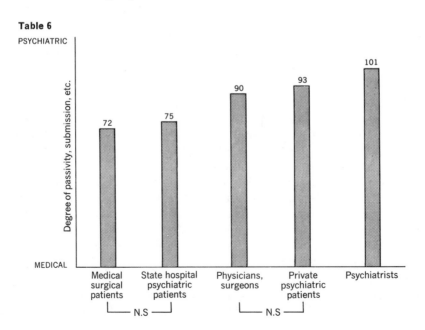

SUMMARY

Certain types of resistance to psychiatric treatment may be explained on the basis of hidden disparities between the expectations of the doctor and the patient regarding the patient's behavior in psychotherapy. Hypothesizing that the traditional role of the medical patient calls for more passive, submissive, and dependent behavior than that of the psychiatric patient, a scale was constructed and was given to medical patients, physicians and surgeons, psychiatric patients and psychiatrists. Significant differences emerged in the different groups' perception of the patients' sick role. A continuum was found regarding these specific attributes with medical patients perceiving their role as most passive, dependent, helpless, and submissive and psychiatrists viewing the same role as calling for more independence, activity, and self-direction. State hospital patients followed the medical role model, whereas private psychiatric patients were closer to the psychiatric role model.

References

1   Tolman, E. C. A Theoretical Analysis of the Relations Between Sociology and Psychology. *J. Abnorm. Soc. Psychol.*, **47**: 291, 1952.

2   Imber, S. E., Nash, E. H., Jr., and Stone, A. R. Social Class and Duration of Treatment. *J. Clin. Psychol.*, **11**: 281, 1955.

3   Frank, J. H., Gliedman, L. H., Imber, S. E., Nash, E. H., Jr., and Stone, A. R. Why Patients Leave Psychotherapy. *A. M. A. Arch. Neurol. Psychiat.*, **77**: 283, 1957.

4   Robinson, H. A., Redlich, F. C., and Meyers, J. K. Social Structure and Psychiatric Treatment. *Am. J. Orthopsychiat.*, **24**: 307, 1954.

5   Kahn, R., Pollack, M., and Fink, M. Social Factors in the Selection of Therapy in a Voluntary Mental Hospital. *J. Hillside Hosp.*, **6**: 216, 1957.

6   Hollingshead, A. B. and Redlich, F. C. *Social Class and Mental Illness: A Community Study*. Wiley & Sons, New York, 1958, pp. 171–193.

7   Overall, B. and Aronson, H. Expectations of Psychotherapy in Patients of Lower Socio-economic Class. *Am. J. Orthopsychiat.*, **33**: 421, 1963.

8   Hollingshead, A. B., and Redlich, F. C. *Social Class and Mental Illness: A Community Study*. Wiley & Sons, New York, 1958, pp. 335–355.

9   Parsons, T. *The Social System*. The Free Press of Glencoe, Ill., 1951, pp. 285–289.

10   Gross, N., Mason, W. S. and McEachern, A. W. *Explorations of the School Superintendency Role*. Wiley & Sons, New York, 1958, pp. 11–75.

11   Sarbin, T. Role Theory. In *Handbook of Social Psychology*, Third Ed. Lindzey, G., Ed. Addison-Wesley, Reading, Mass., 1954, pp. 223–258.

12   Parsons, T. *The Social System*. The Free Press of Glencoe, Ill., 1951, pp. 436–437.

13   Case, R. L. *Life in the Ward*. Michigan State University Press, East Lansing, 1962, pp. 1–148.

14   Mauksch, H. O., Tagliacozzo, D. M., Skipper, J. K., Jr., and Bradley, D. *The Patient's View of the Patient Role: Part I. Analysis of Interviews*. Publication 2. Department of Patient Care Research, Presbyterian St. Luke Hospital, Chicago. Abstract 1–5, March 1962.

15   Mechanic, D. and Volkart, E. H. Illness Behavior and Medical Diagnosis. *J. Health Human Behavior*, **1**: 86, 1960.

16   Lentz, S. How to be a Good Patient. *Today's Health,* January, 1963, pp. 48–50.

17   Sobel, R. Role Conflict or Resistance: A New Look at Certain Phases of Psychotherapy. *Am. J. Psychother.,* **18:** 25, 1964.

18   Gross, N., Mason, W. S. and McEachern, A. W. *Explorations in Role Analysis: Studies of the School Superintendency Role.* Wiley & Sons, New York, 1958, pp. 244–318.

19   Goffman, E. *Asylums.* Doubleday, New York, 1961.

20   See reference #6, pp. 335–355.

32

PATHS TO THE MENTAL HOSPITAL AND STAFF PREDICTIONS OF PATIENT ROLE BEHAVIOR*

Norman K. Denzin and Stephan P. Spitzer

From a host of earlier investigations we have begun to understand the relationship between various background characteristics of patients recruited into psychiatric hospitals, the type of treatment accorded them, and their responses to treatment.[1] Although there is reason to suspect that patterns of institutional recruitment are important variables regulating interpersonal perception and behavior, only a handful of investigations have focused on the various ways in which patients arrive at psychiatric treatment centers.[2] Even fewer have explored

Source: Norman K. Denzin and Stephan P. Spitzer, "Paths to the Mental Hospital and Staff Predictions of Patient Role Behavior," *Journal of Health and Human Behavior,* 7: 265–271, 1966.

* This study was partially financed by National Institute of Mental Health Grant MH-8303-0351 and by funds made available by Dr. Paul Huston, Professor and Head, Dept. of Psychiatry, University of Iowa, and Director, State Psychopathic Hospital.

[1] See especially the following: H. T. Blane, W. F. Overton and M. E. Chafetz, "Social Factors in the Diagnosis of Alcoholism I. Characteristics of the Patient," *Quart. J. Studies on Alcohol,* **24:** 640–663, December, 1963; A. B. Hollingshead and F. C. Redlich, *Social Class and Mental Illness,* New York, Wiley, 1958; J. K. Myers and B. H. Roberts, *Family and Class Dynamics in Mental Illness,* New York, Wiley, 1959; S. Dinitz, *et al.,* "Psychiatric and Social Attributes as Predictors of Case Outcome in Mental Hospitalization," *Social Problems,* **8:** 322–328, Spring, 1961; J. K. Myers and L. Schaffer, "Social Stratification and Psychiatric Practice: A Study of an Outpatient Clinic," *Amer. Soc. Rev.,* **19:** 307–310, June, 1954.

[2] For a discussion of modes of institutional recruitment see: E. Goffman, *Asylums,* New York, Doubleday, 1961; and A. Etzioni, *A Comparative Analysis of Complex Organizations,* Glencoe, Free Press, 1961. The following emphasize the processes preceding and sometimes directly leading to appearance of patients at psychiatric treatment centers: J. A. Clausen and M. R. Yarrow, "The Impact of Mental Illness on the Family," *J. Social Issues,* **11:** 1955, entire issue. One paper in this issue is of especial importance—Clausen and Yarrow, "Paths to the Mental Hospital," pp. 25–32; H. Sampson, S. L. Messinger and R. D. Towne, "Family Processes and Becoming a Mental Patient," *Amer. J. Soc.,* **68:** 88–96, July, 1962; D. Mechanic, "Some Factors in Identifying and Defining Mental Illness," *Mental Hygiene,* **46:** 66–74, Jan., 1962; T. Parsons and R. Fox, "Illness, Therapy and the Modern American Family," *J. Social Issues,* **8:** 31–44, 1952; E. L. Linn, "Agents, Timing, and Events Leading to Mental Hospitalization," *Human Org.,* **20:** 92–98, Summer, 1961; M. Hammer, "Influence of Small Social Networks as Factors on Mental Hospital Admission," *Human Org.,* **22:** 243–251, Winter, 1963; Hollingshead and Redlich, *op. cit.* devote Chapter 6 to the question of who makes the decision to refer disturbed persons to psychiatrists. See also Myers and Roberts, *op. cit.,* especially Chapter 8.

the implications of these pathways.[3] As a result, we know very little about the effects of paths to the hospital on staff attitudes toward patients.

Goffman has suggested the concept of "career" to depict the various phases in the movement of the mentally ill person from his network of community relationships into the mental hospital, and then back into the community.[4] Three distinct phases have been identified: the prepatient phase, the inpatient phase and the postpatient phase. The goal of this research is to examine some implications of the transition from the prepatient to the inpatient phases of the patient career. Specifically, this study investigates the impact of the patient's mode of entry into the hospital on certain staff predictions of patient behavior.

The beginning of the inpatient career represents the conclusion of several processes that had operated during the prepatient phase. Before the patient enters the mental hospital at least four major events have occurred. The first event, here called the *behavioral event* consists of an individual engaging in some public action or set of actions. The second event, called the *definitional event* represents the process whereby the behavior is evaluated and defined as deviant, unacceptable and within the category of disturbed behavior called mental illness. The third event is a *treatment* decision which comes about if the individual fails to adjust his behavior to conform to the expectations of those persons who have defined the behavior as unacceptable. It becomes highly probable that persuasive pressures will be directed toward the individual to leave his present setting and move into an institution created to deal with psychiatric disturbances. Persuasive pressures may stem from the primary groups to which the deviant individual belongs or from secondary groupings such as community social agencies or courts. Sometimes, the individual may recognize the deviancy of his behavior and decide to seek psychiatric help without pressures from others. The fourth and final event in the prepatient career phase is the attachment of a *legalistic* definition to the patient's hospital entry status. While some patients are legally committed other patients gain entry to the hospital upon application for voluntary admission.[5]

One of several basic goals of hospitals is the treatment of illness. In order for the staff members to achieve this goal efficiently it is necessary for the staff members not only to arrive at consensual definitions about such things as the

[3] Mishler E. G., and N. E. Waxler, "Decision Processes in Psychiatric Hospitalization; Patients Referred, Accepted, and Admitted to a Psychiatric Hospital," *Amer. Soc. Rev.*, **28:** 576–587, August, 1963; E. C. Wood, J. M. Rakusin, and E. Morse, "Interpersonal Aspects of Psychiatric Hospitalization," *Arch. Gen. Psychiatry*, **3:** 632–641, December, 1960. These authors took as their main hypothesis that study of the steps leading to psychiatric hospital admission would be ". . . diagnostically and therapeutically useful to the clinician," but they actually studied circumstances leading to admission. Goffman, *op. cit.*, p. 118, alluded to the consequences of characteristic modes of recruitment for organizations when he stated, "Obviously, significant differences in tone will appear in total institutions, depending on whether recruitment is voluntary, semi-voluntary, or involuntary."

[4] Goffman, *op. cit.*, p. 130.

[5] For other similar discussions of this process see the following: H. S. Becker, *Outsiders: Studies in the Sociology of Deviance*, Glencoe, Free Press, 1963; Hollingshead and Redlich, *op. cit.*, p. 171; T. J. Scheff, "The Societal Reaction to Deviance: Ascriptive Elements in the Psychiatric Screening of Mental Patients in a Midwestern State," *Social Problems*, **12:** 401–413, Summer, 1964; Mechanic, *op. cit.*; J. I. Kitsuse, "Societal Reaction to Deviant Behavior: Problems of Theory and Method," in H. S. Becker (ed.), *The Other Side: Perspectives on Deviance*, Glencoe, Free Press, 1964, pp. 87–102.

nature of the patient's illness and the type of treatment to give him, but also for the patient to adhere to staff expectations for patient behavior. A review of several studies conducted in medical settings suggests to us that staff members have at least two types of expectations for patient behavior; expectations highly specific to certain aspects of the role of patient as well as expectations that are more transverse in nature and which pertain to the patient's characteristic demeanor as he encounters various persons and situations in his daily hospital routine. Role specific expectations for patients are illustrated in investigations by Becker, et. al.,[6] and Merton, Reader, and Kendall[7] who found that medical students wanted patients to express clearcut medical symptoms rather than undefined and psychosomatic complaints. The influence of transverse expectations is seen in a study by Spitzer and Sobel which suggests that the overall presentation of self to the medical and nursing staff, regardless of the purpose of the encounter, was associated with attitudes toward the patient.[8] For the purposes of this investigation we have chosen the term *conformity* to refer to role specific expectations and *self-presentation* to refer to the more transverse kind.

Assuming, then, that the attitudes and behavior of patients occupy a place of importance to hospital staff members, the last two steps in the chain of events preceding entry into hospitals are especially important, since the circumstances surrounding the decision of the patient to enter treatment and the legalistic definition with which he enters provide the staff with clues to the patient's future performance as an inmate. For instance, voluntary entry or entry as a result of a family decision suggests that the patient has undergone some degree of anticipatory socialization with respect to the hospital's basic values and definition of illness. At the other extreme, involuntary entry or voluntary entry as a result of coercion by some community agency communicates that the patient is unwilling to acknowledge that he is mentally ill, that psychiatric treatment is beneficial, or that compliance with the demands of the hospital staff is a necessary component of a treatment program.[9]

It seems reasonable, therefore, to hypothesize that psychiatric patients indicating by their mode of entry that they are likely to fulfill expectations for illness behavior and attitudes will be regarded most favorably by the staff. Accordingly, the hypotheses tested in this investigation are as follows:

---

[6] Becker, H. S., et. al., *Boys in White*, Chicago, Univ. of Chicago Press, 1961.

[7] Merton, R. K., G. C. Reader, and P. L. Kendall, *The Student Physician: Introductory Studies in the Sociology of Medical Education*, Cambridge, Harvard Univ. Press, 1957.

[8] Spitzer, S. P., and R. Sobel, "Preferences for Patients and Patient Behavior," *Nursing Research*, **26**: 233–235, 1962.

[9] A distinction related to the ones emplo·ed here is used by Goffman, *op. cit.*, p. 133, who uses the terms "willing" and "unwilling" which ". . . cuts across the legal one of voluntary and committed, since some persons who are glad to come to the mental hospital may be legally committed, and of those who come only because of strong familial pressure, some may sign themselves in as voluntary patients." Here Goffman uses the terms voluntary and involuntary to connote legal status, whereas the terms reflect the standard mode of recruitment of an organization on p. 118, i.e., religious institutions primarily recruit voluntary conscripts while prisons and mental hospitals recruit involuntary conscripts. See footnote 3. Goffman also states on p. 133 that "Once the willing prepatient enters the hospital, he may go through the same routine of experience as do those who enter unwillingly." We disagree with Goffman on this point for it seems highly improbable that patients entering in dissimilar ways would have similar experiences since different entry routes should elicit dissimilar attitudes and responses from the staff.

We have stressed these points since we have been, several times, accused of testing "Goffman's hypotheses." Of course, Goffman's *Asylums* did provide one of several central guides for this investigation.

Legal decision hypothesis: Patients not legally committed to the hospital will be regarded more favorably by staff members than patients legally committed to the hospital.

Prediction: The more voluntary the entry the more favorable the anticipated self-presentation of the patient.

Prediction: The more voluntary the entry the greater the anticipated conformity of the patient to the hospital regime.

Treatment decision hypothesis: Patients referred to the hospital as a result of a self or primary group decision will be regarded more favorably than patients referred as the result of a secondary group decision.

Prediction: The more self or primary group initiated the entry the more favorable the anticipated self-presentation of the patient.

Prediction: The more self or primary group initiated the entry the greater the anticipated conformity of the patient to the hospital regime.

METHOD

Instrument construction. In order to collect a pool of items on which to base the self-presentation measure an open-ended questionnaire was given to 50 psychiatric nurses and aides with instructions to list those traits characterizing the "good" or "ideal" psychiatric patient. Thirty-six adjectives were regularly expressed and with the elimination of synonyms, 18 adjectives remained. Consultations with several psychiatric nurses led to the selection of appropriate antonyms for each adjective. The adjective pairs were: friendly-unfriendly; pleasant-unpleasant; calm-excitable; direct-indirect; cooperative-uncooperative; cheerful-gloomy; appreciative-unappreciative; responsible-irresponsible; understanding-not understanding; open-shy; polite-rude; quiet-loud; considerate-inconsiderate; helpful-nuisance; independent-dependent; self accepting-self pitying; interested-bored; enthusiastic-indifferent. Each adjective pair was then placed on a 7 point bipolar rating scale, following the format of Osgood's work with the semantic differential. Summation of the 18 ratings would yield a global score ranging from a high of 126 (most favorable rating) to a low of 18 (least favorable rating).

The conformity measure was based on a content analysis of 25 case records of patients recently discharged from a local mental hospital. Six statements, each reflecting a rule, regulation, or specific role expectation were chosen from a larger pool of statements that were regularly expressed by nursing staff members.

The statements, beginning with . . . *This patient will* . . . were as follows: dress neatly; have good table manners; offer unsolicited advice to other patients; make unreasonable demands on staff members; take or borrow without permission property belonging to other patients. One statement was worded . . . When asked by the staff members to do something he will do it. Each statement was placed on a 7 point scale with underscored verbal anchors ranging along a continuum from "extremely probable" to "extremely improbable."[10] By summat-

---

[10] The intermediary verbal anchors were probable, slightly probable, may or may not, slightly improbable, improbable.

ing the ratings a global score of 42 (highest probable conformity) to 7 (lowest probable conformity) could be computed.

Subjects and introduction.   Sixty-six psychiatric nursing staff members in a university affiliated teaching and research hospital were presented with a questionnaire which described, using the terminology of the hospital, the legal and motivational decisions that precede hospital entry. "Patients *enter* mental hospitals with one of two possible legal standings: (1) voluntary, i.e., not committed and (2) involuntary, i.e., committed. Patients are *referred* to hospitals in two general ways: (1) through the decision of themselves and/or family, or (2) through the decision of some community agency or institution, such as the courts or social welfare agencies." The respondents were then presented with a brief description of a hypothetical male 35 year old first admission patient with a tentative diagnosis of paranoid schizophrenia.

Experimental design.   As there were two independent variables, each varied in two ways, the patient could be described as having taken four possible routes to the hospital: (1) Voluntary Entry-Self/Family Referral, (2) Involuntary Entry-Family Referral, (3) Voluntary Entry-Community Agency/Court Referral, and (4) Involuntary Entry-Community Agency/Court Referral. The presentation received by each respondent was determined by random assignment.

The questionnaire informed the respondents that . . . "We are interested in the *self-image* that this patient will most likely present to the staff." . . . and that the 18 pairs of adjectives were . . . "descriptive of personality traits shown by hospitalized psychiatric patients." The respondents were instructed to . . . "check that point on each scale which most accurately describes this patient."

After completion of the self-presentation ratings the respondents read the six statements on which the conformity measure was based. The instructions were to . . . "check that point on each scale that most closely approximates the behavior this patient will show in the hospital."

RESULTS

Table 1 shows the mean scores on the self-presentation and conformity dimensions. As expected, the voluntary entry scores are consistently higher than the involuntary entry scores and the self/family referral source scores are equal to or greater than the court referral source scores. An analysis of variance indicated that the legal decision hypothesis was supported at the .025 level ($F=6.22$) when self-presentation was considered. Voluntary entry also led to a greater degree of anticipated conformity although the F ratio did not attain an accepted level of statistical significance ($F=.34$). No statistical confirmation was found for the source of treatment decision hypothesis, either on the self-presentation ($F=1.16$) or conformity ($F=1.06$) dimensions, although the differences between means were in the predicted direction in each case.

Because of the large amount of sociological literature suggesting that the posi-

Table 1
Mean self-presentation and conformity scores*

Dimension	Source of treatment decision	Legal status	
		Voluntary	Involuntary
Self-presentation	Self/family	69.69	63.87
		(N = 16)	(N = 16)
	Community/court	67.71	60.00
		(N = 17)	(N = 17)
Conformity	Self/family	25.31	25.31
		(N = 16)	(N = 16)
	Community/court	24.76	23.41
		(N = 17)	(N = 17)

* The greater the score the more favorable self-presentation and the greater conformity.

tion held by persons within social organizations influences attitudes and behavior, the data were further analyzed in terms of the respondent's hospital roles.

When the responses of nurses and aides are examined separately no new information is found on the self-presentation dimension. The legal decision hypothesis is still supported within both role groups at more than the .025 level ($F=6.17$). Although the main effect of referral source was not significant ($F=1.15$), the observation that the mean differences were in the predicted direction suggests that the source of the treatment decision was not totally unimportant to the respondents.

However, analysis of nurse and aide responses on the conformity dimension led to several additional findings. First, an interaction was found between hospital role and source of the treatment decision ($F=6.19$; $P<.025$). Use of the t-statistic to locate the source of the significant interaction in Table 2 disclosed that the referral source hypothesis was strongly supported by nurses, although not by aids ($t=2.48$; $P<.05$; one-tailed test). A second finding of the analysis by role was a triple interaction between type of role, legal decision and the source of the treatment decision ($F=9.24$; $P<.01$). The means for this analysis are shown in Table 3. Nurses regarded the voluntary self/family referred patient as significantly *more* conforming than aides ($t=3.12$; $P<.01$; two-tailed test), and the voluntary court referred patient as significantly *less* conforming than aides ($t=6.06$; $P<.01$; two-tailed test).

Since it has been demonstrated that the referral source of schizophrenic patients is closely associated with social class and attitudes toward psychiatry, the

Table 2
Mean conformity scores for nurses and aides[a, b]

Role	Source of treatment decision	
	Self/family	Community/court
Nurse	27.59	22.46
Aide	24.00	24.70

[a] The greater the score the greater the conformity.
[b] Legal decision held constant.

Table 3
Mean scores for nurses and aides on perceived conformity*

Role	Source of treatment decision	Legal status	
		Voluntary	Involuntary
Nurse	Self/family	29.17	26.00
		(N = 6)	(N = 5)
	Community/court	19.25	25.67
		(N = 4)	(N = 3)
Aide	Self/family	23.00	25.00
		(N = 10)	(N = 11)
	Community/court	26.46	22.93
		(N = 13)	(N = 14)

* The greater the score the greater the conformity.

question arises as to whether the differences among experimental treatment conditions may not have been biased by staff inferences about the social class of the patient in the entry descriptions.[11] That is, if staff members had categorized the patient according to inferred social class they could have made a number of predictions about the patient's probable attitudes and hospital behavior. For example, patients who aroused the attention of community officials might be regarded as having low social class, unfavorable attitudes toward psychiatry, and an inclination for dangerous, violent, or irresponsible behavior. In order to test the hypothesis that staff members responded to social class inferences rather than paths to the hospital they were requested to estimate the social class of the hypothetical patient on a six point scale ranging from upper-upper to lower-lower class.[12] The differences among the means in Table 4 are small and an analysis of variance not significant.

DISCUSSION

As anticipated, the mean self-presentation and conformity ratings given patients entering under a voluntary legal status were higher than ratings given

[11] Hollingshead and Redlich, op. cit.; Myers and Roberts, op. cit.
[12] The categories were those used in the Yankee City Series. See W. L. Warner and P. S. Lunt, *The Social Life of a Modern Community*, Vol. I, New Haven, Yale Univ. Press, 1941.

Table 4
Social class estimates by entry presentations*

Treatment decision	Legal decision	
	Voluntary	Involuntary
Self/family	3.12	3.19
	(N = 16)	(N = 16)
Community/court	3.18	3.00
	(N = 17)	(N = 17)

* The lower the score the higher the social class.

patients entering under an involuntary legal status; similarly the ratings given primary group referred patients were higher than the ratings of secondary group referred patients. However, the differences between ratings were not always statistically significant. Statistical confirmation for the legal status hypothesis was obtained on the self-presentation dimension. The effects of referral source were not seen to be significant until the analysis took into consideration the role of the respondent; then confirmation for the hypothesis was obtained on the conformity dimension within one role group. In light of the partial confirmation for the hypothesis and the growing body of research literature on mental illness, we suspect that certain of the assumptions that guided our thinking need re-examination, particularly the classic conception of the "sick role."

The concept of the sick role as developed by Parsons and elaborated upon by Sigerist and Mechanic, hypothesizes that once illness has been legitimized by medical sanction the ill person occupies a special role in society.[13] Parsons has stated that there are several institutionalized norms associated with sick persons in American society: (1) the sick person is temporarily exempted from normal social role responsibilities, (2) the sick person is obligated to seek and accept professional treatment, and (3) the sick person is obligated to cooperate with the help source in order to recover from illness as expeditiously as possible. It is tacitly implied that the role is assumed as a result of societal ascription.[14]

The classic formulation of the sick role is concerned with only one type of entry status, the voluntary self or family referral. We had assumed that as psychiatric patients moved away from this status the tendency to assume the sick role would decrease. However, it was observed that while the voluntary self/family patient (who is most similar in entry status to the typical medical patient) tended to receive the most favorable self-presentation and conformity ratings, the involuntary court referred patient (who is least similar in entry status to the typical medical patient) was not always regarded as most nonconforming.

Because of certain unique characteristics of the situation and experiences of the mental patient, *the medical sick role may be inadequate for predicting psychiatric patient role behavior.*

First, three of the four entry statuses on which this investigation focused are very infrequently found in medical illness, although there are instances when medically ill persons with communicable diseases are legally incarcerated against their wishes. Second, there are numerous reasons why there would be a strong reluctance to accept a sick role in the case of mental illness. The uncertainty of diagnosing mental illness as opposed to medical illness, not to mention the stigma of being labeled mentally ill, is certainly likely to mitigate against the patient's willingness to accept a professional definition of mental illness.[15] Similarly, the abandonment and rejection commonly experienced by persons re-

---

[13] Parsons, T., *The Social System*, Glencoe, Free Press, 1951; D. Mechanic, "The Concept of Illness Behavior," *J. Chronic Dis.*, **15:** 189–194, March, 1960; H. E. Sigerist, "The Special Position of the Sick," in *Henry E. Sigerist on the Sociology of Medicine*, M. I. Roemer (ed.), New York, M. D. Publications, 1960.
[14] Actually this is somewhat of an overstatement. Mechanic, *op. cit.*, pp. 190–191, has suggested that fear of physicians and other social and personal characteristics are associated with whether a person does or does not assume the sick role in instances of medical pathology.
[15] Blane, Chafetz and Overton, *op. cit.*, pp. 640–643; Goffman, *op. cit.*, pp. 131–146.

garded as mentally ill (something not included in the classic idea of the sick role) may far outweigh the influence of feelings of family obligation to assume the patient role, at least during the initial stages of psychiatric hospitalization.[16]

In addition, the sick role concept fails to take into careful account the audience of various types of sick role behavior. For example, in a therapeutic hospital, nurses and psychiatrists rather than aides, are the most instrumental for the patient release, and it is not unreasonable to hypothesize that the performances staged for the professional staff are geared toward future goal attainment (recovery from illness, etc.) while performances for the nonprofessional staff are geared largely for immediate need satisfaction.

Using the classic concept of the sick role, we were fairly accurate in predicting the patient's general demeanor but less accurate in predicting his conformity behavior. But because of the different social definitions attached to functional and organically based illnesses, the application of this concept to psychiatric behavior disorders must be made with caution and qualification.[17]

The data are only suggestive in this direction since the present investigation studied staff rather than patient behavior, although there is no reason to assume that staff responses do not accurately reflect patient behavior. The data do suggest however, that the degree to which society allowed the individual to enter into the decision to assume the sick role as well as the locus of the decision had implications for the extent to which the individual was believed to have adopted a sick role.

In the light of these findings it may be tentatively concluded that:

1 the social factors leading to ascription of psychiatric illness are of especial importance in determining the extent or probability that a sick role is accepted or assumed;

2 a patient's legal entry status and source of treatment decision are two variables which influence the attitudinal and perceptual relationships between staff members and patients in mental hospitals;

3 patient role behavior directed toward staff members is determined in part by the hospital role of the staff member; and

4 the dimensions of perceived patient self-presentation and conformity are not as highly interrelated as commonly believed.[18]

---

[16] Yarrow, M. R., J. A. Clausen and P. R. Robbins, "The Social Meaning of Mental Illness," *J. Social Issues*, **11:** 33–48, 1955; Goffman, *op. cit.*, pp. 127–169; E. Goffman, *Stigma*, Englewood Cliffs, N.J., Prentice-Hall, 1964.

[17] It seems popular among social scientists to generalize the notions underlying the sick role concept into research in mental illness. See particularly the following: H. E. Freeman and O. G. Simmons, *The Mental Patient Comes Home*, New York, Wiley, 1963; T. Scheff, "The Role of the Mentally Ill and the Dynamics of Mental Disorder: A Research Framework," *Sociometry*, **26:** 436–453, December, 1963; R. N. Wilson, "Patient-Practitioner Relationships," in H: E. Freeman, S. Levine and L. G. Reeder (eds.), *Handbook of Medical Sociology*, Englewood Cliffs, N. J., Prentice-Hall, 1963, pp. 273–295. Other investigators make this transition with more caution: E. M. Jellinek, "Phases of Alcohol Addiction," in D. J. Pittman and C. R. Snyder (eds.), *Society, Culture and Drinking Patterns*, New York, Wiley, 1962, pp. 356–381; Hollingshead and Redlich, *op. cit.*, pp. 351–353. A paper published after our data had been collected and interpreted also notes a distinction between the roles of surgical and psychiatric patients. See T. R. Sarbin, "Role Theoretical Interpretations of Psychological Change," in P. Worchel and D. Byrne (eds.), *Personality Change*, New York, Wiley, 1964, pp. 176–219.

[18] This statement is based partly on our results and partly on the magnitude of the correlations between self-presentation and conformity in each of the four experimental conditions. Pearson correlation coefficients ranged from —.24 to .70 for nurses and from .15 to .82 for aides.

SUMMARY

Data were gathered from 66 nurses and aides in a university teaching and research hospital to test the hypotheses that knowledge of a psychiatric patient's legal entry status and the source of the decision to enter treatment influenced staff members' predictions of patient self-presentation and conformity.

Some support was found for both hypotheses. Moreover, the respondent's role position within the hospital was associated with differential usage of referral source information on the perceived conformity dimension. The findings support the argument that a patient's legal entry status and source of treatment decision are variables which influence the interactional processes that go on within complex organizations such as mental hospitals. A final consideration of the study was to direct attention to the relevance of the medical model of the sick role for research in the area of mental illness.

33
SOCIAL CLASS, DIAGNOSIS, AND TREATMENT
IN THREE PSYCHIATRIC HOSPITALS
Nathaniel H. Siegel, Robert L. Kahn, Max Pollack, and Max Fink

In 1958, Hollingshead and Redlich reported relationships between social class, diagnosis, and treatment of persons with mental disorders in a community survey in New Haven, Connecticut.[1] Concurrently, at Hillside Hospital, Kahn, Pollack and Fink reported that years of education, as an index of social class, was related to referral for convulsive therapy and to the therapeutic response to this treatment[2] within a hospitalized population, older persons with less education were referred in disproportionate numbers for electroconvulsive therapy and responded more favorably to this treatment modality.

At that time, we thought that it was possible that within the hospital one might find social and treatment relationships which were similar to those reported for the community. Psychiatric patients from the lower socio-economic portion of the scale would thus be more likely to receive diagnoses of psychoses and to receive organic forms of therapy than those from the higher socio-economic groups who would be more likely to be called non-psychotic and to receive the non-organic therapies. In a hospital which primarily treated patients from the lower and middle socio-economic groups, patients from the lower

Source: Nathaniel H. Siegel, Robert L. Kahn, Max Pollack, and Max Fink: "Social Class, Diagnosis, and Treatment in Three Psychiatric Hospitals," Social Problems, 10: 191–196, 1962.
[1] A. B. Hollingshead and F. C. Redlich, Social Class and Mental Illness: A Community Study, New York, John Wiley and Sons, 1958.
[2] R. L. Kahn, M. Pollack, and M. Fink, "Social Factors in Selection of Therapy in a Voluntary Hospital," J. Hillside Hospital, 6 (1957), 216–218.

economic groups would be classified as psychotic and receive organic therapies more often than members of the middle socio-economic group, who would be classified more often as non-psychotic and receive the non-organic therapies. In a hospital treating middle and upper class patients, the lower ranking middle class group would tend to be called psychotic and receive organic therapy, while the upper class group would be classified as non-psychotic and receive the non-organic therapies.

In order to test this hypothesis we decided to repeat the earlier study and to extend it to hospitals where, as at Hillside Hospital, a variety of treatments, *i.e.*, non-organic and organic forms of therapy, were available to patients within the hospital community.

Three training and research hospitals were chosen which were believed to treat somewhat different economic groups. Each hospital offered a range of active therapies, *i.e.*, psychotherapy, convulsive, pharmacological, occupational and milieu therapies. The hospitals were the C. F. Menninger Memorial Hospital in Topeka, Kansas; Hillside Hospital in Glen Oaks, New York; and the Massachusetts Mental Health Center in Boston, Massachusetts. The first two hospitals are non-profit voluntary facilities and the third, the research hospital of a state hospital system. The median ages of patients at each hospital are similar, *i.e.*, MMH, 29; HH, 28; MMHC, 33. In each hospital we studied only those patients who were voluntary admissions.

Two questions were posed in this study:

1   What is the relation of social class of hospitalized patients to their (a) diagnosis, (b) treatment, and (c) length of hospitalization?
2   Are there differences between hospitals treating different class groups in (a) diagnosis, (b) treatment, and (c) length of patient hospitalization?

POPULATION AND METHODOLOGY

During the Winter, 1958–1959, a research team visited each hospital. Historical and demographic data were recorded for each adult in-patient hospitalized on a voluntary certificate for the current hospital census day. At the end of eighteen months (the cut off date), three hundred and seventy-one patients had been discharged from the various hospitals. Type of treatment, length of hospitalization and discharge status were determined and recorded. The Hollingshead two factor index of social class position was employed.[3] It utilizes weighted occupational and educational data for the assignment of class position. Sufficient information was available to classify two hundred and ninety-two patients by social class. These constitute the sample for this study. Unclassifiable cases were most often those where the education of the husband or father of a housewife or minor patient was not known. While these cases were omitted from the following analysis, impressionistic tallies showed that this group resembled the sample in its S.E.S. distribution.

[3] A. B. Hollingshead, *Two Factor Index of Social Class* (Mimeographed, 1958).

Table 1
Social class and hospital diagnosis

Social class	Massachusetts (N = 72)		Hillside (N = 133)		Menninger (N = 87)	
	Psychosis	Neurosis	Psychosis	Neurosis	Psychosis	Neurosis
I, II	17	5	27	9	37	34
III	5	4	35	10	9	6
IV, V	31	10	36	16	—	1
	—	—	—	—	—	—
Total	53	19	98	35	46	41

df = 2	df = 2	* df = 1
X^2 = 1.68	X^2 = 1.10	X^2 = 1.68
p. n.s.	p. n.s.	p. n.s.

* Classes III, IV, V combined

All data were transferred to Hollerith cards, and statistical significance was computed on the $p. < .05$ level.

RESULTS

Hospital class distribution

Viewed in terms of the median class position of its patients, the C. F. Menninger Memorial Hospital patients have the highest status (Class II), Hillside Hospital (Class III) and Massachusetts Mental Health Center patients (Class IV). Our descending class continuum is, therefore, Menninger Memorial Hospital, Hillside Hospital, and the Massachusetts Mental Health Center.

Hospital diagnoses

Comparing the proportion of patients within each hospital classified as either psychotic (i.e., involutional, affective, paranoid, and schizophrenic reactions) or non-psychotic (i.e., psychoneurotic, personality, and transient personality disorders), we found diagnostic differences between institutions. At the Massachusetts Mental Health Center, and at Hillside Hospital, seventy-four per cent of all patients were diagnosed as psychotic, but in the Menninger Hospital, only 53% were thus diagnosed ($Chi^2 = 12.78$; $p. < .01$).

In the combined hospital populations, diagnoses of neuroses were observed in 37% of Class I and II patients, 29% of Class III, and 29% of Classes IV and V.

Within the individual hospitals these proportions varied considerably. At the Menninger Memorial Hospital, 48% of the Class I and II patients were classified as neurotic and 40% of the Class III patients were so viewed. At Hillside Hospital, 25% of the Class I and II patients, 22% of the Class III patients, and 31% of the Class IV and V patients were diagnosed as neurotic. A bell shaped distribution was observed at the Massachusetts Mental Health Center, where 23%

Table 2
Social class and hospital treatment

Social class	Massachusetts (N = 72)		Hillside (N = 133)		Menninger (N = 87)	
	Non-organic[1]	Organic[2]	Non-organic[1]	Organic[2]	Non-organic[1]	Organic[2]
I, II	4	18	15	21	37	34
III	5	4	16	29	10	5
IV, V	13	28	17	35	1	—
Total	22	50	48	85	48	39

df = 2	df = 2	* df = 1
X^2 = 4.13	X^2 = 5.18	X^2 = 1.10
p. n.s.	p. n.s.	p. n.s.
	(.10 > p. > .05)	

[1] Psychotherapy and/or milieu therapies
[2] Psychotropic compounds and/or convulsive therapies
* Classes III, IV, V combined

of the Class I and II patients, 44% of the Class III and 25% of the Class IV and V patients received diagnoses of neuroses.

In none of these hospitals did we observe, therefore, that social class was related to the diagnosis of neuroses or psychoses.

Treatment selection

There were differences in the employment of somatic therapies, *i.e.*, psychotropic compounds and convulsive therapies, in the three institutions ($Chi^2 = 12.12$; df=2; $p.<.01$). Forty-five per cent of the patients at Menninger Hospital received organic treatment, while at Hillside Hospital and the Massachusetts Mental Health Center, 64% and 70% respectively were so treated.

In the combined populations of the three hospitals, the major forms of treatment for psychotic and non-psychotic patients differed ($Chi^2 = 62.7$; df=2; $p.<.001$). In 45% of the non-psychotic cases as compared with 20% of the psychotic cases, psychotherapy and milieu therapies were the dominant treatment modalities. Organic therapies were administered to 32% of the non-psychotic and 75% of the psychotic cases. Patients who received neither organic treatment nor psychotherapy, constituted 23% of the non-psychotic cases and 4% of the psychotic cases.

Within the hospital settings studied, organic forms of therapy were more frequently given to psychotic than non-psychotic patients, but the proportion of lower class patients with diagnoses of psychoses receiving organic forms of treatment was not different from the proportion of upper class subjects so treated. Within each social class group, psychotic patients received organic treatment more frequently than non-psychotic patients. Social class was not significantly related to whether patients diagnosed as either psychotic or non-psychotic would receive organic therapy.

Chi square analyses were also performed, by hospital, to determine whether social class was related to the type of organic treatment received, *i.e.*, drug therapy vs. electroconvulsive therapy either by itself or in combination with a form of drug treatment. No relationship was observed between social class and type of organic therapy.

Length of hospitalization

The mean hospitalization period for the combined populations in the three hospitals for Class I and II patients was 9.2 months, Class III, 9.8 and Class IV and V, 7.2 months. There is no statistical difference between the length of hospitalization of Class I and II combined vs. Class III patients ($t=1.66$; df$=196$; *p*. NS) but there is a significant difference between Class I and II combined and IV and V combined ($t=7.69$; df$=221$; *p*.$<$.001), and Class III and combined IV and V ($t=13.68$; df$=161$; *p*.$<$.001).

These findings probably reflect institutional artifacts, *i.e.*, the hospital treating the largest proportion of Class I, II patients tended to keep most of its patients for the longest period of time (including patients receiving only milieu therapy) while the hospital which treated the largest proportion of Class IV, V patients tended to keep most of its patients the shortest period of time. At the Menninger Memorial Hospital, patients were hospitalized an average of 11.0 months, at Hillside Hospital for 8.9 months, and at the Massachusetts Mental Health Center for 5.4 months.

Within individual hospitals social class was not a significant variable in determining length of hospitalization.

Table 3[4]
Social class and length of hospitalization

Social class	Massachusetts (N = 72)			Hillside (N = 133)			Menninger (N = 87)		
	3 mos.	4–8 mos.	9+ mos.	3 mos.	4–8 mos.	9+ mos.	3 mos.	4–8 mos.	9+ mos.
I, II	7	11	4	1	14	21	9	11	51
III	2	5	2	1	17	27	1	1	13
IV, V	10	23	8	2	25	25		1	
Total	19	39	14	4	56	73	10	13	64

df = 4	df = 4	* df = 2
$\chi^2 = 1.24$	$\chi^2 = 1.75$	$\chi^2 = 0.57$
p. n.s.	*p*. n.s.	*p*. n.s.

* Classes III, IV, V combined

[4] Treatment periods same as earlier Hillside study (Kahn, 1957, *op. cit.*) in which these intervals were used to factor out trial and involutional patients.

DISCUSSION

We have studied the relationship of social class and psychiatric diagnosis and treatment in three hospitals which have comparable treatment facilities available to patients from different socio-economic levels. In effect, we have asked "What is the relation of social class to treatment and diagnosis within hospitals treating varying socio-economic groups where all forms of therapy are equally available?"

Differences in diagnosis, treatment selection, and duration of hospitalization were found in the three hospitals. The hospital treating the highest proportion of its patients as non-psychotic (regardless of individual class position) tended to employ less organic therapy, and its patients remained in treatment for the longest period of time. In contrast, the hospitals which treated higher ratios of patients from the lower socio-economic groups, had larger proportions of patients diagnosed as psychotic and employed organic therapies more often.

The diagnostic categories of psychosis and non-psychosis were found related to the employment of somatic therapies. Patients with diagnoses of psychoses, regardless of social class, had a greater likelihood of receiving somatic treatment.

Class position was also related to the length of time a patient spent in these hospitals. We found that within individual hospitals social class was not a significant variable in effecting length of treatment.

These findings support the observations reported in the earlier Hillside Hospital study[5] when it was found that persons receiving somatic therapy were likely to be hospitalized the shortest periods of time. In that study patients with less education (which was then used as an index of social class) were more likely to receive somatic therapy, i.e., electroconvulsive treatment. Our present study, with psychotropic drugs as the major somatic treatment modality, is not identical to the 1958 experience. This change may be related to the changing attitudes concerning the relations of pharmacotherapy and psychotherapy. The applicability of drug therapy concurrently with psychotherapy has been generally accepted. Such a change in attitude away from the more exclusive views of convulsive therapy may require a revision of the earlier hypothesis that organic treatments are more commonly found among lower S.E.S. persons and psychotherapy among upper S.E.S. hospitalized patients, once we employ the place of hospitalization as a controlling variable.

The personnel of Hillside Hospital, however, like that of the Menninger Memorial Hospital and the Massachusetts Mental Health Center, profess a psychoanalytic allegiance. In institutions with different treatment orientations, it is possible that different relations between these variables may be observed. In hospitals, for example, where treatment types offered are primarily custodial or somatic, or where staff attitude places allegiance on other treatment modes, individual social class may distinguish treatment groups.

We believe that any consideration of patterns of diagnosis and therapy cannot ignore the philosophy of the treatment setting. In these hospitals, patient social class as an intra-hospital factor is less intimately related to diagnosis and type of treatment than the characteristic forms of treatment that the hospital tends to employ, *i.e.*, short vs. long term treatment, and verbal vs. organic therapies.

34
THE SELF-FULFILLING PROPHECY AND PATIENT-THERAPIST INTERACTION[1]
Norman K. Denzin

The purpose of the present paper is to explore certain of the basic social processes which underlie patient-therapist interactions. Specifically, we are interested in accounting for variations in psychiatric treatment as it occurs in one state mental hospital.[2]

One of the more exciting hypotheses which has emerged from Goffman's descriptions of mental hospitals holds that regardless of how ill a patient is upon hospitalization, the therapist accepts "his presence in the hospital as *prima facie* evidence that he is mentally ill."[3] The therapist thus proceeds to set in motion a social act which has as its goal the effective cure of the patient's illness.[4] In order for the therapist to enact his own role as medical practitioner, it is necessary for the patient to publicly accept his status in the hospital and to develop a view of self which is in accord with the therapist's.[5] In short, the patient must learn to view the hospital as a legitimate treatment source. In addition he must learn to view himself as mentally ill and in need of treatment. The therapist is to be defined as his main "help source," and the patient must learn to cooperate in all ways to facilitate his own treatment.[6]

The implication from Goffman's discussion is that variations in patient-therapist interaction are *not* a function of how ill the patient is in any objective sense.

[1] Revision of a paper, "The Self-Fulfilling Prophecy and Patient-Therapist Interaction," presented to the 61st Annual Meetings of the American Sociological Association, Miami Beach, Fla., Aug. 29–Sept. 1, 1966. This research was financed by a grant from the Iowa Mental Health Authority and by National Institute of Mental Health Grant MH-8303-0351.
[2] We take the process of psychiatric treatment to be one of the most important series of interactions the patient engages in during hospitalization. The implication is that once the dynamics of this process are understood, the other encounters the patient engages in will be more meaningful. For an extended discussion of the rationale behind this argument see N. K. Denzin, "An Interactional Analysis of Psychiatric Treatment," unpublished doctoral dissertation, University of Iowa, 1966.
[3] E. Goffman, *Asylums*, Doubleday & Company, Inc., Garden City, N.Y., 1961, p. 380.
[4] *Ibid.*, p. 367.
[5] *Ibid.*
[6] *Ibid.*; see also the following which have identified similar dimensions of the psychiatric line: T. Parsons, "The Mental Hospital as a Type of Organization," in M. Greenblatt, D. J. Levinson, and R. H. Williams, editors, *The Patient and the Mental Hospital*, The Free Press, Glencoe, Illinois, 1957, pp. 108–129; D. Mechanic, "Role Expectations in the Therapist-Patient Relationship," *Journal of Health and Human Behavior*, **4:** 190–198; A. Hollingshead and F. C. Redlich, *Social Class and Mental Illness*, John Wiley & Sons, Inc., New York, 1958; J. H. Thrasher, "The Role-set and Socialization of the Psychiatric Patient," unpublished doctoral dissertation, University of North Carolina, 1961; D. J. Levinson and E. G. Gallagher, *Patienthood in the Mental Hospital*, Houghton-Mifflin Company, Boston, 1964.

Rather they can be attributed to the type of public self the patient presents and to the therapist's interpretation of this presentation. That is, if the patient presents himself in such a way as to communicate his acceptance of the "psychiatric line," the therapist will act toward him in a way which defines him as a good patient and one who will be easy to treat.

In a very real sense what Goffman is describing is the operation of the self-fulfilling prophecy.[7] The therapist assumes the patient is ill by virtue of the fact that he is in the hospital. The patient presents a self to the therapist which communicates either his acceptance or rejection of this identity. The therapist forms an initial definition on the basis of this presentation and proceeds to act toward the patient in a manner which tends to support and validate his initial definitions.[8]

If this explanation is correct, it would be expected that such basic dimensions of psychiatric treatment as initial prognosis, hours of personal therapy per week, and length of hospitalization could all be linked to and explained by the initial definitions the therapist attributes to the patient at the time of hospitalization.[9] More specifically, it would be predicted that patients defined as holding initial favorable attitudes toward the "psychiatric line" would (1) be given more favorable initial prognoses, (2) receive more hours of personal therapy per week, and (3) remain in the hospital a shorter length of time than patients defined as holding initially unfavorable attitudes toward the "psychiatric line."

The converse hypothesis, and the one which Goffman implies is incorrect, states that these dimensions of treatment could be predicted by knowledge of how "ill" the patient is at the time of hospitalization.[10] Thus, if diagnosis were used as an indication of degree of illness, it would be predicted that patients with a psychoneurotic disorder would receive more favorable prognoses, get more hours of personal therapy per week, and remain in the hospital a shorter length of time than patients with either psychoses or personality disorders.[11]

---

[7] See R. K. Merton, *Social Theory and Social Structure*, The Free Press, Glencoe, Illinois, 1957, pp. 421–436. Also, J. L. Simmons, "On Maintaining Deviant Belief Systems: A Case Study," *Social Problems*, **11**: 250–256, 1964. For a more extended statement of Simmons' position see G. J. McCall and J. L. Simmons, *Identities and Interactions*, The Free Press of Glencoe, New York, 1966.

[8] What is at issue here is whether or not the initial impressions of the therapist are so powerful in their effect that they serve to define a patient as a "good" treatment case in spite of the fact that his diagnosis may indicate a severe impairment. If Goffman's hypothesis is correct, a "self-fulfilling prophecy" may be inferred to occur.

[9] These dimensions of treatment are also discussed by Hollingshead and Redlich, *op. cit.*; Mechanic, *op. cit.*, also discusses the treatment act as one in which the patient is continually learning the proper role stance toward the therapist, treatment, illness, hospital, and himself. For a more detailed discussion of these dimensions see Denzin, *op. cit.*, chap. 3.

[10] Goffman, *op. cit.*, pp. 374–375; Denzin, *op. cit.*, chap. 3.

[11] The rationale for treating diagnosis on a continuum of severity of illness is based on research by J. P. Brady, W. W. Zeller, and M. Resnikoff, "Attitudinal Factors Influencing Outcome of Treatment of Hospitalized Psychiatric Patients," *Journal of Clinical and Experimental Psychopathology*, **20**: 326–334, which indicated that patient improvement in symptomatology formed the ordinal scale just described. Actually the "degree of illness" hypothesis contains a slight contradiction. On the one hand it would be predicted that the less severe the diagnosis, the more favorable the prognosis and the shorter the length of hospitalization. On the other hand it might be predicted that the less severe the diagnosis, the fewer the hours of treatment per week. This would be the case if treatment were actually given in accord with how ill a patient was at the time of hospitalization. The other interpretation holds that treatment is a social reward the therapist gives to the patient and that this reward is given when the patient is viewed as a good treatment case. This of course is Goffman's position, as well as our own. See Denzin, *op. cit.*, chap. 3 for an explanation of the position that treatment may in fact be viewed as a social game in which the therapist gives and withholds rewards such as treatment and prognosis in accord with his perceptions of the patient's role enactment.

Research methods and description of samples

The present investigation attempts to test these two alternative hypotheses with data gathered from ten psychiatrists located in a teaching and research oriented state hospital which has, on the average, 500 inpatients. Data were gathered on background characteristics of each therapist.[12] The therapists were between the ages of thirty-one and forty; were eclectic in theoretical orientation; and were predominantly second-year residents at the hospital, since most of them had come directly out of medical school. Four of the ten therapists were not of native American birth. Three of the therapists came to the hospital as either private physicians in other hospitals or from private practice. The therapists, it appears, constitute a nearly homogenous grouping, at least on the basis of these variables.

All therapists were asked to fill out a short questionnaire on each first admission, functionally diagnosed patient they were presently treating. Seventy-three patients were rated by the therapists. The mean number of ratings per therapist was 7.30. Data were gathered from each patient on social class background, as measured by level of education and occupational roles.[13] Hospital records were consulted to learn the diagnosis of each patient. The dominant forms of diagnosis were schizophrenic type, alcoholism, passive-aggressive personality and evaluation. When social class characteristics were considered, it was learned that the majority of the patients had no more than a high school education. The majority of the patients were either unemployed or held occupational roles of unskilled or skilled laborers. From this analysis we conclude that the patients from this hospital are characterized by psychotic disorders, usually of the schizophrenic type, and come from positions in the class structure that are predominantly lower class.

Research instrument

The questionnaire, filled out by all the therapists, consisted of a Psychiatric Sick Role Index containing thirteen items, each of which tapped one or more of the several dimensions of the "psychiatric line."[14] Specifically, five areas were measured: (1) attitudes toward psychiatric hospitals, (2) attitudes toward mental illness, (3) attitudes toward self as ill, (4) attitudes toward mental patients in general, and (5) attitudes toward psychiatrists and psychiatric treatment. These items were selected from a larger pool of questions employed in earlier socio-

[12] This information was gathered through interviews with each therapist. An attempt was made to reestablish the history of the therapist's experiences prior to his arrival at this particular hospital.

[13] The occupational categories were those set forth by the United States Census. See U.S. Department of Labor, Dictionary of Occupational Titles, 2d ed., 1949, vols. I and II. Occupational prestige rankings were determined by the Warner method. See W. L. Warner, Marcia Meeker, and Keneth Eells, "Occupational Composition of Social Class in Sigmund Nosow and William H. Form, editors, Man, Work and Society, Basic Books, Inc., Publishers, New York, 1962, pp. 273–283.

[14] See Denzin, op cit., chap. 4. The therapists made two sets of ratings on each patient. The first was in terms of how they perceived the patient's attitudes at the time of hospitalization and the second, in terms of how they perceived the patient's attitudes at the present time. The data in this paper are based on the *first* set of ratings made by the therapist. Each patient was in approximately the second week of the inpatient career when the therapist made these ratings.

logical, psychological, and psychiatric investigations.[15] After a series of pretests and interviews with hospital supervisors and psychiatrists the following statements were selected for use:

1 *Attitudes toward mental illness*
   a. The patient has an enlightened view of the causation of mental illness.
   b. The patient does not regard mental illness as stigmatizing.
   c. The patient thinks mental illness is only slightly different from physical illness.
2 *Attitudes toward self as mentally ill*
   a. The patient recognizes the fact that he is ill.
   b. The patient accepts his illness.
   c. The patient recognizes the need for treatment by professionals.
3 *Attitudes toward therapist*
   a. The patient shows a great deal of insight into his own illness.
   b. The patient indicates he has trust and faith in his therapist.
   c. The patient wants his therapist to make all his decisions for him.
4 *Attitudes toward hospital life*
   a. The patient willingly gave up the rights and privileges he had in the outside community when he entered the hospital.
   b. The patient seems to conform willingly to hospital rules and regulations.
5 *Attitudes towards treatment*
   a. The patient accepts the treatment that is prescribed for him.
   b. The patient relates well to his psychiatrist in the therapeutic relationship.

Each of the thirteen statements was placed on an agree/disagree format, and each therapist made two sets of ratings on the index, one in terms of his perceptions of the patient's attitudes at the time of hospitalization and another in terms of how he perceived the patient's attitudes at the time of data collection. The index has a range of 13 to 26, with 26 being the highest possible score a patient could receive.

The therapist was also asked to give his initial prognosis for each patient on a good-fair-poor continuum. In addition to this question he was asked the number of hours he spent per week in some form of personal therapy with the patient.[16]

Data were also gathered from the patients rated by each therapist and consisted of a rephrasing of the questions given the therapist. Thus patients were asked their own views about mental illness, self as mentally ill, the therapist, hospital life, and psychiatric treatment. Because essentially the same set of questions were given the patient, they are not presented in this paper. Their exact phrasing is contained in the larger patient questionnaire and is available upon request from the author.[17]

[15] Brady, Zeller, and Resnikoff, *op. cit.;* Hollingshead and Redlich, *op. cit.;* H. E. Freeman and O. G. Simmons, *The Mental Patient Comes Home,* John Wiley & Sons, Inc., New York, 1963; Thrasher, *op. cit.;* N. K. Denzin and S. P. Spitzer, "Paths to the Mental Hospital and Staff Predictions of Patient Role Behavior," *Journal of Health and Human Behavior,* 7: 265–271, 1966.
[16] See Denzin, *op. cit.,* chap. 4 for a more detailed discussion of this instrument.
[17] Patients were interviewed both on and off the wards, most frequently in the recreation area of the ward, or in the therapist's private office (with the therapist absent).

Methods of analysis

Due to the fact that each therapist rated more than one patient, it was not appropriate to employ usual statistical tests of analysis, which rest on the assumption of independent observations.[18] We therefore based the analysis on a computational formula for Goodman and Kruskal's gamma. That is, all the possible pairs of comparison within the therapist ratings were computed. Then, employing the formula for gamma, which is $(S-D)/(S+D)$, we computed for each therapist a summary measure of association.[19] It was not possible to employ the usual tests of significance associated with gamma because of the failure to have independent observation; so the sign test was chosen as our test of significance. This test is appropriate because it is explicitly constructed to deal with pairs of comparisons.[20] The following steps were thus necessary to compute measures of association for each therapist. First, all the possible pairs of comparisons for each therapist were computed. Second, we computed our version of gamma for each therapist. We have chosen to call this measure Hj. Third, the level of significance for each Hj value was determined by consultation of the table of probabilities associated with the sign test. Fourth, we computed a summary version of gamma by combining all Hj values to ascertain the distribution of predicted and unpredicted ratings *across* all the therapists. We call this Value H' and test its level of significance with the sign test. Last, a mean gamma or Mean Hj was computed to indicate the overall level of association for all therapists on the variables under consideration. Mean Hj is computed by the summation of all Hj values divided by the number of Hj values.

RESULTS

Degree of illness hypothesis

For the "degree of illness hypothesis" the method of analysis consisted of introducing into the patient pairs the diagnosis of each patient and predicting that if Patient A (for example) had a psychoneurotic disorder and Patient B had a personality disturbance diagnosis, Patient A would receive a more favorable prognosis than Patient B. This same method was employed for predicting hours of personal therapy and length of hospitalization.

Table 1 (column 1) indicates that when prognosis was predicted by diagnosis, an overall negative relationship existed between the two variables. Of the seven therapists who treated a patient with one of the three major types of diagnosis, only one (405) indicated strong support for the hypothesis.

[18] That is, the assumption of independence of observations was not met, for the number of observations exceeded the number of observers.
[19] Denzin, *op. cit.*, elaborates on this method of analysis. See also Leo A. Goodman and William H. Kruskal, "Measures of Association for Cross Classifications," *Journal of the American Statistical Association*, **49**: 732–764. Based on the Goodman-Kruskal model, S expresses the probability of pairs of ratings falling in the same order, or being concordant, and D expresses the probability of the pairs being discordant.
[20] See Sidney Siegel, *Nonparametric Statistics for the Behavioral Sciences*, McGraw-Hill Book Company, New York, 1956, pp. 68–74.

Table 1
Relationship between the patient diagnosis and initial
prognosis, hours of personal therapy per week, and
length of patient hospitalization*

Prognosis		Personal therapy		Length of hospitalization	
Therapist	Hj†	Therapist	Hj	Therapist	Hj
101	−.50	102	1.00‡	101	1.00‡
102	−1.00‡	104	−1.00‡	103	1.00‡
104	−1.00‡	401	−.20	401	−1.00‡
401	−1.00‡	404	−1.00‡	402	−.71
402	−.73	405	1.00‡	404	1.00‡
404	.00				
405	1.00‡				
Mean Hj§	−.47		−.04		.25
H'¶	−.67		−.20		.20

* The number of raters and ratings varied by dimension and table
because of the problem of tied ratings which arose from comparing
patients with the same diagnosis as well as with the same scores
on either the PSRI or the three dependent variables.
† Hj equals the ratio of correctly predicted ratings minus the number of incorrectly predicted ratings over the total number of ratings
(that is, $(S − D) S+$).
‡ This symbol beside an Hj value indicates that the Hj of H' is
significant at or beyond the .05 level by the signs test.
§ Mean Hj is the sum of Hj values divided by the number of Hj
values.
¶ H' equals the ratio of positive Hj values minus the number of
negative Hj values over the total number of Hj values.

When hours of personal therapy per week were examined (Table 1, column 2),
analysis indicated an overall negative relationship. Mean Hj was −.04 and Hj
was −.20. Thus although it might have been expected that the more ill patients
would have received less treatment, this appears not to have been the case.

Analysis of the relationship between length of hospitalization and diagnosis
showed a low but positive relationship (Mean Hj was .25). However H' was not
significant by the sign test.

From these three analyses it may be concluded that sufficient evidence exists
to cast doubt on the "degree of illness" hypothesis. On only one of the three
dependent variables, length of hospitalization, did diagnosis begin to predict the
observed pattern of interaction between patient and therapist.

Self-fulfilling prophecy hypothesis

Table 2 presents the results of the findings for the first hypothesis. Analysis consisted of introducing into patient pairs the scores on the PSRI and predicting
that the patient with the higher score would receive a more favorable score on
the dependent variable under consideration.

When prognosis was predicted by PSRI score, H' indicated that all H values
were positive, thus confirming the hypothesis. Mean H was .63, suggesting that
a relatively high degree of relationship existed between the two variables.

Table 2
Relationship between psychiatric sick role index score (1) and initial prognosis, hours of personal therapy per week, and length of patient hospitalization

Prognosis		Personal therapy		Actual length	
Rater	H	Rater	H	Rater	H
102	1.00*	104	1.00*	101	.09
104	1.00*	401	.00	102	−.56
105	.60	403	.07	103	.50
401	.83*	404	.33	104	1.00*
402	.11	405	.23	105	−1.00*
403	.55*			401	1.00*
404	.44*			402	.20
405	.11			403	.11
				404	.22
				405	1.00*
Mean Hj .63		.31		.24	
H' 1.00*		1.00*		.60*	

* An asterisk beside an Hj value indicates the Hj of H' is significant at or beyond the .05 level by the signs test.

A similar finding was observed when hours of personal therapy per week were considered. H' was again of the value of 1.00. Mean H was somewhat smaller (.31), indicating a slightly lower degree of relationship.

When length of hospitalization was predicted by the PSRI score, H' was significant at the .05 level. Mean H was .24, suggesting that a mild, but positive relationship existed across all the therapists.

From these results, it may be argued that the data support the "self-fulfilling prophecy" hypothesis. On each of the three predictions analysis indicated support significant beyond the .05 level.

Discussion

Employing patient diagnosis as a perhaps indirect indicator of patient illness, the present study found little support for the "degree of illness" hypothesis.[21] Although the data employed to test the self-fulfilling prophecy hypothesis suffer from the limitation that actual patient-therapist interaction was not observed, the results indicate that this hypothesis is worthy of further consideration.[22]

One implication of this finding is that the following model of patient-therapist interaction may be assumed to exist.[23] The therapist selectively perceives infor-

[21] Actually this statement needs to be modified slightly, for partial support was obtained for the length of hospitalization prediction. Similarly, there was a mild indication that the patients with more severe diagnoses received more personal treatment than patients with less severe diagnoses.

[22] In an extended version of this paper two other interpretations were explored as possible explanations of the observed variations in the present data. The first held that therapists were responding to patients in terms of the social class background of the patient, and the second held that therapists were responding to actual patient attitudes and not to their own interpretations of these attitudes. Analysis of these two hypotheses yielded inconclusive and contradictory results—thus lending perhaps even greater support to the "prophecy" hypothesis. All the findings reported in this paper were also observed in two other state mental hospitals, although they are not reported here. See Denzin, op. cit., chap. 7.

[23] This model of interaction draws heavily upon the views of McCall and Simmons, op. cit., chap. 5.

mation about the patient which he uses to determine how the patient is accepting the "psychiatric line." He then acts toward the patient on the basis of this information and in his actions communicates his impressions of the patient. The patient in turn makes inferences about the therapist and about the therapist's view of him. Possessing something less than complete knowledge about treatment and his role as patient, the inmate will frequently respond to the therapist in terms of these interpretations. This reciprocal response of the patient tends to confirm the therapist's initial inference, and thus the "self-fulfilling prophecy" has run full circle.[24]

More specifically, and in terms of the present data, it appears that a therapist rates a patient in regard to his acceptance or nonacceptance of the "psychiatric line" along some continuum ranging from favorable to unfavorable. Forming this impression he then acts toward the patient as either a potentially "good" or a potentially "bad" treatment case. In his actions he will give the patient a good, fair, or poor prognosis and will either spend a good deal of time with him in personal therapy or spend little time at all. Similarly, he will keep the patient in the hospital for either a long or a short time, depending on this initial definition. By virtue of the fact that he may spend a good deal of time with the patient, the inmate's view of self as a good patient is reinforced; consequently, the patient takes on attitudes and views of self which are in accord with this definition. A similar process may be assumed to occur for the patient who is defined as a "poor" treatment case, who is given a poor prognosis, and who is given little personal treatment by the therapist. In either situation, the initial definitions of the therapist tend to be confirmed by the patient's behavior.

This discussion is not intended to suggest that patient diagnosis—or degree of patient illness—does not also influence the interaction between therapist and patient. As the data in Table 1 indicated, there was some support for the hypothesis that the "less ill" patients remained in the hospital the shorter length of time. It seems likely that there is an "interaction effect" between diagnosis and therapist perceptions. It may well be, for example, that the patients who are best able to communicate their acceptance of the "psychiatric line" are the ones who are least ill (in the sense that they are best able to communicate their views of self to the therapist). If this is the case, therapists are also responding to the degree of illness of the patient when they make estimations about his acceptance of the psychiatric line. Such an argument lends support to the notion that the prophecy concept is multidimensional in the sense that it is based on several aspects of the patient's attitudes and behavior. It might be argued that therapists also have stereotyped views of patient diagnosis and illness behavior. They may assume (and probably correctly) that persons with certain types of diagnoses will respond to hospitalization in certain predictable ways. Thus when they make statements about a patient's view of the psychiatric line, they are also considering the type of behavior they assume persons with certain diagnoses will engage in.

---

[24] It may be argued that therapist and patient are engaged in a social game. The therapist bargains with such variables as prognosis and length of hospitalization, and the patient bargains with his view of self. To receive rewards, the inmate must take a derogatory view of self and learn to enact the humbling role of the socially incompetent and mentally deranged person.

In a very direct way the present investigation has attempted to meet Merton's challenge to identify those social situations in which the self-fulfilling prophecy operates.[25] Following Merton's discussion it appears that the self-fulfilling function of the prophecy is met in the therapeutic relationship. That is, the operation of this process has the latent function of fulfilling the therapist's and hospital's ideological orientation toward mental illness, treatment, and patients, and to this extent it serves the hospital's goals. However, we have modified Merton's notions of the prophecy by suggesting that there is perhaps a degree of "validity" to the therapist's perceptions of the patient. To the extent that degree of patient illness is reflected in length of hospitalization, the therapist's perceptions are reflecting behavior which actually exists for the patient.

It appears also that the operation of the prophecy has self-defeating functions for the hospital. If therapist perceptions override actual conditions of patient behavior, the goal of treating and returning patients to the outside community as rapidly as possible may not be met. (If therapist attention is allocated on the basis of interpretations of the patient's presentation self only, this may be the case.) However, whenever the prophecy operates, hospitals are instituting a latently dysfunctional mechanism which in the long run may serve to deter them from the goal of rapid treatment. If the therapist responds in terms of his initial perceptions of the patient and does not consider degree of diagnosis and actual patient attitudes, patients may not receive equal treatment and attention from the hospital staff. The institutionalization of this stereotype may preclude from intensive treatment those patients who were not fortunate enough in their pre-patient encounters to have undergone the necessary anticipatory socialization which would qualify them to be favorably perceived by the therapist at the time of hospitalization.[26]

For the patient it would appear that this social definitional process works only to the benefit of those who were fortunate enough to have undergone favorable anticipatory socialization toward the "psychiatric line" prior to hospitalization. Similarly, the degree to which the patient is prepared—and able—to clearly present his own views toward self, treatment, therapist, and hospital certainly influences the initial definitions of the therapist. Patients may have developed quite favorable views toward the psychiatric line prior to hospitalization but because of certain factors may not be able to accurately present these views. The Hollingshead-Redlich data suggest, for example, that persons from the lower classes are least well prepared to interact with a psychiatrist.[27] The fear of authority figures—such as a psychiatrist—may inhibit on the part of some patients the expression of their own attitudes. Such inhibitions force the therapist to develop his own version of the patient's attitudes, which may be at wide variance from the actual attitudes of the inmate.

The negative functions of this process for the patient can only be hypothesized at this point. It could be argued, for example, that the stigmatization which

[25] R. K. Merton, Social Theory and Social Structure, The Free Press, Glencoe, Illinois, 1957, pp. 421–436.
[26] See Denzin and Spitzer, op. cit., for a discussion of how this stereotyping process appears to operate for nursing staff members. This same process is also dealt with in N. K. Denzin and S. P. Spitzer, "Patient Entry Patterns in Varied Psychiatric Settings," Mental Hygiene, 50: 257–261.
[27] Hollingshead and Redlich, op. cit

comes from being labeled and treated as mentally ill could either be reduced substantially or be magnified out of proportion, depending on whether a patient remained in the hospital for a few weeks or for months or even years. Furthermore, the patterns of alienation from prepatient significant others, which begin with hospitalization, could be effected by the length of the hospital career as well as by the success of treatment. If the therapist holds the patient in the hospital for an undue length of time and only prescribes organic forms of treatment, it seems likely that the patient will return home essentially unchanged into a hostile and perhaps unreceptive setting.[28]

It remains for future investigations to trace the effect of not having elicited favorable attitudes from the therapist at the time of hospitalization upon post-hospital patterns of interaction with significant others. However, if the "self-fulfilling prophecy" operates in the manner described in the present paper, it would appear that variations in all subsequent phases of the patient career could be traced back to initial therapist expectations and perceptions and the patient's responses to these definitions. Similarly, the present investigation suggests that future studies of patient-therapist interaction *must not* proceed in a fashion which defines treatment as an either/or process. Clearly, multiple factors operate to influence the outcome of treatment, and the focus on one set of variables to the virtual exclusion of others only blinds the investigator to the complexity of patient-therapist interaction.

35
A PRELIMINARY REPORT OF A RESEARCH CONCERNING THE ATTITUDE OF THE FAMILIES OF HOSPITALIZED MENTAL PATIENTS*

Gerassimos Alivisatos and George Lyketsos

On the assumption that moral obligations of the family towards the mentally ill are still strong in Greece, and that the State and special agencies share but a

---

[28] Goffman, op. cit., discusses these alienation patterns. The entire volume of The Journal of Social Issues, **11**, 1955, edited by J. A. Clausen and M. R. Yarrow, deals with the impact of mental illness on the family and the patient. Perhaps the most recent discussion of this topic is to be found in H. Sampson, S. L. Messinger, and R. D. Towne, Schizophrenic Women: Studies in Marital Crisis, Atherton Press, New York, 1964.

The work of J. K. Jackson, "Alcoholism and the Family," in D. J. Pittman and C. R. Snyder, editors, Society, Culture and Drinking Patterns, John Wiley & Sons, Inc., New York, 1962, pp. 472–492, indicates that the longer the patient is removed from his prepatient setting, the greater the alienation from prepatient others and the less the "need" for the patient in the earlier interactional system.

Source: Gerassimos Alivisatos and George Lyketsos, "A Preliminary Report of a Research Concerning the Attitude of the Families of Hospitalized Mental Patients," International Journal of Social Psychiatry, **10**: 37–44, 1964.

* A Panhellenic Union for Mental Hygiene research based on voluntary collaboration: Dr. Patrikios, Professor of Psychiatry, Assistant Professors Koffas and Lyketsos of Athens University and Assistant Professor Zervopoulos of Salonica University have kindly provided material from their hospitals. The following psychiatrists, members of the Panhellenic Union for Mental Hygiene, have collaborated and interviewed the relatives: Drs. Chamogeorgakis and Gianniris, Bachas, Kapelas, Kallitsakis, Kritikos and Vallianatos.

small part of the burden, a research on the understanding of the family's attitude towards the mental illness was planned. Everyday experience of Greek psychiatrists has detected failures and difficulties arising in the families of psychotics since the time of the first appearance of the mental illness up to the time of the rehabilitation of their patients. It was expected that statistical data would correct any individual impressions and provide a clearer picture on such selected major problems. A delay in offering psychiatric treatment, ignorance over mental illness and a cheating attitude towards the patient were found to be important failures of the family during the time that followed the appearance of the disease. Renunciation of chronic patients in the mental hospital and a total desertion by their families—in a country where otherwise nepotism and inter-familial emotional bonds still hold strong through a lifetime—was the insurmountable difficulty for the rehabilitation of these patients.

A statistical survey on such important problems is expected to provide, besides a better understanding of the families' behaviour, advisory material for the interested services of the State, for legal planning, for professional use and for the enlightenment of the public.

Three mental hospitals collaborated in this research: the Athenian University Psychiatric Hospital, the First Division of the Dromokaition Mental Hospital and the Second Division of the State Mental Hospital of Salonica. The above-mentioned hospitals receive patients from all over Greece. Thus the examined sample was taken at random, since no geographical, social or financial selection was taken into consideration.

The responsible relatives† of chronic schizophrenic patients who represent 75 per cent of the population of the above hospitals were interviewed. The interview was based on a questionnaire (see Annexe) which formed the nucleus of the research. General instructions were given to the psychiatrists who interviewed the relatives, but as detailed questions had to be applied according to the personality of the examinees, the questionnaires were completed according to individual conditions.

Approximately 300 satisfactorily completed questionnaires, out of 500 examined cases, formed the material of this research. Incomplete or vague questionnaires were excluded. Since the figures were small, all the results were added together, after a confirmation with the statistical data (Ch²), so that wherever differences occurred amongst the three mental hospitals, they did not have any statistical significance.

The first question of the questionnaire concerned the elapsed time between perception and conviction of the mental illness by the relatives.

As is shown in Table 1, the elapsed time varied from weeks to fifteen years. The average time of eight months and twenty-one days cannot be representative owing to the large standard deviation. In 243 cases, however, representing 85 per cent of the total, the relatives were convinced about the illness of their patients within one year from the time they first suspected it. The average time of the cases is 2.6±0.13 months.

† The relatives who, according to the law, sign the admission of the patient for the hospital and are authorized to act as tutors.

Table 1
Elapsed time between family perception and conviction about mental illness

Time						Total cases
0–1 month	...	...	...	...	...	130
1–6 months	...	...	...	...	...	77
6–12	...	...	...	...	...	36
1–2 years	...	...	...	...	...	18
2–3	...	...	...	...	...	5
3–4	...	...	...	...	...	5
4–5	...	...	...	...	...	4
5–6	...	...	...	...	...	6
6–7	...	...	...	...	...	1
7–8	...	...	...	...	...	—
8–9	...	...	...	...	...	1
9–10	...	...	...	...	...	2
10–11	...	...	...	...	...	—
11–12	...	...	...	...	...	—
12–13	...	...	...	...	...	—
13–14	...	...	...	...	...	—
14–15	...	...	...	...	...	1
						286

In Table 2 the results of the second question are shown.

The elapsed time from the first perception of mental illness by the relatives of the patient, up to the date when the patient was examined by a psychiatrist, varied from a few weeks to fifteen years. The average time, sixteen months and four days, is again not statistically representative, but in 205 cases, representing 71.7 per cent of the total, the patient was examined and put to treatment less

Table 2
Elapsed time between the family's perception of mental illness and the patient's reference to the psychiatrist

Time						Total cases
0–1 month	...	...	...	...	...	79
1–6 months	...	...	...	...	...	84
6–12	...	...	...	...	...	42
1–2 years	...	...	...	...	...	33
2–3	...	...	...	...	...	14
3–4	...	...	...	...	...	3
4–5	...	...	...	...	...	9
5–6	...	...	...	...	...	8
6–7	...	...	...	...	...	3
7–8	...	...	...	...	...	1
8–9	...	...	...	...	...	—
9–10	...	...	...	...	...	1
10–11	...	...	...	...	...	3
11–12	...	...	...	...	...	2
12–13	...	...	...	...	...	—
13–14	...	...	...	...	...	—
14–15	...	...	...	...	...	4
						286

than a year after the relatives first suspected the illness. The average time of these cases is 2.3 ± 0.14 months.

One of the first reactions of the relatives towards mental illness is reflected by the way they succeeded in submitting their patient to psychiatric treatment Table 3 gives the results.

Out of 306 cases, in 50 (16.3 per cent) the patient was voluntarily examined by a psychiatrist, in 29 cases (9.5 per cent) his relatives convinced him that he should be examined, in 131 cases (42.8 per cent) the relatives preferred to cheat him and in 96 cases (31.4 per cent) force had to be used. The larger quota on using force in Northern Greece was not statistically significant. It was not possible to correlate the methods used by the relatives in taking their patient to the psychiatrist, with their intelligence quotient or educational level.

On the assumption that the relatives' postulation about the causes of mental illness influences their attitude, two questions were devoted to this problem, but most of these relatives were unable to distinguish between causation and episodic causes (Table 4).

Out of the 273 cases:

1. One hundred and thirty-nine (51 per cent) of the relatives considered psychic traumata to be the cause of mental illness. These were composed: (a) of 72 cases (26.4 per cent of the total) where mental illness was attributed to psychic traumata: interfamilial conflicts, a steady and extremely hostile and miserable inter-family relationship, extreme jealousies, continuous quarrels and disputes. Unjust incrimination on the part of the family of the patient's immorality, other accusations, pursuit by his parents, family or spouse. Also, patient's moral lassitude, loss of prestige, anxiety due to failure or threatened failure in marriage, school or university; loss of a significant person, separation, abandonment or death of a family member or lover. A sensitive, secluded personality was frequently incriminated due to interfamily emotional traumata and abnormal upbringing (a confused child, unbalanced parental relationship, emotionally deprived, over-spoilt or over-restricted child). (b) Of 67 cases (26.6 per cent of the total) where the mental illness was associated: (i) with extraordinary emotional

Table 3
Patients submitted to treatment

Voluntarily		Convinced		By force		By false pretense		Total
No.	%	No.	%	No.	%	No.	%	No.
50	16.3	29	9.5	96	31.4	131	42.8	306

Table 4
Causation of the mental illness according to the relatives

Psychic traumata		Heredity		Stress due to financial reasons and over fatigue		Other or unknown causes		Total cases
No.	%	No.	%	No.	%	No.	%	No.
139	51	35	12.8	25	9.1	74	27.1	273

stress due to exceptional or catastrophic incidents—life threats to self or someone significant, personal injury or raping, killing of a significant person (accidents, war incidents, bombing, ill-treatment, threatening by outlaws, persecution,
violence and torture by rebels, occupation forces, etc.); (ii) with stress and
inability of adaptation of a sensitive personality in a new environment (marriage,
military environment, merchant marine, exile, immigration).

2. Thirty-five relatives (12.8 per cent) attributed the mental illness to heredity
as there were other mental cases in the family.

3. Twenty-five relatives (9.1 per cent) assigned as cause: financial ruin or
difficulties, unemployment and over-fatigue.

4. Seventy-four relatives (27.1 per cent) attributed the mental illness to odd
(syphilis, alcohol, tobacco, over-religiousness), magic or unknown causes.

The influence of the neighbours and the immediate environment of the relatives is frequently important. The results of dealing with the dominant attitude
of the immediate enviornment according to the relatives are shown in Table 5.

1. In 66 cases out of 312 (21.3 per cent) the dominant attitude of the neighbours and their environment was neutral or indifferent. The neighbours either
did not recognize the mental illness, or if they did they tolerated it.

2. In 102 cases (32.8 per cent) the attitude of the neighbours was positive,
understanding and supportive, an attitude of assistance to the family's misfortune
(moral and financial support, consolation, encouragement, help in the patient's
admission to hospital, visits at the hospital).

3. In the remaining 144 cases (45.9 per cent) the attitude of the neighbours
was negative. These cases were composed of: (a) 55 cases (17.4 per cent of the
total) where the environment was openly aggressive, i.e. in 24 cases (7.5 per
cent of the total) the neighbours participated emotionally and actively in the
interfamilial conflicts and disputes by blaming family members, taking the part
of the one or the other side in the family disputes between family and patient or
spouse or blood relations, etc., and in 31 cases (9.9 per cent) the neighbours
exposed and stigmatized the family, or they mocked the patient and exploited
him; and (b) 89 cases (28.5 per cent of the total) where the environment behaved according to their misinformation and prejudices, over-religious and
magic convictions about mental illness, i.e. in 60 cases (19.2 per cent) they were
afraid of contamination by the mental illness (as if an infective element was
present) or of being attacked by the patient, and they avoided him, and in 29
cases (9.3 per cent of the total) they resorted to religious or magic rites.

A larger quota of the cases in Northern Greece where the neighbours' behaviour depended on their magic prejudices was statistically insignificant ($Ch^2 =$
3.09).

Table 5

Dominant neutral indifferent		Dominant positive supportive		Dominant negative		Total cases
No.	%	No.	%	No.	%	No.
66	21.3	102	32.8	144	45.9	312

The rehabilitation of chronic schizophrenics, who, as already mentioned, form 75 per cent of the population of the mental hospitals, depends mainly on the attitude of the relatives towards the patients and mental illness in Greece. Data about it are included in Tables 6 and 6A.

Out of the 291 cases:

1. Only in 36 (12.4 per cent) did the responsible family relatives want to have their patient back home—four of them because the hospitalization of their patient would become known to their environment and stigmatize the family.

2. In the remaining 255 cases (87.6 per cent) the responsible relatives preferred their patients to remain in hospital.

Out of the latter:

a. One hundred and fifty-eight relatives (62 per cent of the total) were afraid that the patient's residence at home would be unbearable owing to his psychotic behavior, and that difficulties would arise in the application of medical instructions and in controlling his regular medicine administration.‡ They were afraid that the patients would not listen to them as they would to the medical authorities of the hospital, and since no one would be able to take care of them, they would go out of doors uncontrolled and become accident-prone. They also supported their attitude by fears of threatened social implications. Their patients would disturb the neighbours or they would expose the family by their uncontrolled love affairs. A reduced interest in the patient was obvious in this group.

b. Thirty-eight relatives (14.9 per cent) supported their decisions with financial difficulties or with the absence of room in their houses for the patient.

c. Fifty relatives (19.6 per cent) were sure that the patients' return home would create an uncontrolled family disturbance due to strong interfamily conflicts. The patient's misunderstanding, negative, hostile and antagonistic behaviour towards the leader or the members of the family would upset its emotional balance (stability), with only two possible effects: (i) an accident to another member of the family, such as a nervous breakdown or fatal heart attack; or (ii) a relapse of the psychosis of the patient and his rehospitalization.

‡ Although this concerns on-parole patients indicated for rehabilitation.

Table 6
Patient unwanted at home because of:

Prevalent financial reasons		Prevalent inability in applying physician's instructions		Prevalent fear of emotional disturbances in the family		Total denial of the patient		Total cases
No.	%	No.	%	No.	%	No.	%	No.
38	14.9	158	62	50	19.6	9	3.5	255

Wanted at home because of:

Stigma due to hospitalization		Desired home		Total cases
No.	%	No.	%	No.
4	11.1	32	88.9	36

d. A small percentage of relatives, 9 (3.5 per cent), declared frankly that they considered the patient as dead.

Out of the 327 cases:

a. One hundred and fifty-eight (48.3 per cent) of the responsible family members expected their patient to remain in hospital forever. They refused to have their patient back home and declared that under no condition could they be convinced about this. They demanded a total cure of the patient, otherwise they did not wish to live with him and "have the whole family's life endangered because one family member is ill." All these relatives took advantage of the present Act on Mental Hospitals in Greece.§

b. One hundred and sixty-nine of the relatives (51.7 per cent) accepted under conditions to take their patient home. This group was composed of 115 relatives (35.2 per cent) who were satisfied if any aggressive behaviour of the patient towards himself or others could be cured, and 54 relatives (16.5 per cent) who wanted the patient to be able to take care of himself and be capable of doing some sort of part-time work.

Table 7 illustrates the family reaction consequent to the breakdown of one of its members.

§ It must be noted that the clause in the existing law of 1881, in order to protect the patient from any arbitrary retention in the mental hospital, obliges—a moral point of view of the law—the physician to discharge the patient when "cured." This article is misinterpreted by the relatives by a claim that the physician should provide them with a certificate of "complete cure" for their patient and undertake the responsibility for any relapse.

The population of the mental hospitals is composed of chronic mental patients, many of whom were tried for a steady rehabilitation at home repeatedly and unsuccessfully in the past. Their relatives expect a definite "cure" and are unable to accept the patient as a mental invalid and compromise for his life in the community with short rehospitalizations whenever needed.

Table 6A
Relatives' conditions for the patients' rehabilitation at home

Unconvinced by the physician		Convinced by the physician		Total cases
No.	%	No.	%	No.
158	48.3	169	51.7	327

Table 7

Family members	Healthy supportive behaviour		Emotional behaviour within normal limits		Abnormal behaviour		Unconcern		Total cases
	No.	%	No.	%	No.	%	No.	%	No.
Father	10	10	42	42	36	36	12	12	100
Mother	12	8.3	54	37.2	58	40.0	21	14.5	145
Siblings	65	15.3	145	34.2	85	20.1	129	30.4	424
Consorts	6	16.2	14	37.7	12	32.5	5	13.5	37
Children over 16			18	33.3	23	42.6	13	24.1	54
Total	93	12.2	273	35.9	214	28.2	180	23.7	760

Out of 760 relatives of the home environment of the patient, 93 (12.2 per cent) reacted by a healthy supportive behaviour, and 273 (35.9 per cent) reacted emotionally with guilt, shame or hate and acting-out or compensating behaviour.

Two hundred and fourteen (28.2 per cent) of the family members displayed a neurotic or psychotic behaviour (anxiety or depressive reactions in the majority of them). There were also paranoid, dissociate and hysteric reactions and three suicidal attempts. Many of these relatives manifested abnormal neurotic behaviour before or during the illness. The remaining 180 (23.7 per cent) did not show any emotional participation; they were indifferent and left the care and concern of the patient to other family members.

As shown in Table 7, there were two obvious differences in the reaction between parents and siblings: (a) 38.4 per cent of the parents versus 20.1 per cent of the siblings manifested an abnormal reaction. This difference, 18.4 per cent, is statistically significant ($Ch^2 = 25.7$); and (b) 13.4 per cent of the parents versus 30.4 per cent of the siblings were unconcerned. This difference, 17 per cent, is also statistically significant ($Ch^2 = 23.7$).

SUMMARY AND CONCLUSIONS

Quoted below are some results of the present research which would be useful in guiding any future attempt in Greece of a modification of the attitude of the responsible relatives of mental patients towards them and mental disease in general.

1. In most of the cases it took less than one year for the relatives to become convinced that their patient was suffering from a mental illness (85 per cent) and to provide him with psychiatric treatment (71.7 per cent). No delay, or a negligible one, occurred when a physician was the first to examine the patient, as reference to a psychiatrist and treatment soon followed. For the remaining cases, however—corresponding to the 15 per cent and 28.3 per cent of the total —the relatives required from one to fifteen years to become convinced about the mental illness and to have their patient treated by a psychiatrist. These cases are being studied separately in order to distinguish the reasons for the delay.

2. 42 per cent of the relatives preferred to render psychiatric treatment under false pretences to their patient.

3. 51 per cent of the relatives attributed the mental illness to psychological factors and interfamily conflicts.

4. 45.9 per cent of the neighbours and the patient's environment displayed a negative attitude towards the patient and mental illness, i.e. by active participation in the family conflicts, stigmatization, a prejudiced attitude, fear or mockery or exploitation.

5. 28.2 per cent of all the relatives displayed an abnormal behavior as a reaction towards the breakdown of their patient.

6. 87.6 per cent of the responsible relatives preferred their patient to remain in hospital, and about half (48 per cent) of the total of the relatives condemned

their sick relative to a life-long stay in the mental hospital and were strongly resistant towards any psychiatric approach to modify their attitude. These relatives' "show-off" interest was often a compensation of poor emotional ties and it was replaced by a denial and a rejection of the patient out of the family unit. A lack of constructive co-operation and a mercenary spirit dominated their attitude.

Although it is generally accepted that tight bonds hold members of the Greek family united through life, the results of this research showed that in many of the families of mental patients their responsible relatives ceased to consider them as family members. They did not feel any obligation for their care, and their interest was limited to rare visits, if any, to the hospital.

The present research is continuing to collect more cases and, besides other data, to investigate a correlation between the attitude of the relatives and financial factors. It is obvious that such a negative attitude of the relatives, as was found in the present study, is suspending the rehabilitation of their mental patients and loading the State with a heavy financial burden.

Annexe

Panhellenic Union for Mental Hygiene

Questionnaire "A"

1   What is your relationship with the patient?
2   Are you a friend and since when?
3   Since when did you have indications that he was not well and from which incidents?
4   When were you convinced that he was not well and by which incidents?
5   Who first found out that he was mental? Who first expressed a suspicion?
6   To whom did he tell his suspicion and how was this accepted?
7   With which incident do you connect his illness or to what do you attribute it?
8   Under what circumstances did the illness begin?
9   After how long did you take him to a physician?
10 What was the physician's opinion when he first saw the patient?
11 Did he advise you to visit a psychiatrist if he himself was not a psychiatrist, and after how long did you take the patient?
12 During all this time did the patient accept that he was sick, and of what?
13 (i) Did the patient agree to go to the physician for treatment? (ii) Did you have to (a) convince him, (b) cheat him, or (c) take him there by force?
14 What opinion did the neighbours have when he fell sick? How did they act towards him?
15 What do you want to see in order to be convinced that he can live with you?
16 If we told you, would you be convinced?
17 Do you believe that it is better for him to remain in hospital or do you think that he will be better at home?
18 Why do you think that you will harm him if he returns home?
19 How did the outside world react towards your relative's illness?

36

INTEGRATION AND CONFLICT IN SELF-OTHER
CONCEPTIONS AS FACTORS IN MENTAL ILLNESS

Simon Dinitz, A. R. Mangus, and Benjamin Pasamanick

Recently self, or role theory as initiated by Baldwin (1), Cooley (5), Mead (10), and others has been used by sociologists, social psychologists, and psychiatrists as a frame of reference for the study of mental health and mental illness (2, 3, 6, 7). According to this general orientation, a person's conceptions of himself in relation to others significant in his environment arise out of interpersonal role-taking processes. In this interpersonal process interacting persons internalize the cultural and social norms which are valued by the group and thereby define themselves and one another in terms of these norms. The resulting self-other concepts become major factors governing the behavior of each group member. This theory suggests that the greater the disparity in self-other concepts (the way in which persons view themselves and are viewed by others), the greater the impairment in role functioning and in the ability to maintain adequate inter-personal relationships with others (4). In the extreme instance the person's appropriate self-other perceptions give way to private, distorted ones resulting in malfunctioning and often bizarre behavior. From this point of view aberrant behavior may be said to be a manifestation of a failure in the interpersonal role-taking process.

In this paper an attempt is made to test the salient aspects of role or self theory with regard to psychiatric patients. Specifically, this paper deals with the varying patterns of convergences and disparities in self-other profiles of hos-pitalized mental patients. On the one hand, the chief concern is with the pa-tient's conception of himself and significant other persons in his life, and on the other, the reciprocal conceptions that these significant others have of him. The major problem is that of making valid generalizations about the relationship between the characteristics of these self-other conceptions and mental health or illness.

On the basis of this general role perspective a number of research hypotheses were formulated. Some of the more directly salient of these as applied to mental illness are:

1 Admission to a mental hospital is associated with wide discrepancies between patient's image of self and ideal.

2 Admission to a mental hospital is associated with discrepancies between patient's definition of self and others' definition of him.

 a. As a result of differing orientations and training, therapist and nurse view the admitted patient differently from the way he views himself and also differently from the way the patient's relatives see him.

3 Admission to a mental hospital is associated with discrepancies between patient's definition of others and others' definitions of themselves.

Source: Simon Dinitz, A. R. Mangus, and Benjamin Pasamanick, "Integration and Conflict in Self-Other Conceptions as Factors in Mental Illness," *Sociometry*, **22**: 44–55, 1959.

METHOD

This study was conducted at the Columbus Psychiatric Institute and Hospital. This institution is a short-term, intensive-therapy, research and training center. Patients are usually referred by private physicians and with few exceptions are admitted on a voluntary or sign-in basis. As part of the routine intake procedure on each of the five hospital wards (three for females and two for males), 140 of the 302 patients admitted in a four-month period were selected at the discretion of ward personnel as participants in the study largely on the basis of being capable of completing the instruments. These 140 patients were found to typify the hospital population in most respects.[1] They were, however, the less seriously disturbed and confused patients as indicated by the more frequent diagnoses of psychoneurosis and personality trait disorders and the less frequent diagnosis of the psychoses, particularly schizophrenia. There were only half as many psychotics among the 140 patients as in the general hospital population (31 versus 63 per cent) and the respective percentages for the psychoneuroses and personality trait disorders were 43 and 26 in this sample and 20 and 17 in the hospital.

During the first three or four days of his hospitalization, each subject recorded a series of self- and other conceptions by means of an Interpersonal Check List (ICL). In either one or two sittings, the patient used the ICL to describe himself, his ideal self, and his retrospective self. When applicable, he also described his spouse, father, and mother, and his ideals for these roles. The nurse most familiar with the patient ($N=84$) and the patient's therapist (in each instance a psychiatric resident at the hospital) used the same instrument to describe the patient. There were 58 such descriptions of patients by therapists. Finally, the spouse ($N=42$) and parents and relatives ($N=22$), when available, each described the patient and themselves on the ICL.

The ICL, or Interpersonal Check List, was developed by a team of psychologists at the Kaiser Foundation Hospital in Oakland, California, for clinical and research purposes (8). It is currently being utilized by one of the authors as an instrument for evaluating the integrative quality of marriage relationships among young married couples (9).

The ICL contains 128 descriptive adjectives or short phrases about qualities of personality. These items are designed to measure 16 variables of personality centering around two major axes—dominance-submission and love-hostility. In addition to the major axes, all 16 variables of personality are arranged on a circular continuum so that the correlation between any two is a decreasing function of their separation on the perimeter of the circle. The intervariable correlation of the octants for male outpatients in California was found to range from +.56 for the two closest variables to +.06 for the most distant (8).

---

[1] The mean age of the patients was thirty-eight years and their average hospitalization period was two months. Over 72 per cent were first admissions, nearly 90 per cent were voluntary admission cases, 42 per cent were male, all but five per cent were white, and 86 per cent were urban residents. Some 18 per cent had a grade-school education or less while 16 per cent either attended or graduated from college. Nearly 46 per cent were in the white-collar or skilled craftsman occupations and, at the other end, over 20 per cent were jobless. (In the case of married females, the occupation of the husband was used for purposes of classification).

The average test-retest reliability of the ICL has been found to be relatively high. For 77 obesity patients at the Kaiser Foundation Hospital it was +.78 using octant scores (8). Norms based on psychiatric clinic cases are also available for comparative purposes and reference to them is made throughout this paper.

The 128 ICL items were presented alphabetically to the respondents and the raw, unweighted responses were analyzed in terms of a pattern analysis (i.e., general profile of responses). Four sets of scores were derived: the number of items endorsed as being descriptive of self, the dominance-submission and love-hostility vector mean scores, and the vector intensity scores. In each instance the greatest interest was in the discrepancies between comparable scores as, for example, those between self and ideal self, patient and physician, and patient and spouse. As many as 26 such difference patterns were obtained. Both the initial profiles and the difference pattern profiles were also analyzed in terms of diagnosis, course of treatment, and socio-economic variables.

FINDINGS

Before discussing the findings, it is worth noting that the 140 patients in this study (59 male and 81 female) did not differ either in profile or statistically (using the vector mean scores) from the 86 male and 152 female psychiatric outpatients used by the Leary group in one of its early studies (8). They were found to differ, however, from a normal and noncomparable (e.g., age) population of 112 male and 112 female respondents in a study by Mangus in Miami County, Ohio (9). At least in this respect, then, the ICL seems to have some discriminating power.

Self-ideal comparisons

In line with expectations, both the male and female patients defined themselves as being extremely different from the way they would like to be (ideal self), the way they used to be (retrospective self), and from the way they perceive their spouses, fathers, and mothers (see Figure 1). It is particularly significant that both the male and female respondents portray their ideal selves as being outside the normal, standardized range for nonpsychiatrically ill persons. The main difference in the self-ideal images was in the area of dominance-submissiveness. The patients viewed themselves as modest, self-effacing, dependent types and were, as will be indicated, so viewed by significant others. As their ideal, however, they selected what is perhaps the most culturally acceptable image, i.e., the domineering, managerial, forceful, self-confident, responsible but considerate person. This tendency, also as anticipated, was only slightly more pronounced for the male than for the female patients.

The patients' retrospective self-image fell almost exactly between the self- and ideal conceptions except in the case of the females who tended to idealize their former selves on the love dimension and saw themselves as formerly being more responsible, agreeable, cooperative, and considerate persons than they presently were. If, as suggested by some, discrepancies between former, present, and ideal images represent the "insight" component, then these patients were far from lacking in insight and hence at the level of conscious description are probably, from this point of view, not nearly so psychiatrically impaired as their symptomatology and institutionalization would indicate.

Self-other comparisons

Contrary to expectations, the patients generally described themselves in about the same way as they were described by significant others in their lives. Regardless of diagnosis, the patient self-images most closely approximated the images of them held by their spouses and other relatives (Figure 2). Slightly, but not

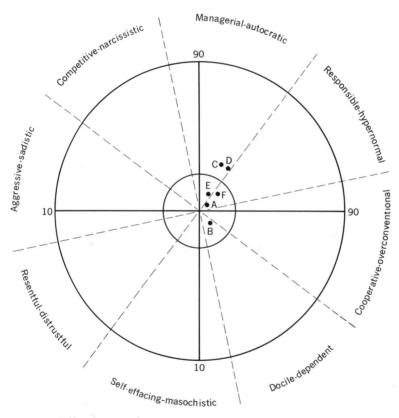

KEY: A = Self-concept, male patients
     B = Self-concept, female patients
     C = Ideal concept, male patients
     D = Ideal concept, female patients
     E = Retrospective concept, male patients
     F = Retrospective concept, female patients

Fig. 1   Vector mean profiles of current and ideal concepts of self of male and female patients.

significantly, different were the nurses' concepts of the patients as is indicated in Figure 3. The nurses portrayed their charges as somewhat more dependent, docile, (i.e., submissive) and more hostile than the patients, both male and female, conceived themselves to be. However, the greatest and only significant statistical and profile differences occurred in the conceptions of therapist and patient (see Figure 3). The therapists were the only group who, at this level of conscious description, saw their patients, particularly the males, as being on the negative or more hostile, distrustful, blunt, exploitive, aggressive end of the continuum. At the same time they also saw the patients as being far more docile and dependent than did the patients themselves.

The extent of these differences between therapist and patient varied considerably with hospital ward and did not vary with the sex of the patients. It is not beyond reason to assume, therefore, that these patient-therapist discrepancies are perhaps mostly a function of the orientation and interpretation of the therapists, who often tend to view conscious behavior as primarily a facade and search for the "real" person at a deeper level. The nurse who is less well trained

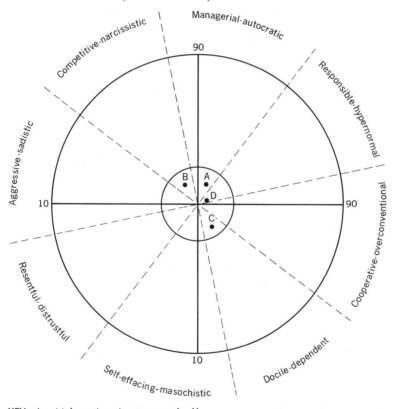

KEY: A = Male patients' concepts of self
      B = Wives' concepts of patients
      C = Female patients' concepts of self
      D = Husbands' concepts of patients

Fig. 2 Vector mean profiles of concepts of self of male and female patients in relation to concepts of them by their respective spouses.

in the intricacies of psychiatric theory tends to reproduce more closely the pa-tient's concept of himself. Those persons with the least training in this area and the greatest amount of contact with the patients such as wives, husbands, parents, and other relatives tend most faithfully to reflect the patients' images of themselves. It should also be noted that despite all these variations, patients were generally described by all these significant others and by themselves as being well within the statistical and profile range for psychiatric cases according to the standardized norms for clinic cases.

Patients' concepts of real and ideal others

The patients' images of their spouses and parents are equally interesting. The male and female patients both described their spouses as more dominant than

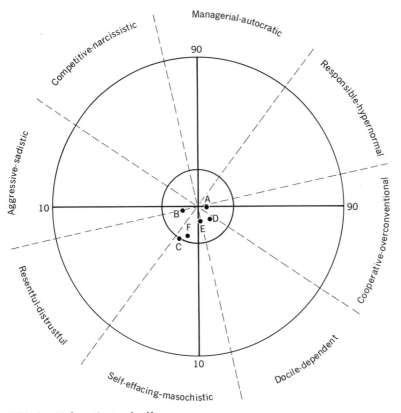

KEY: A = Male patients of self
     B = Nurses of male patients
     C = Therapists of male patients
     D = Female patients of self
     E = Nurses of female patients
     F = Therapists of female patients

Fig. 3   Vector mean profiles of concept of patient by self, by nurse, and by therapist.

those spouses described themselves. On the love dimension, the two concepts (patient of spouse and spouse of self) almost coincided (Figure 4). Suffice it to add that there was less statistical agreement between the patient's concept of the spouse and the spouse's concept of self than between the patient's self-concept and the spouse's concept of the patient.

Finally, both male and female patients, regardless of diagnosis as psychotic or nonpsychotic, visualized their fathers as more dominant and somewhat less co-operative and conventional (love dimension) than their mothers. On the domi-nance axis male and female patients rated these significant others from most to least in this order; spouse, father, and mother. On the love dimension, the de-scending order was mother, spouse, and father. The differences between con-cepts of these important others was not significant on either of the major axes.

As with the patients' ideal concepts of themselves, so the patients' concepts of the qualities of an ideal husband or wife, father, and mother were outside the range of normality for psychiatric cases. The male and female patients almost

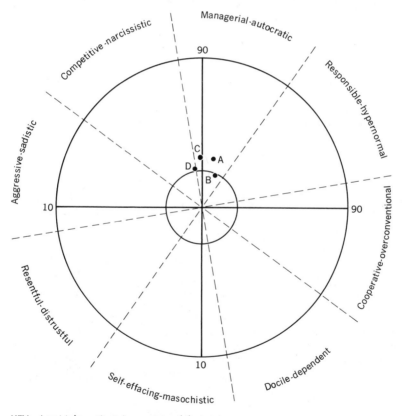

KEY: A = Male patients' concepts of their wives
      B = Wives' self-concepts
      C = Female patients' concepts of their husbands
      D = Husbands' self-concepts

Fig. 4 Vector mean profiles of male and female patients' concepts of their spouses in relation to spouses' concepts of self.

equally idealized significant others as overly dominant, overly loving, responsible persons. It would appear, therefore, that these patients have almost a single concept of the ideal personality and generalize this concept to all significant others regardless of the roles and statuses of these others.

Control factors

These self-concept, ideal concept, and retrospective self-concept profiles and scores were found to be almost totally unrelated to the various criteria against which they were analyzed. Neither the sex, age, education, or occupation of the patient (or of the husband) nor the psychiatric diagnosis, length of hospitalization, number of previous admissions to psychiatric institutions, and the type of release granted (i.e., improved, trial visit, unimproved and A.W.O.L. and/or Against Medical Advice) seemed to bear any significant relationship to the concept profiles and scores or the discrepancies among them (see Table 1). In addition, the discrepancy scores between these concepts were also found to be unrelated to these same criteria.

DISCUSSION

Contrary to expectations, the findings obtained in this study indicate that hospitalized mental patients largely portray themselves in the image which significant others such as spouses, relatives, nurses, and therapists have of them. Not

Table 1
Vector mean standard scores by psychiatric diagnosis, marital status, and admission type

	N	Dom.	S.D.	P	Lov.	S.D.	P
Psychoneurosis*	57	46.6	11.7		53.6	9.8	
Male	14	50.4	9.8	n.s.	53.8	7.9	n.s.
Female	43	45.4	11.9		53.6	10.0	
Married female	29	45.8	12.5	n.s.	53.8	8.9	n.s.
Nonmarried female	14	44.6	10.3		53.2	12.0	
First admission (female)	32	45.6	12.3	n.s.	53.5	8.9	n.s.
Multiple admissions (female)	11	44.7	4.5		54.0	12.1	
Personality trait disturbance*	38	50.7	10.2		50.4	9.9	
Male	23	51.8	10.2	n.s.	49.7	8.9	n.s.
Female	15	49.0	9.8		51.7	10.1	
Married male	13	52.7	11.7	n.s.	50.3	9.4	n.s.
Nonmarried male	10	50.7	7.5		48.8	8.9	
First admission (male)	14	54.1	11.2	n.s.	52.2	8.5	n.s.
Multiple admissions (male)	9	48.3	6.6		45.7	8.8	
Married female	9	52.0	11.1	n.s.	47.4	8.5	n.s.
Nonmarried female	6	44.5	4.7		58.0	9.6	
Schizophrenia*	28	50.2	9.7		54.1	6.7	
Male	10	52.5	10.0	n.s.	55.7	4.3	n.s.
Female	18	48.9	9.4		53.3	7.0	
All other psychoses*	17	52.5	11.3		54.0	10.9	
Male	11	54.7	12.2	n.s.	52.5	10.7	n.s.
Female	6	48.5	7.7		56.7	11.0	

* Diagnostic categories did not significantly differ.

only were the discrepancies in the self-other concepts minimal, but such as did occur (patient-therapist) might perhaps as often be attributed to the special training and viewpoint of the therapist including his interest in the "deeper" qualities of personality and his occasional impatience with the so-called superficial traits which are overtly manifested.

This study is far from a conclusive test of the validity of self-theory as a framework for the understanding of psychiatric impairment. It does point up the possibility that mental patients are deficient not nearly so much in their self-concepts as in their ability (a) to perceive others realistically and (b) to alter their interpersonal and role behavior to conform with the ideal images which they seek and which they would like others to have of them. In short, they may simply be incapable of, or, for other reasons, resistant to relating themselves to significant others in such a manner as is sufficient to warrant altered conceptions of them by significant others and consequently by themselves.

An equally plausible interpretation involves the instrument. The ICL, apart from its other shortcomings, may simply be too insensitive as a research instrument for measuring self-other discrepancies. The evidence for this is chiefly in the lack of relationship between self-concept profiles and summary scores on the one hand and any of the many independent criteria such as age, sex, diagnosis, length of hospital stay, and outcome on the other.

A third possibility concerns the subjects. The patients in this study were not randomly selected and hence were found to overrepresent the less seriously disturbed and confused patients, i.e., those capable of answering the 128 questions shortly after being hospitalized. These patients, however, were probably more disturbed than the clinic cases on whom this instrument was standardized.

On the other hand, the instrument is apparently sufficiently sensitive and the patients sufficiently disturbed to indicate some profile and statistical discrepancies between patients' conceptions of significant others and the self-conceptions of these significant others. Whether these discrepancies are greater than would be expected in a nonmentally ill population is not known since comparable data on this latter population are unavailable.

SUMMARY

This paper reports an attempt to test some hypotheses derived from self-theory as they may apply to the study of mentally ill persons. The specific interest concerned on the one hand the relation between the self-concepts of mental patients and the concepts held of them by significant others and, on the other hand, the patients' conceptions of these significant others in relation to the conceptions of self of these others.

The general findings were derived from a study of 140 institutionalized mental patients using the Interpersonal Check List as the research instrument for evaluating self-other concepts. It was found that:

1. Patient self-concepts do not in general appreciably differ from the concepts of them held by spouses, other relatives, nurses, or therapists (i.e., significant others).

2. Patients tend to view significant others (notably their spouses) differently from the way these persons view themselves. Patients also see their former or retrospective selves as being more within the normal range for psychiatric cases than their present or ideal selves.

3. Patient self-concepts, past, present, and ideal, and the discrepancies among them are almost wholly unrelated to age, sex, diagnosis, length of hospital stay, case outcome, or any of the many other criteria data.

It was suggested that these and the other findings presented indicate that perhaps it is not the self-other discrepancies which are the important problem in mental illness but rather the patient's inability to perceive others realistically and to play his roles in such a manner as to warrant a changing definition of him by others and by himself.

References

1   Baldwin, J. M., *Mental Development in the Child and the Race,* New York: Macmillan, 1895.
2   Bernard, J., *Social Problems at Midcentury,* New York: Dryden Press, 1957.
3   Cameron, N., *The Psychology of Behavior Disorders,* Boston, Mass.: Houghton Mifflin, 1947.
4   Clinard, M. B., *The Sociology of Deviant Behavior,* New York: Rinehart, 1957.
5   Cooley, C. H., *Human Nature and the Social Order,* New York: Scribner, 1902.
6   Foote, N., and L. S. Cottrell, *Identity and Interpersonal Competence,* Chicago: University of Chicago Press, 1955.
7   Jahoda, M., "Toward a Social Psychology of Mental Health" in M. J. E. Senn (ed.), *Problems of Infancy and Childhood,* Transactions of the 4th Conference, Supp. II, New York: Josiah Macy, Jr. Foundation, 1950.
8   Leary, T., *Interpersonal Diagnosis of Personality,* New York: Ronald, 1957.
9   Mangus, A. R., "Family Impacts on Mental Health," *Marriage and Family Living,* 1957, **19,** 256–262.
10   Mead, G. H., *Mind, Self, and Society,* Chicago: University of Chicago Press, 1934.

37
INTERPERSONAL STRAINS IN RELEASE
FROM A MENTAL HOSPITAL

Ozzie G. Simmons, James A. Davis, and Katherine Spencer

In this paper we present evidence on a relationship between doctor, patient, and family characterized by "structured strain." By *strain* we mean the presence of incompatible goals among actors who are under pressures toward consensus.

Source: Ozzie G. Simmons, James A. Davis, and Katherine Spencer, "Interpersonal Strains in Release from a Mental Hospital," *Social Problems* 4: 21–28, 1956.

Strain occurs where actors are subject to cross-pressures toward both consensus and disagreement. *Structured strain* characterizes situations where the strain is produced or increased by the social structure of the relationship. For this analysis, we shall assume the existence of pressures toward consensus in any doctor-patient relationship. (1)

The writers are members of an interdisciplinary research team studying the posthospital experience of released psychotic patients.** In the course of extensive field work, preliminary to a program of long-term interviewing of a sample of released patients, we arrived at the hypothesis that in the days or weeks preceding release from a mental hospital there is a decision-making process involving the three actors, doctor, patient and family, which is characterized by strains, and which is of great importance in understanding the posthospital situation. We shall call this phase the "release process."

In order to test our hypothesis of strain in release, we gathered the following data. We collected the names of the last 25 patients released from each of four services (male reception, female reception, male chronic, female chronic) at a state hospital in an eastern metropolitan area. The sample was then limited to committed patients with a diagnosis of functional psychosis, which left us with 85 cases. The chief of each service was asked, after reviewing his case records, to tell us for each patient: his social or family setting on admission, his social or family setting on release, the disposition plan favored by the patient, the plan favored by the hospital, and the plan favored by the patient's family. Although we do not have independent data from the patient and family, among the three actors in this situation the psychiatrist is in a position to have the most complete information. Moreover, a separate series of cases which included data from all three actors was rated by our staff members and yielded congruent findings.

Analysis of these data yielded three generalizations, which we believe justify our conception of structured strain. First, there is a significant tendency for released mental patients to shift their social setting on release. Second, there is considerable disagreement about release plans among the parties involved. Third, the release situation seems to be characterized by coalitions among the parties and such coalitions seem to determine the decision. We shall discuss these generalizations in order.

CHANGES IN PATIENT'S SOCIAL SETTINGS

Involved in every release decision are two logically separate, but probably interrelated, problems: first, whether the patient should be released; and second, if so, where should he go. Since all the patients in our sample had been released, our data are limited to the second problem. In the release process, there seem to be three basic alternatives. A patient may return to his family and the social

** The research reported on here is being undertaken by the Community Health Project of the Harvard School of Public Health and is supported by a special grant from the National Institute of Mental Health. In addition to the authors, the interdisciplinary team consists of Drs. Stanley H. Cath, Herbert Naboisek, Leota L. Janke, and Miss Dorothy M. Mathews, and any paper emerging from the research is a joint product. We also wish to thank Miss Marilyn A. Lusher for substantial assistance in the statistical tabulations.

milieu from which he came; he may go to some quasi-therapeutic environment such as family care; or, he may go to a new setting, either with other family members or living alone. The latter two involve not only a break with the hospital but a major break with the patient's past. In spite of the difficulties such a transition imposes, this break is not infrequent. Table 1 summarizes the data.

Table 1
Social setting on admission and release*

Admission	Release		
	With kin	Not with kin or with different kin	N
Living with kin	53	11	64
Not living with kin	2	12	14
	—	—	—
	55	23	78

* For 7 cases there was insufficient information. For the statistical test for significant shift in the marginals, .02 > p > .01.

If we look at the diagonal cells, we see that two patients were "reunited" with their families, while 11 patients severed family ties. We may conclude that where there are shifts, release from a mental hospital is associated with the breaking of family ties. (The number of cases, while yielding statistical significance, looks intuitively slender. Therefore, it should be noted that a study in progress using a larger number of cases and analyzing changes for particular types of family composition yields very similar results. We may also note that this trend holds for both sexes, both reception and chronic services, and both schizophrenic and non-schizophrenic diagnoses.)

Diagnosis is the only patient variable which seems to be related to this phenomenon. Schizophrenic patients are more likely than non-schizophrenics to have been living alone on admission (.05 > p > .02). When we examine only those patients living with kin on admission, we find that schizophrenics tend to break family ties more frequently but that statistical significance is not reached. Insignificant trends were also found for more shifts among males than females and chronic than reception patients.

If we assume that the act of breaking family ties is not lightly taken and that such acts are less frequent when there is family harmony, these findings suggest that release from a mental hospital is associated with strain in the patient's interpersonal relationships.

Agreement and disagreement

A more direct measure of strain is provided by the patterns of agreement and disagreement as to where the patient should go on release among the three actors: patient, family, and hospital. When we compare the disposition preferences for the three possible pairings, we get the following results (see Table 2).

There is no significant difference between the proportion of disagreements for

Table 2
Agreement and disagreement among patient, family, and hospital

Pair	No. of cases with sufficient data	Agree-ments	Disagree-ments	Per cent of disagree-ments
Family-Hospital	76	40	36	47
Patient-Hospital	76	48	28	37
Patient-Family	76	54	22	29

the three different pairs, and analysis of the data in terms of the patient charac-teristics of sex, diagnosis, and service (chronic vs. reception) showed only the following: Within all four sex and service groups, there was more disagreement between patient and hospital for schizophrenic than for non-schizophrenic pa-tients $(.05 > p > .02)$.

Because there are no criteria for determining how high levels of disagreement must be to be unusually high, we can draw no firm conclusion. However, we can say that disagreements seem to turn up in about one-third of the compari-sons and that if we look at all three actors at once we find perfect agreement in only 46 per cent of the cases (see Table 3 below). Thus, disagreement by at least one party is as common as consensus. In the following section, we shall analyze patterns of agreement and disagreement among our three actors.

Coalitions and outcomes

In addition to the breaking of family ties and actor disagreement, our data indi-cate a third reason for terming the release situation as one of structured strain. Our analysis reveals that coalitions among the actors are frequent and that the pattern of coalition seems to determine the decision on where the patient should go on release. If so, we have here still another instance of the classically unstable triangular social relationship.

Let us first examine the distribution of patterns of consensus and conflict among the three actors—patient, family, and hospital.

What does this table tell us? First, we may infer that a coalition pattern (two

Table 3
Patterns of consensus and conflict among patient, family, and hospital*

Pattern	N
Patient, family, hospital in agreement	35
Patient and family vs. hospital	19
Patient and hospital vs. family	13
Family and hospital vs. patient	5
Each favors different course	4
	—
	76

* For 9 cases there was no family or insufficient infor-mation.

actors agreeing against the third) occurs about as frequently as consensus; and secondly, that disagreement among all three parties is rather rare. Furthermore, we note that within the coalition pattern the patient is a member of the majority 32 times and of the minority only 5 times. Therefore, we may conclude that the two most frequent patterns are consensus and coalition with the patient. These account for 88 per cent of the cases on which we had sufficient data.

Now, let us turn to the outcome, the actual disposition of the patient, to see whether the pattern of alignment is associated with whether an actor gets his way or not. In the first place, as one would certainly expect, in the case of consensus the outcome is almost always what the three parties wanted. Only one of the 35 cases did not turn out as expected, presumably due to intervening situational factors. However, in the four cases where each actor had a different plan, the patient *always* got his way. The number is very small, but we will see that it fits into a larger pattern. Now, let us turn to the coalition types.

It is quite clear in the first two patterns that the majority got its way and the minority did not. However, in the last case, where we have very small numbers, the minority (the patient) "won" half the time. We suggest that these data support the following generalizations about outcome when there is disagreement:

a The patient almost always gets his way, usually when he is in a coalition, but even in the infrequent cases where he is not (6 out of 9).
b The family and hospital get their way when they are in a coalition with the patient. Otherwise, they do not.

If these conclusions are valid, the question of when the hospital and family get their way resolves itself into two questions: (a) Under what circumstances do coalition patterns emerge? (b) Within the coalition groups, under what circumstances do we find patient-family alliances and when do we find patient-hospital alliances?

Considering our three patient variables (sex, diagnosis and service), we find that while there is no significant difference in the sex and diagnosis comparisons, there is a strong relation with service.

This difference holds for both sexes, both diagnostic groups, and for all three formal types of coalition. Thus, while we may guess that the longer a patient has been in the hospital the more likely it is that his release is associated with a triangular conflict, we still do not know which of our triangles will appear.

Now, if we contrast the two most common forms of coalition (patient and

Table 4
Outcome for coalition patterns

Coalition	Cases where the majority got its way	Cases where the minority got its way	Neither
Patient and family vs. hospital	16	3	
Patient and hospital vs. family	11	1	1
Family and hospital vs. patient	2	2	1

family vs. hospital; patient and hospital vs. family), we find trends, although they are not statistically significant. The patient-family coalition is more common for females, chronic patients, and schizophrenics.

Let us, at this point, introduce a new variable which will show strong trends. This is simply the patient's wish. We find that the form of coalition is strongly associated with the patients preferred disposition plan.

This relation between patient's plan and type of coalition holds up within both sexes, both services, and both diagnostic groups. In spite of the small number of cases, half of the comparisons *within these subgroups* are still significant.

We may make the following generalization: In the case of conflict among the parties, if the patient wishes to return to his family, this will tend to produce a coalition with the family against the hospital. If the patient wishes to live alone, he will tend to be allied with the hospital against the family. Thus, the formation of coalitions, which looms so large in the picture of release, may be a function of conflicting ideologies of family and hospital. We believe that families tend to favor a return to the original social setting, while the hospital tends to oppose this. In this triangular situation, the patient's own preference will swing the balance of power and apparently determine the outcome.

Let us now review the argument from the statistical data. There is a significant tendency for patients to break family ties on release from a mental hospital. There is also a tendency for the three major actors (patient, hospital, and family) to disagree on the optimal plan. The actual outcome seems to be a function of the formation of coalitions among the actors. Such coalitions are generally more common for chronic service than for reception service patients. The choice of coalition pattern seems to be related to the patient's personal preference for returning home or for breaking his family ties.

Thus, *the* structured strain in release may well be the problem of returning to

Table 5*
Coalition and consensus by service

	Coalition	Consensus
Chronic	25	10
Reception	12	25

* .01 $> p. >$ .001

Table 6
Patient's preferred disposition plan
and type of coalition*

Coalition	Plan	
	Return to family	Live alone
Patient and Family vs. Hospital	16	2
Patient and Hospital vs. Family	3	9

Exact probability = .003
* Two patients, whose expressed desire to remain in hospital, are excluded.

an original social milieu or breaking ties with it and living alone. As the patient resolves this conflict, he tends to determine the alignments of all three actors. As these alignments are determined, he also determines where he will go when he leaves the hospital. The strain may be seen as the problem of return or of cutting ties, and the structure may be seen as a triangular instability in the relationships of the patient, family, and hospital.

What may be some of the reasons why strain is so likely to characterize the release process, and why strain is structured in the ways described? With regard to the pervasiveness of strain *per se,* it may be noted that there is considerable uncertainty and ambiguity surrounding release from a mental hospital. In part, this uncertainty is a manifestation of the cognitive unclarity and emotional ambivalence that are prominent components of attitudes toward mental illness in general. Thus, the ambiguity that still characterizes the diagnosis and prognosis of mental illness may be exploited, consciously or not, by the family and patient in pursuit of their own goals. The part that may be played by patient and family in determining the decision about release plans is enhanced by the fact that our society provides few after-care resources or special channels for reintegration of the mentally ill into society. Since none of the three actors has any substantial access to such resources, and no other actors are moved to intervene, the situation must generally be worked out within this triadic relationship.

In this situation, not only are disagreement and conflict generated by ambiguity and uncertainty, but they become structured in certain ways because the roles of the actors are minimally defined. Thus, the direct and indirect exercise of power are critical in determining the outcome. Our data imply that the family, in a substantial number of cases, and the patient, in a majority of cases, use their power to effect the outcome they desire. The data show that where there is a change in the patient's social setting after release, this is usually in the direction of a break with the family. In mental illness, the mutual attitudes of patient and family regarding reunion after hospitalization are likely to be bound up closely with the illness itself, so that whether or not the patient wants to go home or is wanted at home may be directly related to the emotional and material needs of both parties. Hospitalization itself may have represented an attempt by either party, in a sustained intrafamilial conflict, to be rid temporarily or permanently of the other. Thus, patients and families may have motivations and interests that push for a given outcome, and they are frequently able to play an independent role in determining that outcome, whether it is in accord with the hospital's wishes or not.

Paradoxically enough, although the hospital has the greatest formal power and the patient the least, it is clear that the latter's wishes are the best predictor of what the outcome actually will be. The hospital has the formal power, delegated by statute, to release the patient at its own discretion, but it cannot bind either of the other two parties to its wishes. Thus, its legal power cannot guarantee a desired outcome; it can only prevent an undesired one. The family may bring informal pressure on the hospital to release the patient to them. It is probable that most releases against advice (which accounted for six per cent of all releases from this hospital in a recent year) are a consequence of such family pressures.

It may even try to effect its desires by legal action, as by writ of *habeas corpus* to secure the release of the patient. Although the family has less formal power than the hospital to "get its way," it does have great resources for blocking an undesired outcome. If the family is flatly opposed to the patient's return, they may simply refuse to accept him, or they may "leave the field," for example, by desertion or divorce.

Of the three actors, the patient has the least formal power to call upon. At best, he can release himself by escape and is then in a position to make an independent decision, within the limits of the practical possibilities, as to where he will go. However, the patient has a great deal of informal power in that hospital personnel, acting in his interest, will seldom advocate a plan that he strongly resists, and if they judge him ready for release, they have few alternatives but to accede to the patient's preferences even when they do not agree with him. Thus, while "veto power" seems to be characteristic of all three actors, it is the patient who exercises the most powerful veto. The medical aspects of the situation which define all three parties as acting in the patient's interest seem to take precedence over other aspects, and the patient's disagreement thus carries the greatest weight. Under these conditions limits are set on the use of the power available to both hospital and family.

While considerations of ambiguity and structured power differentials apply to all three actors, the position of the hospital is additionally affected by certain "ideological" considerations. While we were not surprised to find the patient getting his way frequently, we were struck by the number of times that the hospital did not. Contrary to the expectations of general medical practice, "doctor's orders" do not always apply in release from mental hospitals. A part of this we attribute to conflicts in the hospital's own beliefs. Prominent in the thinking of hospital personnel are two contradictory beliefs. In the first place, under the impact of current thinking about "institutionalization," "back wards," "total push," etc., the hospital frequently believes that remaining in the institution is paradoxically, not therapeutic. Thus, in case of doubt, the current belief of many personnel is that almost any kind of community setting for the patient is preferable to remaining in the hospital. At the same time, the impact of psycho-dynamic theories of mental illness has been to create great suspicion of the "family." Hospital personnel often tend to view the family as a "pathogenic milieu," a concept which has been most explicitly developed in the notion of the "schizophrenogenic mother." Given such conceptions, hospital personnel often consider the patient's rebellion against family as therapeutic improvement, and the patient's acquiescence to family wishes as unfavorable signs. In short, the hospital has serious doubts about (a) the patient's staying in the hospital, and (b) the patient's returning home. The easiest way out is to favor the patient's leaving the hospital to live alone. Nevertheless, the dearth of community resources for released patients and a reluctance to oppose strongly an outcome which the patient strongly favors frequently result in acquiescence in his return to the family.

This study has singled out for analysis one aspect of the mental patient's hospitalization and convalescence—the "release phase." The analysis has been concerned with demonstrating that considerable strain is imposed on the relations between actors involved in the release process, and that this strain is structured according to systematic power differentials among the actors. Strain is generated by the uncertainty and ambiguity that characterize the process of leaving the mental hospital, and these characteristics in turn afford varying opportunities for exercise of power by the various actors. Although the hospital has the greatest amount of formal power to determine the outcome, it is the patient who seems to have the greatest *de facto* power. In the data analyzed in this paper not only was the hospital the lowest predictor of outcome, but many of its agreements with the other actors were forced by their therapeutic orientations and by ideological and realistic considerations. Thus, in the release process purely medical considerations are often overshadowed by social and interpersonal factors.

Reference

1   Cf. Parsons, Talcott, *The Social System* (Glencoe, Illinois: The Free Press, 1951), Chapter X, "Social Structure and Dynamic Process: The Case of Modern Medical Practice."

PART FIVE

The Patient Career—
Postpatient Phase

A stigmatized person is one with a deeply discrediting identity. As Goffman has indicated, a stigmatized person cannot help but feel "insecure about how normals will identify and receive him."[1] Nor can the stigmatized person avoid the unpleasant sense of not knowing how other persons "really" feel about him. Because of the predominantly unfavorable definition given to mental disorder, the ex-patient and his family members are persons with a stigma. Upon discharge of the patient from the hospital both are confronted with a basically hostile environment, one in which each social contact is a potential source of discomfort for them.

THE STIGMA OF MENTAL ILLNESS

The first series of papers in this section deals with the problem of stigma and mental illness. As a group these papers illustrate the detrimental effects of current attitudes toward mental illness on postpatients and their relatives. In addition, each points to the fact that these effects pose one major barrier to the reintegration of ex-patients into their family and community roles.

Freeman and Simmons examine feelings of stigma among family members of former mental patients. Stigma or sensitivity regarding psychiatric hospitalization of a household member was found to be associated with the degree of inappropriate behavior of the patient after he returned to the home. Stigma was also associated with the social class of the family as well as with certain personality traits of family members. Sensitivity to stigma was most pronounced within upper-class families and among family members characterized by feelings of isolation, frustration, and withdrawal.

In a recent community survey of public attitudes toward mental patients,

Whatley attempted to identify the specific conditions under which rejection was most severe. He found that as long as social distance could be maintained, attitudes toward ex-psychiatric patients were not as unfavorable as had been commonly believed. Specifically, if contact with the ex-patient did not impinge upon primary group values and if contact remained impersonal, community attitudes were relatively neutral.

Although feelings of stigma among relatives of former mental patients have attracted considerable research attention, feelings of stigma among ex-patients, strangely enough, have been almost ignored. Cumming and Cumming show that feelings of stigma are not equally distributed among various segments of two psychiatric populations. In general, high stigma was concentrated within the less severe diagnostic categories such as neurosis, among females not well integrated into family networks, among well-integrated females who had a leadership role within the family, and among the most recently discharged patients.

POSTHOSPITAL ADJUSTMENT OF THE PATIENT

Of all the groups to which an individual belongs, the immediate family is the most important mediator between the individual and the wider society. As such the family provides the major socioemotional environment to which the psychiatric patient returns. The family can add to or detract from the intimate social environment which is needed by a person seeking to return to society. Thus, it might be expected that the posthospital success of the patient would depend in large part upon the kind of family to which he belongs and upon its attitudes, perceptions, and acceptance of him.

A second series of papers in this section deals with the posthospital adjustment of patients. With the exception of one which is concerned with diagnosis and severity of illness as a predictor of posthospital adjustment, these papers focus either directly or indirectly upon the role of the family in adjustment to posthospital life. As a group the studies demonstrate how and why the expectations held for patients, as well as variations in family structure are associated with posthospital patterns of success and failure.

The next Freeman and Simmons paper explores the relationship between social class and (1) posthospital performance levels of ex-patients and (2) family tolerance for deviance. The authors contend that commitment to dominant middle-class norms will be related to the level of posthospital performance of discharged patients, since the expectations for performance among middle-class families are more demanding than expectations among lower-class families. The effect is observed in a higher level of performance among middle-class ex-patients. The authors contend also, that adherence to middle-class values is related to tolerance of deviance, with the middle-class family being less tolerant of nonconformity among former mental patients than the lower classes. Paradoxical as it may seem, the effect of such differential tolerance limits would be a greater propensity among middle-class families to recommit former patients for a given level of deviation than among lower-class families. Data obtained from a sample of males with diagnosed functional psychoses (primarily schizo-

phrenia) confirm the validity of these contentions. In spite of the higher level of performance among middle-class ex-patients their rate of rehospitalization was higher than that of the lower class.

The Freeman and Simmons hypothesis that social class–linked expectations are critical determinants of the behavior of former psychiatric patients was followed up by Lefton et al.[2] The major question asked was: To what extent were the results of Freeman and Simmons applicable to other types of psychiatric in-patients? Rather than testing the hypothesis on male schizophrenic patients, as had been done previously, Lefton, et al. used acutely ill, married female patients, none of whom were organically impaired.[3] (The sample was selected from women discharged from a short-term, intensive-therapy psychiatric installation.) Their data offered partial confirmation for the Freeman and Simmons hypothesis. While the anticipated relationship between social class and expectations for ex-patients was found (middle-class husbands' expectations for performance were higher than lower-class husbands' expectations), the relationship between class expectations and actual posthospital performance levels failed to ma-terialize.

Considering that the general approach to the problem as well as the specific techniques were highly divergent in these two latter studies (i.e., different type of patient, different sex, and different measures of social class and role per-formance), it is remarkable that the results paralleled so closely. The similarities between the results of these two studies attest to the fact that family attitudes and values do have significant consequences for the posthospital fates of psychi-atric patients. The differences imply that the association between role expecta-tions and performances for the two sexes is neither identical nor as simple as previously thought.

Freeman and Simmons, and Lefton et al. were concerned with how class status related to posthospital performance; the following papers are either explicitly or implicitly concerned with how social organization of families bears upon post-hospital performance. Each shows what various aspects of family structure are predictors of case outcomes.

Freeman and Simmons explored the hypothesis that the type of family net-work in which the postpatient resides is related to his level of social perform-ance. On the basis of implications from their earlier pilot studies they contended that parental families have a higher tolerance of former patients as deviants than do members of conjugal families. Furthermore they contend that members of parental families have lower levels of expectations for the patient's social be-havior than do members of conjugal families. Data were gathered from wives and mothers of former male patients. The findings support the hypothesis that the level of posthospital functioning of patients is related to family setting. It was also found that over time, a greater proportion of patients returning to hospitals came from conjugal families, thus supporting the hypothesis that con-jugal families tolerate less deviance among their ex-patient relatives.

The majority of papers included in this collection of readings are quite clear-cut in their findings, and only in several minor ways do they contradict each other. We have included one paper in which the implications and results are somewhat less than clear. Our reading of the paper leads us to rather different conclusions from those reached by the authors. However, it is our opinion that the paper warrants inclusion because it represents one of the few serious attempts to pit psychiatric variables against social variables as predictors of rehospitalization and posthospital behavior of former mental patients.

Dinitz et al. studied the posthospital performance level of former female patients. Ratings of the patient's behavior were obtained from responses given by the patient as well as a family member of the patient. The authors focused specifically on the comparative ability to predict case outcome from certain psychiatric variables (such as type of treatment, diagnostic category, length of illness, and addiction) and certain social variables (such as social class, family structure, age, and residence). It appears that some psychiatric variables were moderately effective predictors of patient posthospital behavior. For example, organic brain damage was almost always associated with ineffective posthospital performance, and patients treated with drugs showed a high rate of return to the hospital.

The data indicate also that several social variables are predictors of case outcome. For example, the performance of patients returning to conjugal households was noticeably superior to those who return to the parental household. In a comparison of females returning to families with and without other adult females, a "significantly" greater proportion of rehospitalization took place among patients returning to families which included another female. Moreover, the percentage of persons of relatively high education who were rehospitalized was greater than the percentage of persons with only a grade school education who were rehospitalized, although the magnitude of the differences between percentages was so small as to raise the question of whether this might not have been a chance occurrence. No differences in case outcome, however, were found by examining age, race, religion, rural-urban residence, and marital status.

While the family is no doubt highly important in the posthospital phase of the patient career, we are uncertain of the credibility of several concluding statements. For example, the authors claim that their results seem to substantiate the hypothesis that "when degree of illness is controlled, familial variables seem to be extremely significant in determining case outcome" (p. 328). This is somewhat puzzling in view of their finding that degree of psychiatric impairment, both at the time of admission and at the time of discharge, was unrelated to the patient's marital status or the type of household to which he returned.

In spite of the authors' attempts to present a strong case against the efficacy of variables traditionally employed for prognosis in psychiatric treatment centers, their results do not seem to wholly corroborate their claim. We are completely in accord with the authors' contention that their findings substantiate the proposition that the posthospital family milieu and the class status of the patient are moderately accurate predictors of case outcome—the results indicate that one can certainly make better than chance predictions by knowledge of social variables. However, we are concerned with their contention that hard psychiatric variables appeared "at best only very poor predictors" of case outcome, for it can be seen that several of the psychiatric variables were found to be associated with the recovery potential and posthospital performance of psychiatric patients.

The adjustment of postpatients while influenced by various factors is, however, not optimum, even for those who are able to avoid rehospitalization. In a follow-up study of discharged psychiatric patients reported elsewhere, Bockoven et al. presented a rigorously developed technique to measure posthospital social adjustment.[4] Social adjustment was evaluated along four dimensions: occupational (job satisfaction, job turnover, employer-employee relations, etc.) economic (rate of pay and financial strain), family (relations with other family members, sexual performance, etc.), and community (friendships and community and recreational activities). Among former patients still in the community at the end of a three-year period, adjustment in these four areas was not optimum. In fact, their degree of social adjustment did not appear to differ significantly from that of the average citizen. However, patients who had been readmitted to the hospital were characterized by an overall level of unsatisfactory adjustment. In none of the four areas did their adjustment scores equal those of the successful ex-patients. It is interesting to note also that one source of economic difficulty among ex-patients, "relapsers" and "nonrelapsers" alike, was their inability to pay the debts incurred during hospitalization.

POSTPATIENT VOLUNTARY ASSOCIATIONS

Aside from alcoholics and drug addicts, mentally ill persons have not in the past been members of specific subcultures and associations which relate to their deviant status in society. Several reasons appear to account for this fact. For example, the stigma associated with mental illness is one inhibiting factor which tends to direct the psychiatric ex-patient away from, rather than toward, others. The former patient attempts to conceal his stigmatizing social identity as much as possible. In the past few years, however, this trend has appeared to change. Associated with the changes in public attitudes toward a greater acceptance of mental illness has been the rise in voluntary associations created specifically for former mental patients. Such organizations provide places where the stigmatized persons can share experiences with others of a like status, in a setting where they will not be ridiculed, pitied, or shamed. The two papers in this section deal with the emerging phenomenon of voluntary associations among former mental patients.

The first paper describes the feelings of many mental patients upon release from the mental hospital. Palmer discusses the fear and stigma associated with mental illness and relates this to a reluctance on the part of the former patient to join clubs. According to Palmer the "club movement" among the mentally ill is still young and in no way compares to the organization of Alcoholics Anonymous. She contends that many former patients are reluctant to announce publicly the fact that they were once mentally ill. This reluctance is related to the fear and stigma associated with hospitalization in the popular mind. Another element that inhibits the formation of clubs is apprehension that such groups might act as unpleasant reminders of past experiences.

The last paper examines the social organization and culture of a club formed by a group of former mental patients. Landy and Singer note that social clubs for former mental patients are based on the assumption that when some patients leave the hospital, they may benefit from being members of a voluntary group with other former mental patients. Such groups provide a therapeutic and rehabilitative atmosphere for the former patients. The dominant culture themes of the club studied by Landy and Singer consisted of group acceptance of former patients, regardless of their illness or past behavior. Furthermore the club provided a permissive atmosphere within which the patients could talk about hospital experiences and about their social and economic failures. Regardless of the positive functions of the clubs, they are not without some dysfunctions. Landy and Singer suggest that because the clubs are deviant subgroups, they tend to perpetuate the former sick role. To the extent that this is the case it may be hypothesized that such clubs are dysfunctional if the club inhibits the return of the patient to the role of a normal functioning individual in the outside community.

References

1   Erving Goffman, *Stigma*, Prentice-Hall, Inc., Englewood Cliffs, N.J., 1963, p. 3.
2   Mark Lefton, Shirley Angrist, Simon Dinitz, and Benjamin Pasamanick, "Social Class, Expectations, and Performance of Mental Patients," *American Journal of Sociology*, **68:** 79–87, 1962.
3   *Ibid.*
4   J. Sanbourne Bockoven, Anna R. Panidscio, and Harry C. Solomon, "Social Adjustment of Patients in the Community Three Years after Commitment to the Boston Psychopathic Hospital," *Mental Hygiene*, **40:** 353–374, 1956.

38

FEELINGS OF STIGMA AMONG RELATIVES
OF FORMER MENTAL PATIENTS

Howard E. Freeman and Ozzie G. Simmons

Despite considerable efforts to remold the public's image of the mental patient, hospitalization for psychiatric reasons continues to result in invidious evaluations of the patient by his community associates.[1] As a consequence of current attitudes toward mental illness, feelings of shame, inferiority, and disgrace on the part of patients and their family members are looked upon as almost inevitable concomitants of hospitalization.[2] The current attitudes toward mental illness that are held by community members, and their resulting detrimental effects on patients and their families, are often regarded as a major barrier to the reintegration of formerly hospitalized persons into the community.[3]

This phenomenon of stigma is the focus of the analysis reported in this paper: specifically, an attempt to identify feelings of stigma among relatives of formerly hospitalized patients by means of structured questions is discussed, and the relationships between feelings of stigma and various social and psychological characteristics of these family members are described. Surprisingly, consideration of the influence of stigma in discussions of the impact of mental illness has not been accompanied by systematic investigation of the phenomenon. A search of the relevant literature indicates that stigma is usually discussed in vague and general terms. In the limited research on the problem, feelings of stigma ordinarily have been inferred from the content of non-directed interviews with a few informants; neither structured scales nor standard probes have been used in previous studies. A noteworthy exception to the unsystematic character of research on stigma is the work of Clausen and his associates, who studied the reactions of wives to the hospitalization of their spouses.[4] They asked specific questions, as part of their study, about the wives' communication with their parents and in-laws, with their children, and with their friends, neighbors, and fellow workers.[5] In the present study, as in the research by Clausen and his associates, stigma refers to the sensitivity of relatives to the reactions of family, friends, and work associates regarding hospitalization for mental illness of a household member.

Source: Howard E. Freeman and Ozzie G. Simmons, "Feelings of Stigma among Relatives of Former Mental Patients," Social Problems, **8**: 312–321, 1961.
This research was undertaken by the Community Health Project, directed by Ozzie G. Simmons. The Project was sponsored by the Social Science Program at the Harvard School of Public Health and supported by grants M-1627 and 3M-9167 from the National Institute of Mental Health.

[1] Robert H. Felix and the members of the Expert Committee on Mental Health, "Social Psychiatry and Community Attitudes," World Health Organization Technical Report Series No. 177, Geneva: World Health Organization, 1959.
[2] Marion R. Yarrow, John A. Clausen, and Paul R. Robbins, "The Social Meaning of Mental Illness," Journal of Social Issues, **11** (1955), pp. 33–48. The other papers in this issue of the Journal of Social Issues also touch upon the problem. Also, see two papers from this study by Charlotte Green Schwartz: "Perspectives on Deviance—Wives' Definition of their Husbands' Mental Illness," Psychiatry, **20** (August, 1957), pp. 275–291; and "The Stigma of Mental Illness," Journal of Rehabilitation, **4** (July–August, 1956), pp. 7–10.
[3] Ernest M. Gruenberg and Seymour S. Bellin, "The Impact of Mental Disease on Society," in Alexander H. Leighton, John A. Clausen, and Robert N. Wilson (eds.), Explorations in Social Psychiatry, New York: Basic Books, 1957, pp. 341–364.
[4] Yarrow, Clausen, and Robbins, loc. cit.
[5] Ibid.

The data discussed in this paper were obtained as part of the first interview in a two-stage investigation of families of former patients. The study design provides for two interviews with relatives residing in the household of former patients. These first interviews were obtained as soon as possible after the patient returned to the community. The second interviews have just been completed; they took place a year after the patient's return to the community, providing he remained there for that period of time. If he was rehospitalized during the year, the second interview took place at that time.

Eventually, feelings of stigma will be used as an independent variable in the investigation of conditions under which patients remain in the community after release from a mental hospital. The analysis reported here, which is viewed as a necessary antecedent to the study of factors associated with the posthospital fate of patients, considers feelings of stigma as the dependent variable. Since the relationships uncovered between feelings of stigma and social and psychological characteristics of patients' relatives were not predicted in advance of the analysis, the findings, most properly, should be regarded as hypotheses to be tested in further investigation.

THE STUDY GROUP

The relatives interviewed were predominantly the mothers and spouses of patients who "left bed" during the first six months of 1959. "Left bed" was defined as remaining in the community for more than 30 days with the expectation on the part of the hospital that in-patient treatment was completed. Many of the patients were technically still "on the books" of the hospitals, either on "trial visit" or "extended leave" status at the time of the first interview. Patients were in the community an average of 41 days at the time of the first interview (standard deviation = 16.5 days).

Every patient with the following characteristics was included in the drawing group: between 20 and 60 years of age, white, native born, living in Boston or adjacent areas, hospitalized for purposes other than observation, not physically handicapped to the extent of being unemployable, not hospitalized primarily for acute alcoholism, and not addicted to narcotics. All were psychotics with non-organic, functional disorders, the majority diagnosed as schizophrenic. Each patient selected was last hospitalized at one of 12 hospitals in eastern Massachusetts, of which nine are state and three Veterans Administration.

The hospital records of all patients meeting these criteria were reviewed. After eliminating patients released to foster homes, half-way houses, and day hospitals, interviews were attempted in all but 12 of the 714 cases in which the patient returned to a family setting. These 12 cases met all the criteria but returned to the hospital before the interview could be accomplished. Of the 702 interviews attempted, 649 (92%) were completed: in 49 of the uncompleted cases, the informants either had severe language problems or were too emotionally disturbed to be interviewed, and in four cases the informants could not be located. Hospital record data were available for all patients, and chi-square goodness of fit comparisons of the completed cases and of the total study group on 48 social and clinical variables revealed that only chance differences exist between completed and uncompleted cases. Likewise, there are only chance differences between completed and uncompleted interviews with respect to the interviewer, the month the patient left bed, and the kin relationship of the informant to the patient.

The completed cases include 280 males and 369 females. The majority of the patients were hospitalized less than six months, although two-thirds were previously hospitalized for over 15 days. Approximately half the patients are married. Interviews were conducted by psychiatric social workers in the home, unless the informant desired otherwise. A standardized interview schedule was employed, and interviews averaged somewhat less than two hours.

ELICITING FEELINGS OF STIGMA

Consistent with the approach utilized in the other sections of the interview schedule, the measurement of feelings of stigma was attempted by means of structured items.[6] In developing these stigma items, the intent was to obtain a set of items which would reflect the sensitivity of the relatives to reactions of family, friends, and work associates regarding the hospitalization of a member of the household. These items were interspersed with others designed to elicit problems that the family felt they were having in managing the patient and the effects on the family of having the patient at home. The section of the interview schedule containing both the five stigma items and the seven items concerned with management problems was introduced by the following statement to informants: "Having a family member who has been in a mental hospital raises problems for the family. Here are some statements that have been made by relatives because someone who was in a mental hospital is living in the house. We would like to know which ones have been problems for your family since (patient's name) has been home." The two response categories read to the informants were "problem" and "not a problem."

The five stigma items were first included in a study of female relatives of male mental patients who were successful in remaining in the community for at least a year.[7] Interviews in that study took place approximately 14 months after patients were returned to the community. In that investigation, 29 per cent of the informants answered that one or more of the five items were a problem. This proportion, although low, was felt to be related at least in part to interviewing only relatives of "successful" patients.

[6] Howard E. Freeman and Ozzie G. Simmons, "The Use of the Survey in Mental Illness Research," *Mental Hygiene*, **34** (July, 1960), pp. 400–410.

[7] Since the N of that study group was only 182, the number of cases in the "with stigma" group was small, and consequently a systematic investigation of correlates of stigma was not undertaken. In an analysis of mobility inclinations, feelings of stigma were included as an independent variable and found to be associated with desire to move to another residence. This finding failed to be replicated in the investigation reported here. Howard E. Freeman, Ozzie G. Simmons, and Bernard J. Bergen, "Residential Mobility Inclinations Among Families of Mental Patients," *Social Forces*, **38** (May, 1960), pp. 320–324.

In Table 1, the proportion of relatives who responded affirmatively to each of the stigma items in this study is reported. With regard to all five items, it appears that only a small proportion of the study group feels stigmatized by having a mental patient in the home. Only one-quarter of the informants answered in the affirmative to one or more of the items and less than 10 per cent of the study group gave two or more affirmative responses.

The issue can be raised, of course, that the structured question approach is not an appropriate way of eliciting feelings of stigma on the part of patients' family members. Although it is not possible to eliminate this completely as a reason for the low proportion of persons expressing feelings of stigma, the items on problems of patients' management do provide a means of evaluating this issue.

As previously mentioned, the management items were interspersed with the stigma items in the same section of the interview schedule. On the average, in comparison with the stigma items, twice as many persons responded affirmatively to the items on management problems. Almost two-thirds of the sample replied affirmatively to at least one of the seven items on management problems. Although it is possible that these items were less extreme than those concerned with stigma, their content suggests that this is not the case. For example, 13 per cent of the study group responded affirmatively to the item "It is like having a ten-year-old child around," and 19 per cent reported "Having him home makes other family members nervous." The proportion of affirmative responses to the management items ranges from 12 per cent for the item "It affects the family's normal ways of life, like eating times and sleeping times" to 35 per cent for the item "Once a person has been mentally ill, he needs more supervision and advice from his family than would otherwise be necessary." It seems likely that if relatives are willing to respond affirmatively to an item such as "It is like having a ten-year-old child around," they would not be reluctant to answer questions reflecting their sensitivity to the reactions of family, friends, and work associates with respect to having a mental patient in the home. The relatively large proportion of the study group willing to acknowledge management problems suggests that the low proportion who express feelings of stigma cannot be accounted for solely in terms of "denial" to structured questions.

In evaluating the low proportion of family members who reported feelings of stigma, it is necessary to take into account the content of the items. By content,

Table 1
Proportion of relatives reporting stigma problems ($N = 649$)

If one wants the respect of his fellow workers, it is much better not to let people know a member of the family has been in a mental hospital.	12.0%
Having him home makes family members less willing to invite people to the house.	10.6
Having him home may cause some neighbors to make remarks about the family.	7.1
Family members sometimes avoid their friends because they are embarrassed.	6.4
I see less of my relatives because I am ashamed.	2.6
Proportion reporting one or more problems.	24.2

the items differentiate, from the rest of the study group, the relatives whose response to being the family member of a mental patient is characterized by withdrawal and concealment. These items would not elicit affirmative responses from those family members who, even in the face of overt negative reactions of community members, do not modify their interpersonal relationships and perhaps intensify them. Actually, our findings are consistent with the research by Clausen and his associates. Although they report that stigma is the "predominant expectation" among patients' spouses, they estimate that only one-third of the study group reacted to the mental illness of their husbands by limiting communication and interaction.[8] Our results, as well as the research of the Clausen group, do suggest that stigma—defined as sensitivity to the reactions of community associates accompanied by withdrawal and concealment—is characteristic of only a minority of families of mental patients.[9]

CORRELATES OF FEELINGS OF STIGMA

Since less than 10 per cent of the relatives gave affirmative answers to more than one of the five stigma items, it was decided to dichotomize the study group, including in the "with stigma" group all informants who answered affirmatively to one or more of the items. Neither the informant's nor the patient's sex is related to feelings of stigma. Throughout the analysis, however, it was deemed wise to control for the sex of the patient, and differences that occur when sex is controlled will be discussed. Three sets of variables—patients' posthospital behavior, relatives' education and class status, and relatives' personality characteristics—were found to be associated with feelings of stigma. In addition, however, a number of variables which failed to correlate with feelings of stigma will also be considered.

By far, the strongest relationships found were between feelings of stigma on the part of relatives and the latters' reports of the posthospital behavior of patients. In Table 2, the direct relationship between patients' posthospital symptomatology and feelings of stigma is presented. This symptom classification was developed from relatives' responses to a check list of twenty-one statements ranging from "tries to commit suicide" to "fails to keep to a time schedule." Informants were offered the response categories "frequently," "occasionally," and "never." In consultation with a psychiatrist, the patients were classified into three groups, taking into account both the severity and frequency of occurrence of the symptoms.[10]

---

[8] Yarrow, Clausen, and Robbins, op. cit., p. 34. As reported below, feelings of stigma are significantly related to social class status and slightly correlated with kin role of the informant. Two-thirds of the wives studied by Clausen and his associates were described as "middle" or "low-middle" class. If our study group were confined to female spouses of patients, and predominantly of the middle class, the proportion of cases feeling stigma would be higher.

[9] We wish to acknowledge the helpful criticisms of Charlotte G. Schwartz to an earlier draft of this paper, as well as those of John A. Clausen and John Cumming.

[10] Although the classification scheme varied somewhat, the procedure for classifying the patients into three symptom groups is essentially that employed in our earlier investigation and described in Howard E. Freeman and Ozzie G. Simmons, "The Social Integration of Former Mental Patients," International Journal of Social Psychiatry, 4 (Spring, 1959), pp. 264–271.

Table 2
Patients' symptomatology and relatives' feelings of stigma

	Proportion feeling stigma	100% equals
Symptoms minor or absent	14.1%	227
Symptoms moderate	22.3	287
Symptoms severe	45.2	135
Total	24.2	649

$\chi^2 = 45.66$, df $= 2$; $p < .001$

Other measures reflecting the posthospital behavior of the patients are also strongly correlated with feelings of stigma on the part of their family members. For example, the scale composed of the items on problems of patient management, discussed in the previous section, is positively correlated with feelings of stigma on the part of relatives.[11] Likewise, a low level of social participation of patients is associated with feelings of stigma and, for male patients, a low level of work performance is also associated with stigma, although this relationship is of considerably lesser magnitude. These findings suggest that rather than being merely the result of having a household member with the *status* of "mental patient," relatives' feelings of stigma are associated with their perception of the patient as still "abnormal" and with their apprehensiveness of a negative evaluation of the family by community members on account of the patient's current bizarre behavior.

The relationship between education, social class, and feelings of stigma appears to be considerably more complex. Education is *not* significantly associated with stigma, although there is a trend for the more educated to cluster in the "with stigma" group. It was anticipated that feelings of stigma would be inversely related to education, since significant relationships were found in this study group between educational level and "enlightened" attitudes toward the etiology of mental illness, mental hospitals, normalcy of patients after hospitalization, and whether patients are to blame for their condition.[12] Significant relationships were also found between informants' scores on a vocabulary test and "enlightened" attitudes toward mental illness. But, like education, verbal ability is *not* significantly associated with feelings of stigma. Although neither education nor verbal skills are related, an objective measure of social class—Warner's I.S.C.—is significantly correlated in a positive direction with feelings of stigma, and the relationship between class self-identification and feelings of stigma is even stronger (See Table 3).[13] These findings are also con-

[11] One possibility that occurred to us at this point in the analysis was that perhaps persons reporting feelings of stigma were those who tended to be willing, on structured items, to indicate any sort of negative experience or feeling. As a means of testing this, we controlled for responses to management problems for all relationships reported in this paper. Controlling in this way does not appear to alter the findings, which suggests that the results are more than a mere reflection of the "givers" and "deniers" within the study group. This is further evidence that the issue of denial cannot account completely for the low proportion of persons reporting stigma.

[12] Howard E. Freeman, "Attitudes Toward Mental Illness Among Relatives of Former Patients," *American Sociological Review*, 26 (February, 1961), pp. 59–66.

[13] W. Lloyd Warner, *Social Class in America*, Gloucester, Mass.: Peter Smith, 1957.

Table 3
Class self-identification and proportion feeling stigma

	Proportion feeling stigma	100% equals
Working class	20.5%	463
Middle or upper class	33.3	186
Total	24.2	649

$x^2 = 11.87$, df $= 1$; $p < .001$

trary to the analysis of attitudes toward mental illness and social class previously reported for this study group: measures of social class that did not include education—such as Warner's I.S.C.—failed to correlate with attitudes toward the etiology of mental illness, the mental hospital, normalcy of patients after hospitalization, and whether patients are to blame for their condition.[14]

The relationships just noted suggest that two contradictory "forces" are operating. On the one hand, relatives with more formal education and greater verbal ability are more likely to be exposed to and influenced by the notions of understanding and tolerance advanced by current mental hygiene and mental health education programs. On the other hand, the more educated informant, by virtue of his higher class status and aspirations, is probably more concerned with a derogatory evaluation of the family by his community associates.

The observation that social class aspirations and education may operate in opposite directions is supported by the relationship between class self-identification and stigma among persons who have and have not attended college (Table 4). Although they are relatively few in number, informants who regard themselves as "working class"—despite some college education—are the least likely to feel stigma, even in comparison with those of high school education who reported they belonged to the "working class." On the other hand, informants who have attended college and who perceive themselves as "middle" or "upper" class are most likely to feel stigma. Of course, the majority of persons with some college education perceive themselves as "middle class." In this sense, the middle class status commitment that is typical among persons exposed to college appears to negate the power of the educational process, which independently

[14] Howard E. Freeman, loc. cit.

Table 4
Class self-identification and proportion feeling stigma among relatives, controlling for college education

	High school or less		At least some college	
	Proportion feeling stigma	100% equals	Proportion feeling stigma	100% equals
Working class	21.2%	433	10.0%	30
Middle and upper class	30.4	125	39.3	61
Total	23.3	558	29.7	91

$x^2 = 4.53$, df $= 1$; $p < .05$ $x^2 = 7.24$, df $= 1$; $p < .01$

Table 5
Bi-serial correlations between
personality characteristics of
relatives and their feelings of stigma

	r(bis)
Withdrawal	.19*
Frustration	.19*
Cycloid thinking	.16*
Self-confidence	—.16*
Nervousness	.15*
Emotionality	.14*
Anomia	.13*
Autism	.11*
Persistence	—.06
Self-sufficiency	—.05
Rigidity	.05
Dominance	.04
Impulsivity-rathymia	.02
Authoritarianism	.01

* $p < .01$

seems to operate in the direction of reducing feelings of stigma. Although the relationship is more complex than they observed, our study does support the finding of Clausen and his associates that feelings of stigma are more likely among relatives who are attempting to maintain a relatively high class status position or who have status aspirations.[15]

The third set of variables associated with feelings of stigma are the personality characteristics of the informants. The personality scales, 14 in number, contain five items each.[16] Of the 14, eight are significantly associated with feelings of stigma (See Table 5). The significant correlations with withdrawal, frustration, lack of self-confidence, autism, and anomia suggest that family members who feel stigma may be characterized as socially incompetent and isolated. This observation is supported by the responses of relatives to items designed to measure identification with the community. For example, one item asked was "How would you say people around here act toward each other? Extremely friendly, just somewhat friendly, or indifferent and unfriendly?"[17] The marked differences in proportions feeling stigma among informants in each of these three response categories are reported in Table 6; feelings of stigma are inversely associated

[15] Yarrow, Clausen, and Robbins, loc. cit.
[16] The items comprising the scales on anomia, authoritarianism, frustration, rigidity, and withdrawal were constructed by Leo Srole and associates for the Midtown Manhattan Mental Health Study, conducted in the Department of Psychiatry, Cornell Medical College, under the direction of the late Dr. T. A. C. Rennie. The items and rationale associated with these scales will appear in a forthcoming monograph on the Midtown Manhattan Mental Health Study. Our categorization of some of the scales as "personality characteristics" is at variance with the manner in which they were originally conceptualized. Srole postulates anomia, for example, as a phenomenon emerging from the interaction of personality and socio-cultural variables, although we have considered it, for our purposes, as a personality characteristic. With respect to anomia in particular, but in terms of all the characteristics discussed, our classification of the scales as individual characteristics makes no reference to their genesis. The other scales were developed by Orville G. Brim and his associates at the Russell Sage Foundation for their Parent Decision Project. This study will be reported in Orville G. Brim, Jr., David C. Glass, and David Lavin, Personality and Decision Processes: Studies in the Social Psychology of Thinking, Stanford: Stanford University Press, forthcoming. Copies of the scales may be obtained from the Community Health Project.
[17] This item was taken from Peter Rossi's Why Families Move, Glencoe, Illinois: Free Press, 1955.

Table 6
Relatives' evaluation of how people act and
proportion feeling stigma

	Proportion feeling stigma	100% equals
Extremely friendly	18.1%	216
Just somewhat friendly	24.3	346
Indifferent and unfriendly	42.4	66
Total	24.0	628*

* No information for 21 informants
$x^2 = 16.45$, df $= 2; p < .001$

with community identification. Clausen and his associates observe that some wives are concerned with "psychological stigma," i.e., they fear that people generally are suspicious, disrespectful, and afraid of mental patients.[18] Our findings suggest that "psychological stigma" is probably a concomitant of general feelings of incompetence, isolation, and distrust on the part of relatives.

The significant relationships between stigma and the other three personality scales—cycloid thinking, nervousness, and emotionality—suggest that feelings of stigma are also associated with personal maladjustment on the part of family members. This point must be made with caution, of course, since it is difficult to place much faith in the sensitivity of structured scales as diagnostic indicators. Another source of data does, however, support this observation. Informants were rated, after the interview, by interviewers who, in all cases, were psychiatric social workers. There are significant correlations betwen stigma and interviewers' ratings of informants for emotionality, tenseness, and nervousness. These additional findings suggest that the relatives' psychiatric status may indeed be related to their feelings of stigma.

A number of other variables were also correlated with feelings of stigma. Although not statistically significant, the findings with respect to kin role relationship between patient and informant are of interest (See Table 7). Patients' wives, more than any other kin group of informants, are likely to feel stigma, probably because their status in the community is so much more dependent upon the patient's evaluation by community members. There is a statistically significant difference in feelings of stigma among sisters who served as informants, depending upon whether the patient is male or female. One possible explanation for this finding may be the anxiety of sisters of patients with regard to anticipated classification by their community associates of all occupants of this family role in the same way. Although the number of cases is too small to place much confidence in the data, it would appear that unmarried sisters of female patients are even more likely than married sisters to feel stigma, perhaps because this group fears that a negative evaluation will deter prospective marriage partners.

In addition to the variables discussed, age and religion were included in the analysis, but were not significantly related to feelings of stigma. Both in terms of variables that did and did not yield significant associations with feelings of

[18] Yarrow, Clausen, and Robbins, loc. cit.

Table 7
Informants' kin role and feelings of stigma

	Male patients		Female patients		Total	
	Proportion feeling stigma	100% equals	Proportion feeling stigma	100% equals	Proportion feeling stigma	100% equals
Patients' mothers	23.3%	116	26.6%	79	24.6%[4]	195
Patients' spouses	28.0	118	20.4	196	23.2[5]	314
Patients' sisters	12.5	24	34.5	55	27.8[6]	79
Total	24.4[1]	258	24.2[2]	330	24.3[3]	588*

* Other informants for 22 male patients and 39 female patients.

[1] $\chi^2 = 2.72$, df $= 2$; $p <$ ns   [4] $\chi^2 = .86$, df $= 1$; $p <$ ns
[2] $\chi^2 = 4.99$, df $= 2$; $p < .10$ [5] $\chi^2 = 2.38$, df $= 1$; $p <$ ns
[3] $\chi^2 = 2.91$, df $= 2$; $p <$ ns   [6] $\chi^2 = 3.97$, df $= 1$; $p < .05$

stigma, we attempted to control for the interaction effects between the independent variables, as well as for the sex of the patient. With the exception of the rather complex findings regarding social class, these operations did not alter the findings.

It should be noted that the analysis is concerned with a cohort of patients recently returned to the community, and the relationships may differ among patients who do and do not succeed in remaining in the community for extended periods of time. Indeed, this may account for the lack of a relationship between residential mobility aspirations and feelings of stigma, a relationship we found in our previous study of families of male patients who succeeded in remaining in the community for over one year.[19] Differences in feelings of stigma when the community tenure of patients is taken into account will be evaluated upon completion of the second stage of this study. In order to do this, the same stigma items are included in the second-wave interviews, and we anticipate that shifts in feelings of stigma can also be analyzed.

SUMMARY

In this paper, we have reported an attempt to identify feelings of stigma among relatives of former patients by means of structured questions and to find correlates of these feelings. Although the proportion reporting feelings of stigma is low, the response rates to items tapping other content suggest that this low proportion is not a function of our particular approach to data collection. Rather, feelings of stigma appear to be characteristic of only a minority of relatives of mental patients, at least at the level of concealment and withdrawal from social contacts. This finding is consistent with the results of a study of hospitalized patients' wives by Clausen and associates. In brief, stigma appears to be associated with the degree of bizarre behavior on the part of the patient, the social class identification of family members, and their personality characteristics.

This research, of course, is only a start toward the thorough examination of the phenomenon of stigma. In order to estimate the "true" parameters of feel-

[19] Freeman, Simmons, and Bergen, loc. cit.

ings of stigma, a comparative investigation is required that utilizes a range of direct and indirect means of measuring the feelings of family members. There is, also, the unanswered "etiological" question of the relative precedence of feelings of stigma and the variables found related to these feelings. Although this research has not dealt with a number of such vital questions, it has been possible to demonstrate systematic variations among families of former patients with respect to feelings of stigma, and the findings should serve as an impetus for further research.

39
SOCIAL ATTITUDES TOWARD
DISCHARGED MENTAL PATIENTS
Charles D. Whatley

This paper reports a study of socially unfavorable attitudes exhibited toward persons who have had a mental illness. It attempts to reveal some of the social factors associated with avoidance reactions toward recuperating patients, and to indicate some of the ways in which these reactions may affect post-hospital adjustment. Both lay and professional observers have pointed out that a lingering social stigma attaches to newly discharged patients, and that consequently their social relations often are characterized by social distance, distrust or denial of employment (5, p. 460). Such patterns of avoidance may constitute a type of social isolation which could have adverse effects on those confronted by it.

One of the implications of the social-isolation hypothesis used in etiological studies is that the presence of intolerant, unfavorable attitudes in the community tends to increase the likelihood of relapse and rehospitalization. Although this study will not directly test this hypothesis, it will present evidence suggesting how such social factors may affect the post-hospital experience of discharged patients.

RESEARCH PROCEDURE

The research is based on the assumption that the attitudes of other persons which impinge on discharged mental patients may be explored by means of an attitude scale. During the summer of 1956, a scale designed for this purpose was administered to a stratified sample of 2001 persons scattered throughout 17 parishes (counties) in Louisiana. The eight items composing the scale (see Table 1) are phrased so as to emphasize the concept of avoidance—i.e., the tendency to shun contacts with persons who have had a mental illness. Collectively, the

Source: Charles D. Whatley, "Social Attitudes toward Discharged Mental Patients," Social Problems, **6**: 313–320, 1959.

items are designed to measure unfavorable reactions which may deny or restrict social interaction opportunities for such persons. Thus, respondents who say they would not hire, associate with, or live near discharged mental patients presumably reveal avoidance attitudes which could have unfavorable, isolating effects.

The items composing the scale were selected from a larger battery of pre-test items having relatively high discrimination values as determined by the Likert method. Professional judges rated each item according to (a) whether agreement or disagreement with it reflected attitudes believed to be unfavorable to the social and psychological adjustment of the patient and (b) the degree of ego-involvement a person would incur in giving a favorable response. Those items with less than 90 per cent consensus were discarded. The retest reliability coefficient, computed from summation scores of 37 persons scattered throughout the city of New Orleans and retested 8 days later is .83 ($p < .01$). For the entire sample of 2001 subjects the reliability coefficient computed by the Kuder-Richardson formula is .87 (3). The test meets the requirements of a Guttman-type scale. It has a coefficient of reproducibility of .91 as determined by the method described by Edwards (2, pp. 184–190).

ANALYSIS OF FINDINGS

For convenience the findings of this study will be presented in two parts. The first concerns sources of variation among unfavorable attitudes toward dis-

Table 1
Keyed favorable responses and ego-involvement ratings of scale items

Ego-involvement rating*	Favorable response	Item
A	Disagree	1. It is best not to associate with people who have been in mental hospitals.
	Agree	2. It is wrong to shy away from people who have had mental disorders.
B	Disagree	3. It would bother me to live near a person who had been in a mental hospital.
	Disagree	4. I would not ride in a taxi driven by someone who had been in a mental hospital.
C	Disagree	5. I would rather not hire a person who had been in a mental hospital.
	Disagree	6. School teachers who have been in mental hospitals should not be allowed to teach.
D	Disagree	7. I would be against any daughter of mine marrying a man who had been to see a psychiatrist about mental problems.
	Agree	8. If I needed a baby sitter, I would be willing to hire a woman who had been going to see a psychiatrist.

* The symbols, A, B, C, and D, are labels for each pair of statements, arranged in a rank order by professional judges according to the amount of ego-involvement a favorable response is likely to call forth. Thus, giving a favorable reply to "A" (items 1 and 2) was judged to make the least demands on the values and interests of the self of the respondent, whereas a favorable reply to "D" (items 7 and 8) was judged to incur the greatest degree of ego-involvement.

charged patients—i.e., the status variables, such as race, occupation, education, and income to which these attitudes may be related. Knowledge of such variations is important in identifying the social environment to which recuperating patients are returned. The second part presents evidence of certain social-psychological determinants of these unfavorable attitudes. Specifically, the purpose will be to show how primary-group values reflected in the ego-involvement ratings of the items are correlated with the tendency to avoid contact with persons who have been treated for mental illness.

Sources of variation

A total of 12 variables were examined for evidence of a relationship with the test scores. Six of these—sex, religion, rural-urban residence, home ownership, having visited a mental hospital, and reported cases of mental illness in the family—showed no correlation whatever with the tendency to avoid social relations with recovering mental patients. Briefly, these findings indicate that in their attitudes toward mental patients, men are no more favorable than women, people living in cities do not differ from their rural counterparts, and Protestants do not differ from Catholics. Nor do Protestants differ among themselves when the effects of education are held constant. Similarly, persons who have visited and seen the inside of a mental hospital are no more favorable in their attitudes than others. This finding fails to support the belief that opening the doors of mental institutions to the public is an effective method of changing social attitudes toward mental patients. Finally, the total lack of any relationship between the test scores and reported cases of mental illness in the family indicates that avoidance attitudes are unaffected by personal knowledge of, and contact with, relatives who have had these disorders.

On the other hand, six sociological variables were found to be associated with avoidance reactions (see Table 2). When the means and correlation coefficients of each are compared, age emerges as the most substantial source of variation. It is followed, in a rank order, by education, race, income, occupation, and marital status. As estimated by the data given in Table 2, the most favorable social environment for recuperating mental patients occurs among young, educated, married whites engaged in relatively well-paid clerical or professional occupations. It is these groups that exhibit the greatest proportion of favorable responses. The differences within each of these variables are significant at or beyond the .01 level of confidence.

One could infer from these differences that patients belonging to such groups would find the social environment more hospitable and thus be able to make a more successful readjustment to the community. Evidence suggesting that this may be true is reported in a study by Adler, et al. (1), who find that patients who are young, married, above average in education, and engaged in white-collar occupations have the highest probability of making successful post-hospital adjustments. With the exception of race, these are the same social groups which have shown the greatest inclination to accept released mental patients. It should

Table 2
Means and correlations of summation scores for age, education, race, income, occupation, and marital status*

Variables	n	$\bar{X}$	F	df	p <	r
Age						
15–35	942	12.2				
36–55	727	13.6				
56-up	332	15.5	86.2	2	.01	.42
Education						
0–9 years	726	14.4				
10–12 years	857	12.9				
13-up	418	12.0	38.1	2	.01	.28
Race						
White	1659	12.9				
Negro	342	14.6	19.4	1	.01	.22
Income						
Over $4,000	904	12.4				
Under $4,000	1097	14.0	38.1	1	.01	.18
Occupation						
Bus. & Prof.	238	13.0				
Clerical	330	12.2				
Skilled	357	13.4				
Unskilled	290	14.6				
Housewife	785	13.4	18.5	4	.01	.15**
Marital Status						
Single	348	13.1				
Married	1521	13.2				
Other	132	14.6	12.3	2	.01	.15**

* The higher the mean the more unfavorable the attitude toward ex-mental patients. The summation score is the sum of the weighted responses to the eight individual items used in the scale. Favorable, undecided, and unfavorable responses were respectively weighted 1, 2, 3. The maximum range of the test scores is from 8 through 24.
** Business and professional dichotomized with other; housewives omitted. Married and other are dichotomized.

be added that whether this apparent correlation has any functional significance remains to be demonstrated by further research.

As noted above, age is the most substantial source of variation in the test scores. The coefficient of correlation is .42, and it accounts for 18 per cent of the variance associated with unfavorable attitudes. When all six variables are combined in a multiple correlation, the predictable variance is raised to 21 per cent ($Ry_{123456}=.46$). This relatively slight increase in predictive validity indicates that the observed differences between the six sociological variables are apparently due to some common factor which is unevenly distributed among them. In other words, the variations associated with race, education, income, occupation, and marital status are probably manifestations of the same factor that is responsible for age differences.

As to what this factor might be, it is likely that some form of culturally generated liberalism is responsible for the variance associated with age. This interpretation would agree well with the findings of Woodward (6), who reports differences among age groups which are highly similar to those found here. Such age variations should be regarded as manifestations of cultural changes in attitudes toward mental illness. The favorable responses among young persons probably reflect liberal attitudes of contemporary society, whereas the relatively unfavorable reactions of older persons reflect learned attitudes carried over from earlier decades. This hypothesis appears more tenable than that which would attribute the unfavorable responses of older persons to psychological conservatism produced by aging. One reason for this is that the multiple correlation shows that age shares a large part of its common factor variance with education, income, and occupation. These variables are usually correlated with liberal, humanitarian attitudes; and it is unlikely that variations among these latter variables are produced by the conservativism of growing old.

Ego-involvement

The status variables described above cast some light on the general picture of unfavorable sentiment toward mental patients who have been returned to the community. This general pattern is useful for descriptive purposes but leaves much to be desired from the standpoint of locating the factors in the social environment that result in avoidance reactions. With the data at hand it can be shown that a more specific social-psychological factor is partly responsible for the somewhat marginal social position of the recovered patient. This factor has been tentatively identified here as ego-involvement (4).

The manner in which ego-involvement comes into play may be determined by considering the distribution of responses for the individual items used in the scale. Table 3 shows that the spread in the per cent of favorable replies varies from a low of 15 to a high of 81. The average person, thus, is able to show sympathetic acceptance of recovered patients in some situations but not in others. Why is this so? A partial answer is provided by considering each item in relation to its ego-involvement rating. The items in Table 3 have been ranked by professional judges according to the degree to which a favorable response would be likely to engage values or interests that are important to the ego of the respondent. They are grouped in pairs, designated by the symbols A, B, C, and D, indicating a rank order from low to high amounts of ego-involvement. Reading from left to right in the column totals of the table, we may observe that there is a steady decrease in the per cent of favorable responses as each item becomes increasingly saturated with ego-involvement. Thus, the more closely social relations with recovered patients tend to involve ego values, the greater the tendency to avoid social contacts with them.

For purposes of illustration, let us consider the first question in each pair of ranked items. Item 1, with a low ego-involvement rating, asks the respondent whether it is best not to associate with ex-mental patients. It has no direct reference to the self, and by disagreeing with it (i.e., giving the favorable response) a person may merely disapprove the practice of shunning persons who have had mental disorders. No immediate demands are made on the individual in terms of his job, his physical safety, or his family, etc. It is "safe" to give a

Table 3
Per cent distribution of favorable replies for each individual item used in the scale*

Variables	Item number and ego-involvement rating								
	A		B		C		D		
	1	2	3	4	5	6	7	8	n
Age									
15–35	85	76	72	66	64	54	44	17	942
36–55	80	72	67	56	56	45	32	14	727
56–up	69	61	61	39	37	28	19	14	332
Education									
0–9 years	72	65	65	42	52	37	31	14	726
10–12 years	85	74	68	62	59	50	37	14	857
13–up	87	79	72	69	61	58	41	18	418
Race									
White	83	75	68	61	58	48	34	15	1659
Negro	68	58	69	42	49	38	42	15	342
Income									
Over $4,000	86	77	71	67	61	54	38	16	904
Under $4,000	76	67	66	50	53	41	34	14	1097
Occupation									
Bus. & Prof.	87	75	73	64	53	50	35	18	239
Clerical	85	77	71	68	66	56	42	17	330
Skilled	80	75	66	61	62	44	36	14	357
Unskilled	72	59	65	46	53	37	36	16	290
Housewife	81	73	68	55	52	47	33	14	785
Marital Status									
Single	79	67	68	59	61	48	40	18	348
Married	82	74	70	59	57	48	35	14	1521
Other	70	64	65	45	43	30	29	16	132
All Groups	81	72	68	58	57	47	36	15	2001

* The item numbers in this table correspond with those in Table 1.

favorable reply because nothing of personal value is committed by doing so. Favorable replies (81 per cent) are higher for this item than for any other in the scale.

Item 3, with a slightly higher ego-involvement rating (B), asks the respondent whether it would bother him to live near a person who had been in a mental hospital. Although no obvious social values of the self are directly implicated by the question, there is the implied possibility of some primary-group interaction with the discharged patient. Favorable replies drop to 68 per cent $(p < .01)$. Items 5 and 7, with ratings of C and D respectively, have considerably more ego-involvement. Here the individual is asked to commit himself in a way that may touch directly upon values of the self. Item 5 asks him to indicate his willingness to employ an ex-mental patient, and item 7 asks him to approve his daughter's marriage to a man who had been undergoing psychiatric treatment. The percentages of favorable replies are 57 and 36 respectively, both significantly less than either of the first two items $(p < .01)$. In short, some persons who are able to act favorably toward mental patients in situations involving relatively abstract values are unable to do so when such action specifically involves the family or

other more immediate values of the self. As to the amount of association between ego-involvement and such unfavorable reactions, an estimate is provided
by a tetrachoric correlation coefficient, computed by dichotomizing the rank
order $(A + B$ against $C + D)$. The resulting value of r is .46.

Table 3 contains an additional category of information which indicates that
ego-involvement may be an important factor in the tendency to avoid social
relations with recuperating patients. This is the response distribution for occupational groups in answer to item 5, which asks the individual about willingness to
hire an ex-mental patient. It is particularly noteworthy that of all occupational
groups, only employers show a significant decrease in favorable replies to this
question. They are no more inclined to hire recovered mental patients than are
unskilled workers, who are the most unfavorably oriented of any occupational
group for all others items in the scale. The most favorable of all groups is composed of persons in clerical work. Two-thirds of them are willing to employ
ex-mental patients as compared with only 53 per cent of both unskilled laborers
and business and professional groups. Relative to other items in the scale, the
white-collar group does not show any decrease in its willingness to employ these
patients.

The findings suggest that persons who are in a position to hire mental patients
are among the ones who are most reluctant to do so. This unexpected result
supports the hypothesis given above—that favorable reactions to returned mental patients are inversely related to the proximity of ego values. Employers are
apparently willing to be favorable toward the recovered patient except in situations which touch directly on their occupational interests. This contrasts with the
situation for white-collar groups, who rarely play the role of employers and who
continue to show the same relatively high proportion of favorable responses to
the question of hiring recovered patients. Presumably, the employer perceives
the hiring of released patients as a threat to his vested interests.

CONCLUSIONS

The measures of avoidance reactions employed in this study may be taken as
tentative indications of socially unhealthy environments for recovering mental
patients. At present, these measures should be regarded as roughly approximate
because of the limitations inherent in polling methods and because they do not
reflect all factors in the social environment to which recuperating patients are
exposed. A more thorough design would require additional measures of relevant
interpersonal factors affecting discharged patients.

With due recognition of these limitations, the chief implications for assessing
the relationship between unfavorable social attitudes and post-hospital adjustment may be stated as follows. Tendencies to shun or to restrict social interaction with ex-patients are most likely to be present in situations which involve
important self values. The r of .46 between ego-involvement and avoidance reactions indicates that freedom of social participation among returned patients is

greatest in secondary groups and least in primary groups. This inference stems from the findings which show that the perception of a discharged patient as a threatening or unwanted social object is partly a function of a defining social context which brings ego values of others into the situation. These ego values may be translated into sociological terms as being somewhat equivalent to primary-group values. When the data in Table 3 are examined in this light, it becomes apparent that favorable responses to scale items are mainly a function of the remoteness of the question to primary group situations. Thus, a tentative conclusion is that attitudes of social acceptance or tolerance of discharged patients are greatest in relatively impersonal situations, and that so long as primary-group values are not implicated the patient is conceived as a relatively neutral, non-threatening object.

From a sociological standpoint this may be regarded as a relatively unhealthy situation for the released and still recovering mental patient. Since most ego-involvements are presumably concerned with dominant value orientations within the community, the pattern of avoidance revealed here suggests that the patient risks a certain amount of social isolation through curtailed interaction opportunities in primary groups.

This interpretation should be given serious attention in evaluating attitude studies which reveal changes toward a more favorable public understanding of mental illness. For example, both Woodward's and the present study provide some evidence of the growth of liberal attitudes toward mental illness. Since social areas other than mental illness have undergone similar degrees of liberalization in recent decades, this evidence is not surprising. There may be some question, however, as to whether the indicated changes have taken place on the primary-group level, where interpersonal relations come into play as possible determinants of personality integration.

Finally, it should be added that the implications of this apparently more basic social factor should be of interest to mental hygienists. To the extent that abstractly learned attitudes have little favorable effect in situations where ego values are involved, there is some doubt as to the ultimate effectiveness of attempts to produce public "understanding" of mental illness as a means of improving the health status of recuperating patients.

References

1 Adler, Leta, et al., *Mental Illness in Washington County, Arkansas* (University of Arkansas: Institute of Science and Technology, Research Series, 1952).

2 Edwards, Allen L., *Techniques of Attitude Scale Construction* (New York: Appleton-Century-Crofts, 1957).

3 Richardson, M. W., and F. Kuder, "The Calculation of Test-Reliability Coefficients," *Journal of Educational Psychology,* **30** (August, 1939), 681–687.

4 Sherif, M. and H. Cantril, *The Psychology of Ego-Involvement* (New York: Wiley, 1947).

5 Weinberg, Kirson, *Society and Personality Disorders* (New York: Prentice Hall, 1952).

6 Woodward, J. W., "Changing Ideas of Mental Illness," *American Sociological Review,* **16** (August, 1951), 443–454.

40
ON THE STIGMA OF MENTAL ILLNESS

John Cumming and Elaine Cumming*

The concept of stigma presented here was developed in the course of a series of studies directed toward illuminating the kinds of social environments most likely to promote ego reintegration after a psychotic illness. Briefly, we propose that the stigma associated with hospitalization for mental illness is a form of ego damage—the loss of a valued attribute; that stigma, unlike some ego-damaging losses, is reversible; and that the circumstances necessary for its reversal can eventually be specified.

STIGMA AS LOSS

The word "stigma" is often used to describe the way in which society stamps those who have been mentally ill. Its literal meaning is "a stain on one's good name," or a "loss of reputation." Originally, the word referred to a mark placed on a slave or a prisoner as a sign of his status. Whether it is a visible mark or an invisible stain, stigma acquires its meaning through the emotion it generates within the person bearing it and the feeling and behavior toward him of those affirming it. These two aspects of stigma are indivisible since they can each act as a cause or effect of the other. For example, the patient may have an inner feeling of shame or inferiority because he has been in a mental hospital, and this may lead him to act in a manner that induces others to respond in ways appropriate to his inner feeling. On the other hand, people may indicate their appraisal of a patient as a stigmatized person by their actions, and he in turn may accept and internalize their estimates. Either way, stigma, like other social definitions, is generated and reinforced in interaction. In a family, or any group tied together by ascriptive bonds, it would not be possible for one member to feel stigmatized, in our sense, without the others being affected.

The stigma that is said to be associated with hospitalization for a mental illness may be similar to the "feeling of unfortunateness" that Dembo attributes to amputees (Dembo, 1956). She believes that the process by which a person becomes defined as "unfortunate" involves the loss, or absence, of something valuable. "Unfortunateness" is most likely to result when that which is lost is an intrinsic attribute of the person, such as health, honor, or reputation; it is less likely to occur when it is merely a possession such as money. Dembo argues

Source: John Cumming and Elaine Cumming, "On the Stigma of Mental Illness," Community Mental Health Journal, 1: 135–143, 1965.

* The data for this analysis were collected under Research Grant Number 6911 Nursing Division, Department of Health, Education and Welfare. We wish to thank Drs. Newton Bigelow and Donald Graves of Marcy State Hospital and Drs. Marc Hollender and Philip Steckler of Syracuse Psychiatric Hospital for helping us to locate our groups of patients. We thank the students of the School of Public Health Nursing of the Upstate Medical Center and their faculty advisors for their collection of the data reported here.

As this research report was completed before the appearance of Erving Goffman's Stigma (Goffman, 1963), no attempt will be made to relate the two different, but probably not incompatible, approaches to the problem.

that devaluation is unlikely to occur when the loss cannot be evaluated by ordinary normative standards. For example, as only the minority value absolute pitch, to be tone deaf, except perhaps in the families of musicians, is *not* to be unfortunate.

The process of "becoming unfortunate," like the process of becoming stigmatized, occurs in interaction. If something generally recognized as valuable is lacking or lost, the person who loses it is expected to suffer and to define himself as unfortunate. If he does not do so, sanctions will be brought to bear upon him automatically because the loser's disregard for his own loss is a direct challenge to the value system of the observer. If he cannot force the loser to an awareness of his loss, he must be prepared to revise his own values. Concretely, a widow must mourn, even if she has been unhappily married; and a spinster, no matter how comfortable, must feel a little disappointed, or the value of marriage is held in question. Some losses, like amputations, are totally irreversible. Some, like spinsterhood, are totally reversible. Some losses seem to require considerable work for reversal.

What can be said to have been lost when a person goes to a mental hospital? We propose, in the light of our own previous work and that of others (Cumming & Cumming, 1957; Clausen & Yarrow, 1955) that, in general, social competence and, in particular, predictability or reliability are lost. Because it is the loss of a *behavioral* attribute, the stigma of mental hospitalization should be reversible through a demonstration of competent and predictable behavior. Nevertheless, many lay people regard mental illness as essentially incurable, and thereby, inadvertently, build into its definition the necessary conditions for irreversible stigmatization. What, then, can be done to clear the reputation of the mentally-ill patient?

THE UNDOING-OF-THE-LOSS

When a patient returns from a mental hospital, he must enter into social interactions that automatically require him to understand the expectations of others and to make his own known. If he can do this, he belies the label "incurable" and is no longer appropriately labeled either incompetent or "unfortunate." It therefore becomes necessary to relabel him in such a way as to restore him to the world of competent, predictable people. However, a redefining of *all* mental illness as curable may be difficult because it would require a shift in a complex set of attitudes toward some grave forms of deviant behavior. One resolution of the paradox of recognizing both a cured patient and the incurability of his illness is to redefine his hospitalization as a mistake. We often hear relatives of patients explaining, "He wasn't like the others in there—the serious cases. It was only a 'nervous breakdown.'" Thus they establish that this "cured" person was never "really crazy," that he was at no time socially incompetent or unpredictable and therefore cannot be now. This reversibility of the process of stigmatization we might call undoing-of-the-loss. Such mechanisms for restoring people to membership in normal society may underlie the reported discrepancies (Olshansky,

1959) between the generally poor *attitudes* people express toward the mentally ill and the fair and generous *treatment* that they so often mete out to them.

On the other hand, there appear to be cases in which those around the patient are apprehensive—both of him and for him—and the patient himself is openly ashamed of his illness and hospitalization. In such cases, where stigma remains, the hospitalization may have brought into focus secondary losses or inadequacies, present before, but now defined as "causes" of hospitalization. For example, a heavy drinker, after he has been hospitalized for schizophrenia, may be defined as "alcoholic." In other words, his stigma "spreads" so that the stain on his character becomes almost the total coloration. In general, we propose that when patients or their families cannot redefine the hospitalization so as to exempt the patient from the imputation of loss of a valued attribute, then stigma is likely to be felt.

These considerations suggest the following question: what kinds of environment favor undoing-of-the-loss, and what kinds favor continued stigmatization?

It seems clear that in any group apprehension about a member's social competence or predictability will create tension. Furthermore, other members of a primary group are implicated in the incompetence of their representative. The undoing mechanism, in a group in which an expatient is a participating member, can be expected to be part of that ongoing flow of integrative activity that prevents it from breaking up under the strain of inner tensions (Cumming & Henry, 1961). The task of lowering tension is usually allocated to specific members in stable groups; and it has been noted that in the ordinary division of labor between men and women, this integrative role is allocated to women (Parsons & Bales, 1955; Strodtbeck & Mann, 1956). These findings suggest that the women closely connected with the former mental patient may undertake the main burden of the undoing-of-the-loss.

Studies have shown, however, that when *male schizophrenics* live with their wives or mothers, they are more prone to relapse than when they live with more distant relatives (Brown, Carstairs & Topping, 1958; Freeman & Simmons, 1963). We might guess that conditions promoting relapse might also promote stigmatization as both are forms of ego damage. Relationships with close female relatives often require a division of labor based on a high level of competence and a clear division of authority, and this may generate too much ambivalence because of the demands of mutual obligation and emotional involvement. The undoing-of-the-loss for this group may best be accomplished by more distant female relatives who can provide sociability and solidarity without the burden of a complex and close relationship. There is some evidence from the work of Brown, Carstairs, and Topping (1958) that the presence of siblings protects schizophrenic men from relapse; studies of our own have shown that the presence of sisters is associated, for schizophrenic men, with a long delay between the onset of the illness and hospitalization (Cumming & Miller, 1961).

There is evidence, however, that non-schizophrenic male patients, living with their mothers or wives, relapse less often than a comparable group in other living arrangements. For these men and for female patients, it might be reasonable to expect that *all* adult female kin would, through the exercise of integrative skills, help the patient to redefine the hospitalization in such ways as to negate the loss of a valued attribute.

This argument is oversimplified but to set it forth in detail would require an excursion into the psychodynamics of sexual relations and the nature of the ego failure in the various mental illnesses. The results of relevant studies have been hard to integrate; for example, Brown et al. (1958) showed that having a wife improves the chance of discharge from hospital, but for chronic schizophrenics it also increases the relapse rate, and all male schizophrenics who live with their mothers have high relapse rates. For women, there are no comparable figures, although theory and general observation would suggest that the mother-daughter relationship should be protective. Among women, marriage raises the incidence of schizophrenia, but does not appear to affect the relapse rate. Manic-depressives, a small group, appear to be uniformly benefited by the availability of close female relatives of all kinds, and thus are different from schizophrenics in an important way.

ILLUSTRATIVE STUDY NO. 1

A cohort of 22 patients consecutively discharged from a state mental hospital was studied. They ranged from 16 to 77 years of age; the median age was 50. There were ten men and twelve women, including seven schizophrenics, two manic-depressives, one involutional psychotic, five arteriosclerotics, six neurotics, and one alcoholic. The unit of analysis was the family. Each patient was interviewed twice; and for the eighteen living in a family setting, a relative who lived in the house with him was also interviewed twice. These relatives included ten spouses, three mothers, three siblings, a daughter and an aunt. We lack comparable information from the families of the four remaining patients, two of whom lived alone, one in a nursing home, and one in a hostel. Interviews took place about eight months after discharge; the first was open-ended and the second structured. The interviewers tried to elicit the problems encountered while the patient was readjusting to the community. No direct questions about stigma were asked; its presence was inferred from the interview material.

Interviews were rated by the authors and an assistant independently. Differences were discussed and a composite rating developed. Instructions for recognizing stigma were worked out, and two raters scored the interviews independently. The authors' composite rating had 86.5% agreement with Rater 2, and 86.5% with Rater 3. Raters 2 and 3 agreed in 72.7% of cases. In the seven cases where there was not total agreement, the opinion of the two agreeing raters was used.

We found two basic evidences of stigmatization: the first an outright expression of shame or inferiority because of the hospitalization, and the second an expectation of discrimination or inferior treatment from others. Shame sometimes permeates an interview; for example, one patient's wife says of him, "My children think he is just lazy. Of course, because of the kind of hospital he was in, the union probably didn't think it was a proper thing to help him financially."

His daughter interjects, "It was hard when he came home because there was all those stories in the paper about crimes and they always turned out to be done by former mental patients."

Expectation of inferior treatment because of having been in a mental hospital shows up in remarks like, "I didn't want anyone to know that I was at a mental hospital and call me crazy." "The fellows I work with didn't know I was there." Of the 22 patients, nine, or 41% felt stigma; of these, four expressed shame and five had a generalized expectation of discrimination. Some complaints of this general sort show a good assessment of reality, however. A sixteen-year old boy wondered if he would have difficulty getting a driver's license because he had been hospitalized; according to New York state law he will have to have a psychiatric certificate of fitness next time he applies for licensing. A woman newly moved to her neighborhood says that she has not told her next door neighbor that she has been in a hospital since, "I don't want everybody knowing I was there—you know what they might think." Such cases may not really constitute stigma in our sense and their inclusion may inflate the number. Where there was doubt of this kind, the respondent was judged to be feeling stigma.

The patients were asked directly whom they visited and how frequently. A person was counted as a significant contact if he was visited once a week or oftener. The reason for hospitalization was not inquired after directly, but almost all of the respondents volunteered at least one. Such reasons as physical illness, overwork, and the stress associated with pregnancy were counted as socially acceptable. The commonest unacceptable reason given was excessive drinking, although two relatives said that hospitalization resulted from generalized incompetence. There is a hint in our material that drinking may be used deliberately to stigmatize some male patients because it may be easier to control them if they are ashamed of their behavior.

The remarks used for establishing the respondent's reasons for hospitalization were in every case different from the remarks used as evidence of the presence of stigma.

As Table 1 shows, an unacceptable reason for hospitalization is always accompanied by stigma, but no one who visits regularly with female kin fails to give an acceptable reason for the hospitalization. Furthermore, redefinitions are usually accompanied by freedom from stigma, and in three of the four cases where there is stigma in spite of there being a redefinition, there is no visiting with female kin. No differences were found by age, sex, work status, education, or household composition.

Because of the small numbers involved in this pilot study, it was planned to repeat it with new populations of patients. The following hypotheses were to be tested:

1 Stigma is related inversely to the rate of interaction with female kin. For schizophrenic men, the presence of mothers and spouses will be expected to be a countervailing force.

2 Destigmatization will be accompanied by reasons for exempting the patient from the label "mentally ill."

3 There may be additional differences between men and women arising from the

Table 1
Number of former mental patients by stigmatization and by visiting with female kin other than mother and giving acceptable reasons for hospitalization

	Total interviewed	Acceptable reasons given		No acceptable reason given	
		Visits kin	Does not	Visits kin	Does not
Total interviewed	22	11	6	0	5
Stigmatized	9	1	3	0	5
Not stigmatized	13	10	3	0	0

Not Visiting Kin is associated with stigma.   *Fisher's Exact Test: P = .008; P = .005; P = .036.*
No Acceptable Reason for Hospitalization is
  associated with stigma.
Acceptable Reason for Hospitalization is
  associated with Visiting with Female Kin.

differences in role demands made of them. Men should be able to prevent the spread of stigmatization by working successfully at an occupation, thus displaying competence. Women can help the undoing process by reassuming the spouse role and by caring adequately for children. Women, however, do not always have to reach a certain minimum of effectiveness in their core roles because others can help them in such matters as caring for children. Some women may only have to refrain from raising tension in the home, and from representing the family in a devalued way outside, in order to begin the undoing process. Men probably do not have as much leeway in the occupational world. It is therefore hypothesized that an adequate work situation, as well as interaction with female kin, will be necessary for the destigmatization of men; and a supportive social system, presumably of female kin, will in itself be sufficient for women.

ILLUSTRATIVE STUDY NO. 2

The second study involves a group of 87 women between 18 and 65 with a median age of 36, who had been consecutively discharged from mental hospital between 12 and 24 months before the interview. Circumstances made it impossible to include men in this study, and the hypotheses regarding work are still untested. Thirty-two were diagnosed as schizophrenic, 14 as depressed, 11 as having other psychoses and 30 as neurotic.

The 87 women were interviewed with a structured instrument designed to assess the level of stigma and the intensity of interaction. The degree of stigma is indicated in this preliminary analysis by the combined score on two separate Guttman Scales of 4 and 5 items each. One scale includes items reflecting the sense of shame or inadequacy identified in the first study and is called self-stigma; the other set reflects expectation of discrimination and is called situation-stigma. Items adapted from a stigma scale developed by Freeman and Simmons (1961) for use with the relatives of patients were also included, and a comparison with their results will be reported elsewhere.

Analysis of these data shows that although our hypotheses about women appear to be generally upheld, they are too simple and too specific. First, the redefinition of the reasons for hospitalization appears to be only one alternative expression of a more general psychological mechanism for undoing-the-loss. Besides having an acceptable reason for hospitalization, the patient can be redefined as changed or transformed through learning or conversion in such a way that she is no longer the person who became mentally ill. "I got sick worrying about my housework; now I have learned not to care if it doesn't get done."

A different type of mechanism is redefinition of the situation so that the "public" is held to be ignorant and prejudiced about those who must go to mental hospitals. In this mechanism, only the initiated know that such people are not crazy at all, but only temporarily ill, or in need of a rest. The relationship between these mechanisms and the two expressions of stigma is still to be explored.

Our prediction concerning the role of female kin appears to have been over-specific. Although it seems to be true that women must be available to play integrative roles if stigma is to be reversed, more generally, it appears, as Table 2 shows, that the integrative role must be embedded in a normatively-governed, consensually-validated social system in which there are both instrumental and integrative roles. Furthermore, the situation seems most propitious if the woman does not have to play a leadership role—that is, assume a role of high power in the family. As Table 2 shows, single women who do not have access, either in the same household or in weekly visits, to a complete nuclear family, including a sibling, are all stigmatized. Separated and divorced women are usually stigmatized no matter whom they interact with. Single women who have at least weekly access to a mother, father, and sibling, that is, a situation permitting role differentiation but not requiring the patient to assume a leadership role, are less often stigmatized. The stigma scores of the married women fall in between these groups, and whether or not they have children seems immaterial.

Table 2 also suggests that not only role differentiation but also position in the system makes a difference: the women in the least stigmatized group are in fully differentiated systems, either daughters in the parental home or widows in the

Table 2
Number of female former mental patients by role position and by stigma score

Role position	Total	Stigma score	
		Low (0–3)	High (4–9)
All women	87	40	47
Full role complement, dependent	12	10	2
Single	10	8	2
Widowed	2	2	0
Full role complement, leader	61	28	33
With children	47	19	28
Without children	14	9	5
Incomplete role complement	14	2	12
Separated and divorced	6	2	4
Single	8	0	8

$x^2 = 12.38$, d.f. $= 2$, $P < .01$.

homes of a married daughter; but they are not in high power positions. At first glance, it may appear that a position of dependency is all that is required; but the most stigmatized group contains young women who live with their mothers and fathers but lack siblings. In other words, the peer role seems to be crucial for the undoing process. The most stigmatized group also includes separated and divorced women. Here the issue is difficult to clarify because of the lack of uniformity in the situations of these women. Among this small group, all have lost the spouse role and hence presumably the role of integrative leader in a complete system. Beyond this, some have returned home, some live with one other family member, others with nonrelatives. Three of the four women with high stigma scores have had to place children in foster homes, while one of the two with low scores lives alone with her four children. The numbers are unfortunately too small for us to reach any conclusions although they suggest that stigma is associated with failure in both the spouse and mother role.

It appears from these findings that the kind of interaction system to which the patient returns is importantly associated with destigmatization, as is the position available in the system for the patient upon her return. As in the first study, no differences were found by age, work status, or education. In this second study, integrative status calculated in terms of the education and occupation of the head of the household is unrelated to stigma and so is the type of treatment received by the patient. Diagnosis, however, is related to stigma as Table 3 shows, with the neurotic group having the highest scores, the schizophrenic group next highest, the depressions next to lowest, and the residual group lowest of all. An adequate discussion of the psychiatric implications of these differences would take us beyond the scope of this paper.

When we combine diagnosis with role context, we see (Table 4) that in spite of the small numbers, the women with diagnoses of neurosis, schizophrenia, or "other" follow the same pattern of stigmatization that we saw in Table 2. Those in a low-power or dependent position in a full role complement have the lowest stigma, those in situations with an incomplete role complement have the highest, and the married group (full role complement, high-power) are intermediary. All

Table 3
Number of female former mental patients by diagnosis and by stigma score

Diagnosis	Total	Stigma score	
		Low (0–3)	High (4–9)
All women	87	40	47
Neuroses	30	7	23
Schizophrenias	32	14	18
Depressions	14	10	4
Remainder	11	9	2
Toxic psychoses	4	3	1
Psychopathic personality	3	3	0
Psychoses in physical illness	2	1	1
Undiagnosed	2	2	0

$\chi^2 = 15.56$, d.f. $= 3$, $P < .01$.

of the depressive illnesses except one, however, are among the married women. Nevertheless, with the depressed women removed, the differences by role complement that we saw in Table 2 remain.

Finally, returning to our hypothesis that women are not required to perform at such clearly specified levels as men, and therefore can make more use of the help of others in the undoing-of-the-loss, we found that the presence of other adult females made no difference to this group. For the married women, however, time out of hospital does make a difference to stigma score. The longer they have been out, the less likely they are to be stigmatized. It is possible that, apart from simply forgetting a disruptive episode, it takes some time for a married woman to reassemble all the parts of her role after hospitalization because some of her duties as integrative leader have fallen to others. Full role participation is, in a sense, necessary for a differentiated system.

This reasoning is supported by the fact that the other groups of women show no association between time out of hospital and stigma score. The unstigmatized may have returned to roles not filled in their absence, and the stigmatized are, as we have shown, in incomplete systems.

When we look at Table 5, however, we see that among the group of married women, diagnoses are not evenly distributed; those with depressive disorders are all among the group longest out of hospital. All of these women but one have been out of hospital between 15 and 22 months; when they are arrayed by the number of months out of the hospital, a Runs Test shows no significant difference. Once again, when this group is removed, the effect of time out of hospital remains significant.

In summary, it appears from these women that some illnesses produce more

Table 4
Number of female former mental patients by diagnosis and role position and by stigma score

Diagnosis and role position	Total	Stigma score	
		Low (0–3)	High (4–9)
All women	87	40	47
Full role complement, low power	12	10	2
Without depressive illness	12	10*	2*
Neurosis	4	3	1
Schizophrenia	4	3	1
Other	4	4	0
Depression	...	...	...
Full role complement, high power	61	28	33
Without depressive illness	48	18*	30*
Neurosis	20	4	16
Schizophrenia	21	9	12
Other	7	5	2
Depression	13	10	3
Incomplete role complement	14	2	12
Without depressive illness	13	2*	11*
Neurosis	6	0	6
Schizophrenia	7	2	5
Other	...	...	...
Depression	1	0	1

* For those women without depressive illness, $\chi^2 = 12.68$, d.f. = 2, $P < .01$.

Table 5
Number of married, female former mental patients by diagnosis and length of time out of hospital and by stigma score

Diagnosis and time out of hospital	Total	Stigma score	
		Low (0–3)	High (4–9)
All married women	61	28	33
Out less than 15 months	20	4	16
Without depressive illness	19	3*	16*
Neurosis	9	0	9
Schizophrenia	8	2	6
Other	2	1	1
Depression	1	1	0
Out more than 15 months	41	24	17
Without depressive illness	29	15*	14*
Neurosis	11	4	6
Schizophrenia	13	7	7
Other	5	4	1
Depression	12	9	3

* Those without depressive illness and out of the hospital more than 15 months are less stigmatized than those more recently discharged.
x^2 (corrected) = 4.88, d.f. = 1, .05 > P > .02.

stigma than others and that the type of role undertaken by the woman upon her return from hospital and the structure in which it is embedded are important in permitting the undoing-of-the-loss of reputation that hospitalization causes. Furthermore, for some women—those in role positions normally defined in terms of integrative leadership—time assists the process.

Finally, if our hypotheses regarding men were to be upheld, it would add credence to these findings because they were generated from the same theoretical base.

References

1   Brown, G. W., Carstairs, G. M., and Topping, G. G. The post-hospital adjustment of chronic mental patients. *Lancet*, 1958, **2**, 685–689.

2   Clausen, J., and Yarrow, M. R. The impact of mental illness on the family. *J. soc. Issues*, 1955, **11** (4) (Whole Issue).

3   Cumming, Elaine, and Cumming, J. *Closed ranks*. Cambridge, Mass.: Harvard Univer. Press, 1957.

4   Cumming, Elaine, and Henry, W. E. *Growing old*. New York: Basic Books, 1961, (Chapter 8).

5   Cumming, J., and Miller, L. Isolation, family structure, and schizophrenia. In *Proc. of the Third World Congr. of Psychiat*. Toronto: Univer. of Toronto Pr., 1961.

6   Dembo, Tamara, Leviton, G. L., and Wright, B. A. Adjustment to misfortune—a problem of social-psychological rehabilitation. *Artificial Limbs*, 1956, **3** (2), 4–62.

7   Freeman, H. E., and Simmons, O. G. Feelings of stigma among relatives of former mental patients. *Soc. Problems*, 1961, **8**, 312–321.

8 Freeman, H. E., and Simmons, O. G. *The mental patient comes home.* New York: John Wiley, 1963.

9 Goffman, E. *Stigma; notes on the management of a spoiled identity.* New York: Prentice Hall, 1963.

10 Olshansky, S. Community aspects of rehabilitation, employer receptivity. In Milton Greenblatt and Benjamin Simon (Eds.), *The rehabilitation of the mentally ill.* AAAS, Publication No. 58, 1959. Pp. 213–222.

11 Parsons, T., and Bales, R. F. *Family, socialization, and interaction process.* Glencoe, Ill: Free Press, 1955.

12 Strodtbeck, F., and Mann, R. D. Sex role differentiation in jury deliberations. *Sociometry*, 1956, **19,** 3–11.

41
SOCIAL CLASS AND POSTHOSPITAL PERFORMANCE LEVELS*
Howard E. Freeman and Ozzie G. Simmons

The relationships of social class to such aspects of mental illness as etiology, epidemiology, diagnosis, acceptance of psychiatric services, and perceptions of illness have been the subject of considerable research.[1] Indeed, social class probably has been employed more frequently than any other sociological variable in mental illness research, as well as in studies in other medical fields.[2] The demonstrated predictive power of this variable led us to include it in a systematic study of the posthospital experience of mental patients who remain in the community for extended periods after release from a hospital. Our major objective was to identify correlates of posthospital levels of occupational and social performance among these patients.

The principal hypothesis examined here is that, among patients who remain in the community for a year or more after hospitalization, a direct relationship exists between their levels of posthospital occupational and social performance and the class status of their families. This hypothesis is one of a series based on the proposition that the tolerance of deviant behavior on the part of family members is a key factor affecting the course of a patient's posthospital experi-

Source: Howard E. Freeman and Ozzie G. Simmons: "Social Class and Posthospital Performance Levels," *American Sociological Review*, 24: 345–351, 1959.

* This research is being undertaken by the Community Health Project, under the direction of Ozzie G. Simmons. The project is sponsored by the Social Science Program at the Harvard School of Public Health, and is supported by a grant (M 1627) from the National Institute of Mental Health.

[1] Perhaps the best example is the research of Hollingshead, Redlich, and their associates. See August B. Hollingshead and Frederick C. Redlich, *Social Class and Mental Illness*, New York: Wiley, 1958.

[2] With respect to public health, for example, see Ozzie G. Simmons, *Social Status and Public Health* (Social Science Research Council Pamphlet 13), New York: Social Science Research Council, 1958.

ence.[3] It was predicted that middle class families are less tolerant than others of deviants and more likely to exclude them from their midst; thus, they should contain proportionately fewer former patients who neither work steadily nor participate regularly in social activities.

The general thesis from which we derived both the working hypothesis and the proposition of an association between social class and tolerance of deviance is that the posthospital fate of the patient is influenced by his family's commitment to the dominant values of the society. Families less committed to these values are more likely to tolerate deviant performance in occupational and other instrumental roles. Although variations in the degree of commitment to the dominant values are manifested in a variety of subcultural identifications and affiliations, social class is perhaps the most prominent and certainly the most frequently employed point of reference for the analysis of value differences in American society.

A number of conceptual formulations regarding the differential behavior and expectations of social classes, as well as various empirical studies, support this point of view.[4] The concern of families with "inadequate" occupational and social performance and consequent definition of the family member as a deviant require awareness of and readiness to act in the ways the dominant culture specifies as "appropriate." Although the power of the mass media has attenuated class differences in awareness of the dominant values of the society, differential exposure to the formal educational process (and to the variety of interpersonal situations for which considerable education is a prerequisite) continues to influence the internalization of values and readiness to act in accordance with them. Moreover, and perhaps most important, the primacy accorded work and other instrumental roles in the value hierarchy of middle class persons severely limits their tolerance of deviant performance in these roles.

In addition, the preoccupation with conformity to the prevailing standards that is more common among middle class persons with respect to the entire gamut of ideological imperatives—including, of course, work and social participation—also restricts their tolerance of deviant behavior. Accompanying these expectations of conformity is an elaborate and specific punitive system for dealing with the member whose behavior deviates from accepted norms. This strong emphasis upon conformity in the middle class has related consequences on the personality level, for example, the tendency to delay gratifications and control impulses.[5] These observations have been integrated in analyses of the socioeconomic aspiration pattern and are considered in a number of general commentaries on American society.[6]

[3] This proposition and the relationship of posthospital performance to other variables have been reported by us in other papers. See "Mental Patients in the Community: Family Settings and Performance Levels," *American Sociological Review*, **23** (April, 1958), pp. 147–154; "Wives, Mothers, and the Posthospital Performance of Mental Patients," *Social Forces*, **37** (December, 1958), pp. 153–159; "Familial Expectations and Posthospital Performance of Mental Patients," *Human Relations* (in press); "The Social Integration of Former Mental Patients," *International Journal of Social Psychiatry* (in press).

[4] For example, the studies reported in R. Bendix and S. H. Lipset, editors, *Class, Status and Power*, Glencoe, Ill.: Free Press, 1953, particularly sections 3 and 4.

[5] Cf. Louis Schneider and Sverre Lysgaard, "The Deferred Gratification Pattern: A Preliminary Study," *American Sociological Review*, **18** (April, 1953), pp. 142–149.

[6] E.g., Robin M. Williams, Jr., *American Society*, New York: Knopf, 1955.

Finally, although perhaps a less direct point, the ability of middle class persons to deal with complex, symbolic processes may also be related to the less frequent retention in these families of patients with low levels of performance. By virtue of the middle class emphasis upon and practice of interpersonal manipulation, these families can more readily mobilize and exploit the outside community so as to facilitate the return of the patient to the hospital. Moreover, the pronounced verbal ability of middle class persons is useful in effecting the rehospitalization of a family member in the face of the frequent reluctance of hospital personnel to readmit the former patient.

No attempt was made to test directly any of these points. Rather, these considerations led to the development of the hypothesis of a direct relationship between the class status of a patient's family and his levels of social and occupational performance. A number of other variables, in addition to social class, were included in the study to amplify the hypothesized relationship and to provide support for the general thesis of a linkage between tolerance of deviance and differential commitment to the dominant values. In addition to measures of objective class status, we have analyzed the relationship between performance levels and three other variables generally held to reflect differential commitment to the dominant values: religion, ethnic background, and class self-identification. We attempted to elicit directly expressions of values in one area, namely, socio-economic aspirations. These data are also included in the analysis.

THE STUDY GROUP

The female informants interviewed were all relatives, predominantly wives and mothers, of male patients who succeeded in remaining in the community since their latest release from a mental hospital sometime between November, 1954 and December, 1955.[7] Every male patient was included in the potential study group who had the following characteristics: between 20 and 60 years of age, white, native born, living in the Boston area at the time of release, hospitalized more than 45 days prior to release, not physically handicapped to the extent of being unemployable, not addicted to narcotics, and not primarily hospitalized for acute alcoholism. By diagnosis, all were psychotics with non-organic disorders, the majority schizophrenic. Patients selected were last hospitalized in one of 13 mental hospitals in the Boston area. Of the 209 interviews attempted, 182 (88 per cent) were completed.

SOCIAL CLASS AND PERFORMANCE LEVELS

Performance level, as employed here, is a combined rating of patients' steadiness of posthospital employment and extent of participation in social activities. Patients who are rated high had worked full time since hospitalization and had participated regularly, and as frequently as other members of their families, in

[7] The study group is more fully described in "Mental Patients in the Community: Family Settings and Performance Levels," *op. cit.*

Table 1
Performance levels and status characteristics

Performance level	Breadwinner's income		I.S.C. score		Rent	
	Under $3900 per year	$3900 and over per year	50 and over	Under 50	$60 and under per month	Over $60 per month
1 (high)	19.0%	48.2%	28.3%	47.7%	28.2%	43.3%
2	28.6	30.6	30.4	31.8	29.1	31.7
3	17.9	7.1	13.8	11.4	13.6	13.3
4	34.5	14.1	27.5	9.1	29.1	11.7
N =	84	85[a]	138	44	117	60[b]
r_{pbs}	.35		.22		.21	

[a] 13 cases not included because of no information.
[b] 5 cases not included because of no information.

formal and informal social activities.[8] Breadwinner's income, rent, and Warner's I.S.C. were selected as measures of social class. Each of these three indexes is significantly associated with the other two. Table 1 shows the relationships of performance levels to the social class variables, and the point biserial correlation coefficients (r_{pbs}) for these relationships. Although reported as dichotomies, the relationships remain stable when more finite categories are employed in ranking families on the three class measures.

There is also a direct relationship between performance levels of patients and the class self-identification of the informants (see Table 2). Indeed, the class self-perceptions of family members appear to be more closely associated with the performance level of the patient than are the objective status characteristics. In Table 3, the families are divided into three groups on the basis of their I.S.C. and self-identification responses. The largest proportion of high level patients is found in families rated middle class both objectively and subjectively. Compared with this group, families rated objectively as lower class have a slightly lower proportion of patients with high performance levels, even if the family member

[8] These scales are more fully described in *Ibid*. Social participation was rated relative to the participation of other family members in order to compensate for class differences in informal and formal social activities. The findings reported here also apply when either work performance or social participation is employed by itself as a criterion of posthospital performance, and also hold when a "social integration scale" is employed as the dependent variable. The latter scale was constructed from the performance measures and a rating on psychiatric symptoms manifested by the patients; cf. "The Social Integration of Former Mental Patients," *op. cit.*

Table 2
Performance levels and class self-identification

Performance level	Class self-identification	
	Labor	Middle-upper
1 (high)	20.0%	39.7%
2	29.1	33.6
3	10.9	12.1
4	40.0	14.6
N	55	116*
r_{pbs}	.28	

* 11 cases not included because of no information.

Table 3
Performance levels and objective-subjective status evaluation

I.S.C.	Class self-identification	Performance level				
		1 (high)	2	3	4	N*
Under 50	Middle and upper	45.9%	35.1	10.8	8.2	37
50 and over	Middle and upper	36.7	32.9	12.7	17.7	79
50 and over	Labor	17.6	29.4	11.8	41.2	51

$r = .28$
* 11 cases not included because of no information about Class Self-Identification; also 4 cases with under 50 I.S.C.—Labor Class Self-Identification are not included.

perceived herself as middle class. But the greatest contrast is between these two groups and families who are rated objectively as lower class *and* whose members identified themselves as laboring class. Almost half the families in this last group have patients in the lowest of the four performance categories.

The thesis that performance levels are associated with differences in the commitment of families to the dominant values of the society is supported by the relationship between performance levels and religion. Families belonging to religious groups who presumably subscribe most fully to the dominant value system—Protestants and Jews—tend to have a disproportionate number of high level patients. Ethnic differences are also related to performance levels. Among patients with foreign-born fathers, 10 of 17 whose fathers were born in Eastern Europe are found in the highest performance category, in comparison with five of 15 patients whose fathers were born in Ireland, and eight out of 21 patients whose fathers were born in Italy. The same relationship holds when the nationality of the mother is employed. Among patients with native-born parents, however, there are less marked differences in performance levels with respect to national origin. Since the study group was restricted to native-born patients, the number with foreign-born parents is small and these findings are somewhat tentative. The clustering of low level patients among Italian and Irish families is consistent with characterizations of their value systems, particularly the relative lack of emphasis on achievement directed activities and on the future.[9] But the seemingly low tolerance of the Eastern European families, who are mostly Polish, is noted only as an interesting question for future research, since we are not aware of empirical data directly relevant to this point.

As noted in our introductory comments, many of the themes of the dominant culture have so pervaded the society that awareness of the dominant values is

[9] *Cf.* Florence Kluckhohn, "Family Diagnosis: Variations in the Basic Values of Family Systems," *Social Case Work*, **39** (February, 1958), pp. 63–72.

Table 4
Performance levels and religion

	Performance level				
	1 (high)	2	3	4	N
Protestant-Jewish	45.5%	36.4%	7.2%	10.9%	55
Catholic	27.3	28.3	15.8	28.3	127

$r_{pba} = .24$

found in all strata. Additional evidence of this situation is our somewhat abortive attempt to measure levels of socio-economic aspirations with a series of direct questions. In the case of several items, almost all the informants gave the most socially approved response. For example, 156 of 182 informants would prefer that a son who graduates from high school go to college rather than do something else. In the case of a few items, however, there is some indication that levels of aspiration are associated with performance levels, although the correlations are quite weak. If only families in which members identified themselves as "laboring class" are considered, the results become more suggestive; for example, among family members of patients in the highest of the four performance categories, six of 11 would take a temporary salary cut in order to get ahead in the community compared with only five of 22 relatives of patients in the lowest performance level category; similarly, seven of 11 relatives of patients with the highest performance level, compared with five of 22 with the lowest, would become more friendly with their supervisors at work so as to get ahead in the community. Admittedly, our attempt to assess levels of aspiration was less than successful, but slight trends indicate that performance levels of former patients are directly associated with the socio-economic aspirations of their families.

Thus, the data support our hypothesis of a direct relationship between performance levels of patients and the class status of their families. In addition, performance levels are directly associated with religious affiliations and with social class self-identifications of patients' families. These relationships, as well as the more tentative associations of ethnic background and level of aspiration with performance levels, suggest that high tolerance of deviance is linked with minimal commitment to the dominant values on the part of families of former mental patients.

COMPARISON WITH THE YALE RESEARCH

Although the relationship reported here between social class and performance levels is not likely to be limited to our particular study group, support for the proposition that differential tolerance of deviance in middle and lower class families underlies this correlation is necessarily restricted by our research emphasis on families of patients who succeeded in remaining in the community. This proposition (of tolerance of deviance) could receive strong additional support by examining the social class of patients returned to the hospital. On the basis of our inference of differential tolerance and the findings presented above, we would expect a higher rate of rehospitalization among middle class than lower class patients.

The study by Hollingshead and Redlich provides data by social class on the proportion of patients who re-enter psychiatric treatment.[10] In discussing their

[10] Hollingshead and Redlich, *op. cit.* Their data are not strictly comparable with ours, in that they employ a different class index. In the discussion that follows we employ the terms and definitions used in their volume. Thus, we refer to "re-entry into treatment" instead of rehospitalization, although, of course, treatment for most psychotic patients involves hospitalization. Professor Hollingshead read the original manuscript, and we wish to express appreciation for his comments. But we should note that they were only partially incorporated in this paper since our interpretations continue to differ in some respects from his own.

patient population, these authors report that while there is no relationship between re-entry into treatment and social class for their total patient group, there is a significant association between social class and re-entry into treatment among those persons diagnosed as schizophrenic. Schizophrenic patients in the highest social class, they indicate, are more than twice as likely to return to treatment within a year than patients in the lowest social class.[11] Since 82 per cent of our study group was diagnosed as schizophrenic, these findings support the proposition of tolerance of deviance, although they suggest that the generality of this proposition may not extend to patients in other diagnostic categories, especially the organic psychoses.

In discussing the re-entry rates of the social classes in comparison with the general population (with age and sex adjusted), however, Hollingshead and Redlich report, even among schizophrenics, an *inverse* relationship between re-entry into treatment and social class.[12] On the basis of our research and their analysis of re-entry rates, we would expect exactly the opposite result, that is, a higher proportion of middle class than of lower class patients re-entering treatment.

Since their finding vitiates the proposition that tolerance of deviance is of central importance, it becomes necessary to examine in some detail the empirical facts upon which Hollingshead and Redlich base their interpretation, and, in particular, one point they note but do not discuss.[13] They did not control for the disproportionate opportunities to re-enter treatment of members of different classes. Unless an inverse relationship between social class and re-entry into treatment can be demonstrated, taking into account the number of persons in each social class who are eligible to re-enter treatment by virtue of once having been a former patient, their interpretation of the data is misleading.

We agree with Hollingshead and Redlich that it is not possible to estimate, with precision, the number of former patients in each social class. But we do not believe that this issue should therefore be ignored. Indeed, the rates of incidence and prevalence they present indicate, relative to the probability of re-entering treatment, a *direct* relationship between class and re-entry rates—as we would expect on the basis of our own study of former mental patients.

An indication of the chances of a member of a particular class to re-enter treatment, relative to the pool of former patients of that class, can be calculated by dividing the re-entry rates by the incidence rates.[14] When this is done, the class differential disappears—except that the re-entry rate of classes 1 and 2 is between 25 and 50 per cent *higher* than those of the other social classes. This new statistic probably still overestimates the relative re-entry rate of the lower classes. For a less conservative estimate, prevalence rates can be used; this procedure underestimates somewhat the proportionate chances of a lower class person to re-enter treatment, since we do not control differences in age at onset of illness and a number of other variables. Using prevalence rates in the same manner as incidence rates were employed, however, results in a marked *direct* relationship between re-entry and social class, suggesting that the re-entry rate of the two

[11] *Ibid.*, p. 295, Table 38, cases categorized "Short Remission."
[12] *Ibid.*, pp. 235–236.
[13] *Ibid.*, p. 219, fn. 26.
[14] *Ibid.*, p. 235, Table 16. The results are similar when all psychotics or only schizophrenics are analyzed.

highest social classes may be as much as four times that of the lowest social class.[15]

The higher tolerance of deviant behavior by the lower class that is indicated by our research as well as the Yale study, if also present prior to hospitalization, serves to amplify certain of the other findings of the latter investigation. For example, it is reported that among patients of private practitioners, as well as among those in clinics and hospitals, a high correlation exists between type of treatment and social class. Characteristically psychotherapy is prescribed for upper class patients and shock treatment for those of the lower class. Undoubtedly, as the Yale group and others have pointed out, this is a function of class differences in the practitioner-patient relationship, types of treatment institutions to which patients of various classes are referred, and ability to pay. If lower classes are more tolerant of deviant behavior, however, patients from these families are probably "sicker," in the sense of manifesting more bizarre behavior, when first referred for treatment. Thus, they may receive shock treatment rather than psychotherapy, partly because of being more acutely ill (in the sense noted above).

Similarly, the findings of Hollingshead and Redlich that lower class psychotic patients are under treatment for more years than higher class patients may, to some extent at least, be a function of the development of graver illness before their more tolerant families sought treatment for them. Indeed, our inference of differential tolerance of deviance strengthens the Hollingshead and Redlich basic thesis of a close relationship between mental illness and social class. If lower class families are more tolerant of deviance, the strong association they report between incidence of psychosis (when only *treated* patients are considered) and social class actually underestimates the proportion of the lower classes who are psychotic, since they must manifest more acute symptoms of illness before being referred for treatment.[16]

SUMMARY

The foregoing discussion was initiated by depiction of the general thesis that the differential commitment of relatives to the dominant values of the society has substantial consequences for the posthospital fate of the mental patient. Evidence has been presented to support the hypothesis of a direct relationship between patients' posthospital performance levels and the social class status of their families. This hypothesis, one of a series specifying relationships between patients' posthospital performance levels and certain variables pertaining to differences in family stucture and in the personality characteristics of family

[15] We are grateful for the advice of Sol Levine and Robert B. Reed concerning this procedure. Of course, they are in no way responsible for the interpretation presented in this paper.

[16] Our research does not control for the influence of prehospital performance level or differential effectiveness of hospitalization. With respect to certain of our other findings, these variables received limited consideration; analysis of the prehospital and hospital conditions do not vitiate our proposition of tolerance as a key factor in the posthospital experience of former mental patients. Cf. "Mental Patients in the Community: Family Settings and Performance Levels," *op. cit.*, pp. 152–153.

members, is based on the proposition that the latter's tolerance of deviant be-havior is a key factor affecting the course of a patient's posthospital experience.[17]

Our findings provide support for the hypothesized relationship between class status and performance levels. In addition to measures of objective class status, the relationships between performance levels and three other variables (class self-identification, religion, and ethnic background) generally believed to reflect degree of commitment to the dominant values are all in the predicted direction. The correlation between peformance levels and ethnic background, however, must be regarded as tentative.

These findings regarding social class, and those of the Yale study considered in this paper, provide further support for the proposition that the differential tolerance of family members is critical to the posthospital fate of the mental patient.

42
MENTAL PATIENTS IN THE COMMUNITY: FAMILY SETTINGS AND PERFORMANCE LEVELS*
Howard E. Freeman and Ozzie G. Simmons

Shorter periods of hospitalization and longer periods of community living be-tween hospitalizations are among the notable trends in the treatment of psy-chotics, particularly those with functional disorders. Although the extensive employment of tranquilizing drugs has discernibly increased the length of com-munity experience of patients, the largest proportion of those ever exposed to hospital treatment remained in the community for substantial periods of time, even prior to the advent of tranquilizers.[1]

There is considerable evidence, however, that improved functioning is not a

---

[17] We have not attempted to relate the findings regarding social class to our previously reported correlates of performance levels. Many of these—reflecting structural differences among families and personality characteristics of family members—are, of course, associated with social class. An examination of the interrelationships between social class and these other correlates indicates that, in a statistical sense, their associations with performance levels are not artifacts of each other. On a conceptual level, however, we have not yet thoroughly exploited the data, and the various findings need to be more fully integrated. We acknowledge therefore the incompleteness of our research task.

Source: Howard E. Freeman and Ozzie G. Simmons, "Mental Patients in the Community: Family Settings and Performance Levels," American Sociological Review, 23: 147–154, 1958.
* The research reported here was undertaken by the Community Health Project of the Harvard School of Public Health, under the direction of Dr. Ozzie G. Simmons, and was supported by a grant (M 1627) from the National Institute of Mental Health. We are grateful for the advice provided during the design phase of the study by Dr. James A. Davis of the University of Chicago. Mrs. Marilyn Plath and Mr. Ber-nard Bergen assisted during data collection and analysis phases of the study.
[1] Adler, for example, found that one year after release from a state hospital, almost three-fourths of the patients in her cohort were still in the community. Leta M. Adler, "Patients of a State Mental Hospital: The Outcome of Their Hospitalization," in Arnold Rose (editor), Mental Health and Mental Disorder, New York: Norton, 1955, pp. 501–523.

necessary requisite for "success," i.e., remaining in the community. The clinical impression that former patients frequently reside in the community while actively psychotic and socially withdrawn is supported by studies employing modes of interpersonal performance as criteria of level of functioning.[2] As Clausen has noted, some released patients are "fully as ill as many patients currently in hospitals."[3]

Explanation of the continued existence in the community of a large number of patients who are less than well must be made with reference to the nature of their interpersonal relations in the posthospital situation. Patients are able to avoid the hospital when their interpersonal performance is within the range of behaviors expected by those with whom they interact. Tolerance of deviant behavior, on the part of the patient's "significant others," is a key factor affecting the process of posthospital experience and crucial to whether or not the patient succeeds in remaining in the community.

By tolerance of deviant behavior we mean the continued acceptance of the former patient by his significant others even when he fails to perform according to the basic prescriptions of his age-sex roles, as these are defined by the society. In our society, access to status is very largely determined by occupational achievement, and the strong emphasis on this factor, and to a lesser extent on other instrumental orientations, tends to be reasonably constant in American society.[4] Consequently, whatever the areas in which deviant behavior is likely to become a critical issue between the patient and those who comprise his world, instrumental performance is one of the most strategic, and acceptance of non-instrumental performance may be said to constitute substantial evidence of high tolerance of deviance.[5]

The familial network in which the patient resides and his status within this network thus assume considerable importance. Not only is tolerance by other household members directly related to "success" in remaining out of the hospital, but since familial expectations affect the patient's participation in other interpersonal networks, acceptance of the patient as a deviant restricts his exposure to others usually less tolerant of non-instrumental performance.[6] If those with whom the patient resides place little emphasis upon his being gainfully em-

---

[2] For example, in Adler's cohort, less than one-fourth of the patients were regularly employed and socially active one year after release. *Ibid.*

[3] John A. Clausen, *Sociology and the Field of Mental Health,* New York: Russell Sage Foundation, 1956, p. 9.

[4] Cf. Talcott Parsons, "An Analytical Approach to the Theory of Social Stratification," *Essays in Sociological Theory: Pure and Applied,* Glencoe, Ill.: Free Press, 1949, p. 174.

[5] In the longitudinal studies of rehabilitative process that constitute one of our principal research activities, we are working with a much broader concept of deviance than that implemented in the survey research reported in this paper. We are here concerned only with the tolerance of non-instrumental performance in role relationships where instrumental behavior is ordinarily prescribed. The objectives of our processual studies are to discern, along a time axis, what becomes viewed as deviant behavior on the part of the patient, by the patient himself as well as by his significant others; how much of this is viewed as problematic and by whom; the ways in which the problems are handled; and the thresholds or points at which deviance is no longer tolerated and cannot be handled within the network. It would be inappropriate to elucidate this statement here, but a paper on the conceptual analysis of deviance for purposes of our research is now in preparation.

[6] This observation is an illustration of the point advanced by Merton that the social structure may tend to insulate the individual from having his activities observed by those who would normally be his peers. Such insulation obviously results in a reduction of pressures for prescribed performance. Robert K. Merton, "The Role Set: Problems in Sociological Theory," *British Journal of Sociology,* 8 (June 1957), pp. 106–121.

ployed and, moreover, make few demands upon him to be socially active, he can exist as if in a one-person chronic ward, insulated from all but those in the highly tolerant household.

Investigation of the relationship between level of performance and structural and status variations in the residential settings of successful patients was a major purpose of a pilot investigation of a small number of patients and their families.[7] One of the principal findings of this exploratory study was that low levels of interpersonal performance are most tolerated in parental families where the patient occupies the status of "child." When patients were divided by level of performance into high and low groups, high level patients clustered in conjugal families or non-familial residences, while those with low levels were concentrated in parental families.[8] Further analysis indicated that this correlation between family type and performance level was not an artifact of associations between family type and either prehospital psychiatric state or psychiatric state at the time of release.

The finding was amplified by comparing, within the same cohort, those low level patients who were successful with those who were rehospitalized. Among the rehospitalized group, about as many came from parental families as there were low level patients living with parental families in the community. In contrast, there were four times as many returned to the hospital from conjugal families or non-familial settings as there were low level patients living in such settings in the community.

The finding that patients with a low level of performance who succeed in remaining in the community cluster in parental families is consistent with the fact that the role of the child in the parental family is the only social-biological role without expectations of instrumental performance. The child's role, regardless of age, consists largely of affective relations with parents and, compared with other family roles, is less concerned with instrumental performance.

To the extent that the grown-up "child" in the parental family has specific prescriptions built into his role, the structure of such families usually provides for alternate actors who can replace or supplement his performance when it is below expectation. Unlike spouses or those who live in non-familial settings, "children" are free of many of the stresses that accompany every other kin or household status.

On the basis of these findings, as well as upon differences in attitudes found to exist between relatives of patients with high and low levels of performance, a large-scale survey of female relatives of successful male patients was undertaken. In this paper, the first report of the survey, we report replication of the association between structural differences in the family settings of patients and performance levels.

---

[7] James A. Davis, Howard E. Freeman, and Ozzie G. Simmons, "Rehospitalization and Performance Level of Former Mental Patients," *Social Problems*, **5** (July, 1957), pp. 37–44.

[8] The patients were dichotomized so that those rated high: (1) worked full time or were solely responsible for the care of the home; (2) participated in informal and social activities about as often as other family members; (3) were able to relate well in the interview situation (as judged by a clinically sophisticated interviewer); and (4) were reported by their relatives to be recovered, active in the life of the family, and without such symptoms as periods of depression or hallucinations.

METHODOLOGY

The female informants interviewed were all relatives, predominantly wives and mothers, of male patients who have succeeded in remaining in the community since their latest release from a mental hospital sometime between November, 1954 and December, 1955. Every male patient with the following characteristics was included in the potential drawing group: between 20 and 60 years of age; white; native-born; living in the Boston area at the time of release; hospitalized more than 45 days prior to release; not physically handicapped to the extent of being unemployable; not addicted to narcotics; and not hospitalized primarily for acute alcoholism. By diagnosis, all were psychotics with non-organic, functional disorders, the majority diagnosed as schizophrenic. Each patient selected was last hospitalized in one of thirteen hospitals in the Boston area, of which nine are State, three Veterans Administration, and one private.

Preliminary screening of the patients was accomplished by examining the discharge forms at the State's central reporting agency.[9] The hospital records of all patients who initially met the criteria were thoroughly reviewed. From this more detailed source of information, it became clear that a number of patients who appeared eligible on the State forms actually did not meet all the criteria, and the drawing group was reduced to 294. We planned to interview a female relative in the household of each patient.[10] Except in cases where the hospital record clearly indicated that the patient was not living with his family, attempts were made to locate a female relative.[11]

Interviews were attempted in 209 of the 294 cases. The remaining cases consisted of five patients who lived in all male households, 64 who lived in non-familial settings, and 16 where the location of neither the patient nor his family could be discovered. It is probable that most of these 16 patients, even if living with families, no longer reside in the interviewing area, which comprises the whole of metropolitan Boston. Of the 209 interviews attempted, 182 were completed.[12] Thus 88 per cent of the attempted interviews were completed and, even if the 16 cases that could not be located are included, the loss rate is still under 20 per cent.[13]

Interviews averaged two hours and were conducted with a standardized schedule which contained items to elicit social data, particularly regarding family

[9] The cooperation of the Massachusetts Department of Mental Health, Dr. Jack Ewalt, Commissioner, is gratefully acknowledged, as is the advice and assistance provided by Dr. Thomas Pugh of the Department and his staff, and by the superintendents of the 13 cooperating hospitals.

[10] The difficulty of rating instrumentality of the "homemaker" role was only one of the reasons for restricting the informants to female relatives of male patients. These requirements also reduced variability in terms of both informants and patients. In addition, as survey research studies indicate, females are more likely to be at home and less likely to refuse to be interviewed.

[11] The informants were notified in advance by mail that they were to be interviewed. The letters were sent ordinary mail but the envelopes were stamped "Postmaster: DO NOT FORWARD, RETURN TO SENDER." Each one returned to us was sent out certified mail with a request for the new address. In this way it was possible to reach all cases in which there was a forwarding address on file. A second source of locating cases was the social service exchange.

[12] The important role of our eighteen interviewers is acknowledged. Most were social workers, though there were two resident psychiatrists and two social scientists.

[13] This loss rate is exceptionally low. In our exploratory study it was 45 per cent and in other cases of interviewing patients and their families, loss rates over 50 per cent are not unusual. Our refusal rate compares favorably with that encountered in studies of normal populations and in marketing research.

structure; attitudes toward mental hospitals, treatment and illness; and "personality" measures such as the F scale. In addition, the schedule included items to obtain information about the patient's pre- and posthospital work history and social life. For each of the 182 completed cases, the data available from the interview and hospital record occupy nearly 1,000 IBM columns. For all the cases, information on 15 background variables is available. There are no differences on these 15 variables between the 182 cases completed and the 27 refusals.

PERFORMANCE LEVEL AND FAMILY SETTING

The relationship between family setting and performance level uncovered in the exploratory study is clearly substantiated in this survey. Two separate measures of performance are employed which are modifications of work and social participation scales originally developed by Adler.[14] The high end of the six-point work performance scale includes those patients who have been continuously employed since their release, the low end those who have never worked since their release. As Table 1 indicates, patients who are husbands are almost exclusively concentrated on the high side and, conversely, patients who are sons cluster on the low side.

When social participation is employed as the measure of interpersonal performance, the same results occur. The highest category is composed of patients who belong to one or more voluntary associations and attend their meetings regularly, and who visit and are visited at least twice a month and at least as often as the rest of the household. Former patients in the lowest category do not belong to any voluntary associations, visit and are visited less than once a month and less frequently than other household members. Once again the results are striking, particularly when the cases are dichotomized.

[14] Adler, op. cit.

Table 1
Relationship between level of work performance and family setting

Level of performance		Family setting*			
		Parental		Conjugal	
		N	%	N	%
(High)	1	20	20.0	45	66.2
	2	11	11.0	14	20.6
	3	7	7.0	2	2.9
	4	5	5.0	4	5.9
	5	13	13.0	1	1.5
(Low)	6	44	44.0	2	2.9
Total		100	100.0	68	100.0

$r_{pbs} = .83$
* 14 cases living with siblings not included.

Table 2
Relationship between level of social participation and family setting

Level of performance		Family setting*			
		Parental		Conjugal	
		N	%	N	%
(High)	1	2	2.0	4	5.9
	2	16	16.0	23	33.8
	3	9	9.0	18	26.4
	4	18	18.0	8	11.8
	5	13	13.0	5	7.4
	6	11	11.0	4	5.9
(Low)	7	31	31.0	6	8.8
Total		100	100.0	68	100.0

$r_{pbs} = .53$
*14 cases living with siblings not included.

The Pearsonian correlation between the work and social participation ratings of interpersonal performance is .51. The magnitude of this correlation indicates that the two ratings are manifestations of a more general mode of interpersonal performance.[15] This is evident when the two ratings are dichotomized and then combined.

Our thesis regarding the relationship between the differential tolerance of family members and variations in levels of performance of patients who succeed in remaining in the community receives additional support when we consider patients from the cohort who were released during the same time period but subsequently rehospitalized. In the course of collecting information on the successful patients in the cohort, a record check was made of the "failures." These failures, it should be noted, include only patients released to the community and returned to the hospital after having been dropped from the hospital's books. Most of the patients not voluntarily committed are so dropped only after leaving bed and successfully remaining on trial visit in the community for one year. There are other variations in the release practices of hospitals. For example, patients whose prognosis is doubtful are sometimes released on extended leaves of absence and then discharged if they succeed in remaining in the community. However, if they "fail," it is not reflected in the records used to select the cohort. The failures whose records are available thus consist of the "best" of the failures in the sense that patients officially discharged are in the community the

---

[15] For purposes of future, more quantitative aspects of data analysis, distributions on the work and social participation ratings have been normalized, added together, and distributed into categories. The intercorrelations of either the raw or normalized work and social participation scores with this combined, standardized level of performance measure range between .80 and .90.

We wish to stress, however, that this study deals with level of performance as defined in terms of performance in work and social participation. The relationship between performance as so defined and the level of functioning of the patients from a psychiatric viewpoint has not been assessed. But it is our belief, based on our exploratory study where patients as well as relatives were interviewed and on the field work experience and judgments of our clinical staff, that the bulk of the "low" patients would be judged seriously disturbed by a psychiatrist, although we cannot present empirical evidence of this.

Table 3
Relationship between combined work and social
level of performance and family setting

Level of performance		Family setting*			
		Parental		Conjugal	
Work	Social	N	%	N	%
High (1–3)	High (1–3)	19	19.0	43	63.2
High (1–3)	Low (4–7)	19	19.0	18	26.5
Low (4–6)	High (1–3)	8	8.0	2	2.9
Low (4–6)	Low (4–7)	54	54.0	5	7.4
Total		100	100.0	68	100.0

$r_{pbs} = .60$
* 14 cases living with siblings not included.

longest time of all hospitalized patients given an opportunity to "leave bed."[16]

In Table 4, the family settings of the low level patients are compared with the settings at the time of rehospitalization of the official failures. Many more patients who last lived with conjugal families are back in the hospital in comparison with successful low level patients presently living with wives. In contrast, few patients whose last residence was with parents are back in the hospital in comparison with low level patients presently living in parental families. Table 4 presents these findings for each rating of performance level.

These results are consistent with our introductory remarks regarding more tolerant expectations toward those who occupy the status of "child." Over time it appears that a greater proportion of patients are returned to hospitals from conjugal families. In their entirety, these findings support the earlier exploratory study.

INFLUENCE OF PRIOR CONDITIONS

Considering the replicative nature of the investigation and the magnitude of the correlation, it is quite certain that the relationship between performance level and family setting is a stable one. Explanation of the differential performance of former patients, however, in terms of tolerance of deviance on the part of their significant others could represent an overemphasis upon the posthospital situation and a neglect of prehospital and hospital conditions. Our analysis of the influence of prior conditions has to depend upon hospital record data and retrospective information from the relative interviewed. Within the limits of accuracy and reliability of these types of data, our explanation of tolerance is not vitiated by this additional information.

[16] The problem of the use of legal definitions as criteria has been amply evaluated by the criminologist, whose comments are directly applicable to the field of mental health. It was possible, in our definition of success, to employ the more realistic one of the date the patient "left bed." It was more difficult to distinguish "failures" from patients not ever returned to the community. The hospitals are required to indicate the "left bed" date only when the case is officially "dropped" from the books.

Table 4
Family setting of patients rehospitalized and those with low level of performance who remain in the community

Rating		Family setting				
		Parental		Conjugal		
		N	%	N	%	r
Work rating						
Low level in						
community	(4–6)	62	65.3	7	25.9	
Rehospitalized		33	34.7	20	74.1	
Total		95	100.0	27	100.0	.33
Social rating						
Low level in						
community	(4–7)	73	68.9	23	53.5	
Rehospitalized		33	31.1	20	46.5	
Total		106	100.0	43	100.0	.15
Combined work-social rating						
Low level in						
community		54	62.1	5	20.0	
Rehospitalized		33	37.9	20	80.0	
Total		87	100.0	25	100.0	.35

Information from the hospital record eliminates the possibility that differences in hospital experience offer a satisfactory alternative explanation. There are no significant differences in performance level which can be accounted for in terms of such variables as type of hospital, diagnosis, type of psychiatric treatment, and ward mobility.

The influence of the prehospital condition of the patient presents a more complex set of relationships for analysis. There is considerable evidence that patients from parental families are more ill when hospitalized than those from conjugal families. Without reference to the data of this study, the argument can be advanced that marriage serves a screening function and "sicker" persons cluster in parental families before hospitalization since the "healthier" of the mentally ill are more likely to marry. Actually, in terms of similar measures of level of performance employed in the previous section of our analysis, but with reference to prehospital history, patients from parental families do have a lower performance level than do those from conjugal families.[17] Furthermore, the obvious point that patients "sicker" when hospitalized are generally "sicker" after release is confirmed by the correlation among patients studied between pre- and posthospital level of performance. On the basis of these findings, is the relationship between level of posthospital performance and family setting perhaps an artifact of differences in prehospital level of functioning of the patients?

While differences in prehospital levels of performance partly explain our find-

[17] Differences in number of times hospitalized and number of months hospitalized since first admitted to a mental hospital also suggest that patients from parental families tend to have lower prehospital levels of performance.

ings, several considerations strongly support the relevance of differential tolerance of deviance as a key variable in accounting for the range of variation in performance of successful patients during the posthospital period. First, the magnitude of the correlations between prehospital level of performance and family setting are substantially lower than those between posthospital level of performance and family setting. Second, if low level patients do cluster in parental families before as well as after hospitalization, a higher proportion of patients should be rehospitalized from parental as compared with conjugal families, unless rehospitalization is associated with differential conditions in posthospital settings. The same proportion are rehospitalized from the two types of settings, however, supporting our explanation of tolerance of deviance on the part of family members in the posthospital period. Moreover, as already reported in Table 4, the number of failures in relation to the number of patients rated "low" is much higher among those from conjugal settings.

Finally, when prehospital level of performance is controlled in the cross-tabulations, posthospital level of performance remains associated with family type, *within* prehospital level of performance groups, indicating that prehospital functioning, in itself, is an insufficient explanation.

Actually, the correlation between prehospital level of performance and family setting is support for our contention that tolerance of deviance is a key variable. While of special significance during the posthospital period, undoubtedly the importance of the tolerance of family members is not unique to this period but crucial to understanding the process of hospitalization as well as rehospitalization. Mothers, compared with wives, are more likely to tolerate deviant performance before the admission of the patient to the hospital, as well as between subsequent readmissions.[18] The person with a low level of interpersonal performance is probably less likely to be hospitalized if living in a parental family, as well as less likely to be rehospitalized if returned to the community in a similar state.

CONCLUSIONS

In this survey of families of male mental patients living in the community, we have found a high correlation between level of performance and family setting. Unlike the exploratory study upon which this survey is based, we have attempted to control variations which might account for the relationship. This replication, with its added controls, convinces us of the stability of the finding. However, several qualifications regarding its generality should be noted:

1. With the exception of the few cases where an interview was refused, the

[18] The tolerance of wives, compared with mothers, probably decreases after the patient's first hospital experience. Wives, emancipated from the patient during hospitalization, are more likely to find, in terms of complementary systems of emotional gratification as well as everyday activities, that they can get along as well or better without their mates. Mothers could not as easily move to such a position. Clausen and Yarrow imply that wives are likely to regard the behavior of husbands, after release, without much tolerance, and the recurrence of the husband's illness as "the last straw." John A. Clausen and Marian Radke Yarrow, "Further Observations and Some Implications," *Journal of Social Issues*, 11 (1955), p. 62.

results are based upon all cases in a preselected cohort of patients. Unlike most survey research, where a sample is interviewed and findings generalized to a population, our findings are limited, in the strict sense, to the cases at hand.

2. Clearly, generalization to groups of patients excluded from the cohort— such as Negroes, foreign-born, and psychotics with organic disorders—is precarious. Although female patients were not included in this research, they were considered in the earlier, exploratory study. On the basis of the results of the earlier study, we believe that the present findings and their implications also apply to female patients.

3. A number of patients who do not live with their families succeed in remaining in the community. Of male patients whose social background and diagnosis are similar to those studied here, probably only seventy or eighty per cent live with their families. Questions regarding the relationship between performance level and residential setting of some twenty to thirty per cent remain unanswered. Nevertheless, we believe that non-familial settings provide functional equivalents in the form of surrogate mothers and wives, and that patterns would be found similar to those depicted in this study of patients with families.

Future reports of the analysis of the survey will amplify the data discussed here by specification of structural distinctions *within* parental and conjugal settings. Though we have confined this report to structural differences, data processing has advanced considerably further. The additional analysis supports the basic proposition underlying the survey, namely that differences in family structure and attitudes, personality, and behavior of family members are associated with level of performance of mental patients who succeed in remaining in the community.

We believe that the findings reported here, in themselves, are of considerable interest from both a psychiatric and sociological point of view. The relationship between family setting and performance level should be of concern to practitioners associated with mental hospitals in planning the release of the patient and in prognosticating his posthospital behavior. If the goal of treatment is only the permanent or semi-permanent separation of hospital and patient, the release of patients to parental families would appear to be an efficient practice. While effective in freeing a hospital bed, however, releasing the patient to the tolerant milieu which tends to predominate in the parental family may be the most inadequate community setting if movement toward instrumental performance is a desired outcome of hospitalization. Return of the patient to the parental family, where there is less likely to be an expectation of instrumental performance, may well occasion regression from, rather than movement toward, better functioning, and eliminate any gains of a therapeutic hospital experience.

The findings are particularly relevant for the sociological study of deviance. In terms of our measures of instrumental performance—work and social participation—the question can be raised whether differences between mothers and wives in tolerance of deviance is peculiar to the perception of the person as a mental patient. Are mothers and wives of, e.g., drug addicts, alcoholics, and the physically handicapped differentially distributed in degree of tolerance when the definition of deviance is with respect to instrumental performance?

Finally, we are convinced that it is the differential *quality* of the role relationships which is critical to understanding the influence of significant others in the posthospital experience of the patient. For example, with respect to the role of the patient in the family, there is the question of the availability of functionally equivalent actors to occupy the normally prescribed roles. Patients who are husbands probably are tolerated more often in non-instrumental roles when there are other adult males in the household to occupy the instrumental roles. Conversely, sons who are patients are probably least tolerated in the parental family when no other male actors are available to take instrumental roles. Such speculations can be partly verified and assessed by further analysis of our survey data, but problems of this order also require longitudinal investigations that employ repeated interviewing. Our research strategy includes cross-sectional surveys, of the kind reported here, and processual studies for observation and assessment of change. Both are necessary for systematic inquiry into the posthospital experience of former mental patients.

43
PSYCHIATRIC AND SOCIAL ATTRIBUTES AS PREDICTORS OF CASE OUTCOME IN MENTAL HOSPITALIZATION

Simon Dinitz, Mark Lefton, Shirley Angrist and Benjamin Pasamanick*

A continuing source of difficulty in mental health research, as in many other aspects of the behavioral sciences, is the chronic inability to predict behavior prospectively. The difficulty in accurately predicting case outcome is particularly acute in the institutional area where an ever increasing number of persons must be cared for and treated and where decisions must constantly be made about readiness for discharge based upon reasonably efficient criteria of outcome.

The difficulty in predicting posthospital adjustment derives in part from the lack of understanding of the etiology of most of the mental diseases. It also derives to a considerable extent, however, from the variety and diversity of objective and subjective factors—prehospital, hospital and posthospital—which seem to play some role, singly and in combination, in determining posthospital success and failure and adequacy of functioning.

These formidable obstacles, fortunately, have not prevented researchers from

Source: Simon Dinitz, Mark Lefton, Shirley S. Angrist, and Benjamin Pasamanick, "Psychiatric and Social Attributes as Predictors of Case Outcome in Mental Hospitalization," *Social Problems*, **8:** 322–328, 1961.
* The outcome study reported in this paper was made possible by a National Institute of Mental Health grant, M-2953. During the course of the study, S. Angrist held a pre-doctoral fellowship from NIMH, United States Public Health Service.

investigating prehospital and posthospital variables as they may relate to case outcome. Simmons and Freeman suggest, by implication, that psychiatric and other medical aspects are less important in determining case outcome than are the attitudes of relatives to whom the patient is returned.[1] Brown has found that the type of living arrangement to which patients were returned was the most significant factor in their success or failure.[2] Others have reasoned that the nature of hospital treatment procedures may be effective in keeping patients out of the hospital and functioning in the community. Related to these findings, although not precisely of the same nature, are the results obtained in incidence and prevalence studies such as those of Rennie and associates,[3] and Hollingshead and Redlich,[4] which emphasize socio-economic variables as determinative of who receives attention, the source of the treatment, the type of treatment, the duration of treatment, psychiatric diagnosis and eventually the re-entry into treatment.

This paper is wholly concerned with the extent to which psychiatric variables on the one hand and objective social attributes on the other are (a) predictive of success or failure in outcome, the latter defined as rehospitalization within six months after discharge, and (b) these same variables can foretell the level of patient functioning of those who remain in the community.

METHOD

The Columbus Psychiatric Institute and Hospital, an intensive therapy, short-term, heavily staffed institution discharged 376 female patients in the period December 1, 1958 through July 31, 1959. Of these released patients, 287 were studied intensively. Hospital and background data were also gathered for the remaining 89 cases who were excluded from the follow-up because they were either (a) returned to communities outside of the thirteen county area served by the hospital, or (b) transferred to another hospital within two weeks after initial hospital release.

The total failure rate for the entire population of 376 cases was 26 per cent including transfers to other hospitals; of the 287 study cases, 41 or 14 per cent were rehospitalized within six months after release.

In order to measure the level of patient functioning after discharge, trained and experienced psychiatric social workers conducted lengthy and structured interviews with the former patients and with a significant other, usually the husband, of each. The quality of posthospital patient performance was derived from responses to three scales in the interview schedules of the significant other.

[1] Howard E. Freeman and Ozzie G. Simmons, "Mental Patients in the Community: Family Settings and Performance Levels," *American Sociological Review*, 23 (April, 1958), pp. 147–154.

[2] George W. Brown, "Experiences of Discharged Chronic Schizophrenic Patients in Various Types of Living Groups," *Milbank Memorial Fund Quarterly*, 37 (April, 1959), pp. 105–131.

[3] Thomas A. C. Rennie and Leo Srole, "Social Class Prevalence and Distribution of Psychosomatic Conditions in an Urban Population," *Psychosomatic Medicine*, 18 (November–December, 1956), pp. 1–21.

[4] August B. Hollingshead and Frederick C. Redlich, *Social Class and Mental Illness*, New York: Wiley, 1958.

These scales consisted of (a) a 32 item index of psychological functioning taken in part from the Lorr Multidimensional Scale for Rating Psychiatric Patients, in part from a similar index utilized by Simmons and Freeman and in part from items developed by us, (b) a domestic functioning scale of nine items dealing with the patient's performance of routine duties customarily associated with the female role, and (c) a social participation index consisting of 11 items.[5]

Together these three indices comprised the total functioning of the patient in the community. On the basis of total scores on the combined index which ranged theoretically from 52 for the poorest possible functioner to 222 for the very best posthospital performer, patients were arbitrarily assigned to three functioning categories—low, medium and high.[6] Approximately one-third of the patients fell into each of these three classifications.

Independent evaluations, comparable to our psychological functioning index were also obtained. Two staff psychiatrists interviewed a total of 65 of the 287 patients. Their evaluations were found to be positively associated with those obtained from the significant others although the assessments of one psychiatrist were closer to those of the husbands than were the assessments of the second psychiatrist.[7]

In order to gather systematic information on the psychiatric and objective social attributes of the patients, a hospital record schedule form was developed which contained 88 different specific questions to be answered from the hospital records. When the records were incomplete on given items, patient charts and nursing and medical notes were consulted. Finally, when possible, comparable information was obtained in the interviews as another method of measuring reliability of patient and significant other responses and of confirming the hospital record information. Very little difference was found in contrasting the information contained in hospital records and in interview responses.

FINDINGS

Two general findings should be noted at the outset of this presentation. First, with only one exception, the various medical-psychiatric attributes of patients, including ward assignments, were less predictive of either rehospitalization or of posthospital level of functioning than were the social background attributes. Second, patients who were successful in remaining in the community but were classified as poor or low level functioners on the basis of their psychological and domestic performance and in their social participation were in some respects more similar to the rehospitalized patients than they were to the moderate or

[5] Copies of the scales can be obtained from the Columbus Psychiatric Institute and Hospital.

[6] The mean scores for these categories are 142.3, 160.5 and 172.2 respectively and are significantly different from each other (CR's $< .01$).

[7] For a more complete report of these relationships see Benjamin Pasamanick and Leonard Ristine, "Differential Assessment of Post-Hospital Psychological Functioning: Evaluations by Psychiatrists and Relatives," *American Journal of Psychiatry*, in press.

high level functioners. This would indicate that additional hospital returnees will probably be drawn from this category of patients.

MEDICAL-PSYCHIATRIC ATTRIBUTES AND CASE OUTCOME

Ward assignment

Ward assignment ordinarily cannot be construed as a relevant psychiatric variable in case outcome. However, when patients are randomly assigned to three hospital wards on the basis of available bed space and are subjected to widely different ward treatment procedures, ward assignment becomes of necessity a meaningful medical factor in predicting outcome. Elsewhere we have tried to indicate that the three hospital wards housing female patients did in fact differ widely in their policies and practices with regard to patient care and treatment.[8] It was shown that these differences seemed to have little bearing on the overt behavior of the patients on the wards; indeed, that overt patient functioning did not differ from one ward to another. It is now possible to indicate that ward differences do not seem to be of much significance for outcome either. The data were analyzed in several ways. First, of all females released from the hospital, including transfers to other hospitals and out-of-area cases, the results indicate that the percentage of successful cases from each of the three wards was 74.2, 77.4 and 68.3 per cent respectively. Second, including only the interview cases, the comparable success percentages were 84.0, 83.0 and 88.6. In other words, once the transfers are excluded from consideration, the wards do not appreciably differ in their success and failure rates. Third, of the patients labelled as successful by dint of their ability to remain in the community at least six months, no differences, by ward, were found in their level of posthospital performance.

Admissions, illness duration, length of hospitalization

Rehospitalized patients could not be differentiated from successful patients nor successful cases from each other by functioning category in terms of their total number of previous admissions, illness duration preceding hospitalization or in their length of hospital stay. Two-thirds of all patients, regardless of outcome, had been first admissions. Illness duration prior to hospitalization varied from 5.4 years for the rehospitalized, 6.8 years for low functioners, 6.2 years for medium outcome cases and 5.6 years for high functioners. These differences were not statistically significant for any two of the groups or for all four groups considered simultaneously. Similarly, the length of hospitalization was greatest for the returnees (58.6 days on the average) and lowest for the low and moderate

[8] Simon Dinitz, Mark Lefton, Jon Simpson, Benjamin Pasamanick, and Ralph Patterson, "The Ward Behavior of Psychiatric Patients," *Social Problems*, 6 (Fall, 1958), pp. 107–115.

functioners (49 days). Nevertheless, even the most extreme differences in this respect were of no statistical consequence.

Diagnosis

There is little doubt that hospital diagnosis is of importance in predicting outcome. Both the returnees (19.5 per cent), and the low functioners (23.1 per cent) were clearly overrepresented among the patients diagnosed as indicating either acute or chronic brain syndromes. When the organic cases were eliminated from consideration, however, the percentages of psychotic and non-psychotic patients did not vary appreciably in the four outcome groups. Hence, a diagnosis of organic damage is an excellent predictor of poor outcome or rehospitalization. Unfortunately, other diagnoses fail to differentiate among outcome groups.

Addiction

As expected, favorable outcome seems to depend on the absence of addictions which are often related to mental disorder. There is, for example, a clear gradient among the outcome categories as regards alcohol and drug complicated cases. Of the returnees, 17.1 per cent had a history of alcoholism or drug addiction. The percentages for the low, medium and high functioners were 12.7, 12.3 and 3.9, respectively. In interviewing the significant others, it was found that a binge or chronic abuse of alcohol was not infrequently the major consideration of the significant other in returning the patient to this or another mental hospital.

Hospital treatment

No significant differences, as already noted, were observed with regard to length of hospitalization and case outcome. Similarly, being subjected to electroconvulsive therapy did not seem to make any appreciable difference in outcome. In general, a smaller percentage of the poorer functioners and returnees received electro-shock treatment probably because of the greater frequency of organic cases among them, than of the moderate and high functioners. On the other hand, a greater percentage of returnees and low functioners (51 per cent) than of moderate and high functioners (34 per cent) were treated with drugs during the course of their hospitalization. The differences in drug treatment were statistically significant.

Release and prognosis at discharge

The type of discharge granted the patients in the four outcome categories did not vary significantly. The only observable discrepancy involved the greater pro-

portion of trial visit discharges in the returnee group (26.8 per cent) as contrasted with the other three groups (14.6 per cent). Discharges contrary to medical advice (AMA) or without leave (AWOL) were lowest in the returnee and
high functioning group (17.1 per cent) and highest for the moderate functioners
(29.2 per cent).

The inability to accurately predict outcome is best demonstrated by the therapists' prognosis ratings of patients at discharge. Favorable prognoses were given
18.2 per cent of the returnees, 10.4 per cent of the low functioners, 24.6 per
cent of the moderate functioners and 31.7 per cent of the high performers. On
the other hand, the percentages of unimproved patients varied from 13.4 per
cent for the low functioners to 7.9 per cent of the high functioners with only
9.1 per cent of the returnees being rated as unimproved.

Using therapists' ratings again, the four outcome groups were seen as being
very similar in the extent of their impairment at admission and also at discharge.
Whatever differences in these ratings did occur seemed to indicate the more
severe impairment of the low performers. It is interesting to find that a third of
all the patients were seen as being moderately or severely impaired at discharge
and that the 43.7 per cent of the low functioners in this category was only very
slightly above the entire group average in this respect.

Finally, data were also obtained on the posthospital treatment of the 287
patients. Approximately one-fifth of them in all outcome categories received no
such posthospital services. Some 30 per cent either received additional outpatient
care from our hospital or from private practitioners. Returnees most frequently
availed themselves of this help (35.1 per cent) and low functioners did so in
lesser numbers (17.9 per cent). On the other hand, three-fifths of the low functioners and two-fifths of the others received non-psychiatric medical attention
after discharge.

OBJECTIVE SOCIAL ATTRIBUTES
AND CASE OUTCOME

Whereas the preceding section has indicated that the medical psychiatric variables, with the exception of diagnosis, are at best only very poor predictors of
outcome, the results to follow indicate that a much stronger case can be made
for the relation of objective social variables and outcome.

Age, race, religion and rural-urban residence

Because of the relative homogeneity of the female patient population, minimal
differences were found in age, race, religion or rural-urban residence of the
patients. Patients in all four outcome groups were approximately 40 years of age,
predominantly white (87 per cent), Protestant (81 per cent) and urban (83 per
cent). On the other hand, marital status, family type, education and social class
were related to case outcome.

Family variables

Simmons and Freeman have previously shown that male ex-patients who are married are better functioners than patients in other marital categories.[9] They interpreted this to mean that wives are less tolerant of deviant behavior than are mothers, for example, and that they expect better performance from the former patients. The patient then is in a situation in which he either lives up to these expectations or is returned to the hospital. A second explanation, i.e., that the sicker patients generally fail to marry, has also been posited. Although these two explanations are not, by any means, incompatible, our data tend to support the former and refute the latter in this instance.

In order to test the thesis that married patients tend to be less ill at both admission and at discharge than are single or divorced and separated female patients, an analysis was made using (a) the therapists' ratings of patient psychiatric impairment at admission and at discharge and also their prognosis of outcome, and (b) four scales—the Schizophrenia, Depression, Psychiasthenia, and Hypochondriasis—of the MMPI, which is routinely administered at admission and discharge. A second analysis compared the MMPI results and the psychiatric impairment at admission and at discharge and prognosis of patients returning to one of eight types of living arrangement, e.g., conjugal, parental, sibling, child, non-kin, alone, etc.

The results of these analyses indicated that the degree of psychiatric disability at admission and at discharge as rated by the therapist as well as his prognosis of outcome was not at all related to the marital status of the patients or the type of household to which they were returned. The same held for the MMPI results.

Thus, marital status and living arrangements after discharge were not selective of differentially impaired patients. Yet these same variables were found to be very highly related to posthospital functioning. Married patients were found to be underrepresented among the low functioners and overrepresented among the high performers. Parental families housed more of the low functioners and few of those rehospitalized. The specific details follow.

Less than half (46.8 per cent) of the low functioners, three-fifths of the moderate functioners and four-fifths of the high performers, were married. On the other hand, seven out of ten of the returnees also were married. Further, 43 per cent of the low, three-fifths of the moderate and three-fourths of the high performers were residing with their spouses as were 59 per cent of the returnees prior to rehospitalization. To make the same point another way, the returnees were very similar to the moderate and high functioners in being married and living with their spouses prior to rehospitalization.

Of the 24 patients who returned to their parents, few (8.3 per cent) were rehospitalized and a great many (41.7 per cent) were low performers. Of the 159 who were returned to their spouses more (14.5 per cent) were rehospitalized

[9] Howard E. Freeman and Ozzie G. Simmons, *op. cit.;* Howard E. Freeman and Ozzie G. Simmons, "Wives, Mothers, and Posthospital Performance Levels," *Social Forces,* **37** (December, 1958), pp. 153–159; Ozzie G. Simmons and Howard E. Freeman, "Familial Expectations and Posthospital Performance of Mental Patients," *Human Relations,* **12** (August, 1959), pp. 233–242.

but far fewer (21.4 per cent) were poor performers. Of the 85 patients who lived in a non-parental, or non-conjugal household or alone, a relatively high proportion (16.5 per cent) were rehospitalized and a high proportion (41.2 per cent) were performing poorly.

Not only will patients returned to a conjugal family perform better, but those returning to households with young children requiring care and attention and devoid of other adult females who can provide this care will do even better. Of the 182 patients who returned to a household in which there were no other adult females only 12.6 per cent were rehospitalized and an additional fourth were poor performers. On the other hand, significantly more of the patients returned to families having other adult females were both rehospitalized and functioned poorly. Again, Simmons and Freeman appear to be correct when they argue that patients do better when role replacements are unavailable.

Social class variables

The data indicate that class variables also seem to play a major role in outcome. Good posthospital performance appears to be related to relatively high educational attainment and socio-economic status. The fewest returnees came from the college educated group (9.4 per cent) and of those who had attended college, two-fifths proved to be high performers. The contrast between the college educated and those patients with only a grade school education was pronounced. Of the latter, 12.8 per cent were rehospitalized, two-fifths functioned poorly and only one-fifth were among the high performers.

Finally, on the basis of a number of social class measures drawn from both the Warner Index of Status Characteristics and Hollingshead's Index of Social Position, low performers were observed to be drawn from the lower socio-economic segments of the hospital discharges, high performers from the highest socio-economic status segment, and returnees and moderate performers were representative of the middle hospital social status category.[10]

DISCUSSION

The findings in this paper lend additional evidence to the proposition that the posthospital family milieu and the socio-economic status of the patient are fairly accurate predictors of case outcome. The hard psychiatric variables, on the other hand, seem to be relatively unimportant in assessing the recovery potential and posthospital performance of former mental patients.

The chief contribution of these data lies in their confirmation of hypotheses and conclusions previously suggested or reached by others. First, these results seem to substantiate the hypothesis that, when the degree of illness is controlled, familial variables seem to be extremely significant in determining case outcome. Married females are better posthospital performers than are single or divorced and separated women. Married women returned to a conjugal or nuclear family

---

[10] These findings will be more fully discussed in a forthcoming paper.

setting are superior functioners. The seemingly best posthospital functioners are married women, of relatively high socio-economic status residing in nuclear households, having relatively young children, and without other adult females to serve as role replacements. It is helpful, too, if they have been diagnosed as non-organic but it makes little difference whether they are classed as psychotic or non-psychotic.

The dynamics underlying the success of patients returned to this type of setting are suggested to be largely subjective (attitudinal) in nature. The significant others of patients in these households are likely to have high expectations for performance, the former patients themselves are also likely to expect more of themselves, their significant others are unlikely to be very tolerant of deviant behavior in the patient and greater external demands are likely to impinge upon them. These greater pressures for success and for a return to "normalcy" and to the fulfillment of the prerequisites of the female role are likely therefore to be translated into better posthospital performance.

One might even interpret these results to mean that the posthospital image by others of the patient as "sick" or not fully recovered or requiring special handling is self-defeating; that the redefinition of the patient as "well" and as one who should perform the routine female role(s) will result in superior functioning. The households containing the better functioners were, by their very nature, those in which the "sick" role could not be maintained.

If this interpretation, admittedly laced with a good deal of speculation but nonetheless consistent with previous findings is realistic, then certain practical consequences for patient care follow. Briefly, those would include minimizing the patients' "sick" role in the hospital by providing hospital tasks for patients to perform consistent with the extent of their disability, broadening of these responsibilities prior to release, and pre-release and posthospital counseling of family members as to the ability of the patient to assume certain obligations and responsibilities. It may even be that patients should be discouraged from returning to parental situations or to those in which role replacements are available. Before recommending these measures, however, a great deal of further inquiry into these matters is mandatory inasmuch as our data are as yet far too limited in scope and range for any but purely hypothetical suggestions to emerge.

44
SOCIAL REHABILITATION FOR MENTAL PATIENTS
Mary B. Palmer

For many patients the day of discharge from a mental hospital is not a joyous homecoming but the beginning of an isolation more complete than that in the

Source: Mary B. Palmer, "Social Rehabilitation for Mental Patients," Mental Hygiene, 42: 24–28, 1958.

hospital they have left. Although they may find jobs, at the end of the day they have no social life. Too many seclude themselves in rented rooms, and live alone, afraid, and sometimes ashamed. Others may confine themselves to the tight family group in which they originally fell ill. They do not know how to go about making friends nor where to look for them. Agencies and clubs in the community exist, but they cannot bring themselves to join.

To meet the need of this kind of patient, clubs for ex-patients have been springing up all over the country in the last few years. (Some also specialize in out-patients or include them as members.) A recent survey[1] reveals at least 24 independent groups, plus Recovery Incorporated with its headquarters in Chicago and some 180 loosely affiliated branches in 20 states. The independent clubs are variously sponsored by the hospitals themselves, mental health associations or state mental health departments or, occasionally, by ex-patients on their own. Although some clubs include therapy groups, vocational help and mental health education for both their members and the public, most focus on recreation. The club becomes the place to meet people, to learn to dance or try a new craft, to set off for a picnic or the local bowling alley. It offers members a chance to develop social confidence in company with others who have similar problems in an environment where they will not be shunned, ridiculed or pitied.

But the club movement is young and rather fragile. Average attendance at meetings seems to range from only 10 to 50, with most clubs somewhere in between. Some have started up only to fade again in a year or two. No national organization exists comparable to Alcoholics Anonymous, although Recovery Incorporated, which goes beyond socialization to offer a kind of self-help system somewhat similar to A.A., appears to be growing steadily.

Apparently mental illness has not yet achieved the social acceptance of alcoholism. There is still fear, folklore and stigma attached to it, especially when it includes hospitalization.

Secondly, mental illness includes a wide range of symptoms in people of diverse personalities. The alcoholic shares drinking as a common symptom with all other alcoholics. Even the epileptic can find affinity with others in his "league." But the mentally and emotionally ill have no specific habit or physical symptom to focus on together. Moreover, the degree of illness and the extent to which it permeates the whole personality differ. And some patients who are among the most isolated do not consider themselves as ill at all.

Finally, many discharged patients want to forget their hospital experience as quickly as they can, or are under pressure to do so from family and friends.

For all these reasons, clubs for mental patients usually adopt ambiguous or innocuous names. Unlike Alcoholics Anonymous, which blatantly announces its membership in its very name, these clubs hide behind such titles as Friendship or Beacon or 103. Even Recovery is not precise as to what its members are recovering from. Social Renascence in Columbus and Fight Against Fears in Chicago are only slightly more explicit.

In England, where the club movement seems to be more firmly entrenched, the generic term is more realistic: "therapeutic social clubs." At least 40 of them

---

[1] The rehabilitation project at the Massachusetts Mental Health Center in Boston under the direction of Dr. Milton Greenblatt, assistant superintendent and research director.

exist today, attached to mental hospitals as part of their after-care program. That they are taken seriously seems to be proved by the number in which a psychiatrist attends as adviser even when meetings are held after working hours. Dr. Joshua Bierer, director of the Marlborough Day Hospital (which alone has 9 clubs), believes that the patient's participation in a social therapeutic club can bring on real changes in his personality—even without conscious insight. Dr. Maxwell Jones of the Belmont Hospital social rehabilitation unit rarely misses a Wednesday evening club meeting of the "graduates" from his largely psychopathic "therapeutic community."

Few American clubs have psychiatrists as closely associated with them as in England, nor such enthusiastic medical backing. Most of the independent clubs have social workers as advisers. The Resthaven Recovery Group in Los Angeles is led by a psychiatrist but this is not so much a social as an educational organization with lectures and movies in mental health. Dr. Melvin F. Blaurock, Chicago neuropsychiatrist, started Fight Against Fears about two years ago, but he and his assistants are only occasional visitors to the club, which otherwise runs under its own steam. The Out-Patient Club at the Menninger Clinic in Topeka has firm clinic backing and employs a social group worker as adviser but encourages the member-officers to plan and organize their own programs as much as possible. Their dances, play-readings and game nights are popular, and members have even put on a skit panning their own propensity for boasting about their symptoms.

In fact, most clubs in this country emphasize self-government and individual responsibility. While the English sometimes express misgivings that too much autonomy may lead to dictatorship by an aggressive minority, most American clubs seem willing to take the chance. A more frequent complaint heard here is that no one emerges in the club with any leadership ability, or that the more capable members leave as they have less need for the club.

Club 103 in Boston is an example of the self-government theory in action. Taking its name from its original street address, the club serves discharged patients from the Massachusetts Mental Health Center (formerly Boston Psychopathic Hospital) from which it draws official support. It originated as the natural sequel to patient government in the hospital. A social worker and psychiatrist are joint advisers to the club, but hospital policy is to encourage the ex-patient members to run their own affairs, without any staff at meetings. Although club fortunes have consequently varied with the leadership, there is a solid core of devoted and enthusiastic members. One young woman member recently put it this way: "The club has given me confidence in facing people. Going to parties here gave me courage to try on the 'outside.'" The club is thought of as a transition between hospital and community, although members may continue to come to meetings as long as they wish. Two ex-patients worked with the staff to start the club. One of these continues with the club, although she no longer holds office, seeing her work as a contribution to mental health.

Fountain House in New York City is probably the best known of the clubs, although it has branched out now to include pre-vocational training, job counseling and group therapy. Started by ex-patients and volunteers, it is now directed by a full-time social worker and psychologist. While most clubs meet in church parlors or the Y, this organization has its own 4-story house on the West Side. Its namesake in Philadelphia is newer and smaller, but also can claim its own quarters. Now carrying on a big public education program with good community backing, it started originally as the single-handed effort of a briefly hospitalized former school teacher.

Recovery Unlimited in Lincoln, Neb., was founded in 1953 by three former patients of the Nebraska State Hospital, one of whom had been hospitalized 18 years. Members now hire a clinical psychologist one evening a week to moderate—but not direct—discussions. At other meetings the general public has been invited in, and the program chairman reports healthy support and interest.

SEARCH is another autonomous club. It originated in a pinochle game in which two ex-patients joked about starting an organization for "crackpots." The president, a patient at Binghampton State Hospital for 19 months, has recently left the club in other hands to devote himself to publishing a mimeographed newsletter of interest to ex-patients across the country. It contains news of club activities, problems of patients in adjusting to life outside the hospital, and a sturdy correspondence from interested people, including professionals. The publication is also called SEARCH.

Recovery Incorporated is more therapeutic than social in intent and uses a system in some ways similar to A.A. Started in 1937 by Chicago neuropsychiatrist Dr. Abraham Low for his own patients, the organization has carried on without medical leadership since his death in 1954.

Recovery meetings are directed by persons who have themselves been mentally or emotionally ill. The leader selects a panel of members each week to discuss the meaning to each individual of one of the chapters in Dr. Low's book *Mental Health through Will Training*. Focus is on everyday experiences and the futility of sick behavior, somewhat reminiscent of the "educational" approach of the late Dr. Austin Riggs of Stockbridge, Mass. Accent is on success, and both leader and group praise the member who has made a step forward.

For example, at a recent meeting in Baltimore, an immigrant woman proudly described her persistence in hunting for work even after being turned down three times. Before joining Recovery a few months before, she said, she would have crawled home to bed to sob to herself that she was persecuted for being "foreign." A factory foreman told how he overcame a crippling resentment toward a newly-hired college boy. At another club, in Stamford, Conn., a storekeeper compared Recovery to "going to school again—only here you graduate when you're ready."

This latter group in Stamford was initiated through the efforts of Dr. Stanley R. Dean, a local psychiatrist, who interested one of his private patients in organizing it, plus a group in Greenwich. He sees Recovery as offering the patient an opportunity to help himself, to give service to others and to have a group experience. He believes it is a very useful adjunct to psychotherapy, and no more of a rival to therapy than church work or service in a useful civic organization. Members of the two clubs include both neurotics and psychotics in remission.

Some clubs for ex-patients invite relatives, and occasionally friends, to visit or actually to join. From this source an English psychiatrist has reported acquiring new patients who might never have sought professional help, or only in the later, and tougher, stage of their illness. The Canadian Mental Health Association in Saskatchewan now operates a rehabilitation center in which both ex-patients and their relatives are active. They have a carefully planned and professionally directed program. The Mental Health Association in Tucson, Ariz., has only married couples in its Friendship Club.

Carrying the club idea a step further are the "half-way houses" in which ex-patients without suitable homes can live until they are ready to establish a place of their own. Usually they are expected to take jobs in the community, but policies are flexible and periods of unemployment tolerated. Three such hostels now are fairly well established in this country. They are Portals House in San Francisco (for male veterans), Rutland Corner House in Boston (for women from the Mental Health Center), and a house for women patients from the Vermont State Hospital sponsored by the Division of Vocational Rehabilitation. In England, the S.O.S. Society runs such an organization for discharged male patients and includes vocational training, while the Marlborough Day Hospital is experimenting with a patient-operated hostel on a small scale. Many mental hospitals in both countries have shown great interest in developing the idea further.

The question naturally arises as to which kinds of patients benefit most from social therapeutic clubs in all their variations, and just how much of a contribution such clubs can make. There has been no definitive research on this, although the Fellowship Club in San Francisco has a special research grant to study the whole question. All that is known now is that existing clubs serve almost every diagnostic category among both neurotic and formerly psychotic patients.

Isolation and loneliness are common in the mentally and emotionally ill. The therapeutic social club in all its variations from recreation to "will-training" offers social rehabilitation, strengthening of self-confidence and an opportunity for responsibility and service. As the movement grows, perhaps members will, in their turn, "rehabilitate" the general public in its outmoded attitude toward mental illness.

45
THE SOCIAL ORGANIZATION AND CULTURE
OF A CLUB FOR FORMER MENTAL PATIENTS[1]

David Landy and Sara E. Singer

Social clubs for former psychiatric patients are based upon the assumption that when some patients leave the hospital they may benefit from being members of

Source: David Landy and Sara E. Singer, "The Social Organization and Culture of a Club for Former Mental Patients," *Human Relations,* **14:** 31–40, 1961.
[1] One of a series of studies on aspects of psychiatric rehabilitation at the Massachusetts Mental Health Center (Boston), under a grant by the Office of Vocational Rehabilitation, U.S. Department of Health, Education, and Welfare.

a voluntary group with other former patients. Sponsors believe that these types of organization have therapeutic and rehabilitative effects that aid the patient over the transition from hospital subculture to community culture, a process fraught with potential cultural and personal discontinuities (Bierer, 1948; Blair, 1955; Landy, 1958b; Mishler, Landy, & Guiness, in press; Wechsler, in press).

Surveys of such clubs over the United States and England revealed that forty-two independent expatient groups exist in the United States, of which the majority were established in the last decade, and over 200 in England (Palmer, 1958; Wechsler, in press). The nature of such clubs varies widely and may be conceptualized as a continuum which at one end is characterized largely by self-governed, usually autonomous bodies, which function with occasional assistance from hospital personnel or community professionals (psychiatrists, social workers, psychologists), usually paid for consultation. The club with which this paper is concerned is an example. At the other end would be the types of clubs which function mainly in England (under Joshua Bierer, Maxwell Jones, and others), organized as an arm or extension of the hospital. These are considered as additional modes of treatment, and recommendations are made by a doctor for a patient to enter club activities as part of his total rehabilitative program (Bierer, 1948; Blair, 1955). (Such prescriptions happen only infrequently in the club under study.)

At times a club movement may reach the proportions of a kind of cult, with highly ritualized and formalized behavior, with a charismatic leader who expounds the Word, and with a dogma and exegesis. An example is Recovery, Incorporated, with its late founder and leader, Dr. Abraham Low, and his book, *Mental health through will training,* which became a kind of "bible" for these clubs (Wechsler, 1960).

At the autonomous end, too, are clubs such as Search, organized by expatients themselves, operating completely free of institutional ties, issuing a mimeographed "newspaper" with an increasingly wide circulation, running a broad campaign against presumed substandard conditions in hospitals and for mental health. Such a club may offer the expatient with feelings against the hospital a weapon by which he may wreak vengeance on all who have "wronged" him. In some cases, also, it may perform a public education function by spreading knowledge concerning mental health and treatment.

Palmer (1958) feels there are three reasons why the social therapeutic club movement has not advanced even further than it has:

1 Apparently mental illness has not yet been accepted widely in the same way as, say, alcoholism, and social stigma is a more pressing problem for the former patient. Thus Alcoholics Anonymous operate with deliberate openness and publicity; social therapeutic clubs tend towards quiet, private anonymity.

2 Mental illness includes a wider range of behavior disorders and symptoms among many diverse individuals; by contrast alcoholics have at least their alcoholism in common.

3 The discharged psychiatric patient often wishes to forget about his experience or is under pressure from relatives to mask his identity.

Additional reasons may be that the therapeutic efficacy of such clubs is still largely a matter of conjecture and difficult to evaluate, and also that they may not appeal to many former patients. We have some inferential evidence to support the last possibility: most persons discharged from most hospitals do not choose to join expatient clubs.

The aim of this paper is to present a rudimentary analysis of the social organization and culture of an expatients' club sponsored by a hospital, where much control has been left in the hands of the members.

METHODS AND TECHNIQUES

The data on which this paper is based were derived by use of the following techniques:

1 Regularly scheduled observations took place in two three-month periods, two years apart, of the meetings and other activities of the club. The first observer visited the club daily, six days a week, spending about two to six hours per day there, and often went on informal outings with small groups of members. She wrote detailed notes, a copy of which was sent to the field supervisor, and her progress and problems were reviewed with him at least twice weekly. The second observer attended all meetings and formal activities, but observation tended to be less intense, as did the review periods with the supervisor.[2]
2 Interviews, most of them taped, were held with all active club members and volunteers, and with hospital staff members interested in the club. These interviews were nonstructured, lasting from one-half to a full hour, and focussed on the meaning the club had for the members, relationships between members, and perceived problems.
3 Semi-structured questionnaires were administered to twenty-two active members and volunteers, covering a number of sociological and psychiatric areas, as well as the areas covered in the interviews.
4 To supplement interview information, hospital case records of interviewees were examined.

Observations and interview and questionnaire findings were checked with hospital personnel for factual accuracy. Findings and impressions of the first observer were compared with those of the second for inter-observer reliability, and close agreement was found. The method of data analysis, essentially similar to that used in ethnographic studies, was nonstatistical content analysis.

HISTORY

About eleven years ago a group of patients who had formed friendships while at the hospital decided to form a club when they were discharged. They met in the

[2] The observer in the first period was Sara E. Singer, anthropologist, in the second period, Henry Wechsler, social psychologist. The study was designed and supervised by David Landy. The present analysis is primarily by the authors of this paper, drawing somewhat upon later findings of Wechsler, for which gratitude is here expressed. Further analyses will appear in a forthcoming number of the *Journal of Social Issues* on "New Pathways from the Mental Hospital" (Wechsler and Landy, issue editors); in a chapter of a book in progress on psychiatric rehabilitation by Landy, B. M. Kramer, and M. Greenblatt; and in Wechsler (in press).

library of the hospital, their first president being a "strong", directive individual whose eventual departure left the club in a weakened state. Much energy had been dissipated in a series of fund-raising schemes. About four years later another club was organized through the efforts of several former patients who, having themselves reached a satisfying rehabilitative status, wanted to help to restore other patients to community life. They were offered room in a "halfway house" (transitional after-care residence) for women (Landy, in press; Landy et al., in press), about one block from the hospital. The hospital administration had become interested in such an organization as a solution to the problem of what to do with scores of expatients who would gather each day in the lobby, participating in sketching classes and group therapy, and maintaining relationships begun on the ward. These gatherings were spontaneous, unsanctioned (though tolerated as a "necessary irritant") by the hospital, and laced with gossip about each other and the staff.

Contacting older members, the new club formed a steering committee including representatives of the hospital, whose function at this time was primarily supportive. The monthly meetings, though attended by hospital personnel, were run by the patients themselves. A system of electing three representatives of the club for staggered three-month terms was developed. Funds were raised by passing the hat at social affairs, by running Chinese or Italian dinners, and in other ways. The hospital supported the club steadily, and membership and activities burgeoned.

Group therapy sessions were shifted from hospital to club, which enhanced its attractiveness for many patients and encouraged discussion of "sticky" club problems in therapy context. They began to publish a mimeographed "newspaper". Volunteers sent by the hospital auxiliary held open house frequently to entertain current and prospective members from the wards, and assisted in money-raising bazaars. But soon they were asked to move owing to expanding needs of the halfway house. By this time the hospital had acquired a three-storey residential building and made one floor available to the club.

The move constituted a blow. Now they would have to move equipment, buy new furniture, entice people to participate in the work required to make the new quarters "presentable." However, a leader began to emerge and the temporary slump changed to a time of high activity. This leader was a highly motivated young woman who in her zeal to make the club a success may have sidetracked potential efforts of less forceful members. Eventually she resumed her occupational role in the community and devoted decreasing time to club affairs, and once again members were mired down in the search for leadership.

SOCIAL ORGANIZATION

We shall call social organization operationally the system of social relationships and grouping arrangements among members of the club, and between them and the volunteers and hospital personnel.

Membership is open to any expatient. There are no formalized rituals of admission—no applications or membership certificates, except a card with the member's name and address which is kept on file. More than 250 names have been accumulated during the lifetime of the club, though during the study periods no more than twenty-seven members could be observed. Of these, fifteen were frequent, twelve somewhat regular, attenders; five or six of the latter constituted a core group whom the observers could count on seeing every day. (Composition of the core group changed between the observation periods but half the original members were still present.) When the club was open in the evenings, they spent as much as six hours a day there, though more recently the club hours have been considerably shortened.

The members, especially the twelve regular attenders, have predominantly chronic-type psychoses and relatively long hospital histories. They frequently lead socially marginal, seemingly lonely, lives among tension-ridden families or in isolated rooms or flats. Economically they derive mainly from low-income families, though a few are from middle-income groups. Often they are jobless, living on public or private welfare and getting small allowances from parents or others. Younger ones may receive such monies without qualms, but for older ones acceptance of "handouts" is not without attendant emotional conflict.

During the observation periods, both of which were viewed as "slumps" by members and hospital, there were few business meetings, newsletters, or scheduled affairs. Elections of representatives were not held. Nevertheless, at the regularly scheduled meetings of the club-hospital steering committee, four to seven members were constant attenders, functioning as *de facto* representatives. Problems like recruitment, leadership, activities, opening and closing the house, and cleaning dirty dishes, were discussed, and some attempt was made by hospital personnel to guide the "representatives" to a solution.

Several community volunteers came on a staggered schedule, acting as hostesses, and bringing coffee, doughnuts, and other food. These women maintained a high degree of interest and motivation and club members appeared to be fond of them. There was no particular ingrouping of volunteers, each usually acting on her own, though occasionally they discussed an activity like a club picnic together; nor did they consult in any systematic or formal way with hospital staff, beyond steering-committee meetings.

During the earlier observation period a leader emerged somewhat reluctantly, a woman to whom the others looked for leadership even though some did not like her personally since they felt she was too verbally hostile. They feared "getting on her bad side," but also felt that she was a safe place to flee to in an interpersonal storm: "If you're on her side, she will protect you." By the time of the second observation stage this leader, while still an active member, had surrendered leadership functions, and the organization once again needed, and was desirous of, an informal head.

An analysis of interactive dyads of the twelve most participating members indicates, in terms of expressed preferences, that, of 132 possible combinations, there were thirty-one cases of members "liking" other members, fifteen instances of "disliking", five instances of "ambivalent" or mixed feelings, and the remainder were simply unexpressed. In other words, eighty-one (or 61 per cent) of the possible preferences of this small, apparently interacting, group of twelve former patients were evidently so unimportant to the individual, or so far outside his ken, that he did not bother to express an interpersonal preference, pro or con. Furthermore, twenty-three (or nearly one-half) of the verbalized likes and dislikes were expressed in vague and ambiguous terms, as if the respondent was unable to make up his mind, or perhaps did not wish to express a sure opinion of something as complex as an interpersonal relationship.

Considering the emotionally impoverished backgrounds of these people, however, and the depth of their illness—some of them had been hospitalized several times and for quite long periods—the striking result is not that 61 per cent of the preferences remained unexpressed, but that 39 per cent could be expressed. Clinard (1957) defines mental illness as occurring when "an individual's mental health has been moderately or severely impaired," and he defines

A mentally healthy person [as] one who is capable of organizing and maintaining adequate relations with other people. Moreover, such a person is capable of deriving satisfactions from these relations. His behavior is socially appropriate in terms of prevailing cultural norms and is not regarded as bizarre. Finally, a mentally healthy person continues his level of social performance in terms of norms current for persons of his age and status.

If we accept these definitions of mental health and ill health, then many of these persons were still seriously ill. They did not usually require institutionalization, though occasionally one became so distressed that he required temporary rehospitalization. In a sense they made the expatients' club a stepping-stone out of the hospital, but for some it seemed to function as a kind of open and unsupervised community ward.

CULTURE

Our operating definition of culture is adapted from Redfield (1941) as the network of common understandings (to which we add values and behavior norms) shared by the members of the club. The culture is analyzed now in terms of "themes" or orientations characterizing these common understandings, values, and behavior norms.

1. *The club accepts mental patients.* It does not ask questions about one's illness or social antecedents. In fact, it makes being mentally ill a prerequisite for membership. Whatever their differences, the members in these terms form a community of kindred spirits.

2. *The club is a place where one may talk about hospital experience and illness symptoms.* It accepts a certain amount of "acting-out" and other behaviors which would be frowned upon as strange and abnormal by family, society, and even the hospital (where, for example, some behavior might be seen as regression and not easily countenanced by therapeutically oriented staff). A member

may not use such behavior modes out of the club, but he is free to do so while in the club.

3. *The member's dependence on the club is accepted.* Members may speak quite openly with each other about how much they need the club. As a member grows out of the club and resumes a normal community role more completely, talking about his dependence upon the club tapers off and it becomes embarrassing to mention it to others. It is a sign that he no longer fully shares the club subculture with other members, and that he is rejecting it in favor of the culture of the larger community.

4. *The club accepts the member's refusal or inability to work.* A person may sit around the club indefinitely, but can hardly do so elsewhere, even in the most tolerating parental or conjugal home. He may say without embarrassment: "I don't know what's so great about going back to work. I have to realize for myself that work is the good thing that everybody says it is." He may take time at the club—outside forces permitting—to "think it out" or, in the psychodynamic vernacular which most of them acquire, "work it through." No one pushes him.

5. *The club accepts economic dependence and need.* Dependence on family and others is commonplace. A man more than thirty years old can admit with equanimity receiving a five-dollar weekly allowance from home. He does not have to fear disapproval or opprobrium within the club, and in turn finds further reward in being able to tolerate the same kinds of thing in his fellow-members. When he begins to be concerned about economic impoverishment, he is losing, albeit unconsciously, the club's culture and learning to accept the values of the larger society.

6. *The club offers freedom from social ranking.* In a class-structured society one's social status becomes an identifying badge and potential source of personal devaluation when the person feels he is in an invidious social position. Despite some divergence in education, family background, and other cultural antecedents (Landy, 1958a), such differences are seldom discussed. True, certain forms of deference are shown to volunteers, who are themselves usually middle class (for example, calling them Mrs. instead of by first name), but this rarely assumes the proportions of rigid dominance-submission relations. Leaders who maintain hegemony for any length of time are usually middle class, relatively highly educated, and interpersonally more competent than the rank and file; yet again deference does not extend to special privileges or other prerogatives (beyond immediate manipulative power). Generally the pervading sense of common experience of illness, hospitalization, and perceived special status produces a leveling effect.[3]

7. *The club offers "freedom" from dating.* Single persons in American society

---

[3] Wechsler (1960) has developed the concept of the "expatient role," to designate the role voluntarily assumed by some patients who tend specifically to identify themselves to themselves and others (for example, in joining expatient clubs) as former patients, in contrast to the patients who wish to forget their patient career and even to mask their identity by "passing" unnoticed into the general population upon discharge. This thinking is a logical extension of the patient role concept in the work of Goffman (1956, 1957, 1959), Parsons (1951, Chapter 10; 1953), and Erikson (1957).

(these comprise the bulk of club membership) are impelled toward the pattern of dating. The fact that the organization is not restricted to either sex is in itself somewhat atypical of social clubs, but relationships within the club are characterized generally by brother-brother, brother-sister, sister-sister modes of behavior. Dating each other would be almost tantamount to breaking an unspoken incest taboo, and happens only rarely. Thus the club seems to be perceived as a substitute family or clan, perhaps even, as some say themselves, as a "home." In any case, it is difficult for the former mental patient, particularly if he is suffering from the desexualizing effects of schizophrenia, to resume with ease former heterosexual relationships or to form new ones. This kind of subculture frees him of the necessity for dating while at the same time placing him in contact with the opposite sex—which may be a source of some psychological conflict, but which may also serve as a prelude to future, more normalized, relationships.

8. *The club has a constant need for new members and new activities.* Members say they are always in need of new members, of "new blood," of new activities that will lend "life" and "spark" to club proceedings. However, they seldom take advantage of situations which would be conducive to the recruitment of members, because of lethargy and interpersonal incompetence, and probably unconsciously because every new member may constitute a powerful threat to the present "cozy" structure of the club. They may sometimes say, "We need more activities. It's terrible just to sit around and chat, play cards, smoke, and chat some more." But extension services offered by the hospital, particularly by the occupational and recreational therapy departments, are seldom taken. They appear to tire easily, to drop activities after brief experience, to hesitate to take initiative, and to become lost in the collective quandary of who will do what.

9. *The club has a constant need for leadership.* The election system, the quick hospital turnover, the apathy of the faithful core, all contribute to an everpresent need for leadership. The members want "someone who can really be a leader to get things done for the club." But when one occasionally attempts to venture into a leadership role, unless he is a particularly ego-strong individual, his fellows are apt to say, "Who does he think he is? What sort of boss is he trying to be?"; or the would-be leader himself will feel he is "sticking my nose too far where I have no business," and soon relinquish his modest show of initiative. Thus freedom from class—or cultural—ranking produces the perhaps unintended consequence of "leveling," so that pressure against being too sharply differentiated from one's fellows may heavily discourage development of indigenous leadership. (It should be noted that in some clubs there are professionally trained leaders, so that not only does the need for leadership become less acute, but the status of professional carries with it expectations for deference and demeanor[4] which include status distinctions.)

10. *The members share a sense of social failure.* All the members think of themseves as having failed socially. They may put this in terms of having talents

---

[4] For a brilliant study of these phenomena as regards patient-patient and staff-patient relations on a psychiatric ward, see Goffman (1956).

which others do not appreciate, or in more self-derogatory terms of simply "not having what it takes." But they feel the very fact of mental illness marks them apart with the stigma, not only of being different, but of not being up to the demands of a competitive, status- and achievement-conscious society.

11. The club is a place where one may find consolation and give support to others. It is an obligation of a member of the club to dispense consolation and support to a member who may be feeling depressed and disconsolate. And it is a right to receive such consolation and support.

12. Club members share a sense of responsibility for each other's fate. This is an attribute of most social organizations, but in the club becomes both more intense and at times much less intense than in "normal" voluntary associations. On the one hand, there have been occasions when the whole larger core group of a dozen or more rallied to the aid of a member who was suddenly rehospitalized, visiting her, bringing her material assistance and gifts, discussing her case, and in at least one instance even intervening with doctors on behalf of the distressed member. On the other, there have been occasions when a member who was unpopular (usually because of one or more irritating social-personal traits) would be outlawed by the entire group, and no one would rise to his defense. We know of two members who were "read out" of the club. Nevertheless, there appeared to be a feeling of mutual responsibility between most members, however fragile its base.

DISCUSSION AND IMPLICATIONS

The social organization of the club may be said to consist of a small inner core of persisting membership, with a somewhat softer core surrounding it of perhaps a score of occasionally participating members, and finally the more or less fuzzy layer of peripheral membership which attends functions only infrequently. The social organization is characterized, with regard to the hard inner core and, to some extent, the second layer, by persisting but loosely formed social relationships, which are built largely around interdependent needs of the members and, on rare occasions, the need for leadership and followership which presages the temporary rise of a leader. As we have elsewhere characterized the social relations of another group of expatients (Landy et al., in press), we might here epitomize the nature of social relations in the club as "equal but separate." That is, there is an understood ethic of equality of rights and privileges (though not necessarily of power in the case of the rare leaders) with regard to the anonymity and commonness of their similar experiences, which effects a "leveling" of social status within the organization. At the same time the social-emotional tone of the relationships is characterized by a kind of separateness of each individual within the group, a hedging of affective commitment even towards others whom one likes and admires. The leveling process makes it difficult for indigenous leadership to assert itself and, once it does occur, to exercise constructively the prerogatives and functions of the leader.

The culture of the club has been shown to consist of common understandings, values, and norms, which may be grouped around characteristic patterns or themes. The club is a place where mental patients are accepted without question as to social or medical antecedents, psychological or economic dependency, and refusal or inability to work. It offers an opportunity to associate with members of both sexes without having to date. It has a constant need for activities, membership, and leadership, but the low motivational level, pressure toward leveling, lack of social experience, and possible threat of new activities and personnel as destructive of the comfortable *status quo,* all militate against the frequent fulfillment of these needs. The members share a sense of social failure, and of stigma because of their illness. They feel it proper to give and receive consolation for these and for other reasons, and to some extent share a sense of mutual responsibility.

The club culture may be expressed in terms of what it means to its members (common understandings), and what it is (values and behavior norms). What it means has been expressed graphically by the members themselves. It is one man's "crutch," which he needs because he is "emotionally crippled." For another, "Maybe this club is my desert island. I'd like to say to hell with society and find me a desert island somewhere." For another, "It's like a cradle. Sometimes one needs a cradle for a while. You might just jump into it if you need it." It becomes a place to escape the pressures of a family life which has become pathological for them, or a society which has been intolerable to, and to some extent intolerant of, them. And since each is in his own way a "lonely one," it is a place to socialize without the ordinary pressures of the community's culture.

Parsons (1951, pp. 477 *et passim*) has termed the sick role

. . . A mechanism which in the first instance channels deviance so that the two most dangerous potentialities, namely group formation and successful establishment of the claim to legitimacy, are avoided. The sick are tied up, not with other deviants to form a "sub-culture" of the sick, but each with a group of non-sick, his personal circle and, above all, physicians. The sick thus become a statistical status class and are deprived of the possibility of forming a solidary collectivity. Furthermore, to be sick is by definition to be in an undesirable state, so that it simply does not "make sense" to assert a claim that the way to deal with the frustrating aspects of the social system is "for everybody to get sick."

One *might* summarize the social organization and culture of the club as being those of an informally organized, deviant sub-group. To the extent that this may be true, the club becomes that potentially dangerous entity that Parsons believes the sick role is culturally designed to avoid. To the extent that the club is a self-perpetuating group for perennially sick people, it may fulfill the qualifications for such a "subculture of the sick" of which Parsons speaks. To the extent that the club serves transitional functions as a bridge between hospital culture and community culture, and for some it does appear to operate in this way, it becomes a midpoint, so to speak, in the process of shedding the sick role for the well role, and so Parsons' "dangerous potentiality" is circumvented.

References

1   Bierer, J. (Ed.) (1948). *Social therapeutic clubs*. London: H. K. Lewis.
2   Blair, D. A. S. (1955). The social therapeutic club, an important measure of social rehabilitation in the treatment of psychiatric cases. *Ment. Hygiene* **39**, 54–62.
3   Clinard, Marshall B. (1957). *Sociology of deviant behavior*. New York: Rinehart. Pp. 315–16 *et passim*.
4   Erikson, Kai T. (1957). Patient role and social uncertainty—a dilemma of the mentally ill. *Psychiatry* **20**, 263–74.
5   Goffman, Erving (1956). The nature of deference and demeanor. *Amer. Anthrop.* **58**, 473–502.
6   Goffman, Erving (1957). Characteristics of total institutions. *Symposium on preventive and social psychiatry*. Washington: Walter Reed Army Institute of Research, Pp. 43–93.
7   Goffman, Erving (1959). The moral career of the mental patient. *Psychiatry* **22**, 123–42.
8   Landy, David (1958a). Cultural antecedents of mental illness in the United States. *Soc. Service Rev.* **32**, 350–61.
9   Landy, David (1958b). Psychiatric rehabilitation: an acculturative process. Paper presented to American Anthropological Association, Washington, November 1958.
10 Landy, David. Exploration in residential after-care of psychiatric patients: a men's halfway house. *Int. J. soc. Psychiat* (in press).
11 Landy, David. A halfway house for women. In proceedings of research conference on *Patterns of transition from hospital to community* (forthcoming).
12 Landy, David, *et al. Halfway home: a sociocultural and clinical study of transitional after-care for female psychiatric patients* (forthcoming monograph).
13 Mishler, A. L., Landy, D., and Guinness, V. Rehabilitation on a mental hospital ward: a process of socialization (in preparation).
14 Palmer, M. B. (1958). Social rehabilitation for mental patients. *Ment. Hygiene* **42**, 24–8.
15 Parsons, Talcott (1951). *The social system*. Glencoe, Ill.: The Free Press.
16 Parsons, Talcott (1953). Illness and the role of the physician. In C. Kluckhohn, H. A. Murray and D. M. Schneider (Eds.), *Personality in nature, society and culture*. New York: Knopf. (2nd ed.)
17 Redfield, Robert (1941). *The folk culture of Yucatan*. Chicago: University of Chicago Press.
18 Wechsler, H. (1960). The self-help organization in the mental health field: Recovery, Inc., a case study. *J. nerv. ment. Dis.* **130**, 297–314.
19 Wechsler, H. The ex-patient group: a general survey and case study. In proceedings of research conference on *Patterns of transition from hospital to community* (in press).

PART SIX

Issues and Problems in the Sociology of Mental Illness

This book of readings began as an exercise in theory development in the area of deviant behavior and mental illness. It has been our intent to demonstrate how the existing body of sociological literature in one area—mental illness—could be reinterpreted and organized around the threads of symbolic interactionism and the recently emerging perspective of deviant behavior as outlined in early chapters of this volume. We return now to our original intent by examining in detail the problems and issues which still remain unresolved in the field of the sociology of mental illness.

One of the first steps toward theory construction necessarily becomes the development of a consistent and workable conceptual framework which, when applied to a body of research findings, will move the behavioral scientist forward in his attempts to arrive at explanation and prediction. This chapter takes up some of the problems and issues which confronted us when we attempted to put this volume together. Central to the symbolic interactionist position are the notions of self, social act, social object, interaction itself, and the notion of the situation. Out of this theoretical perspective, which stresses the fact that persons develop unique views of self which allow them to guide and direct their own behavior through the process of self-indication,[1] grew a perspective on deviant behavior referred to at various times as the "labeling" or "societal reactions" school of deviant behavior. As noted in the introduction to this collection of readings, this particular perspective stresses the fact that deviant behavior is merely the name attached to particular acts by certain sets of others or audiences. Although this approach is not unique in its conceptual orientation, it has stimulated a body of theoretical and research literature which has focused on the processes by which certain types of audiences come to define certain types of behavior as deviant. Adopting this perspective, this book has taken the position that mental illness is a label attached to certain forms of deviant behavior.

461

This view of deviant behavior has quite profitably shifted attention in research to the interactional settings within which the labeling and deviance ascription process occurs; yet, it has deficiencies which may mislead the researcher. Most notable has been a tendency to slight the role played by the deviant or pre-deviant in the actual labeling process. Erikson, Kitsuse, and H. Becker have insightfully noted that the actual province of a sociology of deviant behavior is "audience reactions," but it must be recognized that the actor himself may and in fact quite frequently does play an important determining part in the labeling process.[2] If the burden of theoretical attention is placed upon the audience reaction to social acts, the implication is that the pre-deviant is under the complete control of audience members whenever interpretation of social acts becomes an issue. Thus Scheff has argued that "the most important single factor (but not the only factor) in the stabilization of residual deviance is the societal reaction."[3] It is our position that investigators in the sociology of mental illness, regardless of theoretical orientation, have overlooked the fact that quite frequently persons labeled as mentally ill react to this label and often attempt to dissuade audience members of their allegations. The purposive, striving nature of the human organism is part of the data of several studies in this volume. The patients in the Scheff paper who were presented before court-appointed psychiatrists attempted to answer all the virtually unanswerable questions put to them.[4] The patients attempted to establish their rationality in the face of a social audience which had previously made its interpretation. Similarly, in the Sampson, Messinger, and Towne paper, the reactions of schizophrenic mothers within the family often led husbands to delay pressures for hospitalization, in some cases up to two years.[5] The prepatient actively participated in his own career and was quite successful in determining—at least for a certain period of time—the type of label that would be attached to him.

By ignoring the process of self-indication in social interaction, theorists have presented what at times appears to be an ideological defense for the underdog —e.g., "the poor mental patient."[6] While this defense is seldom if ever explicitly stated, the implication is that the mental patient has virtually no control over his environment and that once he has been so labeled, he will carry for life a deeply discrediting and stigmatizing label. If, as we are arguing, mental patients, like persons who have not shared their experiences, engage in such basic interactional processes as the identification and labeling of social objects in their symbolic environment and engage in the process of locating themselves with respect to others in social situations, then we submit that investigators should shift their focus of interest and examine how the patient conducts himself in daily social interaction. Such a shift in interest might well present a more complete picture of the labeling process. If, after all, the definitions of a person as a deviant entail interaction between deviant and audience, then surely attention should be given to the role played by the deviant in this process.

Although it has been argued by members of the labeling school that the focus of attention should be on audience reactions to deviant acts, a number of unresolved issues still remain. As Clark and Gibbs cogently noted, little attention has been given to the norms which (1) determine how audience reactions are variously organized and (2) determine which audience members will come forth and actually engage in the labeling process.[7] Similarly, little attention has been given to the fact that a large number of undetected deviants or normal deviants are present in society. What actually leads audience members to select only certain persons from this rather large pool of potentially labeled deviants is problematic. Even though little data are available to offer hypotheses of why societal reactions are only infrequently activated or organized in the face of deviancy, it is submitted that such processes as the following may account for differential audience reactions to potential deviant behavior.

First, the behavior of the pre-deviant changes over time and leads to a breakdown in accommodation established between himself and his audience members. Second, the potentially deviant behavior may increase in its frequency and visibility, thus bringing the audience and the pre-deviant to the eyes of outside persons. Third, outside persons may intervene in the interactional relationship established between the pre-deviant and his social others. This intervention may serve to break down the established relationship between the actors, thus leading to the collapse of what had been consensually sustained, accommodative social relationships. Fourth, the action of the pre-deviant may be such that it comes to the eyes of outside legal authorities. The unsuccessful suicide attempt and the behavior of the overt homosexual are but two of several examples. Finally, the norms and standards of conduct of the audience members may change over time while those of the pre-deviant do not.

EPIDEMIOLOGY AND SOCIETAL REACTIONS

Interpretation of epidemiological findings derived from different studies often becomes quite complex. This is so because of the different techniques used in data collection in epidemiological studies, because of variations in statistical compilations, and because of variations in diagnostic standards. It is usually contended that because different results are obtained by different methods, it is difficult to obtain an overall picture of the configuration of illness within a given population. Furthermore, the different results obtained by different methods of data collection often tend to obscure the clues that point to causative factors in mental illness. Three types of rates are generally derived in epidemiological studies: incidence, prevalence, and true prevalence. Incidence is the number of new cases that develop within a given interval of time. Prevalence is the number of cases in treatment on a given date or during a specified interval of time. True prevalence is the number of persons who can be regarded as psychiatrically impaired in a given population, regardless of whether or not they are in treatment. Incidence studies yield the lowest rates and true prevalence studies (sometimes called community or home surveys) yield the highest rates. The reasons for this are obvious, since neither incidence nor prevalence studies include persons who had been in treatment at some earlier time. True prevalence studies, however, do include persons who had been in treatment at some earlier time. Moreover, true prevalence studies include the "undetected" cases of mental disorder. The very fact that different techniques yield varying results may be interpreted, in part, as an indication of different societal reactions to deviant behavior. There are persons in the community whose behavior is just as deviant as the behavior of persons in treatment, but for some reason they have not been rejected. Obviously, accommodation mechanisms have evolved between the "deviant" and his social groupings. Other deviants may successfully avoid the labeling process. And others, who have been labeled successfully, avoid displacement from the community. In this respect it is argued that incidence and prevalence studies are informative about the societal mechanism of rejection, while the true prevalence studies yield, in addition, information about the societal mechanism of accommodation. If epidemiological investigations are reinterpreted from this point of view, the investigator can begin to guide and direct his research in terms of those population clusters which display differential readiness to reject potentially deviant behavior or to accommodate themselves to it. Then epidemiological investigations can begin to reap large rewards for the sociologist interested in developing and testing his theories of societal reactions to deviant behavior and the implications of these reactions for variations in the patient career.

On the conceptual level, problems are still present. The fact that only 18.5 percent of the population in the renowned Midtown Manhattan Study were judged sufficiently free of psychiatric symptoms that they could be classified as well presents a paradox.[8] Freedom from psychiatric symptoms would then be abnormal behavior. Evidently, epidemiological investigations based on true rates of prevalence have rarely constructed their questioning procedures in terms of the frame of reference of societal members, and there are psychiatrists who would argue that the psychiatric perspective was not taken either.

If, as we have argued, variations in research findings may at least in part be attributed to discrepancies between the psychiatric and the social frame of reference, studies should attempt to locate rates of potential mental illness in terms of the categories employed by members of society when they label persons as mentally ill. In short, mental illness should be recognized for what it is —a societal reaction to a certain type of behavior. On another level, epidemiological investigations of the past have tended to abstract behavior from its location in time and space. Failure to consider the fact that deviancy evolves through a career and failure to catch potential deviant behavior in terms of its actual location in society have yielded what appear to be sterile and, at times, theoretically meaningless findings.

SOCIOCULTURAL VARIATIONS AND THE PATIENT CAREER

The emphasis on the patient career in this volume is not meant to imply that the career is a cross-cultural universal. Before the career of a mental patient can be observed, a number of social conditions must be present. It may be argued that all societies have some conceptions of what are and are not acceptable forms of behavior. Through the process of socialization the salient rules of conduct and propriety are learned, and societies' members conduct themselves in terms of these rules. The societal norms carry with them definitions of deviant behavior, and they also define what are proper societal responses for both actor and audience to deviant behavior. Depending on the contour of these rules and norms, societal settings will evolve or create varying types of social mechanisms which influence and organize the behavior of the deviant and the audience members. These definitions give, then, to the actor and the audience a vocabulary of meaning and motives with which they can answer the questions of who the potential deviant is and who they are as audience members.

For the career of the mental patient to exist as we have observed it in American society, it appears that the following prerequisites must be found: (1) a conception of mental illness and a conception of what types of behavior by what types of persons constitute this object called mental illness and (2) a vocabulary of meanings and motives which are translated into social institutions and which serve to organize audience and actor behavior alike when the behavior called mental illness is observed.

It is clear, of course, that many societies have evolved a series of social mechanisms to handle the problem of mental illness. Formalized societal mechanisms have evolved for channeling reactions to persons designated as mentally ill. In Western society we have the mental hospital and other health professionals and treatment centers. Responsibility for reacting to the deviant is channeled to these institutions. In nonliterate cultures the care of the deviant may come under the province of such persons as the sorcerer or witch doctor. In other subcultures which do not avail themselves of the institutions of the majority group and which do not have a division of labor in which a specific person is delegated the task of coping with the mentally ill, responsibility may fall upon the family or, collectively, upon the entire community. The Hutterites and Amish are examples of such groups.

In other societies the conception of mental illness is not present, and what would usually be regarded as mental illness elsewhere is now encompassed under some other rubric. Thus it may be argued that the career of the mental patient is a unique phenomenon observable only when certain social conditions are present. Furthermore, the specific form or course of the career is closely associated with a given society's conception of mental illness and the mechanisms that have been evolved to deal with it within that society. Therefore the career of the mental patient as presented in this volume may be a description of a phenomenon unique to only a relatively small number of societies.

ISSUES IN THE SOCIOLOGY OF THE PATIENT CAREER

The career of the psychiatric patient has, as we have argued, three distinct phases: a prepatient phase, which describes the person in the community prior to hospitalization; an inpatient phase, which describes the person in the treatment center; and a posthospital phase, which describes the person as he is back in the community after the experience of hospitalization. The career perspective was chosen as one of our integrative threads in this volume. We take as problematic the position that changes in attitudes and behavior can be established by examining behavior out of context. Therefore, the cumulative effects of being labeled mentally ill, of being hospitalized, and of subsequently being returned to the outside community must be considered. The career concept necessarily directs attention to two related processes: first, the physical movement of persons in and out of various social networks and second, the concomitant changes in attitudes toward self and other which accompany this movement through time and space. Thus one major intent of this book of readings was to show changes in social psychological processes as the patient moves through the three phases of his career.

The choice of the career concept has not, however, been without some drawbacks. Most notable, perhaps, is the fact that each phase of the career is actually made up of several distinct and quite complex processes.[9] It is often quite difficult to ascertain when one career phase begins and another ends. Does the prepatient phase begin when the label "mentally ill" has been attached and end when a patient enters the hospital? Or is it possible, as Goffman intimates, that the inpatient phase does not begin until the patient has actually expressed changes in attitudes and behavior as a result of hospitalization.[10] There is also the problem of determining when the inpatient phase actually terminates. Persons are released from hospitals on probationary status, make home visits shortly before discharge, and are often transferred to other kinds of institutions, such as prisons, detention homes, and nursing homes. This has led at least one major research group to define the beginning of the postpatient phase on an ad hoc basis, such as having "left bed" for a determinate amount of time.[11]

Similarly, the implication of the readings in this volume has been that once a patient has been released from the hospital, the career has virtually ended. However, it is more appropriate to think of the patient career as a sequence of hospitalizations, where entry into the hospital only signals a longer series of processes in which repeated hospitalizations will occur. To think of the career as an ongoing sequence of events, of which rehospitalization is but one event may have more than conceptual importance. Data to be reported in a forthcoming volume indicate that the most marked changes in self-attitudes and patient-family relationships do not appear until there have been repeated admissions to the mental hospital.[12]

The readings drawn together in this book have been concerned with only one type of patient career—the career which evolves in formal psychiatric hospitals conforming to the total institution model. No attention has been given to career variations as they might occur for persons treated in outpatient clinics or by private practitioners or even as they may occur in the newly emerging community mental health centers. It is quite likely, of course, that such basic processes as changes in self-attitudes and in self-other relationships will vary radically if they occur in these other settings. These are topics in need of further exploration, and it is hoped that the present volume will serve the function of establishing base-line observations to which future studies of the patient career can be compared.

ISSUES IN THE PREPATIENT CAREER PHASE

Although a large proportion of the investigations included in the third part of this book focused explicitly on the processes which bring persons into mental hospitals, a number of unanswered questions still remain. In fact, it may be argued that of the three phases of the patient career, least is known about the prepatient phase. Perhaps of most importance is the issue surrounding the actual decision processes which lead persons into the hospital. We know very little about the actual pathways which a person travels on the way to hospitalization. Hollingshead and Redlich, Wolfrom, Pang, and Courtney, and Clausen and Yarrow have been concerned with referral sources to the hospital.[13] Mills described the various entry statuses (such as forms of legal commitment) that patients may occupy.[14] However, the actual routes to the hospital remain unclear, since it is not enough to know who was involved and what entry status a patient happened to occupy. What is necessary for a clear picture of this process is to identify the various others who are involved at various points along the path to the hospital and the types of influence wielded at various checkpoints.

We have noted that investigators have been most deficient in locating the actual steps which bring about hospitalization, but research on the prepatient phase of the career has suggested the importance of (1) the labeling of the actor as deviant, (2) the visibility of the deviant act, (3) the amount and frequency of the deviant act, and (4) the intervention of outside persons in the hospitalization process. Yet, we still have incomplete answers to the basic question: "What leads certain audience members to decide that hospitalization is necessary?" Similarly, why is it that certain persons make the decision for treatment voluntary, while others have this decision forced upon them? Is it always the case that persons will feel rejection and alienation from those persons who are instrumental in bringing about their institutionalization? Although Goffman seems to imply that this is true, it may well be that certain persons actively cooperate with their relevant social others and come to agree that hospitalization is necessary.[15] Under these conditions the question then becomes "What happens to the social relationships established with such persons after hospitalization occurs?" Alivisatos and Lyketsos submit that such others become alienated from the patient. It may well be that alienation is only one of several types of social relationships which develop before and after hospitalization.[16]

An as yet unanswered question also revolves around the impact of differential images of mental illness and mental hospitals upon the readiness of persons and audiences to attach the label "mentally ill." If it is true that only a small minority of persons who are mentally ill ever become hospitalized, then surely prepatients and their audiences are influenced in some way by their perceptions of mental illness, mental patients, and psychiatric hospitals.[17] To what extent this is the case is still unknown.

The role played by the prepatient himself in the decision to hospitalize also needs further study. Although investigations in the area of medical sociology have noted the differential readiness of certain classes and types of persons to define themselves as ill, few such investigations have been conducted with respect to mental illness.[18] In fact the dominant tendency has been to view the prepatient as an object which is subject to the manipulation of its audience members. Little attention has been given to the actual role played by the patient in his definitional process.

Similarly, little attention has been given to the patterns of interaction between the prepatient and his significant others after the decision for hospitalization has been made but before actual hospital entry has occurred. An entire issue of the Journal of Social Issues was directed to the problem of how mental illness affects the family. The main thrust of the articles in this issue seems to be that wives are slow to "recognize" the spouse's problem as requiring psychiatric care and are often unclear about who should be consulted to bring about hospital entry. It is only by implication that we can infer what happens after a wife has defined her husband as mentally ill and before the husband actually enters the hospital.[19] This period is distinctive, since problems of evaluation and control have been resolved and now other types of problems become imminent.

On a methodological level, the majority of studies on this phase of the patient career have been descriptive or retrospective in nature. Consequentially we have been forced to develop hypotheses and generalizations from data based on unique cases or from data which were subject to distortion and forgetting by the patient and his relevant others. The perennial plea of the sociologist is for longitudinal studies; it would seem, however, that this need is particularly great in the sociology of mental illness. Investigations need to be designed and carried out which follow persons from the time any consideration is given to the label "mentally ill" until the time they arrive at the treatment center. Such investigations would place in proper perspective the role played by the actor as well as that played by the audience in the prepatient phase of the career.

ISSUES ON THE INPATIENT CAREER PHASE

Although the body of research literature on inpatients has begun to resolve a number of important issues and questions dealing with the career of the mental patient, a number of problems still remain. Most notable is the lack of studies which focus on the carry-over of prepatient hospital experiences and relationships into the inpatient career phase. If, as the interactionist argues, man lives in a consensually sustained symbolic environment, it follows that out of this environment the person selects certain persons who are more important than others. Such persons necessarily occupy positions of importance when the actor is removed from their presence. The process of hospitalization of course creates a disjuncture in these relationships; rather oddly, however, investigations that have focused upon the carry-over into the hospital of relationships established prior to hospitalization are difficult to find.[20] The extent to which prehospital socialization differentially prepares inpatients for the treatment experience has been the specific object of only a few investigations.[21] Similarly, the degree to which patients reorient themselves in terms of hospital significant others has only recently been investigated.[22]

In contemporary theory, the mental hospital is viewed as an institution characterized by regimentation and control over all aspects of behavior. As a consequence most studies dealing with the patient and the mental hospital are concerned with the effect of the total institution and variations in its structure on uniform patterns of patient welfare and behavior.

A wealth of data collected in medical settings shows that contrary to the total institution position, there are marked variations in accommodation and behavior patterns among inpatients.[23] This has been less frequently demonstrated for psychiatric inpatients, although there is some evidence that the inpatient is able to and in fact does respond in a number of unique and idiosyncratic ways to the experience of hospitalization. Smith and Thrasher, for example, delineate at least nine distinct role types which emerge out of the hospital experience.[24] Other investigations can be reinterpreted as illustrating variations in adjustment patterns among psychiatric inpatients.[25] Ward social structures may be viewed as a by-product of patient accommodation patterns to institutional living.[26]

It appears then, that the role of the mentally ill is not so stabilized or consensually agreed upon as it is currently contended. Perhaps the main impetus to the position that this role is consensually agreed upon derives from early notions of Parsons and others concerning the medical sick role.[27] Arguing that the ill person is placed in a special status by virtue of his illness, proponents of the medical sick role model have unquestioningly assumed that the norms surrounding this role also hold for the psychiatric patient. Studies by Sobel and Ingalls and by Denzin and Spitzer have noted the unwillingness of mental patients to assume this role. The uncertainty of practitioners surrounding their own behavior toward the psychiatric, as opposed to the medically ill, patient, has also been pointed out.[28] That the amount of stigma, possible social isolation, rejection, and alienation, not to mention differential willingness and readiness to engage in self-diagnosis, varies with the type of illness is apparent. Investigations are clearly needed to focus on these differences for a theory of mental illness.

A portion of the inpatient career which has not been discussed in this volume deals with behavior commonly referred to as "collective behavior" or "collective disturbances" among patients. Although papers have appeared on this topic, each investigation located a different set of assumed causal variables in the disturbance observed.[29] Thus instances of this type of behavior have been observed under such diverse circumstances as (1) lack of staff agreement over ward policy, (2) breakdown of communication between staff and patients (3) turnover of key staff and patient leaders, (4) sudden influx of new types of patients on the ward, and (5) changes in ward normative structures. As pointed out by Denzin, this area is characterized by a singular absence of theoretical orientation or integration.[30] Selections on this topic have not been included because of inconclusiveness and incompatabilities and because of the fact that the large majority of these investigations have tended to be ad hoc reconstructions of past events, rather than rigidly executed and reproducible investigations. Sound empirical investigations are needed which follow such types of occurrences from inception to decline and which view them from the perspectives commonly employed for analyzing such behavior outside institutions.[31] It is our feeling that collective disturbances, when they occur, are important parts of a patient's hospital experience. Not only would we wish to know how frequent such actions are in the hospital, but we would also wish to know what types of patients show propensities to become involved in such disturbances. The impact of such instances of collective behavior upon subsequent career experiences of the patient similarly warrants examination.

ISSUES IN THE POSTPATIENT CAREER PHASE

One problem confronting investigators is how to operationalize postpatient adjustment. The pervasive tendency has been to construct rigid operationalizations of posthospital adjustment based on such diverse measures as numbers of hours worked per week and degree of family and community integration. Such measures deny the fact that human social behavior—be it among mental patients or white-collar workers—involves a continual process of self-adjustment to changing social situations and social others. Granting the assumption that behavior varies by its social context, it may be argued that appropriate operationalizations of such concepts as postpatient adjustment must involve measures that take into account the uniqueness of the situation confronted by the former mental patient. Such concepts, called by Blumer "sensitizing" concepts, allow the investigator to consider what is generically common about different situations as well as what is generically distinctive about each.[32] Viewed from this perspective, measures of postpatient adjustment would involve studying postpatients in a variety of different contexts in an attempt to identify the social mechanisms employed by the former patient and his significant others in adjusting to the hospitalization experience. Such research tactics would obviate the pervasive middle-class bias of existing patient adjustment scales and would allow the investigator to make more meaningful statements about this highly important aspect of the patient career.

Another problem confronting the investigator is that of determining the effect that having been hospitalized in different types of hospital settings has upon posthospital behavior. Although investigators have long recognized that hospitals vary in their goals and methods of treatment, few attempts have been made to assess the relative effects of these differences upon postpatient adjustment.

Little attention has been given to variations in family responses to the postpatient. Freeman and Simmons, and Lefton et al. were notable in their attempts to isolate variations in family responses to the mental patient, but the bulk of their research examined variations in family type and social class setting of the family.[33] The dynamics of family interaction with the postpatient have not received much specific attention. Similarly, few studies have focused upon family interaction patterns other than exclusion and rejection of the postpatient. Although these types of interaction are no doubt important, it is misleading to assume they are the only forms that may develop. Research needs to be directed toward the family's attempts to cooperate with the patient and to reintegrate him into the social situation. Human interaction takes the forms of conflict, cooperation, adaptation, and accommodation. Previous researchers in the area of posthospital adjustment have focused almost entirely upon the processes of conflict, rejection, and exclusion which may develop when the patient returns home. Sampson, Messinger, and Towne were exceptional in their concentration on the role played by accommodative and adjustive processes in the prepatient phase of the patient career.[34] It would seem that similar investigations are needed on the latter phases of the career also.

Investigators have also been guided by the pervasive tendency to accept the argument that having been hospitalized attaches to the ex-patient a highly stigmatizing and socially undesirable label. It seems likely that persons vary in their readiness to view mental illness in this manner, and furthermore, it may be argued that the patient does have something to say about the types of definitions that are attributed to him. If the ex-patient were to be viewed as only one type of social actor who has had a certain set of unique experiences, it must be assumed that the patient also develops the normal techniques of social interaction. Patients do in fact have something to say about how they will be defined, and it seems likely that they will seek out social others who accord them self-definitions most congruent with their own.

Investigations are then needed which follow the patient out of the mental hospital and which focus on the processes by which the patient attempts to bring around him social others who will accord him the types of social support all human actors seem to seek out and desire.

A last area of potential research involves the deterring effect of hospitalization upon reentry into treatment. It may be hypothesized that the process of hospitalization and the social definitions which surround his experience deter some persons from being persuaded to seek hospital treatment or from actively seeking it. To what extent having been hospitalized serves as a mechanism of social control and thus either deters or encourages reentry into a treatment center is not known at the present time. Investigators might do well to consider the effect of this process upon the patient himself.

It is painfully obvious from our concluding discussions that a comprehensive sociological theory of mental illness is still in the formulative stage. It is hoped that readers will share our enthusiasm for the perspective offered in this volume and that future endeavors will pursue in greater depth and detail the implications of a symbolic interactionist framework for the study of mental illness and deviant behavior.

References

1   Herbert Blumer, "Society as Symbolic Interaction," in Arnold M. Rose, editor, *Human Behavior and Social Processes*, Houghton Mifflin Company, Boston, 1962, p. 183. Self-indication refers to the ability of the person to be an object for himself and to act toward himself as others act toward him.

2   Kai T. Erikson, "Notes on the Sociology of Deviance," *Social Problems*, **9:** 307–314, 1962; John I. Kitsuse, "Societal Reaction to Deviant Behavior: Problems of Theory and Method," *Social Problems*, **9:** 247–256, 1962; Howard S. Becker, *Outsiders*, The Free Press of Glencoe, New York, 1963.

3   Thomas J. Scheff, "The Role of the Mentally Ill and the Dynamics of Mental Disorder: A Research Framework," *Sociometry*, **26:** 442, 1963.

4   Thomas J. Scheff, "The Societal Reaction to Deviance: Ascriptive Elements in the Psychiatric Screening of Mental Patients in a Midwestern State," *Social Problems*, **11:** 401–413, 1964.

5   Harold Sampson, Sheldon L. Messinger, and Robert D. Towne, "Family Processes and Becoming a Mental Patient," *American Journal of Sociology*, **68:** 88–96, 1962.

6   See for example the preface to Erving Goffman's *Asylums*, Doubleday & Company,

Inc., Garden City, N.Y., 1961, p. x, where Goffman states: "To describe the patient's situation faithfully is necessarily to present a partisan view. (For this last bias I partly excuse myself by arguing that the imbalance is at least on the right side of the scale, since almost all professional literature on mental patients is written from the point of view of the psychiatrist, and he socially speaking, is on the other side.)"

7   Alexander L. Clark and Jack P. Gibbs, "Social Control: A Reformulation," *Social Problems*, **12**: 398–415, 1965.

8   Leo Srole et al., *Mental Health in the Metropolis: The Midtown Manhattan Study*, McGraw-Hill Book Company, New York, 1962.

9   Howard E. Freeman and Ozzie G. Simmons, *The Mental Patient Comes Home*, John Wiley & Sons, Inc., New York, 1963, discuss this fact, as does Robert Dreeben, "Sociological Aspects of Personality Change: A Study of Mental Hospitalization," paper presented at the annual meetings of the American Sociological Association, Miami Beach, Fla., 1966.

10   Goffman, *op. cit.*, pp. 127–169.

11   Freeman and Simmons, *op. cit.*

12   Stephan P. Spitzer and Norman K. Denzin, *The Career of the Mental Patient*, forthcoming.

13   August B. Hollingshead and Frederick C. Redlich, *Social Class and Mental Illness*, John Wiley & Sons, Inc., New York, 1958; Essey Wolfrom, Lila L. Pang, and Barbara M. Courtney, "Roads to the Mental Hospital," *Mental Hygiene*, **47**: 398–407, 1963; John A. Clausen and Marian R. Yarrow, "Paths to the Mental Hospital," *Journal of Social Issues*, **11**: 25–32, 1955.

14   Enid Mills, *Living with Mental Illness*, Routledge & Kegan Paul Ltd., London, 1962.

15   Goffman, *op. cit.*

16   Gerassimos Alivisatos and George Lyketsos, "A Preliminary Report of a Research Concerning the Attitude of the Families of Hospitalized Mental Patients," *International Journal of Social Psychiatry*, **10**: 37–44, 1964.

17   Figures as low as 1 out of 14 have been suggested. See Thomas J. Scheff, "The Role of the Mentally Ill and the Dynamics of Mental Disorder: A Research Framework," *Sociometry*, **26**: 436–453, 1963.

18   For a study which has directed itself to this problem in medical sociology see David Mechanic and Edmund A. Volkart, "Stress, Illness and the Sick Role," *American Sociological Review*, **26**: 51–58, 1961. See also Gerald Gurin, Joseph Veroff, and Sheila Feld, *Americans View Their Mental Health*, Basic Books, Inc., Publishers, New York, 1960, chap. 10, pp. 255–301.

19   See John A. Clausen and Marian R. Yarrow, editors, "The Impact of Mental Illness on the Family," *Journal of Social Issues*, vol. 11, entire issue, 1955.

20   This topic is explored in Spitzer and Denzin, *op. cit.*

21   For example, Stephan P. Spitzer, Norman K. Denzin, and Richard J. Bealka, "Family Influences on Patient Performance," paper presented at the annual meetings of the Midwest Sociological Society, Madison, Wis., 1966.

22   Kathleen A. Nelson, "The Significant Others of a Psychiatric Population," unpublished M.A. thesis, University of Iowa, 1967.

23   Rose L. Coser, "A Home Away from Home," *Social Problems*, **4**: 3–17, 1956; Mark Zborowski, "Cultural Components in Responses to Pain," *Journal of Social Issues*, **8**: 16–30, 1952; Henry D. Lederer, "How the Sick View Their World," *Journal of Social Issues*, **8**: 4–15, 1952.

24   Harvey L. Smith and Jean Thrasher, "Roles, Cliques and Sanctions: Dimensions of Patient Society," *International Journal of Social Psychiatry*, **9**: 184–191, 1963.

25   S. Kirson Weinberg, *Society and Personality Disorders*, Prentice-Hall, Inc., Englewood Cliffs, N.J., 1952; Richard F. Salisbury, *Structures of Custodial Care*, University of California Press, Berkeley, Calif., 1962.

26 For a compilation of such studies see Milton Greenblatt, Daniel Levinson, and Richard Williams, *The Patient and the Mental Hospital,* The Free Press, Glencoe, Ill., 1957.

27 Talcott Parsons, *The Social System,* The Free Press, Glencoe, Ill., 1951; Mechanic and Volkart, *op. cit.*

28 Raymond Sobel and Ardis Ingalls, "Resistance to Treatment: Explorations of the Patient's Role, *American Journal of Psychotherapy,* **18:** 562–573, 1964; Norman K. Denzin and Stephan P. Spitzer, "Paths to the Mental Hospital and Staff Predictions of Patient Role Behavior," *Journal of Health and Human Behavior,* **7:** 265–271, 1966.

29 See Norman K. Denzin, "Collective Behavior in Total Institutions: The Case of the Mental Hospital and the Prison," *Social Problems* (in press).

30 *Ibid.*

31 *Ibid.*

32 Herbert Blumer, "What's Wrong with Social Theory," *American Sociological Review,* **19:** 3–10, 1954.

33 Freeman and Simmons, *op. cit.;* Mark Lefton et al., "Social Class, Expectations and Performance of Mental Patients," *American Journal of Sociology,* **68:** 79–87, 1962.

34 Sampson, Messinger, and Towne, *op. cit.*

INDEXES

SUBJECT INDEX